FORTRESS ISRAEL

The Inside Story of the Military Elite

Who Run the Country—and Why

They Can't Make Peace

PATRICK TYLER

Portobello
BOOKS

Published by Portobello Books 2012

Portobello Books
12 Addison Avenue
London
W11 4QR
UK

First published in the United States in 2012 by Farrar, Straus and Giroux, New York

A CIP catalogue record for this book is available from the British Library

9 8 7 6 5 4 3 2 1

ISBN 978 1 84627 273 8 (hardback)
ISBN 978 1 84627 274 5 (trade paperback)

www.portobellobooks.com

Designed by Abby Kagan

Offset by Avon DataSet, Bidord on Avon, Warwickshire

Printed and bound by CPI Group (UK) Ltd, Croydon, CR0 4YY

IN MEMORY OF

Michael Timberlake Tyler

and

Einat Tabori

Contents

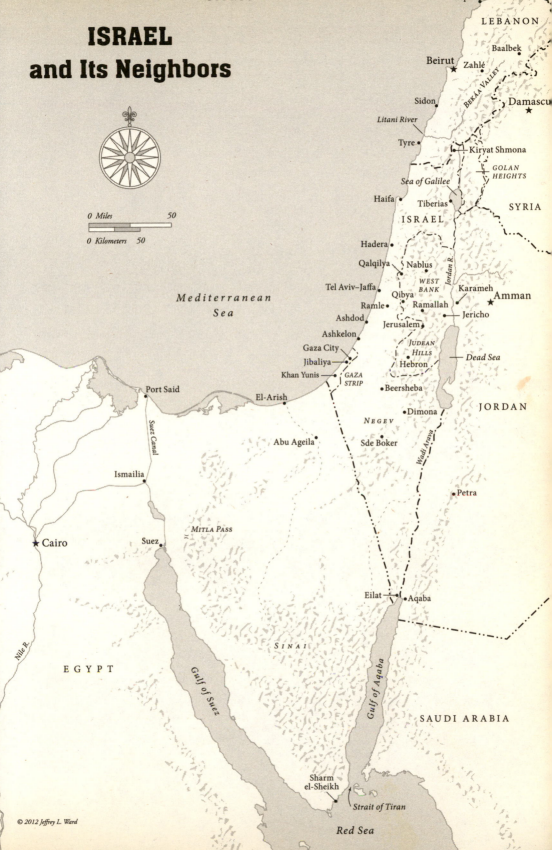

ISRAEL
and Its Neighbors

0 Miles 50
0 Kilometers 50

CYPRUS

LEBANON

Tripoli

Baalbek

Beirut
Zahlé

BEKAA VALLEY

Damascu

Sidon

Litani River

Tyre

Kiryat Shmona

*GOLAN
HEIGHTS*

Sea of Galilee

Haifa
Tiberias

SYRIA

ISRAEL

Hadera

Qalqilya
Nablus

Jordan R.

*WEST
BANK*

Tel Aviv–Jaffa
Qibya
Karameh

Amman

Ramle
Ramallah

Ashdod
Jericho

Ashkelon
Jerusalem

Gaza City
*JUDEAN
HILLS*

Dead Sea

Jibaliya
Hebron

Khan Yunis
*GAZA
STRIP*

Beersheba

JORDAN

Dimona

*Mediterranean
Sea*

Port Said
El-Arish

NEGEV

Sde Boker

Abu Ageila

Suez Canal

Wadi Arava

Ismailia

Petra

MITLA PASS

Cairo
Suez

Nile R.

Eilat
Aqaba

EGYPT

S I N A I

Gulf of Suez

Gulf of Aqaba

SAUDI ARABIA

Sharm
el-Sheikh

Strait of Tiran

Red Sea

© 2012 Jeffrey L. Ward

FORTRESS ISRAEL

Prologue: Murder in Tehran

Tehran's traffic is legendary. Taxi drivers in the Iranian capital have been known to pull a gun to force other motorists to yield. Gridlock and bedlam rule. Even ayatollahs are delayed in their rounds.

Thus important scientists from Iran's military establishment, such as Darioush Rezaeinejad, a weapons engineer, and Mostafa Ahmadi Roshan, a deputy director of the Natanz uranium enrichment facility, were forced to enter the daily snarl like everyone else. That made them vulnerable.

At age thirty-five, Rezaeinejad could have passed for a banker or a deacon. His features were rounded and plump, and under an expansive brow, dark eyes that were youthful and sharp peered out from rectangular spectacles that gave him an aura of experience. His scientific competence included the design of high-speed switches that can be used for the precisely timed explosions that trigger atomic detonations.

His colleague, Roshan, thirty-two, was one of the youngest scientists in Iran's program to develop nuclear technologies for the production of electricity, for medical research, and, if a decision is taken by the country's leadership, for the development of nuclear weapons.

Roshan had not been born, and Rezaeinejad was only a toddler, when the revolution of Ayatollah Ruhollah Khomeini enveloped Iran and when America became—for revolutionary youth—the "Great Satan" and Israel the "Little Satan." The gilded dome of Khomeini's shrine still glows above the layer of dust and pollution in South Tehran, and the national nuclear power program enjoys broad support among young Iranians, who have grown up under sanctions from the West and who see scientific development as a patriotic expression of national achievement.

On the morning of July 23, 2011, Rezaeinejad, along with his wife and four-year-old daughter, was about to launch into the traffic from his home on Bani Hashem Street in East Tehran. One report said their destination was the daughter's kindergarten. Suddenly, two riders on a motorcycle appeared from nowhere. In an instant, one of them pulled a handgun and opened fire. Rezaeinejad, trapped inside his small sedan, went down with a fatal bullet wound to the throat as his daughter looked on stricken with horror. Another bullet seriously wounded his wife. Then it was over. The riders sped away. Rezaeinejad slumped lifeless onto the passenger-side seat.[1]

The killing of Rezaeinejad led to urgent new security procedures. By the time that Mostafa Ahmadi Roshan entered Tehran's morning rush hour six months later, on January 11, 2012, a bodyguard had been assigned to protect him. But as Roshan's Peugeot 405 wheeled down the sloping lanes of North Tehran, another motorcycle appeared, passing close enough to the sedan for the rider to attach a magnetic limpet mine to the vehicle. The riders sped away, and before Roshan understood the danger, the mine detonated and killed him and the bodyguard.

In both cases, the telltales of an Israeli assassination were manifest: the motorcycle approach, the two-man hit team that disappeared into the traffic, the choice of weapons. Prime Minister Yitzhak Rabin had approved an almost identical hit in Malta against the leader of the Islamic Jihad in 1995.

The murders of Roshan and Rezaeinejad appeared to be among the latest in a series of state-directed assassinations by Israel's foreign intelligence services. One former Mossad chief spoke to me about the killings in a tone that conveyed that while he was officially prohibited from stating that Israel was behind them, the entire Western world understood that this was Israel's response to Iran's nuclear threat.

On the day of Rezaeinejad's killing, questions about the Jewish state's involvement were batted down in Tel Aviv. "Israel is not responding," declared Defense Minister Ehud Barak, smiling at journalists.

From a former prime minister and highly decorated retired general, Barak's statement sent a strong message to the Israeli news media: the government expected the media to convey a stance of official ambiguity about the hit in Tehran, an ambiguity that would be enforced, if necessary, by the military censor's office, a large organization within the military that reports directly to Barak.

At least four other Iranian scientists had been killed or injured in similar attacks. In November 2011, an entire weapons depot and base exploded twenty-five miles outside of Tehran, rattling windows like a temblor. Official Iranian sources called it an "accident," but they also announced that Iran's most senior missile scientist, General Hassan Tehrani Moghaddam, had died in the blast, prompting immediate speculation that this, too, was the result of covert action.

The chief of staff of the Israeli Defense Forces, Lieutenant General Benny Gantz, told Israeli parliamentarians in a private session that "unnatural" events would continue to occur in Iran. Gantz said 2012 would be a "critical year" given Iran's continuing "nuclearization."[2]

The war scare seized Western capitals.

European nations, which demanded that Iran demonstrate that it has no illicit program for building nuclear weapons, intensified sanctions on Iranian crude oil exports, hoping to pressure the regime in Tehran to return to the negotiating table and avoid a situation where Israel's armed forces short-circuited the international diplomacy that was under way and ignited a destructive Middle Eastern war.

In Israel, the person who authorizes a state assassination is the prime minister, the final legal authority when it comes to the taking of a life using special units of the army or the intelligence services. In this case, such a decision to kill Rezaeinejad and, later, Roshan, would have been made by Benjamin Netanyahu, the prime minister who came to office in February 2009 with the darkest possible view of the threat from Iran.

Soon after he won the election, Netanyahu told an American interviewer, "You don't want a messianic apocalyptic cult controlling atomic bombs," and, therefore, it was time to do something about Iran. Separately, in an interview for this book, Barak told me that he saw the threat from Iran in a global context: "I can hardly see any stable world order if Iran turns nuclear."

Netanyahu soon put the new administration of President Barack Obama on notice—indeed, he had put the world on notice—that he was prepared to do whatever it took to prevent Iran from obtaining a nuclear weapon, and the implication was that the Israeli prime minister was willing to launch a massive military strike to destroy or degrade the Iranian nuclear complex if sanctions and other coercive steps failed to thwart Iran.

"Since the dawn of the nuclear age, we have not had a fanatic regime that might put its zealotry above its self-interest," Netanyahu warned. "People say that they'll behave like any other nuclear power. Can you take that risk?" he asked.[3]

A year after Netanyahu entered office, it was apparent that the Jewish state was escalating a clandestine war—a campaign of sabotage, intimidation, and assassination—against Iran. It will take some time for all the details to emerge, but the broad outlines of the campaign were clear: Israel was targeting key Iranian scientists—such as Rezaeinejad, Roshan, and others—for elimination. And it was targeting the military and industrial facilities related to a nuclear program.[4]

Netanyahu and Barak hailed from opposite ends of the political spectrum, but they had become close allies and strong advocates for relentless military coercion against Iran—even war, if that became necessary—to deter the Tehran regime from crossing the threshold and becoming a full-fledged nuclear weapons state. Their alliance revealed a common faith in military action as more likely to yield results than diplomacy or negotiation, which they held in low regard.

Few Westerners knew that Netanyahu had served under Barak in the army at a time when Barak's identity had been a state secret. As leader of the elite Israeli military unit Sayeret Matkal, which means "commandos of the general staff," he carried out some of the most dangerous missions of espionage, rescue, and assassination. Benjamin Netanyahu had joined "the unit" in the shadow of his older brother, Jonathan, who led the 1976 raid on Entebbe, Uganda, to free the passengers of a hijacked airliner. Jonathan Netanyahu died in the otherwise successful rescue, which was cheered around the world. Barak delivered the eulogy at Jonathan's funeral, and the younger brother's political career was born in the afterglow of Jonathan's heroism and under the guidance of their father, Benzion Netanyahu, a prominent leader of the right wing of the Zionist movement.

For Netanyahu and Barak, and for much of the Israeli military establish-ment, the undeclared war on Iran was the top priority in national strategy. They had convinced themselves that if there was the slightest risk that Iran might get a nuclear weapon, it followed absolutely that the ayatollahs would launch it against Israel in an attempt at annihilation rivaling the Holocaust—maybe not immediately, but inescapably; and even if Iran was deterred for a time by the threat of a massive Israeli counterstrike that would kill millions of Iranians, the existence of an Iranian bomb would magnify Iran's power to intimidate its neighbors, and it would incite other Middle Eastern powers—Egypt, Turkey, Saudi Arabia—to go nuclear.

Barak asked one interviewer pointedly, "If a nuclear Iran covets and occupies some gulf state, who will liberate it? The bottom line is that we must deal with the problem now."[5]

Barak told me that he had warned Senator Obama when Obama was still a candidate for president that the civilized world was in "a major his-torical struggle" against a triad of challenges: Islamic terror, proliferation of nuclear weapons, and rogue states. In dealing with the threat from Iran, he said, "I told Obama very honestly that we do not remove any option from the table, and when we say it, we mean it."

The astounding thing was that Iran might not have been engaged in clan-destine nuclear weapons development at all. American and Western intel-ligence services believed that Iran's senior leaders, including Ayatollah Ali Khamenei, had decided in 2003, after the American invasion of Iraq, to defer work on nuclear weapons design and fabrication and instead con-centrate their national effort toward building reactors for electric power generation and the production of radioactive elements for medicine and research.[6]

For Netanyahu and Barak, this shift, if true, was at best a tactical ma-neuver. Iran was enriching uranium in volumes that would give Tehran an inventory of fissile material that could be enriched even further to the high level of purity (of uranium 235) needed to produce the cores of the coun-try's first atomic bombs. Just because they had not taken the next enrich-ment steps did not mean they had no intention to do so.

But within the Israeli military establishment, there seemed no recognition of the fact that if Iran *had* deferred or abandoned its quest for an atomic bomb, Israel's covert war on Iran was highly provocative and possibly counterproductive. It might even have led to the self-fulfilling reversal—a resumption of the nuclear weapons effort to deter Israeli aggression.

A new era of undeclared warfare had dawned, and Israel had established itself as its most proficient practitioner. Former Israeli intelligence chief Avi Dichter bragged to an interviewer, "The state of Israel has turned targeted assassinations into an art form. Foreign delegations come here on a weekly basis to learn from us, not just Americans." He called it "the sexiest trend" in modern warfare and asserted that "its effectiveness is overwhelming [and] the precision is amazing."[7]

In the course of research for this book, I met with dozens of Israeli generals, intelligence chiefs, senior officers, and leading political figures, many of whom subscribed to a strong militaristic outlook. In their theory of human behavior, the worst-case scenario was not one of several possible outcomes—it was the *only* possible outcome.

At the same time, I was surprised to find many retired officers who advocated a more diplomatic approach and were deeply concerned that the military establishment was becoming too hard-line, too religious, and too contemptuous of any competing institutions, especially those devoted to diplomacy and negotiation, which might question the military's worldview or national priorities.

Just as America's defense establishment had tended to exaggerate the Soviet threat during the cold war, and just as President Eisenhower had grappled with the influence of what he called the military-industrial complex, Israel seems often to be under the influence of a military elite and an extensive defense bureaucracy, both of which remain extremely reluctant to place their trust in peace or in the processes of engagement or accommodation with the Arab and Muslim worlds. This state of affairs represents one of the greatest challenges for Western policy in the Middle East.

In Israel, the military establishment is the most trusted institution in the country. Civilian political leaders depend on the military system to provide everything from staff support to policy recommendations. The army and the intelligence services dominate the national budget, define external and internal threats, initiate policies, review their own performance, run a large portion of the economy, control vast tracts of land and airspace, and exert immense influence over communications and news media through censorship.

Israelis look to their military leaders as if they were political figures, at times in competition with the civilian leaders of the government. Many Israelis believe that the chief of staff of the Israeli Defense Forces is a figure whose power and influence rival the prime minister's.

"You have to understand that the military in Israel are first and foremost a trade union, they're interested in their own survival," explained Shlomo Gazit, a retired major general in the Israeli army. Gazit was a protégé of Moshe Dayan, Israel's most famous general, and rose to become director of military intelligence after the Yom Kippur War. Gazit grew up in a military system that was deeply skeptical of the possibility for negotiation with the Arabs. In 1977, Gazit even questioned whether Egyptian President Anwar Sadat's dramatic journey to Jerusalem to offer peace was actually a trick to spring another surprise attack.

Late in life, however, Gazit became a tireless advocate of engagement, negotiation, and compromise with the Arabs. In Israel, "whenever a problem is being raised, the military are supposed to provide an answer, and in a trade union they will always say the answer is within our [jurisdiction]."

What was missing, he added, was any strong countervailing institution.

"We have an extremely weak political system that is incapable of standing as a counterweight to the military and that is not capable of coming up with alternatives that are not military alternatives," explained Gazit.[8]

Michael Herzog, a brigadier general from one of the country's founding families who served as chief of staff to two defense ministers, added, "We don't have American culture here. We are still in the process of developing civilian bodies, but for now the whole culture of decision making revolves around the military."[9]

I had come to know Israel as a newspaper correspondent for the *Washington Post* and the *New York Times*. And in the course of researching a book on the American presidents and their experiences in the Middle East, I met a broad cross section of Israel's military elite and was fascinated by the hard realism with which they look out at the world and by their unabashed recognition that the army dominates national life in Israel, where the general staff is called upon to provide policy options to a weak or divided political leadership.

For an American, it was impossible to miss the breathtaking ambition of the Israeli officer corps to lead, instead of follow, U.S. policy in the Middle East. My fascination with this military class and its influence over the political system of the country was the inspiration for this book—a political biography of Israel's ruling elite and the military society that sustains it.

Israeli political history is a story of collaboration, rivalry, and betrayal among a small group of men and a very few women competing for the mandate to secure the Jewish state in perpetuity. David Ben-Gurion and his circle of insiders began the first hotly contested debates over peace with the Arabs in the 1950s; now that they had a state, they argued over the acquisition of nuclear weapons and over how to acquire more land and transfer any war to enemy territory. Those debates have carried forward to the present, where the sons and heirs of that first Ben-Gurion circle, the generals he promoted, cultivated, and influenced, have inherited Israel as a regional superpower, yet one still isolated in the Middle East and still poised incessantly for war.

In relative terms, it is not a great span of time that separates the present generation of leaders in Israel from David Ben-Gurion. The founding prime minister ruled almost continuously from 1948 to 1963 and then struggled to undermine his successors for years afterward, nearly until his death in 1973. Only eleven other Israelis have served as prime minister, and because there is no single figure whose career encompasses the full national narrative of Israel, this must, perforce, be a biography of a class. What defines its members is the competition to control the national security agenda. For whosoever proves himself—or herself—to be the paramount national strategist on national security and survival garners the greatest share of trust and loyalty from the Israelis. The most sought-after label in Israeli politics is that of Mr. Security—*Mar Bitachon*.

My history is drawn from a broad array of sources, declassified documents, personal archives, interviews across a spectrum of Israel's leadership class during my visits to the country over the last six years, memoirs, and secondary sources from the Hebrew- and English-language press.

The broad conclusion that I believe any realistic researcher reaches, and that I explain in depth through this narrative of extraordinary lives, is that Israel, six decades after its founding, remains a nation in thrall to an original martial impulse, the depth of which has given rise to succeeding generations of leaders who are stunted in their capacity to wield or sustain diplomacy as a rival to military strategy, who seem ever on the hair trigger in dealing with their regional rivals, and whose contingency planners embrace worst-case scenarios that often exaggerate complex or ambiguous developments as threats to national existence. They do so, reflexively and instinctively, in order to perpetuate a system of governance where national policy is dominated by the military.

The origins of this martial impulse can be understood only by lifting the layers of secrecy and mythology about the first decades of Israeli statehood, where the aftermath of world war and Holocaust, a precipitous British retreat from Palestine, and the attack by Arab states that greeted Israel's declaration of independence in 1948 profoundly transformed the Zionist movement. The opening of leadership archives makes it possible to understand the personal transformation of Ben-Gurion himself, who within the space of a few years shed whatever romanticism he had once harbored about accommodation with the Arabs and embraced the rugged militarism of the native-born generation of Israelis. These sabras aspired to build a powerful and heavily militarized state that could protect itself and expand its borders in a second and third round of war with the Arabs so as to fulfill the dreams of many Zionists: a state that could accommodate five to ten million Israelis with ample water supplies, agricultural lands, and defensible frontiers. Ben-Gurion dominated the Zionist movement for a half century, leading the Jewish Agency through the dark years of genocide in Europe and through the struggle over British withdrawal from the Holy Land and Arab refusal to partition Palestine as two states—Arab and Israeli—under a United Nations plan. For Ben-Gurion, the founding father and first prime minister, a tough stand toward the Arabs proved to be not just a driving ideology but also good politics.

At the center of Israel's military culture stood the sabras, the class of native-born Israelis who grew up socialized to violence with the local Arabs with whom they jousted over land and grazing rights. The young Israelis who came of age during the world war subsequently acquitted themselves so well in the 1948–49 War of Israeli Independence that military power became the dominant focus of a generation. In a hostile and unstable region, the sabras saw themselves as tough and self-reliant fighters, never as interested in debate as in taking action, less interested in accommodation with the Arabs than in seizing objectives and creating facts on the ground. Moshe Dayan, the one-eyed general who became Ben-Gurion's favorite officer, was the prototype. A thoroughly secular man, Dayan began fighting Arabs with fists and knives as a teenager, and, as he grew older, he read the Old Testament obsessively, though he was nonreligious, because for him it was a manual for war.

Sabra is the tough species of prickly-pear cactus that clings to the Mediterranean coastline. To call oneself a sabra became popular in the wake of World War II, when Jews born in prestate Palestine felt a need to distinguish themselves from the mass of Holocaust survivors and immigrants streaming in from Europe, North Africa, Iraq, Iran, Yemen, and Morocco, most of them strangers to the Zionist pioneers who for decades had been farming and fighting to defend the land in tightly knit communes and urban neighborhoods. Sabras were the new Jews, no longer a caricature of passivism, dependence, and weakness, but a people determined to take its fate into its own hands.

As a description, "sabra" comes as close as any word to defining the outlook of a leadership culture that instinctively reached for military solutions and aligned itself closely to popular sentiments that called for holding on to land at all costs and for meting out retribution after any act of violence perpetrated against Jews.

Today, with the help of the United States and Europe, Israel stands as a regional superpower, but it also continues to respond to its founding configuration of threats as if its vulnerabilities had not changed. It pursues a national strategy of preemptive warfare and covert subversion to weaken potential enemies in a cycle that is not only counterproductive to integration and peace but that also intensifies enmities and feeds Islamic paranoia and extremism.

At a time when the Arab world is reeling with new revolutionary currents that have toppled regimes in Tunisia, Egypt, Libya, and Yemen, and left other rulers teetering in countries where calls for "freedom" and "justice" rise from the streets, Israel sits more isolated than ever, unable to play a constructive role as a partner with Arab states or as an ally of the West. It exists in a steel cage as a regional military hegemon, armed to the teeth and led by a political class that is divided and jaded by its own paralysis.

The legacy of the Zionist revolutionaries who once enraptured the parlors of Europe and America with talk of a Jewish homeland as a moral beacon in a benighted region has instead bequeathed to the Jewish world and the West a highly militarized dependency—a state that has achieved great feats of cultural and economic development but has failed to build strong enough institutions to balance its military zeitgeist with imaginative or engaging diplomacy. It was these institutions that the Zionist founders foresaw as the vehicle by which Israeli statesmen, diplomats, and negotiators would help create a Semitic federation of Arabs, Jews, and Christians in a region that for centuries had hosted and protected Jewish and Christian communities.

If Western nations are to comprehend the difficulties that Israel faces in making peace, they will have to understand and engage Israel's military establishment, which constitutes the most influential component of the country's ruling class. If Israel is to meet the challenges of rapid and unpredictable change sweeping the Middle East, it will be far more likely to succeed if its neighbors perceive that Israel, too, is undergoing a transformation, one dedicated to rebuilding the strategic consensus for peace and accommodation that existed under Prime Minister Yitzhak Rabin. That consensus was founded on Rabin's assertion that Israel was no longer the nation that dwells alone.

Rabin, a sabra, also came to believe after a life of military service that Israel's greatest challenges were less likely to be overcome by military force. He believed a strong military was essential, but he shared the conviction that Israel would have to learn anew to negotiate with its enemies, knowing that human engagement creates its own elixir for compromise. This was the calculated risk that separated Rabin from his forebears and cost him his life. To return to that spirit will require a far more active and constructive diplomacy than Israel has fielded to date, and it will require

Western assistance, support, and resolute determination to protect the architecture of peace.

The Arab states are responsible for their own failures to build democratic institutions for peace, and for the legacy of hatred and incitement against Israel that is a dismal feature of the modern Middle East. From the outset, Arab leaders, with few exceptions, displayed a deep hostility to Israel as a Jewish homeland and Zionist enterprise; they rejected the UN's partition plan in 1947 and showed little or no empathy for a people devastated by annihilation in Europe. But this book seeks to explain with realism and fairness how the martial impulse in Israeli society and among its ruling elite has undermined opportunities for reconciliation, skewed politics toward an agenda of retribution and revenge, and fomented deliberate acts of provocation designed to disrupt international diplomatic efforts to find a formula for peace. As Moshe Sharett, the Jewish state's second prime minister, documented in his meticulous journals, military ambition too often trumped moral aspiration, once the cornerstone of Zionism, to build a homeland that devoted its energy and resources toward integration.

For Westerners, Israel represents a difficult problem of perception. For half a century, we have been encouraged to regard Israel as a tiny embattled democracy in a sea of Arab hostility—Athens under siege. Israel's leaders publicly asserted that their dominant national focus was the pursuit of peace. Leaders of Diaspora Judaism promoted a narrative of "shared values" with the West and projected a high moral skein over the entire Zionist venture. They built formidable constituencies to encourage military and economic assistance to Israel under the rubric that the Jewish state was the last stand in history for a people.

But it was not Athens as much as Sparta that Ben-Gurion turned to as the model for his state, according to a more complete record that has emerged. After witnessing the destruction of European Jewry and the hostile reception to Israel's declaration of statehood, he dramatically shifted his focus during the first decade toward building a different kind of polity, a society organized around the concept of self-reliance and, to that end, continuing warfare and military buildup.

In less than a decade after its founding, Israel had fielded the most agile and powerful army and air force in the Middle East and had made secret plans, with the help of France, to become a nuclear power. By the time the United States got deeply involved in arming Israel during the late 1960s, Israel had already defeated the Arabs in two rounds of war, was preparing to do so for a third time in 1967, and, in utmost secrecy, was also on the threshold of becoming a nuclear weapons state.

Like George Washington, Ben-Gurion founded and led a nation into battle, and the victory of the Jewish militias over the Arab armies in 1948–49 marked the beginning of a new era of militarism in the Middle East. No cross-cultural comparison is completely valid, but both Israel and the United States struggled in their early years to define the nature of their state and the role of the military. Washington and his heirs balanced the powers of government, separated religion from national affairs, and built the institutions of diplomacy under a republic that relegated the military establishment to a highly subservient role.

Ben-Gurion embraced a military model for growth and expansion, and constructed what amounted to a militarized society and a civilianized army, under a military elite that remains wary of putting down the sword. He defeated those political rivals who favored an alternative path and pressed the case for a long war against the Arabs.

Israel's civil society, parliament, supreme court, human rights organizations, and the diplomatic corps within the government have occasionally challenged the power and the policies of the military, but these institutions are no match for its overarching influence.

In a country where every tier of society is connected to the army, it is not clear where the army ends and the government begins. Many government offices, including the prime minister's and those of the Knesset, are served by military staff members. Nearly every Jewish family is a military stakeholder by virtue of service in the active or reserve forces. (Ultra-Orthodox Jews and Arab Israelis are exempted from military service.) Nearly every household sends its high school graduates into the army for three long years of compulsory service. High school students compete vigorously to enter elite military units because, in Israel, one's "unit" becomes a social and business network for life, and the elites reap the greatest rewards.

At Israel's West Point, an officers' academy called Bahad 1 nestled deep in the Negev Desert, the commandant, Colonel Aharon Haliwa, greeted the 2010 class, saying, "The people of Israel don't have anyone who is better than you. There is no one else."[10]

He exhorted them with the law of the jungle. "In the Middle East, you don't get a second chance. We were born here and that's what we have. And it is a strange neighborhood: the stronger one lives, the stronger one survives, the stronger one wins."

He admonished them to ignore those who say there are no more existential threats to Israel. "When a kid is afraid of riding a bus, the danger being existential or not isn't relevant. To the kid's mother, it is an existential danger! She looks at her kid and wants him to live here safely and at peace. And now it's your time to make sure that happens."

For a young Israeli, landing a slot in military intelligence, the paratroopers, or an elite commando unit, or qualifying to fly attack helicopters, fighter jets, or surveillance drones is like winning admission to an Ivy League university in America. The military is the seminal educational experience for acquiring martial skills and for entering adulthood. Its networks open opportunities and reinforce rivalries.

And the rivalries are crucial. Though security unifies the country, the Jewish state is anything but monolithic. Israeli society seethes with competitive clans, ethnic constituencies, and religious bastions. The military has always served as a unifying force, but it was also shaped by rivalries. The Golani (Golan) and Barak (Lightning) brigades are guardians of the North; the Givati Brigade protects southern Israel with units called Samson's Foxes and the Pillar of Fire artillery brigade. The air force squadrons include the Knights of the North, The Hammers, The One, and the Flying Leopard.

Each brigade, each division, each squadron or special forces unit guards its turf and nurtures grievances over battlefield glories unrecognized or denied, over access to budget resources or new weapons, and over mistakes, especially fatal mistakes in battle. Each unit clings to its base, its geographic domain, traditions, songs, and enmities. Seasoned generals refer to their formative years in the paratroopers or the Golani Brigade more than they refer to the army as a whole.

Reuven Merhav, a respected figure who fought as a commando under Ariel Sharon in the 1950s, worked undercover for the Mossad in the 1960s, and practiced diplomacy in the foreign ministry in the 1980s, erupted during an interview when I asked him the effect of "unit loyalty" on Israeli life.

"People go back to the pots where they shit, back to their cliques, their beds, this is incestual! It disarms us from maintaining the ability to judge things objectively."[11]

Once in the military system, Israelis never fully exit. They carry the military identity for life, not just through service in the reserves until age forty-nine, or through social and retirement services, but through lifelong expectations of loyalty and secrecy. Many Israeli officers carry their "top secret" clearances after retirement, reporting back to superiors or to intelligence officers items of interest gleaned from their involvement in business, finance, and interaction with foreigners. For most Israelis, these relationships are natural, along with the power of the military establishment to pull them in on a moment's notice for a special assignment or debriefing.

Israel spends more on its military and intelligence establishments, in proportion to its total economy, than almost any other nation. The military alone receives more than 6 percent of annual gross domestic product. In Tel Aviv, the sprawling commercial capital on the Mediterranean coast, the Ministry of Defense stands as a gleaming seventeen-story cube that seems pinned to the earth by a central shaft that rises through the roof and flares to become a circular heliport. This monolithic headquarters, from where both the defense minister and the chief of staff run the massive military-industrial complex of the country, is the most visible icon of government power. The Defense Ministry complex and the military base that surrounds it in central Tel Aviv are known as the *kirya*—literally, the campus—and Israelis know that its power radiates into space, across deserts and seas, and even underground, where the Israeli general staff meets in the "pit," a sprawling war-room complex that is patterned after America's National Military Command Center beneath the Pentagon.

A few miles to the north of the Defense Ministry lies another large compound of drab white buildings that staircase up a hill near Tel Aviv University. This is the headquarters of Shabak (also called Shin Bet), or General Security Service. Under the motto "Defender that shall not be seen," the Shabak over the decades has monitored almost every facet of Israeli life. In its first decade, beginning in 1948, its existence was not even revealed to the public. And today, the secret networks of its large Arab Affairs division garrison millions of Palestinian Arabs in the occupied territories. A few miles farther north, a large and partially hidden campus of low-slung office buildings sandwiched between the Glilot highway junction, a Cineplex, and a shopping center is the headquarters of the Mossad, or the Institute for Intelligence and Special Operations, whose spymasters run one of the largest and most efficient foreign intelligence agencies in the world.

The roots of these institutions trace back to the prestate Jewish underground, the Haganah. Their leaders were both political and military figures whose identities were shrouded by an official secrets act. They were referred to not by name but by monikers denoting their heft in a small society. Isser Harel, one of the first intelligence chiefs under David Ben-Gurion, was simply known as Memuneh, or "the man in charge." His authority on any question of security was near absolute. His agents bugged the offices of domestic political parties and pulled any Israeli out of bed for extrajudicial interrogations on any matter Harel determined relevant to his mandate to protect the state.

Civil society has evolved since then. There are greater civil rights protections, but the specter of the security state remains a dominant aspect of life. Israeli culture is based on security, not surprising for a small country that began as a nation of watchmen, standing guard over fields, crops, and communes, defending against Arab marauders who resented and feared the encroachment by Jews flooding in from post-Holocaust Europe. As in Sparta, Israel's people were its walls, and boundaries were defined by the tips of their spears. Within this Zionist ethos, six hundred thousand pioneers formed militias, then an army; they seized land, fought and expelled Arabs, and, in order to protect the Zionist enterprise in perpetuity, acquired nuclear weapons to become the most powerful nation in the Middle East. The military *is* the country to a great extent, and it serves as the pervasive national bureaucracy, reflexively working to perpetuate itself, its budget, and its high standing in society. Each generation of new officers feels the pressure to distinguish itself on the battlefield and to validate the expensive weapons systems acquired or developed for new missions or concepts of warfare. Each new class of generals seeks to refine—or expand—the definition of what constitutes an existential threat to the state.

The effect of Israel's success from a half century of militarism has emboldened the military establishment to project itself as a hegemonic power, one independent from but allied with the United States. Some see this as a striking departure from the original goals of Zionism's founders, who imagined a progressive and humanistic state deeply engaged with its Arab and Islamic neighbors and dedicated to lifting all boats in the Middle East. Israel is not the "light unto nations" that many of the romantics of the early Zionist movement had hoped it would be; it stands as a modern Sparta in a region of weak states. Its leaders live on the knife's edge—still—between striking a historic and humanistic bargain with the Muslims or fighting them in another round of war. This is their story.

ONE

Ben-Gurion: The Origins of Militarism

David Ben-Gurion was splayed across his sickbed at the President Hotel in West Jerusalem, down with a miasma of symptoms in late October 1955 as he often was in times of high tension, and, lately, Ben-Gurion appeared to be living on tension. He had complained of lumbago in August but now was suffering from dizziness, and his doctors, fearing an ominous turn, had hospitalized him for a battery of tests.[1] Some thought that he might have suffered a stroke.[2] At sixty-nine, Ben-Gurion, Israel's founding prime minister, seemed to be near the end of his life. Dwight Eisenhower had been leveled by a heart attack the previous month, Winston Churchill had retired in April, Stalin was dead. The passing of a generation appeared to be at hand.

But in Jerusalem, the patient refused to stay down, and the reason Ben-Gurion was too restless and irritable to remain bedridden was the arrival of intelligence reports that Soviet cargo ships were landing in Egypt to deliver—from the Eastern bloc—all manner of heavy weapons: tanks, artillery, fighter jets, bombers, and submarines. Egypt's power under the new military dictator, Colonel Gamal Abdel Nasser, would double or triple within a year. The implication was alarming: Nasser would stand as the colossus of the Arab world.

How could Israel *breathe* with bombers and submarines lurking off its coastline? Ben-Gurion asked. He had been in London during the blitz, and anyone could imagine how totally exposed Tel Aviv stood on the Mediterranean coast, where it could be reduced to rubble in a surprise attack.

Abba Eban, Israel's ambassador to the United Nations, had cabled from New York that it was time to consider a preventive war. Two top intelligence chiefs, Isser Harel of the Mossad, and Yehoshafat Harkabi of military intelligence, had both sent Ben-Gurion secret recommendations that a preemptive strike was necessary to stop Egypt's military breakout. And of course Nasser was stoking Jewish anxiety by having Radio Cairo blare out a staccato of vitriol: "The day of Israel's annihilation is approaching. There will be no peace on the border, for we demand revenge. This means death to Israel."[3]

"Revenge!" Nasser's call rolled across Sinai like the scourge of Pharaoh.

The white tufts of hair rose from Ben-Gurion's balding pate like solar flares, and if his blood pressure was not spiking at that moment, it was under assault by waves of frustration over Israel's failure, in his view, to act more decisively, more aggressively against the Arabs.

From his sickbed, Ben-Gurion called out to Nehemiah Argov, his military aide, instructing him to send a message to Moshe Dayan, the chief of staff of the Israeli Defense Forces. Tell him to cut short his vacation in France, Ben-Gurion instructed. He must return to Israel at once because—and this was not spelled out in the message—Ben-Gurion was ready to go to war even if Moshe Sharett and the rest of the leadership of Mapai, the Workers' Party, were not.[4]

This was the beginning—the origins of Israeli militarism.

In the middle of Israel's first decade, Ben-Gurion, infirm and apocalyptic about the future of the Jewish state, the loss of pioneering spirit among the Jews, the slowing of Jewish immigration, and the erosion of political support for his leadership, began to exhort his defense establishment to think beyond the self-evident tasks of securing the borders, finding weapons, and training recruits who spoke a polyglot of languages.

During an eighteen-month period of semiretirement from mid-1953 to early 1955, Ben-Gurion began thinking and speaking about a more ambitious national military strategy, one that contemplated with certainty a new round of warfare with the Arabs, called for expansion of the Jewish state through preemptive attacks with modern conventional forces, and—it seemed almost impossible for such a small state to think in such terms—the acquisition of atomic bombs as a fail-safe weapon to preserve the Jewish people. The new militant spirit was the culmination of Ben-Gurion's long ferment about the conflict with the Arabs, but also, inescapably, it arose from his deep anxiety about the political lassitude of his people and their flagging support for his leadership. Ben-Gurion understood, or at least hoped, that war—militarism in the face of an Arab threat—might remobilize the Israelis. Faced with the prospect of retirement, Ben-Gurion also came to the conclusion that he had no equal in the Zionist hierarchy, and he seemed therefore determined to extend his political franchise as a paramount leader. He advanced with an irritable self-assurance and visceral compulsion to outmaneuver the stalwarts of his own political party, Mapai, who were treating him, because of his advanced age, like a dead relative.

At that moment in the mid-1950s, only a handful of people knew that the Israeli army—with Ben-Gurion's encouragement and explicit approval—had been conducting clandestine raids into Syria, Jordan, Egypt, and other Arab territories. Despite the fact that he was not—for the time being—prime minister, Ben-Gurion advocated this policy of escalation, but the sitting prime minister, Moshe Sharett, was against the raids in principle.[5]

Ben-Gurion had exhorted the army's commanders to go on the offensive and to do so covertly, to deceive the Americans, the British, and the United Nations, and to avoid the imposition of sanctions. The military had formed a special unit to carry out the cross-border operations. It was headed by a brash young officer named Arik Scheinerman—eventually to be known to the world as Ariel Sharon.

More disturbing for Israel's young democracy, it was painfully obvious within the ruling party that the leaders of the defense establishment, especially Dayan, were making regular visits to Ben-Gurion's retreat in the Negev for consultation and instruction at a time when Ben-Gurion was supposed to be in retirement. From his windswept porch, Ben-Gurion had schemed to circumvent the "old guard" of the Mapai—Sharett, Levi Eshkol, Golda Meir, and their allies—in his quest to put the country back on the attack. In doing so, he relied extensively on the younger generation of sabras and their like-minded comrades throughout the army, where the thirst for combat with the Arabs—a "second round" of war—was far from quenched.

It was there, in the army, that Ben-Gurion had discovered Dayan, a tenacious fighter of the Jewish underground during the world war. (Dayan's father, Shmuel, was among Ben-Gurion's loyalists in the Knesset.) It was there that Ben-Gurion had spotted Yitzhak Rabin, the young officer of the

Palmach militia, the elite fighting force, who had proved his loyalty to the state by attacking a rival militia—the Irgun of Menachem Begin—on the beach in Tel Aviv. (Begin had tried to land arms against Ben-Gurion's order.) And it was there that Ben-Gurion had glimpsed young Arik Scheinerman, the bright-eyed and bullheaded commando who pushed the boundaries of every mission with a brutality that struck fear into the Arab camp.

Prime Minister Moshe Sharett, who since 1933 had worked at Ben-Gurion's side in the Jewish Agency, which helped Diaspora Jews settle in Israel, seemed to be out of the loop in his own government. Before Ben-Gurion slipped away to the desert, he had surrounded Sharett with protégés who ignored or circumvented the acting prime minister's prerogatives. That was the essence of the "plot"—it seemed the only word to describe it—that Ben-Gurion had laid to ensure that Sharett's premiership would fail. And Sharett's failure would, almost certainly, open a political path for Ben-Gurion's return to high office.

Israel's cross-border raids carried a high risk of international condemnation. They were violations of the armistice agreement that had ended the 1948–49 war. Both sides—Arab and Israeli—had agreed to take border disputes and refugee problems to the joint armistice commissions, where officers from both armies were charged by the United Nations to resolve disputes and defuse tensions.

Some of the secret Israeli raids were organized as reprisals for Arab infiltrations or acts of violence because about seven hundred thousand Palestinian Arabs had fled their ancestral homes—many under Israeli coercion—and it was inevitable that some would try to return. The refugees were living in squalid camps in Jordan, Lebanon, and Syria with little food or shelter. From across the frontier, they watched Israelis take over their houses, orchards, and fields. Of those who risked returning, most came to recover property or to harvest crops. But some came to wreak vengeance, and that was a source of fear.

Israeli commandos crossed the borders to commit sabotage, shoot Arabs randomly, and engage in firefights with Arab frontier forces, all to deter the refugees from trying to return. Though these incursions were violations, Ben-Gurion and the most militant commanders in the army believed that the Arabs understood only force. Further, the Israeli army believed that the armistice lines could be changed to improve Israel's position before they became internationally recognized borders.

The Israeli army had managed to seize 78 percent of the territory of the British Mandate as it existed in 1947, but the slender reed of Israel the country—merely nine miles wide just north of Tel Aviv—was far less than what Ben-Gurion believed was needed to support a modern state. No one in the Middle East, least of all Ben-Gurion, believed that the war with the Arabs was over. There would be a second round. He was counting on it.

So was Pinhas Lavon, who at fifty-six saw himself as a leading contender to succeed Ben-Gurion notwithstanding Sharett's seniority in the party. Lavon, born in 1904 in Galicia, studied law at the University of Lvov (in present-day Ukraine) and, with Ben-Gurion and the other leading lights of the Jewish Agency, had built the Mapai Party through years of toil as a grassroots organizer in the Histradut, the Zionist federation of factory and agricultural workers. Lavon had Bogart good looks, bureaucratic skills, and political ambition that put him in contention for higher office, though he lacked the long experience in international affairs that buoyed Sharett's prospects. If Lavon's views on military affairs were known at all, he seemed a moderate figure who had left defense policy to Ben-Gurion.[6]

But when Ben-Gurion appointed Lavon minister of defense in late 1953—at the outset of Ben-Gurion's so-called retirement—Lavon changed; he discovered an inner ferocity. Ben-Gurion had handed him an opportunity to play the role of the man in charge of national security and thereby a chance to pull even with Sharett in the succession sweepstakes. As defense minister, Lavon's stature rivaled that of Dayan, whom many believed Ben-Gurion was grooming as an insurgent candidate for prime minister—a means to bypass the old guard of the party.

In pushing Lavon's appointment through the cabinet, Ben-Gurion, the master manipulator, awakened Lavon's ambition, and the former mild-mannered apparatchik suddenly presented himself to colleagues as the new strongman of Zionist expansion.

Soon after taking office, he shocked his fellow ministers by announcing that his goal was to set the Middle East "on fire" with conflict. His theory was that Israel would profit from serial warfare because the Arab governments were uniformly weak. Any government collapse in Cairo, Damascus,

Beirut, or Amman could be exploited—*should* be exploited, in his view—to expand Israel's frontiers. It was a policy based on mayhem.[7]

Sharett, a veteran diplomat who believed deeply in the new international conventions to prevent war and resolve conflicts, realized that he was up against a wild man in Lavon. The notion of setting the Middle East on fire was repugnant to Sharett, whose strategy for the Zionist state was accommodation with the Arabs.[8] As a boy, Sharett had lived among the Arabs near Ramallah on the West Bank, and then in Jaffa, the old Arab port south of Tel Aviv. He spoke Arabic, and his Zionism—his ambition for a Jewish state and homeland—was suffused with humanist precepts about coexistence.

But Sharett was less in charge than he perceived. Lavon acted as if the Defense Ministry, the army, and the military intelligence service were his exclusive domain. He struggled competitively with Dayan and with Shimon Peres, the young director general of the Defense Ministry whom Ben-Gurion had put in place as his eyes and ears. Lavon went around Dayan by dealing directly with senior generals and he cut Peres out of key decisions on tank purchases from France, where Peres had invested great energy.

The one thing that bound Lavon, Dayan, and Peres together, however, was a deep disdain for Sharett, whom they regarded as a weak sister lacking the credentials to oversee the military and security establishments.

Under the direction of Lavon and Dayan, Israeli commando forces crossed borders and blew up Arab villages, set ambushes, laid mines, and assassinated suspected infiltrators. Their "activist" strategy—that was their euphemism for the new militarism—was popular among Israelis who wanted to strike back every time the newspaper headlines announced that a Jew had been killed or shot at in the border regions. It was especially popular with the right-wing parties, whose members were adamant that Israel become strong enough to seize the whole of biblical Israel.

In the Tripartite Declaration of 1950, the United States, Britain, and France had opposed "the use of force or threat of force" between any of the Middle Eastern states, and, as members of the United Nations, they recognized their obligation to take action to prevent such violations. They condemned Israel's raids as uniformly disproportionate and destabilizing. As a result, in Western capitals, Ben-Gurion was the face of Israeli aggression.

Ben-Gurion had formally returned to government in early 1955 because, despite all of Sharett's efforts to conduct peaceful diplomacy, Lavon had detonated like a time bomb. Within months of his takeover, Lavon embroiled Israel in a major espionage flap in Egypt, which the government dared not acknowledge and which led to the execution of Israeli agents in Cairo in January 1955.

Israel's military intelligence chiefs, with Lavon's encouragement, planning, and approval—though the question of whether he gave a final order to proceed became a matter of lengthy dispute—had activated a network of operatives in Egypt to bomb targets in Cairo and Alexandria where American and British citizens gathered, such as cinemas and libraries. The goal of this scheme of sabotage and terror was to make Nasser's regime look unstable and force Britain to reconsider withdrawing its troops from Egypt. Those troops—eighty thousand of them encamped along the Suez Canal—provided a buffer for Israel against any aggressive move by the Egyptian army, the largest in the Middle East.

Israel's covert operation went awry. No Americans or Britons were killed. Shockingly for the Israeli high command, most members of the Israeli military intelligence team were arrested after Philip Natanson, one of the agents, set his clothing on fire (his explosive device ignited in his pocket). Natanson came running out of a movie theater in agony, and Egyptian police, already on alert, arrested him. Under interrogation and torture, he gave up the rest of the team, whose leader, Avri El-ad, had fled to Europe, an act that prompted Mossad chief Isser Harel to conclude that he had been a double agent all along.[9]

The scandal of Israel's terror campaign against Americans and Britons would have undermined Western support for the Jewish state. That is what made it so sensitive during the twenty years in which it remained a state secret, censored in the Israeli press. Sharett's government, meaning Meir and Eshkol and other ministers, felt they had no choice but to cover it up. Lavon threatened to commit suicide if the cabinet fired him, and it took weeks to negotiate his removal from office because ministers insisted on extracting a pledge that he would not embarrass the cabinet by taking his own life.

The Israeli public did not learn the truth for many years. The incident was referred to in the newspapers as "the mishap." But the terrible reality for Sharett was that Nasser dragged the "Jewish spies" before a military court that convicted them. Two were sentenced to the gallows.

Sharett could do nothing to save those who were thrown into prison or put to death. One female agent committed suicide after torture. Nasser was going to hang Jews. Sharett was forced to lie publicly, protesting the innocence of Israeli saboteurs to an Israeli public fraught with anger and demands for retribution.

This was the tawdry state of affairs when Sharett, in a moment he almost immediately regretted, responded positively to a suggestion from his cabinet that Ben-Gurion be asked to return to government to replace Lavon. With Mapai facing elections in the summer of 1955, Ben-Gurion agreed to come back from his retreat at the Sde Boker kibbutz in the Negev to serve in Sharett's cabinet, but everyone knew that it would be impossible for the older man to play a subordinate role to Sharett after twenty years leading the Zionist movement. And needless to say, Ben-Gurion had no intention of doing so.

In his first week back in February 1955, Ben-Gurion went on the attack. He and Dayan had planned their first move in a tight circle, tapping Sharon to lead an assault and excluding Sharett from all but a vague understanding of what was going on. The plan was to invade the Gaza Strip and to destroy the Egyptian military garrison. Two companies of Israeli paratroopers under Sharon's command shot their way into Gaza City. They laid siege to Nasser's military headquarters and the train station. They engaged in running battles into the evening. By midnight, when the force was ordered to withdraw, the Egyptian base was burning and in ruins. Thirty-eight Egyptian soldiers lay dead, with as many wounded. Eight Israeli paratroopers were among the dead. The ostensible pretext for this military engagement, the largest since the armistice, was the death of a single Israeli who was shot down by an Egyptian intelligence squad that had penetrated the Negev.[10]

The Gaza raid, which the Israeli military called Operation Black Arrow, was a turning point in the Middle East. It sent out a new and bellicose message from Ben-Gurion that he was back and that he preferred war to compromise. The military and its sabra spirit were behind him. The raid locked Israel into an inexorable cycle of escalation. The *New York Times* called it an "overt invasion" and a "ghastly mistake." The newspaper said, "This is precisely the way to alienate world opinion and also to unify the Arab states" in an anti-Israel alliance. "Furthermore, it is taking the inexcusable risk and the onus of setting off the spark of open war in a region that needs peace more than anything else it needs on earth."[11] The *Times* made reference to the hangings in Cairo, but unaware of the truth behind the charges, the newspaper suggested that the executions were not based on any judicial finding of fact but rather on a "political" decision.

Ben-Gurion's aggressive stance was wildly popular at home, fueled as it was by the public anger over the hangings in Cairo. The sabras in the military and throughout the country cheered Ben-Gurion's "activism"; so did the immigrants living in camps on the frontier exposed to the Arabs.

The Gaza raid wrecked the plans of the great powers to impose a new peace in the Middle East. President Eisenhower and British prime minister Anthony Eden had formulated a set of compromises—Project Alpha, they called it—that would require Israel to accept the return of Arab refugees and to give up a wedge of the Negev Desert so as to reconnect the Arab world, which had been split in half by Israel's creation.[12]

Only Ben-Gurion and Sharett and a few others knew of Project Alpha and its threat to hive off part of the Jewish state. The difference between the two men was that Ben-Gurion was prepared to go to war to explode the plans of the great powers. Nasser was hanging Jews in Cairo, and the public believed they were innocent. What better time to attack and throw Nasser off balance and destroy any chance that Project Alpha could succeed?

Ben-Gurion's Gaza assault also wrecked the most promising diplomacy with an Arab state since Israel's founding: Sharett, with the help of the CIA, had opened a secret channel to Nasser. With encouragement from the Eisenhower administration and with logistical support from the CIA, Sharett had exchanged messages with the Egyptian leader; they had agreed to appoint high-level emissaries for talks that Sharett believed might lead to a reduction of tension on the border and, eventually, peace negotiations.

For Nasser, it was a significant risk. He told CIA officials that he would become a target for assassination by his own people if word leaked out that he was in secret talks with the Zionists. Yet he saw in Sharett a potential partner. They had exchanged proposals on gestures each might make, such as allowing Israeli-flag vessels to transit the Suez Canal (a step that would recognize Israel's legitimacy), purchasing Egyptian cotton, lobbying for aid to Egypt in Washington, and curtailing border violence.

It is impossible to say whether the promising back-channel contacts that Sharett and Nasser had initiated the year before might have led to a different and more peaceful future, but it is unmistakable that the carnage that Ben-Gurion inflicted on Egyptian forces that winter profoundly affected Nasser's outlook. Indeed, Egypt's search for a major arms supplier in the Soviet camp began in the immediate aftermath of the assault on Gaza.[13]

Facing the international fury, Ben-Gurion seemed buoyed by new energy. He wasn't oblivious of the negative world opinion about Israel's excessive use of force, but he knew that he had delivered a lethal blow to Eisenhower's and Eden's plans to redraw the map of the region; he also knew the great powers were loath to act against Israel, most of all the United States, where five million Jews and millions of other admirers of the Zionist enterprise functioned like a political shock absorber.

So Ben-Gurion ignored the criticism. "This will be a fighting generation," he had boasted to his military assistant after the Gaza raid. To his colleagues in the government and in the leadership of the ruling party, Mapai, the aging leader had been arguing that there was a window of opportunity for Israel to profit from weakness and disarray in the Arab world—a chance to seize more land and strengthen the Jewish state. He denounced Sharett's moderate approach to the Arabs as cowardly. Sharett bristled at the criticism from the militants. After all, Sharett had embraced the new international order of Eisenhower, John Foster Dulles, and the United Nations following the two most destructive wars in history. The new order stood for conflict resolution by means other than war; it stood for negotiation and compromise. Statehood, as far as Sharett was concerned, required Israel to align its policies with those of the great powers and with the new UN Charter, and central to the charter was the inadmissibility of conquest as a means to resolve disputes.

But Ben-Gurion believed in Zionist exceptionalism, and so he and the youthful sabra military establishment stood to fight.

What motivated them? For the sabras the answer was less intellectual than visceral. They had grown up on the land; they had built a competent army beyond anyone's expectation, and their victory in 1948 propelled them to greater military ambition. Yet Ben-Gurion, a highly developed intellectual who had lived through a century of war and the internal battles of the Zionist movement, seemed motivated by a personal ideology that had been hardened significantly by the Nazi onslaught against European Jews. At minimum, he had succumbed to an innate fear that the catastrophe could be repeated and, therefore, the best defense was a large and well-armed state and a highly mobilized populace. Both were essential to keep the Arabs at bay while Israel acquired the land and water resources it needed. Ben-Gurion's worldview had migrated toward that of his intellectual rival, Vladimir (Ze'ev) Jabotinsky, whose iron-wall philosophy had urged Jewish pioneers to abandon their romantic notions that the Arabs of Palestine would welcome their return to the Holy Land. In a series of essays in 1923, Jabotinsky pointed out that no indigenous people had ever welcomed an invasion, however peaceful.[14]

The father of right-wing Israeli politics, Jabotinsky predicted a long conflict with the Arabs that would end only when the Arabs understood that the iron wall of Israeli defenses could never be breached or defeated. Only then would the Arabs sue for peace.

But thirty years after Jabotinsky's seminal work, Ben-Gurion's vision had expanded to take in a broader perspective of the Zionist state not imagined in Jabotinsky's time. With the advent of the cold war, Ben-Gurion saw that an Israeli declaration of loyalty to the West could transform Israel's status from that of a marginal state outmatched by the influence of thirty million Arabs to a higher, strategic plane as an indispensable ally of the United States and the victorious European powers already engaged in a cold war with the Soviet Union. Indeed, Ben-Gurion made such a declaration of loyalty to CIA director Walter Bedell Smith during a visit to Washington in 1951. Israel, he told the American official, "would pull our weight" in the worldwide struggle against Soviet power.[15] In 1956, he conveyed to the French leadership a willingness to conduct joint, clandestine warfare against Nasser's growing influence in the Middle East.

Thus Israel's natural affinity with millions of Jews in the Americas and Europe created an opportunity for the Jewish state to aspire to a transcendent status: inclusion in the Western camp. Ben-Gurion began to imagine a larger and more powerful Jewish state, one that was more scientifically advanced than many European states and that was integrated with the West economically, technologically, and militarily. In this sense, he reached past Jabotinsky's world; he extended Zionism beyond the romantic vision of its founders, beyond the kibbutznik dream of an agricultural nation ensconced in a Middle Eastern federation with the Arabs.

Moshe Dayan lived and walked the landscape of the Old Testament in awe not of its spiritual narrative but of its martial and human drama.

Most people looked for God in the Bible; to Dayan, the Bible was a text-book, a guide to war, to the battlefields of the ancients, to the vanities, the romances, and the treachery that pervaded the patriarchal clans out of which kings arose—Solomon, Saul, and David.

Self-taught in the topography of war and conflict, Dayan, like most of the sabras of his generation, grew up wholly without the influence of Jewish faith but in the grip of Jewish history nonetheless.

"The patriarchs were independent beings who walked alone," Dayan wrote, and that image became the inspiration for his own life, a life devoted to war and military preparation but ruined for politics by a loner's deep psychological disdain for the diplomatic arts and, as time went on, by a compulsion for his own narcissistic passions: the pursuit of women, money, and antiquities.

Indeed, it was on the flight back from France, rushing to reach Ben-Gurion's side, where Dayan met the Polish-born beauty Rahel, with whom he carried on a public affair for nearly twenty years at the sufferance of Ruth Dayan, the pioneer whom he had married in youth when his greatest ambition was to be a successful farmer and father.

To Ben-Gurion, Dayan was a thing of beauty. Nearly thirty years separated the two men. Dayan's life personified the sabra ethos of tough and practical realism, impervious to criticism. His generation was marked by an ascetic lifestyle, a sensual connection to the land, an idealized self-reliance, and a language that was blunt and spare as if chiseled in the native stone. Dayan was born near the Sea of Galilee but grew up in the Jezreel Valley—that fertile swath that traverses northern Israel—on a farming cooperative called Nahalal. Seen from the air, Nahalal was laid out in a giant circle of greenery, its fields bounded by footpaths that radiated as spokes of a wheel from the hub of the village. There was never enough rain. Harsh winds raked the fields, and the dust sent up an eternal haze. Money was scarce and the cycle of farmwork was brutal. The village design aided defense as the farmers lived in close quarters with their fields, which served as a buffer against Arab marauders. Sabras learned to fight with their fists and, if need be, with a hoe, a rake, or a knife.

The rank poverty of farming life and the conflict with the Arabs, who brandished weapons against the Israelis over land and grazing rights, shaped the adolescent Dayan. During the decade of Arab rebellion in the 1930s, he became a scout, a fighter, and a strategist against the intimate enemy.

Of the Arabs, he wrote, "They would brazenly bring their herds into the cultivated fields among the crops and fodder." The young men of Nahalal would set upon them in wild fistfights. "They were rough fighters and used stones and knives," but as often as not the Arabs would just flee on their camels, leaving younger brothers to steer their herds to safety. Dayan and his comrades would give chase on horseback, beating and humiliating the ones they captured. "There was sheer artistry in the way they fled," Dayan wrote. "They would first prod the camel to get it going, and mount it while it was on the move by first jumping on its neck and then crawling on to its hump; or they would seize one of its hind legs, get a grip on its protruding kneecap with their bare toes, and haul themselves up by their finger nails on to the back of the galloping beast."[16]

Dayan's self-image was that of a rough-hewn farm boy who excelled at combat, and although his military career would open the world to him, his life and outlook were imprinted by the horizons of that valley where the Carmel Ridge runs to Haifa in the west, the Hills of Moreh rise modestly beneath Mount Tabor in the east. And in the near distance, the path at the village end leads to Tel Shimron, the ancient knob where Nahalal's families buried their dead.

When the Arabs of Palestine revolted against Jewish immigration in the mid-1930s, the teenage Dayan—recruited as a guide for British military units—observed at close quarters how an imperial power imposed its will on a restive population. The British assigned him to a Yorkshire Rifles battalion protecting the Iraq petroleum pipeline, which crossed Palestine to reach British tankers in the Mediterranean. Dayan wrote as if he were repulsed by the arrogance and tactics of a great power, but these tactics, too, were imprinted on him.

"They moved in noisy armored cars, and when they waited in ambush, they smoked and cursed," allowing the Arabs to slip past them. The balding British commander, a heavy drinker with brass-colored whiskers, instructed Dayan to present an ultimatum to an Arab chieftain. "Tell the bastard that if there is further sabotage of the pipelines, I'll blow up his house; and if the sabotage is repeated, I'll go on blowing up the rest of the houses of the village."

That night, the pipeline was torched again. The next morning, the British troops blew up the headman's house. To Dayan's suggestion that the Yorkshire Rifles acquire more stealthy tactics, the commander retorted, "I did not come here to teach British soldiers how to crawl in your bloody country. I am here to teach the bloody Arabs how the British operate."[17]

There is a photograph in the Israeli military archives from 1938 of Moshe Dayan and Yigal Allon standing on either side of the Haganah's field commander, Yitzhak Sadeh, a veteran of the Russian army.[18] The young men exude energy, self-confidence, and ambition. Allon went on to command the Palmach, clashing with Ben-Gurion over strategy in 1948 and giving allegiance to Ben-Gurion's political rivals in the Mapam, the left wing of the labor movement. Dayan, on the other hand, devoted himself to Ben-Gurion and to Mapai. He joined the party and became chief of staff of the army. His rivalry with Allon carried over decades, but it arose in the adrenaline of youth.

Dayan's parents had come from Ukraine, like many others in flight from persecution, and in a single generation, they produced offspring who were less worldly, less educated, but fiercely attached to their fields and livestock, the things that sustained their lives. Their world was small and brutal, and their outlook was in the main pessimistic because they, too, foresaw a long conflict with the Arabs.

"There was no God in our lives to pray to," wrote Dayan's daughter, Yaël, in a memoir. "By nature and upbringing, my father was a patriarch. He didn't mind who was in the kitchen, as long as somebody was there, and he didn't resent the idea of women working at anything. He wasn't concerned with questions of equality and took it for granted that the last word would be his."[19]

Dayan identified with biblical heroes, but he evaluated their lives as a realist and a cynic. He relished the story in the Book of Samuel of young David's mercenary instincts in negotiating a king's ransom for slaying the lumbering Philistine, Goliath; he marveled at the contradictions of Samson, a Hebrew warrior who slew, with the jawbone of an ass, a thousand men from the army of Gaza. Yet Samson was "ambivalent" about his enemy, rushing to "pay court to a harlot in Gaza" after "smiting" her kinsmen on the battlefield. And when Delilah's treachery brought Samson low—

his eyes plucked out, his head shorn, and his back bent in slavery at his enemy's granary—he prayed to God "that I may be at once avenged." He stood between the pillars of their temple and cried out in a suicidal rage, "Let me die with the Philistines!" and in the moment pulled down the house on the lords of his enemy. "So the dead which he slew at his death were more than they which he slew in his life" (Judges 16:30).[20]

In Dayan's world, survival was a matter of strength and guile, and these qualities, along with his thirst for combat, drew him into the Jewish militias that formed during World War II and became the core of the Israeli army. In 1941, Dayan slipped into Lebanon as part of the flanking forces supporting the Allied invasion of Syria. Up against the Vichy French, he scouted enemy gun emplacements for Australian soldiers and, while peering through binoculars, he attracted a bullet that smashed through the eyepiece. The fragments destroyed his left eye and splintered the socket. The injury marked his life with pain and fretful reconstructive surgeries that left him with the black slash of an eye patch across his sharp, avian features.

As in everything, Dayan resorted to cynicism about his injury. He bragged that he needed only one good eye to shoot straight, and he once told a policeman who pulled him over for speeding, "I have only one eye. Do you want me to look at the road or at the speedometer?"[21] In truth, he hated the patch and pulled it off as soon as he reached home at the end of the day. Yet it made Dayan instantly recognizable around the world. Together with what seemed a perpetual Dayan sneer, his was the face of Israeli military cunning.

Ben-Gurion had spotted him early. Dayan came from a political family and, when it came to military affairs or strategy, insights flew out of Dayan like switchblades.

The older man was in love with the idea of youth, of young sabras building the Hebrew state, but Ben-Gurion was foremost a political man, and he used them to weaken the Mapai old guard and to perpetuate his own rule.

For Dayan, Ben-Gurion, too, was like a biblical figure. As an architect and a visionary, there was no one like him, or no one left like him. What Ben-Gurion and he shared was an ethnocentric outlook: the Jews were on the land, heavily armed and protected by an undefeated army; let the great powers say what they will. They shared a basic pessimism about the long war, a pessimism that did not extinguish hope or opportunism but girded the senses for the violence that enveloped their lives and bolstered morale in a culture of militancy.

Dayan had never stopped fighting the War of 1948 despite the armistice, which he termed "transitory."

"For a long time we thought we could redraw the armistice lines with lower-scale operations than full-fledged war," he explained years later in a moment of exceptional candor. "In other words, capture a piece of land and hold on to it until the enemy gives up."[22]

The victory over the Arabs in 1948 also had a psychological effect.

"It [the victory] seemed to show the advantages of direct action over negotiation and diplomacy," wrote Nahum Goldmann, the World Zionist Organization chief.[23] After all, the Jews had vanquished the armies of their enemies for the first time in two thousand years. They had triumphed, unexpectedly, in the face of the Arabs' numerical superiority. The psychological impact was pronounced and was especially reflected in the vernacular of the right wing, where one leader who had emerged from the Jewish underground, Menachem Begin, emblazoned his version of the historical exegesis with heroic prose: "Out of blood and fire and tears and ashes a new specimen of human being was born, a specimen completely unknown to the world for over eighteen hundred years, 'the Fighting Jew.' "[24]

The sabra generation looked with discomfort and more than a little contempt at the remnant of European Jewry, the Holocaust survivors who had refused to flee or fight in Europe and who allowed themselves to be led to slaughter.

There were nonsabras, such as Shimon Peres, who spent much of their lives trying to overcome personal histories that left them out of sync with the pioneering core of the country. Born Szymon Perski in Poland in 1923, Peres immigrated to Palestine with his family in 1934, and in the following years, when Dayan and many of his cohorts were fighting Arabs or scouting for the British army, Peres stayed in school, joining the Working Youth of the Mapai. Peres had none of the grit or chiseled features of the sabras. His sweeping brow and aquiline nose conjured a pompous visage accentuated by an equally pompous manner of speech. He was a linguist and an intellectual who exhaled European sophistication. But he lacked personal courage and wilted at the notion of combat. During a climbing outing to Masada near the Dead Sea, he suffered a panic attack during a fall that left him with an intense fear of heights.[25]

In Israel's small society, Peres had caught Ben-Gurion's attention as a talented propagandist. Peres and a group of scouts had made a trek through the Negev in early 1945, and when they returned, Peres rendered a photo album for Ben-Gurion, documenting how the scouts had nearly reached Eilat, proclaiming a kind of manifest destiny over the sandy expanse that Israel conquered three years later in war.

The following year, in December 1946, Ben-Gurion sent Dayan, then thirty-one, and Peres, twenty-three, to the Twenty-second Zionist Congress in Basel, Switzerland. Dayan was already a military veteran who had seen the inside of a British prison and lost an eye, whereas Peres was a service-avoiding neophyte writing flattery and heroic Zionist prose for the party organs.

It took Dayan two days to get back from his vacation in France to Jerusalem, and when he reached Ben-Gurion's bedside, the older man was still profoundly agitated about the news from Egypt. Sharett had departed for Paris to negotiate the purchase of Israel's first modern jet fighters from the French, but before he departed Sharett had made it clear that he opposed an "initiated war" by Israel.[26]

Propped up in bed, Ben-Gurion told Dayan that Israel could not just attack Egypt out of the blue. He, too, was not in favor of an initiated war. They would need a pretext. Nasser's troops were shooting across the border every day, and the shooting had gotten more intense since the February assault into Gaza. Nasser was sending fedayeen ("self-sacrificers") guerrillas over the line to murder and maim. A pretext was taking shape. All they had to do was respond with increasingly large-scale attacks and then escalate to full-scale war.

The immediate goal of the campaign would be to seize the demilitarized zones on the Egyptian frontier in the south and then to move rapidly into the Sinai Peninsula to secure the Strait of Tiran and the Egyptian shore of Sinai along the Gulf of Aqaba. All this was to be prepared so that the moment Ben-Gurion reentered the prime minister's office, Israel would be ready to strike.

Ben-Gurion had come back to government with another vision: Israel as an atomic power. The scientific effort, led by the German-born chemist Ernst Bergmann and Peres, who was serving as director general of the Defense Ministry, was so secret that Ben-Gurion made only oblique references to it in his diary. "It may be that our ultimate security would rest on [science]. But I will not talk about it any further. This could be the last thing that may save us."[27]

Ben-Gurion's intellectual ferment had begun in May 1953. That spring, he began talking openly about his desire to withdraw from public life "for a few years." In truth, he was exhausted. His Ménière's disease induced spells of dizziness. But worse, his political fortunes were sinking. Sharett and the Mapai "old guard" referred to him as "a spent force." The achievement of 1948 had faded. Jewish immigration was falling off rapidly as the realities of nation building had sunk in: repetitive and backbreaking work across waterless vistas of stony, unyielding earth.

Ben-Gurion understood that politics was corrosive; no leader was immune to popular disaffection and leader fatigue. He abruptly announced that he was taking a long vacation in July. Levi Eshkol observed that the older man was in search of a stand-in who could take the heat while Ben-Gurion rested on the sidelines. "Why should I be the guilty party from whose clutches Ben-Gurion will save the country when he returns?" he asked his colleagues.[28] The Mapai leaders nominated Sharett as acting prime minister, disregarding the fact that Ben-Gurion had criticized Sharett's judgment and had insisted that Eshkol, an agronomist who had little worldly experience, was more qualified. Golda Meir called Sharett "the obvious heir," no doubt infuriating her mentor. But Lavon, with Ben-Gurion's encouragement, enthusiastically accepted the Defense Ministry.

In such a small country and in such a small leadership circle, everything was personal, and so when Ben-Gurion withheld Defense from Sharett that summer, giving it to the untested Lavon, it was Ben-Gurion's way of saying that he did not see Sharett as having that combination of political *and* military acumen necessary to lead the country.

Ben-Gurion had said to Nahum Goldmann something that was really directed at Sharett: "The difference between you and me is that I never shrank from giving orders which I knew would mean the death of hundreds of wonderful young men. You would probably have hesitated. And therefore, I can lead a people in war time. You could not." Sharett would have agreed with Goldmann's retort: "You are right, but maybe I could better prevent a war than you, which is still more important."[29]

Sharett took Ben-Gurion's disparagement in stride as just another slight from the man to whom fate had bound him in the Zionist cause. Ben-Gurion and Sharett had worked together for thirty years, but the relationship was complex, and not just because Sharett was eight years younger and subordinate in the hierarchy of the movement (Ben-Gurion was chairman of the Jewish Agency and Sharett headed the political department). More important, there was a broad psychological difference: "I am quiet, reserved, careful," Sharett observed. "Ben-Gurion is impulsive, impetuous, and intuitive. My capital C is Caution; Ben-Gurion's capital C is Courage."[30] But even this description was a gloss on the deeper conflict.

Goldmann best captured the contradictions of Ben-Gurion's character: "The dominant force in Ben-Gurion is his will for power, but not in the banal sense, that is, not power for personal advantage. In this respect he is above reproach. I mean power in the sense of wanting to enforce what he believes to be right, of ruthlessness in pursuing his goals," he wrote in his memoir.[31]

Sharett had mediated the great struggle between Ben-Gurion and Chaim Weizmann, the European Zionist leader, during the crucial years of the world war, when the Zionist dilemma was how to make the transition from supporting the Allied effort against Germany to a postwar goal of declaring Jewish statehood in confrontation with the British.

Weizmann put his faith in British diplomacy. Ben-Gurion did not, and it was during the war that his militancy intensified as the reports of mass extermination of Jews began filtering in from Europe in 1942. Ben-Gurion pushed through the Biltmore Program—named for the meeting at the Biltmore Hotel in New York—that committed the Zionist movement to setting up a state in Palestine even if that meant a violent break with the British and even if the Jews did not get the whole of the biblical Land of Israel.

Weizmann tried to hold Ben-Gurion in check, and the two men clashed in 1943. Sharett aligned himself with Weizmann's diplomatic approach. Ben-Gurion exploded with recrimination and sulked for months. Sharett later told family members that the Weizmann–Ben-Gurion struggle had inflicted a deep wound in his, Sharett's, relationship with Ben-Gurion. Like a cracked crystal vessel, it would never be the same. "[The vessel] remained usable as before, but the crack, an irreparable one, remained."[32] The two men were barely on speaking terms until Ben-Gurion returned to head the Jewish Agency again in 1944.

Weizmann's political base—European Jewry—was all but extinguished.

The war had shifted the center of gravity of the movement to Palestine, where Ben-Gurion was in charge. He had bested all of his rivals. He had co-opted or outmaneuvered fellow travelers from the Socialist camp such as Yitzhak Tabenkin, who leaned toward Moscow's orbit; he had humiliated Menachem Begin, the right-wing underground leader, by shooting up the *Altalena*, the arms supply ship that Begin had landed on Tel Aviv's beach. He had outlived Jabotinsky, Begin's mentor, and Chaim Arlosoroff, the brilliant political strategist of the Jewish Agency, who was murdered in what appeared to be a political assassination on Tel Aviv's waterfront one night in 1933. (Right-wing extremists were suspected.)

Sharett and Ben-Gurion clashed repeatedly in the first years. Sharett was more attuned to great-power diplomacy in the postwar environment. Israel's membership in the United Nations required the abandonment of brute force, which had marked the colonial era. Sharett was deeply committed to normalization of relations with the Arab states. Ben-Gurion was not.

Nonetheless, the Foreign Ministry under Sharett was a hive of diplomatic initiative. And though the differences between Sharett and Ben-Gurion were stark, they both possessed that political gene for collaborative tension, the ability to carry on notwithstanding their profound disagreement.

In the wake of the 1948 victory, Israel faced a cascade of Arab infiltration across the armistice lines. The vast majority—90 percent or more—were desperate civilians seeking to recover homes, property, or crops.[33] Ben-Gurion feared that without a brutal policy on the border, the Arabs would simply return, first as a trickle, then as a flood. Throughout 1950, the Israeli army rounded up Arabs in villages and towns and pushed them across the frontier, but even this was not enough. Soon the IDF escalated the assault, issuing shoot-to-kill orders against returning Arabs along the frontier, mining pathways, and carrying out large-scale cross-border strikes to deter infiltration.[34] To the sabras, these cruel actions were a somber requirement for their generation, and they had to be willing to absorb the world's condemnation without being deflected from the task. Dayan was a leading advocate for roundups and expulsions and, in May 1950, his troops marched 120 Arab infiltrators into the blistering Wadi Arava, firing guns over their heads to make them run and forcing them to walk dozens of miles into Jordan on foot, without food or water. A quarter of them died from dehydration in the scorching wasteland.[35]

When the Jordanians found the survivors, their story set off broad condemnation of the Jewish state. Dayan was called before the cabinet, where Sharett lectured him about Israel's moral standing in the world. Dayan stood defiantly, in effect daring Sharett to say that the army did not have the right to shoot Arabs who crossed the border.

"We shoot at those from among the 200,000 hungry Arabs who cross the line—will this stand up to moral review?" he asked. "Arabs cross to collect the grain that they left in the abandoned villages and we set mines for them and they go back without an arm or a leg." Such brutal facts might not measure up on Sharett's moral yardstick, "but I know of no other method of guarding the borders," Dayan said. "If the Arab shepherds and harvesters are allowed to cross the borders, then tomorrow the State of Israel will have no borders."[36] This was sabra dictum.

In his early years, Dayan mistrusted diplomacy and despised Sharett for pursuing secret contacts with Arab leaders even though these contacts had raised hopes for a modus vivendi with the Arab world.

In 1948, King Farouk had signaled that Egypt would be willing to reach a peace settlement with the Jewish state in exchange for an Arab corridor through the Negev that would reconnect the two halves of the Arab world. Farouk sent a senior court official, Kamal Riad, to Paris to meet with Elias Sasson, Israel's specialist on Arab affairs in the Foreign Ministry. Sasson drafted a peace treaty, which Riad passed to Cairo. Sharett was ready to enter negotiations, but Ben-Gurion remonstrated, refusing to bring the proposal before the cabinet as he plotted with Israel's military chiefs to attack the Egyptian army in early 1949 and drive it out of the Negev altogether.[37]

In 1949, Syria's military strongman Colonel Husni al-Za'im, who had taken power in a bloodless coup, startled the region by proposing that instead of an armistice with Israel to end the fighting, he was ready to conclude a full peace that would include an exchange of ambassadors, open borders, and trade relations. Za'im proved to be a remarkable leader: a member of Syria's Kurdish minority who promoted voting rights for women. American diplomats in Damascus encouraged him to extend his hand to Israel. Za'im responded that he was ready for a personal meeting with Ben-Gurion and made a remarkably generous offer to solve half of the

Palestinian refugee problem by settling at least three hundred thousand of them in northern Syria with Western help. In return, he asked for a share of the Sea of Galilee and the Jordan River.

Ben-Gurion told his negotiators to reject Za'im's offer, demanding that Za'im first sign the armistice that recognized the international border. But Za'im persisted, reiterating his offer through a secret United Nations channel. When Sharett brought the proposal to the cabinet on May 24, he described it as an important breakthrough. But Ben-Gurion would have none of it; he warned of a diplomatic trap and preempted the overture with a letter to the top UN mediator, Ralph Bunche, insisting that Syria first withdraw to the prewar lines.[38]

Israel signed an armistice agreement with Syria on July 20, 1949. It proved to be one of the weakest of the cease-fire instruments. Za'im, for his efforts, was overthrown and executed in another military coup.

Of all the Arab leaders, King Abdullah of Jordan was the most inclined toward an accommodation with Israel, and he carried on secret negotiations with the Jewish state from 1947 to 1951. He had met secretly with Golda Meir in November 1947 to apprise the Jewish Agency leadership that he planned to send Jordan's army, the Arab Legion, across the Jordan River to occupy the West Bank. The king aimed to annex the Arab portion of the West Bank and thus expand his realm to Jerusalem, where he could displace the grand mufti as the protector of the Old City and the Haram al-Sharif, or Noble Sanctuary, the thirty-five-acre central plaza on which stand the Dome of the Rock and the al-Aqsa mosque. This plaza is also sacred to Jews as the Temple Mount, the site of ancient synagogues dating to King Solomon's time. The plaza is girded by the Western Wall, part of the Temple foundations that still exist and where Jews write messages or prayers to God and push them into the cracks.

King Abdullah came out of the war a winner. The Arab Legion defeated Israeli attempts to wrest control of East Jerusalem and the Old City. In armistice negotiations, Abdullah, whose kingdom was flooded with Palestinian refugees, raised the price of peace. He demanded the return of cities—Ramle and Lod among them—whose Arab populations had been driven out; he also sought an Arab corridor connecting Jordan to Gaza. Ben-Gurion blew hot and cold on making any deal with Abdullah, and in the event, the Jordanian leader was gunned down by an Arab assassin in July 1951 on the steps of the al-Aqsa mosque.

There was a biblical quality to Ben-Gurion's retreat to the desert in 1953, for this sabbatical was the genesis of Israel's first national military strategy. At the tiny Sde Boker kibbutz, Ben-Gurion wandered for months in the desert, at times in the company of one of the former Stern Gang assassins, Yehoshua Cohen, who had been pardoned for his role in the death of the Swedish diplomat Count Folke Bernadotte.[39]

Ben-Gurion buried himself in books and briefings about national defense and the theory of war. He read voraciously about tactics and armor on the modern battlefield and the advent of atomic weapons; he examined the problems of the Israeli army in detail, meeting frequently with Dayan and the other generals to hear their views. The problems were formidable: half of the army's conscripts were immigrants who didn't know how to fight; Israel was isolated and still surrounded by thirty million Arabs, and the prospects for an alliance with a great power were bleak.

Israel urgently needed an arms supplier, but most fundamentally, it needed a defense concept that would deflect war from the most vulnerable population centers. Israel needed a nimble and lethal army that could strike across borders in retaliation for any attack, and in the event of war, move the battle quickly to the enemy's territory and inflict disproportionate damage so the Arabs would understand that Israel could not be defeated.

At Sde Boker, Ben-Gurion's wife, Paula, complained about the dust. A guard's tent was pitched in front of their modest house because Ben-Gurion was under threat from Jewish extremists for accepting reparations from Germany as a way to finance the urgent requirements of the Jewish state. But during those months, the older man found a new voice of urgency; he came back to warn his colleagues that war was coming and it was imperative that Israel divert its scarce resources to prepare itself.

The synergy between Ben-Gurion and Dayan was crucial during this period. The young general had become a leading proponent of taking any opportunity to strike the Arabs. A "second round" was inevitable, in his view. To the sabra military establishment, it was the government that was lagging. Ben-Gurion and his intelligence chiefs, Harel and Harkabi, had come to the conclusion that the Arabs would attack as soon as their armed forces were up to it, probably in the summer of 1956. The Israeli army needed an overhaul.

Since 1950, a number of small reprisal raids had been poorly executed against the Arabs. Some had resulted in excessive Israeli casualties. In the summer of 1953, Mordechai Makleff, the British-trained chief of staff who preceded Dayan, had come to Ben-Gurion with the idea of creating a secret commando unit staffed by the best soldiers in the army and to use this force against the Arabs.[40]

The proposal echoed the formation of the "night raiders" under the legendary British officer Orde Wingate, a fundamentalist Christian who became a deep believer in the Zionist cause and who trained Jewish commandos in mobile warfare in the late 1930s. Wingate had been a powerful influence on young fighters such as Makleff, Dayan, and Yigal Allon.

Makleff was a tough and seasoned commander, a sabra who as a boy had witnessed the murder of his family when Arab rioters entered a newly established Jewish settlement outside of Jerusalem in 1929. Makleff escaped by jumping out a second-story window. He had served with the British army in World War II and, during the War of Independence, he commanded Israeli forces that conquered the Galilee and secured much of the northern part of the country.

Makleff and Dayan already had in mind a young officer to lead the commando unit: Ariel Scheinerman, a brash and battle-hungry soldier who had fought in the 1948 war. Scheinerman was at that moment on trial in military court for conduct unbecoming an officer; he had slapped and handcuffed a quartermaster who, instead of promptly delivering new boots for Scheinerman's paratroopers, had dallied for an hour with a girlfriend. Dayan had suspended the trial because the army needed more bulldogs like Scheinerman. Known as Arik, the diminutive with which his Russian-speaking mother had addressed him, Scheinerman quickly assembled an irregular force of volunteers from among his friends and comrades with whom he had fought. It was just a couple dozen fighters, and by summer's end they were ready. The army gave them the secret designation of Unit 101.[41]

In August, Ben-Gurion wrote in his diary that "Contrary to Moshe's [Sharett's] opinion . . . , reprisals are imperative. There is no relying for our security on UN observers and foreign states. If we do not put an end to these murders [by infiltrators] now, the situation will get worse."[42]

It did get worse. On October 12, 1953, Arab infiltrators tossed a grenade into a house in the Yehud settlement east of Tel Aviv, killing a young woman, Susan Kanias, and her two infant children. The perpetrators were believed to have come from the village of Qibya on the ridge north of Jerusalem. When the news came, Ben-Gurion, Lavon, Makleff, and Dayan were in the north of the country observing a military exercise near the Sea of Galilee, where Ben-Gurion had been taking a vacation. The four of them agreed that a major reprisal was in order.

Two nights later, Scheinerman's force of twenty-five commandos from Unit 101 and another one hundred paratroopers assigned to him assembled in a forest opposite the border. He loaded twelve hundred pounds of explosives into trucks, enough to level an entire village.

The least-informed person in the leadership was the acting prime minister, Sharett.

On the day the raid was set to launch, the Israeli-Jordanian armistice commission blamed the grenade attack on Arab guerrillas from Jordan. The commander of Jordan's Arab Legion, Sir John Bagot Glubb, pledged to bring the murderers to justice. He appealed to the Israelis to remain calm in the meantime.

That was enough for Sharett. He told Lavon to call off the attack. "I told Lavon that this will be a grave error . . . that it was never proved that reprisal actions served their declared purpose," Sharett wrote in his diary. "The Jordanians were taking observable steps to stop infiltration." But Lavon had "just smiled" and said that Ben-Gurion "didn't share my view."[43]

Sharett felt the sucker punch. Ben-Gurion had gone around him. He had been running security through his protégés and leaving Sharett to deal with the consequences. Sharett dispatched a message to Ben-Gurion saying that he would resign his position if the IDF carried out the attack.

But Ben-Gurion ignored the threat. The raid went forward. Major Scheinerman and his men shot their way into Qibya late at night. They went house to house, shooting occupants and flinging grenades through windows. Then the sappers began setting explosives, destroying house after house in eruptions of smoke, fire, and plumes of dust while machine gunners laid down a steady rain of covering fire. Many villagers had run away, but many were hiding in their homes as the charges were set and blown. Outside the village, Scheinerman had laid an ambush so that Jordanian legionnaires rushing to intervene were cut down. When the night was over, forty-five houses lay in ruin and seventy civilians were dead, most of them women and children. The cry of "massacre" went out.

The airwaves brought the news to Sharett. "I was simply horrified by the description in Radio Ramallah's broadcast of the destruction of the Arab village." He said he had "walked up and down in my room, helpless and utterly depressed by my feeling of impotence."[44]

Ben-Gurion drove in from Galilee for the reckoning. He was brimming with self-assurance. Europe, the United Nations, and America were all in an uproar. The chargé d'affaires and defense attaché from the American embassy had told Sharett that the raid had stunned the Eisenhower administration, where there was already talk of cutting off aid to Israel. The Americans asked pointedly whether Israel would disavow the action, but Sharett evaded the question. How could he tell them he wasn't really in charge?

Before the cabinet, Sharett "condemned the Qibya affair that exposed us in front of the whole world as a gang of blood-thirsty purveyors of large-scale massacres, unconcerned it seems whether such actions may lead to war."[45]

Ben-Gurion disagreed. He demanded the authority to write the government communiqué on the raid, and when the draft reached Sharett's desk, he was astounded by Ben-Gurion's nerve. He had invented the fiction that the army had nothing to do with the raid: rather, the massacre had been carried out by enraged civilians in the border region who had taken justice into their own hands.

"No one in the world will believe such a story and we shall expose ourselves as liars," Sharett told government ministers. But Sharett also balked at telling the Israeli public and the world the truth. No majority in the cabinet favored confessing to a brutal mission carried out against defenseless civilians by a secret army commando unit. The army was sacrosanct. Ben-Gurion's artifice allowed the cabinet to condemn the violence and protect the military establishment.

On October 19, Ben-Gurion's communiqué, which he read out on national radio, informed Israelis and the world that "we've done a thorough investigation and found that no unit, not even the smallest of the IDF's forces, was AWOL from its base on the night of the attack." It was possible, Ben-Gurion continued, "that a group of civilians, tired of the fedayeen's infiltrations, decided to avenge the blood of the fallen. The government of Israel had no part in the action, wishes to distance itself from such actions, and condemns the citizens who took the law into their own hands."[46]

In the cabinet meeting, Ben-Gurion told the ministers that he had not been informed in advance of the Qibya raid—obviously an untruth given that he had presided over the planning in Galilee—but if he had, he said, he would have approved it. Sharett told the leadership of Mapai that he was going to resign as acting prime minister because it was a sham. Ben-Gurion was deceiving both the public and his colleagues.

The Qibya raid created an atmosphere of deception and duplicity in the upper ranks of the military. Hundreds of Israelis, because they participated in the raid, lived near the border, or knew someone who did, understood that Ben-Gurion was lying when he said on national radio that the army had not been involved in the massacre of civilians. In a small society, such news spread rapidly and invested much of the population in perpetuating a blatant falsehood in the name of security, a trait that would become ingrained in sabra culture. Military censors kept the truth out of the newspapers, and Israelis, as they had during the War of Independence, internalized the lie as part of the propaganda of the state.

At first, Major Scheinerman was offended by Ben-Gurion's disavowal. In the midst of the Qibya outcry, Ben-Gurion had summoned the young soldier to his office in Jerusalem. Ben-Gurion surprised him by inquiring whether the men in his unit were politically reliable: Would they take orders and maintain discipline? In other words, were they loyal to Ben-Gurion and the Mapai? Or did they come from the right-wing underground, which might subject them to other pressures? Scheinerman gave him all the assurances he seemed to need.

When he turned to Qibya, Ben-Gurion said, "It doesn't make any real difference about what will be said about Qibya around the world. The important thing is how it will be looked at here in this region. This is going to give us the possibility of living here."[47] Scheinerman felt that he had been indoctrinated into a great enterprise.

"I knew that Ben-Gurion was talking about the years in which we had had no answer to give to terrorism," he later wrote. "But now we had an answer, a unit that would force those who wanted us dead to take notice and think again about what they were doing."[48]

That was the day Ben-Gurion conferred an even greater honor on

Scheinerman: "I think it's time to give you a Hebrew name." He took note that Scheinerman had grown up in Kfar Malal, part of the lush coastal Sharon Plain that runs to the Mediterranean. "You'll be Sharon," Ben-Gurion declared, pleased that he had connected two things he loved: the geography of Israel and brash sabra leadership. Thus Ariel Sharon was baptized by the father of the state.

TWO

The Destruction of Israel's Second Prime Minister

Ben-Gurion returned that fall as a voice from the wilderness—a voice for war—and when the cabinet rejected his call to mobilize Israeli society and undertake a crash modernization of the military, he seethed with indignation, returning week after week to replay his arguments. Then, in December 1953, he abruptly resigned, telling his colleagues he was going back to the Negev to live in retirement at Sde Boker.

The other leaders of the ruling Mapai Party believed that, at last, the political transition to the second generation of leadership was under way.

"His well has gone dry, we should let him go," Sharett told party leaders in a private conference.[1]

The ruling Mapai installed Sharett as prime minister, despite Ben-Gurion's recommendation to the contrary, because if anyone stood against the war agenda, it was Sharett.

But no sooner had Ben-Gurion stalked out than both Lavon and Dayan came to the new prime minister seeking the political authority to go to war.

Lavon and Dayan both saw the 1949 Armistice as transitory. The great powers were pulling out of the Middle East after World War II, or they were being pushed out by new nationalistic movements such as those that were sweeping Egypt, Algeria, and Morocco. It was going to be up to the army to exploit the turmoil to expand Israel's frontiers to take in more water resources and arable farmland.

Dayan, who was a thirty-eight-year-old general when he took over as chief of staff, wanted to send an Israeli flagship into the Gulf of Aqaba to break the Egyptian constriction on Israel's freedom of navigation. If Egypt fired on the vessel, Israeli forces would attack Egyptian bases in Sinai.

Sharett was taken aback. "Do you realize that this would mean war with Egypt?" he asked Dayan.

"Of course," Dayan replied.[2]

They were sitting in Sharett's living room, where Sharett had invited key Mapai ministers to hear the presentation. But Dayan's brazen lust for combat had put them off. Sharett was pleased because he was galvanizing tangible support to get more active on the diplomatic front. Ever since Ben-Gurion had rattled the cabinet with talk of war, all Sharett could think of was how to prevent it. They needed a strategy—perhaps through a grand offer for settlement, a generous proposal to repatriate Arab refugees, or concessions on the borders. All Sharett knew was that diplomacy was a dire necessity because another war would be a disaster in his view.

Here was the essential tension in Israeli political culture: the clash between Sharett's impulse to engage the Arabs and the military establishment's demand to mobilize for continual war. It is impossible to understand the modern state of Israel without first understanding how these two highly developed and opposing views collided during the formative period of the state, and how early Zionist notions of integration and outreach were undermined by a mythology that Israel had no alternative but war.

The Israeli Defense Forces had swelled to 120,000 soldiers during the War of Independence, but demobilization and the urgent requirements of state building had sapped the army's strength, cohesion, and morale. By 1953, the ranks had tumbled to 37,000, with a reserve force, modeled on the citizen army of Switzerland, that was designed to surge to 200,000 troops in a crisis. Dayan wanted a dominant role for the army, but he was losing the argument.[3]

For a brief period, all of the trend lines appeared to be running in Sharett's direction. During Dayan's presentation in Sharett's living room, the prime minister interpreted the expressions of his colleagues as a vote of no confidence for this first display of sabra exuberance for combat. Dayan took his leave.

Within weeks, however, the target shifted to Syria, which appeared increasingly unstable. Left-wing officers overthrew Adib Shishakli, the dictator who had overthrown Husni Za'im. The leader of the coup was a young Colonel Adnan Malki, a member of the Arab Renaissance Party known as the Ba'ath.

Lavon immediately proposed to Sharett that Israel invade Syria and force an accommodation that would give Israel more land, more water, and more security.[4]

Sharett dismissed the notion out of hand. It was time to put away the sword, he lectured. Lavon complained to other ministers that Sharett lacked vision, but the support was not there for a new military adventure.

Surprisingly, the next intervention came directly from Ben-Gurion, in the form of a letter from the desert. The turmoil in Syria, Ben-Gurion wrote to Sharett, created an opening for Israel to strike next door in Lebanon. The Jewish state should ally itself with the Maronite Christian minority that had dominated the central mountain range of Lebanon for centuries. Here was a chance to cultivate a Christian-Jewish alliance and seize Lebanese territory up to the Litani River, a move that would give Israel strategic depth in the north.

The Lebanese right-wing Phalange movement under Pierre Gemayel, the most dynamic of the patriarchal clans in the Christian community, was ripe for an approach and for clandestine collaboration, in Ben-Gurion's view.

Sharett berated Ben-Gurion's flawed thinking: "In the present circumstances in the Middle East, I cannot imagine that a Christian movement . . . will dare to enter into a conflict with the Moslem World by maintaining friendly ties with Israel. On the contrary . . . so long as the other Arab states persevere in their stubborn policy towards Israel, Lebanon will not be able, even under a friendly Christian government, to give concrete expression to its friendly proclivities."[5]

Lebanon was an Arab state. Why would it isolate itself by establishing ties with Israel? Sharett asked. It had no incentive to do so.

The Syrian turmoil was followed by upheaval in Egypt. Nasser forced General Mohammed Naguib out of the revolutionary council that had carried out the 1952 coup. Naguib's allies rallied. Some of his supporters dispatched tanks into the streets of Cairo. Nasser's control seemed to be ebbing away.

In Israel, Lavon argued that it was time to strike in the north and south simultaneously. In the south, the Israeli army could seize Gaza from Egyptian control, and in the north, other Israeli forces could seize the water-rich demilitarized zones on the Syrian frontier. Dayan was all in favor.[6] Ben-Gurion supported him. But Sharett held his ground and the moderates again prevailed over sabra militarism.

These months in early 1954 were the apogee of Sharett's power.

Sharett aligned his premiership with the goals of Eisenhower and Dulles, who had committed themselves to building a structure for diplomacy and conflict resolution in the wake of devastating world wars. And they signaled their disdain for Ben-Gurion's style of aggression.

"We are not rendering anyone assistance to start a war or to indulge in conflict with others of our friends," the president told reporters at a news conference in April.[7]

The problem was that the Israeli army was not under Sharett's control. In May, Lavon and Dayan authorized reprisal raids, which they did not report to the government. Sharett confronted the war camp in a closed meeting of the Mapai political committee and warned Dayan "to put an end, once and for all, to this unruly behavior of crossing the border every Monday and Thursday, without any consideration for the malignant consequences."[8]

For the military, Jordan was the other target of opportunity. Its government was teetering. Ben-Gurion had come to see Jordan as "an artificial state" created by the British after World War I to reward the Arabs who had fought against the Ottoman Turks. To Ben-Gurion, Jordan had "no future" and ought to be "dissolved" with its lands divided between Israel and Iraq.[9] And if one thing united Israelis—sabras and all others—it was the desire to reclaim all of Jerusalem and the Temple Mount, as Jews had been locked out of their holiest sites since 1948, when Jordan's Arab Legion seized East Jerusalem and the Old City.

King Abdullah had been assassinated in 1951 and his grandson Hussein was on the throne trying to rule a population dominated by Palestinians. Those "subjects" resented the boy monarch (he was seventeen) as a tool of British power, which, to their minds, was most responsible for the creation of the Jewish state and the loss of Palestine. Jordan's army, the Arab Legion, was in fact a British-run force commanded by a British officer, Sir John

Bagot Glubb—Glubb Pasha, as he was known—who had served in Iraq before taking over the legion in 1939.

If Jordan collapsed, if Hussein was overthrown, Ben-Gurion favored a military move into the West Bank to capture the Judean Hills, Samaria, Jericho and the Jordan Valley, and East Jerusalem and the Old City. The large Arab population on the West Bank whose numbers would threaten to overwhelm the Jewish population of Israel did not seem to trouble Ben-Gurion. He had never been one to pause over demographics. The Jews would rule, even as a minority, he had once said privately in his conversations with Arab leaders. That had always been a core principle of the Zionist enterprise as far as he was concerned.[10] Sharett kept Ben-Gurion, Lavon, and the young sabras commanding the military under control by using secret sessions of what he called "the committee of five"—the most senior Mapai ministers, who included Levi Eshkol and Golda Meir. But the extra supervision had only impelled Lavon to deeper levels of intrigue, and from these secret attempts at circumvention came the "mishap."

In the spring of 1954, Lavon and his military intelligence chiefs were searching for the means to stop the British withdrawal from Suez. The British army stood as a critical buffer protecting the southern flank of Israel. British withdrawal, however, had become Nasser's key demand to end British colonial power over Egypt. Here, the Israelis came up with the ill-fated plan to bomb American and British targets in Cairo and Alexandria to freeze the withdrawal.[11] Lavon worked directly with his military intelligence chief, Colonel Benjamin Gibli, cutting Dayan out of the loop. Whatever Dayan knew of the plan, he failed to share with Sharett.

In early July, Colonel Gibli sent the signal to activate the covert team of saboteurs. Bombs soon went off at a cinema and a library where Westerners gathered. Lavon later claimed that he had not given the final authorization, though Gibli asserted until his death in 2008 that he had acted only after developing the operation under Lavon's supervision and after receiving Lavon's permission.

Operation Susannah, as it had been designated, was quickly detected by Egyptian intelligence, and all of the Israeli operatives were arrested after Philip Natanson's capture outside the theater he was to have blown up. Lavon and Gibli covered up all traces of the operation for months while Dayan searched for some diversion, some success that would help them mitigate the catastrophe. Dayan seized on the plan to send an Israeli ship through the Suez Canal, forcing the Egyptians either to allow passage or to detain the vessel. Sharett, still ignorant of Operation Susannah and the arrests in Cairo—Dayan had not bothered to enlighten him—approved the plan because Dayan had agreed that seizure of the vessel would trigger a diplomatic offensive, not a war. They both hoped that any Egyptian assault on freedom of navigation would lead to immediate condemnation by the United Nations Security Council.

The small cargo vessel *Bat Galim* steamed into the Gulf of Suez in the early morning hours of September 28, 1954. The Egyptian navy boarded the ship and arrested ten Israelis. Sharett's diplomats rushed to UN headquarters in New York to protest, but Israel's hope for a clean diplomatic victory over Nasser evaporated. Washington and London both were engaged in secret discussions to draw Egypt into a Western military alliance against the Soviet Union. The *Bat Galim* was all but ignored. Israel's staged confrontation had fallen flat, and now Nasser had ten more Israeli captives.

On October 5, Radio Cairo broadcast the first startling reports about the arrest over the summer of an Israeli sabotage network. Gideon Rafael, one of Sharett's senior aides, broke in to give his boss the news.

"The story was detailed," Rafael later recounted. "It announced the arrested persons would shortly be put on trial and it smacked of authenticity rather than of propaganda."

Sharett gave Rafael a look of total skepticism. He professed no knowledge of the matter, saying that it could not be true because "such operations just could not be ordered without the knowledge of the prime minister, and if a mishap had occurred, he would have been informed immediately." Rafael nonetheless suggested checking with Lavon. Sharett immediately did so and came back "flabbergasted."[12]

From retirement, Ben-Gurion, who also had been kept in the dark, called the episode a case of "criminal recklessness." A distraught Sharett simply could not admit that Israel was to blame, that the Jewish state had been willing to kill and maim American and British citizens all for questionable tactical gain. It was all true, but it was political suicide to utter a word about it. Sharett imposed total censorship on the Israeli press, where rumors were flying. The secrecy had to be explained, and so senior government officials whispered to journalists that there had been a "mishap." With the reports from Cairo about an Israeli sabotage ring, it was not difficult to guess what the mishap might have been.

Sharett had been in office fewer than six months. If the whole story somehow emerged, he saw the destruction of his premiership and perhaps the end of Mapai, all because of the rampant militarism that Ben-Gurion was encouraging. Sharett turned loose the government propaganda organs, which blamed Egypt for inventing crimes against Israel. The espionage trial of the eleven Jews dragged on for months. The Egyptian prosecutor announced he would seek the death penalty, just as he had in the trial of the Muslim Brothers who had tried to assassinate Nasser in Alexandria in October.

While the foreign ministry was working every channel to free the Cairo prisoners, a second mishap occurred. A military commando force of five Israeli soldiers was captured behind enemy lines in Syria during a botched mission to recover wiretap equipment on Syrian telephone lines. Lavon panicked. He ordered the Israeli air force to intercept a Syrian airliner and force it to land in Israel, where its passengers and crew were taken hostage for the return of the commandos.[13] Syria's state media accused Israel of air piracy. The Israeli military spokesman put out a false statement saying the plane had violated Israeli airspace.

Lavon's recklessness left Sharett dumbfounded. He upbraided the defense minister for "military thuggery." Yet Lavon held on to the plane. As international criticism mounted, he released the only American passenger on board, a New Jersey businessman who told reporters that the aircraft had never come close to Israeli airspace.[14] Lavon finally relented, releasing the aircraft, but it took Syria a year to release the Israeli soldiers. By that time, one of them, Private Uri Ilan, twenty, whose father had served in the Knesset, had hanged himself in his prison cell. Hearing of his death, Menachem Begin's Herut Party brought a motion of no confidence against Sharett's government. The motion failed, but political agitation against Sharett's premiership was growing.

The news from Cairo was equally bad.

Two members of the captured Israeli intelligence unit, an Egyptian Jew, Armand Karmona, and Mossad officer Max Bennett, were reported to have killed themselves in prison, though Karmona may have died under torture. A third member, the only woman, Victorine (Marcelle) Ninio, twice tried to take her own life.

Deeply conflicted about the travesty he was covering up, Sharett had addressed the Knesset, accusing the Egyptians of a conspiracy against innocent Jews. But privately, Sharett worked through secret channels to offer Nasser improved relations and to express admiration for the Egyptian revolution if only Egypt would help to put the "mishap" behind them.

"Many of us admire your brave idealism and tenacity of purpose and wish you the fullest success in attaining the emancipation of the Land of the Nile from the last vestiges of foreign domination," Sharett wrote Nasser in December. He asked for the release of the *Bat Galim* and her crew and the easing of the ban on Israeli-flag vessels. On the "urgent" matter of the Cairo trial, Sharett interjected, "I fervently hope that no death sentences will be passed, as demanded by the prosecution. They would inevitably produce a violent crisis, kindle afresh the flames of bitterness and strife and defeat our efforts to curb passion and to lead our people into the ways of peace."[15]

Sharett could have gone public and confessed that Operation Susannah had been a terrible mistake initiated by a military establishment gone temporarily insane, but he could not muster the courage to do so. No one had been killed by the feckless sabotage ring. A candid admission by Sharett might have strengthened him against Ben-Gurion, Dayan, and the sabra cabal in the military, but Sharett seemed to lack the fortitude for direct confrontation. The tragedy was that it was only his fear, his lack of ruthlessness as a politician in an era of ruthlessness, that prevented him from wresting control of national policy.

On the last day of 1954, Nasser sent a reply to Sharett. It was the most promising message Israel had received from the Egyptian leader. Nasser expressed his admiration for Sharett and said that high-level talks between the two countries were possible as long as they were conducted in strict secrecy. He said the *Bat Galim* and crew would be released (it was, the next day), but the ship could not pass through the Suez Canal under Israeli flag. Vessels carrying Israeli cargo under a different flag could. He also pledged to prevent border conflicts and end the propaganda war if Israel would do the same. But with regard to the espionage trial, Nasser pointed out that the defendants were agents of a foreign intelligence service, which had sent them on a mission of terror and violence. He promised they would receive a fair trial but made no commitment on the sentences except that they would not be inflammatory.[16]

Buoyed by this message, Sharett began preparing for secret talks with Egypt. He appointed Yigael Yadin as negotiator. Yadin, an archaeologist, had been the army's first chief of staff. He was an independent thinker with great integrity and had even challenged Ben-Gurion's judgment in military affairs.

Emboldened by the prospect that his diplomacy had defused the crisis, Sharett addressed the Knesset on January 17, 1955, to attack the militarism of the army and to speak the truth—though not the whole truth.

The army, Sharett said, had lied about its mission into Syria. Israel's seizure of the Syrian airliner was not prompted by any violation of Israeli airspace. He spelled out the fraudulent reporting by the military command under Dayan and stated that all Israelis faced a difficult question: "Would Israel be a state of law and order, or of robbery; would it be a state of sound judgment and careful calculation, or one of irresponsible emotional outbursts?"[17]

The speech was a sensational indictment. Sharett bragged in his diary that he had "slaughtered lies and exposed misrepresentations on the right and left." But in Sde Boker, Ben-Gurion was seething. To him, it was a mistake to criticize the Jewish state; enemies would seize on it.

Sharett reveled in his rebellion, and then the dreaded news arrived: Egypt had handed down death sentences for two of the eleven espionage defendants in Cairo, Moshe Marzouk and Shmuel Azar. They were the leaders of the two cells of undercover agents. Within hours, they were marched to the gallows and executed in a prison courtyard.

The news bulletins sent Sharett into shock. He felt betrayed by Nasser and canceled the preparations for secret talks with Egypt. The mood throughout Israel was grim. The public expected the government to consult with Ben-Gurion, and the next day, Sharett and the other Mapai leaders drove to Sde Boker. The older man advised that Lavon had to be jettisoned for the good of the party and the state.

In the middle of it all, the Mapai leaders had come to Sharett and suggested that Ben-Gurion be brought back to run the Defense Ministry. Fearing for the party's fortunes in an election year, Sharett publicly agreed "wholeheartedly" to the suggestion, but privately he had no illusions that the "founder" would be serving under him. When he walked into the Foreign Ministry to brief his top aides, he told them, "You understand, my friends, that this is the end of my political career."[18]

Ben-Gurion returned to power like the wrath of God. The executions in Cairo raised a strong demand in the right-wing press for action. Uri

Ilan's suicide in Syria added to the lust for retribution. Nasser provided the pretext by sending an intelligence patrol from Gaza marauding through Israeli territory and shooting a bicyclist, an orange grove worker, near Rehovot.

That set the stage for Sharon's raid on Gaza in February 1955, Operation Black Arrow, the largest military assault against Egyptian forces since the 1949 Armistice.

The world was distracted by a crisis in China. President Eisenhower had dispatched the Seventh Fleet to protect nationalist Chinese troops on the islands of Quemoy and Matsu from Communist forces on the mainland.

Sharett's diplomacy in Washington was at a crucial stage. He had sent diplomats to the United States, Britain, and France seeking a formal security guarantee from the great powers to protect Israel in the event of an Arab attack and to protect the status quo in the Middle East by balancing arms sales.[19]

With Operation Black Arrow, Ben-Gurion was shredding Sharett's credibility.

The southern sky beyond Tel Aviv rumbled and flashed like Mordor. Dayan drove to the Gaza frontier to wait for Sharon as the battle raged against Nasser's garrison. When Sharon finally appeared out of the darkness, he was leading a silent procession of stretchers carrying the wounded and the dead. Dayan asked him how it had gone. Sharon was hoarse from a cold and from a night of shouting commands in dust and smoke. He had accomplished his mission, he said heavily, but his force had suffered significant losses.[20]

Dayan was cold, his words spare: "The living are alive and the dead are dead." He turned and left.[21]

Where Eisenhower was working assiduously to prevent war from breaking out in the Taiwan Strait, Ben-Gurion appeared, from Washington's perspective, to be stoking war in the Middle East.

The United States and the Soviet Union, for the first time, voted together in the UN Security Council to condemn Israel's action. Anthony Nutting, a senior British official, told an Israeli diplomat, "Surely [Israel] must realize the extreme danger of an organized attack upon the Egyptian Army. Surely they realized the sort of feeling which this would arouse in a country with a military dictatorship."[22]

American secretary of state John Foster Dulles, who for months had been weighing whether to extend a permanent security guarantee to Israel, was deeply affected. He sent a cable to Sharett stating that Ben-Gurion's Old Testament methods made it impossible for Washington to rely on Israel to be restrained in its dealings with its neighbors. Reprisal raids would almost certainly lead to escalation, and that would undermine the greater task of building a regional defense against the Soviets.[23] One of the fighters in Sharon's Unit 101 was a farmer named Meir Har Zion, who seemed to personify all those traits that the Israeli army was trying to inculcate in the many immigrant soldiers who wilted under fire. Har Zion led his men into battle with a "follow me" spirit and with the kind of ferocity that could turn a rout into victory. Dayan called him a warrior of biblical stature.

Like so many other sabras, Har Zion had trekked the length and breadth of the Holy Land, intruding through Arab territory on the sly, skirting Bedouin encampments to see Jordan's magnificent valleys and the soaring spires of the Egyptian Sinai. Suddenly, in March 1955, his younger sister, Shoshana, went missing with her boyfriend in the Jordanian desert.

The couple, both eighteen, had slipped across the frontier to visit Petra, site of the towering sandstone façades of the Nabatean civilization, which flourished on the caravan route that had brought spices and incense from the queen of Sheba's domain in Arabia to King Solomon's realm. Shoshana and her boyfriend, Oved, were murdered by unknown assailants, triggering a crisis that revealed how deeply Sharett was at odds with the military establishment.

When the bodies of the hikers were recovered, Har Zion went into a rage; he told Sharon that he had to avenge his sister's death and was resigning from the army to find her killers. Sharon didn't think he could stop Har Zion. He went to Dayan, who told Sharon to try to talk him out of it. If that failed, "Do everything in your power to make sure he comes back alive."[24]

Sharon outfitted Har Zion with arms and a command car and driver for the small team that volunteered to accompany him. The vigilantes slipped into Jordan. As Sharon described it, they seized six Jordanian Bedouin and "slaughtered five of them." They left one old man alive to return to his village and tell his people that Shoshana's brother had come and taken his debt in blood.

Israel denied any connection with the retribution murders. Har Zion and his cohorts were placed under suspension, pending disciplinary action, but Ben-Gurion and Dayan prevented any action from going forward. Dayan covered up the military's role, and Har Zion was reinstated under Sharon's command.

When Sharett heard about the raid and understood that a code of vengeance was taking root in the army, he wondered how a nation that aspired to stand as a moral beacon could produce a generation of youth who were becoming so enamored with "murdering consciously and in cold blood."

Sharett went to Ben-Gurion in Tel Aviv. The second-floor library was Ben-Gurion's domain, and Paula Ben-Gurion would just send visitors up the stairs at their own risk.

Ben-Gurion surprised Sharett by condoning Har Zion's revenge.

Sharett asked the older man whether he remembered Haganah's policy of *havlagah*—"restraint."

During the Arab uprising of the 1930s, both Ben-Gurion and Sharett had called upon the Jews of Palestine to keep in check the impulse for revenge as Arab bands went on a rampage against the Jewish community. But two decades later, here they were, leaders of the Jewish state, and instead of a culture of forbearance and restraint they were building a culture of violence, revenge, and reprisal.

"Without noticing, we have removed all psychological and moral brakes preventing this burning urge to hurt—which is inherent in the human psyche—and permitted a paratroopers' brigade to [embrace] revenge and turn it into a moral pursuit."[25]

In his diary, Sharett wondered about "the nature and fate of this nation, which is capable of so much gentleness, of such a deep love of all people, and of such craving for beauty and the profound" and at the same time of such brutality. "Which of these two souls, which run through the pages of the Bible, will predominate in this nation?" he asked.[26]

But Ben-Gurion wasn't listening. In the cabinet meeting after the Gaza raid, he had emphasized the importance of demonstrating Israel's military strength. In case anyone missed the political point in an election year, Ben-Gurion said that the thrashing of Egyptian forces in Gaza gave a strong boost to "national morale" in the wake of the Cairo hangings. He disparaged Sharett's diplomatic approach. No matter how accommodating Israel might be, Ben-Gurion said, the great powers were always going to tilt toward the Arabs because of oil.[27]

The strong militarist line also bucked up the Sephardic Jews—tens of thousands of Moroccans and Iraqis who had been trucked into the desert to live in frontier communities. Their political loyalty was up for grabs, and the most important institution in their lives was the army, where their children were growing up as sabras—defenders of the land. In the Knesset, Begin shrieked about the government's incompetence in protecting the borderlands and, as Begin's power grew—drawing strength from the same generation of sabra youth who were coming of age—it inspired fear in the Mapai that the edifice of its power might collapse and pave the way for a right-wing takeover in Israel. Ben-Gurion, though he would be the last to admit it, was aligning himself with the nationalistic forces on the right, who called for seizing more land even if that meant war with the Arabs.

In the months after Operation Black Arrow, Nasser moved with dispatch to acquire arms. Egyptian intelligence purloined a British assessment of the Israeli army and discovered that Israeli forces were better equipped.[28] Nasser made a direct approach to the Soviet ambassador in Cairo: "We want to have arms from you; what will be your answer?"[29] At the Bandung Conference in Indonesia, where the Non-Aligned Movement took shape in early 1955, Zhou Enlai, the Chinese premier, offered to lobby Moscow for arms on Egypt's behalf.

As he waited, Nasser dispatched fedayeen guerrillas to step up their cross-border attacks against Israel. He put hundreds of these fighters under the command of a brutal intelligence chief in Gaza, Colonel Mustafa Hafez. The escalation further weakened Sharett.

Arab raiders struck a wedding party at Moshav Patish, a communal farming village of Iranian Jews in the south, killing Varda Friedman, a young woman who had gone there as a volunteer to help teach farming methods to new immigrants. Many children were injured as well. Eleanor Roosevelt was visiting Israel in March 1955 and witnessed the "deep impression" Friedman's death registered with the public. Ben-Gurion demanded that the cabinet grant him the authority to launch a larger attack on Egypt's army in Gaza. This time he wanted to invade and occupy Gaza. Sharett convened Mapai's committee of five, only to discover that Eshkol and Meir had joined Ben-Gurion, who would not let it go. The debate carried over from one week to the next. Sharett warned that Ben-Gurion's war would incite a demographic catastrophe for Israel, putting three hundred

thousand Arabs under Israeli rule in Gaza. Britain was threatening to in-
voke the 1950 Tripartite Declaration against aggression in the Middle East
if Israel made a move. Sharett asked the CIA to pass a secret message to
Nasser warning him to restrain his forces in Gaza.

Sharett was at his best in the intellectual battle over war. He took the
debate before the full cabinet to regain the advantage, admonishing Ben-
Gurion that Israel could not find its place in the Middle East through the
pursuit of endless militarism. "We cannot repeat whenever we wish what
we succeeded in doing during the crucial year of 1948," he told them. "Now
we must accept the existing borders and concentrate on reducing the
tension in our relations with our neighbors in order to prepare the grounds
for peace with them and the improvement of our relations with the powers, all of which is necessary to promote our security, and also to intensify
the powers' sympathy towards Israel, which is one of the main components of our security."

He went on to argue that the militarists were wrong to assert that they
could achieve results through war; that would require a "decisive victory
in a comprehensive war, that is, by occupying Damascus, Cairo and
Amman. Even then it would not be peace, but an Arab surrender—and
not forever, rather it would be only for a limited period that would be followed by an outburst of rage which might wipe us from the land of Israel."[30]

The cabinet defeated Ben-Gurion in a nine-to-five vote on April 3, 1955.
But he judged that he was not losing. Israel's sabra culture and the right-
wing press cheered Ben-Gurion's tough approach. Israeli militarism and
the new wave of Egyptian aggression were turning public opinion. Ben-
Gurion returned to the cabinet with a proposal to tear up the armistice
agreement with Egypt and reactivate the state of war to confront Egypt's
ongoing blockade of Israeli-flag shipping through the Suez Canal.

Sharett mustered a tie vote against dumping the armistice, but he was
losing the core Mapai ministers. Meir and Eshkol were shifting back to
Ben-Gurion's orbit as it became clear that the older man would lead the
party into the 1955 elections as Mr. Security. Ben-Gurion began speaking
contemptuously to Sharett, stating that he was obliged in his public statements to oppose Sharett's policies. He had not agreed with the government's line since his resignation as prime minister in December 1953.

Sharett flared in anger: "Our ways have parted."[31]

But Ben-Gurion ignored him. He told a special cabinet session in late April that Israel's long-term security could not be based on the guarantees of foreign powers; he alluded to "the future of atomic research" as a priority of the state. Israel, he said, had to rely on its own strength.

Ben-Gurion had a breathtaking capacity to look out across an exhausted landscape and dream of glory. There was a manic quality to his vision, and Sharett, in the midst of his funk over how sabra militancy was undermining a humanistic approach to the Arabs, pummeled himself for a lack of "daring."

"Certainly he is superior to you in imagination," Sharett's wife, Zipora, said one evening in March 1955. "But that is your advantage, your feet are solidly planted on the ground of realism while he floats about in the clouds."[32]

Ben-Gurion increasingly went public to accentuate the contrast between his position and Sharett's. And within Mapai councils, he expressed himself in an electioneering tone: "Nasser-Shmasser!" He must be taught a lesson, and if his crimes against Israel did not cease, "it is definitely possible to topple him, and it is even a sacred obligation [mitzvah] to do so."[33]

In an affront to Sharett's leadership, Ben-Gurion told Mapai Party leaders that Israelis should not "allow ourselves to be influenced by cowardice disguised as pure political logic and purported pragmatism.... Our future does not depend on what the Gentiles would say, but on what the Jews would do!" It was a phrase that would enter the sabra lexicon as a call to arms.[34]

The rhetorical excesses reinforced the call for a more militarist strategy. Dayan told a meeting of Israeli ambassadors to Western capitals that reprisal raids were a "life drug" for the country, forcing the Arabs to police their borders while inciting a high degree of tension in the Israeli populace. During the meeting, Sharett's aide, Gideon Rafael, turned to whisper, "This is how fascism began in Italy and Germany."[35]

Ben-Gurion led the Mapai to victory in the July 20 elections. The party's majority slipped to 40 seats from 45, not enough to rule without coalition partners in the 120-seat Knesset. Ben-Gurion declared he would not serve as prime minister in any coalition government that did not support his militant defense policy, which Nasser was making more popular with incessant fedayeen attacks.

Egyptian raiders were picking off Israeli civilians and soldiers from ambush, blowing up radio towers, water pipelines, and supply convoys. Dayan called the Egyptian base in Gaza the "murderer's battalion." After a deep raid by fedayeen on August 30, Dayan went before the cabinet with a retaliation plan, and when it wasn't immediately approved, he tendered a letter of resignation as chief of staff. Ben-Gurion demanded that the Mapai ministers support Dayan, implying that he, too, might resign if a clear choice was not made to support Ben-Gurion's line over Sharett's.

As the ministers debated, the fedayeen struck again. Finally, even Sharett caved in and the cabinet approved a massive response.

Israeli army units under Major Sharon unleashed an artillery barrage against the Khan Yunis refugee camp in Gaza. Three companies of Israeli paratroopers moved into the strip. The main thrust of mounted infantry was under the command of Mordechai "Motta" Gur, and a blocking force was commanded by Rafael Eitan. Both men had grown up in the army. Israeli sappers blew up houses and other buildings, destroyed railway lines, and pulled down telegraph wires. At the end of the night, more than seventy Egyptians and Palestinians lay dead, with another sixty wounded.

By September 1955, the Egyptian frontier was in a state of low-intensity war. That's when intelligence reports began streaming in about Soviet cargo ships and aircraft landing in Egypt and disgorging their loads of new weaponry. Ben-Gurion had come off his sickbed and Dayan had rushed home from a vacation in France.

The two men were now partners in search of a pretext to launch a full-scale war on Egypt. Dayan assembled the general staff in a special meeting at which he announced that Israel's security dilemma could be relieved only by the destruction of Nasser. That very night, the Egyptian army struck on the border, attacking an Israeli military outpost that had been established in a demilitarized zone near al-Sabha deep in the Negev along the Egyptian frontier. Egyptian troops overpowered the Israeli defenders, killing one, wounding four, and taking two prisoners.

Ben-Gurion and Dayan now had everything they needed by way of pretext. Sharon moved his force immediately into position, and on the night of October 27, he led two hundred paratroopers across the international border. They attacked the Egyptian garrison at Kuntilla, two miles inside Sinai, killed twelve Egyptians, and took twenty-nine prisoners to trade for the Israeli soldiers who had been taken the night before. Sharon's men blew up buildings and virtually destroyed the garrison post. Dayan and Ben-Gurion hoped that the attack would trigger a major response from Nasser, and to that end, Dayan told his generals to stand ready with an Israeli strike force of eight thousand soldiers to conquer the northern Sinai.

Without consulting the government further, Ben-Gurion authorized Dayan to attack all the way to the Suez Canal if Egypt mounted a challenge. But Egyptian forces held their fire.

Sharett was in Geneva, begging arms from John Foster Dulles and the other Western leaders assembled for an international conference. In Sharett's absence, Ben-Gurion bullied the Mapai leadership to agree to an all-out attack on Egyptian garrisons surrounding the demilitarized zone in Sinai. It took several days because Levi Eshkol, the acting prime minister while Sharett was away and until Ben-Gurion presented his new government, wanted to wait until Sharett's return. Sharett came back from Europe on November 2 with the promise of French arms. He cautioned Ben-Gurion to hold off on the attack until after a new government was seated.

Ben-Gurion walked into the Knesset and all but claimed that Israel was entering a state of war. "The Egyptian representatives at the UN have openly declared that a state of war persists between Egypt and Israel," Ben-Gurion grimly told the members. "The government of Egypt has violated basic international law," he added, in closing the sea lanes to Israeli shipping. "This one-sided war will have to stop, for it cannot remain one-sided forever."[36]

He foreshadowed what was coming: "If our rights are assailed by the acts of violence on land or sea, we shall reserve freedom of action to defend those rights in the most effective manner. We seek peace—but not suicide."

Sharon launched a night attack into Sinai from multiple directions, catching the Egyptians off guard despite the high alert. He destroyed camps and fortifications along a broad swath of frontier. When Sharon was done, he held all of his objectives and counted eighty-one Egyptian dead. His troops took fifty prisoners.

The assault into Sinai surpassed all previous cross-border operations in the scale of forces involved and destruction inflicted on the Egyptian army. At dawn, as black smoke rose through the mist over the battlefield, Dayan arrived in a jeep and ascended Jebel Sabha, the outcropping that offers a strategic view of the border region. Now it was in Israeli hands, and Dayan looked across the desert as if he hoped to see Nasser's forces regrouping, but the Egyptians were in disarray. He sent a message to Ben-Gurion: "We are now inside Egypt. Let us stay there."[37]

But Ben-Gurion would not allow it. He told Dayan to pull back. Without an Egyptian counterattack, they had no pretext. They had failed to provoke Nasser into a major fight. It was necessary to avoid international condemnation, Ben-Gurion said. So Dayan pulled back. One of his aides, Uzi Narkiss, suggested they tell Sharon to just keep the battle going and move deeper into Egypt, but Dayan pulled them up. Here was his loyalty to Ben-Gurion: "I wouldn't do anything against his will," he said.[38]

Dayan returned to military headquarters in Tel Aviv and regrouped. After huddling with the general staff, he sent Ben-Gurion a memorandum on November 10 calling for "an early confrontation with the Egyptian regime in order to bring about a change of the regime or a change in its policy."[39]

But Sharett now intervened, claiming to be on the verge of a diplomatic breakthrough. Buoyed by his meeting with John Foster Dulles in Geneva, Sharett, serving once again as foreign minister in Ben-Gurion's new government, said there was a real possibility of obtaining arms from the United States.

Dulles was in the midst of last-ditch diplomacy to bring Nasser's Egypt into the Western camp by helping to finance a high dam at Aswan on the Nile River that would meet Nasser's goal of stabilizing the annual flood and opening up massive new tracts of farmland for the Egyptian people. Sharett, however, had zeroed in on Nasser's arms purchases from the Soviet bloc. Dulles would surely balance those Soviet arms by selling arms to Israel, Sharett believed.

Yet Dulles's price was high. The Western powers—Britain and the United States—expected Israel to give up those wedges of land in the Negev to reconnect the Arab world. They wanted Israel to take back one hundred thousand Arab refugees, a step that seemed to Western leaders eminently reasonable given that seven hundred thousand Arabs had been displaced in 1948.

Dayan came to Ben-Gurion during this diplomatic interregnum with Operation Omer, a plan to send an army down the eastern coastline of Sinai to seize Sharm el-Sheikh and the Strait of Tiran. Dayan had built a new elite unit under Chaim Bar-Lev to take the maritime territory. The only problem was that Sharon discovered the plan and was furious. Bar-Lev was the officer who had presided over Sharon's aborted court-martial in 1953. Sharon detested Bar-Lev and threatened to resign. It took all of Dayan's considerable charm to convince Sharon that Bar-Lev's appointment was a one-off deal. He promised that Sharon would be back in charge of the paratroopers for the next major operation.[40] Dayan told Ben-Gurion that the army was prepared for an all-out war.

But suddenly Operation Omer was aborted. Nasser had moved reinforcements to Sharm el-Sheikh. Geopolitics had also shifted. Ben-Gurion was under pressure to stand down. In November 1955, Sharett seemed genuinely on the verge of a breakthrough with the Americans for arms and a security guarantee. Anthony Eden, the British prime minister, had gone public with Project Alpha—the year-old peace plan that called for Israeli territorial concessions.

Eden's address at Guildhall in London caught Ben-Gurion by surprise. He held council for several days before answering. From the rostrum of the Knesset on November 15, Ben-Gurion rejected the Eden-Eisenhower proposal "to truncate the territory of Israel for the benefit of her neighbors." He asserted that the U.S.-British peace proposal had "no legal, moral or logical foundation and cannot be considered."[41]

No Israeli leader had ever spoken so defiantly or contemptuously of compromise. For Ben-Gurion, the Arabs had squandered their chance for statehood by rejecting the UN Partition resolution; they had attacked Israel after it declared its own statehood; they had lost the first round of war in which six thousand Israelis had sacrificed their lives. There was no going back as far as he was concerned. And the country—especially the sabra military establishment—was behind him.

Nasser had signed a mutual defense treaty with Syria, as had Saudi Arabia, which agreed to set up a joint military command with Damascus. Dayan reasoned that if Israel attacked on the northern front, Nasser would be obligated to launch a war to defend Arab honor alongside the Syrian army.

In Operation Olive Leaves, the Israeli army sent a police boat across the Sea of Galilee to the northeastern shore, where Syrian gunners opened fire.

Major Sharon was standing by with two paratrooper battalions. The night attack unfolded as a series of Israeli artillery and mortar barrages followed by assaults by land and sea against Syrian positions. Sharon directed the battle from a small plane circling over the sound and light of unfolding battle—the largest military engagement undertaken on the Syrian front since the signing of the armistice agreement. Sharon's forces killed fifty-six Syrian soldiers and wounded many more. They also took thirty prisoners as leverage for the release of Israeli soldiers still in captivity. Again, the unprovoked Israeli assault across the armistice lines shocked the Israeli cabinet, which had been kept in the dark. It drew expressions of outrage from the international community and prompted a new wave of condemnation against Ben-Gurion's government.[42]

But Nasser made no move to strike Israel. He denied Ben-Gurion any new pretext for all-out war.

Sharett was beside himself with anger. Still in Washington, close to clinching a deal with the Eisenhower administration for arms and a security guarantee, he called the raid "a dastardly act." One of Dayan's aides—Uzi Narkiss—observed that it was obvious that part of Dayan's motivation was "to deliver a body blow to Sharett," in hopes that it would destroy him politically.[43]

The December 11 attack on Syria roused the Israeli cabinet against Ben-Gurion's autocratic rule. He might as well have blindfolded them. He had made a mockery of the democratic process. He had trashed Sharett's diplomacy and once again sent the UN Security Council into session to condemn the Jewish state for unwarranted aggression. The newspaper *Ha'aretz* decried the state of affairs in a lead article titled "The Prime Minister's Dictatorship."

Two days after the attack, the State Department notified Abba Eban at the United Nations that Israel's request for arms had been deferred as a result of the raid. Sharett flew home and confronted Ben-Gurion in private where, astoundingly, Ben-Gurion asserted that he had not approved the attack on Syria.[44] But his mendacity did not survive Sharett's reconstruction of events, in which Ben-Gurion's personal assistants, Teddy Kollek and Yaacov Herzog, both confirmed that their boss had approved the raid.

Ben-Gurion called Dayan and Sharon to the prime minister's office to congratulate them, and his only complaint—and they both knew that it was not really a complaint—was that the operation had been "too success-ful" because Israel was facing threats of international sanctions.

Sharett vented his indignation to Mapai's leadership council. He told them how close he had been to clinching a deal in Washington. The *New York Times* columnist James Reston had whispered to him that he would not be disappointed with Dulles's decision.

Ben-Gurion had entered the hall where Sharett was speaking in Jeru-salem but refused to sit at the head table, a sign of disrespect to Sharett. Ben-Gurion took a seat between Yitzhak Navon, his political secretary, and Gideon Rafael, Sharett's aide. Sharett was in high dudgeon.

"This operation has been like the eclipse of the sun," he told them. "Satan himself could not have chosen a worse timing." The word "Satan" reverberated through the hall. Rafael noticed that Ben-Gurion "jerked as if he had been hit by a bullet, and then leaned back without uttering a sound. I could physically feel how the word had hurt him. The audience gasped, as if witnessing a tightrope walker losing his balance."[45]

Sharett accused Dayan of subverting the democratic process. He had told his military chiefs that even though the government opposed a war against Egypt, the military could trigger such a war by continuing its esca-latory policy of border raids.

"I am against preventative war because it can turn into general war, to a ring of fire all around us, rather than be restricted to war with Egypt," Sharett continued. "I am against preventative war because that which did not occur in the War of Independence may occur, namely, intervention by a foreign power against us. . . . I am against preventative war because it means measures by the UN against us. I am against preventative war be-cause it means injury and damage at home, the destruction of settlements, and the spilling of much blood."[46]

He addressed the sabras: "There is an urgent need to subjugate our im-mediate defense considerations to the more comprehensive and long-term considerations of security. And this means strengthening Israel through closer connections with the Western powers and pursuing a peace process with Egypt."[47]

The Mapai chairman invited Ben-Gurion to take the floor, but he de-clined. A sense of gloom prevailed as the party leaders filed out—everyone could see that Sharett's relationship with Ben-Gurion had reached a break-ing point.[48] Ben-Gurion spoke for the popular will and for the army; Sharett represented a shrinking political consensus in the Mapai leader-ship. A majority of the cabinet supported his call for declaring an end to Ben-Gurion's war policy, but Sharett had lost the support of his own party.

The planning for war continued in Dayan's general staff. Sharon records in his memoir that ten days after the raid on Syrian forces, Dayan called him to headquarters and asked him to lead a new invasion of the Gaza Strip, this one designed to seize and hold the northern half of the territory and to destroy all of Nasser's forces around Gaza City. Sharon massed his forces and said they were sitting in their half-tracks at H-hour when an order came down to abort.[49]

Ben-Gurion, forced to make a tactical pause, went before the generals and explained to them the dilemma Israel faced. On the one hand, it seemed crucial to strike Egypt quickly before its army could absorb the Soviet arms, but on the other hand, doing so would bring on a destructive war. Britain might intervene on the side of the Arabs (due to its defense treaties with Jordan and Iraq), and the great powers might turn irretrievably against the Jewish state as a threat to international peace, thus denying Israel the chance to obtain arms for its long-term defense against the Arab armies.[50] Ben-Gurion said the cabinet was correct in opposing a preventa-tive war. He used Sharett's arguments, but Sharett had little confidence that Ben-Gurion truly embraced them.

The older man had left himself a sizable out. His militarism had put Nasser on the path to war, and all Ben-Gurion had to do was wait for the next opportunity—a hostile action from Egypt—and that would be enough to break Sharett's crumbling wall of resistance in the Mapai, where Eshkol, Meir, and the others could see that Ben-Gurion had fully restored his power. The "succession" was off the table. Sharett had lost control of the future the moment that Ben-Gurion had reentered government. The most important item on the older man's agenda was weaponry.

Eisenhower had mostly recovered from the heart attack that had struck with the news that Soviet weapons were landing in Egypt.

Ben-Gurion sent his Mossad chief, Isser Harel, privately to Washing-ton in January 1956 to tell CIA director Allen Dulles that the United States had grievously erred in not opposing the Soviet arms sale to Nasser. The Soviet bloc was gaining a foothold in the Middle East while the leaders of the free world stood idle. Harel, of course, spun the threat in geostrategic terms without mentioning how Ben-Gurion's militarism had contributed to Nasser's quest for arms.

Instead, Harel, a strong Ben-Gurion loyalist, told Eisenhower's aides that Israel would not wait for the Arabs to gain the upper hand in weaponry.

"If you give us arms," Harel told Dulles, "there will be no war. Nasser won't dare attack us, and Israel will be preserved. But if Israel gets no arms, there will be a war!"[51]

Speaking to the Knesset on January 2, 1956, Ben-Gurion seemed to be preparing the country.

"We knew that after a victory on our part in one war, there would be a second round, and even after our victory in the second round there could be a third, and there would be no end to it," he said. He blamed everything on the Arabs: the armistice agreements "were violated by our neighbors." Egypt "deliberately organized fedayeen" to attack Israel. Nasser had "also blocked passage of Israeli shipping" in the Suez Canal and through the Strait of Tiran.

"We shall only be able to hold our ground if from now onward we prepare for whatever is in store and muster all our strength—moral, economic and military—to forestall the blow," Ben-Gurion concluded.[52]

Eisenhower was becoming more alarmed: Ben-Gurion's militarism and Arab nationalism were feeding off each other. The president needed a more robust diplomacy. Operation Gamma was Eisenhower's response, a round of secret visits to Cairo and Tel Aviv by Robert B. Anderson, a Texas oilman who had served in the Pentagon and was soon to become Eisenhower's treasury secretary.

Anderson knew the region and its leaders, and he probably reflected the bias of the Eisenhower men, who tended to see Nasser as the most important figure in the Middle East. This was certainly the reason why Washington had not broken relations with Cairo over the Soviet arms deal, and why the White House was working assiduously with the World Bank to line up funding for the Aswan Dam. Washington still hoped to pull Nasser into the Western orbit.

The problem for Anderson was that, after the bloodletting that had occurred throughout 1955, neither Nasser nor Ben-Gurion was in a peacemaking mood. Nasser demanded that the Arab world be reconnected at
Israel's territorial expense. Ben-Gurion demanded arms from Washington
to match Nasser's.

Speaking in private to Anderson on January 23—Sharett was also
present—Ben-Gurion told the Texan, "I want you to understand the depth
of our anxiety. We are facing a position which, so far as we are concerned,
is one of life or death. If the Egyptian army invades our country and
defeats our army, that is the end of our people."

Sharett joined in, demonstrating how he and Ben-Gurion could still
work in tandem despite their rift: "The leaders of Egypt are driving their
people into a frenzy," denouncing Israel "as blacker than the devil." In this
way, "they make their people slaves to hatred."[53]

Sharett cataloged all of his diplomacy aimed at engaging Nasser in
peace talks, but when he came to the Lavon Affair, the sabotage operations
in Cairo, and the hangings in Cairo that had incited the Israeli assault on
Gaza, he was less than honest.

"A number of Egyptian Jews were arrested in Cairo and we worked to
save them from the scaffold," Sharett said. "We did not succeed: our operation in Gaza at the beginning of 1955 had no connection with the death
penalties in Cairo; it was a reply to the fedayeen operations from the Gaza
Strip. I approached Nasser several times through an emissary to get these
operations stopped—but I received no response."

Sharett's mendacity in front of the American envoy reflected his Israeli
loyalties but also his paralysis. He was living with a massive lie and struggling to find a path around it. That spring, Sharett even probed Moscow
for arms to see if that might jolt Washington.[54]

When Anderson shuttled to Cairo, Nasser told him to warn the Israelis
not to launch a preventative war. He said that he was ready to negotiate on
the basis of Project Alpha, but Nasser appeared to be maneuvering for
time. "I blame Ben-Gurion for this situation," Nasser said, referring to the
Gaza raid and the escalation that followed. "Such severe clashes did not
occur when Sharett was Israel's prime minister."

Anderson could not induce the two leaders to enter negotiations.

"I can see only one way to prevent war," Ben-Gurion told him in their
final meeting in March 1956. "To bring about peace is almost impossible,

but there is a way to prevent war," he said. "The only way to prevent war is for Israel to have defensive arms."[55]

Ben-Gurion concluded, "It depends on you. I do not see how you, seeing the danger, can morally refuse to give us arms. Perhaps I should not say this, because it is a question of conscience for you." Ben-Gurion made it personal, battering Anderson toward the end of their session, referring to American policy as the same kind of "appeasement" that had occurred in 1938 in the face of Nazi aggression. He belittled the Tripartite Declaration, asking Anderson, "Can we be confident that Britain will go to war against Egypt or Jordan if Israel is attacked?" If the Arabs rushed in, even the United States might move cautiously, he asserted. "The United States government would need time to consult Congress, while Nasser's planes can bomb us within ten minutes—I do not believe that you would go to war against Egypt if they attacked us."[56]

Thus Anderson's mission failed. Eisenhower and Dulles rightly feared the consequences of arming Ben-Gurion. Sharett sent John Foster Dulles a message: "I am authorized by my Government to state that, if given adequate arms, they will be used only for defensive purposes and that the avoidance of war and of any further deterioration in the stability of the area will be a primary consideration in our policy and action."

But Sharett's offer was not credible enough to convince Washington or London that Israel had abandoned Ben-Gurion's line. Sharett even suggested that the Mapai leadership was discussing a package deal to reconnect the Arab world and compensate Arab refugees for property left behind. Needless to say, Ben-Gurion was against these proposals. He was clearly in charge, and the military establishment was behind him.[57]

On January 19, the UN Security Council had condemned Israel's December raid into Syria as a "flagrant" violation of the armistice and of Israel's obligations under the charter. The condemnation carried an explicit threat that the United Nations would consider "further measures"—there was talk of sanctions—if Israel did not restrain its militarists.[58] But there was no restraining Israel, for Nasser was indeed becoming a military threat. He believed he had no choice.

Eisenhower, writing in his diary on March 8, wrestled with the changing perception of Nasser that spring: "We have reached the point where it looks as if Egypt, under Nasser, is going to make no move whatsoever to meet the Israelites in an effort to settle outstanding differences. Moreover, the Arabs, absorbing major consignments of arms from the Soviets, are daily growing more arrogant and disregarding the interests of Western Europe and of the United States."

Eisenhower thought that it was time to consider entering into a defense treaty with Israel and to recruit other Arab allies—perhaps Saudi Arabia—to isolate Nasser.

"I am certain of one thing," the president wrote. "If Egypt finds herself thus isolated from the rest of the Arab world, and with no ally in sight except Soviet Russia, she would very quickly get sick of that prospect and would join us in the search for a just and decent peace in that region."[59]

Facing a reelection campaign, Eisenhower was out of new ideas. The Arabs were flocking to Nasser. At the beginning of March, the young Jordanian monarch, King Hussein, sacked Sir John Bagot Glubb and put Jordan's Arab Legion under Arab command for the first time.

The British response was volcanic: "I don't want Nasser neutralized, I want him destroyed!" Eden shouted in front of his aides.[60] News of this hardening of views in London encouraged Ben-Gurion. He ridiculed the American refusal to provide arms to Israel as a "base hypocrisy."[61] He authorized Dayan and Shimon Peres to make direct contacts with the new Socialist government in France in hopes of finding a new ally against Nasser. Sharett, shunned in Western capitals, lost his leverage over the sabras.

And the growing violence on the border reflected Nasser's new militarism. Three Israelis were killed on April 4 when Egyptians opened fire on an IDF patrol. In response, Dayan ordered an artillery barrage against Gaza City that killed fifty people and wounded a hundred more, mostly civilians.[62]

Britain plotted Nasser's overthrow and Eden endeavored to bring a reluctant Eisenhower along in the enterprise. John Foster Dulles and his brother, Allen, the CIA director, were under orders not to target Nasser directly—as they had Mossadegh in Iran. Eisenhower feared that a Western move to topple Nasser would blow up in their faces. So Dulles came up with Operation Omega, whose loosely defined mission was to prevent revolutionary nationalism from spreading across the Middle East.

The imminent threat of war saturated the Israeli media.

And between April and June 1956, Ben-Gurion mounted a campaign within the Mapai leadership to remove Sharett. There was no question that the political momentum had shifted. Nasser had played into Ben-Gurion's hands after Gaza by turning up the volume of the border violence and flaunting Egypt's new status as the recipient of Soviet weapons. Ben-Gurion threatened to resign unless the government backed a more militant line. The public and the army were with Ben-Gurion.

When an Egyptian fedayeen raid in April killed five Israeli children gathered at a synagogue near Tel Aviv, Ben-Gurion ordered the military to prepare for a major attack. The cabinet balked, however, over launching a war while UN secretary-general Dag Hammarskjöld—with the blessings of Eisenhower and Dulles—was shuttling between Cairo and Jerusalem in another frantic effort to prevent war from breaking out. The cabinet restrained Ben-Gurion but gave him the authority to launch a major strike in the event of renewed fedayeen attacks. A more militant public mood shifted the political balance toward Ben-Gurion. Dayan said publicly that it was not a matter of whether there would be war, but whether it would begin with an Israeli attack into Gaza or across the Sinai Peninsula.

At that moment, a breakthrough came in Paris that profoundly changed the course of events.

The French Socialists had come to power under Prime Minister Guy Mollet and his militant defense minister, Maurice Bourgès-Maunoury. Both were eager to strike against Nasser. French intelligence had discovered that Egypt was supplying weapons and training to Algerian nationalists who had rebelled against French colonial rule in North Africa.

Ben-Gurion sent Shimon Peres secretly to Mollet in April 1956, with a letter asserting that Nasser intended to attack Israel with his "huge" arsenal of Soviet weapons. He begged the French leaders, who had fought in the underground against the Nazis, to sell arms to Israel "in order to guarantee the survival of our state."[63]

Nothing happened until June, when Ben-Gurion's chief of military intelligence, Yehoshafat Harkabi, returned from Paris to report that the French were interested in forming a secret alliance to conduct military operations against Egypt. If Israel would join, France would sell substantial quantities of arms.

"France will give us arms," Dayan told Ben-Gurion, "only if we give it serious help in the Algerian matter. Serious help means killing Egyptians, nothing less."[64]

What was more astounding was that the French were willing to cooperate in the field of nuclear power. Between April and June 1956, the Israeli leader decided to activate a full-scale program, a scientific and industrial collaboration with the French that would provide Israel with atomic weapons in a decade's time. According to French officials, Bourgès-Maunoury among them, Israel undertook to obtain from Jewish American nuclear scientists the information that both countries needed to build their first atomic bombs.[65] Though decision making on the Israeli nuclear program was closely held by Ben-Gurion himself, the decision to move the program into the development stage circulated among the most senior members of Mapai, including Sharett, Levi Eshkol, and Golda Meir.

Ben-Gurion never submitted the nuclear program to the cabinet or the Knesset. While several senior leaders expressed deep reservations in private over how Israel would pay for such a large-scale enterprise, and some senior scientists questioned the morality of the Jewish state bringing nuclear arms into the Middle East, Ben-Gurion arrogated unto himself the strategic judgment to undertake the massive endeavor. In doing so, he set himself apart as the indispensable leader—at least in his own mind—who was willing to undertake a fateful gamble on behalf of the Jewish state, a gamble which, if it paid off, would catapult Israel to a new status among the great powers—a member of the nuclear club and a force to be reckoned with.

Sharett could not compete. His feckless pandering to Eisenhower and Dulles for weapons had achieved nothing. Ben-Gurion, with little effort, had profited beyond all imagination from the change of governments in France and a convergence of national strategy with French Socialists determined to hold on to France's colonial possessions in North Africa.

Ben-Gurion's allies in the defense establishment leaked to the press that Sharett was finished and that Golda Meir would replace him as foreign minister. It was apparent that his support in the cabinet had diminished, along with his stature.

Sharett announced his resignation on June 17. Most of the country knew the nature of Sharett's clash with the older man, but Ben-Gurion worked fiendishly to prevent full disclosure of the conflict because Ben-Gurion's record of false statements and misreporting would have damaged his credibility. Only in the privacy of his diary did Sharett construct the indictment: Ben-Gurion's "distortion and suppression of information" and the cover-up of "Israel's own misconduct . . . as well as actions by our people that resulted in grave disasters, some of which have influenced the entire train of events and contributed to the security crisis we are now facing."[66] He mentioned the Gaza raid in particular.

The newspaper *Ha'aretz* asked, "What policy failed? Is it the policy based on the sincere belief that it is possible to bring the Arabs to make peace . . . , or that policy which, supported by most of the parties, has refused to pay for peace with any concession?"[67]

THREE

Suez Crisis: Ben-Gurion Goes to War

In Israel, Nasser had become "Hitler on the Nile."

For Ben-Gurion, destroying the Egyptian leader and his military junta would yield a profound victory against the largest Arab state whose very power and enmity threatened the Jewish state's existence. But the risks were great—if for no other reason than Ben-Gurion and his coconspirators were keeping the leader of the free world, President Eisenhower, completely in the dark.

They were calling it Operation Musketeer. Ben-Gurion and Dayan were betting all their chips—going to war with Egypt in secret alliance with France and Great Britain.

Nasser's decision in July 1956 to nationalize the Anglo-French Suez Canal Company created, in a single instant it seemed, a congruence of interests between Israel and Europe's great powers to topple the Egyptian dictator. The canal's revenue stream was crucial to the beleaguered postwar economies of Britain and France. Riding the anticolonial wave sweeping the region, Nasser was supporting anti-French rebels in Algeria and subverting pro-British monarchies in Iraq and Jordan.

The new French government had taken the first step, offering Israel large volumes of heavy weapons—tanks and combat aircraft—to balance Egypt's power. And secretly, they were providing the industrial base needed for nuclear weapons production.

The conspiracy unfolded in private meetings at French safe houses, where Ben-Gurion dropped the veil to reveal his ambition to seize the Sinai Peninsula—and its oil—for the state of Israel.

Ben-Gurion had been probing the French ever since the Socialists came to power in the spring with a new militancy to protect France's colonial possessions in North Africa. In June, he had dispatched Dayan, Peres, and Harkabi, the military intelligence chief, to meet with Mollet's top military advisers. In a castle at Vermars, they had parried their views on Nasser and the Soviet threat to the Middle East. Dayan spoke for the Jewish state: Nasser would eventually turn the region into a Soviet bastion against the West; only his destruction could prevent it.

The Israelis were leaning on an open door. The Vermars Conference came to the conclusion that Ben-Gurion had been yearning for: the French were willing to sell on favorable terms $100 million worth of weapons—modern jets, tanks, and artillery—if Israel would take the lead in mounting commando attacks on Egyptian and Algerian targets across North Africa. They discussed blowing up the Voice of the Arabs radio station that Nasser used to spread his anti-Western message from Cairo. There was talk of assassinating Nasser himself.[1]

French and Israeli military planners were still working on their covert action plan when Nasser took over the Suez Canal Company in a lightning operation.

Nasser shouted out to his people: "We Egyptians will not allow any colonizer or despot to dominate us politically, economically or militarily. Choke with rage, but you will never succeed in ordering us about or in exercising your tyranny over us!"[2]

Though the Western powers were furious, Ben-Gurion wrote in his diary: "I am afraid they will not do anything."[3]

But Peres, who was in Paris following Nasser's thunderbolt, cabled home that the French defense minister, Bourgès-Maunoury, had asked him an astounding question: "How long would it take the Israeli army to fight its way across the Sinai and reach the canal?"[4]

The Franco-Israeli alliance rapidly took shape. In a matter of weeks, French cargo ships were docked in Haifa secretly unloading the arms that had been promised at the Vermars Conference, but there was no more talk of pinpricks or covert action. The game had changed. And Ben-Gurion made sure that his cabinet ministers saw with their own eyes the miracle of arms he had produced. He spirited them at night to be dazzled by the sight of French warplanes landing at Israeli bases.

Peres took the Israeli poet Nathan Alterman to see the tanks rolling off the ships. Alterman penned a heroic tribute to the "chains of steel" with which Ben-Gurion was girding the Jewish state.

It fell to Dayan to come up with a war plan.

One of the first things he did was to relieve Sharon of his command, transferring the egotistical officer to a staff job at army headquarters. Dayan gave no explanation, but anyone on the general staff could see that it was difficult to advance other talented officers while Sharon monopolized the role as the nation's "commando" in chief.

Moreover, Sharon's power was growing.

Not only was he an uncontrollable force on the battlefield, he had also insinuated himself into Ben-Gurion's good graces. In the small world of Israel, many officers lived in the same army-built subdivisions around Tel Aviv, where Sharon stood out for self-promotion. He bullied rivals, cultivated admirers, and trafficked in gossip and intelligence about what was going on at headquarters; he fed information to journalists, who lionized his military exploits. He rivaled even Dayan in bureaucratic skill, and the perception spread that he was the prime minister's favorite warrior.

Dayan was a realist. Israel needed Sharon's roar on the battlefield, but Dayan wanted to get it under greater control. Sharon was good at everything except taking direction or calibrating the violence of battle. Promoting a more controllable officer to command the paratroopers thus became essential. But before Dayan could act, Sharon picked up the rumor of what was about to transpire and rushed to Tel Aviv to confront the chief of staff. Dayan was suddenly unavailable for a meeting. All Sharon got was a stern rebuke from an adjutant: "Maybe there is no room for an officer like you in the Israeli army."[5]

Enraged, Sharon drove to the prime minister's office and tearfully vented his anger. Here Ben-Gurion was at his manipulative best. He soothed Sharon with a story about a Chinese fisherman who found the body of a drowned peasant. The fisherman brought the body to the family and asked for money for his trouble. The family did not want to say no, but they had no money, so they consulted a monk who told them to wait. Just wait.

Ben-Gurion was signaling that he needed time. Soon they were laughing about the oriental mind. And soon, Dayan reversed his decision.[6]

The bigger problem was that the great powers had put their war plans on hold under pressure from Washington. Dulles had been engaged in protracted negotiations to find a face-saving compromise with Nasser.

Ben-Gurion wanted action.

On October 9, two Israeli orange grove workers were killed and their bodies mutilated. Ben-Gurion approved a large-scale attack on the Jordanian military headquarters in Qalqilya, a major Arab city northwest of Jerusalem.

Dayan and Sharon quarreled throughout the planning. Sharon intended to go in with tanks, but Dayan feared that too large an attack might cause Britain to activate its mutual defense treaty with Jordan.

There was no stopping Sharon. His armored formation moved out on the night of October 10. The battle quickly deteriorated as Israeli forces came under heavy assault by the Jordanian counterattack. Dayan drove to Sharon's forward command post. There, in the middle of the night, the two men shouted at each other over Sharon's decision to commit an armored column to relieve his trapped forces. Dayan wanted a lighter force.

Sharon wheeled on the chief of staff: "Moshe, if we don't do this we are going to get their bodies out tomorrow from the UN Armistice Commission."[7]

Dayan glared at Sharon with his one eye. Sharon ordered the armored column into the battle, defying his superior. Dayan just turned on his heel and walked out.

When sunrise came, eighteen Israeli soldiers had been killed and sixty wounded. Jordanian losses were put at one hundred dead and two hundred wounded. From Qalqilya, another cry of massacre went out.

Palestinians in Jordan rioted over the failure of King Hussein and the Arab Legion to defend Arab honor. Nasser called for revenge. He paraded new Soviet weapons for the whole region to see.

Dayan was furious over the number of Israeli dead and wounded. But Sharon blamed Dayan. In a postmortem with his commanders, Sharon alleged that interference from above—from Dayan—was responsible for the deaths of so many of his men. When word of this meeting reached Dayan, he summoned Sharon and all of his officers to Tel Aviv.

At army headquarters, Dayan walked in with Meir Amit, a meticulously organized sabra officer and Dayan's chief of operations. The two men ripped into Sharon for deflecting responsibility, insubordination, and incessant blame shifting. If it weren't for Ben-Gurion, that might have ended Sharon's career. Dayan wanted to dismiss Sharon, but Ben-Gurion intervened, again, to prevent it. The older man saw Sharon's martial skills as decisive. It was also plain—certainly Sharon sensed it—that Dayan was threatened by such a powerful officer who was doted on by the prime minister. Ben-Gurion thrived on this creative tension and was not about to give up an instrument as lethal as Sharon, so long as his loyalty to Ben-Gurion and the state was not in question.

The American-sponsored mediation with Nasser collapsed in September 1956, triggering the French and British decision to finalize their war plans. They invited Ben-Gurion to meet clandestinely, and on October 22, the Israeli prime minister flew to Paris.

At a villa in the suburb of Sèvres, Ben-Gurion put his cards on the table. Speaking in Hebrew through an interpreter, he told the French leaders that it was time to redraw the map of the Middle East. He warned them that what he was about to say might seem fantastic or naïve, but it was based on a comprehensive plan—Ben-Gurion's plan—and he would need their help to take this plan to the Americans in order to sell Eisenhower on its merits.

It *was* fantastic. Here was the Israeli prime minister trying to incite an even grander conspiracy of war and dismemberment than that which was on the table. Under his plan, one country would disappear (Jordan) and another would be swallowed up by Syria and Israel (Lebanon), leaving only a tiny canton of Maronite Christians to raise the Lebanese flag.

Jordan was a failed state under a weak king, Ben-Gurion argued. It should be broken up and divided between Israel and Iraq.

Lebanon did not work as a country. The Maronite Christians on Mount Lebanon should become a Christian state, while the rest of the country should be divvied up.

Egypt did not need the Sinai Peninsula, Ben-Gurion argued, but Israel did. And Sinai contained substantial oil deposits, Ben-Gurion said. Israel would be willing to share these with the French.[8]

Here was a plot worthy of a conqueror. Ben-Gurion said they should take their time and seek a "joint policy" with the United States.

The French, however, were not interested in reinventing the Middle East, only in destroying Nasser's power, and if that meant hiving off a piece of Sinai to pay for Israeli participation, they were willing to consider it, but Israel would have to play its part.

The Israeli role, as both the French and the British envisioned it, was to be the aggressor. Israel would launch an unprovoked attack. The French and British forces would intervene as peacekeepers in a contrived war between Israel and Egypt. In doing so, they would return the Suez Canal to Western control and eliminate Nasser.

The first day at Sèvres settled nothing. At lunch on the second day, the French general in charge of the military planning suggested that Israel stage a phony bombing raid on its own territory and call it an Egyptian attack.

Ben-Gurion erupted in anger: "I cannot lie, either to the world public opinion or to anybody else."[9] Ben-Gurion's self-righteous display did not impress the French. They knew that Ben-Gurion had been lying in the face of world opinion for some time. They also knew that he was prepared to lie in order to obtain nuclear weapons technology. What was the point of the outburst?

Dayan and Peres were puzzled as well. The Israeli leader's mood had turned foul because it was becoming clear that the French saw Israel less as a partner than as an instrument—a Middle Eastern army chosen to carry out Western objectives. The powers intended to capitalize on Ben-Gurion's reputation as a militarist to touch off a war whose conclusion they would orchestrate for their own ends. They were not planning to defend Israeli aggression or territorial acquisition before the world or at the UN Security Council. They would stand on the high moral ground, while Israel would be in the dock.

Despite the affront, it was soon clear that Ben-Gurion was not going to walk away from the opportunities that the plot offered. Peres suggested that war could be triggered by sending another Israeli ship into the Suez Canal. But this idea had been tried once, unsuccessfully, with the *Bat Galim* in 1954.

Dayan finally came up with a solution. They didn't really need a pretext, he said. They could parachute Israeli commandos deep into Sinai to make Nasser think they were going to seize the canal. That would draw out

Egyptian forces for a battle and provide the trigger for the French and British to "intervene." In doing so, the conspirators would gain control of the canal and Nasser's fate. Israel could then occupy Sinai.

Ben-Gurion liked the idea because the insertion of the small commando force gave him the flexibility to pull his troops back quickly in the event of a double cross. He mistrusted the British, who might encourage Iraq and Jordan to strike Israel once its army moved into Sinai.[10]

For all his bluster and anxiety, Ben-Gurion never wavered at Sèvres. Dayan knew his mentor and fashioned an option the older man could accept. That night in Paris, they all went out to a strip club to break the tension, and then Dayan and Peres, unable to sleep, reviewed the day's amazing events at a sidewalk café.[11]

Ben-Gurion returned to Israel in a mood of exuberance and high anxiety that would drive him back into his sickbed while Dayan and General Amit took over the final planning for the war. The Soviets chose that week in late October to invade Hungary and put down rebellion in Eastern Europe. Eisenhower was in the last days of his reelection campaign against the Democratic senator Adlai Stevenson.

Under pressure to move quickly, Dayan told his generals that the battle plan was to be changed dramatically. "I cannot even explain to you, the reason," he told them. "You have just to take orders and one day you'll know, but I can't explain it to you now."[12]

Dayan said the new plan would call for a single parachute drop about thirty miles from the Suez Canal near the Mitla Pass. A column of mounted infantry would then race across Sinai to reinforce the paratroopers. That was the plan. Dayan did not go further, because he had pledged to Ben-Gurion that he would not tell the army that Ben-Gurion still suspected British treachery and, if the moment came, he intended to execute a full retreat.

Sharon later wrote that Dayan let him in on the secret just before the operation began. Sharon was at headquarters, and Dayan reportedly said to him that if the British double-crossed them, "it will be a very complicated situation . . . you'll have to bring back your forces [because] . . . you might be the only ones in Sinai."[13]

The call-up went out to Israeli paratroopers on the army radio station a day in advance. They came by bus or hitchhiked to Tel Nof air base in the desert near the Egyptian frontier. In Shekem Hall, Major Rafael Eitan stood before the four hundred soldiers and told them that Israeli forces for the first time in two thousand years were going to parachute into enemy territory.

The men roared with pleasure and sang a traditional battle song, "Why Didn't You Tell Me Before?"[14]

Eitan—known to his men as "Raful"—was going to lead the jump. Born in Afula in the Jezreel Valley, Eitan had been fighting Arabs since he was a boy. His father was one of the founders of Hashomer, the Jewish defense league created at the beginning of the century to guard the fields around Jewish settlements from Arab marauders. A wiry sabra with dark hirsute features, Eitan was one of Sharon's most loyal and courageous commanders. Six months earlier, during the attack on the Syrian army in Galilee, Eitan had taken a machine gun round in the chest, and for his bravery on the battlefield, Sharon had put him in for the Medal of Courage.

H-hour was set for the next day, Monday, October 29, 1956.

Sharon walked resolutely among the soldiers, exhorting them with profanity and patriotic slogans. He arranged for a sturdy meal of meat and rice, and briefed them on the battle plan, making each feel that he was part of a great enterprise of the Jewish people.

"Every time he would tell the same joke about the old bull and the young bull," recalled Reuven Merhav, who was one of two Merhav brothers who served under Sharon. "The young bull says to the old bull as they survey the herd, 'Let's run and fuck a few.' And the old bull replies, 'Let's go slow and fuck them all!' "[15]

Late on Monday afternoon, Major Eitan and 394 paratroopers climbed with their weapons and heavy packs into sixteen DC-3 Dakotas, all thirty-two engines roaring as they muscled slowly into the air, turning west toward the sun. Israeli pilots in a dozen French-made jet fighters rose into the warm air to escort the Dakotas to their destination 150 miles to the west.

The drop zone had been shifted back a few miles from the Mitla Pass because a reconnaissance flight had detected Egyptian tents and vehicles near the pass itself. In the last hour of light, the Suez Canal appeared as a blue ribbon of seawater incongruously laid across the desert. Mitla Pass was visible as a cleft in the low hills to the east of the canal.

In each plane, the men clipped on to the static line that would deploy their canopies. The jump signal tensed their muscles like electric current. One by one, the paratroopers leaped into the dusk over enemy territory, silently drifting down, thankful for the element of surprise.

Sharon and the rest of his brigade, mounted on tanks, half-tracks, and trucks, burst across the frontier at Kuntilla and made a beeline across Sinai to join up with the paratroopers. As they raced through the desert, Sharon and his men heard over the radio net that the military spokesman was describing the operation as a raid to eliminate terrorist bases in Sinai. By the next morning, Sharon rolled into the perimeter where Eitan's paratroopers had settled. Sharon was ready to fight, but there were no Egyptians.

He and his men had no military objective other than to hold this ground and wait for orders. By the end of the day, as Ben-Gurion grew increasingly furious at the delays of the British and French entry into the war, Sharon could not stand still. He sent a message to headquarters that he was going to proceed to take the Mitla Pass.

A blunt message came back denying air support for such a move. Sharon decided he could attack without air cover and formed an assault force. But just before 6:00 a.m., an order arrived to stand down. The high command did not approve his plan; he should sit tight. Soon thereafter, Egyptian warplanes strafed Sharon's dug-in force. Israeli jets rallied to chase them away and pilots reported that the Mitla Pass looked clear. They also reported that an Egyptian force appeared to be advancing on Sharon from forty miles out.

Sharon was on the radio protesting his orders when a light plane landed and the deputy head of the southern command, General Rehavam Ze'evi, stepped out and greeted Sharon. Everyone knew Ze'evi as "Gandhi," a strange nickname for a skinny young militia fighter. But as he walked from the showers dressed in a towel, Ze'evi's shaved head and spectacles had conjured up the image of the Indian leader. Ze'evi listened to Sharon's complaint that his forces were too exposed, that the Mitla Pass seemed to be clear, and that as the commander on the ground, this should be his call.

Ze'evi compromised, agreeing that Sharon could send a reconnaissance patrol into the pass to see if it was clear. "You can go as deep as possible, just don't get involved in a battle."[16]

As soon as Ze'evi's small plane disappeared over the horizon, Sharon disregarded the limitations. He ordered one-third of his twelve-hundred-man force to form up under Motta Gur, the wavy-haired sabra from Jerusalem who had distinguished himself during the Qalqilya raid and at Khan Yunis, where he was wounded in action and where Dayan had put him in for a citation of honor. Sharon had only three tanks in his force, but he sent all of them into the pass with Gur along with two companies of men in half-tracks.

The Mitla Pass was a natural ambush site, yet Sharon ignored the elementary tactical requirement: reconnaissance. There was every reason to believe that the Egyptians were hidden in the rocky slopes that rose on either side of the road as it snaked into the pass. After all, Sharon had moved the drop site at the beginning of the operation because air reconnaissance had seen Egyptian tents and vehicles. Sharon was sending his men—the majority of his force—into a perfect shooting gallery without scouting the terrain.

The Egyptians were there with a force twice the size of Sharon's. They allowed the Israeli column to advance deep into the pass before they opened fire with heavy machine guns, mortars, and rocket-propelled grenades. The stone walls of the pass reverberated with deafening explosions and the cries of men yelling orders or screaming for medics. In the first minutes of the attack, Gur shouted into the radio for reinforcements. They had walked into a trap: "Get me out of here!" he said.

Gur tried to keep the column moving, thinking that he could reach the western exit of the pass, near where Yitzhak "Hakka" Hofi, another of Sharon's battle-tested officers, was pinned down with his company. Gur's advance was halted by withering fire, which shredded the half-tracks and forced the Israeli paratroopers to scramble for cover. The Egyptians had them in crossfire, blistering them with hot lead from the heights. The French-made tanks were useless. They could not maneuver in the narrow pass or elevate their guns high enough to fire on the Egyptian positions.

For the second time that month, Gur had been sent into an ambush by Sharon and was again unable to extract himself because the operation had been planned so poorly. At Qalqilya, Sharon had blamed the disaster on Dayan, but here there was no excuse: Sharon, the great tactical planner, had failed to reconnoiter the ground.

Sharon also failed to personally direct the counterattack, leaving the task of extricating a third of his men to his deputy, Aharon Davidi, whose unit had managed to fight its way out of the entrance to the pass. Sharon supervised the construction of an airstrip because they were going to need transports to evacuate the grievously wounded soldiers who lay bleeding in the pass.

For the next five hours, all of Sharon's officers were either fighting in the pass or trying to extract their comrades, but Sharon stayed a safe distance away. This was not the "follow me" code of the Israeli army; Sharon's men were dying, but his battlefield courage seemed to wilt, and his absence from the fray registered on many of his soldiers.

Motta Gur and Hakka Hofi realized that they would have to scale the walls of the pass and fight for every inch of high ground.

Outside the pass, Davidi called to his men. He needed a driver to race into the pass and draw Egyptian fire so the counterattacking force could pinpoint the Egyptian gun emplacements. Accounts differ on what was said in response to Davidi's call, but he finally turned to his own driver, Yehuda Kan Dror, and told him what needed to be done. Kan Dror went pale; his lips pursed. Everyone standing around him knew it was a suicide mission. He had every reason to decline. His brother had been killed in the War of Independence. Yet he didn't. He quietly mounted his jeep, revved the engine, and sped into the pass, careening around the smoking hulks of abandoned trucks. He was not even hundred yards in when he ran into a hail of bullets. Dozens of hits ripped his torso. He lost control of the jeep, which lurched onto its side. Mortally wounded, Kan Dror rolled into a ditch for cover. He lay there bleeding until nightfall and then crawled dozens of yards, calling out weakly to his comrades. Once he was pulled to safety, Kan Dror's torn frame was loaded by stretcher onto the first flight out. He died six weeks later.[17]

Inside the pass, Lieutenant Oved Ladijinsky led one contingent of the rescue force. A sabra farmer's son from the Rehovot area, he had won a citation a year earlier for taking out a Syrian machine gun nest that was spraying soldiers who had stumbled into a barbed-wire barrier near Kursi on the shore of the Sea of Galilee.

Now he was leading his men up the treacherous slope of the Mitla Pass, trying to take out another Egyptian machine gun position. Picking his target, Ladijinsky pulled the pin on a grenade and lobbed it over his head, hoping it would drop on the Egyptians, but instead the grenade came bounding back down among Ladijinsky's men. In an instant, he dove to protect them and died from the blast.[18]

After more than five hours of fighting, Gur's trapped battalion reinforced by Davidi's men overcame the Egyptian defenders in the Mitla Pass, but Sharon's paratroopers had suffered nearly 40 dead and 150 wounded.

The Suez campaign was in full swing. British and French paratroopers landed in northern Sinai while British marines slogged ashore at Port Said on the northern coast. British and French bombers flying out of bases on Cyprus and Malta descended on Cairo and other major targets, terrorizing civilians and touching off a firestorm in the residential neighborhoods of Port Said, where thousands died.

Eisenhower was as mad as a hornet. James Reston of the *New York Times* wrote that not "since the days of General Grant" had the corridors of the White House rung with "barracks-room" language. Sharon's forces pulled out of Mitla and rushed south with orders to conquer the southern tip of Sinai and the promontory that faces the Strait of Tiran. Over the next several days of fighting, as Sinai easily tumbled into Israeli hands, a number of Sharon's officers privately seethed over the lives Sharon had needlessly expended in the Mitla Pass. It was a completely unnecessary battle over an objective that was immediately abandoned.[19]

The complaints about Sharon's performance reached Ben-Gurion, who received Sharon on November 4. Ben-Gurion was still in bed with fever. Sharon acted as if the Egyptians had done "something extraordinary" in fortifying the Mitla Pass.

"They did not disperse on the hilltops but entered the cliffs and built burrows in them, so that from the air nothing could be seen," he told the prime minister, claiming that it was "very unusual for Arabs to do something like that: inside the walls of the rocks, at different heights, they dug holes, and there are also natural cavities there, and they moved in a force of 600, and there was terrible fire from there."[20]

Of course there was nothing unusual about what the Egyptians had done; what was unusual was that Sharon had failed to scout the terrain before sending his men into a trap.

Gur and Hofi, whose battalions had borne the brunt of the attack in Mitla, never forgave Sharon. Some officers considered Sharon a coward for failing to lead the counterattack. A number of junior officers, among them Lieutenant Dov Tamari, a platoon commander who lost ten men, openly criticized Sharon. The episode marked all of them for the rest of their lives.[21]

Dayan was embittered, but he knew that Ben-Gurion, who was exultant over the Israeli performance on the battlefield (indeed, in his own words, he was "drunk with victory"), was unwilling to pass judgment on Sharon's dereliction of duty—or loss of nerve—at Mitla.[22] In public, where the death toll from Mitla incited anguished cries against Sharon, Dayan defused the criticism with an aphorism that lionized Sharon's impetuousness: as a commander, he said, "I would rather have to restrain dashing horses, than prod lazy oxen."[23]

Many years later, however, Dayan wrote in his memoir, "I regretted that I had not succeeded in molding such relations of mutual trust that if they had wished to defy my orders, they would have done so directly and openly."[24]

It was as close as he ever came to publicly calling Sharon an insubordinate liar.

Ben-Gurion went before the Knesset a day after Eisenhower won reelection in a landslide and described the Suez campaign as "the greatest and most glorious operation in the annals of our people and one of the most remarkable in world history."[25] He brazenly asserted Israeli sovereign rights to Sharm el-Sheikh by saying it was the site of an ancient Jewish kingdom, a claim of questionable foundation.

Ben-Gurion's militarism had reached too far. He had underestimated the impact on both the Soviet Union and the United States. The Soviet response was a mordant warning from Premier Nikolai Bulganin: "The GOI [Government of Israel] is criminally and irresponsibly playing with the fate of the world and with the fate of its own people." The allusion to a nuclear threat from Moscow was none too subtle when Bulganin said that Israel was "sowing hatred of the SOI [State of Israel] among the Eastern peoples, such as cannot but leave its mark on the future of Israel and places in question the very existence of Israel as a state." He added ominously that "the Soviet government is at this moment taking steps to put an end to the war and to restrain the aggressors."[26]

Ben-Gurion complained that Bulganin's message "could have been written by Adolf Hitler,"[27] and even though Moscow was likely engaging in strategic bluster, there was no other power willing to stand up to the combined fury of both superpowers, for Eisenhower, as soon as he figured out what had happened, immediately signaled his outrage that Britain and France had conspired behind Washington's back to encourage Israeli militarism—naked aggression in this instance—in the Middle East. They had subverted the principles of the Tripartite Declaration, the Charter of the United Nations, and the very spirit of the transatlantic alliance, which was based on trust and concerted action.

Ben-Gurion was not one to give up easily a prize as great as Sinai. He dispatched Golda Meir and Peres to Paris for a crisis meeting. Christian Pineau, the French foreign minister, stated that his government was forced to take the Soviet threat seriously and that Paris was in the process of "drawing conclusions" about the folly of the whole enterprise. At that moment, Meir clumsily broached the question that Ben-Gurion had earlier raised—the oil resources of Sinai. It seemed a desperate attempt to offer the French some financial incentive to stay the course, but Pineau just looked at her as if she was crazy. "Soviet pilots are flying over Syria, the Soviets want to intervene in the Middle East and you still think of the oil in Sinai?"[28]

By November 7, 1956, it was over. British and French troops on the beach in Sinai marched back aboard their ships, leaving only the Israelis still deployed and hoping to hang on to their gains.

In Washington, Eban made the rounds in Congress, the State Department, and the CIA. None of Israel's close friends, not even Senator Lyndon Johnson, the Democratic leader, could rationalize the brazen military conspiracy that Israel had joined. Herbert Hoover, Jr., standing in for stricken Secretary of State Dulles, warned Eban's deputy that Israel risked "expulsion from the United Nations" for violating the UN Charter if it did not withdraw from Egyptian territory. Internationally, the mood had turned strongly against Israel. Canadian prime minister Lester Pearson told Eban that Ben-Gurion's speech was "offensive" both to the Arabs and to Europeans. "If you people persist with this, you run the risk of losing all your friends."[29]

The war had cost Anthony Eden his premiership and put the French government in turmoil, but the Israeli prime minister was the last of the conspirators to come to the conclusion that he had to give up what had been achieved, and that was substantial. A small and embattled military society had demonstrated its prowess in combat for the second time in a decade; it had seized the Sinai Peninsula—an area three times the size of Israel. Sparta had prevailed over Athens with spectacular results. No society, especially one so closely entrenched in the military as Israel's, could walk away from such a victory.

Ben-Gurion thus refused to budge. Dayan and much of the sabra military establishment were adamant that Israel not give up its territorial conquest, which had cost 160 battle deaths—40 of them in the Mitla Pass—and hundreds more wounded. When Ben-Gurion announced a withdrawal of Israeli forces on November 9, it was clear that Israel was still trying to hang on to the eastern shore and tip of Sinai as well as the Gaza Strip. Ben-Gurion resisted and resisted. He told Eban to fend off the attacks at the United Nations, and Eban maneuvered, employing formidable oratorical skills.

Dayan, disgusted with diplomacy, took off his uniform and appeared before the leadership of the Mapai on November 14 to argue against the withdrawal; Ben-Gurion orchestrated the appearance to demonstrate to the political class just how strongly the military establishment and the sabra bedrock of the country were committed to defying the world.[30] At one point, Ben-Gurion asked Minister of Finance Levi Eshkol to do some quick calculations on how long the country could hold out if the United Nations imposed sanctions and cut off food and fuel supplies. Eshkol crunched the numbers for half an hour and reported that the Jewish state could survive about five months under total blockade.[31]

What the world could not see was that Ben-Gurion was still caught up in the euphoria. In mid-December, he signed the first secret nuclear agreement for "technical and industrial assistance" in building a large atomic reactor and for a French commitment to supply it with 385 tons of uranium by 1960.[32] The afterglow was so intense that one of Sharon's most vivid memories that winter was of the party that Ben-Gurion hosted for the commanders of the Sinai campaign.

Here was the assembled elite of the officer corps, most of them battle-hardened sabras from families that Ben-Gurion had known since the earliest days of Zionist Palestine and that had helped to build and defend the *yishuv*, the prestate community of Jews under the British Mandate. They were all now under Ben-Gurion's roof, and as the hall filled, Sharon could hear Ben-Gurion calling out, "Is Arik [Sharon] here? Where is he? I want him sitting here with me."[33]

Stomachs were churning at the mention of Sharon's name. Most officers present knew what had happened at Mitla. Some were furious over the wasted deaths, but here was Ben-Gurion fawning. What conclusion could they draw?

Sharon, then twenty-eight years old, said the other officers in the room exchanged "dark looks" over Ben-Gurion's attention to him, but Sharon just lapped it up. His father lay dying in the hospital and his wife was at home with their newborn son, Gur. But Sharon could not resist reveling in Ben-Gurion's high esteem.

The memory of these warriors jostling for favor before their leader was, for Sharon, an erotic experience; he recalled most specifically the effect on Ben-Gurion of the actress Orna Porat. The older man could not take his eyes off of her during her performance. He tapped his chair to the rhythm of her song, and it was plain to Sharon that "his desire [was] smoldering." When Ben-Gurion summoned the actress to his table, the officers applauded.

"Suddenly, I saw for the first time Ben-Gurion as a man of blood and flesh," Sharon wrote, but only much later would the country learn that the founding leader had extramarital affairs, as had Dayan and Meir. And though Sharon was not known as a womanizer, as a number of senior officers were, he was rumored to have carried on an affair with his wife's younger sister, Lily (whom he married after his wife died). In those days, the military and political elites were protected from exposure by the timely interventions of the army censor. "In that generation," Sharon said, referring to 1956, "secrets were kept, the mysteries of life were closely hidden."[34]

Into this cocoon, the world intruded. Eisenhower's initial anger had subsided and he focused on how America would repair the damage wrought by British, French, and Israeli deception in fomenting a war of conquest and regime change as if it were still the colonial era. And it did not help that by way of comparison, Soviet troops had rampaged through Hungary to put down rebellion in the Eastern bloc. Whom was Eisenhower to blame? The Soviet "missile threat" hung in the air, and in the middle of it all, John Foster Dulles was rushed to the hospital where exploratory surgery revealed abdominal cancer.

Eisenhower never openly turned on his allies. His political advisers convinced him that doing so would only benefit the Soviets. He was clever enough to let events develop against the conspirators. With the Suez Canal closed, oil shipments to Europe slowed. There was a run on the British currency in financial markets. Anthony Eden and Guy Mollet, the British and French leaders, were forced to withdraw their armies. Against Ben-Gurion's formidable determination to hold on to part of Sinai, Eisenhower's only real leverage was the threat of UN sanctions—even expulsion—and the loss of legitimacy that would entail.

To a joint session of Congress, the president laid out the Eisenhower Doctrine in the Middle East, a declaration of American policy that would stand in for the Tripartite Declaration of 1950, which now lay in tatters because two of its three signatories had undermined the core principle of nonaggression. But Eisenhower did not single out his wayward allies as the enemy. The enemy, he said, was international communism, and he asked Congress for the tools to confront it.

But Eisenhower had not forgotten Ben-Gurion. The United Nations was moving to impose sanctions that would be devastating to the Jewish state if it refused to withdraw.

Lyndon Johnson, the Senate majority leader, told Eisenhower on February 20, 1957, that it was unfair to chastise Israel for its actions in Sinai when Russia had invaded Hungary with impunity.[35] But Eisenhower, who was reelected in a landslide in which the Jewish vote had gone to his opponent, seemed impervious to pressure. He went over Johnson's head, addressing the American people directly on the relatively new medium of television. Eisenhower told the country that Israel's conquest in Sinai put the high principles of the UN Charter at risk. The United Nations was not yet a decade old and, in Eisenhower's mind, it was the essential institution to carry the burden of conflict resolution in a century of war and destruction.

"The United Nations must not fail," he said, and therefore the international community "has no choice but to exert pressure upon Israel to comply with the withdrawal resolutions."

It was the first time an American president had characterized Israel not as a tiny embattled democracy but as a military aggressor whose invasion and occupation scheme was a violation of international law.

From the moral high ground, Eisenhower—the commander who had succeeded in keeping America out of war since he came to office—said that in the new world, he as president could not accept "the proposition that a nation which invades another should be permitted to exact conditions for withdrawal."[36]

But when the television lights dimmed, Eisenhower worked in secret channels to offer Ben-Gurion an inducement to end the standoff.

After cancer surgery, Dulles summoned Eban to his home in Washington and showed the Israeli envoy the draft of a statement the United States was willing to support regarding Israel's rights to free navigation. It was a significant American offer, and Dulles warned Eban that if Ben-Gurion refused to take it, if he refused to withdraw from Sinai, Israel was risking a rupture in its relations with the United States.[37]

Israel was "on the verge of a catastrophe," Dulles warned. "If Israel is not interested in taking up the American initiative, the matter will go back to the United Nations, where I doubt that you could get any worthwhile guarantees at all."[38]

Eban caught a plane back to the Middle East, and when he got to Jerusalem, he told Ben-Gurion that they were out of time. No one in the Senate, not even Johnson, could stand up to the president on this issue. The mood among American Jewish leaders was no better. "Your chief is carrying stubbornness too far," Eban quoted one of them as saying. But Ben-Gurion still faced the united opposition of the military establishment, especially Dayan and Sharon, who also had begun to protest any move to leave Sinai. Ben-Gurion did not want his victory spoiled by a sabra rebellion.

He instructed Eban to banish the word "withdrawal" from his vocabulary at the United Nations but instructed him to lock up the strongest American declaration supporting freedom of navigation for Israeli shipping through the Red Sea and Gulf of Aqaba that he could get.

The diplomatic compromise provided Ben-Gurion with a concrete concession and, in late March, Israel agreed to withdraw from Sinai and from the Gaza Strip. This was not the victory that Ben-Gurion had hoped for, but it was enough for him to face the sabras and their allies throughout the military establishment. The Sinai War was over.

Dayan bitterly reproached Ben-Gurion. If Israel could hold out against sanctions for half a year, "why do we have to kneel down before we have to?"[39] Why not wait until the oil and food supplies were exhausted and the electrical plants were forced to shut down, and then surrender if that was still necessary? Dayan asked. But Ben-Gurion was not willing to put everything at risk, least of all the nuclear project, as well as the strong new arms relationship with France, which had given Israel a modern military arsenal for the first time.

On March 7, after 125 days of occupation, Israeli forces marched out of the Gaza Strip, and the Israeli flag was lowered over the military governor's house in el-Arish, the Egyptian regional capital in eastern Sinai. Dayan was in an angry and sullen mood. He told reporters that "officers have to eat army rations, the sweet as well as the bitter."

Dayan boarded a small airplane with Ezer Weizman, his brother-in-law at the time and an influential sabra whose uncle Chaim had led the Zionist movement. They flew out into the Sinai for the last time so Dayan, as chief of staff, could join the retreating column of Israeli soldiers. It was an uncharacteristic act of dissent: Dayan as the last soldier reluctantly leaving the land into which a new generation of sabras had poured its blood.[40]

Israel's strategic goals in the Suez campaign, to seize part of the Sinai Peninsula and to contribute to the overthrow of Nasser, were never realized. Still, Israel had demonstrated that it was willing to go on the offensive, in the absence of any imminent threat, to seize territory or to weaken an enemy through preventative war. The precedent of the Suez Crisis was "activism"—the euphemism for Israeli militarism—on a grand scale.

There were tangible benefits: Israel had allied itself with France against the largest and most powerful Arab state, Israel had gained a conventional arms supply at a critical moment in history, and it had gained a strategic partner in the development of an atomic weapons complex that would place Israel in a league of its own in the Middle East.

At that crucial moment, both French and Israeli leaders had understood that they had no response to Soviet nuclear bullying. Whatever reticence still existed toward the development of atomic weapons disappeared in those heated hours of brinksmanship with Moscow.

The war also activated the United Nations to deploy peacekeeping forces to Gaza and along the Egyptian frontier all the way to Sharm el-Sheikh. This had the felicitous effect of opening the Gulf of Aqaba for

Israeli shipping just as Israel was developing plans for a large port facility at Eilat. Within a few years, Israel's growing relationship with Iran (under the shah) would transform Eilat into a major port for Iranian crude.

Moshe Sharett's vision of another path—toward peace with the Arabs—was all but buried by the war, and this was the most tragic consequence. Nasser decried what he called the "Tripartite Aggression" and rallied the Arabs to unite behind his leadership to fight neocolonialism, imperialism, and their "stooges" in the Middle East. Israel was now the main enemy. Its defeat by a collective Arab effort became the organizing principle that animated Arab politics from then on.

Nasser emerged as a savior of his people. Egypt had won full control of the Suez Canal and its revenues; Nasser was able to boast to the Soviet leadership that Egyptian forces had prevented the West from turning Egypt into a "missile base" against the Soviet Union; Israel had clashed with Eisenhower, making Nasser's point about Ben-Gurion's militaristic character.[41]

What was remarkable was that the brief period when all of the trend lines had been running in the direction of Sharett's diplomacy, toward accommodation and against Ben-Gurion's militarism, vanished almost without a trace. It was covered over by layers of classification and buried by the new mythology that Israel had no alternatives to the military option. With Sharett in forced retirement, no Israeli leader dared plot a strategy to try to salvage relations with the Arab world or reopen the secret dialogue with Nasser and other Arab leaders, as the Americans had once promoted. The Middle East had tipped beyond the constraints of the immediate post–world war period. Escalation toward another round of war seemed inevitable.

The Suez Crisis was the new Genesis. It affirmed Israel as a military society in which preparation for war—mobilization, training, acquisition of weaponry, building of military industries, and a willingness to strike—returned to the forefront of national strategy as Ben-Gurion had been arguing since his long sabbatical in the desert in 1953.

The civilian economy would continue to develop, but the war had delivered benefits that even Ben-Gurion had not imagined. The war brought quiet to the frontiers of the Jewish state for the first time, an achievement whose political impact could not be understated. Though the endgame was messy and fretful, Israel had emerged stronger, more secure, and more devoted than ever to the efficacy of military power over concession and compromise. The lesson taken was that war created unforeseen opportunities for those who had the courage to exploit them. And Ben-Gurion's "capital C," as Sharett had ruefully said, was courage.

Sharett's caution in matters of war was at the heart of Ben-Gurion's disdain for him as an intellect and a leader; the older man was contemptuous of anyone who saw the Arab enemy in humanistic terms. These were the elements that had compelled Ben-Gurion forward—to mobilize Sparta and to persist against all odds as its paramount leader.

FOUR

Israel as "Detonator"

It looked like the return of Alexander the Great's armada, not against Israel's sandy shores but farther north off the coast of Lebanon.

In the late afternoon of July 15, 1958, three American aircraft carriers of the Sixth Fleet—the *Essex*, *Wasp*, and *Saratoga*—bore down on Lebanon's coast with two hundred combat aircraft and, one after another, they sent their warbirds catapulting off flight decks.

The combat jets roared skyward as fourteen thousand U.S. marines churned up wakes in the eastern Mediterranean. Their landing craft and gunships headed for the beach, where the swarm of stern-faced marines bounded ashore along the waterfront of the Lebanese capital, Beirut.

"The first boat touched the beach at exactly 3 p.m., and a wave of amphibious vehicles chugged in behind it," observed a Western journalist who dashed to the water's edge. "Within five minutes the Marines were pouring across the beach, flanked by crowds of admiring Lebanese."[1]

An entire fleet stretching across the sea had assembled to support the landing, which President Eisenhower compared to a small-scale D-day invasion because the "potential consequences," if things went wrong, "were chilling," just as they had been at Normandy in 1944. Seen from the belly of each landing craft, the folds of Mount Lebanon rose as a brooding Leviathan overlooking the coast.[2]

The triggering event for the massive American military landing was the violent coup in Baghdad on July 14, where pro-Nasser army officers slaughtered King Faisal II and the royal family, and dragged the body of the murdered prime minister, Nuri al-Said, through the streets of the capital.

Pro-Nasser forces were on the verge of insurrection in Lebanon, where the government of Camille Chamoun, a Maronite Christian, was under pressure from Arab nationalists to share power with Lebanon's growing Muslim population. The Lebanese army's loyalty was in doubt and Muslim militias ruled south of Beirut.

Eisenhower feared chaos and anarchy, exactly what the Israelis had at times hoped to exploit in the Middle East.

"Until stable governments are set up and supported locally, the Middle East will never calm down," the president told his advisers. Even though he was risking "the deep resentment of nearly all of the Arab world" and "general war with the Soviet Union," the worst thing, Eisenhower later reflected, would have been "to do nothing."[3]

Ben-Gurion and Israel's military establishment monitored short-wave radio reports as the landing unfolded. It was only a year after the Suez Crisis, and he must have been astounded to witness such an act of super-power resolve in peacetime and so close to Israel's frontier. After all, Ben-Gurion had been arguing that even America could not be relied upon to come over the horizon in a crisis.

Yet here it was. Eisenhower, as if he were still in uniform, had summoned a military display of global proportions. U.S. airborne forces in West Germany were on alert to move into the Middle East, the Sixth Fleet had swelled to more than seventy ships, and the president, with great deliberation, had elevated the readiness of U.S. nuclear forces—eleven hundred aircraft in the Strategic Air Command—and sent refueling tankers aloft around the world as a warning to the Soviet Union not to interfere.[4]

On the beach in Lebanon, the marines who splashed ashore in mid-summer were sweaty, irritable, and uncertain of their mission, but to many observers in the Middle East and beyond, Eisenhower had finally taken a huge step toward taming the Arab nationalism that was rampant in the region, where Nasser exhorted the masses to overthrow pro-Western monarchies and other allies such as Lebanon's Maronite Christian government.

All Ben-Gurion could do was watch as a churlish spectator, disappointed that Israel was not allied with such great power, keen to profit somehow from these events, and hopeful that they would lead to a decision in Washington to supply arms to Israel.

The Jewish state had no formal security guarantee from the United States, and here was Eisenhower rushing in to defend an Arab regime. Even King Hussein in Jordan, who was also under threat from Nasser's subversion, was receiving flights of British military transports, but none of the great powers seemed too concerned about Israel, exposed to any Arab backlash. Ben-Gurion complained that the British were overflying Israeli territory and he sent word to Eisenhower through intelligence channels that "if Hussein falls," Israel would move to seize the West Bank, where nearly one million Arabs lived.[5]

The American incursion in Lebanon in 1958, along with a similar British deployment to Jordan, lasted only three months as an elaborate show of force that was heavily criticized in some quarters, but it showed convincingly that the United States was now the dominant power in the region, replacing Great Britain, and that Washington would no longer tolerate Nasser's intimidation of pro-Western governments, a message that could not be lost on Ben-Gurion and the Israelis.

If the American leader was willing to dispatch such a massive force into the Middle East to preempt Egyptian or Soviet subversion, the implication was that Eisenhower might also act forcefully to block Israeli aggression. All the regional powers could draw their own conclusions, but Ben-Gurion had to consider that he would soon be hiding an illicit nuclear reactor under construction in the Negev Desert. His worst nightmare would be that one of the superpowers discovered it, then confronted Israel and, with a show of force, demanded that it be dismantled or put under international supervision.

In retrospect, there was also a powerful irony.

Had this projection of American power into the region come a decade earlier, the British collapse in Palestine might have been averted and the creation of Jewish and Arab states might have proceeded without major incident under UN resolutions. Here was Eisenhower standing against "international communism" in Lebanon, but at the same time he seemed powerless to address—right next door—the long-standing failure of the international community to create an equitable architecture of nation-states for the Arabs and Jews in the Holy Land.

For Ben-Gurion, the lesson of 1958 was the emphatic reiteration of American military strength, a muscular reminder that Israel's military ambition was constrained by the overarching dominance of U.S. forces in the Middle East. Whether Eisenhower intended it or not—he never addressed the question—the projection of raw American power threatened the very freedom of military action that Israel had just demonstrated in the Suez campaign. Israel may have been heavily engaged in secret military cooperation with France, but there was no ignoring the enormity of America's display. And so Ben-Gurion set out in the aftermath of the crisis to find a role for Israel in the American orbit. He pushed for Israel's association with the NATO alliance; he dispatched his Mossad chief, Isser Harel, to CIA headquarters to propose joint covert operations in the Arab world; and he sought to interest the State Department in Israel's "alliance of the periphery"—building Israeli relations with Iran, Turkey, Sudan, and Ethiopia—to keep the Arab world off-balance. In the wake of Lebanon, Ben-Gurion sent Abba Eban and Shimon Peres to Washington to make the case—again—for arms, and he warned that any new attempt by the great powers to truncate the territory of Israel to appease Nasser "will be met with the entire military force of the state of Israel."[6]

Egypt was rearming after the Suez Crisis. The decision by the Soviet Union to replace weapons that had been destroyed or captured begged the question of how the United States would maintain a balance of power. Eisenhower no longer had any illusions about Nasser, but at the same time he did not want to become Israel's visible arms supplier.

So Eisenhower made a fateful decision: he decided to arm Israel—mostly through American allies—on the logic that a more secure Jewish state would be more confident in making concessions for peace, a logic that collided with the very nature of Israel's military ambition and the character of the sabra military establishment. In Sparta, arms did not moderate ambition; they incited it.[7]

The breakthrough came after Meir and Peres visited London that summer. Prime Minister Harold Macmillan told them privately that Britain, having been encouraged by Eisenhower, was willing to sell heavy Centurion tanks, submarines, and some other items to build up Israeli forces. Separately, Washington opened a funding channel to assist Israel in making arms purchases, and Eisenhower sent one thousand recoilless rifles directly to the IDF. These were significant first steps in the inexorable escalation that was coming.[8]

Dayan told a group of officers that the Suez War had shown that Israel's power in the Middle East was that of a "detonator."

"Israel is not merely a Jewish state whose existence is morally justified," he told them, but in any confrontation, "when someone wishes to force on us things which are detrimental to our existence, there will be an explosion which will shake up wider areas, and realizing this, such elements in the international system will do their utmost to prevent damage to us."

Dayan added that the great powers are not "motivated by sympathy for the Jews," or for Israel, "but by the realization that we are such a state with such a power that if anyone tries to harm us—the explosion will do damage to others too."

"This is not a constructive thesis," he continued. "It is a thesis advocating that we should be a kind of biting beast, capable of developing a crisis beyond our borders and expanding it to far wider areas" when Israel perceived its interests under threat.[9] For the leading military thinker of his day, Dayan's worldview was brutally frank: Israel as a biting beast, a reckless detonator that eschewed diplomacy in favor of some Hobbesian concept of calculated mayhem. Such a strategy evoked Dayan's biblical obsession with primordial combat. It was a strategy worthy of Samson against the Philistines, but in the post–world war environment of the modern Middle East, where the great powers were trying to enforce war prevention under the UN Charter, it was a prescription for unceasing war.

Peres, too, sought to define the new parameters of Israeli security in the post-Suez period. "We have to aspire to alter the state of Israel's borders," he told a closed meeting of senior government officials in 1957. The Jewish state need not seek reconciliation with the Arabs, he said. "I am not an ardent admirer of the Middle East culture and I don't need music records from Yemen or books from Egypt." Israel, he said, "should follow the world's big blocs and the only natural place for us—distance wise—is Europe."[10]

From retirement, Sharett mounted a rearguard assault on the militarism that Dayan and Peres were espousing as national policy. He told a seminar of Mapai leaders that the Suez War had been unnecessary. Whatever gains that had come from battle could have been achieved through diplomacy, he asserted.

"The activists believe that the Arabs understand only the language of force," he said. They believe Israel must "from time to time prove clearly that it is strong . . . in a devastating and highly effective way. If it does not prove this, it will be swallowed up, and perhaps wiped off the face of the earth."[11]

There was another approach, he argued. "The question of peace must not be lost sight of for one single moment. This is not only a political consideration; in the long view, it is decisive from a military point of view. . . . We must always bring the question of peace into our overall calculations. We have to curb our reactions [to Arab violence]" and especially disproportionate reactions, which Ben-Gurion had embraced.

"When military reactions outstrip in their severity the events that caused them, grave processes are set in motion that widen the gulf and thrust our neighbors into the extremist camp," Sharett warned.[12]

The journalist Amos Elon heard of Sharett's internal dissent and pleaded with him to go public so that the country might better understand the debate that had raged in private and that had cost Sharett his premiership, but Sharett refused. His stoicism was connected to some unstated view of what was best for the country, or the party. Elon considered Sharett's silence a form of cowardice.

Ben-Gurion emerged from the Suez War fully restored as the preeminent national leader. He held the lion's share of power as both prime minister and defense minister, ruling almost as an autocrat unrestrained by any other intellectual force in the Israeli establishment. When right-wing members of the Knesset sought to bring home the body of Vladimir Jabotinsky, their ideological leader who had died in New York in 1940, Ben-Gurion blocked the transfer, an act of spite against his onetime bitter rival.* Even on the cultural scene, Ben-Gurion delayed for more than a decade the advent of television in Israel, claiming it would undermine the

---

* Vladimir Jabotinsky's remains, and those of his wife, Jeanne, were finally repatriated to Israel in 1964 under Prime Minister Levi Eshkol.

pioneering spirit of youth. Most of the country got its news, carefully censored, from Kol Israel (The Voice of Israel) and, later, the IDF radio station, Galei Zahal.

Having driven Sharett from government, Ben-Gurion kept all talk of political succession at bay. He relegated the old guard of the Mapai to a subservient, advisory role. Eshkol moved up as presumptive heir, and Golda Meir became foreign minister and the essential spokesperson for Israel abroad. Her quiet insistence on the idea of an embattled Jewish state on the knife's edge of existence was a crucial palliative for a Diaspora troubled by Eisenhower's disapproval of Israeli militarism.

With Meir in charge of diplomacy, it was soon apparent that the search for an opening to the Arabs would recede. If Meir was anything, she was a Ben-Gurion loyalist with little pretense of competing vision. She wanted the American portfolio because she had lived in Milwaukee and in Colorado as a girl and had proved to be the most effective fund-raiser of anyone in Ben-Gurion's circle. American Jews responded to her unpretentious, motherly approach, which also provided a counterpose to Ben-Gurion's militancy.

In truth, the opportunities for engaging the Arabs were diminishing. Syria had embraced Nasser's leadership, and in 1958 the two governments approved a "total union" to become the United Arab Republic. Nasser, in theory, commanded armies on Israel's northern and southern flanks, though even in combination they were no match for the Israeli army, whose modern French arsenal had swelled with all the arms captured in Sinai and the new British tanks.

Reflexively, Jordan and Iraq had created their own Arab Union as a counter to Nasser, but the coup in Baghdad had put an end to that. Moreover, Moscow, with arms and propaganda, had fully embraced the Arab cause as a means to isolate Israel and weaken the United States.

Within the Mapai Party, Ben-Gurion introduced a new generation of leaders, Dayan being the most prominent as a sabra military hero. He resigned as chief of staff and entered the cabinet in 1959 as minister of agriculture. Peres also entered the Knesset in the 1959 election, beginning his political career as deputy minister of defense. The younger men believed that Ben-Gurion's goal was to eventually overthrow the Mapai leadership and make way for a new generation. But as young lions, Dayan and Peres failed to realize that Ben-Gurion was going to use them mostly as leverage against the old guard, whose power as stalwarts of the trade union movement in Israel was greater, collectively, than Ben-Gurion's.

Still, Dayan epitomized the sabra rebellion against the old guard. The very mention of his name spawned fear and revulsion in the upper ranks of Mapai. He entered the cabinet chambers as if wearing a dorsal fin.

Dayan once asked an interviewer how it could be said "that Israeli youth who in the past 15 years have crawled among the thorns and rocks with rifle in hand, fought in planes, and destroyers in the War of Independence and the Sinai campaign" were somehow inferior to "those who have been sitting for 25 years [in the party headquarters]?"[13]

The Mapai ministers busied themselves with the socialist-labor machinery that ran Israel's civilian economy, leaving national security to Ben-Gurion and his military chiefs.

But no one shared Ben-Gurion's decision-making authority over the covert atomic project. Ben-Gurion acted alone, with Shimon Peres as his secret envoy to the French. On October 3, 1957, a day before the Soviet Union astounded the world with its launch of Sputnik, the first satellite, France and Israel signed a secret agreement to construct, over five years, the Dimona reactor in the Negev. The agreement called for equipping the plant with a clandestine underground plutonium separation facility where nuclear weapons could be fabricated. Ben-Gurion never presented the nuclear project to the cabinet, in part because there was so much opposition to it. Many members of the political elite feared that the "nuclearization" of the Arab-Israeli conflict would be a disaster for the region and the world.

Meir and Eban feared the consequences of deceiving the Americans about Dimona. How could they look the Americans in the eye and call it a textile plant or the like?[14]

Others saw the construction of a large reactor as a white elephant that would bankrupt the country. Eban privately referred to Dimona as "an enormous alligator stranded on dry land." Opposition was stated on moral, economic, and security grounds. Generals feared that funding for conventional military forces would suffer. Intelligence chiefs worried that the Soviet Union or the United States might invade Israel to shut down the illicit reactor. And some just hated the program because Peres, whom they regarded as a pretentious thirty-year-old sycophant, was connected to the project under Ben-Gurion's supervision. Peres was using it, along with his other arms activities, to run Israel's relations with France and Germany, leaving Meir and the foreign ministry out of the loop.[15]

Nevertheless, Dimona went forward because Ben-Gurion willed it so. No one dared challenge him for fear of being accused of treason against the Jewish people, because that was how Ben-Gurion had framed the issue in the wake of the Holocaust. To him, the bomb meant: never again.

Amos Elon, who learned of the atomic project as a young Israeli journalist, recalled the way pervasive fear that statehood would fail bent many Israelis to Ben-Gurion's will. "Nearly everybody in the power elite was seized by the fragility of it all. And for this they wanted an atom bomb. I suppose they thought this would be a deterrent, that it would reassure them."[16]

The prime minister raised funds for Dimona's construction working outside the budget with the help of Jewish American businessmen. He enforced a stringent level of national secrecy—thousands of Israeli scientists, members of the military, construction workers, and political figures knew about Dimona—through a robust internal security network that functioned like secret police.

Anyone could be taken in the middle of the night for an interrogation by internal security; even Dayan's fourteen-year-old daughter, Yaël, would be yanked out of her home over her friendship with a foreigner.[17]

The cold war descended on Israel with a terrible complexity: so many Israelis had fled the Soviet Union; many left relatives behind, and some came as agents of the KGB, Soviet intelligence. Israel's sheer diversity created problems of espionage and opportunities to spy on Moscow for the West, and one of Israel's first big intelligence breaks occurred when Nikita Khrushchev's speech denouncing Stalin to the 20th Congress of the Communist Party fell into Israeli hands through a friendly Polish diplomat.

Isser Harel, the Mossad chief, and Amos Manor, head of Shabak, ran national surveillance programs to detect espionage penetrations, but they also protected Mapai's preeminence on the domestic political scene. Harel and Manor passed on political gossip and useful intelligence to Ben-Gurion, especially in cases where rival political camps strayed beyond the bounds of what Harel considered loyal opposition.

After Suez, Sharon showed no immediate ambition outside the army. He was not among the sabras rallying around Dayan as a potential successor to Ben-Gurion. The truth was that Sharon was sulking, bitter over the withdrawal from Sinai and defensive about his performance at the Mitla Pass. Just months after the war, Amos Ben-Gurion, the prime minister's son and police chief of Tel Aviv, told one of Sharon's friends over lunch to pass the word that Sharon should stop making public statements that the withdrawal from Sinai was "bad for the Jews."

"People already envy him his military success," the younger Ben-Gurion said of Sharon. "This jealousy could turn to hatred if he continues to show contempt for his superiors." On the other hand, he added, "if he can hold his tongue, he has a good chance of being promoted to chief of staff by my father."[18]

This was how Ben-Gurion manipulated the young bulls of the defense establishment, defining the requirements of loyalty and reinforcing them with promises of advancement that could be kept or abandoned according to his whim. Sharon's criticism of the Sinai withdrawal soon ceased, and he was selected to travel to England for senior officers' training at the British army's staff college at Camberley.

The winter of 1959–60 brought depressing news in Israel that agriculture had come up against the limits of growth without more water. Funding for a National Water Carrier, a pipeline to tap the Sea of Galilee and transport water to the arid south, was severely strained. German war reparation payments were declining, and revenue from Israel bonds sold in the United States would soon be diverted to repay interest on the bonds coming due.

Water was life, and there was not enough of it. Every sabra who had been raised on the land felt the mixture of pain and pleasure when the winter storms rolled in from Mediterranean, pelting some fields with showers and passing others by.[19]

If the Jewish state was to accommodate a doubling of the population, which is what Ben-Gurion hoped for, the army would have to seize more territory and water resources. The 1949 Armistice had left fertile lands along the Syrian border in disputed demilitarized zones. Israel's claim to the headwaters of the Jordan River and other small rivers remained contested. For Ben-Gurion, military "activism"—expansion of the frontiers—

was given a humanitarian rationale: it would make it possible for the Jewish state to grow and put food on the table.

Ben-Gurion had promoted Chaim Laskov as Dayan's replacement as chief of staff. Laskov, a pugnacious soldier who had never been one of Dayan's favorites, issued orders to the army to begin shooting at Syrian farmers who crossed into the disputed demilitarized zones to plant or harvest crops.

Laskov had earned his war-fighting credentials against the Nazis in the British army. After serving as an officer in the Jewish brigade, he organized vigilante squads to hunt down and execute German officers who had doffed their uniforms, and collaborators who had assisted them. He also helped organize the boat lifts of displaced Jews trying to reach Palestine despite the British blockade.

Laskov had grown up fighting. He had come from an impoverished family that had settled in Haifa after fleeing Barisov in present-day Belarus. His father was killed by Arabs in 1930, and within a few years, Laskov was hunting down Arab gangs as part of the special night squads organized by the British officer Orde Wingate, under whom Dayan and Yigal Allon also served.

Ben-Gurion admired Laskov and had protected him in the rivalry that had developed when Dayan wanted Meir Amit, a sabra ally, to succeed him as chief of staff.

Now Laskov was in charge, directing the army's mobilization on the Syrian frontier. The skirmishing was developing toward a full-scale clash. Ben-Gurion approved a cross-border raid to destroy a Syrian outpost in the village of Tawfiq, southeast of Galilee. After a night of battle, the Syrian army brought up reinforcements. The Soviet Union warned of a "Zionist-Imperialist" plot to overthrow the regime in Damascus. Nasser rushed to the Syrian capital and, as president of the United Arab Republic, he vowed to defend his Syrian brothers.

In early February 1960, Israeli intelligence picked up signals of troop movements on the Egyptian front. An armored division equipped with Soviet tanks was moving out from its base near Cairo and heading east toward the Suez Canal. Laskov and his chief of military intelligence, Chaim Herzog, ordered an air force reconnaissance mission, whose pilot found nothing. The Israeli command realized that the Egyptian armored force might have crossed the canal and continued east. They sent a second reconnaissance flight deep into Sinai, where the pilot made a shocking discovery: Nasser had sent almost his entire army—five hundred tanks and fifty thousand soldiers—to the Israeli border.[20]

The enemy was at the gates.

The Jewish state lay naked—with only twenty to thirty tanks defending its territory—in front of a military force that could be in Tel Aviv before anyone could stop it. Here was the nightmare that Ben-Gurion and Dayan had long feared.

Yitzhak Rabin was chief of operations on the general staff.

"We have gotten caught with our pants down," Rabin said to Ezer Weizman, the air force chief, when the general staff assembled in Tel Aviv. Until tanks could be deployed from the north, "Everything depends on the air force," he said in a note he pushed into Weizman's hand.[21]

Yet surprisingly, Ben-Gurion did not go public and declare a national emergency. He deployed Israel's only armored brigade to the Negev and asked friendly intelligence services to send Nasser a message that Israel had no intention of invading Syria or Egypt. He then waited for Nasser's next move.

Nasser's army sat there out in the open, exposed in the desert, and the last thing Ben-Gurion seemed interested in doing was attacking it. No one argued that Israel could not afford to stay mobilized in a defensive posture; there was no discussion that Israeli deterrence would be devastated if it failed to wipe out the Egyptian force. There was just silence.

After weeks of high tension, Nasser began to call the army back, taking credit in the Arab world for his willingness to confront the Zionist enemy and for preventing an Israeli invasion of Arab lands. And the most obvious lesson that could be drawn from what the Israelis called Operation Rotem was that Ben-Gurion saw no advantage in fomenting all-out war with Egypt. For the older man and for the military establishment that he still dominated, the unintended gains that had come from the Suez Crisis were worth preserving: a military status quo enforced by UN peacekeepers in Gaza and Sinai all the way to Sharm el-Sheikh.

The challenge at the outset of a new decade was to quietly build out the Israeli military while secretly working to complete the Dimona project at all costs, for Dimona would be the core of Israeli self-reliance for generations to come. The last thing Ben-Gurion wanted was a war that might bring attention to the huge construction project in the desert. And, there was an open question in Ben-Gurion's circle about Eisenhower—if the American president discovered the illicit nuclear weapons project, would he send U.S. marines to shut it down?

For Ben-Gurion, obsessed by the notion that he was the indispensable leader at a time when the Jews were making their last stand in history, the atom bomb was a fail-safe device. No Arab enemy, not even Egypt with its potential to put a million soldiers in the field, could withstand the deterrent power of atomic weapons.

On February 13, 1960, France detonated its first nuclear explosive in the Sahara Desert in Algeria. Soon there were CIA reports that Israeli observers had been spotted at the test site. The following month, the French cabinet was informed that Israel might use the Dimona reactor and French uranium supplies to build nuclear weapons. Charles de Gaulle, back in charge of France, told his government that he would terminate French nuclear cooperation with Israel. In May, the French foreign minister, Maurice Couve de Murville, summoned the Israeli ambassador in Paris and demanded that Israel lift the secrecy over Dimona and submit the facility to international inspection. France would withhold the supply of uranium until these conditions were met, he said.

In one stroke, the French seemed poised to renege. The strain on Ben-Gurion was formidable. The invasion scare with the Egyptian army had motivated the Israeli leader to travel to Washington to implore Eisenhower to sell early-warning radars, antiaircraft missiles, and other weapons to the Jewish state.

For nearly two hours, Ben-Gurion briefed Eisenhower on threats to Israel's existence in the Middle East, and though the secret of Dimona did not pass his lips, he was really making the case for Israel's becoming a nuclear power.

"Israel has only two alternatives," Ben-Gurion told Eisenhower. "Either Israel remains free and independent or Israel will be exterminated just as Hitler exterminated the Jews in Germany." Ben-Gurion's tone was apocalyptic, and though he deeply felt the threat of annihilation, he put a gloss on his own militarism by exaggerating the threat from Nasser.

It was not possible to believe that Israel could simply be defeated, Ben-Gurion told the president. If Nasser won, he would feel compelled to cut every throat in Israel. The Jewish state was "our last stand after fighting for survival for the last 4,000 years. I don't believe we deserve to be destroyed the way Hitler destroyed all but 300,000 of the six million Jews of Europe."[22]

Ben-Gurion's rhetorical approach was to portray the Arabs as the aggressors though he and Eisenhower knew that Israel had gone on the offensive starting in the mid-1950s; it had launched a war of aggression into Sinai and pressed the French at Sèvres to persuade Eisenhower to redraw the Middle East—to break up Jordan, Lebanon, and Egypt for Israel's territorial benefit. Eisenhower had no illusions about the Arabs and he didn't mind being pitched, but he was not blind to Ben-Gurion's aggressive policies.

After an hour and forty minutes of Ben-Gurion's monologue, Eisenhower dispatched the Israeli leader with a five-minute rebuttal. He did not want to become the principal arms supplier to the Middle East. "This is because we desire to be friends with all countries there—to be in a position to act as mediators." He cut off Ben-Gurion's appeal by saying, "Of course you deserve to exist," but security, he said, cannot rest solely on the possession of arms, especially in these days of terrible nuclear weapons. He suggested that Israel continue to meet its needs by purchasing arms in Europe (with American support). Moscow, he said, was not likely to complicate Israel's security by providing nuclear weapons to Nasser, so there was no reason for apocalyptic thinking.[23]

Ben-Gurion knew that he had lost. He went home empty-handed and alarmed, perhaps, that Eisenhower could, at any moment, discover the Israeli atomic secret in the desert.

After Nasser pulled the Egyptian army back in early 1960, Ben-Gurion sent a message to Isser Harel, his Mossad chief, to come home because he was needed. Harel was off in Argentina on what Ben-Gurion may have thought was a fruitless search for Adolf Eichmann and Josef Mengele, two of Hitler's most notorious henchmen. Eichmann had run the massive industrial enterprise that exterminated six million Jews. Mengele, as an SS physician—the Angel of Death—had carried out gruesome experiments on Jews interred at Auschwitz-Birkenau. Both had so far escaped justice.

After months of silence, Harel suddenly landed in May 1960 at Israel's main airport with a sedated Eichmann on board his plane. News of the sensational clandestine capture swept the media, along with accounts of Mossad's daring operation that had been personally directed by Harel. Ben-Gurion was astounded. He invited Harel, whose face and identity were a state secret, to sit behind the prime minister as Ben-Gurion announced to the Knesset on May 23 that the architect of Hitler's final solution had been arrested and would stand trial for crimes against humanity.

Israel's reputation in the world soared as Ben-Gurion stood on high moral ground, embracing the rule of law—even for Eichmann—to accentuate Israel's status as a sovereign nation. Israel would not drag the war criminal through the streets but would put him on trial and give him the right to present a defense.

The trial of Eichmann in 1961 and his execution by hanging in 1962 served as a dramatic two-year backdrop for the other sensational development that was unfolding: the discovery by American and Western intelligence that Israel was building a large nuclear reactor in the desert.

Due to Israeli secrecy and censorship, it has been impossible to see the world as Ben-Gurion saw it at that moment until the veil of classification lifted, but here was the inescapable nexus between Israel's atomic project and the Eichmann saga—the Jews had suffered one massive attempt at genocide in the Nazi era and, therefore, could never rely on any other power, no matter how great, to protect the embattled nation from another attempt at annihilation.

Eichmann's capture fortified Ben-Gurion's case through the grim vortex of memory. With Eichmann, Israeli militarism found irrefutable justification.

Full of righteousness in the wake of the capture, Ben-Gurion flew to France to confront de Gaulle in secret over the French leader's decision to cut off uranium supplies Israel needed to start Dimona when the reactor reached completion. De Gaulle greeted Ben-Gurion with the news that France was seeking relations with the Arab world. He would end the war in Algeria and resume trade links across the region. The last thing he wanted was for France to be associated with an Israeli nuclear project that seemed to be veering from peaceful research to a bomb-making endeavor.

Ben-Gurion pleaded that Israel had just survived a dress rehearsal for invasion by Nasser's entire army. If the Egyptian leader had pulled the trigger, no power could have rescued the Jewish state from a catastrophic outcome. Surely de Gaulle, Ben-Gurion must have been thinking, whose country had been overrun by the Nazi blitzkrieg, could understand that each nation had to rely on itself for its ultimate security.

But when de Gaulle leaned close in their final session, what he really wanted was candor from the Israeli leader who had gotten so much from France: "Tell me, truthfully, why do you need a nuclear reactor?" he asked. Ben-Gurion may have felt that his only recourse was a lie. He replied that the Jewish state was not out to develop nuclear weapons. The reactor would be used only for peaceful research.[24]

The atomic secret reached American ears that same month. The U.S. embassy in Tel Aviv reported that rumors were circulating that France was collaborating with Israel on an atomic energy project near Beersheba in the Negev, but when U.S. diplomats queried the Israeli government, they were told that the industrial facility under construction at Dimona was a "textile plant." American and British spies and diplomats were dispatched to Beersheba to find the site and provide photography while Eisenhower tasked the CIA to get overhead photography using one of the top secret U-2 spy planes.

By August 1960, the CIA was certain that Dimona was a large-scale production reactor, the kind used to produce plutonium for nuclear weapons. On August 21, the French defense minister bluntly informed the Israelis that the entire nuclear cooperation agreement under which the two countries had been working since 1957 was canceled.[25]

The abruptness of the French reversal stunned Ben-Gurion, but after three months of high anxiety, the Israelis hit upon a strategy. Ben-Gurion sent Peres to see Couve de Murville. Peres told the French minister that if France pulled out of Dimona, Israel would go public with the names of the French companies contributing to the project, exposing them to attacks in the Arab world and a boycott of French products. Sitting there representing Ben-Gurion, Peres, the effete Europeanist, played poker like a sabra, tough and bloodless in a bluff that proved to be one of the most important performances of his career.

Couve de Murville icily returned the gaze of the young Israeli envoy and asked, "What do you suggest?"[26]

Out of this encounter came compromise. The French government withdrew official sponsorship for the Dimona project but allowed French firms to complete the work for which they had contracted. France dropped all of its demands for international inspection of the secret facility, and Israel agreed to affirm the peaceful intent of the project in a public statement.

Peres was still engaged in the details when he was urgently recalled. He reached Ben-Gurion at Sde Boker, where Meir and Harel were huddled with the prime minister. The Mossad chief had startling news: the Americans had overflown Dimona with a U-2 spy plane. The secret was out. Worse, the Soviet foreign minister, Andrei Gromyko, was on his way to Washington, and this could only mean that the two superpowers were going to expose Dimona and demand that it be shut down or placed under international inspection.

Peres saw the power play; Meir and Harel were out to cut his throat. If Ben-Gurion panicked, the whole atomic project might be abandoned, dismantled as a white elephant and Peres blamed for inflicting delusions of grandeur on the state.

Peres pushed back. It was too soon to draw dire conclusions, he told them. Gromyko could be traveling to Washington for any number of reasons not associated with the American discovery of Dimona. And a U-2 could not see inside buildings.

Ben-Gurion refused to panic; he too understood the power play. Both Harel and Meir opposed the project as too provocative.

But the truth was out. The CIA had produced a "special national intelligence estimate" for Eisenhower detailing its suspicions about Dimona. In mid-December, *Time* magazine disclosed that a "small power" that was not Communist or part of NATO was developing nuclear weapons. Three days later, a British newspaper reported that Israel was the mystery country, forcing Ben-Gurion to respond. On December 21, he issued a statement to the Knesset asserting that the Dimona reactor was not a military project; it was there to serve "the needs of industry, agriculture, health and science."

The report that Israel was secretly engaged in acquiring nuclear weapons, Ben-Gurion said, "is either a deliberate or an unconscious untruth." The reactor, he added, "is intended exclusively for peaceful purposes."[27] Every time Ben-Gurion lied to protect the atomic secret, Meir and Eshkol cringed, wondering what the Americans would think when they found out.

John F. Kennedy had been elected president in November. During the transition, Christian Herter, who had succeeded Dulles as secretary of state, peppered the Israelis with demands for information. The American ambassador, Ogden Reid, jousted with Ben-Gurion over Washington's right to know.

Then, as if to save Ben-Gurion from these intrusions, a domestic crisis intervened. A sudden new eruption of the Lavon Affair afforded Ben-Gurion the opportunity to evade American pressure. Lavon had come to Ben-Gurion with proof that aides to Colonel Benjamin Gibli, the military intelligence chief who planned the 1954 sabotage operation in Cairo, had backdated Lavon's approval to launch the operation.

Ben-Gurion, adept at sidestepping any bureaucratic tar baby, just looked at Lavon and said, "I didn't condemn you then, and I don't condemn you now. But I am not authorized or empowered to clear you, because I am neither judge nor investigator."[28] Ben-Gurion maintained that the only way Lavon could be exonerated was if there was a full judicial inquiry that took evidence and examined witnesses under oath. But the party's old guard, led now by Eshkol and Meir, wanted to be rid of the Lavon Affair.

Despite Ben-Gurion's opposition, a committee of seven, headed by Eshkol, reviewed the new evidence and on December 25, 1960, declared: "We hereby conclude that Lavon did not give the order to the senior officer and that the mishap was carried out without his knowledge."

The Lavon verdict came the day after the American ambassador had demanded access to Dimona for American scientists.

Ben-Gurion chose that moment to resign.

"I am not your partner; I am not a member of this government," Ben-Gurion told Eshkol. His resignation threw the government into chaos. The Americans were informed that it would take six months and new elections before things settled down; there was no way to deal with a request for access to Dimona. Ben-Gurion would continue as interim prime minister, but he sheltered behind the political crisis.

Here was the fallacy of Israel's democracy: it could be undemocratically manipulated by an autocratic act—a "detonation" in the political realm. There was no reason whatsoever that Ben-Gurion's decision to resign in January 1961 and call late-summer elections should have rendered the government dysfunctional. After all, when he left office in 1953 and 1954, Sharett had stepped in to carry on diplomacy and domestic affairs. The

Mapai leadership could have effortlessly put an interim government in place, but Ben-Gurion did not allow it. He owned the nuclear project as a military autocrat whose power on this issue could not be challenged. He also had every reason to believe that he would prevail in the coming election. There was no Sharett to challenge him. And so Israel's representatives abroad argued that Ben-Gurion's decision to step down relieved the government of responsibility to address the urgent issue that Eisenhower and, more insistently, the incoming Kennedy administration had put forward.

Instead, Ben-Gurion told Washington that he had no idea whether he would be the next prime minister, but if he were, he would be happy to invite some American scientists to Dimona. He had just bought himself the better part of a year to get the French shipments of uranium restarted and to accelerate construction of the reactor.

The day before Kennedy was sworn in, he met Eisenhower alone and then the two leaders were joined by advisers. Kennedy asked about countries that were close to obtaining atomic weapons. Outgoing secretary of state Christian Herter replied: Israel and India. In a matter of weeks after his inauguration, Kennedy let it be known that he was determined to roll back the Israeli program.[29]

In March, Kennedy learned from the CIA that the Dimona reactor was likely twice as powerful as earlier estimated and therefore able to produce substantial quantities of plutonium. Kennedy told James Reston of the *New York Times* that Ben-Gurion was a "wild man." He had sent the Israeli leader a message that he had thirty days in which to allow a thorough inspection of the Dimona reactor, and the deadline had passed. Dean Rusk, the new secretary of state, told Kennedy in a memorandum that "Israel's acquisition of nuclear weapons would have grave repercussions in the Middle East, not the least of which might be the probable stationing of Soviet nuclear weapons on the soil of Israel's embittered Arab neighbors."[30]

When the State Department summoned the Israeli ambassador, Avraham Harman, and told him the president wanted an early date for an inspection of Dimona, Harman replied, "In Israel, no one is thinking about anything else except the political crisis."[31]

Kennedy invited Ben-Gurion to the United States, and under the new president's charm offensive, the older man was forced to relent. He accepted.

The first inspection of Dimona, in May 1961, was a meticulously executed charade. Israeli scientists carefully rehearsed how they would lead two American scientists from the Atomic Energy Commission through the construction site, steering them away from hidden doors and cosmetic barriers to prevent them from discovering the large underground laboratory whose purpose was the separation of plutonium from irradiated fuel. Instead of evidence of a military program, all the Americans found was a large reactor unconnected to the national electrical grid. They were sold a fiction that Dimona was all about research for seawater desalination, for medicine—anything but military purposes.

The two AEC scientists returned to Washington and reported that "there is no present evidence that the Israelis have weapons production in mind" at Dimona. Ben-Gurion was ecstatic. At the White House, Myer Feldman, Kennedy's liaison to both Israel and the Jewish community in the United States, asserted that the inspection "confirmed the peaceful purposes of the reactor."[32]

Kennedy remained skeptical. Anyone could see that Israel was a threat to Kennedy's policy to control the spread of nuclear weapons.

Ben-Gurion traveled to New York to see if he could moderate a new president's zeal. On May 30, he was ushered into the presidential suite on the thirtieth floor of the Waldorf-Astoria in New York. After initial brief amenities, Kennedy plunged into his concerns. His CIA briefing material for the meeting included a five-page history of "the French-Israeli relationship." Though the document did not assert categorically that Israel was building an atomic bomb, it made the case that this was likely. It quoted one source as saying that in September 1957, "then French premier, Bourgès-Maunoury, and the French army chief of staff had decided that France could furnish 'complete information concerning atomic energy' to aid Israel in constructing an atomic bomb."[33] Kennedy was not exactly blunt or tough. He spoke to Ben-Gurion about Caesar's wife.

"On the theory that a woman should not only be virtuous but also have the appearance of virtue, our problem," he said, was how to disseminate information about the nature of the Israeli reactor in such a way as to remove any doubts other nations might have as to Israel's peaceful purposes.[34]

Kennedy wanted, and got, Ben-Gurion's permission to tell Nasser about the results of the Dimona inspection. Ben-Gurion said Kennedy could inform whomever he pleased. Ben-Gurion said Dimona had to be understood in the context of Israel's problems, the greatest of which was the shortage of water in the Negev Desert, which Israel was keen to develop. Even if they successfully diverted part of the flow of the Jordan River, there would still not be enough water, and therefore the only recourse was desalination of seawater, a huge undertaking that could be done economically only through the use of nuclear power for massive electricity generation.

The Israeli leader acknowledged that France had helped with the project. He looked at Kennedy and said that was the full story. Israel had consulted experts in India and Great Britain and, with the help of France, had built the nuclear reactor in the desert southeast of Beersheba. Israel's main purpose—and for the time being, only purpose—was using nuclear power to make electricity to produce fresh water in large volumes.

The words "for the time being" hung in the room, and then Ben-Gurion added quite pointedly: "We are asked if it is for peaceful purposes. As of now, the only purpose is peaceful. Not at present, but in another three or four years' time, we might have a need for a plant to process plutonium." In one version of this conversation, Ben-Gurion was said to have asserted that plutonium separation, which creates bomb-grade material, is "necessary for every nuclear power plant reactor.

"We have no such intention at the moment, and we won't do it during the next four or five years. But we shall see what happens in the Middle East, it doesn't depend on us. Perhaps Russia will give bombs to China or Egypt, or perhaps Egypt will develop them by itself."[35]

Now, unmistakably, they were talking about nuclear weapons, and all of Ben-Gurion's assertions of peaceful intent seemed suddenly conditional upon developments in the Middle East. The implication of his analysis was that Israel saw nuclear weapons coming on the Arab side and, therefore, Israel had no choice but to precede the Arabs into the nuclear club, all explanations of peaceful intent to the contrary.

But also, here was Ben-Gurion laying the predicate for withdrawing his lie to two presidents. To Kennedy he now disclosed what he had never disclosed to Eisenhower, that a plutonium-separation facility was part of Dimona. In fact, it was already secretly under construction. It was not true that plutonium separation was "necessary for every nuclear" reactor. Spent uranium fuel can be stored indefinitely or sent abroad for reprocessing. Ben-Gurion had confessed the possibility that he would give the green light to his scientists for atomic weapons, but Kennedy failed to take up this crucial thread of logic.

Kennedy told Ben-Gurion that while his estimate of Egypt's nuclear ambition might be correct, "we do not want by our actions to increase tensions in the Middle East." It was in the "common interest" of the United States and Israel, he added, "that no country believes that Israel is contributing to the proliferation of atomic weapons." It was obvious, he said, that Nasser would not permit Israel to get ahead in this field without responding.

Kennedy had argued that the security nightmare of the cold war made America's predicament more dire than Israel's. But Ben-Gurion replied that the "difference, Mr. President, is that we are the only remnants of a people that have been fighting for survival for the past 4,000 years. If Nasser defeats us, we are destroyed."

Both leaders seemed less than satisfied by the conversation and the undertone that neither could give assurances most desired by the other. When both delegations stood, Kennedy's aides exited the sitting room, but Kennedy lingered with Ben-Gurion. "You know that I was elected by the Jews . . . of New York," Kennedy reportedly said. "What do you think I should do?" he asked, suggesting that he was willing to do something "for them," or "for you."[36] "Do what is good for the United States," Ben-Gurion replied, according to his own reconstruction of the event.

In later years, Ben-Gurion disparaged Kennedy for his solicitous approach, calling him a mere "politician," not a statesman. The older man desperately wanted Hawk antiaircraft missiles to defend Tel Aviv and Dimona because Nasser had warned that he would go to war to prevent Israel from going nuclear. It may have suited Ben-Gurion's political vanities to dismiss Kennedy, but it would not have surprised any Israeli leader that an American president might acknowledge the importance of the Jewish vote to his election.

Ben-Gurion could only have been delighted that Kennedy was seeking some means to demonstrate his gratitude, and if Ben-Gurion restrained himself from taking the opportunity, again, to appeal for missiles, he might well have believed that such a solicitous president would come to the right decision in good time.

Soon after Ben-Gurion returned home, Israel received intelligence from its embassy in Washington that Egypt had purchased ballistic missile technology from a California firm. The news was a great surprise in Israel, not because the technology was advanced—it was not—but because with Israeli elections just a month away, Nasser was threatening to embarrass Israel with a Sputnik-style sensation.

Ben-Gurion's determination never to be upstaged by Nasser on the security front was at risk. He summoned Israel's rocket scientists and instructed them to prepare a test launch of whatever rocket they had in development. In great haste, the scientists assembled a small meteorological missile they called Shavit-2—there had been no Shavit-1—and erected it on the beach south of Tel Aviv. On the morning of July 5, 1961, they fired it into the atmosphere. It reached an altitude of forty-seven miles and was declared a great success by Ben-Gurion, who made sure that a photo was released to the domestic newspapers showing that the prime minister had personally been on hand to observe the launch while standing on a sand dune, flanked by the chief of staff of the army, Zvi Zur, and the chief of weapons development.

The Israeli launch probably boosted Mapai's performance at the polls that summer, though its parliamentary base slipped by another five seats. But what the missile incident demonstrated more than anything was Ben-Gurion's intense sensitivity to how his leadership was being perceived by the sabra establishment—the core of the military and a rising political class, more nationalistic and right wing than the old Socialist order of the European Jews who built Mapai. He knew he had to stand as a warrior and project Israel's military power. The election once again restored him as paramount leader.

Nasser waited until the following summer to deliver his own surprise. On the tenth anniversary of the 1952 Egyptian Revolution, Nasser's military establishment launched four ballistic missiles with ranges up to 350 miles. Nasser boasted that the al-Kaher (Conqueror) missile could strike any target "south of Beirut," meaning that all of Israel was now imperiled by this new weapon. But worse, after an intense investigation by Mossad agents across the Middle East and Europe, Harel reported to Ben-Gurion by mid-August that Nasser had been employing West German scientists since 1959 to build factories capable of producing hundreds of surface-to-surface missiles. Harel cited one Mossad source who asserted that Nasser was buying up supplies of radioactive cobalt 60 to produce a "dirty bomb" that could be mounted on a rocket and fired to disperse contamination across Israel's urban areas.

The failure to detect Nasser's project subjected Harel and the Mossad to intense criticism. Harel had been off in Argentina chasing Adolf Eichmann and, after that, he had deployed Mossad's resources—at Ben-Gurion's request—to the hunt for Yossele Schumacher, a young Israeli boy whose kidnapping by an ultra-Orthodox Jewish sect was a test of secular law over religious authority. It took months and dozens of agents scouring Europe, Africa, and the United States to find the boy—who was found alive in Brooklyn. So Nasser's missile surprise raised questions about how the program had escaped Mossad's detection.

Harel did not tarry. In a few weeks, the spy chief was in Ben-Gurion's office with a detailed history of the Egyptian rocket program. Harel was outraged—so was Golda Meir—that the German government seemed to be looking the other way as its scientists helped create weapons that might be used to terrorize Jews. They counseled a tough frontal approach to German chancellor Konrad Adenauer, demanding that he discipline the errant scientists.

But here Ben-Gurion demurred. Adenauer had pledged $500 million in loans and a transfer of American-made heavy tanks and aircraft to show that there was a "new Germany" in Europe. Peres—upstaging Meir with Ben-Gurion's support—was negotiating favorable terms with Adenauer's defense minister, Franz Joseph Strauss.

Ben-Gurion's solution was indirect. He told Peres to lodge a private complaint to the German government through Strauss in hopes that a nonconfrontational plea might spur Adenauer to action. But at the same time, Ben-Gurion authorized Operation Damocles, an intelligence war aimed at killing or intimidating the German scientists who were behind the Egyptian program. Over the next three months, seven people associated with the program disappeared, were murdered, or died in suspicious circumstances. Dr. Heinz Krug, one of the program's managers, was last seen leaving his office in Vienna in the company of a dark-skinned man. His body was never found.[37]

Another scientist survived an assassination attempt by a gunman who fired at him and missed. Parcel bombs mailed to the Egyptian missile factories blew up, killing six Egyptians, blinding and disfiguring a secretary.

European governments were up in arms, especially over the violation of their sovereignty and the indiscriminate violence.

Kennedy had told Ben-Gurion at their Waldorf meeting that the United States would not be the first to introduce advanced missile systems into the Middle East, but Nasser's big display was enough to justify the sale of Hawk air defense missiles to Israel in August 1962.

Ben-Gurion was getting everything he wanted: the Dimona reactor, Hawk missiles, and the cover of the United States, all based on the solemn assurance that the nuclear project was peaceful and that Israel's growing arsenal of conventional weapons was for defensive purposes only.

It was a year of missile crises. In October 1962, Kennedy confronted the Soviet Union over its missile installations in Cuba. Kennedy showed courage, diplomatic skill, and restraint in bringing the world back from the brink, and when the crisis was over, it was clear that the control of nuclear weapons was going to be the centerpiece of Kennedy's foreign policy and an important campaign theme for his reelection.

Two months later, while vacationing in Florida, Kennedy met with Meir to discuss the problems in the Middle East.

The State Department had developed a proposal to resettle the Palestinian refugees still living in misery in the camps of Jordan, Syria, and Lebanon. It was going on fifteen years since they had fled or been forced out of their homes in Israel. Kennedy told her that he also hoped progress could be made in dividing the water resources of the Jordan River. And he wanted to press the nuclear question because it was ever on his mind. Nasser's behavior that fall—he had sent his army into Yemen in support of a nationalist coup—gave Kennedy little hope that he could achieve reconciliation in the Middle East. But he seemed increasingly anxious—and solicitous to both sides. At minimum, Kennedy hoped to prevent a new regional war from breaking out. He had set his sights on a broad foreign policy based on arms control with the Soviets and stability in Europe.

For Meir, the audience with Kennedy was a coup in her struggle with Ben-Gurion over Germany. *She* was getting the audience; *she* would describe the threat from the German scientists and air her grievance that Adenauer's dereliction was giving rein to these rogues.

All during the fall, she had pressed Dean Rusk and other Kennedy aides for additional sales of American weaponry to meet the perceived Egyptian threat. Her list included tanks and ground-to-ground missiles capable of striking Egyptian cities. If she could just bring home a new American commitment, it would help undermine the pro-German policy that Ben-Gurion and Peres had embarked on.

Seated on Kennedy's couch at the family compound in Palm Beach, Meir first complimented Kennedy on his performance in the Cuban missile crisis and then drew the obvious comparison to the threat the Soviets posed to Israel's existence. She accused Egypt of developing a radiological weapon—a dirty bomb on a missile—with the help of the Soviets. She passed on Harel's full brief on Egyptian missile developments. She complained that Egypt's submarine force was a menace to Israel's seaports.

"This is how the people of Israel live," she pleaded. "There is a constant shadow of Nasser's ambitions in the Middle East."[38]

Though Kennedy's notebook for the meeting contained a laundry list of Israeli obstructions to U.S. policies in the Middle East, Kennedy had decided to take a conciliatory tack with Meir, perhaps because she had such a large American following, or perhaps because he sensed she needed a successful visit. But Kennedy also knew that there was no point in making a frontal assault on such a fortress. The political reality, as Kennedy had stated to Ben-Gurion, was that American Jews had voted Democratic in 1960 and he would need them again in 1964.

So Kennedy was reassuring in a manner he had never shown an Israeli leader, and here was a precedent that would be imitated and embellished by many presidents who followed. Kennedy told Meir that Israel's relationship with the United States was "special." He compared it to that of Great Britain, and in doing so impressed on Meir that such a relationship required a cooperative and understanding attitude toward America's other interests in the Middle East.

"I think it is quite clear that in case of an invasion, the United States would come to the support of Israel," he told her. "We have that capacity and it is growing," he added, referring to the U.S. Sixth Fleet, stationed nearby in Italy. According to the Pentagon, its forces could respond to an attack on Israel within thirty hours.

Finally he bore in on the main point. Given all that America was willing to do, he hoped "that Israel could give consideration to our problems on this atomic reactor. We are opposed to nuclear proliferation."[39]

Meir's hand must have been in the air and her head nodding, because she quickly interjected that America would not have any difficulty with Israel over Dimona. She was not telling the truth, but Kennedy didn't challenge her.

Meir returned to Israel armed with the most explicit security guarantee the United States had ever uttered with regard to Israel. She had every reason to believe that such goodwill could be converted to a new arms supply relationship with Washington. In the Knesset, she rose to defy Ben-Gurion's complacency about Germany. She declared publicly that hundreds of German scientists and technicians were engaged in Nasser's missile factories developing "weapons forbidden by international agreements" and "that serve the exclusive purpose of the extermination of any living being."

Menachem Begin's Herut Party railed against relations with Germany. He accused Ben-Gurion of carrying on business as usual while "the Germans send microbes to our enemies!"

What soon became clear, however, was that the German-Egyptian missile program represented a hollow threat; its missiles performed poorly with outdated technology and primitive design. The Germans had not been able to develop a workable guidance system, and thus the accuracy of the Egyptian missiles could not be assured even if aimed at a large city. Some of Harel's most sensational information, about dirty bombs and other unconventional warheads under development in the German-run Egyptian laboratories, simply could not be verified by other sources such as the CIA. Yet the German scientist scare created a frenzy in the Israeli press, where there were invented reports of "death ray" weapons and other fantasies.

The anti-German hysteria in Israel was working against Ben-Gurion's desire to tap German guilt and generosity to bolster the Israeli military establishment and the civilian economy. But Harel for some reason could not let it go. He briefed newspaper editors, inciting sensational press coverage. And though Ben-Gurion had put an end to the assassination of German scientists—Mossad's terror campaign had aroused fear and outrage across Europe—Harel was slow to call off his troops. In early March 1963, Mossad sent agents to Basel, Switzerland, to threaten the family of one scientist who was working on the missile guidance system problem. The message was that he should desist or face presumably violent consequences. But the Swiss police pounced on the agents, and the story burst into the

European press, intensifying the focus on and criticism of Israel's terror campaign.

Ben-Gurion ordered his military intelligence chief, Meir Amit, to examine the raw intelligence underlying Mossad's claims. Separately, Peres picked apart Harel's information. Yes, Nasser had new ballistic missiles, but Egypt had no supplies of cobalt 60 for dirty bombs and no prospect of putting anything other than conventional explosives on the missiles. The missiles thus had little or no military utility because they could not hit their targets for lack of a workable guidance system. Amit and Peres drew on American or British intelligence, which also discounted the threat.

Ben-Gurion called in Harel and confronted him with the new assessments. Since the founding of the state, Harel had been one of Ben-Gurion's most loyal servants, but as Harel's reputation had grown, so had the vanities of "the man in charge." In the world of intelligence, through which Israel had come to conduct so much of its foreign policy, he truly was one of the leaders of the state, accountable to no one except Ben-Gurion.

Harel had exceeded his brief. His attack on the scientists of West Germany was inspired by the same revulsion for the unexpurgated strains of Nazism that he and Meir and many other Jews believed still lurked in German society. As far as he was concerned, Adenauer, Strauss, and the whole German security establishment had known about the scientists helping Nasser, notwithstanding their claims of ignorance.[40] Harel could not abide Ben-Gurion's attack on his veracity. He submitted his resignation and walked out of Mossad headquarters. Ben-Gurion had to move quickly, and his first choice for a new Mossad chief was Amos Manor, the deputy Shabak director, but Manor was traveling and out of touch. Ben-Gurion turned to Meir Amit, the military intelligence chief and Dayan ally whose careful analysis of the missile threat had undermined Harel's credibility.

Amit was an unpretentious man who had lived since childhood in the same apartment building in Ramat Gan, the eastern suburb of Tel Aviv where winding, tree-lined streets connected markets, schools, and storefront businesses. Amit swam laps every morning to stay fit and, if he had any vanities, it was that he believed that he could win people over with guile, dedication, and an engaging management style. Gregarious and open, Amit was not the sphinx that Harel presented to his staff. And Amit displayed that strong sabra loyalty to Ben-Gurion and to those beside whom he had fought, Dayan foremost.

Less than a year away from his reelection campaign, Kennedy issued a presidential directive to the State Department, Pentagon, and CIA to conduct an exhaustive review of countries that were engaged in secret nuclear weapons research and to develop a plan to head them off through a robust program of implementing safeguards or other means. Israel was prominently on the list, along with China and India.

The depth of Kennedy's resolve was reflected in his query to the Soviet leadership on how Washington and Moscow might cooperate in preventing China from carrying out its first atomic test. The Pentagon was examining how surgical military strikes might set China back.

When Kennedy found out that Peres was in Washington lobbying for new weapons sales, he called him to the Oval Office and grilled him about Dimona.

"You know that we follow very closely the discovery of any nuclear development in the region. This could create a very dangerous situation," Kennedy said. "For this reason, we kept in touch with your nuclear effort. What can you tell me about this?"

Peres was forced to ad-lib. He had no instructions for evasion. He responded with the words that Ben-Gurion had used to privately brief Israeli newspaper editors, who were trusted with the secret. "I can tell you most clearly that we will not introduce nuclear weapons to the region, and certainly we will not be the first. Our interest is in reducing armaments, even in complete disarmament."[41]

Kennedy easily recognized the nonanswer. He issued new instructions to draw up a plan for an international agreement preventing the spread of nuclear weapons and advanced missile technology in the Middle East. He wanted Israel and Egypt to sign it.

Time was running out for Ben-Gurion. Dimona was virtually completed. The reactor would be ready for start-up operations by the end of the year. Ben-Gurion looked out at the world and realized that getting other nations to accept Israel as a nuclear power would be difficult at best, but it would be less difficult if there was a sense of urgent threat to the Jewish state's very existence. The German-Egyptian missile scare had, to some extent, played into his hands. The Israeli public was at an elevated state of fear for its survival. Yet Ben-Gurion needed a stronger case.

So when the leaders of Egypt, Syria, and Iraq signed an agreement in April 1963 calling for the three countries to unite as a federation with a goal of liberating Palestine, Ben-Gurion sounded an alarm. Some ministers thought he had gone mad with an "apocalyptic spirit." Others saw the outburst as the ravings of an old man who exhibited a "deep, almost irrational anxiety."[42] Yet only Ben-Gurion, at age seventy-seven, was carrying full responsibility for the atomic project and, in order to see it to completion, he mobilized the foreign ministry, with Gideon Rafael as his assistant, to write nearly one hundred letters to presidents, prime ministers, and other heads of state laying out the sources of his anxiety.

To Kennedy, he wrote a seven-page valediction at the end of April, citing the "danger of a serious conflagration in the Middle East."

He asserted that "the liberation of Palestine is impossible without the total destruction of the people in Israel, but the people of Israel are not in the hapless situation of six million defenseless Jews who were wiped out by Nazi Germany." He reminded Kennedy that at that time, "the civilized world, in Europe and America" treated Hitler's declarations against the Jews "with indifference and equanimity. A Holocaust unequaled in human history was the result."

Ben-Gurion's personal anxiety, his fear that Israel might not be able to withstand exposure or the pressure that Kennedy seemed prepared to apply, was apparent in one sentence that leaped off the page: "It may not happen today or tomorrow, but I am not sure whether the state will continue to exist after my life has come to an end." No one could read the sentence without shuddering over the magnitude of Ben-Gurion's vanity and his sense of proprietorship over the entire Zionist enterprise. He addressed an incredulous president of the United States, invoking a wild sense of danger in the world, imploring Kennedy to look the other way as Ben-Gurion perpetuated his personal rule by arming himself with atomic bombs for Armageddon.

Ben-Gurion said he wanted to fly to the United States urgently to discuss the looming threat with Kennedy. But the CIA could discern no threat, leaving Kennedy to wonder at the intensity of Ben-Gurion's excitation. Kennedy worried that Ben-Gurion had worked himself into such a state that Israel might invade Jordan, or seize the West Bank.

In the end, Kennedy responded with restraint. He bluntly explained in a May 4 letter that the real danger in the Middle East "is not so much that of an early Arab attack as that of a successful development of advanced offensive systems" that would "dangerously threaten the stability of the area." Kennedy sent his ambassador, Walworth Barbour, to deliver the letter with a strong demand not just for the resumption of U.S. inspections at Dimona but also for a fixed program of twice-yearly inspections.

Two days later, Kennedy hosted the French foreign minister, Couve de Murville, and confided that "the Israeli problem causes me great concern." When the French official tried to soothe him by saying that at best, the Israelis would be able to produce a couple of crude atomic weapons, Kennedy replied bluntly that "if Israel obtains atomic weapons we and you would be blamed: you for providing her with uranium and we because of our financial aid to Israel."[43]

On May 10, Kennedy again sent Ambassador Barbour to see Ben-Gurion, stressing the "intensity of presidential concern for the promptest" reply "to our proposals for semi-annual Dimona visits, with the first visit this month." Kennedy was escalating the pressure at an alarming rate, citing his "global responsibility" to halt the spread of nuclear weapons. This responsibility transcended the give-and-take of "day-to-day bi-lateral relations," he said.

But Kennedy's escalation led to an even longer letter from Ben-Gurion. It was essential, he replied, that one or both superpowers guarantee the borders in the region and vital that America sell arms to Israel to match the Soviet deliveries to the Arabs.

"Mr. President, my people have the right to exist, both in Israel and wherever they may live, and this existence is in danger," he concluded.

There was no arguing with Ben-Gurion when his blood was up. Ambassador Barbour returned four days later and told Ben-Gurion in the most direct terms: "We need to see Dimona."

Ben-Gurion replied that it was better for the world and for Nasser to be a "little afraid" of what Israel was up to.

Kennedy now understood that he was being diddled. In the twilight of Ben-Gurion's life, the old warrior was being asked to give up his weapons, to abandon the atomic fail-safe that his military society craved. It was no wonder, as Kennedy considered his options, that Ben-Gurion resisted.

On May 18, Kennedy reminded Ben-Gurion of Golda Meir's pledge that there would be no trouble between the two countries over Dimona. Kennedy professed a "deep commitment to the security of Israel," but, he added, "this commitment and this support would be seriously jeopardized in the public opinion of this country and in the West, if it should be thought that this government was unable to obtain reliable information on a subject as vital to peace as the question of Israel's efforts in the nuclear field."

Kennedy's letter was a harsh and alarming rebuke. It took Ben-Gurion more than a week to consider his options. He finally replied on May 27 with a letter full of obfuscation and delay.

"I fully understand the dangers involved in the proliferation of nuclear weapons," he wrote, "and I sympathize with your efforts to avoid such a development. I fear that in the absence of an agreement between the Great Powers on general disarmament there is little doubt that these weapons will, sooner or later, find their way into the arsenals of China, and then of the European states and India."

In other words, proliferation was inevitable. Ben-Gurion was arguing that Israel's drive to obtain nuclear weapons was not a breach of the relationship, just a recognition of current realities.

He talked around Kennedy's demand for immediate inspection of Dimona and for a semiannual inspection regime and then reinflated the apocalyptic vision that he hoped would serve as sufficient grounds for Kennedy and the rest of the world to accept an Israeli bomb.

"We in Israel cannot be blind to the more actual danger now confronting us," he wrote. "I refer to the danger arising from destructive 'conventional' weapons in the hands of neighboring governments which openly proclaim their intention to attempt the annihilation of Israel. This is our people's major anxiety."

As the exchange between Kennedy and Ben-Gurion escalated, Kennedy sent John J. McCloy, a pillar of the American establishment and his chief disarmament adviser, with a draft agreement to suspend the Arab-Israeli arms race.

It would be easy to dismiss this U.S. initiative as naïve, but given the confrontation Kennedy had weathered with the Soviets over missiles in Cuba and the blockade in Berlin, he was in fact working feverishly with the diplomatic tools that were available to him. As a first-term president elected by the narrowest of margins, he could not afford a confrontation with Israel that radiated into domestic politics. But he had to find a balance between two things: the newly enlarged mission of his presidency—controlling the burgeoning threat of nuclear weapons in the world—and the political reality he faced at home: support for Israel within the Democratic Party and Congress.

Kennedy's path to reelection would be paved with feats of diplomacy and statesmanship in the wake of his finest hours in the Cuban missile crisis. He would work to end nuclear testing in the atmosphere and to head off, if possible, the Chinese and Indian nuclear programs. Kennedy knew that these efforts would fail—they simply would not pass the credibility test—if Ben-Gurion declared Israel a nuclear power. Yet Kennedy knew there were limits to the amount of pressure he could apply without risking a backlash from the American Jewish establishment.

Americans, and most Israelis, were not even aware that Israel was about to join the nuclear club and that America was trying to stop it. The Kennedy–Ben-Gurion exchanges, the debate and assessment within the American government, and most Israeli records remained classified for decades. Important pieces of the record are still classified. What is known, however, is that in mid-June 1963, Kennedy went all in with a final set of demands for Israel to open Dimona for a thorough investigation whose findings the United States could share with the world. The letter was transmitted to Ambassador Barbour on the Jewish Sabbath, Saturday, for him to hand-deliver on Sunday morning. It is certain that Ben-Gurion got word that a brutal message was coming and that failure to comply with American demands for inspection would put U.S.-Israeli relations in jeopardy.

The pressure on Ben-Gurion had now reached maximum intensity. If there was one strong consensus in Israel, it was that Israel's relationship with America was the greatest hope to protect the Jewish state for the long term. Increasingly isolated at the top of his party, Ben-Gurion was now vulnerable on a crucial issue: he had put the American relationship at risk. That Saturday, Golda Meir was remonstrating in private over the related issue of Germany. She had discovered that Israeli soldiers were training in Germany on tanks and other weapons; this had reignited her anger over Ben-Gurion's rapprochement with Adenauer's "New Germany."

The confrontation with Kennedy over Dimona was reckless, in her view; full disclosure was her policy. She believed that the Americans would understand that the Jewish state needed the reassurance of a bomb in the basement, that this would calm the fears of the Holocaust generation. But Meir could never explain how she would handle the Americans if they demanded that Dimona be dismantled.

Meir walked to Ben-Gurion's house to vent her feelings. She wanted Ben-Gurion to instruct the military censor to ban the news of Israeli soldiers training in Germany. The image of Israeli soldiers cooperating with Germany, even a new one, was still too much for the death-camp survivors. It roiled sensibilities. Ben-Gurion refused.

By various accounts, it was a day of bile and recrimination; Ben-Gurion's stubborn dominance, Meir's opposition to the German policy, the heated debate in the Knesset that stirred up Begin and the right-wing opposition, and, now, the mishandling of the American relationship. Ben-Gurion showed his irritation, but he was not one to explain himself to subordinates and he certainly did not regard Meir as his equal. Meir returned late that night, this time with Ben-Gurion's chief of staff, Teddy Kollek, in tow, and they hashed and rehashed their quarrel in Ben-Gurion's kitchen, but he refused to accommodate her.

They knew that Kennedy's letter would arrive the next morning. Ben-Gurion had no more room to maneuver. Meir stayed up late banging on his eardrums, but his mind went to the heart of the matter: he was at the end of his political string and the only strategic card he had left to play, again, was resignation. He must have realized that night, perhaps while he was venting to his diary about the stinging words of his adversaries—Begin, Lavon, and Harel—that the time had arrived: the only way to stop Kennedy was once again to throw the government of Israel into chaos.

Due to the heavy censorship in Israel over nuclear issues, Israeli historians have distorted Ben-Gurion's underlying motivation for this career-ending act. The secret atomic bomb project meant at least as much to Israel as the Manhattan Project had meant to the United States in World War II. Dimona was a few months away from going critical. Sufficient uranium stores had been delivered to fuel the reactor for several years, and the underground plutonium separation facility, which had been kept hidden from the Americans on each of their visits, was being readied to extract the first quantities of weapons-grade fissile material.

So on Sunday morning, June 16, 1963, Ben-Gurion announced to his cabinet and to the country that he was resigning at the age of seventy-seven. He told his ministers that he could no longer carry the burden, but in fact, he had. A great outcry went up from the young men he had promoted—Dayan and Peres—for they would have to fend for themselves.

But among the old guard of the Mapai, there was nothing but relief. Ben-Gurion would get his due as the founder of the state, the visionary, and all of that, but the era of unchallengeable autocracy was over.

The American ambassador never got to deliver Kennedy's letter. Everything in the relationship was put on hold, which is what Ben-Gurion had most wanted.

FIVE

The Rise of the Generals

Nothing mobilized the Arabs like hatred for Israel and support for the Palestinians who had lost their homes and lands in 1948. In January 1964, Egypt's President Nasser summoned the Arab leaders to the banks of the Nile for what amounted to a council of war on how to stop Israel from diverting the waters of the Sea of Galilee to make the Negev Desert bloom with new Israeli towns and cities.

Nasser was at the Cairo Airport to greet each of the Arab heads of state.

"Thank God you have come safe," he said to Saudi Arabia's King Saud, whose plane landed on the shimmering tarmac just before noon.

"May God help us to succeed," the sixty-one-year-old Saudi monarch, dressed in traditional robes, replied as he leaned on a cane at the head of a retinue of forty princes and aides.[1]

King Hassan II of Morocco brought dates and milk to share with Nasser as a sign of greeting. He also told Nasser that he had just released five Egyptian officers whom he had caught spying on Moroccan forces along the Algerian border.

To Syria's strongman, Major General Amin al-Hafez, Nasser offered only a polite handshake, since the Cairo press had been calling Hafez a "fascist butcher" for having crushed a pro-Egyptian rebellion in Syria.[2]

More than a decade into the Egyptian revolution, Nasser was desperate to restore unity in the Arab world, which had been sundered by Egypt's "liberation" war in Yemen and by Nasser's assault on the Middle East's traditional monarchies and pro-Western governments.

Not yet prepared to confront the Israeli army in a climactic battle over the fate of Zionism, the Arab heads of state fell upon a strategy to prevent

Israeli growth—and the immigration of more Jews—by starving the Jewish state of its main water sources, which rose in Syria's arid watersheds and fed the Jordan River Valley and the bountiful Sea of Galilee.

The pipeline from the Galilee to the Negev was Levi Eshkol's life's work. He had served as the director of the national water company and had supervised its construction as finance minister under Ben-Gurion. Now as prime minister, Eshkol, the avuncular technocrat who disliked confrontation and who worked by consensus, was facing his first concrete threat to Israel's national security from the convocation of Arab leaders in Cairo.

Israel's military establishment reacted sharply to the Arab summit. A seasoned young general, Yitzhak Rabin, who during the War of Independence had fought tenaciously on the road to Jerusalem before taking on the Egyptian army for the final campaign that preceded the 1949 Armistice, became chief of staff in December. Rabin saw the summit as a dramatic turning point. The reason, he explained, was that the Arab leaders were constructing a strategy that would "constitute the . . . means for the final liquidation of Israel."[3]

In Cairo, the Arabs also announced the formation of the Palestine Liberation Organization, not yet a lethal guerrilla force and under Nasser's tight control but a symbol of increasingly militant policies on the Arab side.

Eshkol was cautious and by nature averse to war. And Ben-Gurion feared having a nonwarrior as his successor.[4]

The Dimona reactor had been activated in December 1963 and Eshkol had consented in January 1964 to the inspection postponed by Kennedy's assassination. His decision to accommodate the Americans drew private criticism from the Ben-Gurion camp over whether Eshkol was sufficiently tough or resolute to complete the atomic project.

The clash between John F. Kennedy and David Ben-Gurion over the Dimona reactor proved to be the last gasp of the Ben-Gurion era, but the "old man," as many referred to him, seemed never to give up on the possibility of yet another political comeback. He remained a member of the Knesset and, as the months passed, he became a frequent critic of Eshkol within the Mapai.

Eshkol's only defense, as an untested prime minister with no substantial military background, was to run the government skillfully by seeking consensus and compromise from ministers, many of whom were also eager to move beyond the Ben-Gurion era. One of Eshkol's first gestures to the right-wing parties was to allow Jabotinsky's body to come home from New York for burial on Mount Herzl.

Ben-Gurion's retirement from the paramount political role in the country and Eshkol's ascent prompted an immediate stocktaking of how the great event would affect the lives of so many.

The sabra generation—the sons and daughters of pioneers who had fought the war in 1948 as teenagers—was coming of age. The new generation carried little of the ideological baggage of its parents, who had come to British Palestine when the world was heaving with war and revolutionary currents. For young Israelis, formative experiences were everything. They were blank slates written on by family, farm, and school, but the most profound imprint was soldiering and war.

The military unit in Israel was nearly as strong as family. In the early years, military experience created rival clans because the militias arose from political parties within the Zionist movement.

The mainstream Jewish Agency had established the Haganah as the preeminent underground militia, but Ben-Gurion also encouraged Jews to serve in the British army during World War II so they could bring home martial skills and combat experience after the war. The British-trained officers tended to see their service as superior to all others.

After the world war and the establishment of the state, Ben-Gurion had faced the threat of competing militia forces. That was the backdrop for the *Altalena* incident in June 1948, when Ben-Gurion demanded that the right-wing militia under the command of Menachem Begin surrender a shipload of weapons due to land north of Tel Aviv.[5]

The right-wing militia, the Irgun Zevai Leumi, or National Military Organization, had been founded by Ben-Gurion's nemesis, Jabotinsky.

Ben-Gurion had turned to Yigal Allon to discipline Begin and the Irgun. Allon was the commander of the Palmach, or "strike forces," an elite corps carved out of the Haganah in 1941 when so many Haganah fighters headed off to war in British uniforms. The Palmach fighters stayed home; they worked the fields of the kibbutz movement half the time and trained, during their free time, to fight on the home front against the British or the Arabs.

The Palmach favored hit-and-run guerrilla warfare and had little respect for British army tactics. And the Palmach commanders, especially Yigal Allon, leaned toward the pro-Soviet politics of the kibbutz movement.

To subdue Begin's right-wing mutiny, Allon called on a young deputy commander, Yitzhak Rabin, who was about to make his military and political debut before the whole country. It was a military debut due to the task at hand, but it was political because Rabin fought as a political instrument of Ben-Gurion to consolidate the power of the new state.

In Rabin, Ben-Gurion observed an apolitical soldier, a cautious tribune who took orders without question.

Begin ultimately ran his arms ship aground on the main Tel Aviv beach in defiance of Ben-Gurion's order to surrender the cargo. Israelis came out onto balconies to watch as a searing battle unfolded.

Rabin and his men killed more than a dozen Irgun fighters before Begin surrendered the ship and its cargo. The lesson of the brutal internal purging of Irgun's power was lost on no one. The state of Israel was going to be Ben-Gurion's version of a Mapai-dominated polity protected by a unified national army, the Israeli Defense Forces.

The country was now a fully militarized state where nearly every able-bodied person—male and female—was mobilized for battle or for some supporting role.

Ben-Gurion dissolved the Palmach in early 1949, in the midst of the Israeli campaign to drive Egyptian forces out of the Negev. He merged the Palmach headquarters with the IDF and, after Allon had secured the victory over the Egyptian army, Ben-Gurion relieved him of his command and put Dayan in charge of the southern front. It was shocking treatment of a popular war hero, but Ben-Gurion mistrusted Allon for his allegiance to the pro-Soviet kibbutz movement and the breakaway Mapam Party, whose leaders, Yitzhak Tabenkin and Israel Galili, represented the hard left of the labor movement.[6]

The question for Ben-Gurion was whether Yitzhak Rabin could be weaned away from the Palmach and Allon's strong influence.

Ben-Gurion had known both of Rabin's parents and claimed to have recruited Rabin's father into the British army's Jewish Legion in World War I. Rabin's parents had met in 1920, when his father, deactivated from the British army, rushed to Jerusalem to defend the city during a period of

Arab unrest, and there he met Rosa Cohen, a volunteer nurse. Rabin's mother had run a munitions factory in Russia during the revolution but suffered from a weak heart. Anyone who knew the family understood that young Rabin spent his adolescence fearing for his mother's health.

Rabin described how his mother's chest pains would send him running for a doctor, not knowing if when he returned he would find her dead. She died in 1937, when Rabin was sixteen. It seems clear that the terror of losing his mother instilled in Rabin a deep sense of vigilance and caution along with the psychological armor with which he girded himself to face catastrophe. Many years later, he told an American diplomat in the middle of a crisis, "Expect anything."[7] It was how he had lived his life.

Rabin was not in awe of politicians.

He was wary of Ben-Gurion because he had seen how Ben-Gurion had targeted Allon for extinction in the midst of the 1948 war, in which Allon was instrumental in Israel's victory. Rabin's father had known Jabotinsky, Ben-Gurion's great rival, and so Rabin had grown up with an appreciation of the competitive side of politics. As a soldier, he believed in loyalty to his unit. He had resented Ben-Gurion's attempt, after the 1949 Armistice, to forbid officers serving in the new Israeli army to attend a farewell rally for the disbanded Palmach.

Rabin was determined to go. Ben-Gurion summoned him to his home in Tel Aviv for a long political discussion on the afternoon of the rally. Rabin was the highest-ranking Palmach veteran still in uniform. Ben-Gurion told him that it was inappropriate for him to show divided loyalty. Rabin explained to Ben-Gurion why he was wrong. The rally was about tribute and remembrance for those who had served and died.

As the hour of the rally approached, Ben-Gurion invited Rabin to stay for dinner, but Rabin excused himself. They both knew why: Rabin was going to the rally.

Ben-Gurion never fully forgave Rabin. Dayan promoted Rabin to general in 1953 and sent him off for senior officer training at Camberley, where the British thought Rabin was an unimaginative dolt. What was clearer, however, was that Dayan saw Rabin as a protégé of Allon and therefore a rival because Allon and Dayan had been rivals since youth.

When the Suez War came, Dayan transferred Rabin north to the Syrian front where it would be certain he would see no action.

Rabin felt that his allegiance to the Palmach and to Allon had been held against him and retarded his military career. But in 1959, Ben-Gurion shook up the military command over a botched mobilization drill that panicked the country. Suddenly, Rabin was vaulted into the second-highest post: chief of operations for the general staff.

In January 1960, Rabin mobilized Israeli tank and air forces in Operation Rotem. But a year later, Ben-Gurion passed him over and appointed a former commander of the Haganah, Zvi Zur, as chief of staff. Ben-Gurion summoned Rabin and explained that he had appointed Zur because he was certain Zur would resign if Rabin was advanced in front of him. But Ben-Gurion added that there were other factors. "On one occasion you did disobey orders. And you are cautious," Ben-Gurion said to him.

The comment infuriated Rabin. He said that he had been serving in the army out of a sense of duty, but if Ben-Gurion wanted him to leave, he would.

"Wherever did you get that idea?" Ben-Gurion flared. "I want you to remain in the army. It is imperative that you stay. What can I do to convince you of that?"[8]

Rabin had feared that Peres was behind a whispering campaign that sought to portray him as overly cautious, and so Ben-Gurion's words of reassurance meant everything, and they steeled Rabin for combat with Peres, who positioned himself as Rabin's main rival in the defense establishment.

The foundation of the Rabin-Peres rivalry was both personal and esoteric. The men came from rival camps. Rabin, a relentlessly pragmatic thinker, wanted to spend the state's limited budget on muscular conventional forces—tanks, planes, and artillery—as the backbone of military power. Since Israel's Armored Corps had received its first heavy tanks, the fifty-ton Centurions, from Britain in 1959, the general staff had focused on building an army of one thousand tanks that could be distributed along the three enemy fronts against Soviet tanks in Syria and Egypt, and British armor in Jordan. Under Ezer Weizman, the Israeli air force was seeking new Mirage fighters from France, and A-4 Skyhawks from the Johnson administration to balance the superior numbers in the combined Arab air forces.

Eshkol's lack of military experience made Rabin the most influential member of the country's military establishment, and Rabin was not enamored of nuclear weapons and missiles as the key to the Jewish state's defense.

Here was a new rivalry: exotic weapons versus conventional forces. For Peres, the atomic project was everything. It had made his career. To Rabin, the sabra general, power came from well-trained soldiers, modern aircraft, and the barrel of a gun.

But beyond the professional debate, Rabin could not stand Peres's haughty manner or Parisian tastes. To many who observed both men closely, the largest part of their long enmity sprang from mutual envy: Rabin envied Peres's sophistication while Peres envied Rabin's sabra legitimacy. Peres had never worn the uniform, and in Rabin he saw a battle-hardened soldier, now a general, who commanded the respect of the army. Rabin was visceral; Peres cerebral. Rabin communicated more with a grunt or a snort than Peres could with rhetorical flourish. Peres had worked assiduously to convince Ben-Gurion that Rabin would make a poor chief of the army, but Ben-Gurion had kept his word, and Eshkol had followed through.

"Yitzhak, I promised that you'd be chief of staff, and you are going to be the next chief of staff," Ben-Gurion had said in March 1963. But then he had added that the appointment would not be announced for a year, because Zur had asked for an additional twelve months. Rabin was elated. He flew off to France for a round of official meetings and bumped into Peres in Paris.

"I understand you had a talk with Ben-Gurion. How did it go?" Peres asked.

"Very well," Rabin replied dryly.

"What happened?" Peres pushed.

"Ben-Gurion told me that I am going to be the next chief of staff," Rabin said, enjoying Peres's glare.

"Did he say it in so many words?" Peres asked.

"In just so many words," Rabin replied.[9]

Eshkol's approach to the Arabs was not manifestly different from Ben-Gurion's. He supported the Israeli military buildup with the help of German financing and British and American weaponry, a match for the Soviet arms that were flowing into the Arab world.

He accepted the notion that intermittent war with the Arabs might be necessary as a form of deterrence, but he was more determined to avoid war. Though he had harbored reservations about the cost of the secret atomic project, as prime minister he showed total dedication to completing the enormous undertaking. In what seemed to be a stab at burnishing a military profile, he absurdly wore a black beret, a symbol of Israel's elite commando and paratrooper forces.

But even if Eshkol had been inclined to take a different course with the Arabs, Israel's military establishment and Ben-Gurion's legacy as its chief strategist left him little room for maneuver. By 1963, it was a well-established dictum that Israel had moved beyond the Sharett approach: concession and accommodation with the Arabs. Two wars had demonstrated that the military impulse was predominant, that military power was far more efficacious in delivering Zionist goals of expanding borders and enforcing rough deterrence in a brutal neighborhood.

Any leader suggesting diplomacy and concessions—allowing Arab refugees to return to their homes in Israel—was committing political suicide. The military state had fully taken hold. The conventional view was that the army, and Israeli families, had paid for every acre of land in blood. The Zionist orthodoxy, which Eshkol had helped to establish, held that if the Israelis were going to build a state to accommodate five to ten million Jews, they would need every bit of land and every drop of water they could seize. Therefore, all eyes had to be directed forward, toward conquest and the next round of war.

As Eshkol assembled his government, some of the younger members of Mapai pressed him to elevate Dayan to defense minister, but Eshkol knew better. He had seen how Dayan had undermined Sharett in 1954, and he was not about to expose himself to political treachery. Eshkol kept the defense minister's portfolio in the prime minister's office, and Dayan remained neutered as minister of agriculture.

With Ben-Gurion out of office, no one had a larger target on his back than Peres.

Golda Meir hated the young Ben-Gurion acolyte and hoped that Eshkol would drive him out of government for his many usurpations of Meir's prerogatives as foreign minister. But Eshkol needed Peres for the sake of continuity, on the nuclear project in particular. He kept Peres on as deputy defense minister, promising him that he would "try to bridge things with Golda."

Peres's terms for staying on were minimal, but, most important, he asked that he keep his role as the secret emissary to the West German defense establishment. He would remain as a key adviser on Dimona and the parallel effort to build a French-designed ballistic missile system to deliver Israel's first nuclear warheads. Eshkol agreed, but like a Yiddish grandfather, he admonished Peres *not* to consider himself a free agent.

"I'd like to be involved in the running of things," he told Peres.[10]

And just to be sure that he could protect himself from any Peres double-dealing, Eshkol balanced the young man's power by reaffirming Rabin's appointment as chief of staff.

With Eshkol fully in charge, the reckoning with Kennedy could be put off no longer. The back-channel message from Washington was that "Israel must come clean."[11] On August 5, 1963, the United States and the Soviet Union signed the limited Nuclear Test Ban Treaty, covering atmospheric detonations, in a ceremony that highlighted the strong sense of mission that Kennedy was undertaking to control nuclear arms. Behind the scenes, Kennedy was pressing Soviet leader Nikita Khrushchev to consider joint action to stop the Chinese atomic bomb from becoming a reality. If Kennedy was thinking that big, how could Israel defy him?

On August 19, after much drafting and consultation with Golda Meir, Eshkol had dispatched a reply to Kennedy with the key phrase "I believe we shall be able to reach agreement on the future schedule of visits."

Kennedy decided to accept Eshkol's wording as an explicit agreement—though it was not—for an American inspection regime over the Dimona reactor and the uranium stockpile that would pass through the reactor. Kennedy warmly congratulated Eshkol for "generously agreeing" to the American demands. "You have acted from a deep wisdom regarding Israel's security in the longer term and the awesome realities which the atomic age imposes on the community of men."[12]

Eshkol had passed his first test. He had defused the Dimona crisis with clever draftsmanship but in reality had given up nothing. The secret of the bomb project and the deception of the Americans now formed the core of Israeli policy. The centerpiece of Israel's national strategy was based on lying to its most important patron and ally.

Golda Meir pressed her colleagues to level with the Americans; this would help in convincing the United States to become Israel's chief arms supplier. Dayan, ever skeptical of reliance on America, warned Eshkol that Washington would try to use financial aid or any other "leverage" it could find to force Israel to give up Dimona.

Eshkol was conflicted. He wanted to tell the Americans because he feared that with all of their intelligence resources, they would find out anyway, and the discovery would put him in confrontation with Kennedy.[13]

"The question is how important it is to us that [Kennedy] will know that the prime minister, or the foreign minister or the whole government [of Israel] does not lie to him?" Eshkol asked.[14] He continued to drag his feet on Dimona as he pressed for a greater commitment from the United States to guarantee Israel's security and to sell modern battle tanks, warplanes, and missiles to counter the Arab buildup.

In frustration, Kennedy's Middle East expert at the White House, Robert Komer, complained to a senior Israeli diplomat that Americans "were expected to subsidize Israel, both privately and publicly, to support her to the hilt on every issue, to meet all of her security requirements, and to defend her if attacked. In return, we did not even know what she intended to do in such critical fields as missiles and nuclear weapons. . . . What kind of a relationship was this?"[15]

This question was still hanging when the news of Kennedy's death reached Israel. Whatever sense of relief Israel's leaders felt—the tragedy, after all, averted a confrontation—they were buoyed by the realization that one of Israel's most powerful supporters in Washington, Lyndon Johnson, had assumed the presidency, a twist of fate that promised incalculable gains for the Jewish state in its quest to strengthen the military and political cooperation between Israel and the United States. Of course, nothing was certain. Johnson would be constrained by Kennedy's policies that he was inheriting, but almost everyone who knew the Texan understood that he harbored a strong personal and sentimental bias for Israel and a basic mistrust of the Arabs.

In June, Johnson invited Eshkol to Washington and treated him to a formal state visit, the first ever for an Israeli leader and an honor that had been pointedly denied to Ben-Gurion.

Johnson's aides had warned for months that "the good relations we've built up with the Arabs are increasingly in jeopardy, primarily because of their frustration over the inability to stop Israel's water diversion." Robert Komer recommended that Johnson "reassure Nasser that our recent inspection of Israel's Dimona reactors shows that Israel isn't going nuclear."[16]

At the White House, Eshkol and Johnson got on extremely well, talking for hours about the Arabs and Israel. Mathilde Krim, a former member of the Irgun and the wife of Arthur Krim, one of Johnson's biggest fund-raisers, had told the president that he would like Eshkol because they were both farmers.

Johnson was no expert on the Middle East, but his Senate career had drawn him close to American Jews who were part of the brain trust of the liberal wing of the Democratic Party. Still, anyone could see that the cold war was heating up in the Middle East.

The previous month, Premier Khrushchev made his first trip to Africa and was greeted in Cairo by hundreds of thousands of cheering Egyptians. Nasser hailed the Soviet leader as a "courageous warrior." Khrushchev told the Egyptian national assembly that Israel had "robbed Arabs of their own sources of water" by building the pipeline to the Negev. He referred to the Israelis as "stooges of imperialism."

Eshkol was delighted to be lumped into the "imperialist" camp because it made it easier to plead for direct American sales of tanks and aircraft to the Jewish state.

"We cannot afford to lose," he told Johnson in their private meeting. "This may be our last stand in history." Here was the face of Eshkol but the voice of Ben-Gurion.[17]

Johnson pledged to Eshkol that for the duration of his presidency, America would be Israel's most reliable friend. Within the administration, Johnson's senior advisers had convinced themselves that they had few options but to begin direct arms sales to Israel. The stronger Israel stood with conventional arms, the more likely the Jewish state might be persuaded to forgo the development of nuclear weapons. But Johnson had misperceived the iron resolve of the sabra military establishment to become the first atomic power in the Middle East.

No sooner had Eshkol returned home than the Arabs confronted him. At a second summit at Alexandria, they issued a communiqué calling for an "immediate start on Arab projects" to block the Israeli water diversion scheme. An Egyptian general was placed in charge of a "United Arab command," and in the final weeks of 1964, Syria sent a phalanx of giant earth-moving bulldozers to begin a two-year project that would include the construction of two dams to divert the headwaters of the Jordan River through an eighty-mile canal and into Jordan's Yarmuk River system.[18]

Israel's military spokesman warned that Arab interference with Israel's water supply would be considered a military attack on the Jewish state.

Eshkol gathered his inner cabinet. Dayan said that if Syria went forward with the plan, war was inevitable. Israel Galili and other senior ministers urged Eshkol to seize Syrian territory to prevent the advance.

Eshkol turned to Rabin for an option short of war. The cautious chief of staff came up with a plan to fire long-range artillery at the Syrian bulldozers to force them to abandon their work. Israel was ill equipped to hit distant targets, so Rabin called in Israel Tal, the chief of the Armored Corps, and asked him if he could devise a method to fire a tank round at long range with pinpoint accuracy.

With Tal's innovations for stabilizing 105mm tank guns, coupled with precision targeting, Israeli tank gunners managed to fire artillery rounds more than five miles with sufficient accuracy to harass the Syrian earth movers. In March 1965, the Israeli army began sending armored tractors into a demilitarized zone to provoke a battle. On March 17, Israeli troops backed by tanks pushed across the border to destroy Syrian bulldozers. One Syrian driver was killed, but what the action showed was that Syria was on its own; Arab states did almost nothing to come to its aid.

The Syrian leader chastised his peers. Speaking to journalists in Damascus, he said, "At the last summit meeting, I told them, 'If you look in the mirror, you will see shame written on your foreheads.'" If the full power of the Arabs were mobilized, he said, "Israel would be eliminated in a matter of weeks."[19]

By early 1965, Israel's harassing tactics forced the Arabs to abandon their plan for a counterdiversion project. The defeat of a plan so prominently associated with Nasser's leadership contributed to the tension that was building toward war in the Middle East.

Eshkol felt no respite from Ben-Gurion's behind-the-scenes criticism, which had seriously escalated as the Mapai Party prepared for national elections in November. Peres, acting as Ben-Gurion's consigliore, was at the forefront of the whispering campaign.

"It is hard to accept the fact that colleagues in the government are engaged in relentless efforts to topple their prime minister," Eshkol penned in a blunt note to Peres.[20]

To protect themselves, Eshkol and Meir had been working to broaden the political base of Mapai, and in late 1964, they orchestrated a political merger for a larger labor alignment. The political shake-up had the effect of driving Ben-Gurion out of Mapai altogether. In 1965, he formed a rival party, Rafi (Israel Worker List), and took Dayan and Peres with him, forcing them to resign from Eshkol's cabinet.[21]

The power struggle extended beyond politics.

Mossad under Meir Amit was still an independent power base. In the wake of the Suez War, the Israeli security services had grown rapidly. The Eichmann kidnapping had also enhanced Mossad's reputation.

Amit was out to prove himself a worthy successor to Harel. He expanded Israel's secret ties to governments in Africa and Asia. He established strong relationships through intelligence channels with Iran, Turkey, and Morocco, and built an alliance with the Kurdish chieftain of northern Iraq, Mullah Mustafa Barzani. Tens of thousands of Moroccan Jews immigrated to Israel through a clandestine underground that Mossad erected despite the opposition of the monarch, King Hassan II.

But in mid-1965, the young Moroccan monarchy, fearing the rise of a national opposition movement in parliament, turned to Israel for help in eliminating the most prominent opposition leader, Mehdi Ben Barka. The request landed on Amit's desk, and what astounded Eshkol, when he discovered later what had happened, was Amit's decision to involve the state of Israel in the assassination of a foreign political figure as if the security establishment could act unilaterally without consulting the prime minister.

From his exile home in Geneva, Ben Barka had aligned himself with revolutionary movements around the world. He was working to include Moroccan dissidents in a "Tricontinental Conference" to be held in Cuba in early 1966. The Moroccan interior minister, General Mohammed Oufkir, turned to his allies in the Mossad for help in stopping Ben Barka. It was Mossad's task to "set up" the dissident politician by luring him out of Geneva to Paris. There, Mossad operatives could turn him over to a group of rogue French intelligence agents and underworld figures who were part of the plot.[22]

The hook that got Ben Barka to Paris was a fake invitation to meet a prominent French film director. The rendezvous was set for October 29, 1965, at the Brasserie Lipp in St. Germain des Prés, a fashionable district for left-wing artists and intellectuals.

But before Ben Barka entered the restaurant, a kidnap squad seized him, pushed him into a car, and drove him to the villa of a French underworld figure. Waiting for Ben Barka was General Oufkir, who executed him. Ben Barka's corpse was said to have been buried on the banks of the Seine, but it was never recovered.

De Gaulle was outraged by the assassination on French soil with the participation of rogue French agents and an Israeli intelligence team. In Israel, Amit could not keep the secret bottled up for long. When Eshkol found out, he insisted that Amit never informed him of the assassination plan or of Mossad's role in making it possible. Amit claimed that he conveyed the essence of the Moroccan request in a letter and had received Eshkol's blessing to proceed.

Given Amit's loyalties to Ben-Gurion and Dayan, Eshkol could only suspect the worst about his motives in acting alone. Eshkol's first step was to bring Isser Harel out of retirement and appoint him as his personal intelligence adviser. Harel, who had been fired by Ben-Gurion and replaced by Amit, must have savored the opportunity to help Eshkol "monitor" those who seemed out to bring down the prime minister. Amit protested Harel's appointment, but the hero of the Eichmann case was back fighting again for influence, which he never really regained.

Whatever the truth about the depth of Mossad's involvement in the Ben Barka murder, Eshkol feared that he was sitting on a scandal greater than the Lavon Affair, and it had occurred just days before the Israeli elections—set for November 1—which would test whether Eshkol had a firm grip on the country. Public knowledge of Mossad's role in the Ben Barka murder might bring down his government. One sure thing was that Eshkol had lost all confidence in Amit. Harel demanded that Amit be fired. But Amit refused to go. Dayan and Peres threatened to bring Eshkol down if he fired Amit, and Amit all but dared Eshkol to risk exposure of the Ben Barka Affair by sacking his Mossad chief.

Amit stood there as a sabra general who had run the Suez War under

Dayan, who had served as chief of military intelligence, and who had restored order in Mossad after Harel's confrontation with Ben-Gurion over
the German rocket scientists.

Eshkol ordered a top secret investigation by a special commission,
which concluded that Eshkol had effectively given his approval in the
Ben Barka hit. Suddenly, Eshkol's neck was exposed. Meir, Allon, and
Galili stepped in and reversed the commission's secret findings. When a
popular magazine, *Bul*, went to press with a story about Ben Barka's
assassination, Eshkol employed all of the resources of Shabak to seize copies of the publication before it reached newsstands. The military censor
imposed a total blackout, even sending a message directly to the *New York
Times* stating that its correspondent in Israel would not be allowed to respond to certain queries from his editors about the case; the ban appears
to exist to this day.[23]

With war clouds gathering in the Arab world, Eshkol's leadership had suffered a terrible blow, one that had revealed the extent to which he could be
intimidated by the sabra establishment in the army, where Amit had many
supporters; even Eshkol's young wife, Miriam, his third, was an ardent
admirer. Eshkol may have feared Ben-Gurion's and Dayan's power to manipulate the facts of the Ben Barka affair in their whispering campaign. He
wanted to bury it and sent out notice to the censor that any Israeli newspaper editor who dared to mention an Israeli connection to the assassination
risked imprisonment, as the editors of *Bul* had learned from their own secret arrest and incarceration.

But the one true thing that Eshkol could not bury was that the military
elite had rolled over him; Amit had done as he pleased. Eshkol looked
the fool for not knowing what he had authorized in the Ben Barka affair. The
return of Isser Harel as an enforcer had failed because neither he nor the
prime minister could muster the political coin to fire the Mossad chief, who
was Ben-Gurion's man and Dayan's ally and a hero of the military establishment. Any insider had to ask, Who really was running the country?
Israel had become a poisonous political landscape where only a small elite at
the top of the military and among the political leaders knew the secrets
that were being covered up to prevent political collapse. Though the sabras
no longer were a monolithic force behind Ben-Gurion, Eshkol's hold on

power was never as tenacious as Ben-Gurion's had been because Eshkol was not as skillful a manipulator. Indeed, he was a weak figure who believed he could command a military society by political consensus. Amit survived the Ben Barka affair because Eshkol could not risk alienating the sabra base in the army, whose leaders regarded Amit as a tough and dedicated officer whose purported sin—setting up for murder a political enemy of King Hassan II, one of the very few Arab heads of state willing to carry on relations with Israel secretly—was not great enough to overcome Amit's record of wartime service.

The climactic battle with Ben-Gurion came at the Mapai congress in February 1965, where Ben-Gurion mounted a frontal assault on his successor. He demanded a judicial inquiry into the Lavon Affair. He told the party leaders that Eshkol was not worthy to serve as prime minister, and the subtext, which could not be spelled out in public, was that Eshkol could not stand up to the Americans on Dimona.

Ever since Eshkol's visit to Washington, President Johnson had been pressing—not as hard as he could have—to put Dimona under the inspection regime of the International Atomic Energy Agency, which was set up by the United Nations to assist nations developing peaceful nuclear power. Its other role was preventing illicit diversion of nuclear materials. The truth was that Eshkol was resisting this pressure with the same tenacity Ben-Gurion had summoned.

In front of the assembled party leaders, Golda Meir rose to speak in opposition to Ben-Gurion. She faced her mentor menacingly. The hall hushed. Her Hebrew was bitingly harsh in the stale air: "The first curse lying over the threshold of our home occurred when people began to talk of favorites and non-favorites."[24]

Even Moshe Sharett, who was dying of cancer, entered the auditorium to impale Ben-Gurion one last time, saying the older man had climbed to "dizzying heights" as the "hero of the great historical epic," but that he had taken on such a "tremendously heavy load" that it was "perhaps too heavy to bear.

"And when such a contradiction appears," he added, "tragedy is the result." There on the stage, Meir walked over and kissed Sharett on the forehead.[25]

After all the heat and fire from the podium, Ben-Gurion's motion for a judicial inquiry on Lavon failed, 841 votes to 1,246. The seventy-eight-year-old leader could no longer dominate the party; he could not eject Eshkol from the prime minister's chair. He had exhorted the military elite to turn against the nonwarrior prime minister, but he had succeeded only in weakening his successor for the crucial battles that were to come.

That should have been the end of it, but in June, Ben-Gurion called a group of supporters to his home in Tel Aviv and surprised them with an announcement that they were forming a new political party: Rafi, Israel Workers List. Dayan was despondent. He owed everything to Ben-Gurion and could not refuse him, but he confided to his daughter that Rafi, as an insurgent political force, could never overcome the well-oiled machine of the labor movement, with its extensive union network and collective farms. Mapai was unbeatable.

Still, Rafi's new triumvirate—Ben-Gurion, Dayan, and Peres—hammered away at Eshkol. Ben-Gurion bragged to one audience about the secret military operations he authorized in the 1950s (the Qibya massacre), and Eshkol, angry over the breach, dispatched a private letter to Peres, asking, "Are you out of your minds? What is Ben-Gurion doing by speaking about Qibya, what are you doing by speaking about Dimona? I even received information . . . from different sources that you say I intended to sell Dimona! Is there no limit to setting fires and poisoning wells?"[26]

The November 1965 elections were a strong endorsement of Eshkol's stewardship, and the labor alignment between Mapai and Ahdut Ha'avoda (Labor Unity) won forty-five seats, leaving Ben-Gurion humbled with only ten seats for Rafi. Even Begin and the right-wing parties trounced Ben-Gurion with twenty-six seats for their new Gahal bloc, an alliance of Begin's Herut (Freedom) Party and the Liberal Party. Begin was gaining legitimacy in Israeli politics.

Eshkol, the hand-wringing consensus builder, had won big with the electorate, but the military establishment saw only his weaknesses. He had demonstrated to the generals that he was working hard on their behalf to build up the conventional army while also acquiring the atomic bomb. His warm relations with Lyndon Johnson made it possible to send Ezer Weizman, the brash Israeli air force commander, to Washington seeking more than two hundred combat aircraft to supplement the two hundred French-made jets in the air force.

The Israelis had aided their case by presenting Johnson, in August 1966, with a Soviet MiG-21 fighter from the Iraqi air force. Mossad operatives had coaxed a disgruntled Iraqi officer to defect with his aircraft from a base near Mosul.

Meir Amit got much of the credit, and the transformative powers of a grand intelligence play could not have been lost on the Mossad chief, who had seen how the Eichmann case had immortalized Harel.

During this same period, Amit gathered his staff to examine whether Israel might open a secret channel to Nasser, whose army was mired in Yemen the same way Johnson was mired in Vietnam.

"What kind of candy can we offer him?" Amit asked the experts gathered around his conference table in Tel Aviv.[27] It was obvious that the Egyptian economy was tanking. The ground was crumbling under Nasser, and Amit saw an opportunity to open a dialogue that might lead to rapprochement.

What if Israel offered to help Nasser win more aid from Washington? What if Israel bought part of the Egyptian cotton crop? These were the questions of the day at Mossad headquarters. In return, Israel could ask for some of the same concessions that Moshe Sharett had requested a decade earlier—opening the Suez Canal to Israeli shipping, a cooling of the rhetoric that had so polarized the region.

Amit traveled to Paris and met with the head of Egyptian intelligence, General Abdel-Moneim Khalil. Out of this meeting came an invitation for the Mossad chief to visit Cairo secretly to meet Abdel Hakim Amer, the supreme military commander who was at Nasser's right hand. If Amer was willing to see him, Amit understood that it was almost certain he would meet Nasser, too.

It was a grand play. Spymaster as peace negotiator with Israel's greatest enemy.

When Amit presented Eshkol with a proposal that the chief of the Mossad travel to Cairo for a secret parley with Nasser, Eshkol punted. He turned to his colleagues for some consensus. Some said it was worth a try. But Harel stepped forward and advised Eshkol that it was a terrible idea, a likely trap. Egyptian treachery might expose the most intimate state secrets. He didn't have to say "Dimona." Moreover, Mossad had been operating spies at high levels in both Cairo and Damascus, and the Arabs had scored some success in ferreting them out, most notably Eli Cohen, who had reached the inner circle of the Syrian presidency before he was captured and hanged.

Much was at risk for Amit.

Most of the details of Amit's offer and the debate over whether he should meet Nasser remain secret, but Amit told me before he died that the accounts of the attempted opening to Nasser were accurate, though he did not want to talk about the motives for Harel's opposition or Eshkol's ultimate decision to walk away from the initiative. But some of the motives were obvious. Harel was a hard-liner unconcerned about Nasser's collapse. He may have hoped for Nasser's fall simply because the great powers would be compelled to intervene to support a pro-Western leader in Egypt.

Harel may also have begrudged Amit any leading role as a secret envoy to the largest Arab country and Israel's main enemy.

For the military elite, things were going Israel's way: Johnson's top advisers had come to the conclusion that the "controlled" and "judicious" sale of U.S. arms to Israel was in America's best interests, and even though such arms could not be directly leveraged to prevent Israel from building an atomic bomb, it was "as good an inhibitor as we've got."[28]

This strategy proved to be an illusion. The notion that the United States should begin selling large quantities of conventional arms to Israel as a strategy to induce the Jewish state to forgo the nuclear option revealed a fundamental misunderstanding of the sabra ethos of self-reliance, which Ben-Gurion and Dayan had so deeply inculcated into the military elite with a decade of "activism"—the euphemism for militarism—and doctrinal immersions in "detonator" theory and the like. By the mid-1960s, the inevitability of an Israeli atomic bomb had registered within the military elite as an unparalleled national achievement, proof that Ben-Gurion, whatever his flaws, had been a farsighted visionary when he set the nation on a path to obtain the ultimate deterrent against an Arab onslaught or a Soviet surprise attack. Becoming a nuclear power, even an undeclared nuclear power, would increase the self-confidence of Israel's Holocaust survivors and add a new measure of stability and permanence to the Jewish state.

After Johnson approved the first tank and aircraft sales in 1966, Eshkol reneged on his pledge to establish regular visits to Dimona by American scientists. He steadfastly refused to put Dimona under any kind of safeguards program and rejected Johnson's request to share information about Dimona with Nasser, who told the United States that if Israel crossed the nuclear threshold, the Arabs would go to war.

The reason for Eshkol's reversal was straightforward: the entire military establishment and the political elite had embraced the nuclear project as it neared completion. At the same time, Eshkol was under constant hyperactive political surveillance by the Ben-Gurion camp for any telltale that the prime minister was wilting in the face of American pressure. Whatever he had thought in the past about the Dimona project, Eshkol had come to realize that he had to see it through, and in doing so establish his own credentials as the leader of the military establishment.

During this period, Mordechai Gazit, a diplomat who served Ben-Gurion and, later, Meir, told the U.S. State Department experts on the Middle East that the "common [view] accepted by the overwhelming majority" of Israelis was that "the Arabs will come to accept Israel's existence only when they finally realize that they can never surpass Israel's power." Whether the conflict continued for another ten years or twenty years, "Israel will stay ahead by whatever means are necessary." For Washington, he concluded, "there must be an appreciation of the fact that Israel cannot make concessions."[29] Here was the code of the sabra military elite whose outlook had hardened significantly in the ten years since Ben-Gurion had undermined the alternative approach for which Sharett had built a majority in the Mapai leadership.

In 1966, the Israeli military establishment had not abandoned its assessment that the Arabs were arming for another round of war, but with Nasser's army still tied down in Yemen, the Middle East was enjoying a fragile stability that had become the norm since the Suez Crisis ten years earlier. The interregnum had given Rabin time to build out the army, which fully mobilized could put 250,000 soldiers into battle—more than 10 percent of the population—with a dozen armored and mechanized brigades supported by paratroopers and ten or more infantry brigades, all under the umbrella of an air force comprising more than two hundred modern warplanes. The army's doctrine was to strike quickly and ferociously to make short work of defeating an enemy, because the Suez Crisis had demonstrated how quickly the great powers could intervene to prevent an all-out Israeli victory.[30]

The air force under Weizman and the military intelligence apparatus under General Aharon Yariv had mapped the combined Arab air forces—much greater in number than Israel's air force—so that when the day came, Israeli pilots would be able to launch a surprise attack.

Though Israel was not looking for war, when the prospect of war appeared, Eshkol lost control in a way he and most of the country had never imagined. Eshkol simply had not realized how difficult it would be to modulate the pace and the scale of escalation, or contain the rapacious second-guessing by the sabra officer corps.

On the Arab side, a new and more radical regime had come to power in Syria under Nureddin al-Atassi. The commander of the air force was General Hafez al-Assad, a rising power broker. The new radicalism coming out of Damascus called for a "people's war" to eradicate Israel. Syria offered training camps, arms, and forward bases to Palestinian guerrillas eager to attack the Zionist state.

For the first time since the mid-1950s, Arab guerrillas—the fedayeen—were back, among them a young Yasser Arafat, staging raids on Israeli territory and inflicting military and civilian casualties. In the spring of 1966, four Israeli soldiers died in clashes with Palestinians, and soon thereafter, Rabin launched an aerial attack on Syrian earth movers, destroying five of them in the southern Golan Heights. A month later, Syrian air force jets dive-bombed an Israeli patrol boat that had run aground near the northeastern shore of the Sea of Galilee. Soon an air battle was under way and Rabin sent Israeli bombers north to pummel Syrian targets on the Mediterranean coast.

This no longer was the "cautious" Rabin. Israel's military establishment was in the midst of the most important modernization since the Suez War. After the air battle, Rabin, in an interview with an army magazine, spelled out what sounded like a new Israeli doctrine. "The reaction to Syrian acts, whether they be terrorism, diversion or aggression on the border, must be aimed at the perpetrators of that terrorism and at the regime that supports it," he said. "The problem with Syria is, therefore, essentially a clash with its leadership."[31] Rabin was entering his final year as chief of staff, and the conflict with Syria seemed to provoke him beyond the caution for which he was known.

Eshkol immediately walked Rabin's statement back, explaining to the cabinet that the chief of staff had been misinterpreted. But the episode was indicative of the excessive self-confidence that had taken hold at the top of the military. Rabin's old Palmach comrades Yigal Allon and Israel Galili had joined Eshkol's cabinet, another bulwark against Ben-Gurion's pressure. But these were men of the military elite who believed in pushing Israel's frontiers to the Jordan River and expanding the state to achieve more defensible borders.

Now Syria was spouting Arab bombast. Yet Syria was something of a sitting duck in military terms. Its modest arsenal of Soviet-supplied weaponry was no match for Israel's. Nasser complained that he was supporting fifty thousand troops in Yemen and, therefore, was not about to go to war over a Syrian tractor.

"What's next?" he asked in Cairo. "If Syria is attacked, then I should attack Israel? The result is that the Israelis can dictate to me when I must hit them."

Just as Ben-Gurion, Dayan, and Lavon had been tempted to goad Syria into war in 1955, Rabin looked out to his northern frontier and saw a weak and isolated regime whose antics in stirring up the Palestinian fedayeen were not to be tolerated.

The Arabs swelled with pride over the fedayeen attacks. To appease public opinion, Nasser offered Syria a mutual defense treaty. No sooner had the two countries signed the pact than fedayeen militants placed a mine that struck an Israeli border patrol, killing three soldiers. Rabin pressed Eshkol for authority to stage a large reprisal raid, one that would threaten the stability of the new Syrian regime and expose Nasser to ridicule. Eshkol reluctantly approved, but he insisted that the raid not be launched at Syria, which might provoke the Soviets.

An Israeli armored column—fifty vehicles led by eight Centurion tanks and more than three thousand soldiers—rolled into Jordanian territory on the West Bank on November 13, 1966. There in hills south of Hebron, far from the Syrian frontier, the column entered the town of Samu. Under the morning sun, the Israeli commanders called out the residents and herded them into the central plaza while sappers laid explosives and began blowing up homes and other buildings. For hours, the hills rumbled with explosions as smoke and dust rose from the town that was systematically being turned into rubble in the largest Israeli military operation since the Suez War.

A UN survey put the number of demolished homes at more than a hundred. In the midst of the raid, the Jordanian army mobilized from a nearby base and raced toward Samu only to run into an ambush the Israeli force had laid for it. The Jordanians were overwhelmed; fifteen of its soldiers were killed, along with three civilians. More than a hundred Arabs were wounded in the devastation wrought by the Israeli army, whose actions were condemned by the United Nations.

By almost any measure, the Samu raid was a disaster, an act of unbridled militarism that revealed Rabin as lacking any subtle grasp of how to conduct military policy beyond the blind retribution of the Ben-Gurion era. But it also demonstrated to the Syrians that they could continue to foment guerrilla attacks across the northern borders of Israel with relative impunity because Israel seemed too cautious to mount a direct counterattack on Moscow's client.

In Jordan, the raid touched off riots against King Hussein, still regarded as a weakling who could not defend his people. Hussein responded by stepping up his verbal attacks on Nasser for "hiding" behind the United Nations force on his frontier with Israel. Nasser looked complacent if only because he was doing nothing to oppose Israeli militarism; in effect, he was deflecting violence to the territories of his Arab brothers while UN peacekeepers protected the Egyptian frontier.

Rabin, stung by criticism of the Samu raid, appeared before the Knesset and said, "I had no way of knowing that the Jordanians would be foolish enough to try and shoot at such a strong opposing force."[32] This, of course, was evasion: What army would not defend against invaders?

A nervous Eshkol sought to preempt American anger with a letter to Johnson explaining the raid as an overreaction. Johnson did not reply.

Internally, the harsh military response to the killing of Israeli soldiers played well in the press and quieted the political opposition that had questioned Eshkol's fitness as a national leader. After Samu, Eshkol told his

Mapai Party colleagues, "The Arab countries will understand that we mean *business*," saying "business" in English.[33]

The venomous triangle of Arab politics dominated the region in early 1967. The Arabs were weakened by Egypt's diversion in Yemen's civil war, now in its fifth year. What stands out in these months, as Dayan was to point out later, is that the Israeli military establishment seemed to be trying to goad Syria into a major fight—either to topple the regime in Damascus or humiliate Egypt by forcing Nasser to make good on his pledge to defend Syria, a step that would expose his military weakness. The prospect of humiliating the Arabs undoubtedly propelled Rabin and the generals forward.

Every time Israel sent a tractor into the demilitarized zone in the north, it was a provocation orchestrated by the army, according to Dayan. In early April 1967, Rabin presided over a new probe. Two Israeli tractors rumbled into the DMZ near the shores of the Sea of Galilee, and the Syrians let loose with armor-piercing rounds—bullets as big as Coke bottles—as tracers streaked across the landscape. Israeli tanks opened up on the Syrian positions with long-range artillery and the Syrians started firing mortar rounds into every Israeli town within their range. The ground battle was raging when Rabin got Eshkol's approval to send in the air force. Soon both Israeli and Syrian warplanes were engaged in dogfights over the Golan Heights. Two Syrian MiGs were shot down and, as more French-made Israeli fighters rose for the battle, the Syrian air force broke off with the Israeli jets giving chase all the way back to Damascus, where a large air battle involving more than a hundred aircraft ensued. Four more Syrian jets were shot down before the Israelis broke off. Before they returned to base, some of them buzzed Damascus.

Rabin had taken the battle to Syria. The downing of six Soviet-made Syrian jets was trumpeted throughout the military establishment. Israeli defense chiefs bragged to American friends that they could outmaneuver the best fighters that the Soviet air force could put in the air.

The air war of April 1967 and the bellicose rhetoric that followed proved to be a tipping point.

Neither side expected it, despite the escalation that both incited in an international environment charged by the Vietnam War and the ascent in

Moscow of Leonid Brezhnev and Andrei Grechko, the hard-line Soviet defense minister.

Rabin and the Israeli military establishment believed they were sending a strong message to the new Syrian regime. By fomenting a "people's liberation war" using Palestinian guerrillas, Damascus risked a devastating military strike.

"We must make it clear to the Syrians that they cannot continue in this way, and I think that the only way to make it clear to the Syrians is by using force," said Israel's chief of military intelligence, Aharon Yariv. He briefed foreign correspondents in Israel following statements by Eshkol and Rabin indicating that Syria was setting itself up for an even larger confrontation.

Yariv had never been a man to mince words. He said that the only "sure and safe answer" to the Syrian challenge was a "military operation of great size and strength," but he qualified this assessment by stating that "not everything that is sure is possible," an allusion to international constraints. Yariv expressed confidence that Israel could calibrate a military action in the right proportion that would convince Syria that it faced the risk—if it persisted in fomenting the "people's war"—of an "imminent all-out confrontation" with Israel. Such a confrontation would force Israel to consider the whole range of responses, including an "all-out invasion of Syria and the conquest of Damascus."[34]

Nasser read the reports of this briefing as new intelligence reached him from Moscow alleging that the Israeli army was massing troops in the north for an attack on Syria. The Soviet intelligence was mostly disinformation, though it was clear that the Israeli army was in a heightened state of alert along the northern frontier.

Still, it was impossible for Nasser to ignore the intelligence reports that came to him from the Soviet ambassador, the KGB chief in Cairo, and vice president Anwar Sadat, who was leading an Egyptian delegation on a visit to Moscow.

For Nasser, it didn't matter whether the intelligence reports were false. Israel, after all, was telegraphing militaristic intentions to chasten the radical Syrian regime. What mattered was that Nasser was in an untenable spot as the putative leader of the Arab world. He had called King Hussein a whore for the West on Radio Cairo, and Jordanian radio had fired back that Nasser was hiding behind the "skirts" of UN peacekeepers.

On May 13, Nasser convened the Supreme Executive Council and ordered the Egyptian army into Sinai. This was no stealthy move.

The army mounted up on its trucks, which roared down the Nile highway in full view of crowds that reveled in Nasser's determination to threaten the Israelis with war. All over the Middle East, the Arabs cheered Nasser's bravado, even though Egypt's treasury was nearly empty and much of his army was still in Yemen.[35]

It was as if diplomacy was dead.

Six-Day War: The Military Revolts

Without doubt, it was wartime in the Middle East.

Each day's newspapers in Cairo and Tel Aviv displayed images of mobilization, of tanks and soldiers marching toward battle lines in the desert. The roads were choked with reservists heading for their units. The chief of the Egyptian general staff on May 16 requested that the United Nations withdraw its peacekeeping forces from Gaza and Sinai, and to the surprise of many governments, Secretary-General U Thant complied without trying to stall for diplomatic intervention.

When the blue-helmeted UN peacekeepers pulled out in a matter of days, suddenly no buffer force stood between the Egyptian and Israeli armies, and the threat of war mounted rapidly. Nasser flew to the Abu Suweir air base in Sinai on May 22. By then, eighty thousand Egyptian soldiers were facing Israel. Nasser delighted his air force commanders by announcing that he was closing the Strait of Tiran to Israeli shipping. Cairo's *Al-Ahram* daily reported that the Egyptian navy had mined the entrance to the Gulf of Aqaba.

"The Jews threatened war. We tell them—*Ahlan wa-sahlan!* [Welcome!] We are ready for war. Our armed forces and all of our people are ready for war, but under no circumstances will we abandon any of our rights—this water is ours."[1]

No battle plan survives contact with the enemy.

War overcomes logic, and Levi Eshkol began to understand after the army's clash with Syria that events were slipping the bonds of control. It would be up to him, the nonsabra prime minister who had never served in the army, to restrain the generals and quell the surge of enthusiasm for war that was becoming more and more pronounced in the officer corps. This spirit was buoyed by an inchoate notion that the time had come for the IDF to demonstrate its standing as the most potent military force in the region and to prevent, through some kind of military humiliation, Nasser's attempt to unify the Arab world behind his leadership once again. Flush with new American armor, warplanes, and battlefield weaponry, the Israeli army had spent a decade building out the Armored Corps: the air force, the paratroopers, and the navy. The logic that now weighed on the officer corps was: If not now, when?

Eshkol was desperate to deescalate.

He called Soviet ambassador Dimitri Chuvakin to the prime minister's office and offered personally to escort the envoy to the northern border to see that the intelligence reports of Israeli buildup there were false.

Chuvakin drily declined, saying that it was *not* his job to observe facts on the ground, only to convey the views of his government.[2]

On May 22, the day Nasser closed the Strait of Tiran, Eshkol went up to Jerusalem to open the summer session of the Knesset. In a major address, he blamed the Arabs for the crisis: the young radicals in Damascus, Nasser, Palestinian guerrillas who had stepped up infiltration attacks. Eshkol called on the great powers to "remove the danger of a conflagration."

Speaking to the Arabs, Eshkol said, "We do not intend launching an attack. We have no interest in violating their security, their territory or their legitimate rights. Nor shall we interfere in any way in their internal affairs, their regimes or their regional or international relations."[3]

But Nasser had already pushed in his chips for a big military display, even greater than the one he made in 1960 during Operation Rotem. He would rally the Arab world, extricate himself from the Yemen quagmire and, if necessary, absorb an Israeli military strike, as he did in 1956, because he was certain Israel would be condemned for it.

"Israel today is not backed by Britain and France as was the case in 1956," Nasser told his officers. "It has the United States, which supports it and supplies it with arms. But the world cannot again accept the plotting which took place in 1956."[4]

Richard Nixon, preparing to run for the Republican nomination for president, called on the Johnson administration during a stop in Chicago to take strong measures to prevent the use of force by either Israel or Egypt.

"The past record of the United States should give pause to any potential aggressor in the Near East," he said.[5]

Former president Eisenhower, speaking to reporters near his retirement home in Gettysburg, Pennsylvania, warned that "it would be a serious mistake" for any single nation to try to resolve the crisis. "We should have a whole concert of nations in this matter," he went on, cautioning against "unilateral" actions by either Moscow or the United States.[6]

At first, Moshe Dayan thought Eshkol and Rabin had acted foolishly. Dayan acidly suggested, during a meeting of the Knesset committee on defense, that Nasser's move into Sinai was predictable given the Israeli provocation. The Samu raid and the April 7 air battle over Damascus had forced the Arabs to escalate dramatically. Dayan's initial judgment seemed to be that the crisis smelled like an Israeli miscalculation.

Ben-Gurion agreed. The country was facing a real danger of Arab mobilization with Soviet backing. Why had Rabin and Eshkol stirred up the hornets' nest? he wanted to know.

"I very much doubt whether Nasser wanted to go to war, and now we are in serious trouble," Ben-Gurion said to Rabin when the chief of staff called at his home. "You have led the nation into a grave situation. We must not go to war. We are isolated. You bear the responsibility."[7]

With the Americans tied up in Vietnam, who would come to Israel's rescue? Ben-Gurion asked. He agreed with Nasser. This crisis was not like 1956, when Israel had allied itself with Britain and France. Now they were risking everything.

Peres parroted the older man's line. To a gathering of Rafi leaders, he said that what the country needed was a "prime minister and a defense minister who in spite of everybody saying 'Yes!' to going to war, can be brave enough to say, 'Not now!'"[8]

Yet as the Egyptian divisions poured into Sinai, Dayan was the first to shift ground when it became clearer that Nasser was gambling with a weak hand. The Israeli army was far more powerful in 1967 than in 1960, while the Egyptian army was overextended in Yemen.

At eight the morning after Nasser's declaration closing the strait, Aharon Yariv, the Israeli director of military intelligence, announced to the general staff that the decade of tranquillity—the post-Suez period—was over. As the generals assembled in the "pit" beneath the Defense Ministry in Tel Aviv, Yariv established himself as a leading hawk.* If Israel did not respond to the closing of the strait, he told the generals, the psychological deterrent value of Israel's military power would disappear. The Arabs would smell weakness and mount an even greater threat to Israel's security. Ezer Weizman, the architect of the contingency plans to wipe out the Arab air forces, wanted to attack immediately.[9]

Eshkol convened the Knesset defense committee. He invited Menachem Begin and Dayan to join. Meir was there to support Eshkol as Rabin laid out the difficulties of a war on three fronts without allies. "We're not talking about a stroll in the park," he warned them. There was a lot of posturing in the meeting, with Eshkol, Eban, and others making statements they knew would be repeated in the press: "A nation that could not protect its basic maritime interests . . . ," and so on.[10]

But when it got down to decisions, Eshkol was not ready to commit to war, and Dayan was the first to sense this and to accentuate the risk of too much delay.

Sitting there at the cabinet table with that slash of black eye patch, Dayan looked at his colleagues and framed the issue in his characteristically brutal manner. "We are not England here, with its tradition of losing big battles first," he said. Nasser had given them an opportunity. They should recognize it. "We should destroy hundreds of tanks in a two-to-three-day battle," he said. Dayan's calculus was simple: if they struck quickly, they

---

* Though Yariv was a hard-line intelligence chief, he was among the first high-ranking officers among the military elite to propose negotiations with any Palestinian group that was willing to forswear violence and work for a peaceful resolution to the Palestinian problem. The proposal followed Yariv's service to Golda Meir's government in supervising Operation Wrath of God to track down Arab militants in the wake of the Munich massacre of 1972. The Shemtov-Yariv Formula of 1974, made jointly with Victor Shemtov, the Mapam Party chief with the Labor bloc, was vigorously criticized from the center and right as a perceived overture to the PLO. It effectively ended Yariv's prospects for a political career.

could shred the Egyptian army. Nasser was vulnerable. He had put a force into the desert that could easily be defeated. What hung in the air was whether the current leadership was up to it.[11]

Eshkol could see that Dayan, speaking from the opposition benches of parliament, had shifted the focus to the prime minister. Dayan was no longer in uniform, but he was the unofficial voice of the sabra military establishment. On a question of war, he carried more weight at that moment than anyone else, even Ben-Gurion. And there was a new factor that added to the pressure on Eshkol: Dimona. The reactor, into which Israel had sunk so much treasure, was now a possible target. The Egyptians had flown a high-altitude reconnaissance mission over the Negev a few days earlier. They were obviously scouting the deployment of Israeli ground forces, but they were also doubtless gathering targeting data for their bombers. Eshkol had placed the atomic bomb project under his direct command at the beginning of the year and had tasked the nuclear scientists to fabricate two nuclear explosives in case they were needed. The design of these bombs would not be elegant, but Eshkol had been persuaded by the small group of experts that Israel should prepare the option of exploding a nuclear device within sight of Egyptian forces as the ultimate deterrent against attack. A so-called demonstration shot could also be fired to stop an Arab army that had already broken through Israel's defenses.[12]

Before any decisions could be made, Eshkol said they must consult President Johnson. He would dispatch Eban to Washington. Before the end of the day, Eban had added Paris and London to his diplomatic itinerary. The generals were frustrated. The diplomatic pause would undermine the momentum for an immediate strike.

After the meeting, Rabin had been accosted by Moshe Chaim Shapira, the tough-minded minister of interior from the National Religious Party. Shapira lit into him. He accused Rabin and the prime minister of provoking a war to enhance their position in the history books. Why start a war? Who would provide ammunition if they ran short? the minister asked. "If we're attacked, of course, we'll fight for our lives, but to take the initiative? To bring this curse down on us with our own hands? Do you want to bear the responsibility for endangering Israel? I shall resist it as long as I draw breath!"[13]

Rabin was shaken. The vigilant soldier, the military guardian of the Jewish state, suffered a massive loss of confidence. He tried to argue with Shapira. "Nasser has threatened Israel's standing," he protested. "His army will threaten Israel's very existence. I don't want to go to war either, but there's no way out if the American political efforts fail." Yet Rabin was not sure he believed his own words. He had been working around the clock for weeks, using coffee, whiskey, and cigarettes to keep him going. That night, when Rabin got home, he slumped into a chair and succumbed to waves of anxiety and depression. The weight seemed crushing and he had lost the vise with which he usually gripped the certainties of his life. He could barely speak when Yariv came to his house to buck him up, and soon even Yariv left despondent.

That evening, Rabin called Weizman and spoke in deepest confidence about his fears. The two men had come up together through the ranks. They had faced Nasser's army in 1960 together. Now Rabin was accused of being a warmonger. "Am I to blame?" he asked Weizman that night. "Should I relinquish my post?"[14]

Weizman may have thought Rabin was falling apart, but he told him to hang on. In the event of Rabin's incapacitation, Weizman was keenly aware that he would become chief of staff.

Leah Rabin stepped in at that moment. She called the family doctor, who told Rabin he needed a night's sleep and gave him a sleeping pill. That was it for Israel's top soldier. He was out of action. If Nasser had chosen that moment to attack, Rabin would have gone down in history as the wimp who went to bed.

The next morning, Weizman called the entire general staff together. He was acting on his own authority. He put the air force on alert and instructed the commanders of the northern, central, and southern fronts to complete their mobilization and move their units into battle formation. A number of generals exchanged worried glances. "Where was Rabin?" Weizman offered no information, but he rattled them further by instructing them not to communicate with the chief of staff.

After the meeting, Weizman went to the prime minister's office and informed Eshkol that he had been acting in Rabin's place, that he had convened the general staff and issued several important orders. There he stood, trying to contain his own emotions about whether the mantle was about to be placed on his shoulders, but Eshkol just looked at him and thanked him, adding that he had done the right thing. That afternoon, Eshkol went to the Defense Ministry in Tel Aviv and summoned Rabin's doctor and asked him what the chief of staff was suffering from.

"Acute anxiety," the doctor reported and was sent away. Eshkol could only smile. What a surprise. The sabras were human.

Close friends went to Rabin that afternoon and found him trying to rally. General Avraham Yoffe, who was also Rabin's brother-in-law, came to the house and told Rabin that morale was high and that the commanders all favored launching a preemptive strike on Nasser's army. Rabin replied that he was going to return to work the next morning. He explained his collapse by saying he had been smoking too much, and from this would come the legend that he had suffered from "nicotine poisoning," though the public heard nothing about it because the military censor kept everything about Rabin's collapse out of the press.

Israel was in the period called "the waiting," which for the public was a time of fear, dread, and uncertainty. Trenches for mass graves appeared in city parks, where rabbis blessed the ground because word had leaked that thousands of battle deaths were expected. A popular song on radio—there was still no television in Israel—was "Nasser Waits for Rabin," but in reality, Rabin was waiting for Eshkol and Eshkol was waiting for Lyndon Johnson, who was enmeshed in the Vietnam War. Key senators had told him that the country could not fight two wars at once, but Johnson seemed certain that Congress would come around as the Arab threat to Israel intensified.

His idea was to organize a group of maritime countries in the United Nations to reassert freedom of navigation in the Strait of Tiran. It would take weeks to organize, but Johnson believed he had time. The CIA and the Pentagon believed that Israel could defeat any collection of Arab armies that attacked it. The Pentagon also believed that Israel could stay mobilized for two months without damaging its economy, while Egypt could not stay mobilized in the desert for more than a few weeks.

Eshkol had chosen a course of restraint. He was determined to show the American president that Israel was a trustworthy ally.

Yet throughout these tense weeks, the Israeli public never understood the scale of back-channel efforts that Johnson was making to avert war. Johnson did not want news of his actions to leak out lest it antagonize the Arabs. The reason was painfully obvious. In the spring of 1967, Johnson knew he had less than a year to turn things around in Vietnam, or he would be facing a reelection campaign with the stinking corpse of failure in Southeast Asia on his shoulders.

Johnson was desperately trying to engage Nasser to find out what was in the Egyptian leader's mind, and he needed a little time. On May 17, he warned Eshkol not to act precipitously. "I cannot accept any responsibilities on behalf of the United States for situations which arise as a result of actions on which we are not consulted."[15]

The Israeli public also did not know that Israel had its first crude nuclear bombs and that the general staff's secret military unit was standing guard over the devices, ready to transport them on half-tracks or trucks out to the frontier to stop an onslaught or, if need be, to put the Arabs into a massive fright.*

Abba Eban meanwhile was on a fool's errand: a diplomat trying to head off a war that the generals increasingly wanted to fight, which meant that diplomacy and, therefore, Eban himself would become the enemy of the generals' ambition. The military establishment did not trust Eban; the generals—especially the sabras—saw him as a silver-tongued Cambridge man who had spent most of his life out of the country. He was all rhetoric and parlor games with skills that appealed to the sophisticates of the Ministry of Foreign Affairs—the house that Moshe Sharett had built. To the military establishment, diplomacy was the art of saying whatever was necessary to enable the Israeli army to realize its goals.

Eshkol, of course, did not see it that way, nor did he regard Eban's mission or diplomacy in general as a wasted effort. The problem was that by May 25, the generals were pressing for immediate military action. Intelligence reports indicated that Abdel Hakim Amer, Nasser's supreme military commander, had ordered what looked like the beginning of offensive

---

* It is widely believed in Israel's military and intelligence establishments that Brigadier General Yitzhak Yaakov, a leading Israeli weapons scientist and former chief of research and development in the Defense Ministry, was in charge of the deployment of Israel's first atomic explosives in 1967. In early 2001, the retired general, known as Yatza to his friends, was living in New York as an American citizen when he showed a draft manuscript of his memoir to an Israeli journalist. The journalist's article about Yaakov's role in overseeing the atomic explosives of 1967 was censored. When Yaakov returned to Israel that year for his 75th birthday celebration, he was arrested, charged and tried in secret, and convicted for breaching Israel's security. He was not allowed to return to the United States. According to a June 20, 2002, report in *Ha'aretz*, Yaakov ultimately received a two-year suspended sentence.

operations to commence the next day. Yariv, the director of military intelligence, told Rabin that the Egyptian air force was poised to strike and he feared that the attack was coming within hours. Rabin took Yariv with him to convince Eshkol that the Israeli army was losing the strategic and tactical edge the longer they delayed. If Eban was not going to get an iron-clad commitment from Johnson to treat an attack on Israel as an attack on the United States, what was the point of waiting?

Two of the leading hawks for war, Yariv and Weizman, now the army's chief of operations, had gone to Rabin's home to press for a surprise attack on the Egyptian forces. But Rabin, still on the defensive following his breakdown, could not overcome Eshkol's resistance. "The IDF will not attack before the political options have been exhausted," Eshkol declared.[16] Eban had to be given a chance to meet with Johnson, but Eshkol authorized Rabin to draft an urgent cable to Washington instructing Eban to seek an immediate meeting at the highest level to inform Johnson that an attack was imminent and asking whether the "United States would regard an attack on Israel as an attack on itself."[17] This was language straight out of the NATO alliance, of which Israel was not a member.

Eban thought the cable the height of lunacy and panic, but he was not privy to the intelligence that had incited it, intelligence that would later show that Amer may have tried to launch a war on his own authority but was overruled by Nasser.

Still, when the attack did not materialize the next day, Israel's credibility with Johnson suffered a blow. The CIA told Johnson that there were no indications that the Egyptian army was moving out of its defensive formation in Sinai. Johnson asked British prime minister Harold Wilson "whether your intelligence people share our judgment that the Israeli assessment is overdrawn and, indeed, what is your estimate of Nasser's intentions." Word came back that British intelligence shared the CIA view.[18] Johnson conveyed this information to Eshkol. By the morning of Friday, May 26, Yariv and the military establishment had egg on their faces. They had missed something.

Eshkol got only a brief reprieve from the sabra rush to war. He knew he needed to broaden the leadership circle to build unity and to neutralize all of the sniping from the sidelines, especially Ben-Gurion's. Eshkol's idea was to create a committee of leaders whose judgment the military and the country would respect. The key was to somehow co-opt Dayan.

Eshkol called Dayan back from the southern front, where the former general had been reviewing the frontline brigades and talking with the disgruntled commanders who were eager to strike. Dayan's first stop upon reaching the city was Weizman's office. Weizman told him that war would likely commence within hours. After years in the wilderness, Dayan more than anything wanted to get back into uniform and go to war. He asked Weizman to help him, to use his authority to reinstate him as a general to lead one of the divisions on the southern front or, failing that, to advise the general staff from the field.

Both men knew that only Rabin or Eshkol could make that decision. Dayan then went to Mossad headquarters to see Meir Amit, who briefed him on everything else he had missed regarding Eban's mission, the mood around Eshkol, and rumblings in the Knesset. The two men discussed how Dayan could get reinstated so he could participate in the war, and Amit agreed to take a handwritten note to Eshkol.

Dayan moved swiftly. He thought diplomacy and dialogue with Nasser were nothing short of appeasement.[19] Though Rabin was walking a fine line between reluctant politicians and hell-bent generals, for Dayan there was only one role: leading the militarist camp.

Dayan had flown in a small plane back to the southern front when Eshkol's message reached him. He immediately returned to Tel Aviv, where he found Eshkol at the Dan Hotel on the waterfront. Dayan offered his assessment of what Israel was facing—eighty thousand Egyptian troops now in Sinai with eight hundred or more tanks. Israel should destroy the Egyptian army without delay, he said. They could buy a decade or more of security by wiping out the core of the Egyptian army.

Eshkol told Dayan that they needed a war council to make the big decisions. He wanted to expand the Knesset's defense and foreign affairs committee from five to seven members, bringing in Dayan and Begin as representatives of the opposition parties. Israel would be united. He was offering Dayan a seat at the leadership table. But Dayan had come to ask for a field command. They parted with Eshkol promising to respond within twenty-four hours.

On Friday evening, May 26, in Washington, Eban rode the White House elevator to the second-floor residence. Johnson told the Israeli envoy that he could not act precipitously without Congress. He was willing to stand up for Israel in the United Nations. He was willing to organize a naval flotilla to open the strait. If more was needed, he would go to Congress, but if Israel acted on its own, he would not be able to help. He echoed the advice de Gaulle had given Eban: "I think it is a necessity that Israel should never make itself seem responsible in the eyes of America and the world for making war. Israel will not be alone unless it decides to go it alone," he said.

Eban left the White House feeling that he had gotten a commitment from Johnson to take concrete and immediate steps to open the Strait of Tiran, but Eban's mission was already a lost cause. Dayan, Rabin, and others had made the point that the freedom-of-navigation issue had been overtaken by the imperatives of destroying Nasser's army. Yes, the closure of the strait was a cause for war, but the focus had shifted to the Egyptian divisions ripe for the plucking on the Israeli frontier.

"The waiting" had also impelled Menachem Begin into action against Eshkol. He and his Herut Party elders, among the strongest hawks for going to war, went to Ben-Gurion's house expecting the eighty-one-year-old leader to be willing to lead the war camp. But Ben-Gurion's response shocked them. He thought war would be Eshkol's greatest blunder. It was putting everything that Ben-Gurion had built at risk. Perhaps the older man had taken this position reflexively—due to his hatred for Eshkol—and was unable to shift ground as nimbly as Dayan. Not even the prospect of destroying Nasser, his old nemesis, had moved Ben-Gurion off his position that Israel should not act without a major power as an ally. Whatever his motive, Ben-Gurion abandoned the sabra militarists and, though it was not immediately apparent, the break with his protégés ended his influence over the military elite.

Eban's plane landed that same evening and Eshkol's secretary was dispatched to pick him up and drive him to Tel Aviv where the cabinet was meeting. Tough messages warning Israel not to rush to war had come in from Soviet premier Kosygin and from de Gaulle. But neither of these was as influential as Johnson's message: the American president wanted three weeks to organize international opposition to Nasser's closure of the Strait of Tiran.

Eban found Eshkol and his ministers surrounded by generals: Rabin, Chaim Bar-Lev, Weizman, and Yariv. They were there to witness the split in the cabinet; their presence would bolster the war camp. During the heated debate, Eshkol passed Rabin a note saying that Moshe Chaim Shapira, head of the National Religious Party, was threatening to resign if the cabinet voted for war. That would cause the collapse of Eshkol's coalition, and the last thing he needed was paralysis. Eshkol polled the cabinet on the choice: war now to preempt Nasser or wait for the Americans. The tally was nine ministers in favor and nine opposed.

The next morning, nothing could relieve the deadlock. The war camp was stymied by a new message from Johnson. The Soviets believed that Israel was preparing to strike. Kosygin was warning Britain and the United States that Moscow would "render assistance" to the Arab states if they fell under attack. Johnson was in Texas, but he dispatched a cable to Eshkol saying, "As your friend, I repeat even more strongly what I said yesterday to Mr. Eban. Israel must not take any pre-emptive military action and thereby make itself responsible for the initiation of hostilities."[20]

Eshkol was fighting to keep control over events. He accompanied Rabin to meet the generals and explain the cabinet's decision—or lack of decision. There, in a conference room of the defense complex, Eshkol faced an attack that he had not seen coming. One by one, these sons of Israel told Eshkol that he was making a terrible mistake by waiting for America.

Ariel Sharon was the most brutal. "Today, we have shredded with our bare hands the deterrence power of the IDF." The army, he continued, was "ready like never before to totally destroy the Egyptian forces." Relying on diplomacy made Israel seem weak and incompetent. "Who if not us is authorized to come and tell you that the army is ready for war?" His point could not have been clearer: in a crisis, the army was the superior power, and no prime minister should lightly stand in its way. With the enemy so close, how could civilians arrogate unto themselves the powers of life and death for the Jewish state? Only the military was capable of acting.

Eshkol was loath to let this challenge go unanswered because he knew that Sharon was mouthing a raw sabra ultimatum.

"Nobody said we are a pre-emptive army," Eshkol fired back. Just because Egypt had moved its army into Sinai did not mean that Israel had to jump up and destroy it. And where did Sharon think all those fine weapons that were now in his hands had come from? "You wanted one-hundred aircraft. You got it. You got tanks as well. You got everything so that we can win if we have to."

Diplomacy, Eshkol pointed out to him, all that needless running around that Sharon ridiculed, had delivered the very instruments that the national security now depended upon. If they had to fight a war, how would they rearm? Where would they get the weapons to rebuild the army?

"Will we have an ally to help [us]?" he asked, drilling into Sharon's head why the relationship with the Americans was so important. Victory or no victory, "the Arabs will still be there," Eshkol said. But would Johnson?

With that, Eshkol turned and walked out. Weizman was furious. He looked at his colleagues and read mutiny in their faces. "This forum must find a solution as to how to bring [the government] to decide." Sharon was more than ready to lock the civilians in a room and launch the war, or so he said in the aftermath.

Rabin said little. He was torn. He might have thought that the government would remain deadlocked and the army would have to make a fateful decision to go to war on its own. He later said he felt that the politicians were waiting for the generals to tell them what to do. That was the heart of the sabra disillusionment with Eshkol, for with each new intelligence report of Arab mobilization, Eshkol rushed to consult his coalition ministers with no result. The sabras wanted action.

Still, Eshkol pushed forward, consulting with the party leaders who were terrified of inviting a disaster.

That afternoon, Eshkol was sharing a meal and private conversation with one colleague when Weizman burst into the room. "The state is being destroyed, Eshkol! Why waste your time with Moshe Dayan? Who needs Yigal Allon? Give the order and we will win . . . and you'll be the prime minister of victory." Weizman was out of control. He stood there menacingly and then reached up to rip the epaulets off his shoulders and threw his general's insignia to the floor. He stormed out, leaving Eshkol aghast.[21]

Shaken by such encounters, it was no wonder that Eshkol stuttered when he went on national radio that night to speak to the Israelis. Virtually every home was tuned in. Soldiers at the front stopped what they were doing and reached for dials to find the main news frequency. Suddenly there was the voice of Eshkol. He sounded tired and confused. He stumbled here and there, and stopped at one point and whispered to an aide. There were handwritten changes on his text and he was obviously having trouble reading it; he had undergone surgery for cataracts. His wife,

Miriam, was listening, irritated at his staff over the messy text. But what the country heard was a leader who was unsure of himself. His was not the voice of commanding self-assurance that Israelis desperately needed after weeks of anxiety. Hundreds of thousands of Israelis were mobilized for war. The feeling that swept the national consciousness was that Israel was prepared in every way but at the top. The prime minister was not a warrior. Eshkol's wilting performance deepened the loss of confidence, and the sabra war camp seized on it to bring Eshkol down.[22]

Nothing brought Ben-Gurion back to the fore like the smell of Eshkol's demise. Ben-Gurion dispatched Peres to see Golda Meir, who now served as secretary general of Mapai. She must have enjoyed watching Peres grovel. The Rafi Party, he told her, was willing to forget all past political differences and rejoin Mapai in a national unity government. Dayan should be made minister of defense, he said, stripping Eshkol of his control over the military establishment and the imminent war.

But Meir was unwilling to weaken or betray Eshkol. She made no deal with Peres, though she knew that was not the end of it.

The next morning, one of the major newspapers called for Eshkol to step down. "If we could believe that Eshkol was really capable of navigating the ship of state in these critical days, we would willingly follow him. But we have no such belief."[23] The editorial called for Ben-Gurion and Dayan to return to government as prime minister and minister of defense, with Eshkol relegated to domestic policy. Ze'ev Schiff, the military correspondent for *Ha'aretz* whose views were those of many in the military establishment, wrote, "It is amazing how a people who suffered a Holocaust is willing to . . . endanger itself once again."[24]

Here was the sabra indictment: waiting for foreigners, even for the Americans, was a betrayal of Jewish self-reliance. Here was an impulse in Israeli society that was overpowering, but Eshkol was still raging against the notion that the military elite could take the country to war while ignoring the importance of allies, especially the United States.

A CIA report delivered to Johnson on the morning of May 29 documented the sabra revolt. "[The] militant factions of the IDF [are] growing increasingly restive" and "Dayan [is] emerging as the national army candidate."[25]

The Israeli press pounded the drum for Eshkol's removal from military decision making. Though fear of the consequences of war was driving the cabinet, so was the realization that Ben-Gurion and his allies were exploiting the crisis to accomplish what they had failed to achieve in the previous four years: toppling Eshkol. The struggle sustained Eshkol, but Nasser's strength was growing, too. The crisis was uniting the Arabs.

On May 30, King Hussein suddenly flew to Cairo and signed a defense pact with Nasser, pledging to come to Egypt's aid if Israel attacked into Sinai. An Egyptian general was placed in charge of Jordan's army as part of the United Arab Command.

Eshkol was feeling the heat of delay. The newspapers reported that Eban's trip to Washington had failed to produce a plan to immediately open the Strait of Tiran. Eshkol sent Eban in front of the press to say that if international action was not effective in breaking the Arab blockade in the Gulf of Aqaba, Israel would act alone. Eshkol refused to set a time limit. Johnson's request for a few weeks was looking impossibly long. An Israeli diplomat in Washington told the White House that Eshkol probably had only ten days. "We will act alone if we must, but with others if we can," Eban said. His words were reported to Johnson in the daily CIA situation report.[26]

Johnson had ordered the aircraft carrier *Intrepid* through the Suez Canal so it would be on station in the Red Sea to operate against the Egyptian blockade. The United States also circulated a proposed declaration by maritime nations against the Egyptian blockade. The Joint Chiefs of Staff were assembling a naval force to open the strait. All of these moves were secret, thus not alleviating the press-fed anxieties in Israel that "nothing" was being done. One of the dailies carried a front-page advertisement that called for "changing the present bankrupt government to a government of national unity before it is too late."[27]

What Eshkol needed was some tangible sign from Johnson that he could use against the onslaught at home. Before the day was out, he wrote to Johnson saying that the U.S.-led maritime force needed to act within a week or two. Israelis needed to see American warships, but more important, the American Sixth Fleet needed to start coordinating its movements and communications with the Israeli military command. "Without such concrete measures the American commitment to Israel's security will remain less credible and effective than it should." Eshkol confided to Johnson about the "difficulties that I face" in maintaining public confidence "without being able to reveal American commitments."[28] But Johnson kept the lid on while he plied Congress for support and put lines out to Nasser.

Eshkol's coalition cracked on May 31 when he lost a key ally against the war camp. Moshe Chaim Shapira, the head of the National Religious Party, said it was time to bring Dayan into the government as defense minister. Shapira said he still hoped to avoid war, but the Israelis needed reassurance of a strong military figure in charge of defense.

Eshkol was flabbergasted. "Let me understand you," he said to Shapira, "you want Dayan and you *don't* want war?"[29]

The prime minister knew he was finished as commander in chief, trumped by the military elite for not being warlike enough.

Dayan was not immediately aware. He had still been focusing on getting command of the southern front, which would require Rabin to relieve the veteran general Yeshayahu Gavish of his command, something Rabin hated to do.

Rabin grilled Dayan. "Are you prepared to submit to my authority as chief of staff? Do you want to replace me as chief of staff?"

"No!" Dayan protested. "I merely want to take part in the war, rather than watch it from the sidelines."[30]

No one, including Rabin, expected that he could control Dayan once he was put in charge of the front.

On the morning of June 1, the Pentagon's national military command center flashed a message to the White House Situation Room that the USS *Intrepid* had cleared the Suez Canal at 6:39 a.m. and was headed for the tip of Sinai and the Strait of Tiran. But as Johnson made contingency plans—he refused to move until there was support in the Senate—they were overtaken by events.

Johnson told the Israeli embassy to tell Eshkol to stop referring to the "U.S. commitment" to Israel's security. He sent another message to Eshkol: "We are exploring on an urgent basis the British suggestion of an international naval presence in the area of the Straits of Tiran. As I said to Mr. Eban, there is, however, doubt that a number of other maritime powers will be willing to take steps of this nature unless and until the United Nations processes have been exhausted."[31]

To that end, the State Department was circulating a draft declaration of the maritime powers calling on Egypt to end the blockade. Johnson was protecting his political flanks. He knew that pressure would build in the Senate to protect Israel, but he had to wait for it.[32]

A great deal of intelligence indicated that Nasser was in no position to initiate a war. Still, he seemed determined not to back down. Had he lost his reason? Were the Soviets whispering they would support him? No one knew.

Yet Israel's militarism was an advantage to Egypt. Nasser figured that he simply could not lose: either the Israelis would strike and that would turn the world against them as it had in 1956, or the great powers would intervene and Nasser would lead the Arab world in negotiations for a settlement. It seems almost certain that Nasser saw no downside to letting the crisis build.

Johnson sent Eisenhower's troubleshooter, Robert B. Anderson, to meet personally with Nasser and discern what he could of the Egyptian leader's intentions. Anderson reached Cairo on the night of May 31 and spent two hours with the Egyptian leader, who repeatedly assured him that Egypt would not initiate a war but would wait for the Israelis to strike.

Nasser asserted Egypt's rights over the Strait of Tiran but said he might be willing to submit the issue to the World Court. Asked if he was prepared to accept Israel as a matter of fact in the Middle East, Nasser said he did not believe stable and lasting peace with Israel could be achieved without disposing of the refugee problem.

"If the policy was for Arabs and Israelis to live together harmoniously," Nasser told the envoy, then "Israel should allow a million refugees to come back to Palestine, which would solve the refugee problem and still the Israelis would have two million of their own citizens in the same country." This, he added, would be true "living together."

Nasser offered to send his vice president to meet with President Johnson the following week, but if war came in the meantime, he said, it would not be like the Suez humiliation for Egypt. "We are prepared. We've got the Jordanians under our control. We've got the Iraqis and others lined up." Nasser's only worry, Anderson said, was the Syrians, who were not under the Egyptian command. If Syria launched the war, Egypt would have to fight.[33]

Eshkol desperately needed something from Johnson, some tangible proof that the Americans were going to back Nasser down, by force if necessary.

But by June 1, Eshkol had almost nothing from his friend Johnson. Both John Foster Dulles and Kennedy had pointedly said the Sixth Fleet would go into action against any military threat to Israel. Well, here it was. Where was the American patron of the Jewish state?

Then a cable arrived from Ephraim "Eppie" Evron, the Israeli diplomat who was considered closest to Johnson personally. Evron reported that Johnson's national security adviser had called him to the White House to say that the Israelis were overinterpreting what Johnson had pledged in the meeting with Eban. He had *not* pledged to use "all and every measure" to open the Strait of Tiran. What he had said was that he would make "every effort." He was doing what he had said he would do, working with the maritime powers for a United Nations statement on freedom of navigation and then a show of force by several nations willing to put their warships in harm's way to break the blockade.[34]

Evron's cable landed in Tel Aviv with devastating effect. It looked as if Johnson was pulling back, although nothing had changed. Rabin and the military establishment argued that Evron's report showed that Eban's mission had been a failure dressed up as success. The Sixth Fleet was refusing to coordinate with the Israeli military. That was taken as a sign of American duplicity.

That night, Eshkol felt he could not sustain the rebellion. General Yariv, the hawkish director of military intelligence, suggested sending Meir Amit to Washington to find out the true status of the antiblockade efforts and to probe Johnson's attitude toward Israeli action. The Mossad chief was firmly in the war camp, and so Eshkol might have predicted the outcome. After Eban's suspect performance, the sabras wanted their own man to go.

The record of Amit's visit to Washington on the eve of war is still murky, but one important document has emerged that shows how single-mindedly Amit used the trip to bolster the war option and increase the pressure on Eshkol.

Amit went straight to Langley with James Angleton, the CIA counterintelligence chief who also managed the day-to-day intelligence liaison with Israel. Angleton arranged for Amit to see Richard Helms, the CIA director. Amit learned, if he didn't already know it, that the Egyptian vice president was coming to see Johnson.

Amit told Helms that it was a "mistake" for Washington to continue focusing on freedom of navigation in the Strait of Tiran as the real issue. "It is only a pretext to Nasser's moves to dominate the Middle East." Amit's message was that the failure to defeat Nasser would mean nothing less than the "loss"—to the Soviet Union—of the Middle East as the United States had "lost" China in the 1950s.[35]

Speaking the language of the cold war, Amit added that "the first sign of the 'domino' effect was Jordan's forced accommodation with Egypt." It had put its army under Nasser's command.

Helms tried to sum up Amit's message in a memorandum to the president. "Amit thinks the Israelis' decision will be to strike." An Israeli victory would take "three to four weeks, with Israeli losses of about 4,000 military personnel."

Helms said an internal struggle was under way in Israel. "Eban's mission," he reported, "was seen by [Amit] and the Israeli nation as a failure." Amit said Eshkol was in trouble for having delayed an attack on Egypt and for making "false political assumptions" about Washington's position.

Helms's memo revealed a brutal warning from the Mossad chief that a day of reckoning would come for anyone who sought to delay the Israeli rush to destroy Nasser. "The lives that will be lost in any action by Israel will be placed against the account of those who urged Israel not to react earlier," Amit had said ominously. The threat seemed to apply not only to Eban, of whose diplomacy Amit was contemptuous, but also to the Johnson administration.

Helms pointed out to the president that Amit's view likely reflected Dayan's. "Both are sabras—men born in Israel—and their past careers have been closely connected." Theirs was the view of "tough" Israelis, who were "driving hard for a forceful solution, with us and with their own government.

"Amit said Israel wants nothing from the U.S.—except to continue to supply weapons already arranged for, to give diplomatic support, and to keep the USSR out of the ring," Helms reported.

The Mossad chief seemed confident that "Nasser will not attack Israel on the ground for the moment; however, if Israel continues to do nothing, a surprise Egyptian air strike against Dimona or airfields is very possible." Nasser, Helms added, "would prefer to provoke Israel so that he could point to Israel as the aggressor."[36]

As Amit briefed the Americans, Eshkol had run out of time at home. The wave of anxiety created by his "stumbling" speech convinced the political and military elites that a stronger figure had to be in charge of warmaking decisions. Surrender for Eshkol meant forming a national unity government and giving up the Defense Ministry. Eshkol would remain prime minister, but Ben-Gurion would not return to government. That was Eshkol's only condition. "Those two horses [Eshkol and Ben-Gurion] could no longer pull together," Eshkol said over and over. But Eshkol would accept Dayan as minister of defense and he would also invite Begin and Yosef Sapir from the right-wing bloc to join the unity cabinet. In taking these steps, Eshkol knew he was giving up the ability to avert war. Dayan and Begin would vote for war. The cabinet's deadlock would be tilted toward attack. It was just a matter of days.

The military had won.

It had fallen to Shimon Peres to tell Ben-Gurion that his bid to return to power one last time had failed. Peres stepped gently into Ben-Gurion's house on Keren Kayemet Boulevard and broke the news to his mentor.

"And Eshkol will remain as prime minister?" Ben-Gurion was asking.

"Yes" was all that Peres could manage as a response.

Ben-Gurion's face darkened. "I thought you were a friend—and you are not," he erupted. "I thought you were a statesman—and you are not. I thought you knew how to negotiate—and you do not! How could you give up the most important change that had to be made, Eshkol's replacement?"[37]

Peres was shaken. Ben-Gurion had never turned on him so bitterly. The older man later apologized, but Peres was never able to forget the force of Ben-Gurion's rage.

Now that Israel was committed to war, it had to make sure it would win—and with American support. Amit's final meeting in Washington was with Robert McNamara. The Mossad chief walked in and was soon holding up his hand, indicating that he was not there to listen to the American secretary of defense but rather to explain to him why Amit would return to Israel that very day with a recommendation to launch the war.

Israel could not remain mobilized, he said. Nasser was getting too powerful. The fight was no longer about freedom of navigation.

Amit understood that a decision to go to war would negate American diplomacy. But it was clear from his voice that Israel was not interested in diplomacy. The sabras were interested only in an immediate and devastating strike. Amit said the decision was hours away. The news had broken that Dayan had joined the cabinet. Abe Harman, the Israeli ambassador in Washington, was being called home.

What was astounding was how Amit had undermined his prime minister and his government. He had disparaged the efforts of Washington to avert war and he had tarnished the name of diplomacy by suggesting that the death of any Israeli would be laid at the feet of anyone who had delayed the jump to war. With Egyptians in Sinai, Amit said, Israel's mobilization would bring the economy to a standstill. "There are no workers in the fields, and the harvest is still standing."[38] This, of course, was hyperbole. Israel could withstand full mobilization longer than Egypt, whose economy was nearly bankrupt. In 1960, Israel had stayed mobilized—without excessive harm to its economy—until Egypt withdrew. Amit, in these conversations, spoke with little authority or accountability and with the overarching aim of convincing the Johnson administration that it was wasting its time—the war decision had been made.[39]

"It is better to die fighting than from starving," he had said to Helms.[40]

On that note, Amit flew back to Tel Aviv and went straight to Eshkol to tell him that the Americans were doing little or nothing and that they did not object to Israel's going to war.[41] This was an exaggeration, at the very least; at the most, it was a calculated lie.

If Eban's mission had been a failure of clarity, Amit's mission was a failure of honesty, for he thereafter indulged the myth that Washington had given Israel a green light to launch an unwanted war in the Middle East.

Amit joined Eshkol and the war council in session. The Mossad chief stated, erroneously, that the American plan for an armada was going nowhere. He told the ministers and generals that the White House, Pentagon, and CIA raised no objection to Israel's acting on its own.

Eshkol and Eban had nothing to stand on. How could they counter the

Mossad chief's report? Nothing in the diplomatic channel had given them hope that American forces were on the way. The Sixth Fleet was unresponsive to Israeli requests for coordination. Eppie Evron reported that he had floated the idea in the White House of Israel's sending one of its ships through the strait to see whether Nasser would give them a stronger pretext by opening fire on the vessel. Walt Rostow had taken this proposal straight to Johnson, and though nothing had come back, the senior Jewish American advisers around the president, including the Supreme Court justice Abe Fortas, were reporting that Johnson understood that Israel was alone. In other words, if Israel was not willing to wait for Johnson, that was Israel's decision. As a gesture, McNamara had arranged for Amit to load his chartered flight with U.S. army gas masks because the CIA and Israeli intelligence had hard information that Nasser's army was equipped with poison gas munitions. The CIA also reported that Israel "probably has some offensive CW [chemical weapons] capability themselves."[42]

Eshkol and the cabinet shifted to war mode. They used the weekend of June 3–4 to prepare for the preemptive strike. Eshkol presumably issued further secret orders to ready the first two nuclear explosives to be deployed by ground transport if necessary to the southern front. Peres had pressed Eshkol to consider setting off a "test" that would convince the Arabs that it was futile to think they could win, but Eshkol held the fail-safe weapons in reserve.[43]

Friday night was the beginning of the Sabbath, and Dayan went home to have dinner with his family. The familiar smell of chicken soup filled the home. Dayan's daughter, Yaël, recalled that the house was "full of flowers, chocolates and baskets of fruit," all sent by well-wishers—the sabra elites—delighted that Dayan was back in charge of the military. Dayan was just coming out of the shower when Yaël walked in.

"Father walked out of the bathroom in his underpants and slippers, and without his eye patch. He hardly fit the confidence-inspiring image" that had gone out to the military establishment. Yet, she added, "It was all there. The brightness in his direct look, the youthful stride as if a burden had been shed, the seriousness of a tremendous responsibility, and the bemused half-smile." Dayan was chattering about the fast pace of events. He spoke admiringly about Sharon and the other commanders in the field.

"He talked about being endowed for the first time with the highest authority," she recounted, and what a contrast that was to the Suez War, where Ben-Gurion had run the show. Now it was all up to him. He had worked out a very specific secret agreement with Eshkol: the two men would consult on the big questions—going to war, bombing cities, and expanding the war to other countries—but the basic war plan was all Dayan's to manage. After consulting with Rabin, Sharon, and others, he adjusted the attack plan to a massive armored thrust into Sinai to destroy the Egyptian army. There would be no dallying in Gaza.

"For good or for ill, I will be on my own," he told his daughter.[44]

On Sunday morning, June 4, Eshkol addressed the inner cabinet.

The sabra impulse for war, an unnecessary war given the realities of Egypt's decrepit economic state, prevailed in the room.

"I'm convinced that today we must give the orders to the IDF to choose the time and the manner to act," Eshkol said. He could not seem to speak the word "war."

Dayan gave the justification. "Nasser must fulfill the process he started. We must do what he wants us to do. It's our last chance to win, to wage this war our way."[45]

Moshe Chaim Shapira, head of the National Religious Party, still had a doubt. Ben-Gurion, he said, insisted that Israel must act in alliance with a great power.

"Then let Ben-Gurion go and find us an ally," Dayan said cuttingly at the invoking of his mentor's name. By the time an ally could be found, he said, "I'm not sure we'll be alive!"[46]

Dayan thus inflated the threat to genocidal proportions and declared his independence from Ben-Gurion, who was "living in a world that had passed. He still admired de Gaulle," he had "an exaggerated opinion of Nasser's power," and he "underrated the strength of the Israeli Defense Forces." Dayan spoke harshly, drilling his words irrevocably. In that room of military and political leaders, Dayan now held the mantle as commander more profoundly than Eshkol.[47]

Thucydides had written of the Peloponnesian War: "What made war inevitable was the growth of Athenian power and the fear which this caused in Sparta." But in this case there was no growth of Athenian power. Nasser's strength was declining, his army a spent force. It was Israel—Sparta—whose power had grown with the arrival of new American, British, and French weapons in large quantities. Moreover, Israel had become an atomic power in the weeks leading up to war. Eshkol had his finger on the button of a fail-safe weapon that could rescue any military catastrophe.

Israel's decision to launch a preemptive war in 1967 cannot be explained solely by the actions of its enemies. Beginning in January 1964, the Arabs had gathered to cut off Israel's water supplies and stifle its growth. Soon thereafter, the first Palestinian militant groups, among them Yasser Arafat's Fatah, began a guerrilla campaign that triggered large-scale Israeli reprisal raids. And in an effort to humiliate the Syrians, the Israelis began a campaign to provoke Damascus by pushing Israeli tractors into the demilitarized zone in the north, hoping for an attack that would justify a massive Israeli response, like the raid on Samu. Only Dayan, in retrospect, was honest in later acknowledging the provocative nature of this policy. Nasser's move into Sinai, however, created an opening for Dayan and his allies in the military establishment—sabras such as Amit, Rabin, Sharon, and other tough-minded generals such as Yariv (born in Russia)—to overwhelm the diplomatic approach that Eshkol had chosen. They overran Eshkol's strategy in the same manner that Ben-Gurion had overrun Sharett, who believed in a broader devotion to statesmanship as a means to avoid war and resolve conflicts through diplomacy, negotiation, and compromise. Instead, with its preemptive war on June 5, 1967, Israel set a precedent that is still being followed a half century later.

The Six-Day War began with a devastating strike against the Egyptian air force, a surprise attack by nearly two hundred Israeli warplanes that flew out over the Mediterranean to assault Egypt's air bases from the west, catching most pilots after they had flown their dawn patrols and then landed for breakfast.

Despite a high level of alert, the attack caught Egyptian commanders off guard as Israeli bombers cratered Egyptian runways, trapping warplanes on taxiways and aprons, where they were shredded by machine-gun fire and shrapnel.

Dayan had risen at dawn and breakfasted with his wife, Ruth, chatting about her plans to go to Jerusalem for a meeting and without telling her or other members of the family about the momentous events that were about to unfold. Dayan was driven from his home in Zahala northeast of Tel Aviv to "the pit" under the Defense Ministry, where he made a brief appearance among the generals before slipping out to a nearby café to meet his mistress, Rahel, with whom he shared coffee and croissants. She, too, was unaware that soon all hell would break loose.

Dayan's daughter, Yaël, was assigned to Ariel Sharon's division. Once the air force had launched into Egypt, Sharon came on the radio net from his mobile command vehicle and shouted forcefully into his microphone, "*Nua! Nua!*" Move!

As the tanks and armored vehicles pushed into Sinai, Dayan's voice could be heard on transistor radio: "Soldiers of Israel, we have no aim of conquest. Our purpose is to bring to naught the attempts of the Arab armies to conquer our land, and to break the ring of blockade and aggression which threatens us. . . ."[48]

In Washington, Johnson had been preparing to receive Egyptian vice president Zakaria Mohieddin on Wednesday, June 7. He had dispatched a final letter to Eshkol admonishing him not to resort to war while urgent efforts were under way to break the Egyptian blockade. Secretary of State Dean Rusk had just reported that eight maritime countries were willing to join the United States in a declaration against Egypt's restrictions on freedom of navigation.[49]

But Eshkol wasn't listening. His reliance on Johnson had cost him at home. He had lost the confidence of the country without being able to explain the commitments Johnson had made to Israel's security. One of Johnson's political aides, Harry McPherson, was in Israel when the war broke out. He and the American ambassador, Walworth Barbour, were summoned by the Mossad chief, Amit, who was riding high after playing a crucial role. Amit asserted to the Americans that Egyptian forces had attacked first along the front line. This was a lie, a lie that Eshkol, Dayan, Meir, Eban, Rabin, and the other members of the war council had agreed to disseminate in order to create a fog around the opening hours of the war. The fear was that the great powers might react strongly to an unambiguous Israeli strike, and the war council wanted to prevent any intervention by the powers until it had achieved its objectives.[50]

But the Mossad chief did more than just ply the Americans with disinformation. He castigated American policy, alleging that Johnson's efforts to restrain Israel had aided Nasser's war preparations and would make Israel's task much more difficult. Having sought to put the Americans on the defensive, Amit said that Washington could mitigate the damage by contributing arms and money and by keeping the Soviets at bay.[51]

The American public never understood the extent to which information about the onset and prosecution of the Six-Day War was manipulated by the Israeli defense establishment. And the Israeli deception was soon overtaken by Arab assertions that the United States and Britain had joined in the bombing attacks on Egypt, and this "big lie" became the focus of Israeli propaganda.[52]

Once the war was under way, Dayan's notion of a crushing blow lasting two to three days gave way to opportunism. Dayan had cautioned Rabin and his commanders against pushing all the way to the Suez Canal, fearing this would "internationalize" the war. But he soon gave ground to sabra field commanders—Sharon among them—who, like those of a decade earlier, saw a chance to seize all of Sinai in a blaze of glory for the army. The zeal of militarism trumped the rational restraints of the war planner.

On the eastern front it was the same. After Jordanian artillery batteries had opened fire on Jewish neighborhoods in Jerusalem, Yigal Allon and Menachem Begin joined in proposing to the Israeli cabinet, which was meeting in the Knesset basement, that the shelling gave Israel the pretext it needed to liberate Arab East Jerusalem, including the Old City and the Western Wall.

Motta Gur, the paratrooper commander who had fought under Sharon in numerous reprisal raids in the 1950s, and who had nearly perished at Mitla Pass, now led his men into Arab territory once again, taking heavy casualties in battles for Ammunition Hill and other bastions around the Old City. The cabinet feared the Vatican's reaction if the holy sites of Christendom suffered damage, but Dayan was more worried that Israeli forces might get caught short by a cease-fire imposed by the powers. On June 7, he authorized Gur's force to take the Old City.

"The Temple Mount is ours!" Gur soon reported over the military radio net.[53]

Capturing Jerusalem fulfilled a millennial ambition, and Dayan scampered toward the limelight. He told Eshkol that it was too dangerous for the prime minister to go personally and witness the most important episode of the war, yet Dayan himself raced to Jerusalem for the photo op. He, Rabin, and Uzi Narkiss, head of the Central Command, staged their own entrance into the Old City through Lion's Gate. Dayan and Rabin wore helmets, Narkiss just a cap, and they strode toward a row of photographers for the snapshot that became an icon of the war. The chief rabbi of the army, Shlomo Goren, declared that the Israelis had "come to this place never to leave it again." Then Goren pulled Narkiss aside. "Uzi, this is the time to put a hundred kilograms of explosives in the Mosque of Omar—and that's it, we'll get rid of it once and for all." Goren was referring to the Dome of the Rock, the shrine whose gilded dome is the most recognizable feature on the elevated plaza that Muslims call the Noble Sanctuary and that for Jews has been the Temple Mount since King Solomon's time.

Rabbi Goren pressed further: "Uzi, you'll enter the history books by virtue of this deed."[54]

To his credit, Narkiss resisted the call of overwrought Hebrew nationalism. To a pragmatic sabra, possession was better than desecration and what would have been seen worldwide as an ideological assault on Islam. In truth, neither Narkiss, Dayan, nor Rabin—nor most Israelis—would have condoned the destruction, but the rabbi's urgent suggestion reflected the religious nationalism that was embedded in the army and Israeli society. Even Dayan, the model of secular restraint throughout his life, gave voice to that nationalism. After being photographed as the liberator of the Old City, Dayan—upstaging Eshkol again—told national radio, "We have returned to the holiest of our sites, and will never again be separated from it." Israel, he said, "extends the hand of peace" to its Arab neighbors, "and to the peoples of all faiths we guarantee freedom of worship and our religious rights."[55]

Dayan had been reluctant to attack beyond Jerusalem, but when Nasser urged King Hussein to pull the Jordanian army back across the Jordan River to the East Bank, Dayan gave the order to fill the vacuum and occupy the entire West Bank. That meant that all of biblical Judea and Samaria and the Jordan Valley, with its large Arab population, were now in Israeli hands.

Dayan ran the war like Caesar, which is to say that he took into account the general wishes of the war council, but at the same time he did not hesitate to seize opportunities when they arose without bothering to consult. In doing so, he gave enormous latitude to his commanders, so much so that when they clashed or disobeyed orders, he was reluctant to discipline them. Dayan had warned that he would personally court-martial any officer who drove his army to the banks of the Suez Canal, but when Sharon and Avraham Yoffe did just that, Dayan acquiesced, telling his daughter that he had been presented with "facts in the field" by the army and had to accept the actions of generals who felt they had been "robbed" of glory when other units captured East Jerusalem.[56]

Such was the sabra code as Dayan practiced it.

Somehow, all of the territorial ambitions that had been denied Ben-Gurion and Dayan in the 1950s tumbled into the army's hands. The conquest of Arab territory succeeded beyond all expectations, inciting a wave of nationalistic ambition to press on. Here in the middle of the Six-Day War, the symbiosis that characterized relations between the civilian and military authorities blurred their distinctions. Neither was fully in charge. The country was in the grip of a nationalistic juggernaut, no longer suppressed or inchoate, as it had been in 1948. The sabras made up the inner circle, but the bandwagon had filled dramatically with nonsabras and recent arrivals, including American Jews, who were attracted to Israel's rugged self-reliance, its military exploits, and its social cohesion.

The arguments of generals—even blatantly political arguments—carried as much weight as the arguments of ministers. The question that seized them was how to set the boundaries of victory. Should the army take all of Sinai? Should it mop up all of the West Bank? Should Syria be punished for starting the war? If so, should the army take the Golan Heights, or move on to Damascus and topple the regime?

The generals' answers were invariably yes. The IDF should take as much land as possible and flaunt the power of its military to the entire region.

On June 8, the fourth day of the war, Israel's political and military elites were engaged in a raucous debate. The kibbutz leaders from the collective farms around the Sea of Galilee—those who lived in the shadow of the Golan Heights—rushed to Jerusalem to lobby for broader war aims. Syria, they argued, had provoked the war. It had shelled Israeli towns and provided bases for Yasser Arafat's Palestinian guerrillas. General David

Elazar, the commander of the northern front, argued vociferously that if Syria was allowed to get away unscathed, its radical leaders would simply resume the low-intensity war after any cease-fire took effect.

Eshkol and Dayan both initially opposed taking the war into Syria without a new provocation. They had to consider the risk that the Soviet Union would enter the war to protect its client. Eshkol stayed on the fence. Dayan at first seemed more repulsed by the greed of the farmers who had come to plead their special interests. They had looked across the Syrian frontier and "saw this fertile land" on the banks of the Jordan River and "fantasized" about taking it away from Syria. "They didn't even try to hide their greed," Dayan later said.[57]

As far as Dayan was concerned, it was not necessary for Israel to attack Syria. The whole issue of security for the border towns could be solved by moving the collective farms back from the frontier. But Dayan's opposition, like most things in his life, was tactical. On the strategic level, he had always favored a major blow to Damascus. But the Egyptian front was not yet stabilized. He did not want to be diverted prematurely.

Miriam Eshkol told General Elazar that she had a birthday coming up and wished him to seize one of the most beautiful springs in Syrian territory, the Banias, as a gift to her. It was like something out of the Bible, but she wasn't kidding.[58] Elazar said that he would try, but she would have to do her part, too, meaning that she needed to change Eshkol's mind, or at least his vote.

The marathon debate was interrupted during the day by the news that Israeli torpedo boats and warplanes had raced out into the Mediterranean to attack a U.S. navy intelligence vessel, the *Liberty*, as she was steaming in international waters with an onboard contingent of Arabic- and Hebrew-language specialists from the National Security Agency. The attack on the vessel, which was flying the American flag and whose hull markings were in English, continued for more than an hour despite the fact that Israeli military controllers advised over the radio net that the ship might be American. The assault left 34 Americans dead and 170 wounded. The Israelis soon apologized, pleading that it was a case of mistaken identity, but the residue of doubt and recrimination over what many still believe was a deliberate or grossly negligent attack lingered for decades.[59]

At the end of a momentous day, Dayan remained in the pit, taking in the reports that both the Egyptian and Jordanian fronts had stabilized.

Sometime after midnight, Dayan received an intelligence report—an intercepted telephone call from Nasser to the Syrian leader Atassi. Nasser warned his colleague that Israel was in the process of concentrating "all of its forces" to eliminate the Syrian army. He advised Atassi to accept a UN cease-fire resolution immediately.[60]

Yariv's military intelligence analysts confirmed that the Syrian army was preparing to pull back on the Heights, affording Israel an opportunity to strike, and he became a vocal advocate for expanding the war. Both he and Dayan could sense the opportunity. It is not clear with whom Dayan consulted during the night, if anyone, except that he did not consult with Eshkol or with Rabin, who was awakened at 7:00 a.m. by a telephone call from Weizman.

"Fifteen minutes ago, Dayan contacted Dado [Elazar] and ordered him to attack the Syrians immediately."[61]

Rabin rushed to the pit so as not to look entirely out of the loop, but Dayan once again had preempted the political leadership with a blaze of sabra entitlement that was breathtaking. His unilateral decision to open a third front violated his agreement with Eshkol over decision making.

Dayan scrawled a handwritten note to Eshkol on the margins of the Nasser-Atassi intercept. Here, he said, was evidence of the Egyptian-Syrian collapse. "It must be exploited to the full. A Great Day.—Moshe Dayan."[62]

Eshkol erupted. "That's despicable!" he exclaimed. Dayan and the military had again preempted him. The prime minister was like a beached whale while Dayan and the generals were all motion and dorsal fins, slashing at the enemy and flaunting the military's prerogative.

Eshkol had been shunted aside. He even had to ask his military assistant if he could cancel Dayan's attack order. But after a moment, he reconsidered. He had lost his nerve for confrontation. What could he do? The army was against him. The army was not only running the country, it was running roughshod over Israel's neighbors with no thought whatsoever about the day after the war ended. All Eshkol could do was accept the humiliation.

"What a vile man," he said to his military aide, referring to Dayan. "If he thinks he can do whatever he wants, let him do it." Here was Eshkol's weakness: the same lack of courage that had hobbled Sharett in crisis and in confrontation.[63]

When the war council met later in the morning, Begin was the first to excuse Dayan, calling his unilateral decision to open a new front an "aesthetic" violation of the Knesset committee's guidelines but within the prerogative of the prime minister and minister of defense. But, of course, the prime minister had not even participated in the decision. Eshkol lamely said that he "was really in favor" of an attack on Syria and was "sorry that it was postponed" due to Dayan's opposition. But what could they do now?

"How can we stop now that we're in the middle of the operation? I cannot say."[64]

Elazar's forces attacked hard up the slopes and across the plain of the Golan, fighting intense tank battles and pushing the Syrians back until Israel was forced by pressure at the United Nations and a specific threat from Moscow to accept a cease-fire.

But it was done. The Golan Heights were in Israel's hands.

When the guns went silent, Israelis looked around and blinked. The Middle East was never going to be the same. Israel had tripled its size by conquest. It was as if the militarism that had characterized the Suez War and that had been chastened by Eisenhower's muscular response had been liberated. All in one week.

"Now we had the capability not to take crap from anybody; we'll take care of ourselves." That was how Moshe Arens, who later served as foreign minister and defense minister, put it.[65]

SEVEN

War as Policy: Nasser and the PLO

After Waterloo, Wellington said, "Nothing except a battle lost can be half so melancholy as a battle won."

The tragedy of the Six-Day War arose from the law of unintended consequences. Dayan had led the military establishment on a rout through Arab lands without considering what it would mean to hold Arab territory for a single day—let alone decades—afterward. He had set out to destroy the core of the Egyptian army, but having done that and more, he found no compelling need to bring the army home—from Egypt, Syria, or the West Bank. In tripling Israel's area, the victory had triggered a powerful Zionist impulse to hold on to as much of the land as was possible. And, of course, the seizure of so much territory gave the Arabs a new cause for war.

A decade earlier, Eisenhower had said that the United Nations could not survive if Israel were allowed to change its borders through conquest. He went on national television and forced Israel, with the threat of sanctions, to withdraw from Sinai.

But Johnson was not inclined to roll back Israeli gains. With America mired in Vietnam, the Israeli victory was a novelty. To the American public, Israel had not engaged in naked aggression so much as it had responded to a large and threatening Arab buildup.

After the smoke cleared on the battlefield, Johnson told his senior advisers that he doubted that anything good would come from Israel's victory, but he did nothing to stand up for the principles of the UN Charter. Instead, he took the advice of those prominent American Jews who were among his close political advisers—Abe Fortas, ambassador to the United Nations Arthur Goldberg, the lawyer David Ginsberg, the banker Abe Feinberg, and Arthur and Mathilde Krim—and he chose not to make any demand for Israel to return the Arab territories it had seized.[1] This fateful development allowed Israel to assert that it would return the Arab territories only in return for formal peace treaties.

Dayan put it succinctly: Israel was waiting for a telephone call from the Arabs.

This was the formula for paralysis. The Arab leaders demanded that Israel withdraw from all conquered territories without conditions.[2]

"The Arabs would like the projectionist to roll the film back," Arthur Goldberg told Eban.[3]

One of the most secret discussions the Israeli cabinet undertook related to the burning question of land. On June 19, Eshkol, Meir, and Dayan convinced the other members of the unity government that they should at least offer to return some of the Arab territories if they could do so on favorable terms. They asked the Americans to convey private proposals to Egypt and Syria to enter formal negotiations for peace treaties. (Nothing was offered with respect to the West Bank, which many Israelis wanted to annex.)

Israel kept this proposal secret for many years simply because Eshkol and the military elite feared a backlash from Israelis across the political spectrum who were applauding the army's achievement.

At summer's end, the Arab heads of state met in Khartoum and issued their three no's—no recognition of Israel, no negotiation, and no compromise. Arab rigidity fed the Israeli desire to hold on to its conquest. The world had changed. With Johnson in the White House, the United Nations would not be allowed to pressure Israel. Five months after the end of the war, the Security Council reached a consensus on Resolution 242, whose preamble referred to the "inadmissibility of the acquisition of territory by war" and called for the "withdrawal of Israel's armed forces from territories occupied in the recent conflict."[4]

But the paralysis had already set in.

"The victory of the Israeli Defense Forces in the Six-Day War has brought the nation and the state into a new and fateful era." With these words, the

Movement for Greater Israel was born as a broad-based coalition, formed in September 1967 and dedicated to holding on to the gains of the war.[5]

The manifesto was true in every respect. The Six-Day War, because it *seemed* so successful, had reaffirmed the most important precept of military society: that military solutions were paramount. "Activism"—meaning sabra militarism—was national policy. The other broad sentiment that unified sabras and nonsabras was that of Zionist fulfillment. For many Zionists, Israel was about heritage, a way of life for Jews gathered in a homeland, but for the military elite, Israel was not about religion or democracy—it was about territory, about rebuilding the contours of biblical Israel and defeating the Arabs so completely that they would have to accept peace on Israel's terms.

For all of his efforts, Eshkol got little credit for anything. He was tarred with wearing the mantle of indecision and diplomacy, as if he were another Sharett.

Eban was privately vilified by the sabras as a poseur who put Israeli lives at risk while he strutted through European and American capitals, misrepresenting to his colleagues at home Johnson's "commitment" to Israel's security.[6]

Generals began for the first time to openly promote political views, as if they had earned a right to share in governing.[7] Sharon stated publicly that he opposed the return of the occupied territories.

"These boundaries are not indeed peace borders, but they are borders that prevent war," he said. "Today we are in an ideal position. There will be no normalization [with the Arabs] for decades." He declared he was against any withdrawal "that does not guarantee us total military control over the territory. That obviously means hold on to the present situation."[8]

Sharon said he had no reservations about speaking out. "We the generals have every right not only to express our opinions, but also to influence opinion. What will largely dictate public opinion in Israel is the attitude of the IDF."[9]

It was as if the sabra military establishment had declared itself a rump government. The generals had proved that the provenance of state power was the military itself and, therefore, the military chiefs had earned a seat at the table.

Out of the Six-Day War, new stars arose and a new migration of army officers into the political realm began. Rabin, whose term was up as chief of staff, startled Eshkol by walking into the prime minister's office and asking for an appointment as ambassador to the United States. Weizman, embittered that neither Rabin nor Dayan recommended him to become the next chief of staff, retired and entered politics on the right, joining Begin's Gahal bloc.

But Dayan's star shone brighter than all others in the aftermath of the war, for in the eyes of the public he had rescued Eshkol from faintheartedness and transformed a potential disaster into a triumph. And because his image had become the face of Israeli military excellence, the old guard of Mapai once again feared that he would try to usurp their power by demanding to lead the party's ticket in the next election. Eshkol soon elevated Yigal Allon and Israel Galili, long-standing rivals of Dayan, as key advisers to the prime minister.

Eshkol and the old guard also insisted on their choice for chief of staff to replace Rabin. They picked Chaim Bar-Lev, the Palmach veteran who had helped to build the Armored Corps and who had been brought out of retirement to be Rabin's deputy. Bar-Lev was loyal to Mapai but also close to Allon, Galili, and the left wing of the labor movement. What Bar-Lev lacked in charisma he made up for with steady nerves and professionalism. Born in Vienna in 1924, Bar-Lev grew up in Yugoslavia and fled Europe in 1939. He spoke Hebrew with a slow, methodical eastern European drawl. On the battlefield he showed the dash of Montgomery and the calculation of Patton. In 1949, he had convinced Egyptian tank crews to abandon their vehicles and flee on foot. Bar-Lev had shown political sophistication throughout his career, which made him a reliable military adviser.

And the army he inherited was no longer just a fighting force.

The Israeli Defense Forces were suddenly in charge of a vast new landscape with more than one million Arabs. No other institution in Israel could control and administer these new territories. Eshkol and his allies feared that Dayan would build an empire for the army; they fought to preserve a role for civilians, but Dayan set up the military administration bureaucracies for Sinai, Gaza, the West Bank, and the Golan Heights. Soon the military was deeply involved in governing the much-expanded country. The chief of staff and his top aides became frequent and familiar participants in cabinet sessions; they attended and often prepared the agenda for key committees of the Knesset. The military controlled the registration of Palestinians entering Israel to work and the flow of Palestinian goods across borders into Jordan and Syria as well as the collection of intelligence. In short, they performed all the duties of a military occupation. The Western news media datelined its stories from "Occupied West Bank" or "Occupied Sinai" to denote that Israel was operating outside of international law.

From the outset, there was resistance.

The Palestinian territories were laced with underground networks. Yasser Arafat and his Fatah guerrillas entered this labyrinth to gather recruits and organize the "armed struggle" that was not so much a threat at first but was taken deadly seriously by the Israeli military elites who feared that the docile Arab population of the West Bank and Gaza could be radicalized by infiltrators.

Arafat was then largely unknown in the West. A firebrand whose political awakening had occurred at Cairo University in the 1950s, Arafat had come of age in Nasser's Egypt and his language was that of Palestinian nationalism.

After the Israelis humiliated the combined Arab armies, Fatah announced that it was moving its headquarters from Damascus into the occupied territories in order to take the armed struggle to the Israelis, who responded by carrying out military operations focused on capturing or killing Arafat.

Israel's intelligence agencies also emerged as more powerful after the war. The Arab Affairs department of the Shabak was assigned the task of penetrating Arab society in the West Bank and Gaza Strip, and conducting surveillance of anyone suspected of being connected with the Palestinian national movement.

Jacob Peri, a young sabra from Tel Aviv who had given up a career in music to enter the domestic intelligence service, was a Shabak division chief on the West Bank when Arafat burst on the scene.

"A group of intelligence officers brought [a report] that there is a guy by the name of Yasser Arafat and he is living in the hills of Nablus and preparing cells for terrorist activity," Peri explained to me in an interview. Shabak tracked Arafat to an apartment between Jerusalem and Ramallah, and when the Israeli agents rushed in to arrest him, Arafat managed to slip

away. Peri said they found "the mattress still warm and his radio still playing with Arab songs."[10]

The new militancy Arafat brought to the West Bank—land mines and
ambushes against Israeli civilians and soldiers—was a contagion that had
to be nipped in the bud, Peri said, but Arafat continued to elude Israel's
military and intelligence squads.

In March 1968, after a roadside explosive destroyed an Israeli school bus
and killed two children in the Negev, Eshkol could not ignore the military's demand for retribution. Dayan and the military chiefs sent an invasion force of more than one hundred tanks and artillery pieces into Jordan
to attack the PLO's main training base and kill hundreds of Palestinian
militants stationed there. When the Jordanian army saw the size of the
Israeli force massing on the Jordan River, its commanders assumed Israel
was going to storm the Jordanian capital, Amman. Jordan moved up one
hundred American-made tanks and eighty-eight artillery pieces in defense.

But the target was Arafat's base at Karameh, a town fifteen miles northeast of Jericho in the Jordan Valley. Dayan told the military chiefs that the
government authorized a mission to destroy Fatah, capture or kill Arafat,
and level the base.

It may have been hubris or just bad planning—or both—but the Israeli
invasion force literally ran into the mud after rolling across the Jordan River
Bridge and then into the low wadis around Karameh, which had been
washed by spring rains. There was fog that morning, and when it began to
clear, the Israeli force was greeted by an eruption of gunfire that crackled
in the air. Hot lead zipped down from the hillsides like a plague from well-
entrenched Jordanian and PLO fighters.

On the eastern side of Karameh, one of the paratroopers whose unit
flew deep into Jordanian territory that morning was Muki Betser. A tall,
good-natured sabra farm boy, Betser was married to Dayan's niece and
had grown up on tales of Sharon's commando exploits. Highly regarded as
one of the most formidable fighters in Captain Matan Vilnai's reconnaissance unit, Betser was eager to get into the battle. The fog had delayed the
eight helicopters that were the paratrooper force, whose mission was to cut
off any escape from Karameh.

"Nobody warned us that we lost the element of surprise," Betser explained to me. "But barely a dozen strides into the hour's run carrying full gear across the wadis east of Karameh, we ran into the enemy. I don't know who was more surprised."[11]

The sea of mud mired the Israeli tanks, and soon the ragtag PLO fighters opened up with rocket-propelled grenades. Israeli tanks burst into flames as others fired on Jordanian tanks, destroying a third of the Jordanian force. Israeli warplanes shredded Jordanian armor and covered the extraction of wounded soldiers and damaged tanks.

Betser's paratrooper force was tied down. "It took almost five hours to move five miles, instead of the hour we had planned," he said. And then Betser himself was taken out of action when a bullet hit him in the face.

"A blast exploded inside my head," he recalled. "The impact jerked me upright, while teeth flew out of my mouth. Instinctively, I grabbed my throat . . . but as the blood poured out, so did my strength." Betser was down, and so were dozens of Israeli soldiers.

Jordanian artillery units zeroed in on the Israeli infantry. Israeli jets roared through the hills bombing and strafing the PLO and Jordanian positions. But by the end of the day, it was a disaster for the IDF. Nearly thirty Israeli soldiers had died and seventy were wounded, many of them, like Betser, seriously. More than thirty Israeli tanks had taken hits; four were destroyed and one was abandoned on the battlefield, giving the Palestinians a trophy for their "victory." They had taken far more casualties than the Israelis—two hundred Palestinians dead and more than one hundred captured—and their base was blood-soaked rubble.

But here were Palestinians taking on the vaunted Israeli army and driving its elite forces back across the river. *Karameh!* The word became a battle cry.

After Karameh, Nasser invited Arafat to Cairo as the new face of Palestinian nationalism. Nasser allowed the Palestinians to set up a radio station to broadcast news and propaganda to their people living under occupation. In July, Nasser took Arafat on his personal jet to Moscow and introduced him to the Soviet leadership.

The battle made Arafat's reputation as the leader of the Palestinian liberation movement and as the main enemy of Israel's military establishment.[12]

———

Dayan had missed the battle of Karameh. He had checked in at defense headquarters in Tel Aviv during the final planning, and then he had raced off to an archaeological site near Azur just south of Tel Aviv to indulge his obsession for digging up antiquities. Archaeology touched deep chords in Dayan's character: a fascination with history and art but also the greed that is engendered by discovering ancient treasure. His use of state assets to dig on public lands raised many eyebrows, but in Israel's tribal culture of the time, Dayan—still defense minister—acted with sabra entitlement.

The morning of the battle, while Israeli soldiers waged a desperate fight, he pushed himself into a narrow cave whose walls were not supported. He was alone when the structure collapsed and hundreds of pounds of earth and rock came crashing down on him.

All Dayan could remember was that he couldn't move, couldn't see or breathe. "This must be the end," he thought as he fell unconscious. Frantic digging soon uncovered him, but his ribs and vertebrae were crushed, a vocal cord severed. He lay in traction for three weeks with his health irreparably damaged. The epitome of sabra fitness and strength could now not sleep or cope with his pain without barbiturates.

"He would never from then on be totally well," his daughter observed.[13]

He was not alone in declining health.

In September 1968, the Egyptians unleashed an artillery barrage along the Suez Canal that caught Eshkol by surprise, just as he learned that he was facing terminal cancer. The news of his illness was suppressed. But fearing for Mapai's hold on political power, Pinhas Sapir, a senior Mapai minister, flew to Switzerland to find Golda Meir, who also was fighting cancer. She was convalescing in alpine Europe and Sapir intruded on her privacy to inform her that Eshkol had less than a year to live. The Mapai leaders insisted that Meir return to prepare to assume the post of prime minister in order to avoid a damaging battle for succession. Dayan's supporters had already formed a movement to promote his candidacy; Yigal Allon was positioning himself to run against Dayan and keep the premiership for Mapai.

"You have to step in to avoid a suicidal clash between Allon and Dayan," Sapir told Meir.

She said little, but Sapir sensed that she would not turn down the mantle of Ben-Gurion for which she had waited all her life.

"As long as Eshkol lives, what do you want from me?" she asked him.[14]
It was her way of saying yes.

Arafat made his debut on the cover of *Time* magazine in late 1968. He was called a "Fedayeen Leader" under the headline "The Arab Commandos—A Defiant New Force in the Middle East."

"To the Israelis, the raiders are terrorists and thugs, inept and indiscriminate in their missions," *Time* said. "To the Arabs, they are freedom fighters in the best guerrilla tradition, skilled in the arts of the commando and the saboteur. The world knows them best as the fedayeen, meaning 'men of sacrifice,' a disparate group of clandestine plotters often at odds with one another, who play a large part in keeping the Middle East on the edge of war."[15]

This was the beginning of recognition in the West that the Six-Day War was going to have serious, long-term consequences. In America, where the backdrop for the 1968 presidential contest was the Vietnam War and the Soviet move to crush the Prague Spring uprising in Czechoslovakia, the Middle East conflict was increasingly seen through the lens of the cold war. This was a boon to Israel's military establishment because it cast Israel as an indispensable ally against the Soviets, a circumstance that would prevail for the next two decades, and that, by then, would be very difficult to untangle.

Richard Nixon, running for president against Hubert Humphrey—in March, Johnson had announced that he would not seek reelection—criticized the Johnson administration for failing to understand the "scope and the seriousness of the Soviet threat in the Middle East." Moscow, he said, had "systematically rebuilt the armed forces" of Egypt and Syria and, in doing so, fostered a new ambition to wage "a war of revenge and drive Israel into the sea."[16]

"As long as the threat of Arab attack remains direct and imminent," Nixon told a B'nai B'rith convention, "the balance [of power] must be tipped in Israel's favor" with additional arms deliveries from the United States.

Nixon was not the first American president to pander to Jewish voters. Harry Truman had called for Britain to allow a hundred thousand Holocaust survivors to enter Palestine in 1946, and he threw American support behind Israel's declaration of independence in 1948. But the 1968 presidential campaign was the first time American leaders began vying for Jewish votes by proposing ever greater levels of military support for Israel. By politicizing the sales of arms, the United States, beginning with the Nixon administration, surrendered much of the leverage that it had maintained under the more cautious approaches of Eisenhower, Kennedy, and Johnson, all of whom sought to ensure Israel's security through the deterrent power of the U.S. Sixth Fleet and by maintaining Israel's parity of arms with the Arabs.

Over the long term, nothing incited the ambitions of Israel's military establishment—and made diplomacy more problematical—than escalating sales of American weaponry that put the Jewish state on the path to becoming a military superpower in the Middle East, bereft of any national diplomatic strategy for peace.

Militant Palestinian leaders believed that Nasser and the Arab heads of state had forfeited the fight against Israel. Without armed forces, the Palestinian militants believed that the world would pay attention to their cause only if confronted with sensational acts of terrorism.

One of the most brazen Palestinian militants was George Habash, a Christian who abandoned a medical career and formed the Popular Front for the Liberation of Palestine, or PFLP, to make war on Israel. On Christmas Day 1968, a PFLP team attacked an El Al airliner at the Athens airport, killing two Israeli passengers.

Palestinian militarism then collided with Israeli militarism. Dayan and most of the Israeli military establishment believed that sensational terrorism could be met only with overwhelming acts of retribution.

In the wake of the Athens attack, Dayan and Bar-Lev recommended mounting an assault on Beirut's international airport, a facility that had no connection to military affairs or to any armed group. But Dayan wanted a dramatic reprisal raid, one that would get the world's attention like a "detonator." He got the cabinet's approval for a commando raid that would blow up four or five Lebanese airliners as they sat parked and empty.

The ministers approved, but when Dayan arrived at military headquarters on December 28, air force reconnaissance reported that there were twice as many airliners on the ground as expected. Bar-Lev turned to Dayan for instructions. Dayan just looked back and said, "Blow them all up."[17]

That night, a flight of Israeli helicopters used the cover of darkness to reach Beirut and drop demolition teams onto the airport tarmac. The night sky brightened with a series of explosions; jet fuel eruptions added to the inferno that destroyed thirteen airliners belonging to Middle East Airlines.

The lame duck Johnson administration protested the violence in the "strongest possible terms." The president was embarrassed, having just announced that the United States would sell fifty supersonic Phantom jets to Israel, with deliveries scheduled for 1969.

The ailing Eshkol had been caught unawares by the scale of the attack, but Dayan made no apology.

"Our main purpose in this action," he told the nation, "is to make clear to the Arabs of Lebanon that they should avoid the employment of Fatah against our civil aviation services. The plane which brought the Fatah people to Athens came from Lebanon. The terrorists trained in this state. If the government of Lebanon allows the Fatah to train in its territory they must be punished." Finally, Dayan said that "the Lebanese will think twice before they carry out such operations against our planes."[18]

Of course, the Lebanese had not carried out the operation and neither had Arafat's Fatah organization. The PFLP was based in Damascus, and its training camp was in Jordan. The PFLP team that reached Athens might just as easily have departed from Istanbul or Cairo. But it didn't matter.

Dayan's rationale was the logic of collective punishment: the Arabs, in general, would suffer whenever Jews were attacked.

This principle was becoming ingrained in Israel's military establishment, just as it had been ingrained in Dayan's character ever since he had seen the British blowing up Arab villages in retaliation for attacks on the British oil pipelines during the Mandate years.

An Arab diplomat in Beirut told the *New York Times* that the assault on Beirut would only "harden" the militancy of the Arabs. "It will also bring Lebanon closer into the struggle. That's why it was a mistake for Israel to act this way."[19]

Yitzhak Rabin knew that he had no future in the army under Dayan, so he had doffed his uniform and headed for Washington as ambassador.

At first blush he seemed an unlikely envoy. He spoke English poorly and had none of the social skills required for diplomacy, but he admired America, where his father had lived after fleeing Ukraine. And, like most in the military establishment, he saw the American relationship as crucial.

Rabin arrived in Washington at a time when the Israeli embassy was under siege because the White House wanted Eshkol to sign the Nuclear Non-Proliferation Treaty, part of Johnson's eleventh-hour attempt to create a peace legacy as a counterweight to Vietnam.

Rabin's job was to head off Johnson's effort and keep the focus on the acquisition of American arms, which was all the more important now because Charles de Gaulle had imposed an arms embargo on Israel. The French leader was peeved because Israel had ignored his advice not to "fire the first shot" in the Six-Day War. The Israeli military establishment had its sights on Phantom jets because these supersonic fighter-bombers could take the war deep into Egypt, or almost anywhere in the Middle East.

A year before his death, Eshkol made a pilgrimage to Johnson's ranch in Texas to lobby for the Phantoms and for help in rearming after the war. Johnson played coy, refusing to make a commitment on the airplane while pressing Eshkol to sign the non-proliferation treaty. At one point in the talks at the ranch, Johnson stood and said, "I'm going to the bathroom. Let's all go to the bathroom."

In the lavatory, Johnson waited until the last man had relieved himself before taking his turn, and when he wheeled around to wash his hands, there stood the Israeli diplomat Eppie Evron, Johnson's favorite, with his head down standing in the corner.

"Why are you looking so blue? What's wrong with you?" Johnson asked.

"Mr. President, my prime minister has come all the way from Israel to make this request of you, and it's clear that it's going to be denied. And I've had him come. And it's just going to be a tremendous disappointment to him and to Israel."

"Goddamn it, Eppie," Johnson replied, "you're going to get the F-4s, but don't you tell him that yet. There's some things I want from him."[20]

It is impossible to imagine what Johnson was trying to accomplish in sharing this confidence with a foreign diplomat who most certainly shared it with his prime minister. Suffice it to say that the contradictions of Johnson's character might have allowed for a belief that his Israeli friend Evron would not betray him, giving Johnson time to apply a little more pressure on Eshkol to conclude a reasonable quid quo pro: America would supply conventional arms to the Jewish state in exchange for an irrevocable pledge not to develop nuclear weapons.

Johnson soon wrote to the dying Eshkol as a "close personal friend," arguing that it would be an "irreversible tragedy" for a nuclear arms race to break out in the Middle East. It didn't matter how often Israel reiterated that it would not be the first to introduce nuclear weapons into the region, "only Israel's adherence to that [non-proliferation] Treaty can give the world confidence that Israel does not intend to develop nuclear weapons."[21]

From all declassified accounts, Johnson didn't know that the horse, as it were, was out of the barn. Israel already was a nuclear power, by any measure, and Johnson's desire for a peace legacy was never going to overcome the sabra ambition to obtain the ultimate self-reliance, which the Jewish state was achieving with the completion of its first atomic bomb.

Levi Eshkol died of a heart attack on February 26, 1969, a month after Richard Nixon had been sworn in as president.

Eshkol was laid out on a bier in the Knesset, and the big question among the political and military elites was whether Ben-Gurion would come to say goodbye. Dayan went to see his aged patron and urged him to do so for the sake of Zionist solidarity after so many years. But Ben-Gurion told Dayan that though he was sorry to hear of Eshkol's death, he would not pay any last respects in public.

"Respect for Eshkol?" Ben-Gurion asked. "No."[22]

Dayan looked into the older man's eyes and saw the bitterness and anger. Was it really over Eshkol's decision to bury the Lavon Affair, or disagreement over the bomb project? Or was it just rage against mortality because, more than anything, Ben-Gurion hated losing power?

Golda Meir was seventy-one years old, the last of the old guard to become prime minister, which was bittersweet since she, too, was suffering from cancer.

But real power also accrued to military figures. Sharon came out of the Six-Day War as one of the golden generals, popular with the public, a headstrong commander who got things done. Sharon's division had obliterated the Egyptian army at Abu Ageila in a textbook display of maneuver war-fare. Sharon's performance incited great jealousy among the other stand-outs of the war, most notably Israel Tal, the innovator of Israel's Armored Corps, whose tank forces stormed el-Arish, the Egyptian headquarters in Sinai.[23]

The arrival of Bar-Lev as chief of staff was disastrous for Sharon. Ever since Bar-Lev had sat on the court-martial panel that put Sharon on trial in the summer of 1953, Sharon had nurtured ill feelings for him. The fact that Bar-Lev had distinguished himself in the 1948 war long before anyone had heard of Sharon probably inflamed a strong rivalry.

In staff meetings or in the field, Sharon refused to accept Bar-Lev's lead-ership and treated him with contempt. He had always ignored the chain of command when he disagreed with instructions. In an interview with *Ma'ariv* on January 25, 1974, Sharon was asked whether he had ever dis-obeyed an order. "Yes," he replied. "When I receive an order I treat it accord-ing to three values: the first, and most important, is the good of the state. The state is the supreme thing. The second value is my obligation to my subordinates, and the third value is my obligation to my superiors. I wouldn't change the priority of these three values in any way." Sharon's problem now was that Ben-Gurion was no longer there to protect him. He served at the whim of the chief of staff—Bar-Lev—and so his relations with his superiors seemed all the more reckless.[24]

The conflict intensified when Bar-Lev convened the general staff to decide on the best means to defend the front line along the Suez Canal, where Egyptian artillery held the advantage with its concentration of fire-power. Bar-Lev proposed building a static line of fortresses on the eastern shore of the canal. Using bulldozers and sandbags, the army could erect a wall of well-defended positions that could withstand artillery strikes.

Sharon derided the plan as foolish. His vehemence and contempt were so blatantly insubordinate that Bar-Lev could scarcely stand to be in the same room. It didn't matter that Sharon's argument had some merit: the Bar-Lev Line would become an easy target for Egyptian gunners, putting Israeli soldiers at risk each time they stepped outside and putting others at risk when supply trucks had to make the dangerous approach to the canal. Sharon's idea was to pull back several miles from the canal, out of artillery range, and defend the front line with a mobile force of tanks, infantry, and air support, which could rush forward at any moment to repel an Egyptian attempt to cross the canal.

But Bar-Lev had the prime minister's ear. Meir was concerned that pulling back from the canal would look like a territorial concession. At last Sharon's hotheaded approach to Bar-Lev, which included scornful comments fed to the press, came to a head in early 1969. In one Monday morning general staff meeting, Sharon had lacerated his superior with such intensity that Bar-Lev decided to orchestrate a showdown. He called the generals back, this time with Dayan in attendance, and they were all there waiting when Sharon walked in the door.

"I saw Moshe Dayan sitting there together with his deputy," Sharon recalled. "Alongside them were Bar-Lev and every single one of my most vehement critics. . . . As I sat down, the tension was so thick you could cut it."[25]

The head of the Southern Command, General Yeshayahu Gavish, began the litany of complaints: Sharon's bad attitude, his insulting behavior, etc. Sharon was suddenly out of his chair. He wasn't going to accept the criticism of these men, even though they were his superiors. He would just "send them all to hell and walk out."

Then Dayan spoke out. "Arik, you've been invited to a general headquarters meeting. It's not up to you to decide what's going to be discussed."

Sharon made it clear he did not care. "If you proceed with this, it's going to be without me," he fired back, retaking his seat.

Gavish just picked up where he had left off, and Sharon again was out of his chair heading for the door.

Dayan called after him. "Arik, you can't do that. You have to come back. Come back!" But Sharon had flung the door closed behind him.

Soon thereafter, the army's personnel office notified Sharon that his appointment as a divisional commander was not being extended. He was being mustered out of the army on a technical procedure. Sharon went to Dayan, who must have smiled. "Bar-Lev doesn't want you," he told Sharon. How could Sharon be surprised? "I don't see how I can interfere in it," Dayan added.

Sharon then went to the prime minister. But why would Meir stick her neck out for a roguish general whom the army commanders loathed and who was already flirting with opposition parties?

"I make it a point never to intervene in matters like this," she said coldly.

Sharon was out and, in no time, he had arranged a meeting with Menachem Begin. To Sharon, joining a right-wing party seemed an appropriate act of revenge. The press erupted with headlines that Sharon was going over to the opposition. It was too much for Pinhas Sapir, the behind-the-scenes kingmaker of Mapai. Sapir pulled the party leaders into a conference and asked whether they really wanted a bull elephant like Sharon to join Begin and Weizman on the right. Their political survival was already at risk.

The Mapai ministers agreed. Sapir prevailed on Bar-Lev to swallow his pride and take Sharon back. It was difficult, but the army decided to send Sharon on a world tour to cool things off. By the end of the year, he was handed the Southern Command when Gavish retired. Sharon was in charge of the Egyptian front and the Bar-Lev Line along the Suez Canal. Sharon had won, over the prime minister; a powerful and popular military figure had trumped his rivals and the political realm.

The triumph of the Six-Day War was now giving way to a realization that Israel had not defeated the Arabs, or, most important, Nasser. Soviet weapons were flooding into Egypt and Syria. Low-intensity warfare was going to be the new norm unless Nasser could be destroyed by other means.

Rabin's mission as ambassador to the United States suddenly took on elevated importance as the military establishment escalated its requirements for new weapons to match the Soviet resupply. Most important, Israel needed a larger and more capable air force, and the Phantoms would be the centerpiece.

Rabin wanted to use those planes to "screw" Nasser. That was the word he had used in 1967 and it still applied because Nasser had come out of the war stronger than ever. The Egyptians were ready to blame everyone, except *El Rais*—the boss.[26]

Egyptian snipers and artillery commanders daily peppered the Israeli defenses along the canal, forcing Israel to keep the army partially mobilized.

The army mounted its first postwar attack into Egypt in October 1968, sending helicopters across the Gulf of Suez and inland all the way to the Nile, where Israeli commandos destroyed a power station and blew up a bridge. Each day the Israeli air force prowled the front lines looking for signs of Egyptian troops massing for another round of war.

Then in early 1969, Egyptian artillery gunners unleashed their largest fusillade since the cease-fire, ravaging the Bar-Lev Line with high-explosive rounds. Day after day, the bombardments continued and, by July, Egyptian forces had killed dozens of Israeli soldiers and wounded more than a hundred.

The Israeli high command realized that it would have to win this war of attrition or withdraw from Sinai. The generals first sent in special forces. A mixed team of Israeli commandos—Sayeret Matkal and navy frogmen—attacked the heavily defended Green Island fortress in July, knocking out radar and antiaircraft batteries that defended the entire Canal Zone. Two months later, an armored Israeli force—using captured Soviet tanks and APCs—crossed the Gulf of Suez and shot up Egyptian defenses along a thirty-mile stretch of sand, killing a visiting Soviet general and his Egyptian counterpart.[27] In December, another commando force shot its way ashore and dismantled a seven-ton Soviet-made radar installation and hauled it back to Israeli lines by helicopter.

Yet none of these spectacular raids threatened Nasser's standing or Egyptian morale. Here Rabin intervened.

He had arrived in Washington as a parochial figure. But it was fortunate that he had once lavished time and attention on Nixon during the candidate's visit to Israel. Nixon had not forgotten the kindness and gave Rabin immediate access to the White House. There Rabin found Henry Kissinger, a sympathetic figure, in charge of Nixon's foreign policy team. Kissinger's profound attachment to Israel and his ignorance of the Middle East—he had never visited the region—formed the basis of a strong and lasting relationship in which each man mentored the other.

The Kissinger-Rabin relationship established a new symbiosis that inverted the old Eisenhower axiom. Ike had focused on restraining Israel so that it might find accommodation with its neighbors. But Nixon's inclination to play a tougher hand against the Soviets encouraged new thinking that Israel could be employed—with American arms—as an instrument of the cold war.

As Rabin attached himself to Kissinger, Efraim Halevy, the new

Mossad station chief in Washington in 1970, attached himself to Richard Helms, the CIA director, and to James Angleton, the CIA counterintelligence chief who had run the CIA's liaison with Israel since the early 1950s. Angleton had first encountered the Mossad in Italy during World War II.

These relationships—Kissinger and Rabin, Halevy and Angleton—were critical to the policies that flowed from them. Kissinger opened a new world of geostrategy for Rabin; Angleton, seventeen years older than Halevy, tutored the younger man on the cold war and U.S. intelligence strategy; they would carry on a correspondence for many years.[28] Famous for his mole-hunting obsessions at CIA headquarters, Angleton pursued a theory—which extended long after he had left the CIA—that Yasser Arafat was an "asset" of Soviet intelligence.

Once a month, Halevy and Angleton would invite Rabin to join them at Rive Gauche, a stylish eatery near the White House, where they exchanged political gossip about Washington and Tel Aviv.

Rabin's determination to destroy Nasser converged with Kissinger's desire to expand Israel's role as an American ally in the Middle East, which Kissinger regarded as a cold war battleground. It is impossible to read Rabin's cables home during this period without hearing the echoes of Kissinger.

In September 1969, for instance, Rabin reported to Meir that "the National Security Council is considering the impact of Israeli military operations against Egypt, and the Americans are giving careful consideration to their possible effect on the stability of Nasser's regime." Rabin reported that "lines of thought" were beginning "to emerge" in Washington that "continuation of Israeli military operations, including air attacks, is likely to lead to far-reaching results. Nasser's standing could be undermined, and that would in turn weaken the Soviet position in the region."[29]

Rabin reported to Abba Eban, the foreign minister, but he directed his advocacy for action to Meir. "Some sources have informed me that our military operations are the most encouraging breath of fresh air the American administration has enjoyed recently. A man would have to be blind, deaf and dumb not to sense how much the administration favors our military operations, and there is a growing likelihood that the United States would be interested in an escalation of our military activity with the aim of undermining Nasser's standing."

There was a manic quality to Rabin's description of official thinking in Washington. "Some circles were considering the possibility of Israel destroying the Egyptian army in a large-scale offensive action; and certainly no one here is dismayed by such a prospect . . . thus the willingness to supply us with additional arms depends more on stepping up our military activity against Egypt than on reducing it," Rabin wrote.[30]

From the CIA, Helms seemed to cheer Israel's militarism. In a memo to Nixon, he suggested that Israeli attacks on Egypt should be encouraged "since it benefits the West as well as Israel." If Nasser were toppled by relentless Israeli pressure, no successor could possibly be worse, Kissinger added in a cover note, because he "will not have Nasser's personal charisma in the Arab and Moslem world."[31]

There was little or nothing in Rabin's cables about a peace strategy, and when a peace plan did emerge from Secretary of State William Rogers, no one worked harder to undermine it than Rabin in collusion with Kissinger. If one thing was clear, it was that Rabin was still at war.[32]

As for Meir, she couldn't tell whether Nixon wanted Israel to make war or make peace. She traveled to Washington to meet Nixon in September 1969 and came away with a sense that relations with the United States were going to be easier than the last time Nixon was in the White House as Eisenhower's vice president. Still, she got mixed signals on where Nixon was going. One side of his administration was talking about linking weapons sales to movement on the peace front; this was Nixon's "hardware for software" formula. But others in the administration, including Kissinger, told Meir that Nixon would never pressure her. Israel's secret atomic bomb project was barely mentioned and, if it was, it was in the context that Nixon had not determined his policy on nuclear proliferation; he was kicking it down the road.[33]

Meir sailed through Israeli national elections the following month, having coaxed Mapam back into a Labor alignment with Mapai, which served to strengthen Yigal Allon, a popular figure with the public. Dayan had tried to block the merger and, during the postelection maneuvering, Meir allowed Dayan to draft the new government's platform.

Dayan imposed a new militant orthodoxy on the political establishment, declaring that the definition of "secure borders" meant, in effect, confiscating in perpetuity—annexing, in other words—Arab lands. The Golan Heights would remain in Israel's hands, along with a strip of the Sinai down to the Strait of Tiran; Gaza would remain in Israel's hands as well as the West Bank of the Jordan, which would become the eastern boundary of modern Israel.

Dayan preened in front of the political establishment, laying down the bedrock of a new sabra dictum for national security policy. Even Begin and the right wing could not fault his expansionism. It seemed that with few exceptions, everyone in Israel had embraced a creed that envisioned a Greater Israel, from the Mediterranean to the Jordan. There were differences over how to achieve it, but these were subordinated to the sense of national destiny that was propelling the country.

But Nixon also was in search of his own destiny. He told his aides that he wanted "big plays" in foreign policy, and in late 1969, he suddenly encouraged Secretary of State William Rogers to put forward a major peace plan that would roll back Israel's military gains in the region.

Rabin was the first to pick up a piece of intelligence that the U.S. State Department was about to propose that Israel withdraw from its forward positions along the Suez Canal. Rogers was sending Joseph Sisco, an assistant secretary, to Moscow to inform the Soviets that a larger American peace initiative was coming.

The so-called Rogers Plan of 1969 represented the first major diplomatic intervention by the United States in the Middle East since Eisenhower's Project Alpha. Its scope was comprehensive in seeking to roll back the gains of conquest and to negotiate secure borders for the Jewish state along the pre-1967 lines. The Israeli leadership regarded the American proposal as dire and threatening. Yet Golda Meir seemed blinded to the obvious opportunity for diplomacy, and there was no voice within her circle, with the possible exception of Eban's, that could penetrate the psychological resistance to engaging the Arabs. Instead, almost as soon as the Israeli leadership learned of the impending American initiative, its members resolved to undermine it by launching a new phase of war.

The quest for expanded borders and the strong martial impulse ingrained in the military establishment impelled not only Meir's ambition to strike but also that of a majority of the political class.

Rabin told his prime minister that now was the time to "undertake deep penetration bombing raids and strike military targets in the Egyptian heartland . . . delivering a sharp blow to Nasser." This, he said—as if he were America's cold war strategist—"would help to shore up America's status in the region and thus prevent America from having to back down in talks with the Soviet Union." Rabin fostered stories in the Israeli press quoting "diplomatic sources" in Washington that Israel's military pressure on Egypt was insufficient. Eban confronted Rabin: Why was he planting false stories? Rabin, to his credit, admitted that he had planted the stories, but he asserted that since everyone else was leaking to the media, he might as well promote his own agenda.[34]

Meir saw the Rogers Plan as a potential disaster. It cut deeply into Zionist ambitions to hold the gains of the war. Rabin flew home for the cabinet session that declared that peace under the Rogers Plan would be a "grave danger" to Israel. Rabin's plan for a strategic bombing campaign suddenly had a thousand fathers, including Dayan.[35]

Only Eban challenged the militarist line, especially Rabin's assertion that the Nixon administration favored an escalation of the war. How could Nixon, who had come into office claiming that the Middle East was a "powder keg," favor expanding the conflict and risking a superpower clash? Eban's logic made eminent good sense, but it was dismissed, a reflection of how little influence he retained after the generals had undermined and disparaged his diplomacy in 1967.

Israel's strategic bombing campaign commenced on January 7, 1970. The air force launched more than three thousand sorties in thirty-four major raids, dropping an estimated eight thousand tons of bombs on military and civilian targets over three months. For the first time, American bombers played the most prominent role—U.S.-made F-4 Phantoms terrorized Egyptian cities. Hundreds of Egyptians died in the raids, including forty-seven children in one mistaken attack on an elementary school. Seventy civilian workers were killed in one factory. Nasser told an American diplomat visiting Cairo, "For the first time I feel bitterness. There was no bitterness in the time of Dulles and the Baghdad Pact, but now, with the killing of children and workers and civilians, there is."[36] The bombing campaign did not weaken Nasser or incite a coup against him. But the Egyptian leader was under pressure to do something. He flew to Moscow, where he told Leonid Brezhnev that he would not allow the Egyptian army to be destroyed. If Moscow failed to act decisively, he said, he would resign and turn the country over to a pro-American leader.[37]

Brezhnev summoned the Politburo and forced a decision. Egypt was too important to lose. The Soviet military agreed to take over Egypt's air defense, sending fifteen thousand soldiers, airmen, and trainers. Ships arrived bearing the latest radars and missiles. And Soviet air force pilots landed 150 advanced aircraft at Egyptian bases ready to take on the Israeli air force.

Here were the consequences of which Eban had warned. Israeli militarism, secretly encouraged by Rabin's "sources"—Kissinger and his deputy, Alexander M. Haig, Jr.—resulted in the largest breakout of Soviet military force in the Middle East since World War II.

Rabin's attempt to destroy Nasser failed utterly; hundreds of lives were lost on the battlefield and Egypt suffered grievous civilian casualties from the bombing campaign, which aroused the Soviet leadership to effectively enter the war in the Middle East. Rabin seemed undeterred. He went to Capitol Hill with a request for fifty more Phantoms and told Nixon that if the president refused a new Israeli arms request, the Soviets would see it "as a sign of weakness."[38]

Nixon hated to be squeezed, but he also knew there was a limit to the amount of pressure he could exert on Meir and her government.

The arrival of Russian forces in Egypt changed the military balance in the Middle East. The Soviet air force sent its own pilots with modern jet fighters and shot down a half dozen Israeli Phantoms and captured three pilots.

In April 1970, Israel was forced to suspend its strategic bombing campaign due to the influx of Soviet weapons and air defenses.

Rabin wanted his government to ask the Americans for one hundred more Phantoms to escalate the conflict, but Meir was running into resistance at home.

Out of the blue, Nahum Goldmann, the president of the World Jewish Congress and an old ally of Moshe Sharett, received an invitation from

Nasser to visit Cairo and hold talks on the prospects for peace. Meir surprised many Israelis by curtly refusing Goldmann's request to travel to Cairo as an official envoy. To many Israelis, especially young people facing military service, her refusal did not square with public assertions that Israel yearned for peace. Hadn't Ben-Gurion and Meir spent their lives telling the public that they would go to the ends of the earth to talk with the Arabs? Hadn't they schooled the young on the notion that Israelis were "doomed" to struggle because—*ein breira*—there was *no alternative*?

In a letter to Meir that received saturation coverage in the Israeli media, a group of high school students who were facing their compulsory military service wrote that "after the government rejected the prospect of peace by refusing Dr. Nahum Goldmann's trip, we do not know whether we would be capable of carrying out our duty in the army under the slogan of *ein breira*."[39]

The letter struck a nerve in that heavily militarized society. Was there no end to conflict? It seemed inevitable that a rising generation would ask: Would military triumph actually deliver peace?

In May, Nixon met with Eban and Rabin at the White House. According to Rabin's account of the meeting, the president said, "In view of the Soviet involvement, is Israel's position still—as I once heard Ambassador Rabin say—'Give us the tools and we'll do the job'?" Before Eban could answer, Rabin jumped in with an emphatic "Yes!"

"Good, that's all I wanted to know," Nixon said.

Nixon went on about how he loved it every time he received reports that the Israelis were pounding the Egyptians and Syrians. Part of him screamed, "Let 'em have it! Hit 'em as hard as you can!" he said, but there was more to the Middle East agenda than just pulverizing the enemy, he admonished.

"We will back you militarily, but the military escalation can't be allowed to go on endlessly," Nixon said. "We must do something politically."[40]

Eban was heartened. The president was pushing diplomacy and negotiation. But each person heard what he wanted to hear; that was the effect of Nixon's contradictory approach. "I am a political man," Nixon said many years later in an off-the-record session with *New York Times* reporters, as if to excuse the duplicity with which he approached competing constituencies. He believed that every political figure had to play two hands at once, until one showed winning cards.

Nixon believed that Eban and Rabin had gotten the message: Israel should climb down from the triumphalism of the Six-Day War and start working on a strategy of accommodation in the Middle East. But Rabin heard Nixon's bellicose preamble and asserted that he and Eban had witnessed the "most openly pro-Israeli statements ever uttered by an American president." Rabin said he was "deeply moved."[41]

But Eban, the more astute analyst at the time, had taken Nixon's message differently: "Both Nixon and Secretary Rogers believed, not without justification, that exclusive Israeli preoccupation with its own military strength"—and the role of war—"was exaggerated. The main objective," in Nixon's view as Eban saw it, "was to end the fighting that was increasingly liable to involve the U.S. in an unwanted confrontation with the Soviet Union."[42]

Nixon and Rogers followed up with a cease-fire plan that called for the parties to stop shooting and to start negotiating under the terms of UN Security Council Resolution 242 of 1967, which called for Israeli withdrawal and security for all states.[43] Meir resisted for weeks. Meanwhile, the Israeli military staff came up with a plan to lure a flight of Soviet fighters out over the Sinai after a series of skirmishes. Israeli Phantoms successfully sprang the trap and shot down five Soviet MiG-21 jets on July 31, 1970, raising concerns that a larger clash with Soviet forces could come.

By the time the American-sponsored cease-fire went into effect in August 1970, the War of Attrition had proved costly to Israel. Seven hundred Israelis had died, and an equal number were wounded. The proposal, which the Israeli cabinet adopted, called for negotiations with Egypt and Jordan to return Arab territories under Resolution 242, a step that incited Menachem Begin to resign from the national unity government. He opposed giving up anything. Negotiations stalled.

The synergy between Kissinger and Rabin seemed profound. Another opportunity for proxy warfare came quickly. In September, the PLO declared war on King Hussein, and the Jordanian monarch struck back brutally, accusing Arafat of seeking to overthrow the government. The Jordanian army shelled Palestinian refugee camps, and the confrontation came to be known as Black September. A week into the army's crackdown, Palestinian militants loyal to George Habash and his PFLP went on a hijacking spree, seizing Western airliners and forcing them to fly to a remote airfield in Jordan. Passengers were marched off the planes, into which explosives were packed and detonated on September 11, sending up towering plumes over the desert.

Alarmed over King Hussein's assault on the Palestinians, Syria launched a column of tanks and Palestinian irregulars into northern Jordan, a gesture meant to show solidarity with the PLO. But this minor battlefield intervention, which was not large enough to threaten Jordan's control of the situation, nonetheless sent Kissinger into motion. He portrayed the Syrian move as a Soviet-inspired challenge to the West, though it was neither Soviet inspired nor militarily potent.[44]

Meir was in New York with Rabin at a United Jewish Appeal function. Kissinger telephoned to ask if Israel would be willing to intervene in Jordan to block the Syrian force. For Rabin, the most important thing was to act with American backing. He demanded a formal presidential request and Kissinger soon delivered it.

Rabin's mobilization, however, was sharply opposed by Dayan and Sharon. Both favored allowing the PLO to topple King Hussein. They wanted Jordan to become a Palestinian state, a home for all of the refugees living in camps and a destination for the remaining Palestinians in the West Bank and Gaza if Israel moved to annex those territories.

"I argued as hard as I could against Israeli intervention in Jordan," Sharon later wrote, adding, "Dayan was also against it. But the majority felt differently."[45]

Israeli troops never went into action because the Syrians pulled back. And Nasser called Arab leaders to Cairo to negotiate a cease-fire between Jordan and the PLO. But just as the crisis was ending, Nasser, who had driven to the airport to see off the emir of Kuwait, suddenly fell ill and died of a heart attack.

Israel's nemesis was dead, the voice of the Arabs silenced. After all Israel's efforts to topple him by military means, Nasser succumbed to a heart weakened by diabetes, heavy smoking, and the strain of leading Egypt.

The tragedy was that although the passing of Nasser would create an opening for a new chapter between Israel and Egypt and a strategic move toward peace, Meir proved unequal to the task of marshaling the case to seize the opportunity.

Under Meir there was no such thing as a peace camp, no intellectual base in the government or the army to foment a peace strategy. There were party factions adhering to competing lines of militancy: Meir's sought to convince the Americans to declare that the Rogers Plan was dead; Rabin focused on obtaining new American arms and enhancing Israel's role in the region as a U.S. military proxy; Dayan and Allon's concern was how to redraw the West Bank so both Arabs and Jews could live there under the security of the Israeli army.

Diplomatic stalemate was good policy because the Arabs had no military ability to overcome the most modern air force in the region backed by a highly maneuverable land army and a nuclear deterrence force. In Israel, conflict with the Arabs had entered the realm of doctrine. A biting satire on an endless war of attrition called *The Bathroom Queen* appeared on the stage at this time, spoofing Meir with didactic monologues, including a complaint that it was exhausting to be right all the time: "I'm only a human being!"

Meir was of the Jordanist school, meaning that she saw the best solution of the Palestinian problem as long-term association between the West Bank Arabs and the Hashemite Kingdom of Jordan, with Israel as the de facto sovereign power through annexation. That meant no Palestinian state. Ever.

"There is no such thing as a Palestinian people," Meir had told the *Sunday Times* of London. "It is not as if we came and threw them out and took their country. They didn't exist."[46]

So it was inevitable, as the occupation dragged on, that the passivity of the people under occupation would begin to wear. Palestinian nationalism was growing, as were incidents of violence and "armed struggle" against the occupation.

During this period, Kissinger secretly took note of new CIA estimates that showed the Jewish state was in the process of fully entering the club of nuclear nations. Its scientists had built a small arsenal of ten to twelve operational atomic bombs that could be delivered by aircraft or missiles, and another dozen Jericho missiles were due for delivery.

In private conversations with Kissinger, Rabin—both implicitly and explicitly—indicated that Israel wanted nuclear weapons for two reasons: "first to deter the Arabs from striking Israel, and second, if deterrence fails and Israel were about to be overrun, to destroy the Arabs in a nuclear Armageddon."[47]

Meir's Israel had become the invincible state, about which she bragged to Nixon, "We never had it so good."[48]

As commander of the southern front facing the main enemy, Ariel Sharon was eager to show that there was a military solution for even the intractable problem of Palestinian terrorism.

Arab militants in January 1971 had thrown a grenade into the car of an Israeli family that was visiting Gaza, where Arabs and Jews intermixed in the markets along the sea. The couple's two children were killed instantly by the blast, and the parents suffered serious wounds. Dayan came down to Sharon's headquarters to talk about terrorism as they inspected the former Egyptian base at Bir Gafgafa.

This was a low point in Dayan's life. He was minister of defense, but Meir and her allies in the cabinet tied him down with a thousand filaments. He knew that the old guard would never allow him to become prime minister. Though he was still married to Ruth and romantically involved with Rahel, Dayan sought refuge with other women, conducting a number of affairs that led to newspaper accounts of taped conversations by one paramour and blackmail threats. In his turmoil, he was abusing sleeping pills, which made him groggy and subjected him to mood swings. Ruth Dayan eventually asked for a divorce, telling family members that Dayan was no longer the man she had married, that he had succumbed to fame. The divorce cleared the way for Dayan's marriage to Rahel, who doted on Dayan and who had also tolerated his dalliances. In these later years, the iconic general became obsessed with making money, and he demanded thousands of dollars for interviews from the foreign periodicals that were enthralled by his legend.[49]

When his father died, Dayan called his daughter at two in the morning rambling with slurred speech about how his parents, his brother and sister were all in the cemetery, waiting for him. So were the worms, he said.[50]

Touring with Sharon, Dayan was in his element out in the wilderness of Sinai, surrounded by soldiers. The talk turned to terrorism. Sharon wanted to hit hard in Gaza after the grenade attack.

"Moshe, if we don't take action now, we are going to lose control there, without any question," Sharon recalled saying.

"Dayan just looked at me and said quietly, 'You can start.'"[51]

This was the sabra code, the same code that Sharon and Dayan had been using for twenty years, going back to that day when Dayan had told the young paratrooper that the reason he got all the assignments for reprisal raids on the Arabs was that he never asked for his orders in writing. Now Sharon interpreted Dayan's meaning this way: "Do what you want. If you succeed, fine. If it backfires, don't start looking to me for support."[52]

Sharon's army entered Gaza. He looked across the twenty thousand acres of orange groves bounded by dense urban neighborhoods and refugee camps and decided he would conduct what he called "anti-terrorist guerrilla warfare." He divided Gaza into grid sections, each one a mile or two square. Each of his junior officers took a section; each was to conduct surveillance, recruit informants, and extract information by any means to identify and locate PLO and PFLP militants.

If Dayan was paying attention, he wasn't paying close attention. Sharon claimed that he got permission to widen the narrow passageways of the refugee camps so that armored vehicles could be used to chase militants. Perhaps Dayan had not imagined what such "widening" would look like when Sharon's forces descended on the camps with bulldozers that crushed rows of ramshackle homes and sent Palestinian women and children fleeing for their lives. Sharon seemed to revel in the negative publicity—they were calling him "The Bulldozer." But Meir and the cabinet recoiled in the face of the international reaction.[53]

As the rubble was being cleared, Sharon took the next step of bringing in one of the elite commando units, and that was where Meir Dagan got his reputation as one of the most efficient killers in the unit called Sayeret Rimon. Suddenly, Palestinian militants began showing up dead, their bodies dumped in alleys or fields. The liquidations went on for nearly a year and stopped only after the Gazan elders pledged to help control the streets if Sharon stopped the extrajudicial killings. From July 1971 to February 1972, Sharon claimed that his force killed 104 Palestinians—he called them all terrorists—and imprisoned more than 740.[54]

Sharon gained an international reputation as a no-nonsense brute of the Israeli military. As the occupation authority, he was bound by the Geneva Conventions to protect the population living under occupation in Gaza. Yet there was never an accounting of the process by which Sharon and his commanders carried out over many months a series of unsupervised executions based on intelligence that was not subject to judicial review.

Dayan escaped all scrutiny in the episode.

He had approved and enabled Sharon's assault on Gaza, knowing that his methods would be brutal and destructive. Under pressure to bring the campaign to an end, however, Dayan issued an order transferring responsibility for Gaza from the Southern to the Central Command. Sharon heard about it on television, which finally had been introduced after the Six-Day War.

The Americans had scarcely noticed the drama in Gaza. David Rockefeller, the Chase Manhattan bank chairman and friend to Nixon and Kissinger, visited Israel during this time and focused exclusively on whether Anwar Sadat, the new Egyptian leader, was bluffing with his "year-of-decision" threat of renewed warfare if there was no progress on Israeli withdrawal from Sinai. All Rockefeller could do was observe the sclerosis of the Israeli political and military elite. Sadat, who had been Nasser's vice president, was considered a lightweight who would be swept away by one or more of Nasser's circle, but Sadat was beginning to show some tenacity. He had used the Americans to send Israel a peace feeler—the two sides should pull their armies back from the Suez Canal so the cities along the waterway could return to normal life. The canal had been closed since 1967.

But Meir had refused to respond, saying only that Israel would not return to the 1967 borders. Full stop.

Nixon was frustrated. Why did the Israelis have to be so stubborn? he asked.

Rockefeller put that question to Yigal Allon, who responded, "If we don't get better borders, there will be another war." Then Allon ticked off the Arab lands that Israel would like to keep: the Golan, a third of the West Bank, part of Sinai.

"Do you in your judgment need peace?" Rockefeller asked.

"Of course, morally, economically, politically," Allon replied.

"Then I come back to the same point: this is a good time to start," Rockefeller said.[55]

An astute judge of character, Rockefeller tried to lead Allon and his colleagues to the conclusion that peace has to have a starting point.

He asked Meir why the government had made a categorical statement that Israel would not go back to the 1967 borders.

"What do we have to do, Mr. Rockefeller? Most people who interpret us this way do so out of ignorance or malice. I almost think we made a great mistake after the war. We should have said, 'These are our borders. We will keep them.'

"Then, when there was great pressure, we would have negotiated," she said.

Rockefeller could only shake his head. But he pressed on: What was keeping Israel from negotiating with Sadat?

Meir got up and took a book off the shelf. "We have four of these volumes. The fifth is coming out and I hope there won't be a sixth. It carries a short biography of every boy and girl who fell in the war. It has pictures, poems, paintings, etc. All I want is that there shouldn't be ten volumes. I think if Egypt had volumes of this kind, they wouldn't want war."[56]

That was Meir, rigid to a fault, unable to engage the concept of negotiating with her enemy.

Sadat's persistence in offering something concrete—withdrawal from the canal to a distance of twenty-five miles—motivated Dayan, however, to make a political proposal. In March 1971, he convinced a number of cabinet members that Israel should respond to the Egyptian leader, because peace along the canal would relieve the threat of renewed hostilities.

But Meir and her allies rose in opposition. Bar-Lev, the chief of staff, said he opposed a deep withdrawal; so did Allon, Galili, and Sapir, leaving Dayan dead in the water. In late March, Eban cabled from Washington, where he was visiting. No one in Washington could figure out whether Meir's government wanted 70 percent of Sinai or 7 percent, he said.[57]

Walworth Barbour, the dowdy American ambassador, pleaded with Meir to consider how many times in Zionist history there had been a leader like Sadat who had actually said something as positive as that he might someday sign a peace agreement with Israel.[58]

In Washington, Kissinger admonished Eban: "There is serious fear that all you *really* want is to evade any settlement that requires concessions on your part so that you can remain along the lines you hold at present!"[59]

Sharon watched the struggle in the cabinet over whether to respond to Sadat's peace initiative and, without cabinet authority, he expelled five thousand Egyptian herders—the Bedouin of northern Sinai—from their ancestral lands. Sharon then invited Israeli settlers to move into the territory he had cleared along the coast between Gaza and el-Arish and establish an Israeli presence. In his own brutish way, Sharon—no fan of Meir—was stiffening her spine to hold on to a significant portion of Sinai. No Israeli prime minister could lightly consider uprooting Zionist settlers once they had put down their tent stakes.[60]

The paralysis within the Israeli political and military establishments reflected not only the domestic power struggle but also the deeply embedded martial impulse that impelled Israel through its most rigid period following the 1967 War and undermined the first promising breakthrough for diplomacy that followed the death of Nasser. Sadat's probe and Dayan's proposal for a pullback could have drawn Egyptians and Israelis into a negotiation on how to stand down their respective armies, a worthy enough goal, but much more important, it would have led to human contact and the insights that arise from engaging and trying to understand an enemy.

This was the wisdom that Sharett had tried to impart to his colleagues before he died—the strategic importance of never for a single moment losing sight of opportunities for peace.

Sharon and Israel Tal, interestingly, had both agreed with Dayan about negotiating a significant pullback, but Meir's top generals—Bar-Lev and Elazar—preferred only a token pullback, which Sadat could not accept.

Then the Soviets came up with their own diplomatic strategy.

In late 1971, Leonid Brezhnev laid out in secret to the Nixon White House a detailed peace proposal for the Middle East that called for reopening the Suez Canal, withdrawal of major Soviet forces in Egypt, and an overall Arab-Israeli settlement that—like the Rogers Plan—would be based roughly on the 1967 lines.[61]

Here was a significant development of the cold war—a tangible effort at constructive superpower cooperation that Nixon had promoted as a policy of détente.

But when Rabin flew home and presented the proposal to Meir and the cabinet, the knives came out again. Since Ben-Gurion's time, the orthodoxy of the military establishment was never to allow the great powers to become the arbiters of peace. After all, what had the great powers tried to do under Eisenhower but carve out part of the Negev from Israel to reconnect the Arab world? The UN partition resolution of 1947 was a disaster that would have created a Jewish state even smaller than the one they had. What Ben-Gurion had learned in the 1948–49 fighting was that it was better to rely on the army to take the land that was needed. After the Six-Day War, the military elites had come to believe that if Israel just held out long enough, the Golan Heights, part of the Sinai, all of Jerusalem, and much of the West Bank could be annexed without major international blowback or UN sanctions.

No Eisenhower was standing in Meir's way. She did not want to go down in history as the Zionist leader who gave up land for which Israeli soldiers had died, even though her mentor, Ben-Gurion, had done that very thing in 1957. And though Nixon was keen to make détente work in the Middle East, Kissinger had sent the message to Meir that Israel would not be blamed if it rejected Brezhnev's initiative.

Yet Nixon did blame Israel for its intransigence because the debates within the Israeli cabinet were not about accommodation with the Arabs; they were about finding the best strategy to exploit Israel's military superiority.

Meir finally confided to Rabin in January 1972 her motivation for resisting Nixon's entreaties so tenaciously: "Israel's policy aims toward a considerable change in her border with Egypt," Meir told her ambassador. "That means a change in sovereignty, not just an Israeli presence. We do not employ the term 'annexation' because of its negative connotation."[62]

There it was: finally Meir had come out and said it. Israel was more intent on expanding its territory (through force if necessary) than in making peace.

The idea that the Israelis wanted to keep Arab lands infuriated Nixon, but in an election year, the last thing he was going to do was take on Meir. He would give her arms to keep her satisfied. As it happened, she didn't need them. The Soviets were slowing the pace of arms deliveries to Egypt as Brezhnev sought to engage Nixon in a policy of détente to reduce the risk of proxy wars and superpower confrontation. But Sadat felt betrayed, and so he summoned the Soviet ambassador and announced in July 1972 that he was sending fifteen thousand Soviet advisers home.[63]

The young generation of Israelis was growing up on the art of war; there were no heroes of Israeli diplomacy, no statesmen who stood as visionaries of long-term accommodation with the Arabs. In the mythology of the sabra majority, only weaklings and appeasers stood for engagement with the enemy. Israel had built the most agile special forces in the region, and the military elite was straining to employ them to keep the enemy off guard.

By 1972, a young officer named Ehud Barak had risen to be commander of Sayeret Matkal, the secret commando unit that reported directly to the general staff. Almost everyone who laid eyes on Barak, or heard him speak in highly literate Hebrew about history, art, science, or classical music—he was an accomplished pianist—believed that he would one day be chief of staff or even prime minister.

Barak took on every task with forethought and planning, especially in recruiting exceptional soldiers for the "unit." Barak's officers were the best and brightest; they included Jonathan Netanyahu, whose father, Benzion Netanyahu, had served as Jabotinsky's chief of staff in the 1930s, and whose younger brothers, Benjamin and Iddo, would follow him into the unit. Barak personally recruited Muki Betser, the paratrooper who had been shot in the jaw during the battle at Karameh in 1968. It took more than a year for Betser to get his health back, and then the army had sent him off to Uganda to train the security forces of Idi Amin, Africa's most brutal dictator.[64]

Many of Sayeret Matkal's operations have yet to be declassified by the Israelis, in part because they involved bugging and electronic surveillance operations whose location and technique are still relevant. By 1972, for instance, Israeli intelligence had found a way to place a listening device in the Egyptian military command center.

The secret unit's responsibilities were broad and included many missions into Egypt, Syria, Lebanon, and Jordan, sometimes to kill, but most often to bug or collect intelligence on Arab formations, weapons, communications, radar systems, and air defenses. The unit also ran rescue missions.

In 1970, Israel had lost three pilots over Syria during raids against the Syrian army, and for two years, Meir's government had failed to negotiate their release, even after thirty-seven Syrian soldiers were captured during one raid staged for the purpose of taking hostages for an exchange.

The unit got involved in June 1972, when Israeli intelligence learned that high-ranking Syrian officers from the air force and intelligence corps were making regular inspection tours by car along the northern border. Generals David Elazar and Motta Gur, the chief of staff and the head of the Northern Command, respectively, traveled to the border to supervise Barak's ambush operation from a grove of trees.

Three groups of soldiers mounted American-made armored personnel carriers and rolled across the border, waving laconically at UN peacekeepers monitoring the area. Barak's team would make the grab. Betser was stationed with a second team in case the Syrians got past Barak. A third team would close off the road after the convoy passed.

They didn't have to wait long. Betser heard Barak on the radio: "Two sedans . . . one Land Rover . . . two jeeps . . . an armored personnel carrier."

"Halt!" came a command over the radio. It was Gur. No one had said anything about an armored escort.

"It's okay," Barak insisted. "It's no problem for us."

Then Elazar came on the speaker: "No."

"I can jump them now," Barak protested. They were only a few yards away from his hidden position in the rocks. "I request authorization to proceed."

"No," Elazar said again. "No authorization."

The hidden Israeli force let the Syrians pass. The adrenaline had surged without release. When they got back to the grove where Elazar and Gur were waiting, Barak addressed his superiors in the blunt style of the army.

"I never expected that the presence of an APC would make you decide not to act," he told them in front of his men. He said they had been prepared to handle an armored personnel carrier. "But the worst thing about your decision is that you created a situation where next time, we might not report all the information we have, worried that you might make a decision like today's."

Betser, who witnessed this rebuke from the Sayeret commander, said the generals looked like "schoolkids being reproached by an angry teacher." Elazar had a stick in his hand, and with his head tilted to the ground, he scratched patterns in the flinty soil. After a moment, he looked up at Barak and his officers. "Maybe I was wrong," he said. "I just hope we get another chance."

In the ethos of the Israeli army, the field commander has a special status. As leader of the commando force, Barak exhibited an aura of self-assurance that was impossible to ignore.

A few days later, reports indicated the Syrian convoy would return the next day. Barak announced to his men that this time he was going to stay in the grove with the generals to make sure they did not go wobbly over some surprise. He turned over command of the ambush to Jonathan Netanyahu. They used two decoy cars with their hoods up to look like civilians with engine trouble.

Just before noon, the convoy appeared. Almost nothing went according to plan. The Syrian cars stopped short. A civilian car raced forward and its driver spoke to the convoy drivers, who then began to turn around. Were they tipped off? Netanyahu and his men burst forward. The blocking force jumped from its hiding place, and after a brief exchange of fire, the convoy, with its Syrian general and two colonels from air force intelligence, was taken into custody. Eight months later, the Israeli pilots were released in a trade.[65]

Yet as Israel sharpened the tip of its spear, the Arabs also escalated.

In September 1972, a squad of Palestinian guerrillas stormed the Israeli dormitory during the Summer Olympic Games in Munich, West Germany, killing two athletes and taking nine others hostage. The drama unfolded on worldwide television, as millions of viewers had tuned in to follow the swimming exploits of Mark Spitz and the tumbling of Soviet gymnast Olga Korbut.

But suddenly the play-by-play coming out of control booths focused on the demands of the Black September terrorists, who had come seeking recognition for their cause and for the release of their comrades from jails.

A frantic German effort to free the hostages after they were transported to a military base by helicopter ended horribly when the terrorists discovered they had been led into a trap, and German sharpshooters, poorly prepared for their mission, failed to immobilize the heavily armed militants before they turned their guns on the defenseless athletes. Most died from multiple gunshot wounds, and the terrorist squad also threw grenades into the helicopters to incinerate the bodies.

All of Israel was frozen by fear and anxiety over the athletes; at the Knesset, Dayan sat alone at a table, staring out the window of the sun-drenched dining room awaiting updates during the day.

The ABC sports announcer Jim McKay broke the news in the middle of the night: "They're all dead." The cabinet gathered. Barak and the Sayeret Matkal team were poised to fly to Europe, where Mossad chief Zvi Zamir had been frantically trying to prevent the terrible ending that unfolded at one thirty in the morning.

Nothing the Palestinian nationalists had ever done delivered a blow as heavy as Black September did in Munich. That they did so in Germany was particularly painful to many Israelis. The Germans released the three surviving Black September gunmen after hijackers seized a German air-liner weeks later. Arafat's intelligence chief, Salah Khalaf—believed to be the architect of the Black September terror program—wrote that Munich forced the world "to take note of the Palestinian drama" in the Middle East, and through the terror at Munich, "the Palestinian people imposed their presence on an international gathering that had sought to exclude them."[66]

The Palestinian militant and poet Mahmoud Darwish wrote defiantly, "The one who has turned me into a refugee has made a bomb of me."

Many in the world, even many Palestinians, were repulsed by this new era of grand terrorism. For the Israeli military establishment, there was nothing to debate: retribution was coming. The only question was how many would die; deterrence, at least in the conception of the Israeli mili-tary, demanded a devastating blow or Munich would become another Karameh, a victory for the PLO.

Meir stood before parliament a week later and said that Israel had de-clared war on those who were behind what was being called the Munich massacre. Israel would hunt them down "with all the zeal, self-dedication and skill our people are capable of. . . . We must deploy ourselves for this warfare even more than we have done up till now—methodically, in knowledge and resolution."[67]

The first response came within days, when two squadrons of Israeli warplanes flew north to strike PLO camps in Lebanon and Syria. Meir brought back the retired chief of military intelligence Aharon Yariv, one of the hawks of the 1967 War, and put him in charge of coordinating the efforts of Mossad, military intelligence, and domestic intelligence for a retaliation campaign—Operation Wrath of God—that would range across the landscape of Europe and the Middle East. Arafat estimated that sixty of his people were killed or maimed by Israeli assassins, exploding packages, or exploding telephones, or in commando raids.

Barak's unit was assigned the most high-profile strike of the campaign, Operation Spring of Youth, a nighttime infiltration into a fashionable neighborhood in the heart of Beirut in April 1973 to gun down senior Black September and PLO operatives. It was a joint operation with paratroopers under the command of Amnon Lipkin-Shahak, who was to attack the headquarters of George Habash's PFLP. Lipkin-Shahak was a sabra who had risen through the paratrooper brigade and had won a medal of valor for bravery in action against Arafat's forces at Karameh. Like Barak a standout soldier, Lipkin-Shahak had an easy manner and Cary Grant looks; he had everything Barak had except the ability to project himself as a prodigy. Barak spoke powerfully and cut the profile of a political figure, as if he were a young Ben-Gurion, and he exuded self-assurance that was almost stifling.

It was a night of legends for the Israeli commandos. Barak, dressed as a woman in a blond wig, landed in a rubber boat on the Beirut beach with his small commando force. His "date" and partner was Muki Betser.[68] They climbed into an American sedan rented by Mossad agents and sped through the streets of the city. The Mossad driver warned that there were Lebanese gendarmes in the target neighborhood. Barak didn't respond at first, but when the Mossad man repeated the warning, Barak just snapped, "I heard you. Go."

The cars followed the winding streets into the hills overlooking the sea, and when they reached one of their main targets, Betser led the team that raced up six flights of stairs and burst into the apartment of Mohammed Youssef al-Najjar, also known as Abu Youssef, Black September's chief of operations.

"Four strides and I reached my target's office," Betser wrote later. According to the diagram of the apartment Mossad had acquired, the master bedroom was to the right. Just as Betser swung his Uzi submachine gun in that direction, "the door flew open.

"The face I knew from three weeks of carrying his picture in my shirt pocket looked at me as I raised my gun," said Betser. Al-Najjar, seeing that he was under attack, slammed the door. Betser and one of his team members opened fire, shredding the door and everything behind it, including al-Najjar and his wife.[69]

The other teams struck methodically and simultaneously, killing dozens of PLO and PFLP militants.

In this new war, Meir and the military establishment would give no quarter, just as they had given no concessions during the diplomatic season that now had passed.

Israel was striking back.

EIGHT

The High Price of Militarism: Yom Kippur

Ashraf Marwan was no ordinary spy.

He was Nasser's son-in-law, married to the Egyptian leader's daughter Mona. On their honeymoon in 1966, they were guests of President and Lady Bird Johnson at the White House. Within a few years, Marwan had telephoned an Israeli embassy in Europe to set up a meeting where he offered to sell Mossad political and military intelligence.[1]

After Nasser's death in 1970, Marwan became an intimate of President Anwar Sadat. The new Egyptian leader considered Marwan part of the family, treating him as an adviser and sharing with him the transcripts and reports of Sadat's meetings with heads of state, including the Soviet leadership. For Mossad, Marwan was a gold mine, and even Henry Kissinger had been impressed when Rabin showed him a transcript of Leonid Brezhnev's private conversations with Egyptian envoys. Kissinger wanted to know if Mossad was intercepting *his* conversations with Brezhnev, too.

In early 1973, Marwan reported to his Mossad control officer in Europe that large-scale maneuvers set for May 1973 were a mask for an all-out attack across the Suez Canal on May 19. Marwan's warning was soon partially confirmed by the Egyptian announcement that they would begin a training maneuver designated as Tahrir-35 at midmonth.[2]

America was distracted by Watergate. The Senate investigations committee under the chairmanship of Sam Ervin of North Carolina was gearing up for a summer of televised hearings. The *New York Times* reported that even though Nixon was being politically savaged at home, he still commanded great respect in foreign capitals. "Anything that threatens Nixon's prestige and influence threatens us," an unidentified Israeli official was quoted as saying.[3]

Nixon was preparing for a summit in June with the Soviet leader, and both Israel and Egypt feared a superpower deal that might affect them adversely. Israeli leaders worried they might have to give up territory in a settlement imposed by the powers; Egyptians suspected that Nixon and Brezhnev might propose some diplomatic delaying tactic that would prevent Egypt from going to war.

Sadat called new American feelers for an interim agreement along the Suez Canal a "fraud" and urged Brezhnev to reject them.

"Beware of that American settlement," Sadat told a crowd in a Nile Delta textile town as he was preparing his army for attack. "Beware of that myth."[4]

As commander of the southern front, Sharon was among the first to get the word that war was imminent in the spring of 1973. "When the evaluations indicated that this was a serious threat, I moved into Sinai with the forward headquarters," he wrote later. "We brought in additional troops, put the finishing touches on our plans, and held exercises, bringing the entire command to the state of readiness."[5]

The Bar-Lev Line was the main defense. It consisted of forty-four fortresses along the hundred-mile front, each built with sandbags and concrete and protected by a massive sand berm dense enough to withstand artillery fire. With thirty men in each fortress, the line stood as an impressive defensive array. Sharon suspected that Dayan, too, believed this Maginot Line was a mistake—any army worth its salt can find a way around fixed positions, as Hitler did when he stormed France—but Dayan refused to overrule or criticize Bar-Lev. Dayan flew to the south with Sharon to inspect the front. As they arrived, the Egyptians opened up with harassing artillery fire.

Dayan lay down in the courtyard of the fortress. Shells burst in the near distance. Sharon could not abandon Dayan, so he lay down beside him. There on the ground, they faced each other.

Dayan turned his head toward Sharon and said, "Arik, this is a bad mistake," referring to the Bar-Lev Line. "You must convince them."

Earlier in the day, Sharon had clashed again with Bar-Lev over how to defend Sinai. Sharon made the case to pull back and defend the canal from a depth of ten miles with mobile armored forces and jet fighters that could throw back any invasion force. Dayan, listening, had said nothing. Now he wanted Sharon to take the initiative at further risk to his career.

"Why don't you just give them an order?" Sharon asked.

"No," Dayan replied. And then he looked at Sharon with that single eye and that smirk and added, "Just keep at it."[6]

Sharon had to smile at Dayan's deviousness. He wanted Sharon to be the blunt instrument—and to take the heat.

Kissinger had been named secretary of state to replace William Rogers. But to almost anyone he met, Kissinger said that the United States would make no new moves on the diplomatic front in the Middle East during 1973, at least until after the Israeli elections set for November. Kissinger believed that the Arabs, having lost the 1967 War, were just going to have to accept the status quo dictated by Israel.

"No conceivable solution is going to be all that acceptable to the Arab governments," Kissinger explained to one Middle Eastern ambassador. "Why not let the Egyptians take the heat?"

And Kissinger confided to another Middle Eastern envoy that he would not get involved in a high-risk diplomatic initiative in the Middle East at such a delicate time domestically. "I'd be the first one to be assassinated by both the Jews and the Arabs!"[7]

The Soviets, however, were eager to show that superpower collaboration—détente—could reduce the risk of war. In early May, Brezhnev hosted Kissinger at the Politburo's private boar-hunting lodge at Zavidovo. During their talks, the Soviet leader delivered the first of several warnings that war in the Middle East was imminent. To head it off, Brezhnev suggested a superpower-sponsored negotiation based on a set of "principles"—including security for Israel but also withdrawal from Arab lands.[8]

Brezhnev's dilemma was that he and Sadat were barely on speaking terms. During Sadat's visit to the Nile Delta, he had damned Brezhnev with faint praise. "Our friends in the Soviet Union only go to a certain point with us," he said, referring to Soviet arms supplies. But Israel was getting "all-out" support from the United States.[9]

Within days of these comments, Moscow learned that Sadat was preparing an attack across the Suez Canal on May 19. The Soviet leader sent an urgent message, through the Syrians, asking Sadat to call off the attack. The reason: Brezhnev was due to travel to Washington for the summit with Nixon. They planned to sign an Agreement on the Prevention of Nuclear War. An Egyptian attack and the eruption of war in the Middle East would spoil the aura of superpower détente.[10]

Brezhnev's intervention succeeded. Egypt stood down, leaving the Israelis heavily mobilized for war and wondering what had occurred. Some questioned whether the superspy, Marwan, was a fraud or a double agent.

In America, Brezhnev visited Nixon in late June as the Watergate hearings weighed on Nixon's presidency. John Dean, the former White House counsel, had told investigators that he had discussed a cover-up of Watergate crimes with Nixon dozens of times.

The Agreement on the Prevention of Nuclear War, signed in Washington on June 22, scarcely got a headline. The two leaders flew to Nixon's California home at San Clemente the next day. That night, after Nixon had gone to bed, Brezhnev awakened the house, sending word that he had to discuss the Middle East with the president.

War was coming unless the superpowers did something to prevent it, Brezhnev told Nixon when they were settled in Nixon's study overlooking the Pacific.

"The Arabs cannot hold direct talks with Israel without knowing the principles on which to proceed. We must have a discussion on these principles. If there is no clarity about the principles we will have difficulty keeping the military situation from flaring up," Brezhnev said.[11]

The Soviet leader pressed Nixon late into the night for a commitment to some basic standards for Middle East peace: "security for Israel," the return of Arab lands, opening the Suez Canal, etc.

But Nixon feared the blowback from Israel's supporters in Congress. "On a subject as difficult as this, we cannot say anything definitive. I'm not trying to put you off. It is easy to put down principles," but even putting down principles could create enormous problems, he told the Soviet leader.

Brezhnev pushed and pushed. At one point, he told Nixon that without principles to present to the contending parties, "we have no basis for using our influence" as superpowers.

Nixon fought off the effort, at one point propping his head with pillows as Brezhnev hammered on. Nixon simply would not chance the effort, even if it meant that war would break out. And what could he really do while Golda Meir was talking about annexing the lands Israel had seized? Israel's militarism had paralyzed America, too.

Nixon and Kissinger decided to do nothing in the Middle East; they assumed Israel would once again prevail on the battlefield. It was not a high moment of statesmanship, but with the Watergate scandal raging, it was survival politics. Nixon could not afford to lose a single vote in the Senate because the Senate would become the court of his impeachment trial, if it came to that.

The truth was that Israel, too, was preoccupied with the domestic battle over who would succeed Golda Meir, who was struggling against lymphoma and a host of other ailments endemic to a chain-smoking, overweight, and sleep-deprived matriarch.

Dayan accused the old guard of lacking Zionist verve to go forward with de facto annexation. The problem, he said, was that Meir "viewed Israel's presence in the Territories as a passing phenomenon." They were afraid of making "any attempt to establish strong ties between Israel and the Territories. They refuse to invest there. They refuse to settle there."[12]

"The Territories are not a deposit," Dayan admonished the Labor leaders. "We have to build industries and urban centers there." He was preaching to an audience that he believed arched across the political spectrum, from left-wing kibbutzniks to right-wing settlers, from Ben-Gurion followers to Begin followers.[13]

Dayan's colonizing zeal extended into Sinai, where he wanted to build a new deep-water port at Yamit, the settlement carved out of Egypt's Mediterranean coastline. Sadat called the idea a knife in his heart. Indeed, he said that "if it was only for that one statement of Dayan's I think we should go to war." Dayan praised Sharon for moving military-training bases into the West Bank, creating more "facts on the ground."[14]

Despite Dayan's humanistic sentiments about the Palestinian Arabs, he saw them essentially as a conquered people. He told a Western interviewer that summer, "There is no more Palestine. Finished." And when he had unveiled his program for territorial expansion in April of that year, it was a blueprint for permanent occupation. The Arabs, he argued, could be *induced* to accept "a kind of arrangement of two peoples living in one area" under Israeli sovereignty. The Arabs would be the junior partners, a subjugated population.[15]

Dayan told his supporters that he envisioned "a new state of Israel with broad frontiers, strong and solid, with the authority of the Israeli government extending from the Jordan [River] to the Suez Canal." It was a Zionist declaration of a new colonial era enforced by the militarism Dayan believed Meir and the remnants of the old guard would have to accept.[16]

In these crucial months of 1973, with Arab armies gathering their strength ominously on the borders, Israel's ruling elite seemed unable to come to any precise agreement on national policy. The differences were not great. Israel's leaders were debating *how* to permanently annex Arab lands, not *whether* to incorporate them; they were debating *how* to rule the Palestinian Arabs, not *whether* to rule them.

Israel's military success in the Six-Day War had become the most emphatic set of facts on the ground in the history of the state and was becoming more significant with each passing day.

Meir's policy had devolved to speaking softly to the Americans and harshly to the Arabs, while maintaining a firm grip on territory and political power. She seemed more moderate than Dayan, but she was after essentially the same things. She just wanted to leave the party and the country in the hands of men she trusted, and few were left.

Dayan had regained much of his strength and was a rapacious political figure that summer as war clouds gathered. He lashed out at his rivals and threatened to leave the Labor Party coalition if it did not adopt his program. Meir countered by asking Israel Galili, a veteran of the Haganah, to come up with a unifying campaign manifesto for Labor—one whose tone was *un*-Dayan.

Galili did so, but his program was a distinction without a difference. He, too, provided a blueprint for colonization of the occupied territories. Existing settlements would be strengthened; new ones would be built. Israeli industrialists would be encouraged to move their factories into Sinai and the West Bank. Israelis would be allowed to buy land in the occupied territories—a key Dayan demand. Even Dayan's deepwater port at Yamit made it into the Galili plan.[17]

The right-wing parties went further. Begin called openly for broad annexation of Arab lands. And thus Israel overall—the military and political elites—was deeply mired in Zionist revanchism, re-creating by war, conquest, and occupation the biblical contours of the Land of Israel under a warrior caste. And it was this endeavor that animated bitter rivalries over who would emerge as *Mar Bitachon*—Mr. Security.

Sharon stayed mobilized for war for as long as he could after the false alarm of May 1973. His tour as southern commander was up, and he discovered that after all of his bruising battles with Bar-Lev and his successor, David Elazar, the army did not want him. They mustered him out on a technicality—he had not filed a reenlistment request—and all of his appeals to Dayan and Meir were fruitless. The only concession he could wangle out of Dayan was to be assigned as a "reserve" general in charge of a tank division in time of war. With that, Sharon turned the Southern Command over to his subordinate, General Shmuel Gonen.

Sharon went back to private life, this time as a politician. To him, the question facing the army and the country had not changed: Was Israel bold enough to take the land and expand the state in the face of worldwide condemnation? Could they live out the Ben-Gurion admonishment that it doesn't matter what foreigners say, it only matters what Jews do?

Sharon went back to Begin and made the case for uniting the right-wing parties under one umbrella—Unity, or *Likud* in Hebrew. That would make the right wing more competitive against the Labor Party federation.

In one sense, Sharon and Begin were like family. Back in Poland, Sharon's grandmother was the midwife at Begin's birth. Begin had made an appearance at the funeral of Sharon's firstborn, Gur, who died of a gun accident just after the Six-Day War. Begin arrived late to the service and Sharon caught a glimpse of him from the car window as the funeral procession was leaving for the cemetery. Begin was just standing there on the sidewalk, "a look of profound grief on his face.

"He did not see me, and I never mentioned it to him afterward, but it was something I never forgot," Sharon said.[18]

There was something about Begin that elicited in Sharon contradictory feelings—awe, fear, and admiration—the same feelings that Sharon's father had instilled in him. Both Begin and Sharon's father, Samuil

Scheinerman, exhibited austere, obsessive, and stubborn personalities. And though Sharon was willful and obsessive in his own way, these two authoritarians triggered deep insecurities that Sharon was loath to explain.[19]

"Begin inspired in me a sort of instinctive fear," Sharon wrote. "I, who had never been frightened of anything, was trembling before the intense willpower that emanated from this slight man."[20]

Sitting in Begin's sparse living room, Sharon appealed to Begin's vanities. He compared Begin to Ben-Gurion as a visionary and intellectual.

Like Ben-Gurion, Begin was "fascinated by the idea of Jewish fighters," Sharon recounted. Both leaders were Polish immigrants who had seen what European militarism had done to the Jews. Both were grateful that, in Israel, the Jews had spawned a generation of warriors.

On Saturday, September 29, Sharon was in Sinai, not as a general but as a Likud campaign manager making a television commercial for use by the party in the election campaign. He had brought along Lily and his sons, Gilad and Omri, for what proved to be a festive Sabbath picnic on the banks of the Suez Canal. The commercial was an attack on the Labor Party and its policies. After Sharon had said his lines for the camera, he and the family spread themselves out on the sand to enjoy lunch.

Sharon could see the Egyptian positions across the canal.

"The Egyptians were working like crazy, adding height to their already towering ramparts just as they had been doing three months before when I last saw them." Sharon recalled that some of the Egyptians looked across at their picnic and "made some gesture at us—a greeting from Egypt," no doubt obscene. Sharon just lay there and looked at the front that was seven days away from full-scale eruption and thought that "even with all the military preparations, it had seemed so peaceful."[21]

After the May war scare, there was a natural tendency to avoid crying wolf again. Ashraf Marwan's reputation as Mossad's superspy had diminished. Dayan had taken to hedging his own predictions. He disparaged the Egyptian army while at the same time stating that war would break out before the end of the year. He once explained to a relative that if he was wrong, people would feel relieved, and if he was right, he would look prescient.[22]

During a meeting with Nicholas Veliotes, an American diplomat in

Israel, Dayan said the Arab armies were like rusting freighters at anchor, "slowly sinking into the sand."[23] When Veliotes had gone to see the Egyptian forces arrayed along the canal, an Israeli general said to him, "If the Egyptians attack, they may cross over at night, but in the morning they will die."

Under Dayan, Israeli intelligence had put a low probability on the chances for war simply because the Arabs knew they could not achieve air superiority over the battlefield, without which they could not overpower Israel's tank forces or take the war to Israel. This became known as Israel's intelligence "concept." The Arabs would not risk another humiliation until they had built up their air power. The chief of military intelligence, Eliahu Zeira, was the strongest adherent of this view, but it was widely shared by Dado Elazar, the chief of staff, and Zvi Zamir, the Mossad chief.

None of them understood Sadat.

The Israelis misinterpreted nearly all of the telltales of the war that was nearly upon them. Up and down the chain of command, Zeira's and Dayan's rigid adherence to the "concept" of Arab inferiority—the lack of air power and those rusting armies sinking into the sand—blinded the country.[24]

Zeira had the authority to activate the bugging device that had been placed at the Egyptian army's headquarters. The device operated on batteries and so its capacity for monitoring for long periods of time was limited. Zeira was asked during those crucial days of late September and early October whether he had turned on the device to determine whether the military exercise called Tahrir 41 that was being planned for the first week of October was indeed an exercise or a cover for a surprise attack. Zeira, unwilling to waste this precious asset, lied to his peers. He said he had turned on the listening device and confirmed that there were no indications of war. He was still clinging to his "conception."[25]

Then came the warning that could not be ignored. On October 5, Ashraf Marwan telephoned his Mossad contact in London and told him that he had just returned from Cairo, where Sadat and Syria's Hafez al-Assad had set the H-hour for a two-front attack at 6:00 p.m. on October 6. Zvi Zamir personally flew to London to question Marwan since so much—again—was riding on a spy's word. They met late in the day on October 5. Zamir became convinced that Marwan was genuine and that war was at hand. Meir did not receive the Mossad report until early the next morning.

As it turned out, Marwan's information was off by four hours. He had left Cairo before the final adjustment in the H-hour was made—from 6:00 p.m. to 2:00 p.m. The two fronts came to life unexpectedly in the early afternoon as Israeli commanders were rushing armored forces forward in a desperate attempt to stanch the onslaught.[26]

When it came, all of the hubris of the Israeli military establishment was swept away. Sadat struck on Yom Kippur, the holiest day of the Jewish calendar, the Day of Atonement. The one-hundred-mile front opened up with one of the most intense artillery assaults in history. The Egyptian air force roared across Sinai, bombing Israeli rear bases. Giant fire hoses, wielded by Egyptian engineers, cut through the Bar-Lev Line.

Israel's military elite had not foreseen the impact of new Russian weapons in the Arab arsenals, especially antitank and antiaircraft weapons with which Egyptians were knocking Israeli Phantoms out of the sky and shattering Israeli tank armor.

The war raged for nearly three weeks as a savage battle of armor, infantry, and air forces.

In the opening forty-eight hours, Dayan performed poorly, arguing with Elazar over whether a total mobilization of the reserves was necessary when it was obvious that it was. Dayan fell into a black mood, fearing that nothing could stop the Egyptian army's advance into Israel and anticipating the collapse of Israeli forces on the Golan Heights. In a meeting with newspaper editors, Dayan warned darkly of the "destruction of the Third Temple." A number of sources have suggested that Meir put Israel's nuclear forces on alert in case the Syrians or Egyptians broke through. Dayan infected so many people with his gloom that Meir forbade him from appearing on television lest his mood incite panic in the country.[27]

On the battlefield, the southern front commander who had succeeded Sharon, Shmuel Gonen, performed so erratically in the opening three days that Meir brought Chaim Bar-Lev back from retirement and put him in Gonen's headquarters to oversee the decision making. The Southern Command was a scene of frayed nerves and bouts of shouting. Gonen's first tactical response to the Egyptian crossing was to order two divisions—

Albert Mandler's and Sharon's—to make lateral attacks along the Egyptian front lines, which was a complete failure. The maneuver left Sharon frustrated and exhausted. Mandler was killed by an Egyptian artillery shell that hit his command vehicle.[28]

Sharon raged against Gonen's whole approach to the front. And Gonen was frantic to control Sharon, who wanted to throw all of the reserve tanks into a desperate and probably suicidal effort to rescue the Israeli defenders in those forty-four fortresses of the Bar-Lev Line. Sharon thought the fortresses should have been evacuated, but there they stood, surrounded by Egyptians. The Israeli soldiers within were fighting for their lives. Many were slaughtered; others surrendered. Everyone who was on the southern front remembered their cries coming over the radio network. Those few who escaped joined the ranks of the deeply embittered after the war.

Israeli losses were heavy, but the army managed after the first week to stop the advance and turn the tide of the battle. That cleared the way for two divisions, one of them commanded by Sharon and one commanded by Avraham "Bren" Adan, to cross the Suez Canal. Once across, Adan's division swung south along the western side of the canal, enveloping the rear area of the Egyptian Third Army, which was dug in on the eastern side. Sharon's division attacked to the north and west toward Ismailia and did not figure in the final drama of encircling the Third Army, though that became part of the mythology of the war.

Meanwhile, on the northern front, where Yitzhak Hofi and Raful Eitan were in command, the clash of armor had brought the Syrian army to within striking distance of the Sea of Galilee region before the Syrian front line began to break and Israeli tanks went on the offensive. The counterattack was a slogging battle that penetrated deep into Syrian territory before it met such fierce resistance that the Israeli forces ground to a halt, unable to close on Damascus.

The Yom Kippur War was a catastrophe that should have been averted, if not by the diplomacy aimed at pushing the armies back from the canal then by a superpower intervention that Leonid Brezhnev had proposed to Nixon at San Clemente. Israel's military elite had been hoist on its own illusions and rigidities. It had failed to analyze Sadat in depth and refused to believe that an Arab leader, for the first time since 1949, was honestly talking about long-term peace with Israel. Here the legacy of Ben-Gurion, the militaristic state that lived apart from the Arabs, was blinded by a martial impulse and a false intelligence "conception" of the enemy, all of which undermined any diplomatic strategy toward accommodation or peace. Sharett had admonished his countrymen to keep the question of peace at the forefront of national focus, but Meir had led the country into an orthodoxy obsessed with the fruits of war.

Only in one sense was it Meir's finest hour: the stubborn and doctrinaire party apparatchik, age seventy-five, suffering from cancer and heart disease, held together the military establishment even though centrifugal forces were pulling it apart. She overcame Dayan's misjudgment and gloom, she strengthened the Southern Command leadership, and she managed to give Sharon—already known as the commander of the "Likud division"—enough leash to perform while constraining his most counterproductive impulses. And she handled Israel's erratic ally—the Americans—as well as anyone could by taking Kissinger's advice most of the time but by going around him to Nixon and to Congress when he failed to deliver as rapidly as promised on the resupply of weapons and munitions. But her performance notwithstanding, Meir, in so many ways, had barred the door to negotiation and compromise that might have prevented it all.[29]

Israelis were psychologically devastated by the war, which in only nineteen days killed nearly three thousand soldiers and wounded thousands more. The pace and intensity of combat surpassed all previous wars. Even the battle-hardened Sharon wrote that he had witnessed scenes of battle and death that had numbed the senses unlike anything he had seen before. All of the tales of missed warnings, poor preparations, and miscalculation of enemy weapons and tactics came home with an embittered army. The disillusionment washed into the parliamentary election campaign of December 1973.

Within the Labor coalition, Dayan led the militarist camp and still had the support of a significant portion of the political establishment, though he was the last one to fully grasp how rapidly the rank and file—and therefore the public—was turning against him. The hero of Suez and the Six-Day War, who had scoffed at Arab capabilities, afterward showed no remorse whatsoever for having led the country to believe that the Arabs would not attack. He was unwilling to accept any responsibility.

Instead, Dayan exuded his customary glib bravado, which now rang hollow to all of those still in shock. In the wake of the cease-fire, Dayan postured himself as eager to go back on the attack. He threatened to re-start the war, using any Egyptian cease-fire violation as a provocation. He wanted to destroy the Third Army and achieve a more demonstrable vic-tory given all the costs of the war, especially to his reputation. And here Dayan's hypermilitarism ran afoul of Meir, who opted to conduct face-to-face negotiations with the Egyptians at Kilometer 101 on the Cairo-Suez Highway. Meir wanted prisoners of war repatriated quickly. The families of those being held constituted a powerful political force on the eve of elections.

General Israel Tal, the flinty sabra who had been Israel's premier strat-egist of tank warfare, was put in charge of the southern front, where Sha-ron and the other frontline generals had stayed in place in case combat resumed. Tal attended the cabinet session where Meir and a majority of ministers decided to keep the front quiet so negotiations could commence. Nonetheless, afterward Dayan issued orders to frontline forces to open fire if provoked. Tal countermanded Dayan's order and reportedly asked Dayan directly, "Has the government's policy changed since we were both present at the cabinet meeting that decided to keep the area quiet?"

"Leave the government to me," Dayan snapped, implying that as de-fense minister, he was in charge of interpreting the cabinet's decision.

But Tal would not accept it. "If that's what you have to say, then my com-mander is the chief of staff—from him I take orders and not from you."[30]

Meir also was plagued by dissent. Protesters followed her wherever she went. They camped outside her home and office. Their ranks included fam-ily members of dead and wounded soldiers. They called for her resignation or shouted, "Murderer!" One of the surviving officers from the Bar-Lev Line, Motti Ashkenazi, who had commanded the northernmost strong-hold, called Budapest, the only one that had not fallen to the Egyptians, planted himself in front of the prime minister's office through the cold weeks of winter, calling on her to take responsibility. He held up a sign saying, "Grandma, your defense minister is a failure and 3,000 of your grandchild-ren are dead."[31]

Dayan was the focus of even stronger protests.

Meir determined that she had to keep Dayan in the Labor tent and be-lieved she could prevail one last time because the electorate was not ready to put an extremist like Begin into the prime minister's chair.

She skillfully put off the reckoning over the war by appointing a commission of inquiry headed by Shimon Agranat, the president of Israel's Supreme Court. The appointment meant that an official verdict would take months of examination of testimony in secret before the results were published.

David Ben-Gurion died on December 1, 1973, at age eighty-seven, and Israelis went to the polls on December 31. They voted the Labor Party back into office, but with a thin plurality. The right-wing coalition that Begin and Sharon put together increased its representation from 32 to 39 seats (out of 120).

The one thing Meir did that showed she was thinking ahead was to bring Rabin home from Washington. She made him minister of labor, which put him in a holding pattern for higher office. Rabin was now a unique figure—a military hero untarnished by the Yom Kippur War.

Meir's wounded government set a record for brevity, for when the Agranat Commission published its interim report on April 1, 1974, the country erupted in recriminations over its findings. The commission blamed only the uniformed army officers—the chief of staff and the director of military intelligence and some of their subordinates—for all of the failures and miscalculations. Agranat absolved Meir, Dayan, and all the civilian authorities of any blame. The verdict deeply offended the military elite and much of Israeli society, which understood that the cabinet was at the top of the chain of command whether or not it was written down. Who other than Dayan had arrogated to himself decisions to attack Syria and seize the Golan Heights in 1967? Who visited the front constantly and gave orders as if he still was a general? If Dayan was not responsible for creating the aura of security from 1971 to 1973, who was?

Generals Elazar and Zeira may have shared the blame for unforgivable miscalculations, but in Israel, where leaders—military and civilian—are judged on how they take responsibility for failure, the Agranat Commission results seemed a massive breach of faith.

"After 1973, everything we had thought of him [Dayan] fell like a house of cards because he didn't take the responsibility," said Muki Betser. "I was never in battle with Moshe Dayan. I was a child. But what a soldier remembers from the battlefield is the behavior of his commander under fire."[32]

Dayan failed the test. Ben-Gurion was gone, unable to deflect the blow or rescue Dayan's reputation. Dayan refused to heed the grassroots calls for his resignation. That left only Meir to bring down the government herself—forcing Dayan and the entire cabinet to resign—for the good of the country.

No one knew how sick Meir actually was. Each day she rose before dawn to slip into Hadassah Hospital for cobalt treatments against the cancer she was still battling. On April 10, ten days after the Agranat explosion, she stood before party leaders wearing a plain black coat and looked out at them with an implacable gaze and said that five years was enough.

"It is beyond my strength to continue carrying this burden. I don't belong to any circle or faction within the party. I have only a circle of one to consult, myself. And this time my decision is final, irrevocable."[33]

Didactic in surrender, Meir knew that the party kingmakers would orchestrate a succession that would appeal to the rank and file, one that was based on a softer, pro-American Zionism that avoided contentious words like "annexation" but that accomplished the same thing. She felt that she had saved the party from Ben-Gurion, from Dayan and, she hoped, from Peres. She would let the others—the sabras—sort out the rest.

NINE

Rabin: From General to Prime Minister

In Israel, the harshest impact of the war came afterward. Israel became a land of funeral processions.

Ben-Gurion had died in the immediate aftermath of battle, as if to lead the dead to the cemetery. Crowds of Israelis—European Jews from eastern Europe; Oriental Jews from Morocco, Yemen, and Iraq; soldiers, students, and sabras young and old filed past his flag-draped coffin on Knesset Hill in Jerusalem, two hundred thousand in all by the official estimate.

One old man in shabby clothes with stubble on his face planted himself in front of Ben-Gurion's casket and fought off the guards who tried to move him along.

"Don't push me. I knew this man!"

The guards withdrew and the man stood frozen in the shuffling throng, speaking occasionally to the dead leader, and after a quarter hour, he waved one hand toward Ben-Gurion's bier and said, "Shalom," before turning to leave.[1]

The country seemed draped in black.

Throughout 1974, the bodies of soldiers released by the army or retrieved from battlefields months after the end of the war were still coming home. Many of the grievously wounded succumbed to their injuries. Amputees walked stoically on the beaches, nursing psychological and physical wounds.

Over nearly three decades, the sabras had sought to make Israel an unrivaled military power, and they had succeeded, but all Israelis faced the consequences.

As if the gloom were not deep enough, a month before Yitzhak Rabin presented his government to the Knesset, a squad of Arab militants dressed in Israeli army uniforms sneaked through a wildlife refuge on the northern border and burst into a village, shooting their way up a hill and taking over an elementary school at Ma'alot. When Israeli commandos tried to storm the building the next day, the militants triggered explosives and opened fire, killing twenty-five children and wounding more than sixty.

Capturing the sense of despair, Rabin rose in parliament in June 1974 to say, "Something has happened to this country since the Yom Kippur War. Even though we scored one of our greatest victories in that war, many of us have deeply troubled hearts."[2]

"We must shake off our despondency," he said in a rising voice. He told the Israelis that if they looked around, they were not doomed to a vale of tears. Their cause was still just and their strength growing.

But the words failed to rouse so many whose sons or daughters had come home in coffins.

Richard Nixon also arrived in Israel during Rabin's first month in office on what proved to be a farewell tour. Huge crowds had greeted him in Egypt, and Israelis turned out to show their gratitude to the president who had resupplied them with arms during the war. For Rabin, the association with Nixon was no longer the boon it had been because Nixon was so heavily marked at home for impeachment or resignation.

During Nixon's visit, the public learned that the United States had discussed assisting Egypt in the peaceful uses of atomic energy. Rabin privately expressed his anxieties to Nixon, who reassured him that any sharing of nuclear technology would be accompanied by safeguards ensuring that no fissile material could be diverted to a military program. Nonetheless, Menachem Begin brought a motion of no confidence against Rabin's government, accusing Rabin of showing an "irresponsible and light-hearted" attitude about a possible effort by Egypt to acquire atomic weapons.[3]

The measure failed by only ten votes. It was an inauspicious beginning.

Yitzhak Rabin had a simple and familiar persona. He stood without pretense as a sabra son of Israel, into whose experienced hands the Israelis seemed ready to entrust themselves after five years of near constant warfare.

He had no discernible political skills, much less any charisma. He had not joined Ben-Gurion's party as a young officer. His military career had started in the Palmach, which Ben-Gurion had held against him.

Yet while Rabin may have been dull and introverted, a hard drinker with an explosive temper, and overall not well suited to politics, he possessed the most important qualification of all: he had been out of uniform during the disastrous failures of the Yom Kippur War.

Meir and the party stalwarts were not wild for Rabin. He was cautious, though this was now an asset. They remembered his mother fondly as a committed Socialist revolutionary from Russia and a labor Zionist. And putting their weight behind him was the best way for the old guard to prevent Peres from ascending and thus providing a pathway for Dayan to worm his way back to power.

Rabin was not without political ambition. After all, he had parlayed his role in the Six-Day War to become Israel's envoy to Washington, a high-profile political posting that had introduced him to Nixon's inner circle and also to many world leaders and media barons. He may not have been as politically astute, or as glib, as Peres, but he had the one thing that Peres would never have: military heft.

Though Rabin came out unblemished in the wake of the Agranat Commission's indictment of wartime mismanagement, Peres also was emboldened to throw his hat into the political ring as soon as Meir announced her resignation. Over the next two weeks, Peres lobbied more than 400 members of the Labor Party central committee, whose 560 delegates would choose the next prime minister.

The Peres camp hoped it could overcome the party's bias for Rabin and, in the midst of the intense April campaign, Weizman surfaced with the secret that he hoped would sink Rabin: he revealed that the former chief of staff had suffered a nervous breakdown in the critical days leading up to the Six-Day War.

For six years Weizman had been sitting on this bombshell. Among the few people to whom Weizman had confided his secret was Dayan, who had encouraged him to write a detailed memo on the episode and keep it in his desk drawer for the right moment.

Weizman's motivation was transparent. First, he and Peres were friends, but more important, Weizman was bitter that Rabin and the Labor stalwarts had not seen fit to make him chief of staff, the job to which he felt entitled.

Rabin had humiliated him on the eve of the 1967 War by inserting Bar-Lev in the chain of command above Weizman. Passed over for chief of staff, Weizman had resigned and joined Begin's right-wing Gahal bloc, but he had failed to find a satisfying role in national politics. Rabin's sudden emergence as the leading candidate to become prime minister incited Weizman's impulse for revenge.

What followed was not a proud moment in Israeli politics. Weizman went secretly to Pinhas Sapir, the Labor kingmaker, and told him that unless Sapir threw the party's support behind Peres, the story of Rabin's collapse would explode in the press. The naked attempt at extortion convinced Sapir that Rabin was the right man to lead the country, assuming he survived the onslaught.[4]

When Rabin got word that the story was about to break, he called his family doctor to preview what he would say; the doctor assured him that he would describe the incident as a case of acute exhaustion that required a sedative and a long sleep. Rabin tried and failed to convince the newspapers to hold off, but when the story hit, a number of commanders from the Six-Day War, including Sharon, came forward with testimonials that blunted the negative tide that Weizman—and Peres—hoped would sweep Rabin out of the race.

Meir denounced the personal attack. Rabin had figured he was ahead of Peres by one hundred votes in the central committee before the story broke. But in the event, Rabin's margin tanked: he won by forty-four votes.

Lacking the mandate of a general election, Rabin entered office as a political weakling in a climate still marked by postwar anger and disillusionment. If there was any spark to his premiership it was that he was the first native-born Israeli—the first sabra—to step into Ben-Gurion's shoes. And he was the first military man to take the political helm. He stood where Dayan had long lusted to stand, where Peres and Weizman believed they deserved to be, and where Sharon had begun to imagine himself. Rabin was no Ben-Gurion. He had worried himself into a state of collapse in 1967, but most Israelis also knew that even Ben-Gurion had taken to his sickbed in times of war.

The military establishment had never welcomed a prime minister so committed to its interests. Rabin saw his most important task as rebuilding the army and its arsenal. But the greatest liability with which Rabin started his political career was that he was forced to accept Peres as his defense minister. Otherwise Peres and the remnant of the Rafi Party would bolt the Labor coalition, which could not afford to lose a single vote in parliament.

Nothing epitomized Rabin's political fragility as much as this decision to appoint Peres to defense instead of Yigal Allon, the former Palmach commander who was like an older brother to Rabin. Having Peres at the top of the military establishment was like a snake against Rabin's breast.

When it came to Peres, Rabin was irrationally dismissive of and paranoid about the "service avoider" in his cabinet; when it came to Rabin, Peres was a Machiavellian out to remove the cautious dolt who did not deserve, in Peres's view, to be prime minister.

Peres was a master leaker, a skill that Rabin had only begun to develop, and Peres's long years as a Ben-Gurion understudy had given him a strategic outlook that equaled Rabin's education under Nixon and Kissinger. If they had been able to overcome their rivalry, Rabin and Peres would have been a formidable duo and could have avoided the inestimable damage their competition inflicted on the party and on the country. But they could not.

Rabin made sure that Israel maintained its militarist outlook. Rabin was no breath of fresh air in these years, and Meir was looking over his shoulder. The real question was whether Rabin could become a viable politician. He lacked Meir's skill at both oratory and party discipline. He believed in a long struggle with the Arabs, whom he did not trust or well understand. He lived and breathed the concept of military deterrence as it had been handed down by Ben-Gurion and Dayan. In that sense, Rabin, Peres, Dayan, and Allon were all variations on the same theme. In truth, it seemed to many Israelis that their philosophy had been vindicated by the long fight with Egypt and Syria, but few of them knew the full story of the opportunities that had been lost to engage the Arabs. So they followed the party line: superior arms and the certainty of retaliation—disproportionate retaliation—were essential to prevent Arab aggression.

In forming his cabinet, Rabin pushed aside Abba Eban, the last of Sharett's brain trust, a formidable voice for Israel in international affairs and the last one left in the cabinet to stand up for diplomatic principles. Eban's success was in large part due to his ability to conjure a heroic narrative for the Jewish state. For most of his career, he had been able to read Ben-Gurion's mind and to align himself with the political winds at home, but from 1967 onward, he was out of sync with the military elite. His greatest sin was to have labored so intensely in 1967 to prevent war when war was the very thing the sabras had wanted.[5]

Rabin gave the Foreign Ministry to Yigal Allon and offered Eban the Ministry of Information, knowing that Eban would reject it, thus paving the way for the exit of one of Israel's most experienced statesmen, one who might have been useful to an inexperienced prime minister.

The orthodoxy of Israel's military establishment baffled Gerald Ford, who succeeded Nixon in August 1974 and who had worked earnestly over two decades to support Israel and the American efforts to bring peace to the Middle East.

"For the past 25 years, the philosophical underpinning of U.S. policy toward Israel had been our conviction—and certainly my own—that if we gave Israel an ample supply of economic aid and weapons, she would feel strong and confident, more flexible and more willing to discuss a lasting peace." But after four wars, Ford continued, "I began to question the rationale for our policy."[6]

After Nixon's resignation, Ford promptly urged Rabin to get more active on the peace front.

The new American president tried and failed to persuade the Israelis to consider a broad engagement of the Arabs, starting with Sadat, who was more than ready for bold diplomacy. If anything, Sadat was desperate, though he always managed to project a kind of imperial serenity by puffing on his pipe and arranging himself on an elegant lawn under jacaranda trees to meet visiting dignitaries such as Kissinger. But in reality, Cairo had become the Calcutta of North Africa, with millions of Egyptians slipping deeper into poverty. After the 1973 war, hailed in Cairo as a great victory, the Egyptian leader styled himself as the "Hero of the Crossing," but as peace failed to deliver either prosperity or the return of lands, the admonishment heard on the street was "Hero of the Crossing, where is our breakfast?"[7]

Sadat was gambling that only the Americans could apply the pressure needed to dislodge Israel from Arab lands. He supported Ford's activism and hoped that he could push the Americans beyond Kissinger's "shuttle" diplomacy to making a commitment for a full Israeli withdrawal.

"We do not ask the Americans to abandon Israel," Sadat told an interviewer, but he insisted that the Americans come to some definition of what they meant by "Israel." Was it Israel as it existed in 1967? If so, Sadat was ready to do business. But if America accepted the lines of conquest in Sinai, Golan, and the West Bank, there was going to be another war.[8]

Unfortunately, the politically timid Rabin wrapped himself in the party's orthodoxy. He said repeatedly that Israel would never return to the 1967 borders, not just because he believed it, but because to say otherwise would trigger a rebuke from Meir or a challenge from Peres. To President Ford, Rabin absurdly argued that insecure borders had been the cause of the Six-Day War. And he refused to withdraw beyond the strategic passes of central Sinai—Mitla and Gidi—or give up the Abu Rudeis oil field unless Egypt signed a "nonbelligerency" pledge as part of a second disengagement agreement.

Sadat steadfastly refused and, when Ford and Kissinger threatened Rabin with a broad "reassessment" of U.S.-Israeli relations, a step that might freeze the delivery of $2.5 billion in arms and economic aid, Rabin activated Israel's defenders in the U.S. Senate, where seventy-six members signed a letter to Ford demanding full support for Israel. Ford and Kissinger caved, and the disengagement agreement was signed in September 1975, paving the way for a reopening of the Suez Canal but leaving most of Sinai still in Israeli hands.

The Americans believed that peace might also be possible between Israel and Jordan. King Hussein had stayed out of the 1973 war, and in its aftermath, the Palestinians on the West Bank were more restive than ever.

Kissinger had told Rabin that he could deal with King Hussein now or with Yasser Arafat later, because it was clear that Palestinian nationalism was gathering momentum.

The problem was that Rabin had little to offer Hussein. Jordan's army had lost the West Bank and East Jerusalem in 1967. The king was demanding that Israel return every inch of it. Even if Rabin had wanted to be accommodating, he was blocked internally. He was trying to coax the National Religious Party—with its 10 Knesset seats—to join his governing coalition, which had a razor-thin majority of 61 seats out of 120. The NRP vehemently opposed any concessions to Jordan over the West Bank and Gaza.

Rabin, like Meir, considered himself a Jordanist. He favored a solution under which the Palestinians lived under limited self-rule in a federation with Jordan. Rabin was a realist about power: the Palestinians had none and, in his view, they would eventually have to accept the Jordan option.

A new settler insurgency—largely religious and awakened by the victory of 1967—showed its first anarchic tendencies under Rabin, a conspicuously nonreligious man like many of his generation who looked askance at the religious establishment. Religious parties, infused with money and immigrants—many eventually from the United States—forged alliances with secular leaders as diverse as Sharon and Peres, creating an insurgent force in Israeli society whose goal was to stampede politicians, the army, and the government to establish a broad new landscape of settlement for millions of Jews. The messianic theme of this would-be citizen army had always lain dormant in Jewish life: that God willed the return of the Jews to the lands of biblical Israel as a means to advance the appearance of the Messiah and the Day of Judgment.

And so they came, tens of thousands of new settlers responding to faith and large cash advances from the government and from Hasidic communities around Jerusalem and, eventually, from as far away as Brooklyn and Queens, New York.

Religion had a place in Jewish culture and tradition, but Rabin believed the rabbis should devote themselves to spiritual affairs.

After Rabin had worked so diligently to coax the National Religious Party into his coalition, a settler group known as the Bloc of the Faithful—Gush Emunim—chose that moment to rush into the West Bank and establish the first illegal settlement at an abandoned Ottoman railway station in Sebastia. Prominent members of the Knesset, including Menachem Begin, accompanied the settlers and cheered their defiance of the government. But what infuriated Rabin was Peres egging them on with public statements

such as "The hills of Samaria are no less lofty than the hills of Golan"—
meaning that the military establishment supported Gush Emunim.[9]

Rabin ordered the military to remove the settlers, but after a series of
confrontations, the chief of staff, Mordechai Gur, balked. He refused to
send the army against them.

Motta Gur was a national hero, having helped to liberate Jerusalem in
1967. Rabin had never imagined that Gur would take a political stand in
the face of an order from his prime minister, but there it was.

Removing the settlers would result in bloodshed, Gur argued; his soldiers might disobey their orders; it would be a disaster for the army and
the country. He implied that if Rabin insisted on his order, he would
resign.[10]

In the face of Gur's opposition, Rabin relented, allowing a compromise
for the Sebastia settlers. They could relocate a short distance away to a
military camp, where they built their houses and schools and laid their
perimeter of concertina wire. It was the first step in a long tragedy of illegal colonization that carried through the ensuing decades, bringing bulldozers and hundreds of thousands of Jews into occupied Palestinian lands
to create a new set of facts on the ground and establish a base of resistance
to Palestinian statehood.

Years later, Rabin justified his decisions by telling an interviewer that
his actions would have been "entirely different" if he had only had a stronger Labor majority. "I don't believe that any prime minister in the past has
had to act with such a narrow margin, or been so dependent on a coalition
among parties that are not close to the mainstream of Labor government
as I have been," he said.[11]

Here was the rationalization that Rabin and his successors employed to
excuse their failure: politicians had no choice; it was either indulge the
settlement binge and protect it with a colonizing military spirit, or confront the religious parties and risk the collapse of government, new elections, and the prospect of extremists coming to power under Begin.

All of this frustrated Rabin and exacerbated his rivalry with Peres.
Their tension exploded during a trip to Washington in January 1976 when
Rabin accused Peres of adding outlandish items to Israel's shopping list of
weapons.

Rabin called Peres's list "exaggerated and pretentious" because it included a spy satellite system equal to those of the superpowers. At a gath-

ering of Israeli reporters across from the White House, Rabin stepped up to the microphone trembling with fury.

"Peres is sabotaging my visit," he exclaimed. Rabin said he had been forced to scale back Israel's request in the face of awkward questions from Congress.

"He does this on purpose!" Rabin accused. Some journalists thought he was drunk.

"The president and secretary of state will laugh at me," he continued. "I'm going back to Israel and I am going to throw him out."[12]

Though he later retracted his statements, those close to Rabin understood that he was not bearing up under the pressure of office and was near the breaking point with Peres.[13]

To humiliate his rival, Rabin brought Sharon in as a military adviser, diminishing Peres's role as defense minister.[14]

In truth, Rabin needed sound military advice. Lebanon was disintegrating into civil war. In early 1976, Christian militia forces had laid siege to Palestinian refugee camps and slaughtered PLO fighters. PLO forces retaliated against Christian villages in the south. The Arab world was up in arms over the plight of Palestinians and the fate of Lebanon. Arab leaders, with the blessing of the Ford administration, authorized the Syrian army in May to intervene in Lebanon and restore calm. Sharon had tried to convince Rabin to oppose Syria's move because, he argued, once Syria established itself as the dominant force in Lebanon, it would never willingly leave.

But Rabin was too cautious to go to war against Syria over a police action that much of the world supported. Still, he knew there would be consequences. The arrival of the Syrian army would push the PLO guerrilla armies farther south toward the Israeli frontier.

The PLO was profiting from Lebanon's disintegration.

Arafat's guerrilla army had acquired tanks and artillery, and West Beirut bristled with weapons. The Palestinian cause was gaining recognition. Arafat had traveled to New York in November 1974 to address the United Nations General Assembly.

"I am a rebel and freedom is my cause," Arafat told the delegates from more than a hundred countries. "I know well that many of you present here today once stood in exactly the same resistance position as I now occupy and from which I must fight. You once had to convert dreams into reality by your struggle. Therefore you must now share my dream."[15]

Support for the PLO in the West Bank and Gaza was increasing. Local elections brought to power a generation of mayors openly sympathetic to the PLO. Peres had encouraged the elections, arguing that new, more pragmatic leaders would emerge, but he was wrong. Jacob Peri, the Shabak division chief for the West Bank, said that every Friday when he reported to Rabin on developments in the Palestinian territories, Rabin would flush at the mention of Peres's name: "He would call to his aides to bring whiskey," Peri recalled.[16]

Arafat's ministate in Lebanon was antagonizing Maronite Christian leaders who had governed the country in delicate balance with the Sunni, Shiite, and Druze populations since 1943. Lebanon's civil war offered Israel the first opportunity for a regional power play since the 1950s.

Ben-Gurion had dreamed of a "minority alliance" with Lebanon—Jews and Christians staving off Syrian power and PLO influence on Israel's northern border. Dayan had spoken of the need to "purchase" the right Lebanese politician or military man to begin building such an alliance.

No one fell harder for this vision than David Kimche, a senior Mossad division chief.[17]

Kimche was a tall and erudite spy. Born in Britain and educated at the Sorbonne in Paris, he had come to Israel at age eighteen to fight in the War of Independence. Afterward, he had joined Mossad under Isser Harel and built an espionage career across Africa, Europe, and the Middle East. His cover name was David Sharon, and as a young agent, he had traveled clandestinely to northern Iraq to meet Mulla Mustafa Barzani, the Kurdish chieftain, and helped organize the training of his *peshmerga* forces that led the rebellion against Baghdad in the early 1970s. Every subsequent Israeli spy chief had promoted Kimche, and by the mid-1970s he was a contender to succeed Yitzhak Hofi as Mossad director.

Kimche had come to the conclusion that Lebanon's Maronite Christian clans were the natural enemy of Arafat's ministate, which had overplayed its hand by trying to act like a regular army. "As the military infrastructure of the PLO grew in strength, it became increasingly clear to Israel's political and defense establishment that [Israel's] army sooner or later would destroy it," he said.[18]

These were the years when no member of the military or intelligence elite could concede the existence of Palestinian nationalism as anything other than a threat, so any expression of it was targeted for destruction.

As an expert practitioner of espionage and secret diplomacy, Kimche saw the opportunity to revive Ben-Gurion's dream of the Israeli-Christian alliance by offering the Christians a chance to engage the Jewish state as "the enemy of my enemy . . ." Kimche's enthusiasm infected or was shared by senior leaders, among them Peres, Allon, Weizman and, eventually, Begin and Sharon.

Camille Chamoun, the former Lebanese president, and Pierre Gemayel were two of the leading Christian patriarchs. Kimche had built a close relationship with Gemayel's youngest son, Bashir, who was helping his father build a strong militia under the right-wing Phalange Party, founded in the 1940s. Kimche believed that Bashir had the brains, the charisma, and the brutality to prevail in Lebanon.

In February 1976, Peres was the first to bring the Christian leaders secretly to Tel Aviv for a lavish dinner at his home. There, he toasted Dany Chamoun (Camille's son) and young Bashir, exhorting them as sons of Lebanon to consolidate their power at home and to regard Israel as an ally.[19]

Rabin was notably absent from the dinner. A few days earlier, Israel's largest daily newspaper, *Yedioth Ahronoth*, reported that tension between Rabin and Peres was disrupting almost every government meeting. Peres's initiative on Lebanon forced the methodical Rabin to call for a review of Israeli policy. He dispatched a Mossad and military intelligence team under Colonel Binyamin Ben-Eliezer to Beirut to meet with the major Christian clans and assess their reliability as potential allies, their military needs, and their ambition.

What the team discovered was the murderous rivalry among the Christians, a profoundly atavistic brutality. Camille Chamoun, who had been the Lebanese president when President Eisenhower had sent the marines to secure the country against Nasser's subversion, invited Ben-Eliezer to step into the garden of his villa to inspect a group of female fighters. To Ben-Eliezer's surprise, the women produced plastic bags filled with human fingers and ears—"trophies" that they had sliced off the corpses of their Palestinian victims.[20] The Maronite clan leaders said they were willing to put their personal rivalries aside and unite, but there were many doubters. In Israel's military establishment, Christian unity seemed a chimera to those who knew the fierce competition among the clans for territory and for the smuggling and import trade on which each prospered. There were many other questions. Would they refuse to make peace with Israel, as Sharett had warned Ben-Gurion many years earlier?

Most important: Were they simply trying to induce Israel to fight their war?

When Ben-Eliezer returned to Tel Aviv, Rabin presided over a special meeting of the military establishment along with Peres and Allon. Gur represented the military and Hofi the intelligence agencies. Ben-Eliezer presented a realistic assessment of the treacherous landscape of Lebnon. The consensus was that it might be worthwhile to provide training and arms to the Christians as a way to encourage Christian unity and to build up an alternative power base as the Lebanese army continued to dis-integrate.

Hofi, the battle-tested general whose judgment Rabin trusted most in the Mossad hierarchy, cautioned strongly against Israeli intervention in the Lebanese morass. The Christian clans were notoriously unreliable and brutish. Hofi believed they would try to drag Israel into war with Syria so they could profit from the outcome. They showed little leadership outside their own enclave in Lebanon's central mountains, where each clan had been fiercely guarding its turf for centuries.

Out of this review came Rabin's policy of helping the Christians to help themselves, but he was determined to keep Israel out of the Lebanese civil war and to prevent a confrontation with Syria. Yet that was not the end of it. Kimche took the decision by Rabin's government as a victory. Mossad began sending arms to Christian Beirut under Hofi's tight constraints.

It was in the midst of this initial ferment over Lebanon that a dramatic hijacking unfolded. Palestinian and West German militants seized an Air France flight from Tel Aviv to Paris on June 27, 1976, throwing the Rabin government into turmoil over the fate of 248 passengers and crew, many of them Israelis.

The Airbus A300 was seized in Athens and diverted to Libya before it landed at Entebbe airport in Uganda, where the hijackers placed themselves under the protection of the dictator, Idi Amin, and demanded the release from prison of more than fifty of their comrades. During the seven days of high tension that followed, the Israeli military establishment functioned under the enormous static of the Rabin-Peres power struggle.

In the first twenty-four hours, Peres and Rabin argued over whether Peres was derelict in failing to order up a viable rescue plan. Peres criticized Rabin for suggesting that Israel might surrender to the demands of the hijackers in order to win freedom for the hostages. When Peres's posturing in the cabinet session became intolerable, Rabin snapped, "Our problem at the moment is not rhetoric. If you have a better proposal, go ahead! What do you suggest?"[21]

Peres had no immediate plan. But from the first report of the hijacking, Muki Betser, the Sayeret Matkal deputy commander, had gone into action. Betser was in charge that week because his thirty-year-old boss, Jonathan Netanyahu, was on a highly secretive mission to penetrate the Egyptian zone in Sinai, presumably to plant new listening devices that would serve as early warning against an Egyptian surprise attack.

Netanyahu's mission was judged too important to call off, and so Dan Shomron, the paratroop commander who oversaw Sayeret Matkal, appointed Ehud Barak to reassume command of the unit and prepare for a rescue. Barak's appointment did not last long; it rang like a vote of no confidence in the unit's existing command. Barak was soon dispatched to Kenya to manage the advance reconnaissance for a possible raid. Much of the planning for Entebbe was inspired by Betser's experience in Uganda, where he and other Israeli officers had trained Idi Amin's commando forces.

The Air France hostages were being held in the old British-built terminal at the airport. Betser thought that the obvious way to make an approach was to put a black Mercedes on the tarmac—the kind that Amin used—and fill it with men with guns. The sentries would simply think that Amin was making a late-night inspection.

The unit had only days to refine a plan, and General Gur, the chief of staff, told the cabinet that the military would not go ahead with a rescue unless he was sure that it would succeed. Mossad agents flew a small plane close enough to the Entebbe airport to get good photos of the layout and defenses, and the team devised a flight path to send the unit into Entebbe on C130 military transports that would follow closely behind a commercial airliner, dropping down at the far end of the airport. There, the unit would offload a black Mercedes and chase car. Paratroopers would block any Ugandan reinforcements while also blowing up thirty Soviet-made jets of the Ugandan air force.

"We knew the control tower was a sensitive spot," Betser recalled. Its five stories loomed over the airport with a squad of Ugandan soldiers perched on its balcony with machine guns. Those guns represented the greatest threat to the attacking force. For that reason, surprise was crucial. Imitating an approach by Idi Amin's staff car should have done the trick.[22]

The only mistake in the operation proved to be Netanyahu's—and it was fatal. He had barely made the Entebbe team after emerging from his secret mission in Sinai. Now, as the Mercedes was crossing the tarmac, a lone Ugandan sentry stood in the middle of the sea of concrete, and when the black sedan and chase car approached, the sentry snapped to attention and shouted out for the car to declare itself.

"Cut to the right and we'll finish him off," Netanyahu said into his headset.

"Leave it, Yoni," Betser said emphatically. "It's just his drill." Betser knew the protocols of the Ugandan army. The sentry challenge was like a salute. If the Mercedes roared past, the sentry would just resume his position.

There was only an instant to decide. Netanyahu wanted to shoot the sentry. Betser refused, not taking time to explain. So Netanyahu fired his weapon, not thinking what the effect would be on the machine gun nest they were approaching.

The sentry went down, but soon the night erupted with gunfire and panic as the Sayeret Matkal team arrived under fire. One soldier took a bullet in the spine that would paralyze him for life. The Israelis returned fire on the control tower and finally silenced it; Betser led the force inside the building, where the militants were quickly killed, along with an Israeli who jumped up at the wrong moment.

The world would judge the raid an amazing success, another feat of Israeli daring and bravado, but within the military, the tragedy that was felt most deeply was Netanyahu's fatal mistake. He had taken a bullet in the neck from the control tower and was dead by the time they got him back to the C130 for the long ride home.

Netanyahu's error in judgment remained a secret until Betser revealed it in 1996 in a war memoir, which was roundly criticized by members of

Netanyahu's family and by others who felt that Betser had tarnished the dead hero of the Entebbe raid.[23] The damage of Betser's revelation, in Israeli terms, had to be judged not just as the unfortunate disclosure that revealed a very human error that can occur in any complex military operation but also as a political threat to the Netanyahu political brand, which was on the ascent. Netanyahu's father harbored political ambitions for his second son, Bibi, who had followed his brother into Sayeret Matkal.

Over the next two decades, no one traded on Jonathan's legend as the hero of Entebbe more than Bibi. He established The Jonathan Institute on terrorism and published a carefully edited book of his brother's letters, which Herman Wouk described as a "remarkable work of literature."

Rabin had told his wife when the planes had taken off for Entebbe that "tomorrow morning—either Israel's shares will be sky high, or I will be hanged in Kikar Medina [the public square]." But the huge success incited Peres to make a grand play for the credit. He sent his spokesman out to say that Rabin had consistently opposed military action and it was due only to his own efforts that the government decided to attempt the dramatic rescue.[24]

Despite Rabin's cautious stewardship, his premiership was failing.

The arrival of the first four American-made F-15 Eagles in December 1976 turned into a political disaster when the planes flew in on a Friday evening, the eve of the Sabbath. Speeches ran late. Not all members of the audience reached their homes before sundown. This minor violation of the Sabbath had meaning only for the small religious parties that were part of Rabin's governing coalition. Suddenly, an ultra-Orthodox group that controlled two Knesset seats in Rabin's coalition entered a motion of no confidence, citing the "desecration of the Sabbath." A no-confidence vote requires the prime minister's coalition to muster all of its votes to defend itself, but the National Religious Party ministers abstained. Rabin could not tolerate the breach of discipline: they were undermining the government in which they were serving. He fired them and called for elections. Here was an opportunity, Rabin calculated, to throw the religious right and its smothering agenda out of his government and, with new elections, broaden the mandate of the Labor Party by regaining seats that had been lost to the right-wing parties.[25]

But the Israeli electorate was in a churlish mood. Menachem Begin put Ezer Weizman in charge of the Likud campaign. Sharon was stalking the political outskirts, looking for a path to power. Likud prepared for a strong nationalistic campaign, gathering a phalanx of sabra war heroes, Irgun hard-liners, and religious zealots all coming together to promise better government, better housing, and a better economy. They made a strong appeal to the "dispossessed"—the Yemeni, Moroccan, and Iraqi Jews seething with grievances against the Ashkenazi elite who had dominated the country since its establishment.

Rabin's political advisers were frustrated by his prickly insouciance. He had always traded on his strong ties to America, but the luster faded when it became known that he had used the military censor to squelch the publication of a book unflattering to Henry Kissinger. Rabin no longer seemed a paragon of virtue. His central bank appointee, Asher Yadlin, was on trial for taking kickbacks totaling hundreds of thousands of dollars, and the housing minister, Avraham Ofer, under investigation for embezzlement, had driven to a Tel Aviv beach in January 1977 where he committed suicide with a revolver. If that was not enough, inflation was running at 35 percent.

The wheels were coming off.

In February, Rabin barely prevailed over Peres in Labor Party voting over who would lead the left-of-center bloc into elections. Rabin tallied 1,445 votes to Peres's 1,404 and then traveled to Washington to meet the new American president, a former governor and peanut farmer from Georgia.

In April 1977, when the "scandal" broke about the American bank account that Leah Rabin maintained after her husband had left Washington, Rabin felt compelled to resign, both as prime minister and as head of the Labor Party. The bank account was a technical violation of the law. It should have been closed when they came home from the United States in 1974. But for Rabin, the fact that his wife was going to be prosecuted by the government he headed was too much.

Some saw his resignation as a gesture that was unique to Rabin's personality. But it also seemed that he had lost the will to serve, that his premiership was at a dead end. He told aides that the integrity of the prime minister's office demanded that he step down, though it wasn't really so.

But it also seemed that the only way Rabin could recapture some semblance of personal dignity was to demonstrate that he was not a craven politician who would cling to power at all cost. So he invented the principle that a prime minister could not continue to serve while his wife was in the dock. The resignation garnered Rabin some credit, but it was eclipsed by the ugly public mood.[26]

Rabin went into seclusion, his political career in tatters. But as the leader of Israel's military establishment, he had presided over a doubling of Israel's overall military strength. Greater access to American arms also spurred the growth of the Israeli defense industry. The cadres of the military state expanded. And, as it would turn out, Israeli military capability created ambition within the military elite.

Israel also drew closer to the apartheid regime of South Africa, selling arms and sharing nuclear technology that the Pretoria government needed to develop its own illicit nuclear weapons program.

Alon Liel, an Israeli diplomat who served in South Africa during these years, told me in an interview that there were two sides of the Israeli embassy in Pretoria: one was populated by diplomats, who went through one door, and the other, far larger wing was populated by Israeli military personnel carrying on an entirely secret liaison related to sharing weapons research and nuclear technology.

The diplomats were walled off from Israel's military relationship with South Africa. Yet in public they denied allegations that Israel was sharing nuclear technology.

"We lied," Liel told me.* "We didn't know we were lying, and when we asked the Ministry of Defense, they said, 'No, nothing is going on.' So when I look back, I lied many times to the press without knowing that I lied. When I came back and realized that we lied, we were very furious at our ministry."[27]

The imperatives of the military state had once again trumped diplomacy.

The military establishment had orchestrated Israel's foreign policy in South Africa around the parochial interests of the military elite—the secret sharing of nuclear technologies, a policy that ignored or rejected the

---

* Liel later went on to become the Israeli government spokesman and also served as ambassador to Turkey.

worldwide condemnation of apartheid rule by South Africa's white minority. In the course of doing so, the military elite had not only relegated diplomacy to a subservient role; they had also excluded seasoned diplomats from any useful participation in national strategy.

Jimmy Carter came into office speaking out about the Palestinians; he referred to their national "rights," their need for a "homeland," and a return to 1967 borders. No American president had spoken in such terms, which were deeply alarming to Israel's military elite. The sudden shift of American emphasis to the Palestinian agenda undermined the perception that the stalwarts of the Labor Party had a strong grip on the American portfolio.[28]

It didn't matter. Change was coming.

TEN

Begin: A Peace to Enable War

Menachem Begin had been waiting for twenty-nine years to lead Israel.

Many Israelis exulted that, finally, democracy had delivered a new kind of prime minister: a warrior who had broken the stranglehold of Ben-Gurion's party over Israeli society; a leader who stood apart from the most powerful institutions of labor, industry, and the army; one unbeholden to the codes and loyalties of the military establishment; a commander of the Irgun in the war against the British and against the Arabs; a man whose patriotism was unassailable for a large part of the population disillusioned with Ashkenazi, the European Jews who formed a social elite and whose sons dominated the officer corps of the army.

So many disaffected Israelis had been waiting for a candidate who could overthrow the arrogance and corruption of the ruling party and empower the disenfranchised—the Moroccans, Yemenis, Iraqis, and other Sephardic Jews who flocked to Begin's call for a more equitable society.

Begin's victory on May 18, 1977, overthrew a political epoch.

The frail ideologue of the right, the man many regarded as a terrorist from his Irgun days when his men blew up the King David Hotel, had won a mandate to form the next government. The world could scarcely believe it.

"So now they have brought the terrorists to power," gasped one Arab commentator.[1]

Though deeply ideological, Begin comported himself as a Polish gentleman with a lawyer's devotion to language and a warlord's appreciation for the trappings of military power. He had lost most of his family in the Holocaust, and this had engendered in Begin a deep admiration for men in uniform and for the concept of the "fighting Jew," hence his reverence for the sabra military establishment even though it was not his natural base. Though Begin was hardly imposing—a slight figure with Coke-bottle glasses and a congenitally weak heart—he disconcerted many Israelis with his exaggerated sense of righteousness, as if he personally spoke for the six million Jews who had perished.[2]

Begin's victory was no landslide. To many, it seemed a fluke. Begin's Likud bloc won 43 seats in the 120-seat parliament, far short of a majority. But Labor's support had collapsed, dropping from 51 to 32 seats. Labor's strength was sapped by an insurgent clean-government party called the Democratic Movement for Change headed by Professor Yigael Yadin, the eminent archaeologist who had deciphered the Dead Sea Scrolls.

Yadin's fifteen seats, however, did not make him the power broker. Begin assembled a coalition of right-wing and religious parties to reach a sixty-three-vote majority. *Then* he invited Yadin to join the ruling coalition.

What nearly defeated Begin, age sixty-three, was his health. A month before the election, he suffered a major heart attack. Yet the burgeoning right-of-center bloc of voters refused to abandon him.

At the White House, Jimmy Carter's aides were ordering copies of *Terror out of Zion*, a history of Begin's life in the Irgun underground.

The *New York Times* pointed out that Begin was a leader who would never return the West Bank, or perhaps any other portion of the occupied territories, in exchange for peace. When asked about those Arab lands, Begin replied they were not "occupied" but "liberated."

"There is trouble ahead," the *Times* concluded.[3]

Begin's greatest challenge was to prove to the Israelis and to the world that he was no longer a wild man, no longer the reckless warrior whom Ben-Gurion had humbled by shooting up the arms ship *Altalena* on Tel Aviv's beach in 1948. Some members of the military establishment still wondered whether Begin could be a suitable guardian of the Jewish state.

Begin represented a strong ideological commitment to the "third stage" of Zionism—"military Zionism." He had clashed with his mentor, Vladimir Jabotinsky, a year before the older man's death and was in the process of wresting control of the right-wing movement from him. Jabotinsky had admonished young Jews to "learn to shoot" but retained a strong faith in diplomacy and in the British commitment to a Jewish homeland. Still, with the onset of world war followed by Jabotinsky's fatal heart attack in 1940, Begin and the "maximalists" of the right ordained the wave of Irgun violence that helped to define Jewish "terrorism."[4]

Born in Poland in 1913 and trained as a lawyer in Warsaw, Begin had been Jabotinsky's most devoted adjutant and had run the Revisionist Party's youth movement, Betar, with energy and a flair for propagandistic displays. The caricature of Begin sketched by his critics was that of a strutting Betar commandant, in love with martial displays, uniforms, and the heroic rhetoric of the nationalist movements rampant across Europe's prewar landscape.

For all the zeal that Begin exuded in the 1930s for dispatching young Jews from Poland to fight in Palestine, Begin himself did not rush to battle. He tarried in Europe until after World War II broke out. He fled into Russia, spent two years in an internment camp, and finally made it to Tel Aviv in the company of Polish army exiles.

He arrived to the news that Jabotinsky had died in New York from a heart attack; the Revisionists were rudderless until Begin took control of the Irgun and directed the underground campaign that made him a national figure. His fighters blew up the King David Hotel in Jerusalem, executed British soldiers, and would become infamous during the 1948 War of Independence for the massacre of Palestinian civilians in the village of Deir Yassin near Jerusalem. Begin spent most of his time in hiding from the British and from the mainstream Jewish Agency, where Ben-Gurion frequently called for his arrest following acts of terror.

After the war, Begin emerged as the man in the Knesset whose name Ben-Gurion refused to utter and could not abide due to Begin's shrieking tirades against the government. But during his long service on opposition benches, Begin had gained legitimacy for his movement. Eshkol had brought him into the national unity government during the Six-Day War, along with Dayan, and though Begin returned to the opposition a few years later, he matured as a politician.

When he stood before parliament on June 21, Begin looked frail. Chest pains had sent him back to the hospital after the election. He walked slowly to the lectern and looked up at the gallery where his wife, Aliza, was seated.

He called on Arab leaders to meet with him without precondition but warned that if they refused, "We shall make a note of Arab intransigence." And though Israel wanted the Arab states to recognize Israel's sovereignty, he summoned a militant tone to say, "I wish to declare that the government of Israel will not ask any nation, be it near or far, mighty or small, to recognize our right to exist. We were granted our right to exist by the God of our fathers, at the glimmer of the dawn of human civilization nearly four thousand years ago."[5]

To reassure the military establishment that he was no longer reckless, Begin named prominent military stars—Weizman, Sharon, and Dayan— all of them sabra war heroes, to his cabinet. He wanted ministers with deep roots in the army and security services. Besides Yadin, who was given the honorific title of deputy prime minister, he named Yadin's ally Meir Amit, the former Mossad chief, as transportation minister.

As an enticement to Sharon, whose Shlomzion (Peace-Zion) Party had made a poor showing at the polls, Begin offered to appoint the ex-general as minister without portfolio, but in fact he would be in charge of overseeing Mossad and the intelligence services. Here Yadin and Dayan persuaded him to withdraw the offer. It would be courting disaster to put Sharon in charge of Mossad, they argued, given his penchant for deception and stretching his orders. Still, Sharon got a key ministry, agriculture, which he transformed into an economic engine in support of the settler movement.[6]

The bold stroke had been the selection of Dayan.

Begin reached across party lines and named Ben-Gurion's favorite general and onetime protégé as foreign minister. Still in fragile health himself and out of favor with the public, Dayan was in search of a role that would restore his stature. Labor Party stalwarts accused Dayan of rank betrayal of his roots. But Begin yearned for Dayan's old star power and was willing to meet Dayan's minimal condition: that the government would not annex the West Bank while negotiations with the Americans and the Arabs were under way.[7] This was easy, for Begin had already begun to say that Israel need not annex that which already belonged to the Jewish state from history.

"I believe Judea and Samaria are an integral part of Israel liberated in the Six-Day War," Begin told an American audience.[8]

The awkward task for Rabin and Peres was to brief Begin on the secrets of the state. The first thing that Peres told him was that war was coming again with Egypt.

Peres's "personal guess" was that Egypt would attack across the Suez Canal by October–November 1977. The intelligence chiefs believed that Sadat, who had achieved no measurable gains from his surprise attack in 1973, was getting ready to resume combat to force the great powers to intervene and impose a settlement more favorable to Cairo.[9]

Also from Peres, Begin would learn that the Israeli military was engaged in secret nuclear cooperation with South Africa's apartheid regime and that France was selling a large nuclear reactor to Saddam Hussein in Iraq.

Begin named his campaign chief, Ezer Weizman, as minister of defense, which was sweet victory for the impetuous former general, who had once been denied the post of chief of staff. Now the Israeli army reported to Weizman and through him to the cabinet.

Weizman, a tall, handsome, sandy-haired fighter pilot, had built the Israeli air force that flew to victory in 1967. He had grown up in Haifa in the shadow of his world-famous uncle and Zionist founder, Chaim Weizmann, Israel's first president, but like so many young sabras, he had eschewed the intellectualism of his uncle's generation for a raw and pugnacious outlook. Weizman had joined the British Royal Air Force at eighteen but saw no action. He returned to Palestine to fly Messerschmitts and Spitfires against the Egyptian army in 1948–49.

Weizman cut the profile of a hard-drinking and overly confident fly-boy who had joined Begin's Irgun, plotted assassinations of British officers, and dedicated his life to building the Israeli air force. His hair-trigger personality was well known, and he was prone to excessive displays of aggression or affection. His visceral combativeness during his youthful piloting years had led to table-smashing brawls that were the terror of Tel Aviv's drinking establishments. Though he swore like a sailor, he was unquestionably bright, but what was always missing in Weizman was the gravitas of judgment. In the early years, Weizman and Dayan were related by marriage, and Weizman had advanced through the ranks of the military not only on the strength of a famous name but also because he proved to be a skilled pilot and a clever strategist.[10]

The high moment of the 1967 victory was followed by tragedy for

Weizman: an Egyptian sniper shot his son, Shaul, on the front line in Sinai, leaving him disabled for life.

After the 1977 election, Weizman walked into the Defense Ministry and told a room full of major generals and their aides that they should be prepared for the magnitude of change coming under Begin.

"We will not agree to withdraw from any territory," he told them. "There will be a different settlement policy. We believe Jews have the right to settle everywhere in the land of Israel."[11]

Then Begin arrived and told the military leadership that the new political guidance for their planning was that Israel's permanent borders would extend into Egypt, absorbing part of Sinai up to a line from el-Arish in the north to Sharm el-Sheikh in the south. Likewise, Israel's eastern frontier would be the Jordan River. They should adjust their thinking and operational planning to take account of the new reality.

Motta Gur, the chief of staff, asked Begin to put what he had told them in writing and Begin soon did so.[12]

Weizman's first act as defense minister was to reinforce Israeli troops in Sinai, fearing that Sadat might strike a preemptive blow to surprise Begin's new government.

The sabra military regarded Anwar Sadat as an implacable enemy, bent on the destruction of Israel. Yet there were obvious telltales that Sadat had given up on war and shifted his strategy. He had welcomed President Jimmy Carter's proposal to convene a Middle East peace conference in Geneva, at which he and Begin would meet to negotiate the return of Sinai and other Arab lands without preconditions.

"Begin or no Begin, it is the United States that counts," Sadat told one interviewer.[13]

Sadat had applauded Carter's decision to publish a Middle East policy statement even before Begin made his first trip to Washington. The statement called on Israel to "withdraw from occupied territories" and to make progress toward a negotiated peace with the Arabs as an "essential" step "if future disaster is to be avoided. . . . This means no territories, including the West Bank, are automatically excluded from the items to be negotiated," the statement said.[14]

But the change of thinking in Cairo and Washington was not registering with Israel's military establishment.

Shlomo Gazit, the director of military intelligence, was obsessed by the prospect of a surprise Egyptian attack. In September, Gazit ordered a major psychological analysis of the Egyptian leader and his ruling circle. Gazit presented its conclusion to Weizman: Egypt was planning to achieve its political objectives through war.[15]

Gazit, however, did not possess one crucial piece of information: Israel was already engaged in a secret dialogue with Egypt about peace.

Dayan had slipped out of the country in disguise during September to meet secretly in Morocco with Sadat's personal emissary, Hassan Tuhamy. The Egyptian envoy told Dayan that Sadat was ready to negotiate a comprehensive peace agreement with Israel provided that Israel give prior commitment to full withdrawal from all Arab lands taken in 1967. Dayan couldn't make such a commitment, but he desperately wanted to believe that Sadat was ready to make peace on terms that Israel might be able to accept.[16]

Begin did not share Dayan's dramatic overture with the military establishment. Mossad and military intelligence were in the dark, but Begin, armed with the disturbing assessment of Sadat's intentions from his analysts, decided to order up a large-scale military exercise in occupied Sinai. Hundreds of tanks stirred the desert and the air force swarmed the skies. The effect on Sadat was immediate. He mobilized the Egyptian army and prepared to defend the Suez Canal against an anticipated Israeli invasion. The level of tension at the beginning of November 1977 was so high that it seemed that any spark might touch off a new war.

At that moment, Sadat did something so surprising, it changed everything.

Speaking in Cairo to his national assembly, with Yasser Arafat as a guest in the front row, Sadat said, "I know that Israel will be astounded when I say that I am ready to go to their very home, to the Knesset, to debate with them" about peace.

Sadat's words, delivered as a single line to his ruling party, at first were not taken seriously in Arab capitals. But in Israel, the speech sounded a klaxon of alarm to the military elite. Motta Gur and his intelligence chief, Gazit, suspected that Sadat was setting Israel up for a surprise attack.

Gur told Israel's largest newspaper, "It should be clear to President Sadat that if he is planning additional deception of the type he engaged in during the Yom Kippur War, his intentions are clear to us; we know that the Egyptian military is in the midst of preparations to commence war against Israel."[17]

The Israeli military establishment had it wrong again, badly wrong. The obsessive fear of surprise, the intense focus on the worst-case scenario had driven the military elite to believe what it needed to believe—that war was always imminent.

Even if the military had known about Dayan's secret contacts in Morocco with Sadat's envoy, it might not have changed the minds of generals whose careers were constantly on the line over the possibility of a grand deception like the one in 1973.

Still, it seemed as if the world was paying attention only to Sadat. Even Walter Cronkite, the CBS News anchorman, conducted on-air diplomacy urging Sadat to make the journey and checking with Begin to confirm that an invitation had been extended to the Egyptian leader.

Millions of television viewers followed Sadat's daring flight. After a sharp warning from Syria's president to call it off, Sadat's plane descended to Ben-Gurion airport on November 19, where a red carpet awaited him along with Begin's outstretched hand. Trumpets sounded and cannons thundered. Sadat asked to meet Sharon and Golda Meir. They all were nervous under the lights with cameras rolling. The first Arab leader had come to offer peace. What should they say?

Sadat told Meir that in Egypt she was known as "the strongest man in Israel," and that made her laugh.[18]

"I take that as a compliment, Mr. President," she replied.

To Sharon, Sadat said that if the general tried to cross the Suez Canal again, "I will put you in jail!"[19]

In the Knesset, Sadat implored the Israelis to break the psychological barriers to peace and, for the first time in years, many Israelis, including prominent members of the military and political elites, began to entertain the notion that there was another path.

Sadat said he was prepared to build a "huge edifice of peace," if the Israelis recognized that peace could not emerge from the continued occupation of the lands seized in 1967.

"Peace cannot be worth its name unless it is based on justice and not on the occupation of the land of others," he said, adding, "with all frankness and in the spirit that has prompted me to come to you today, I tell you: you have to give up once and for all the dreams of conquest and give up the belief that force is the best method for dealing with the Arabs."[20]

Sadat's visit created a prominent fissure in Begin's cabinet.

Weizman, all trussed up and on crutches from a serious car accident on the road to Jerusalem, became a convert to Sadat's sincerity. At first, Weizman had resisted. During Sadat's speech, he passed a note to Dayan saying, "We have to prepare for war."[21]

But in the course of observing Sadat in public and in private conversation, Weizman became deeply impressed by the Egyptian's personal courage and statesmanship. Weizman talked through the night with Sadat's advisers, all of them from prominent Egyptian families, and he came to understand the enormous risk the Egyptian leader had taken and the importance he attached to a meaningful Israeli response. For Weizman, Sadat's act radiated integrity.

Not all Israelis looked at it this way, certainly not Sharon, who believed that Weizman had gone soft.

By January 1978, Sharon was worried that peace negotiations with Sadat would put a halt to his grand settlement project, which envisioned two million Israelis in new homes on the West Bank, Gaza, and Sinai. Sharon had presented the plan in September, touching off an international furor. President Carter wrote Begin a letter of stinging rebuke, and Begin tried to lay most of the blame off on Sharon.[22]

But Dayan egged him on, with the clever aphorism "I would rather have Sharm el-Sheikh without peace than peace without Sharm el-Sheikh."

Both men told Begin and the cabinet that the settlements were not an obstacle to peace, but of course they were.[23]

Begin felt that Israel had to stage a tactical retreat in the face of negative world opinion. He told the cabinet they should abandon the ambitious building plan and just strengthen the settlements that already existed.

But Sharon used the issue to rally his base on the far right. "That is a change of our former decision," he said in a challenging tone to Begin.

It was a "new" decision, not a change, Begin said.

Sharon would not let it go. He wanted the cabinet to know that he had the courage to face down the world.

"I did not come on January 3rd just to get a decision written into the minutes for history. I came to get it implemented," Sharon said. "I don't think there are people around this table who are not Zionists. But there are some people here who make decisions, and there are some people who implement them."

Sharon was full of stubborn resolve. Begin was offended. Dayan stepped in, taking Sharon's side on the point that the cabinet had approved the plan. They had all agreed, he said, but now they had to back down given the international reaction, but they had to do so without appearing weak. The pullback, Dayan said, would be "oral torah" not "written torah."[24]

Begin's unwillingness to offer anything to the Palestinians strengthened Sadat's standing in the West while the Israeli prime minister denied the existence of Palestinian nationalism.

"Palestine is a foreign translation of the historic word Israel," he said, and as for the Arabs of the West Bank and Gaza who called themselves Palestinians, "They will live here with us in peace."[25] He didn't say it, but the meaning was plain: they would live in a kind of perpetual subjugation.

At the end of 1977, Begin had gone to Washington with his version of autonomy for the Palestinians: the Arabs would rule themselves in their towns and villages, but Israel would have the right to overrule their decisions and the Israeli army would remain in charge of security in the West Bank and Gaza. Essentially, it was the same military-style rule that the Allies had imposed on postwar Japan.

Begin's intransigence awakened a new political movement in Israel, one that advocated a return to peace as a national strategy. And the importance of it was that it arose in great measure from the military establishment. Nearly 350 reserve army officers issued a public letter in early 1978: "A government that prefers . . . 'Greater Israel' to . . . peace with good neighborliness [with the Arabs] will be difficult for us to accept."

The manifesto said that it was wrong for Begin to prefer settlements to "normalization" with the Arabs. The officers and academics argued that control over a million Arabs in the occupied territories "will hurt the Jewish-democratic character of the state."

For the first time in Israel's history, a significant mainstream movement had arisen to challenge the "military Zionism" that had overtaken the humanistic Zionism of the founders. Here was a grassroots movement elaborating the risks of building a "fortress Israel" to subjugate the Arabs instead of integrating with them.

"The power of the IDF," they said in an ominous conclusion, "is in the identification of its soldiers with the path of the State of Israel." Begin was putting that identification in jeopardy. It was a none too subtle reminder that the civilian government was out of sync with a large portion of the army, the military establishment, and the country.[26]

The spirit of Moshe Sharett had found a new voice in a new generation of officers who had come around to the logic of peace. The movement would come to be known as Peace Now.

As had happened so many times in the past, just as the Israeli peace camp was gaining some traction, Palestinian militants intervened to undermine their momentum. On March 11, 1978, a PLO squad comprising eleven Fatah commandos landed in rubber dinghies on the beach fifteen miles south of Haifa and threw the country into turmoil.

The militants were under the command of a woman, Dalal Mughrabi, a nineteen-year-old refugee from Jaffa. The first person her squad encountered on the beach was an American nature photographer, Gail Rubin, the niece of Abraham Ribicoff, a senator from Connecticut. They cut her down with a burst of gunfire and dashed to the coastal highway, where they hijacked a tour bus and made a run toward Tel Aviv, shooting Israelis in their cars along the way. After a fiery crash into a police barricade and a cascade of gunfire, Israeli security forces subdued the assault squad.

The country was stunned. Thirty-four Israelis were dead and eighty-four wounded. Nine PLO commandos, including Mughrabi, had been killed.[27]

The brazenness of the attack on the country's main highway gave rise to boisterous calls for retribution. Within three days, Begin sent an invasion force of the Israeli army across the northern border, joining with a renegade Christian militia (under Major Saad Haddad) that had taken over on the Lebanon side to protect Christian villages. Israeli tanks rolled nearly twenty miles to the Litani River, attacking PLO redoubts, bombing training camps and villages, and exchanging fire with PLO militants as civilians fled.

Operation Litani was a return to large-scale reprisal.

The logic, however, was difficult to understand. Lebanon had been mired in civil war for three years. Central authority had broken down. The efficacy of collective punishment was open to question. Yet a large segment of the Israeli public, particularly Begin's hard-line base and much of the military leadership, demanded action.

Since Ben-Gurion's time, it was understood that any politician who ignored the impulse to strike back did so at his peril. Operation Litani became the template for violence against Lebanon, a course of action that the Israeli military establishment viewed as carrying the least risk of provoking a response from Syria, Egypt, or the Soviet Union.

It may have been cynical, but it was also ruthlessly pragmatic to the sabra military elite.[28]

The miniwar lasted a few days. Israeli warplanes with U.S.-made cluster bombs, together with artillery strikes, left an estimated one thousand Lebanese civilians dead and more than one hundred thousand homeless across a landscape where poor Shiite Muslims saw themselves increasingly as victims. Carter told Begin that the United States regarded the incursion as an overreaction. He warned Begin, for the second time in a year, that the use of American-made weapons in offensive military operations against a neighboring state was a violation of U.S. law.

Begin pulled his army back, but he chafed at Carter's attempt to constrain his use of military power.

Carter's bold strategy to go for comprehensive peace in the Middle East was at a dead end in the summer of 1978 when the American president decided to invite Begin and Sadat to Camp David to try to break the impasse.

Begin knew he could not refuse the invitation. But before he left for the United States, he had an urgent and fateful item on his calendar: What to do about Iraq?

France had been courting Saddam Hussein in order to expand its markets in the Middle East for French weapons and technology. Prime Minister Jacques Chirac had agreed and encouraged French firms to build a nuclear reactor south of Baghdad. France had covered its diplomatic flanks regarding the safety of nuclear materials because Iraq had signed the Nuclear Non-Proliferation Treaty. But there were deep concerns in Israel that the uranium fuel, after it was delivered and activated in the reactor, could be reprocessed clandestinely to reclaim plutonium for atomic bombs.

The record of Begin's meeting with his military and intelligence chiefs is still classified, but Sharon, who was there, has asserted that he pressed the government to make a public declaration that Israel would regard any attempt by an Arab state to obtain nuclear weapons as a cause for war.

Yadin, the former chief of staff and deputy prime minister, spoke out strongly against Sharon's formulation. He opposed military action. Unlike Israel, Iraq had signed the Non-Proliferation Treaty. Was it Israel's place to attack an Arab country that was developing a nuclear industry under the direct supervision of the International Atomic Energy Agency? Yadin's answer was no, and he was supported by Mossad's Hofi as well as Gazit, the head of military intelligence.[29]

In Begin's conference room that day, the military and political leadership began a debate that would have a profound effect on Israel's national outlook for decades. Israel was building the military infrastructure to sustain hegemonic military power while neglecting the infrastructure for diplomacy, negotiation, and compromise.

For Begin, the Iraqi reactor was an existential threat to the Jewish people. Here there could be no question of reliance on the international system. Begin declared within this closed circle of military and political elites that he possessed an unshakable resolve to prevent Iraq, a long and bitter enemy, from even approaching the nuclear threshold.

Looking out at the world, Begin saw that the nuclear era and the advent of the Jewish state had created the potential for another catastrophe: with 20 percent of the world's Jews gathered in their own nation—the fulfillment of the Zionist dream—an enemy armed with weapons of mass annihilation could repeat Hitler's onslaught with a genocidal strike.

The meeting ended with a decision not to follow Sharon's recommendation to go public with a national warning, but Begin found a consensus to turn the intelligence community loose on the Iraqi nuclear project. The goal was to sabotage the European industries where components of the

Osirak reactor were being manufactured. At the same time the army and air force began studying whether it was possible to insert commando teams into Iraq to destroy the reactor if Begin and the cabinet made a decision to do so. Here was the beginning of a new phase of militarism.

Begin emerged from this heady internal discussion and made haste to the United States for his rendezvous with Carter and Sadat.

Over the next thirteen days at Camp David, the hard-line Israeli prime minister became something that he had perhaps never imagined: a peacemaker.

The zealot of the right, the former Irgun commander and "terrorist" loathed by Ben-Gurion, had managed to do what Ben-Gurion and his political heirs had never accomplished—conclude a peace with an Arab state. And not just any state, but the main enemy and the largest Arab nation.

And he did it with full support of the military elite.

Marveling at the irony, Yitzhak Rabin was said to have blurted out in reaction to Begin's achievement, "If this had happened while I was prime minister of a Labor government, there would have been blood spilled in the streets."[30]

In signing the Camp David Accords, Begin agreed to give up Israel's largest conquest of the Six-Day War, a step that shocked his right-wing ministers and the leaders of the opposing Labor Party. He agreed to return every inch of the vast Sinai Peninsula, sending a powerful message that registered with the Arab states—that it was possible to return to the 1967 borders.

Though there was worldwide celebration and a shared Nobel Peace Prize for Begin and Sadat, the peace treaty that was signed at the White House in March 1979 opened a new fissure in Israel's military culture.

Begin had arrived at Camp David in the company of Dayan, Weizman, and a host of military and political aides representing the sabra establishment. For Dayan, Camp David was an opportunity—perhaps his last opportunity—to etch a more positive imprint of his life. And while he didn't believe that Camp David could settle the Palestinian problem, Dayan regarded his own approach to crafting an autonomy deal as more humane than Begin's. His greatest concern was that whatever they achieved for the Palestinians in negotiations, Begin would not follow through.

Of all the Israelis at the meeting, Sadat trusted only Weizman and called him "Ezra," the Arab version of his name.

The human connection was palpable to all who observed them, and Sadat hoped that if peace failed, Begin's government would fall and Weizman might replace him as prime minister. Weizman had changed, that was certain. The rapacious hawk had come to see that the intelligence about Sadat had been wrong. Egypt was not a lion in the weeds waiting to pounce. Sadat was a leader trying to change the fortunes of his people.

But Begin at Camp David was rigid and parsimonious. He wanted to keep el-Arish, Yamit, and Sharm el-Sheikh. He wanted to lease the air bases Israel had built in Egyptian territory. In contrast, Weizman and Dayan grasped early on that the price of peace would be returning *all* of Sinai. If that was done—if Sadat got all the land back—they would find him more pliable on the Palestinian front, where all Sadat wanted was a credible framework for negotiating self-rule for the inhabitants of the West Bank and Gaza.

At times, it was Begin against everyone else.

He may have cultivated the image of a Polish gentleman, but as a party leader, Begin was a hard-bitten autocrat, intolerant of questions or debate when he had settled on a course. Dayan chafed under his constant glare because Begin never measured up to Dayan's standard for leadership; only Ben-Gurion had.

"There were times when only by clenching teeth and fists could I stop myself from exploding," Dayan wrote. "No one disputed Begin's right, as prime minister and head of our delegation, to be the final and authorized arbiter of Israel's position in all matters under review. But none of us was disposed to accept, as though they were the Sinai tablets [of Moses] those of his views which seemed to us extreme and unreasonable. We were not always at odds, and indeed, on most issues we held identical opinions. But on those occasions when I disagreed with him and questioned his proposals, he got angry, and would dismiss any suggestion that did not appeal to him as likely to cause inestimable harm to Israel."[31]

Few Israelis had believed that Begin would make any compromise at Camp David, and as the days dragged on, many blamed him for intransigence.

It wasn't only Sadat's insistence on recovering all Egyptian territory that wore Begin down. When Begin buckled, it was due to his changing perception of what the military establishment would support and how that might affect the public. He had steeled himself to give up nothing. Sharon and the other hard-line members of his coalition had seemed prepared to bring down his government if he ceded too much.

On the final day of the Camp David marathon, when Begin and Sadat were on the horns of deadlock, a pragmatic general on the Israeli negotiating team, Avraham Tamir, had the idea of getting Sharon's endorsement to give up the Sinai settlements. If Sharon, the self-styled architect of settler ambition, agreed to make the eleventh-hour concession, it would have a big impact on Begin. Tamir convinced Weizman and Dayan that it was worth a try, and soon they had Sharon on the telephone.

When Sharon showed pragmatism, stating that he could support the compromise, it changed Begin's view of how the peace treaty would sell to the military elite and to the country.[32]

Indeed, the Camp David peace was a political watershed in Israel, with polls showing more than 80 percent of the public in favor of the accords, a strong affirmation that the martial impulse could be overpowered by a strategy based on accommodation with the Arabs.

Some Likud supporters greeted Begin with black umbrellas, signifying that Begin's surrender of the Sinai settlements was the equivalent of Neville Chamberlain's surrender to Nazi power in 1938.

Yet the Camp David Accords stood there like juridical instruments, signed at a White House ceremony and endorsed by most of the world. They recognized Palestinian national rights the same way British foreign secretary Lord Arthur Balfour had recognized the need for a Jewish homeland in his 1917 letter to the Zionist leadership.

Inevitably, Camp David triggered a new internal Israeli struggle: Begin feared that he had gone too far in accepting the modalities for a "self-governing authority" in the West Bank and Gaza. What would self-rule mean for the Palestinians? Could it turn into a viper?

Sharon's support was not unconditional. He questioned whether Begin had planted the seeds for a Palestinian state by recognizing the rights of the Palestinians to self-rule in the West Bank and Gaza. This was a grave accusation. In a cabinet session, he cited the dangers inherent in the treaty. "It could easily become a Balfour Declaration for the Palestinians and

The origins of Israel's martial impulse can be understood only by lifting the layers of secrecy and mythology about the first decade of Israeli statehood, when the aftermath of World War II and the Holocaust, a precipitous British retreat from Palestine, and the attack by Arab states that greeted Israel's declaration of independence in 1948 profoundly transformed the Zionist movement. Here, Jewish soldiers in the British Army march in Tel Aviv in 1942 (*top*), and Israeli women volunteers drill (*bottom left*). Future leaders such as Moshe Dayan and Yigal Allon (*bottom right*) trained in guerrilla tactics with Yitzhak Sadeh of the Haganah, the main Jewish militia force. (Top and bottom left: Kluger Zoltan, Government Press Office, State of Israel; bottom right: Jewish National Fund, 1983)

David Ben-Gurion (*top*, with Golda Meir) sought to undermine his successor, Moshe Sharett, seen here with Ben-Gurion at Sde Boker (*bottom right*). Ben-Gurion regarded Sharett as a coward interested more in diplomacy and accommodation with the Arabs than in building an indomitable military power in the region. Ben-Gurion promoted Pinhas Lavon to be defense minister, and Lavon (*bottom left*, with Moshe Dayan and Shimon Peres) wanted to set the Middle East "on fire" to exploit the weaknesses of the Arabs. (Top: Fritz Cohen, Government Press Office, State of Israel; bottom left: Government Press Office, State of Israel; bottom right: Paul Goodman, courtesy of the Moshe Sharett Heritage Society)

Moshe Sharett (*top*), Israel's second prime minister, seen here in Geneva after a meeting with John Foster Dulles, resigned from government after clashing with Ben-Gurion, who had returned to power with a plan to attack Egypt and to obtain atomic weapons for the Jewish state. Golda Meir reassured President John F. Kennedy (*bottom left*) that Washington would have no difficulties from Israel over the Dimona reactor, which the CIA suspected was part of an illicit nuclear weapons program. But with the capture, trial, and execution of Adolf Eichmann (*bottom right*), the Nazi war criminal and architect of the "final solution," Ben-Gurion argued to world leaders that Israel desperately needed a stronger defense. (Top: Rene Jarland, INP, courtesy of the Moshe Sharett Heritage Society; bottom left: courtesy of the John Fitzgerald Kennedy Library; bottom right: Government Press Office, State of Israel)

By the time Israel triumphed over the Arab armies during the Six-Day War of 1967, the Jewish state had already crossed the nuclear threshold by constructing its first crude nuclear explosives at the Dimona reactor complex (*top*). Moshe Dayan and Yitzhak Rabin upstaged Prime Minister Levi Eshkol by marching into the liberated Old City of Jerusalem (*left*) and informing Eshkol after the fact of major military decisions (*bottom*). (Top: courtesy of Mordechai Vanunu; left and bottom: Ilan Bruner, Government Press Office, State of Israel)

Golda Meir (*top*, surrounded by soldiers during the 1973 Yom Kippur War) might have headed off war with Egypt had Israel's military establishment been willing to engage in the diplomacy offered by the United States to pull back from the Suez Canal and give up the territorial gains of 1967. Ariel Sharon (*bottom right*, with Chaim Bar-Lev) commanded the "Likud Division" and bullied his way across the Canal, setting the stage for his political career. The military establishment built an architectural icon of its power in the center of Tel Aviv (*bottom left*). (Top: Frenkel Ron, Government Press Office, State of Israel; bottom left: © Dana Kopel; bottom right: Yossi Greenberg, Government Press Office, State of Israel)

The Israeli military is the seminal educational experience for acquiring martial skills and for entering adulthood. Landing a slot in military intelligence, with the paratroopers, or in an elite commando unit opens opportunities and creates networks that flow into business, government, and politics. Jonathan Netanyahu (*top right*), the hero of the 1976 raid at Entebbe International Airport in Uganda (*top left*), came from a prominent right-wing political family; his brother, Benjamin Netanyahu, would become prime minister. Prime Minister Menachem Begin (*middle left*, with Yitzhak Shamir, his foreign minister) deeply admired the military and backed General Raful Eitan's (*middle right*) plan to invade Lebanon and bombard its capital, Beirut (*bottom*), in hopes of destroying the PLO. (Top left and right: Government Press Office, State of Israel; middle left: Saar Yaacov, Government Press Office, State of Israel; middle right: Han Micha, Government Press Office, State of Israel; bottom: © Roth Yossi)

The Old City of Jerusalem, the citadel of religious symbolism. Dividing Jerusalem remains one of the great challenges of peace. (Herman Chananya, Government Press Office, State of Israel)

Prime Minister Ehud Barak's strategy in 2000 was to get the Palestinian leader Yasser Arafat (*right*, with President Bill Clinton) into a room and offer him the best deal that might be accepted by Israeli voters. When Arafat refused, he was "unmasked" as incapable of making peace. Ariel Sharon (*top*) was determined to block Barak's offer of concessions to the Palestinians as Benjamin Netanyahu (*bottom*) also took aim at returning to power. (Top: Harnik Nati, Government Press Office, State of Israel; right and bottom: Avi Ohayon, Government Press Office, State of Israel)

might well lead to a second Palestinian state [Jordan being the first], something that no Israeli with any regard for the country's safety could agree to."[33]

One thing was clear: peace would remove Egypt's million-man army—the largest military threat to Israel—from the battlefield.

The balance of power, which had been tilting heavily in Israel's favor since the mid-1950s, now shifted beyond all proportion. Like nothing before it, the treaty conferred on Israel the status of regional superpower, armed with nuclear weapons, American-equipped air forces, and tank divisions far beyond the capabilities of any combination of rivals. And the military establishment was in the hands of a right-wing government, far more inclined to employ military force to achieve its objectives.

Begin understood that Israel's newfound strength was something to be exploited. In his private councils, the prime minister did not regard himself as a peacemaker as much as a tribune of Israeli power. His thoughts ranged toward the broad application of military force—north into Lebanon against the PLO and Syria, east into Iraq against Saddam Hussein—to strike at threats developing far beyond the horizon. Diplomacy was not even in the equation.

Most of all, Begin came to the realization that if Israel was to ensure that there would never be a PLO state in the West Bank and Gaza, the country would have to go to war to destroy Yasser Arafat. For Israel's military elite, there were plenty of other reasons to do so, the Munich massacre being the most intensely felt.

Just at that moment, Begin's Mossad chief walked in with the news that the agency had located the PLO's most notorious Black September terrorist, Ali Hassan Salameh, who had planned the Munich assault.

He was the one who got away.

Salameh, an Arafat favorite, was living openly in Beirut. He was the scion of a prominent Jerusalem family. His father had been an Arab military commander in the 1948 war and was killed by the Haganah. Young Salameh had always been a playboy militant, married to a former Miss Universe, Georgina Rizk, and known as Abu Hassan throughout Beirut.

Crucially for Arafat, Salameh had established close contacts with the American CIA station in the Lebanese capital. The dialogue was mostly about security for U.S. citizens living in the city. Arafat had used Salameh to build confidence between the PLO and American diplomats, whose safety was constantly under threat. But the channel was open for political messages as well.

The Israelis learned of Salameh's channel to the Americans and became infuriated that Washington was meddling in Palestinian politics. If the Americans did anything to bolster the legitimacy of the PLO, it would undermine Israeli efforts to cultivate an alternative or "tame" Palestinian leadership in the territories.[34]

An earlier Mossad attempt to kill Salameh had turned into a catastrophe. An Israeli assassination team, believing they had identified Salameh, gunned down an innocent Moroccan waiter who was strolling down a sidewalk with his pregnant wife in Lillehammer, Norway. This case of mistaken identity led also to the capture and long incarceration of Mossad operatives.

Thus Begin's decision to order a new assassination attempt in January 1979 could not have been taken lightly. For one thing, he was in the midst of sensitive negotiations with Carter and Sadat to complete the Camp David treaty. How would it look if it became known that he was making peace with one hand and ordering an assassination with the other?

And though Salameh was on the Mossad hit list, the decision to kill him while he was in the midst of building the PLO's new link to the Americans could not have been coincidental. Mossad officials had queried the Americans about contacts with Salameh, but the Americans had shielded the relationship, seeing Salameh as a useful conduit to Arafat.[35]

War-torn Beirut was still a haven for espionage and agents of influence.

The Mossad hit team members arrived separately and over several months, using forged British and Canadian passports.

Salameh had gotten careless. He often used the same route along the rue Verdun to travel from his PLO safe house to his wife's apartment.

With little notice, a Mossad officer identified as Erika Mary Chambers moved into a West Beirut flat overlooking rue Verdun in the fall of 1978. Her neighbors recalled that the free-spirited artist perched in her window every day for months, fussing over a sketchpad as if she were recording the street life below.

Once Salameh's identity was confirmed, Begin gave the final go-ahead.

There has never been reference to any discussion of whether it might have been possible to kidnap Salameh—as Eichmann had been kidnapped—and bring him to Israel for trial. It was obvious that such a trial would have turned into a forum on Palestinian national rights. The rule of law that Ben-Gurion had so enjoined during the Kennedy administration had given way to an unambiguous form of retribution.

On the afternoon of January 22, 1979, Salameh was riding with his bodyguards in his Chevrolet station wagon along the familiar boulevard when a parked Volkswagen loaded with plastic explosives detonated just as they were passing.

Salameh's four bodyguards died instantly. Salameh lingered with mortal wounds before dying in a hospital later that day.

The blast killed four innocent bystanders, including a German nun and an English student. Another eighteen people were injured. Most foreign intelligence agencies believed that Salameh's death represented a belated and final shot connecting him back to the Munich massacre, but in Israel, in the circle around Begin, it was inescapable that the assassination would serve as a warning to the Americans: first, peace accords would not stop Israel from striking out when it saw fit and, second, Arafat and his men were still in the crosshairs of the Jewish state.

Defense minister Weizman had set out to find a new chief of staff who was strictly a professional soldier, and he had settled on Rafael Eitan in March 1978. Raful was a soldier's soldier, a courageous sabra, both resolute and earthy. He had none of the diabolical tendencies of Sharon, but he had passed all the tests of military leadership and bore the scars to prove it.

As a young paratroop commander, Eitan had led the 1956 jump at the Mitla Pass with Motta Gur and Hakka Hofi. He served under Hofi on the Golan Heights in some of the most savage fighting of the Yom Kippur War. He did not share Hofi's hatred for Sharon. Eitan reserved all of his passions for the enemy, and the regime in Damascus figured most prominently on Eitan's enemies' list.

For Begin and Weizman, however, the destruction of the PLO was paramount. Only then could Israel force the captive Palestinian population on the West Bank to accept Israeli terms.

In 1979, Weizman and Eitan put the military through an urgent war-planning process. The "intent paragraph" of their headquarters' exercise stated: "The IDF will occupy south Lebanon up to the Jounieh-Zahlé line [meaning as far as Beirut], [and] will destroy the terrorist [PLO] forces so as to create a new situation in the area [and] will destroy Syrian and Lebanese forces as may be necessary in executing the mission."

The "mission" was clear.

As Sharon later put it, "Any operation strong enough to deal with the PLO state within a state would almost inevitably also put us in conflict with Syrian occupation forces in the south Bekáa [Valley] and in West Beirut, which had become the Palestinian terrorist capital."[36]

The secret plan was given the name Oranim (Pines).

Weizman and Eitan had thus conceptualized a major invasion of Lebanon. But Begin pulled them up short. He upbraided Weizman for overstepping his power.[37]

In reality, Begin was not ready to go to war. The peace with Egypt was not yet complete. The United States was transferring billions of dollars in new aid to Israel and to Egypt to solidify the Camp David treaty. The Israeli and Egyptian armies were still facing each other in Sinai; they would withdraw on a precise schedule. The two countries were also exchanging ambassadors and opening embassies. Begin could not take the risk of invading Lebanon while so many tangible benefits of the peace were flowing in.

Begin was also under pressure from Carter to open negotiations with the Palestinians, but with every step he took, Begin showed that Palestinian autonomy was going nowhere.

There was a struggle for the soul of Israel under Begin, and it was splitting the sabra establishment because Begin offered contradiction as policy: he professed to be advancing the cause of peace while also confiscating Arab lands. He worked both openly and covertly to encourage Gush Emunim to increasing levels of boldness in establishing new settlements.

Weizman accused Sharon of encouraging the settlers "to steal out under cover of night" to seize their foothold in the West Bank, where they erected their tents and water towers and draped the perimeter with concertina wire. They demanded protection, which Weizman was forced to give them because the military was not only the occupation authority, it was also the protector of Jewish settlers. Despite opposition from Dayan, Weizman, and Yadin, Begin ran interference for the settlers. And Sharon just shrugged off the personal attacks over his role, knowing that Begin would protect him.

"This man and this Gush are forcing the cabinet into situations that endanger its survival," Weizman complained in one June 1979 cabinet session. "This is a cabinet that doesn't make decisions. Instead, it is dragged along."

Begin demanded to know what "man" Weizman referred to.

"Sharon!" he replied.[38]

But Begin just ignored him. He patronized Weizman, using a diminutive, Ezerkeh, to address him.

Dayan, too, was disillusioned. Begin's government commenced expropriating private Arab land on the West Bank for Israeli settlements, violating Dayan's principles.

"I did not feel that I could remain in the government," Dayan later said.[39]

His health had taken another turn for the worse: he was diagnosed with colon cancer. He had no leverage over the Palestinian autonomy portfolio, which Begin had entrusted to Yosef Burg of the National Religious Party, cutting Dayan out of the process. So he tendered his resignation in October 1979, telling President Carter privately a few months later that Begin would not keep the promises made to the Palestinians that were implicit in the Camp David Accords.[40]

It was as if an ill wind was roiling the Middle East, feeding off the voices of Palestinian grievance that television was sending around the world. At the same time, the latent power of Islamic revival was bursting through barriers that had long contained it, and this, too, infused a renewed passion into the Palestinian cause.

Revolution in Iran had swept Shah Mohammad Reza Pahlavi from his throne and Israel had lost a powerful friend in the Muslim world. Israeli diplomats and spies had been forced into hiding in Tehran. The Ayatollah Khomeini hosted Yasser Arafat in the Iranian capital and turned over the Israeli diplomatic compound to the PLO in a humiliating spectacle for Israel's ruling elite. All that Israel had built with the shah vanished in a matter of weeks, including Israel's access to Iranian crude oil.

When radical students overran the American embassy, taking fifty-two Americans hostage in November, the Israeli military elite looked on in disbelief, and many wondered why the shah had not employed his military arsenal to put down the rebellion by force.

Begin's popularity, meanwhile, was plummeting.

The Likud government had lost control of the economy, and Begin seemed powerless to get inflation under control, so much so that even Eitan, the army chief, felt compelled to criticize the government for incompetence in economic affairs. Few Israelis understood where Begin was taking the country, and Begin, in his public statements, did little to clarify matters.

In March 1980, he appointed Yitzhak Shamir to replace Dayan as foreign minister. Shamir's arrival meant that the peace process, such as it was after Camp David, was dead. Shamir walked in as a hardened relic from the fringe; he had voted against the treaty with Egypt. A former career Mossad operative, he was a man of few words and seldom telegraphed his moves. He was uncomfortable with exposure to the public.

A former leader of the underground Stern Gang during the British Mandate, Shamir had approved some of the most shocking assassinations, including the killing of Count Folke Bernadotte, the UN envoy who had come to Jerusalem in 1948 to help end the war.

Shamir had been rehabilitated like many underground extremists who had once been hunted by Ben-Gurion's security forces. The Mossad recruited him for intelligence work, and he spent ten years as a covert operative in Europe.

Shamir arrived in office just in time for a new crisis with Lebanon.

On April 7, five Palestinian militants belonging to a small PLO faction that was funded by Saddam Hussein crossed Israel's northern border and slipped into a kibbutz late at night. They shot dead the secretary and took refuge in the nursery, where they held six children hostage. Israelis awoke to news bulletins about the violent drama. Begin authorized commandos to storm the nursery, and a two-year-old boy and an Israeli soldier died in the firefight. Eleven other soldiers were wounded.

The horror of the attack on a nursery at Kibbutz Misgav-am sent Begin and the military establishment into a frenzy of retribution planning. Weizman, with strong support from Sharon in the cabinet meeting, told Begin on April 8 that the military was ready to invade Lebanon to wipe out all PLO networks.

The invasion plan—Operation Pines—was on the shelf. Weizman called for a "meaningful" strike, by which he meant that the army would take control of "a large part of Lebanon" all the way "up to the Zahrani [River] and to Beirut."[41]

Eitan was ready, but Begin was uncertain.

The Israeli army's withdrawal from Egypt would take another twelve months, and a major strike into Lebanon might trigger negative reactions in Cairo and Washington. Jimmy Carter was quietly struggling to free the American hostages in Iran. Begin might have been aware, through intelligence channels, of the extensive American military preparation to mount a mission to rescue the hostages, which underscored Carter's call for restraint at a very delicate moment.

So Begin deferred. Israel would not invade Lebanon in April 1980. Instead, the military establishment was authorized to unleash a series of air strikes against PLO targets across southern Lebanon, hitting training camps and hideouts, thus slaking the public demand for retribution.

But what was abundantly clear that spring was that two lines of military planning were ripe for execution, and important constituencies within the military establishment were competing for Begin's attention. The first called for an attack on Iraq to destroy the Osirak reactor; the second was a large-scale invasion of Lebanon to destroy the PLO.

In Beirut, the project to create a Christian state under Bashir Gemayel had become increasingly bloody.

David Kimche, a Mossad division chief, had put together his own team with a goal of turning the Phalange Party and Gemayel's Christian militia into the core of a new national army. And this was done in the face of mounting skepticism from Hakka Hofi, the Mossad chief.

One member of Kimche's team was the veteran Israeli diplomat Avi Primor, with whom I spoke in Tel Aviv about the Mossad's work in Lebanon.[42]

"The concept was [to build] a Phalangist Lebanon," Primor told me. So much of the policy was riding on Kimche's personal relationship with young Bashir Gemayel. "Bashir loved this fellow [Kimche]. Really trusted him and liked him. When they met, they hugged like a couple of gays."[43]

Primor ran a seminar for Gemayel's men on "politics and propaganda," while Kimche briefed senior members of the political elites to promote his concept.

"David had contact with top politicians like Begin and Weizman," Primor said. "Weizman was totally convinced."

But Hofi was not convinced and more than once called Primor to Mossad headquarters to express his doubts.

Instead of uniting, the Christian warlords were fighting each other as intensely as they were striking out at the PLO and its allies. Mossad officers looked on as Gemayel's men bombed, ambushed, and targeted for assassination rival Christian leaders. Among those killed by Phalangist gunmen was Tony Franjieh, the son of the Christian Lebanese president, Suleiman Franjieh.

At Mossad headquarters, Hofi was offended by Gemayel's brutal campaign of consolidation. His standing order to Kimche had been to withhold financial and military support from the Christians whenever they fought among themselves. To Hofi, Christian unity was the goal of Israeli policy, and that's where he trapped his subordinate. Kimche had continued to ship weapons to Gemayel even as his Phalange militia savagely attacked its Christian rivals.

In April, Hofi and his deputy, Nahum Admoni, assembled the evidence and called Kimche before the directorate of the Mossad, where Hofi read out the indictment of Kimche's breach of orders. All of Mossad's division chiefs were there, many of whom regarded Kimche as a contender to become the next chief. Hofi announced that he had lost confidence in Kimche and, in front of his assembled peers, dismissed him. Kimche's dream of running Mossad was over.[44]

The firing rattled the intelligence establishment but failed to thwart the Lebanon project. Shamir quickly offered Kimche a post as director general of the Foreign Ministry, from where Kimche continued to advocate Israeli support for Gemayel.

The high-level shake-up in Mossad was followed by a more significant change at the top of the military establishment. Weizman's political ambition had been awakened by Begin's drop in the polls. He found Begin's political circle suffocating.

"I have never seen people so immersed in the past," he later wrote of Begin's followers. "There were some you could wake in the middle of the night and with their eyes still closed, they could reel off the minutest detail of events in Plonsk in 1910—but they had not the slightest inkling of what went on in an Arab village within Israel last week."[45]

Weizman had commented in public that a new election in Israel would be a good thing to sweep the cobwebs out of government. His political daring had escalated as opinion polls showed that his popularity had surpassed Begin's. Weizman was in favor of a change, he said, even if that meant the Labor Party's returning to power.

With elections a year away, Weizman was shopping for a suitable issue over which to resign, and when the economic crisis prompted Begin's finance minister to freeze all government contracts, including those in the Defense Ministry, Weizman declared that he would not tolerate cuts in defense.

He strode into Begin's office and threw down his resignation letter in the face of Begin's sour expression and, on the way out, he ripped a poster extolling peace off the prime minister's wall saying, "No one here is interested in peace."[46]

Without a defense minister, Begin had two choices: give the defense portfolio to Sharon, or keep it himself.

Begin was not ready for Sharon, and neither were some members of his coalition. So many people had warned Begin that Sharon could not be trusted. Even Begin had called Sharon a "danger to democracy" who might someday surround the prime minister's office with tanks to get his way.[47]

Like Ben-Gurion, Begin served as both prime minister and defense minister, but he relied heavily on Raful Eitan, the chief of staff, to run the military establishment.

Throughout the fall of 1980, Begin kept the Osirak reactor threat on the cabinet's agenda. Begin felt that he could strike Iraq only with a broad consensus. With Sharon as his ally, Begin pressed ministers to authorize a strike into Iraq. Yadin had not budged from his opposition when Saddam Hussein surprised the world by invading Iran in September. In the first week of the war, the Iranian air force launched American-made Phantom jets to bomb Osirak, inflicting minor damage. The Iranian attack demonstrated that Israel was not the only country whose government feared Hussein's nuclear ambition.

Yadin began to reconsider his position.

Within the military establishment, David Ivry was among the sabras who favored action in Iraq.

As air force commander, Ivry was instrumental in developing the plan to destroy the Iraqi reactor. When I went to see him in Tel Aviv, he told me that during those crucial months of planning, he played on Begin's Holocaust sensibilities to encourage him to keep up the pressure on reluctant ministers.

"I came up with the big image of the Holocaust and the children of Israel," Ivry told me, "and this was, in his mind, the most critical issue—that Saddam Hussein is a guy who can use a bomb against Israel."[48]

A straw vote in the Knesset's committee on military and defense affairs was six to four in favor of a strike, but Begin wanted a stronger front of sabra support to inoculate himself against political blowback if something went wrong.[49]

Begin kept pushing. At the end of 1980, he was a vale of exhaustion, depression, and ill health. The national economy was facing runaway inflation and the government had been forced to impose punishing austerity measures. Begin's weak heart added to the sense of deterioration. The prime minister sat through government meetings with a vacant stare from sallow features.

The opposition's power was growing. Peres and Rabin had fought a highly personal battle over who would lead the Labor Party ticket. Peres had won with a margin of more than 70 percent. For the first time in his political career, Peres looked like a winner. The polls showed him towering over Begin, who was forced by the economic crisis to advance national elections from November to June 1981.

Peres publicly expressed the sense of national alarm over Begin's physical and mental deterioration. "It is out of the question to put the fate of the nation in the hands of a person whose mood fluctuates so violently from unrestrained and complete euphoria to the deepest depression."[50]

Faced with almost certain defeat, Begin miraculously rallied.

In early 1981, he emerged from his depression with a missionary spirit, setting out on what he knew was to be his final election campaign. It may well have been Peres's candidacy that energized him, for Begin regarded

Peres as lacking in courage and ideological principle. Indeed, Begin was sure that if Peres won the election, he would shrink from bombing the Iraqi reactor.

Begin's campaign strategy focused on three targets: Iraq's reactor, Syria and the PLO in Lebanon, and the sagging economy at home.

Yoram Aridor, his new finance minister, was a lawyer with no training in economics, but he soon implemented a wildly popular program of price reductions, especially for imported cars and appliances, that sent the Israelis on a shopping spree.

Suddenly Begin was a populist hero. He was greeted by enthusiastic crowds chanting, "Begin! King of Israel!"

When Begin and Peres campaigned before Moroccan Israelis in April, the throng chanted for Begin while Peres was pelted with tomatoes, forcing him to flee the stage.[51]

On Lebanon, Begin made it increasingly clear that he saw the fate of Lebanese Christians the same way he saw the fate of the Jews. In one interview, Begin said that every time he read *While Six Million Died*, Arthur D. Morse's account of the Holocaust, "I am not ashamed that my eyes are filled with tears when I think how our people were left to themselves. The Germans murdered, but the world left us to our own devices. I want to tell you that we are a Jewish state, with our own experiences, and under no circumstances are we going to acquiesce in the Syrians' attempt to reduce the Christians in Lebanon in the 1980s to the status of the Jews in Europe in the 1940s."[52]

The Christian warlords chose that moment, in early 1981, to foment the crisis at Zahlé.

Nestled in the Bekáa Valley about twenty miles east of Beirut, Zahlé is a city of two hundred thousand people that sits perched on strategic ground along the main cross-country highway to Damascus. Gemayel and his Phalange commanders sent their artillery to the mountainous heights above Zahlé to extend Christian control and provoke the Syrian army, which regarded the Beirut-Damascus highway as its most crucial supply line. Syria responded by raining its own artillery fire on Zahlé and sending airborne troops and assault helicopters against the Christian positions.[53]

Bashir Gemayel and Camille Chamoun flew urgently and secretly to Israel to plead for Israeli intervention to rescue the garrison at Zahlé, and Begin went before the cabinet and said it was no longer a matter of helping the Christians to help themselves. It was time to intervene to ensure that a small people was not extinguished by a brutal dictator. Some Labor Party ministers, including Chaim Bar-Lev, the former chief of staff, spoke in favor of helping the Christians, but others, Yigael Yadin in particular, warned Begin that he was losing control of the military establishment, which was pursuing its own agenda in Lebanon.[54]

Yadin's subtext was: Raful wanted his war with Syria.

The Syrians were ferrying commandos using transport helicopters to the Sannine Heights above Zahlé. Moments after the Israeli cabinet approved intervention, General Eitan stepped out of the room, and within minutes he returned to report that Israeli jet fighters had shot down two Syrian transports, killing dozens of enemy soldiers.

Hafez al-Assad, the Syrian dictator whose army was in Lebanon under an Arab League mandate, could not leave an Israeli attack unanswered. Within days, the Syrians began moving Soviet air-defense missiles into the Bekáa Valley to protect its forces and challenge Israeli warplanes seeking to control the airspace over Lebanon.

Begin entered war mode. The Arabs had crossed his red lines on two fronts. The Iraqi reactor was due to receive its final load of highly enriched uranium from France by summer, and the Syrians were threatening to push the Israeli air force out of its position of dominance in Lebanon. Begin was ready to strike in both directions at once, but his coalition members warned that Israel might exceed the tolerance of the international community.

Peres accused Begin of whipping up the Lebanese crisis as a campaign strategy to unify the country behind his candidacy. Begin must have smiled—he had observed Ben-Gurion in his day doing the same thing. As in Sparta, a military society lines up together when the leader declares an imminent threat.

Looking back, David Kimche wrote that there was little doubt that Begin and the military elite allowed themselves to be manipulated by Bashir Gemayel. "Bashir had, from the outset of the Syrian occupation of Lebanon, believed that only by the direct intervention of Israel could the Lebanese free themselves from the Syrian presence. He was astute enough to realize that Begin would not remain passive in response to such a cry for help and the threat of a Christian massacre."[55]

Begin's military moves were doing wonders to rejuvenate his political prospects for reelection. From the end of April and throughout May, the Israeli public waited as Begin prepared to strike in Lebanon or Iraq. On the Lebanese front, the Reagan administration sent a special envoy, Philip Habib, to cool down the artillery duel around Zahlé. Begin was forced to defer an attack on the Syrian air defense sites.

But the Americans were in the dark about the plan for Iraq.

Washington had asked Israel if it would take early delivery on several squadrons of F-16 fighters that had been promised to the shah of Iran before he fell. Here was another arms windfall for the Israeli military, for these American warplanes made up the strike force that the Israeli air force assembled in the final months of planning. The rise of the ayatollahs was already bolstering the Israeli arsenal.[56]

Begin won cabinet approval for a strike on Osirak May 9. But Peres, fearing a political boost for Begin, tried to head it off. He told Begin that François Mitterrand had privately pledged to him during a meeting in Paris that France would halt the delivery of enriched uranium to Iraq if he was elected president. In a handwritten letter to Begin marked "personal and top secret," Peres argued that the attack was ill considered and highly provocative. He implied that Begin was acting rashly, that there was still time to allow a new French president to withhold nuclear fuel from the reactor. And he warned in veiled terms that Israel would be isolated and that its own nuclear capability at Dimona might be called into question: "We would be like a tree in the desert—and we also have to be concerned about that."[57]

Begin handled Peres deftly.

He postponed the raid for two weeks, infuriating the military command but allowing a decent interval for Mitterrand to act and moving H-hour for the attack ever closer to the Israeli elections.

With a strong majority in the cabinet, Begin authorized the air force to strike on the afternoon of June 7. During the countdown, the French leader failed to take any immediate steps to shut down French cooperation with Osirak.

The warplanes had the sun at their backs when they took off from the Etzion Air Base in occupied Sinai and streaked low over Jordan toward the

Iraqi desert. Flying in radio silence, the F-16s raced across the Euphrates River and then popped up to four thousand feet to release their unguided two-thousand-pound bombs.

Where the Iranian air force had failed, Israeli pilots succeeded in destroying the Osirak reactor, sending up a huge plume of smoke visible across much of central Iraq. An Arab state had been denied nuclear power by Israel. The doctrine of Israeli nuclear exclusivity that Sharon had advocated was carried out in muted kinetics.

The successful destruction of Osirak dramatically lifted Begin's political fortunes and put Peres perilously on the defensive. When it leaked that Peres had tried to convince Begin not to undertake the attack, Peres asserted that he had objected only to the timing. But Begin would not let Peres off the hook. The prime minister personally brought Peres's secret handwritten letter to the Knesset committee so its members could see that Peres opposed more than the timing. The letter leaked to the press, and its contents contributed to Peres's image as a political manipulator. It also diverted attention from Begin's own political motives.

Campaigning in Netanya, Begin sounded the jingoistic themes that had once marked him as a dangerous extremist. He shouted out a warning to Hafez al-Assad: "Beware! Yanosh and Raful are waiting for you!"[58]

He was referring to General Avigdor "Yanosh" Ben-Gal, the northern commander, and General Eitan, the chief of staff. Begin told the crowd that if Philip Habib did not get the Syrian missiles out of the Bekáa Valley, the Israeli army would do the job.

To President Reagan, who criticized the raid on Iraq, Begin replied that "a million and a half children were poisoned by the Ziklon gas during the Holocaust. Now Israel's children were about to be poisoned by radioactivity. For two years we have lived in the shadow of the danger awaiting Israel. This would have been a new Holocaust. It was prevented by the heroism of our pilots to whom we owe so much."[59]

The right wing turned out for Begin.

An eleventh-hour attempt by Peres and Rabin to join forces was not enough to stop the juggernaut. Begin had infused a demoralized government with a potent stimulus of militarism abroad and easy money at home. Begin won what proved to be one of Israel's ugliest political campaigns, in which he again benefited from populist anger in the Sephardic community against the Ashkenazi elite who dominated the Labor Party.

Sabras were overturning sabras as a new divide pitted hard-line militarists against a burgeoning peace camp that was attracting many officers, academics, and civic leaders. Peace as a strategic objective was an explosive new idea on the streets, on campuses, and in the barracks, where the stirrings of Moshe Sharett's old admonition never to lose sight of peace, not for one single moment, could be heard once again in reaction to Begin.

There was a new sense in the country that war in Lebanon would be part of the national agenda in Begin's second term, and those who were standing in the way began to feel the heat. At Mossad headquarters, Hofi read with what could only be a sense of foreboding the attack in the right-wing newspaper *Ma'ariv*, suggesting that he had voiced strong opposition to the Osirak raid for "blatantly political reasons."

The story questioned Hofi's integrity. The author of the attack was Uri Dan, Sharon's ally and propagandist. It did not take much imagination to see that since Hofi opposed a deepening involvement in Lebanon, Sharon and Eitan saw him as an obstacle that had to be neutralized.[60]

Despite the boost from the Osirak raid, Begin and the Likud won by a whisker in the June 30 elections. Likud took 48 seats to Labor's 47. Labor had no allies with which to form a coalition, while Begin had the small religious and nationalist parties on the right to give him a 61-member working majority in the 120-seat Knesset.

Absent from Begin's second government was any overlay of national unity: Dayan, Weizman, and Yadin all were gone. Begin rewarded Sharon for his strong support on the Osirak raid by making him defense minister.

Shamir stayed as foreign minister, and Begin extended Raful Eitan's tenure as chief of staff for another year. Never had an Israeli cabinet been led by such a triumvirate of hard-liners, each of them alienated from any concept of accommodation with the Arabs, each of them deeply committed to a militaristic agenda: war with Syria and the destruction of the PLO ministate in Lebanon.

The Israeli air force stepped up the war against the PLO as soon as Sharon took over the Defense Ministry. They no longer waited for a specific PLO attack but launched random bombing missions that triggered a massive PLO response, which surprised the Israeli general staff. The Palestinian militants unleashed two weeks of artillery and rocket fire that thundered across the region with such intensity that it drove, for the first time, tens of thousands of frightened Israelis out of their homes in Kiryat Shmona and neighboring towns. Israel had never witnessed such an exodus from the border, and the scenes of civilians huddled in dark bunkers affected Begin profoundly.[61]

The War of the Katyushas—the primitive rockets fired into Israeli towns—triggered Sharon's first declarations in the cabinet that aerial bombardments and artillery strikes against the PLO were not enough. "The complete elimination of the issue can only be brought about if the terrorists' political-military infrastructure no longer exists," he said. If the cabinet was ready for the complete solution, Sharon was ready to expand the Pines war plan, but he made clear that "it should take in the entire area" of PLO operations, "including Beirut." People started calling it Big Pines.[62]

In the meantime, Israeli bombers streaked north on Friday, July 17, at the peak of rush hour in Beirut. The mosques had emptied and the Fakhani district of West Beirut was bustling with shoppers. With no warning except the sudden noise of jet engines in the distance, the neighborhood erupted with explosions, collapsing apartment blocks in smoke and fire.[63]

Israel had brought the war to the Lebanese capital to deliver a crushing blow to the PLO headquarters that stood in the center of the busy civilian district. When the concussions stopped, 150 civilians lay dead, and 600 wounded walked or were carried into hospitals. The bombing killed about thirty PLO militants. The scenes of civilian casualties and suffering shocked President Reagan, and he dispatched a written message to Begin saying as much.

Begin responded, "I feel as a prime minister empowered to instruct a valiant army facing Berlin, where, among innocent civilians, Hitler and his henchmen hide in a bunker deep beneath the surface."[64]

Begin told those close to him that he was determined to root out Arafat and kill him. "We shall catch the devil in his bunker."[65]

Ariel Sharon had finally reached the pinnacle of military power.

He swept into the Defense Ministry that summer, purging old enemies and elevating loyalists.

He promoted Ehud Barak, the brilliant young commander who had led Sayeret Matkal, to major general. He canceled the promotion of Dov Tamari, an outstanding staff officer who, as a young lieutenant, was among those who sharply rebuked Sharon for his failure of courage at the Mitla Pass in 1956. Though Tamari had lost ten soldiers from his platoon in the battle, Sharon had never forgotten his criticism and, without explanation, he forced Tamari to retire without promotion.

Sharon was out to remake Israel as a regional superpower—allied with but not under the control of Washington—and capable of blocking a Soviet invasion into the region or of policing the radical Arab states. Wherever he went, including the White House and Pentagon, he carried a bundle of maps, which he spread out to show the Soviet invasion routes into the Middle East and how Israel could be counted on to block them. He told Reagan's national security adviser, Robert McFarlane, that there was no need for America to court Egypt or Saudi Arabia, for they were unreliable allies and only Israel could stand off Moscow.[66]

To witness these lectures, as President Reagan did during one Sharon visit to the White House, was to understand how Israel's military establishment was in the hands of a hard-line junta, whose leaders were intoxicated by the power that America had bestowed upon them. Israel's military potential had grown beyond anyone's expectations, first through America's unmoderated supply of sophisticated weaponry and then through the growth of Israeli military industries.

Though many Israelis would come to believe that Sharon was leading Begin to war, it was Begin who warned the Americans in the fall of 1981 that Israel was planning to go into Lebanon decisively.

Sadat's assassination at the hands of Islamic extremists on October 6, 1981, brought a great convocation of world leaders to Cairo to mourn the death of the Egyptian peacemaker. Begin was there to show that Israel was still Egypt's partner, and during the day he had a long conversation with Secretary of State Alexander Haig, informing him almost casually that the Israeli army was prepared to go into Lebanon and clean out the PLO ministate.

"Does that make sense to you, Al?" Begin had asked.

Haig was never opposed to the notion of destroying Arafat and the PLO, which he considered a pawn of the Soviet Union in the Middle East. But Haig said Washington was worried how the world would perceive such an operation. If Israel moved in response to an internationally recognized provocation, the United States would be at Israel's side, but if Israel acted unilaterally, without a major provocation, "you move alone," Haig responded.[67]

Haig's comment was not so much a warning as an admonition to Begin to find an adequate pretext for war. And Haig's remarks were later interpreted for what he had not said. He made no threat to cut off financial aid or the flow of arms.

Days after Sadat was buried, Moshe Dayan died of heart failure and cancer. Begin had just returned from Cairo and the country uneasily said goodbye to one of its most complicated leaders.

They buried Dayan where his parents, his brother, and his sister awaited him: at the end of the path that leads out of Nahalal to the hill of Shimron in the Jezreel Valley.[68]

Dayan's long descent, his greed, and his scandalous philandering in a conservative society rendered him as a formless shape, like the antiquities he had scratched from the desert. There was a barely discernible original image—handwrought by idealism and high principle—which had not withstood the corrosion of fame, power, and ambition. Only his belief in Israel had persisted unchanged. He had lived his life as a biblical figure, a conqueror and a lover with more lust for acquisition than faith in a goal. And on the Sabbath, as his daughter recalled in her memoir, "god was absent from our lives, as from our education," and on the day of rest, "the imposed quiet that descends on the land had a disquieting, enervating effect on us all."[69]

Ezer Weizman wrote of Dayan that he had taken too much of the blame for Israel's failures. "Israelis love idols, but they also display an unrestrained lust in demolishing them."[70]

Whatever Begin felt, he kept to himself. He, too, was under the pressure of time. He pushed his cabinet ploddingly toward a consensus for war. In December, he flew into a rage over something Syria's president said about the impossibility of peace with Israel, prompting him to summon his cabinet to his bedroom (he had fallen and broken his hip), where he announced that Israel would formally annex the Golan Heights. Why give it back if Hafez al-Assad says there will be no peace? he asked.[71]

When the United States protested, Begin called in the American ambassador and ranted that Israel was not some "banana republic" that Washington could censure at its whim. He sent the ambassador, Samuel Lewis, packing. On the way out, Lewis was surprised to find the ministers of the government in the outer room. Something was up.[72]

Sharon had completed the refinements to Operation Big Pines by the first of December, and over two days he briefed the generals at headquarters and the northern commanders on its details, which stressed a massive thrust all the way to Beirut. Sharon had cleverly taken his cue from Haig, telling his commanders that the invasion scenario was a "contingency plan" and would not be implemented unless the PLO resumed its shelling of the northern towns. In Sharon's mind, that would be the "clearly recognizable provocation."[73]

With the cabinet members in his bedroom on December 20, Begin invited General Eitan to brief the ministers for the first time. They were uniformly astounded, blindsided by the scale and scope of the invasion plan that Eitan unfolded for them. It seemed like an undertaking as extensive as the Yom Kippur War, and Begin had not prepared them for it. The arrows on his maps showed massive Israeli armored assaults up the coast, up the center, and up the eastern flank of Lebanon, linking up with the Christian militia in Beirut and squeezing the Syrian army so hard that it was difficult to imagine that an Israeli-Syrian war was not also part of the plan.

Several of the startled ministers spoke against what they saw, and from the furrowed brows and shaking heads, Begin realized that if he asked for a vote, he would lose. "The atmosphere is quite clear and there is no point in continuing," he said, adjourning the meeting.[74]

Sharon's testing of the invasion plan with the Americans drew similar expressions of shock and alarm. He told Philip Habib, President Reagan's envoy, that if the PLO continued to violate the cease-fire, "We will have no choice but to wipe them out completely in Lebanon, destroy the PLO's infrastructure there." Habib was alarmed by Sharon's bellicose tone.

"General Sharon, this is the twentieth century and times have changed. You can't go around invading countries just like that, spreading destruction and killing civilians," Habib said. "In the end, your invasion will grow into a war with Syria, and the entire region will be engulfed in flames!"[75]

The Mossad handlers had not told Bashir Gemayel exactly which senior Israeli official was coming to see him in January 1982, but when the rotund Sharon hoisted himself down from a helicopter that landed in Jounieh, the Christian-controlled port serving East Beirut, Gemayel gushed: "I knew you would be the one to come."

Sharon had flown to Beirut because he wanted to meet the Christian leadership and impress upon them the enormity of Israel's military preparation and the high stakes for all of them.

They spent the day touring the Christian sector of the capital. There were already one hundred thousand dead in the Lebanese civil war, and Sharon looked out over West Beirut from the safety of a Christian promontory and surveyed the lair where Arafat was hiding.

"In case there is a war, what would you expect of us?" Gemayel asked.

Sharon replied that the Christians first and foremost needed to defend their territory because the Israeli army would not be able to invade Beirut itself. It was an Arab capital with foreign embassies, and he would not get bogged down in a complicated urban war. But Sharon then motioned out toward the hill in Muslim West Beirut where the defense ministry stood at Yarze, overlooking the Beirut-Damascus highway.

"You see that hill there, the defense ministry hill? That hill is vital. If there is a war, take that hill," Sharon said.[76]

Sharon had brought along his chief of military intelligence, Yehoshua Saguy, and the deputy chief of staff, Moshe Levy. The Mossad contingent was headed by Nachik Navot, a good-natured and slightly hyperactive operator who was trying to establish the same rapport with the Lebanese that Kimche had enjoyed—without much success.

What was clear to the Mossad men on the ground, however, was that Sharon was taking charge of policy in Lebanon and that Mossad was no longer taking the lead. Mossad's director, Hofi, told his operatives to stand aside. Hofi told Navot that once the military was involved, it was time for Mossad to back away, play whatever supporting role was requested, but not to try to run the show; that was the army's job.[77]

The Christian leaders hosted Sharon at a sumptuous luncheon feast. The patriarch Pierre Gemayel made the case for desperate measures—a forceful invasion by Israel to wipe out the PLO. The elder Gemayel openly wept when he described the death toll of the civil war. Camille Chamoun hissed under his breath, "Don't cry!"

The Christians were there to gauge how serious Sharon was about bringing the Israeli army to Beirut, and Sharon was there to gauge how committed the Christians were to an alliance with Israel. Thanks to Kimche, Begin was under the impression that the Christians were a willing partner; they would make peace with the Jewish state if Israel cleared their land of PLO and Syrian oppressors.

But Chamoun, for the first time in Sharon's hearing, dispelled the notion of an open alliance. Lebanon, he said, could not conclude a separate peace with Israel. The Christians were Arabs, after all, and the Lebanese were part of the Arab family, which had collective demands for peace.

Sharon took in this admonition without comment. He understood that Chamoun, as a former president, spoke with great authority, but he also knew that the old man's rigid resistance to an Israeli-Lebanese peace was not the final word.

If Israel installed young Gemayel as president, Israel, by virtue of its invasion army, would have overwhelming influence. Still, Chamoun's words hung in the air as Sharon's delegation boarded helicopters for the return flight.

Sharon had no illusions about the task in front of him. When his wife asked him his impression of the Lebanese, he replied cynically, "The impression I got was that they are a people who kiss ladies' hands—and murder."[78]

Over the next two months, Begin, Sharon, and Eitan frenetically worked to construct a passable foundation for war against the PLO.

Sharon traveled to Egypt during this period to oversee negotiations for the final withdrawal of Israeli troops from Sinai. In Cairo, he broached the idea with senior Egyptians of an Israeli-Egyptian-Lebanese alliance.

But the Egyptians were not buying anything that Sharon was selling. Egypt was not interested in taking another leap of faith until Begin delivered on the promises of Camp David.[79]

At the same time, Begin sent General Saguy, the military intelligence chief, to Washington to catalog for President Reagan's aides the litany of Palestinian violations of the cease-fire. Meanwhile Sharon met with Habib and argued that Israel's goal in invading Lebanon would be to create a new democracy in the Middle East.[80]

Begin, too, was grasping for the right pretext. In early March, he summoned some of the senior ministers of his coalition to his home, where Sharon and Eitan expressed concern that, with the death of Sadat, Egypt under Hosni Mubarak might renege on the Camp David peace treaty.[81]

Israel was due to make its final pullout on April 26, 1982.

Sharon suggested that the invasion of Lebanon by Israel would be a good test to see whether Egypt's new leader was really committed to the peace treaty.

The ministers—Shamir, Yosef Burg, and Simcha Ehrlich—balked; they were unwilling to vote for war without pretext, but Begin and Sharon were gradually winning them over.[82]

Next, the cabinet ministers wanted to hear from Hofi and Saguy. The intelligence chiefs warned that it was naïve to think that the Israeli army could manipulate Lebanon's internal political system by elevating Bashir Gemayel to the presidency and then withdraw. The foundation they were planning to construct under Gemayel would collapse under pressure from Syria, the Muslim majority, and Gemayel's Christian rivals. The implication was that Israel would be in for a long and costly occupation.[83]

Israel's military establishment was divided, yet the doubts and concerns that were being expressed by the professionals were simply overpowered by the ideological advocates for war.

Begin was obsessed with crushing the PLO.

Sharon and Eitan may have harbored different motivations—Eitan wanted to defeat Syria; Sharon wanted to push the Palestinians into Jordan—but together they were an unstoppable force. They silenced General Saguy by telling him that it was an act of disloyalty for him to contradict their assessments when speaking to cabinet ministers. Saguy's job, they said, was to advise the military chiefs; it was Sharon's job, he asserted, to advise the civilians.[84]

At Mossad, Hofi retreated into silence, telling his division chiefs that the military was in charge of Lebanon policy.

The Israeli cabinet was inescapably aware of the deep reservations that existed among the intelligence chiefs, but the ministers allowed themselves to be persuaded by Sharon's forceful assertion that *he* also was an expert on Lebanon, and along with Eitan, Sharon told them that the army's hierarchy was confident that it could prevail against the PLO and Syria. But behind these careful statements to the cabinet was the larger aspiration—or delusion—that a victory in Lebanon could change the shape of the Middle East to Israel's advantage.

General Eitan betrayed the naked overconfidence of the military establishment. "Now that I've built a military machine which costs billions of dollars I have to use it. It's possible that I will be in Beirut tomorrow."[85]

Sharon's last chore for Begin before they could launch the war was the delicate task of removing several thousand settlers from Yamit in Sinai.

The settlers had to return to Israel under the Camp David treaty. Begin feared bloodshed or images of settlers clinging to their homes. Any incident could trigger a major political backlash among Begin's right-wing supporters. But Sharon had become the ultimate Begin loyalist, working assiduously to coax the settlers into an orderly retreat and promising them new homes in choice settlements on the West Bank.

And to show them how much he hated giving up any settlement, Sharon moved his forces into Yamit, after it was cleared of civilians, and dynamited it to the ground. His pernicious act contravened all of the understandings with Egypt. The dust and smoke hung over Sinai like a cloud of hostility toward the Egyptians. But to the settlers, and thus to Begin, it was a wildly popular statement that Israelis, especially those devoted to the concept of Greater Israel, do not give up ground lightly.

In the weeks following the Israeli withdrawal from Sinai, the Israeli army made final preparations, moving hundreds of tanks, mobile artillery, and armored personnel carriers to the northern border. In Washington, a young National Security Council aide, Howard Teicher, wrote a report to his boss, Robert McFarlane, warning that war was inevitable and that the Reagan administration had a limited amount of time to head it off, but McFarlane evinced no inclination to mobilize the president. This was Haig's turf and Haig was dealing directly with Begin and Sharon.

Indeed, Sharon flew to Washington on May 25 to personally brief Haig, who was impressed by the battle plan. Haig continued to caution that there had to be an internationally recognized provocation for any war, but he also conveyed that the United States would not try to thwart an Israeli invasion. No evidence has emerged to date that Reagan was even informed by Haig of the Sharon briefing and its implications for imminent war in the Middle East. Reagan's published diary for the period contains no reference to Sharon's visit.

In late May 1982, the PLO and Israeli gunners were trading fire along Israel's northern border when the PLO announced that it would no longer respect the cease-fire. Arafat, too, had succumbed to his militants.

Begin told the cabinet that Israel now faced the same dilemma that John Kennedy had faced during the Cuban missile crisis. "The Americans had not waited until they were hit by the first Soviet missile from Cuba." The PLO, in effect, had declared war on the people of Israel, he said. Begin did not call for an immediate response; he was still waiting for the right moment in order to satisfy the Americans.[86]

That moment came on June 3, when a Palestinian gunman stepped out of the shadows near London's Hyde Park and shot the Israeli ambassador, Shlomo Argov, in the head as he emerged from a reception at the Dorchester Hotel.*

British and Israeli intelligence services came quickly to the conclusion that Argov's assailants were members of the radical PLO splinter group of Abu Nidal that had been sent by Iraqi intelligence as provocateurs seeking a war to weaken its rivals. This distinction was of no interest to Begin, who silenced any doubters with one of his withering Holocaust metaphors.[87]

"The hour of decision has arrived. You know what I have done, and what all of us have done, to prevent war and bereavement. But our fate is that in the Land of Israel there is no escape from fighting in the spirit of self-defense. Believe me, the alternative to fighting is Treblinka, and we have resolved that there would be no more Treblinkas. This is the moment in which a courageous choice has to be made. The criminal terrorists and the world must know that the Jewish people have a right to self-defense, just like any other people."[88]

In such a psychological state, Sparta, nursing a terrible wound from history, tumbled toward war.

---

* Argov did not die from his wound, but the bullet in his brain rendered him an invalid. He died in 2003 at the age of seventy-three.

ELEVEN

The Sabra Caesar: Sharon in Lebanon

The northern coastal plain of Israel shuddered as if Caesar's legions had returned.

A great nimbus of dust and exhaust filled the sky between the mountains and the sea as the columns of Israeli tanks, artillery, and infantry—thousands of vehicles—moved northward across a rock-strewn landscape of ancient Crusader forts and Arab villages.

The 1982 invasion of Lebanon, launched on June 6, three days after the shooting of the Israeli ambassador in London, was Israel's largest military undertaking since the Yom Kippur War.

Five years after he had come to office, Begin was taking the strategic gamble of his life—the gamble that had taunted and plagued him since Camp David: Could he deliver a knockout blow to the PLO before anyone could stop him?[1]

The military establishment, however divided within the ranks about the necessity of war, had saluted Raful Eitan and Sharon and prepared to demonstrate the power of an arsenal that had more than doubled in size in a decade and was arrayed against Soviet-backed clients—Syria and the PLO—who were ill prepared for large-scale combat.

At the last minute, Ronald Reagan, who had just landed in Europe for an economic summit, a visit to the Berlin Wall, NATO meetings, and an audience with the pope, was outraged that Begin had diverted the world's attention from American diplomacy by starting a war. Fecklessly, Reagan tried to halt the onslaught with a letter, but Begin just put it aside, preening at the martial display he had set in motion.

Henry Kissinger, writing in the *Washington Post*, hailed the "strategic rationale" of Begin's power play because, Kissinger said, it had always been a "mirage" that the PLO could moderate its behavior.[2]

From the outset, the war was an exercise in national deception. Seldom had a military enterprise so large and so ambitious been launched with such a modest description of its purpose. Begin and Sharon had come up with the name Operation Peace for the Galilee to convey to the world that Israel was doing no more than cleaning out the nest of PLO artillery gunners and rocketeers who were raining fire down on the women and children of Israel's northern settlements.

Begin pledged that the army would push no farther than twenty-five miles into Lebanon to accomplish its mission of creating a security zone. Israeli troops would sanitize southern Lebanon, avoid the Syrian army, and come home. He was even overheard telling his wife that it would all be over in a couple of days. One of Begin's biographers excused Begin's mendacity by calling it "Begin-ese," a carefully crafted truth to cover a lie.[3]

The truth was that Begin and his cabinet were willingly "deceived," for one had only to see the scale of the invasion forces to understand that this was an army that had been assembled to take a country.

Sharon and Eitan sent nearly ninety thousand soldiers mounted in armored columns led by nearly eight hundred tanks and fifteen hundred armored personnel carriers. The invasion force exceeded seven divisions—more than Israel had thrown against the Egyptian army in 1973—and was arrayed against a ragtag force of fifteen thousand Palestinian militants and the unimpressive forward elements of the Syrian army, which was eager to avoid a clash.[4]

As Eitan was soothing government ministers, saying that that his troops would not cross the twenty-five-mile line, he was landing one part of his invasion force well north of that line, at Sidon, in a flanking maneuver aimed at surrounding Beirut. On the eastern path of the invasion route, the twenty-five-mile line fell within the Syrian army's forward deployment area, yet Sharon was able to convince the cabinet that he could attack the PLO inside the Syrian lines without triggering a larger war. It was as if the cabinet had suspended its judgment, but this was Begin's Israel: the right wing of the political elite aligned with a right-wing military elite.

Sharon deftly and relentlessly moved the army north by informing the cabinet of daily tactical adjustments. By the end of June, the Israeli army had reached the outskirts of Beirut, ignoring every cease-fire along the way, which the Americans had brokered with Syria's dictator, Hafez al-Assad. Sharon laid siege to Beirut: he cut the main highway to Damascus, trapping the PLO and part of the Syrian army. For the first time, the Israeli army stood poised at the gates of an Arab capital.

Begin, euphoric at the pace of the military advance, issued an order to the Sayeret Matkal commando unit to find Arafat and kill him. Now it was clear: Peace for the Galilee aimed at decapitating the PLO; destroying its infrastructure, weapons, ammo dumps, and headquarters; flushing the Palestinian population out of Lebanon; and, according to Sharon's thinking, sending the Palestinians back to Jordan, where they could declare their Palestinian state.[5]

Sharon announced to Reagan's frantic Middle East envoy, Philip Habib, that Arafat and all the ten thousand PLO militants holed up in the capital had to leave—or "they will be destroyed."[6]

There was a sensation in the news media about the speed with which Sharon had executed the invasion and, back in Israel, it dawned on the Labor Party leaders that Begin was in the midst of pulling off a major achievement, bigger than the destruction of the Iraqi reactor. This strutting Polish gentleman was stealing Labor's thunder.

Rabin was the first to mobilize. He flew north with Sharon to have his picture taken on a rooftop overlooking Beirut. All of Israel knew that Rabin, as chief of staff, had made Sharon a general. On military matters, the two men shared many views, one of which was that warfare creates opportunities. Rabin would not have initiated the war in Lebanon, but he believed that once war begins, it should be exploited quickly so that Israel can claim some success and get out. Sharon was preparing to cut off the water and electricity, and he was contemplating a massive bombardment of Beirut to force the PLO's surrender. Rabin advised Sharon to "tighten up" the siege. "I can live with a 24-hour bombardment of Beirut," he said. He could also live with cutting off the water to the civilian population.[7]

The Americans stood back appalled, especially Ronald Reagan, who had seen television coverage of a Palestinian girl whose arms were blown off, an image the president could not shake. But Sharon, with Begin's consent, continued to escalate the bombardment of civilian neighborhoods in a city already suffering the effects of six years of civil war. Sharon was doing nothing to the Lebanese that they had not done to themselves, but from an invader whose agents had manipulated the civil war almost from the outset, Israel's affront to the Arab world was injurious beyond calculation.[8]

Sharon refused to buckle to international pressure.

When some Labor voices criticized Begin for conducting an "aggressive war," Begin seethed at the opposition benches: "If you who are responsible for the Yom Kippur War will defame us, will libel us, will supply our enemies with material, [are] we not permitted to answer back?"[9]

As the columns of smoke from Israeli air strikes rose above the Beirut skyline, Sharon sent a message to Arafat through the Egyptians that if he chose to collect his troops and his people and make an exodus to Jordan, it would take only a word from Sharon to force King Hussein to abdicate his throne.

"One speech by me will make King Hussein realize that the time has come to pack his bags," Sharon said.[10]

Five days later, Israeli intelligence pinpointed Arafat's location, and the air force flew in a massive bomb that leveled a seven-story apartment block where the PLO leader had been hiding. An estimated two hundred people were killed or wounded by the blast, but Arafat narrowly escaped. He moved about the city frantically to keep one step ahead of the Israeli agents who were feeding tips and rumors to the assassination team.[11]

Sharon told the Italian journalist Oriana Fallaci that Henry Kissinger had called him and said that a "new era is starting in this region, new possibilities are opening for the solution of the Palestinian problem"—Sharon's solution. After pummeling the city for weeks, he averred that he had never wanted to enter Beirut, where hundreds of thousands of civilians would be exposed to danger. But he just as sharply said that when it came to winning, he did not care who got in the way.

"And believe me, had I been convinced that we had to enter Beirut, nobody in the world would have stopped me," he admitted. "Democracy or not, I would have entered even if my government didn't like it. I mean I would have persuaded them. And I would have done it."[12]

The siege of Beirut raged until August 12 after the saturation bombing of the city that killed six hundred civilians, wounded thousands more, and added to the humanitarian crisis. Reagan witnessed Sharon's final onslaught on television and decried the "Holocaust" that he believed Begin was perpetrating on another country.[13]

Arafat had no choice but to succumb to the pressure. He received assurances from the Americans that a multinational force would protect Palestinian civilians left behind in the city. He and fifteen thousand PLO fighters and Syrian soldiers boarded ships in Beirut's harbor and departed, firing their guns into the air. An Israeli sniper had Arafat's head in his crosshairs as he boarded the ship, but Begin had promised Reagan that no attempt on the PLO leader's life would be made during the evacuation. Sharon's supporters later blamed Begin and the Mossad for letting Arafat escape.[14]

Still, Sharon had won. Or so it seemed.

On August 23, Mossad officers and Israeli military teams fanned out across Lebanon and rounded up sixty-two deputies of the ninety-two-member Lebanese parliament and assembled them in a basement. Muslim deputies boycotted; one was shot allegedly for refusing to participate in the Israeli-orchestrated election. On the second ballot, fifty-seven deputies voted Bashir Gemayel into the presidency. The thirty-four-year-old warlord was the leader of a deeply divided people, but it was only the strength of Israeli militarism that protected him.

Begin was ecstatic. He declared a "triangle of peace"—from Israel to Egypt and Lebanon. He telegrammed warm salutations to Gemayel as if he were a son. Sharon was supremely confident that he finally would realize Ben-Gurion's dream. He left the region to take a victory lap through America, raising money for Israel Bonds and stopping off in Washington to admonish Secretary of Defense Caspar Weinberger that if he did not help Gemayel establish the Christian government's authority over Muslim West Beirut, "We will see a return of the previous state of affairs."[15]

But the sweet taste of victory did not last. The Arabs denounced Gemayel's bloodless coup. President Reagan chose that moment to put a peace plan on the table that would grant Palestinian independence in a federation with Jordan. The Reagan Plan—actually the invention of George Shultz, the new American secretary of state—was seen by the Israelis as a shocking attempt to undermine everything they had just achieved.

They had expelled Arafat and the PLO, and now Reagan was trying to offer the Palestinians a de facto state on the West Bank and Gaza? The Americans were directly challenging the Greater Israel concept, which held that these lands belonged to Israel—the very principle that had motivated Begin to go to war.

The news of the Reagan Plan reached the prime minister as he was visiting Nahariya near the Lebanese border.

"It was the saddest day of my life," he later said. "We have been betrayed by the Americans, the biggest betrayal since the state was established," Begin told his aides. "They have stabbed us in the back."[16]

Begin was desperate for a countermove.

The American initiative had no realistic prospect of success since Begin wanted nothing to do with it, and the Palestinians had long since decided that they would not subordinate their dream of statehood by becoming subjects of the Hashemite monarchy in Jordan. But still, America might as well have planted a Palestinian flag on the West Bank.

Begin summoned President-elect Gemayel to Nahariya. He kept the younger man waiting for two hours—because the American ambassador had also arrived with the Reagan Plan—and when Begin walked in, with Sharon at his side, he made it clear who was in charge. Israel had just put Gemayel on his throne. Begin said the price of Israel's support was a peace treaty under which Lebanon would become the second Arab country to recognize the Jewish state. Israel and Lebanon would exchange ambassadors, open borders, and coordinate policy.

Begin had already made public statements about "the basis for the peace treaty between our two countries," and Sharon had just declared in an essay in the *New York Times* that "there will be peace between Lebanon and Israel."[17]

Now, three days later, Gemayel stood before Begin and told him that there could be no immediate peace treaty. He needed time to bring the Muslim communities into the new government and to convince the Arab states that his government was legitimate. Otherwise he had no chance of expelling the Syrian army or of leading the Lebanese.

Suddenly, Begin the autocrat was scowling at his young charge, whose answer was unacceptable. Begin said that Gemayel ought to reflect more deeply on who had made his presidency possible. Begin reminded him that Israel had already purchased the loyalty of Major Haddad in the south. The mention of Haddad's name triggered Gemayel's anger. He said Haddad was a deserter from the Lebanese army and he would like to put him on trial.

Why not make him chief of staff? Begin shot back.[18]

Tempers flared and Sharon was soon shouting at Gemayel that the

Israeli army owned Lebanon at that moment and he had better come to terms with those who were in command.

Gemayel could not believe that the Israeli leadership seemed to have no understanding of Arab politics. Gemayel thrust his arms out in front of him. "Put the handcuffs on! I am your vassal!" he sneered.[19]

That was the end of the meeting, and the end of a crude attempt by Begin and Sharon to dictate terms to a client for whom they had little actual respect. David Kimche was appalled when he heard what had happened in Nahariya. But the failure was not Begin's abusive treatment of his ally. The central failure of the whole scheme was Israel's belief that it could project its power into Lebanon, subjugate the Arabs, dictate political results, and then leave.

Begin told an interviewer during those days in Nahariya that "the P.L.O. is a beaten organization. . . . They are dispersed in eight countries. Everybody disarms them. . . . What can they do? . . . They can't fight any more. They don't have the arms, they don't have the bases, they don't have their headquarters."[20]

In his mind, he had launched the army against a Hitler-like evil in order to save the Christian population of Lebanon from annihilation and then to kill Arafat in his bunker. The Israeli writer Amos Oz called this "a typical Jabotinskyian fantasy" and added, "This urge to revive Hitler, only to kill him again and again, is the result of pain that poets can permit themselves to use, but not statesmen." He admonished Begin that "Hitler is dead and burned to ashes."[21]

But Begin, for all his political skill, had failed to master the politics of Lebanon or of the Arabs more generally.

All of Begin's illusions about dominating Lebanon were sundered by a deafening blast on September 14, when a massive explosion tore through Gemayel's headquarters and killed the young president-elect. Bashir's body was barely recognizable in the rubble. The bomb, planted by Syrian agents, utterly destroyed Israel's plan for a vassal state on its border and set in motion another long Lebanese descent into civil war, terrorism, and hostage taking. Sharon's first response was to react militarily. He ordered the Israeli army into West Beirut to preempt any other power from filling the vacuum. Then he and his officers stood by as vengeful Phalange militia forces moved into the Palestinian refugee camps of Sabra and Shatila, where they slaughtered 850 Palestinian old men, women, and children. Eitan told American diplomats that Gemayel's troops were "obsessed with the idea of revenge" for the death of their leader. They blamed the Palestinians—the PLO—as much as they blamed Syria.

"I could see it in their eyes," Eitan acknowledged, but he and Sharon and the other Israeli officers on the ground let it happen.[22]

Nachik Navot, the top Mossad official in Beirut, got a call from his son when news of the massacre was being reported. "What the hell is going on up there?" he asked indignantly. Navot claimed not to know.[23]

The outcry was intense, but Begin seemed strangely subdued. "Goyim kill goyim, and they immediately come to hang the Jews," he said.[24] But within days, hundreds of thousands of Israelis took to the streets to protest the affront to Jewish morality that the IDF's passive acquiescence in the massacre represented. The whole country bore down on the government's role, especially Sharon, Eitan, and the other military commanders who had stood by as Gemayel's henchmen drenched themselves with blood.

Begin resisted and resisted, calling the charges of Israeli complicity a "blood libel," but he was forced by public pressure to relent and impaneled the Kahan Commission on September 28 under the Supreme Court justice Yitzhak Kahan, knowing that its judgment might lead to the end of his political career. The clouds had gathered. The massacre unhinged Begin psychologically. He had gone to rescue Christians and now stood accused of complicity in mass murder. The throng in the streets called for his resignation, and he saw his grand enterprise—something that not even Ben-Gurion had been able to accomplish—crumbling. Only Sharon was still fighting, lobbying the Americans to declare Israel's invasion a victory over Soviet-backed forces.

Sharon argued and bullied and pleaded with Philip Habib, warning that if the Americans tried to use Lebanon to bring the Syrians closer and resolve the Palestinian question, "they would watch the whole thing slip through their fingers."

If not for Israel, he declared, the Soviets would have overrun the region; they would be sitting on the Suez Canal. "You have the possibility of making Lebanon an integral part of the free world," Sharon preached to American congressmen and anyone else who would listen.[25]

But the massacre blotted out everything else. When Begin's wife, Aliza, died suddenly in November, Sharon had a premonition that it all was going to turn out wretchedly for him. Begin had decided to bury Aliza in the old Mount of Olives cemetery in Jerusalem behind the graves of Meir Feinstein of the Irgun and Moshe Barzani of the Stern Gang. They had killed themselves in prison with a grenade when the British were preparing to hang them for plotting the murder of a British general.

Begin reserved a burial site for himself next to Aliza. Sharon arrived with the mourners. Sharon's great-great-grandfather was buried in this cemetery. The weather was raw and cold, and as the Begin family made its way to the grave, Sharon saw two men staring grimly at him. They were all in black, and he realized that this was Kahan and Aharon Barak, two of the three members of the commission investigating Sabra and Shatila. Their gaze was intense, "unfriendly," Sharon thought. They were perched "like two black ravens" there in the cemetery and again later that day in the Knesset, when they glared at him from the visitors' gallery.[26]

Time was short, Sharon realized. In his mind, the real tragedy was that his "victory" in Lebanon was being squandered. He couldn't convince the Gemayels, either the old man, Pierre, or Amin, Bashir's older brother who was taking over, to finish the job, clean out West Beirut and push the Syrians back. It was as if Sharon was still holding to Dayan's "detonator" theory: Israel could force the great powers to respond to its demands by "detonating" a new crisis. Sharon, up to the last, wanted to expand the war until it got settled to his satisfaction, meaning: Palestinians out, Syrians out, pliable Christians in, Israel in charge.

Sharon's premonition about the Kahan Commission was more than confirmed on February 8, when its members handed down a scathing report on Israel's "indirect responsibility" for the massacre. Kahan and his colleagues recommended that the government remove Sharon from his post, send Eitan into early retirement, and remove the chief of military intelligence along with the commanding general on the scene in Beirut, Amos Yaron.

But Sharon bore the brunt of the condemnation. "As a politician responsible for Israel's security affairs," the commission wrote, "it was the duty of the Defense Minister to take into account all the reasonable considerations for and against having the Phalangists enter the camps, and not to disregard entirely the serious consideration mitigating against such an action, namely that the Phalangists were liable to commit atrocities. . . .

"From the Defense Minister himself we know that this consideration did not concern him in the least."[27]

The Kahan report also exposed the cynicism and duplicity at the heart of Begin's government. Begin had been incurious. Generals and intelligence officials had appeared to suspend their judgment. The foreign minister, Yitzhak Shamir, had received a telephone call from a fellow minister indicating that a "slaughter" might be under way in Beirut, and Shamir reacted by doing nothing, writing off the phone call to his colleague's dislike of Sharon.[28]

The battle moved to the cabinet, where Sharon fought for nearly a week against the growing calls for his resignation, and when the vote came, he lost sixteen to one, with Sharon himself casting the single no vote. Begin had refused to fight for Sharon, and this was the deepest wound.

To Sharon, Begin had come to represent an authority figure much like Sharon's father, the uncompromising dictator of his youth. Sharon had never been ruled by the painful memories of his life in Kfar Malal, but he had not forgotten that day when he was seventeen and his father had told him that as far as he was concerned, the boy could join the Palmach, which at that moment was engaged in hunting Irgun extremists such as Menachem Begin. The elder Scheinerman had pulled the boy close and said, "Arik, anything you decide to do with your life is all right with me. But you have to promise me one thing: Never, never participate in turning Jews over to non-Jews. You must promise me that you will never do that."[29]

Sharon had taken so little from his father, but he had held on to that admonition, perhaps because it seemed a noble impulse, unlike so many of the irrational obsessions of his father's life. And that was what Sharon was holding on to when he went, finally, to Begin's office after he had cleared out his desk at the Defense Ministry and prepared for life as the pariah of Israeli politics, a minister without portfolio.

Sharon went to sit with Begin during these tumultuous days of change and said, "I want to tell you something. I don't know how you see what has happened. But I want you to know how I feel about it."

Begin looked at him calmly through his thick spectacles. Sharon told him what his father had said that day in the orange grove and how, at that time, Begin was being hunted and how the notion of Jews turning on Jews had so repulsed Sharon's father.

And look what had happened, Sharon said. A cabinet dominated by

Irgun men who knew what it was like to be hunted had turned Sharon over to the "mob."

"Menachem, it was you who handed me over to them. You are the one who did it."[30]

The anguish and rage of the Jewish state's most controversial soldier reflected Sharon's deep sense of alienation from his own people. But Sharon's incapacity for introspection about what he and Begin had wrought in Lebanon revealed a deeply callous disregard for Arab suffering that repulsed many Israelis, sabras and nonsabras alike.

The failed Israeli invasion of Lebanon had demonstrated the limits of militarism. Israel was a small state with finite resources to sustain an occupation army in the field without massive resupply and financial support from the United States. For all of Begin's assertions that Israel must have freedom of action, the military elite saw that Begin and Sharon had overreached; they had endangered the country's relations with its most crucial patron and gained none of the strategic objectives that had danced in their imaginations. Israel's military society, which had sacrificed so much, had developed a growing intolerance for casualties, and in Lebanon, more than 650 Israeli soldiers had perished and another 2,400 were wounded, many seriously. Young Israelis asked more defiantly than ever what they had been fighting for in Lebanon. To much of the country, it seemed an unnecessary war.

With Sharon out of action, Lebanon reverted to a battleground. Reagan decided to keep the contingent of U.S. marines in Beirut, part of a multinational force with the French that was supposed to have prevented Sabra and Shatila. But all notions of military efficacy were being blown up. A truck bomber destroyed the American embassy in April, killing sixty-three people, including Robert Ames, the CIA's leading expert on the Middle East, and a group of CIA officers who were meeting with Ames in a conference room just above the entrance of the embassy where the bomber's truck came to a halt a moment before detonation.

Shamir sent Kimche to Beirut to secure the best agreement Israel could get from postinvasion negotiations, which were organized by the Americans. Amin Gemayel, Bashir's older brother, spoke for Lebanon, and Syria was excluded—a fatal decision by George Shultz. When the American secretary of state emerged with an agreement on May 17, 1983, the accord tilted heavily toward Israel. The Syrians denounced it and threatened to terrorize Lebanon until the Christians disavowed it. Syria, rearmed by the Soviet Union and brimming with confidence, shot down an American jet on a reconnaissance mission, further embarrassing the Reagan administration.[31]

Damascus moved closer to Iran—in large measure to counter Saddam Hussein's growing power in Iraq—and Iran dispatched the first contingent of Revolutionary Guards to Syria from where they entered Lebanon's Bekáa Valley. There they recruited young Shiites and trained and equipped a new force of Iranian-backed fighters that would open a second front against the West. Among the new Shiite soldiers of terror was Imad Mughniyeh, a militant Shiite who had served in Arafat's Force 17 protection unit. With the PLO gone, Mughniyeh helped to organize the new underground army that functioned as the military wing of the Shiite political awakening, soon to be called the Party of God, or Hezbollah.

It didn't take long to demonstrate that a new power was rising in Lebanon, one that the sabras had not seen coming. On October 23, 1983, Mughniyeh organized simultaneous attacks on the U.S. and French bases in Beirut with massive truck bombs whose explosions that morning were so devastating that they collapsed buildings and killed three hundred American and French soldiers. Twelve days later, a third truck bomber hit the Israeli base farther south at Tyre, killing twenty-nine Israeli soldiers and dozens of Lebanese.

The military establishment had suffered a devastating blow, stampeded by Begin's false vision and Sharon's ambition. They had proceeded with no political or diplomatic constraints of the kind that had hemmed in Ben-Gurion in 1955 when Lebanon stirred his imagination. And Sharett's caution about Lebanon had been vindicated, though almost no one in the country seemed to recognize this.

The judgment of the Kahan Commission, like the judgment of the Agranat Commission after the Yom Kippur War, demonstrated that blame fixing was now intrinsic to Israel's political and military culture. This would set up conditions for even greater reliance on the military establishment to provide detailed guidance and policy recommendations about potential threats to national security. For the political elite, the military establishment was mitigating the political risk of governing, or of taking chances on diplomacy, negotiation, and compromise. It was easier just to let the military run the country.

The catastrophe in Lebanon broke Menachem Begin.

The Kahan Commission's judgment effectively rendered his premiership a failure, not just of leadership but also of Jewish morality. It was true that the Camp David treaty stood out as Begin's monument, but Israelis came to see what the Egyptians saw: that Begin's peacemaking was in the service of war. A new militarism had been directed at the Palestinians, at Syria, and at the whole Arab world.

The judgment of failure sent Begin into the well-known psychological tailspin of depression and withdrawal, deeper this time perhaps because Aliza, his partner since their youth in Poland, was not there to provide the reassurance that had been the bulwark of his life.

"He didn't break with Sharon, he broke with himself," said Arye Naor, one of Begin's closest aides and, later, biographer. "After the Kahan Commission report, which criticized him—from that moment on, he never returned to himself."[32]

More than 650 Israeli soldiers had died in a senseless military campaign. Israel's bereaved parents, most of whom had themselves served in the army, focused their rage at Begin for demanding a life-shattering sacrifice in pursuit of martial folly.

In August 1983, Begin, looking listless and depressed, surprised his fellow cabinet ministers by saying, "I cannot go on." He announced his retirement from public life and walked away.[33]

Ronald Reagan also walked away.

After promising Amin Gemayel that America would stand behind his new government, Reagan pulled the marines out of Beirut in early 1984 and turned toward his reelection campaign. Under pressure from Syria, Gemayel abrogated the May 17 accord and turned his back on Israel.

With Sharon and Eitan disgraced, the IDF went into self-protection mode.

The general staff recommended a staged withdrawal across southern Lebanon and, as the army moved back, the Druze, the Syrians, and the

Shiites filled the vacuum and resumed their internecine war. Hezbollah's power grew, strengthened by new weapons and missiles shipped from Iran to Syria and then trucked into the Bekáa Valley. Bereft of hope, Lebanon again lapsed into a period of sectarian fighting, terrorism, and hostage taking that ensnared a large number of Americans and other Westerners.

The Israeli dead and wounded came home to a country that had begun to ask what had been the point of invading Lebanon. And since the country was the army, the introspection was marked by a new wave of disillusionment as broad as or broader than the one that followed the Yom Kippur War.

If Begin's vision had failed, what was the correct path?

No one really expected Yitzhak Shamir, the interim prime minister, to provide the answers.

Shamir was less a man of vision than he was a scion of the security establishment, trusted by many of the sabras and the military intelligence professionals as one of them. His grip on popular sentiments had never been strong. Like Begin, he was a refugee from Europe who had never escaped the psychology of the Holocaust. When Sharon challenged Shamir for leadership of the Likud Party in May 1984, Shamir won, but the political establishment took note that Sharon captured 42.5 percent of the vote among Likud members, a strong showing for a supposedly discredited militarist.

It reminded Israelis of the cries by Sharon supporters that if the country did not want him as defense minister, it might just get him as prime minister.

The failure in Lebanon energized the Labor Party and the new peace movement.

Six months after he had appeared with Sharon overlooking Beirut, Rabin stood at a lectern at Hebrew University in Jerusalem, calling on Begin to admit that it had been a dangerous illusion to think Israel could impose a new political order in Lebanon by military means. Rabin called Lebanon a "quagmire."[34]

Shimon Peres and the leaders of the Labor establishment saw that a centrist majority of Israelis was deeply interested in peace. The Peace Now organization had grown dramatically since its inception in 1977 when 348 reserve officers signed the letter to Begin. Peres, whose entire history had shaped him as a Ben-Gurion militarist and a champion of the settler movement, suddenly reversed course and began working to transform Labor into the party of peace. Few who knew Peres believed that his transformation was anything other than opportunistic, but it didn't matter since he brought a powerful voice to the effort.

In late 1985 and again in late 1986, Peres seemed on the verge of a diplomatic breakthrough for peace with Jordan's King Hussein, but on each occasion he failed to close the deal. His self-aggrandizing style of diplomacy simply never met the expectations of his Arab partners for the return of lands, the sharing of Jerusalem, or the recognition of true Palestinian self-rule. And within the two-headed government, Shamir outmaneuvered him.

Rabin was more cautious and more concerned about the damage that Begin and Sharon had done to the army. He wanted to bring the troops home from Lebanon. And he was not enamored of the prospects for peace as long as Arafat owned the sympathies of the Arab street.

By all rights, the Labor Party with Peres and Rabin heading the ticket should have trounced the Likud slate headed by Shamir in July 1984, but the campaign proved that any prolonged examination of Peres revealed a man that Israelis—especially sabras—liked to mistrust, a man of clever aphorisms who lacked any connection to the land or to military service.

Labor won forty-four seats, enough to best Shamir and the Likud (forty-one seats), but Peres failed to find coalition partners to reach a working majority of sixty-one deputies. He was forced to turn to Shamir to form a two-headed national unity government, Labor and Likud, with the two men alternating as prime minister. For the first two years, Peres would serve as prime minister, with Shamir as foreign minister, and for the final two years they would reverse roles. Rabin would serve as defense minister under both leaders.

The importance of the 1984 election is that it ushered in nearly a decade of political paralysis during which none of the three top leaders—Peres, Shamir, Rabin—could galvanize a sufficient majority of Israelis to impose a new national strategy. The military and political elites were almost evenly divided.

One thing was clear: with Rabin's return to the Defense Ministry, Israel resumed a more cautious posture. Rabin's strategic focus was weakening the PLO's influence in the West Bank, deterring Syria, completing a withdrawal from Lebanon, and improving ties with Washington.

By the middle of 1985, the Israeli army under Rabin had completed a withdrawal from most of Lebanon save for the security zone in the border region policed jointly with the Christian force known as the South Lebanese Army. The Likud ministers in the national unity government—Shamir, Sharon, and Moshe Arens—all opposed Rabin's withdrawal plan, but the vote carried when one Likud minister, David Levy, sided with Labor.

"I don't want to be the policeman of Lebanon," Rabin told an American interviewer in early 1985. "It's not the business of Israel. Israel was not created to serve as a policeman of the region."[35]

How much had changed.

Syria was once again the dominant power in Lebanon. The dictator Assad had bested the Israelis.

"[If] they want to stay in Lebanon," Rabin said of the Syrians, "let them stay. I know that whoever sets his foot in Lebanon has sunk into the Lebanese muck. [If] they want it, let them enjoy it."[36]

Looking back on Lebanon much later, Efraim Halevy, the Mossad chief who had watched his colleagues tear each other apart over the misadventure with the Phalange, said: "In retrospect, what happened in Lebanon is that we misjudged the future; in other words, we didn't realize that the future was not going to be the Christians, but rather the Shiites."[37]

But the military elite had also misjudged the past.

The martial impulse that impelled Begin, Sharon, and the army into Lebanon ignored all of the warnings from history—Sharett's most prominently, but also those of key intelligence chiefs—that military power could not rearrange the complex political order of Lebanon. The Arabs of Lebanon—Christian and Muslim alike—shared common principles with the Arabs of Egypt and Jordan and, increasingly, throughout the region: the foundations of peace and coexistence with Israel could arise only from a settlement of the Palestinian question and even then it would take time, patient diplomacy, negotiation, and compromise, the least developed weapons in Israel's arsenal.

For Begin and Sharon, the simple fact was that all restraints on their power had disappeared when the opportunity to make a grand play in

Lebanon presented itself. The temptation had been too great for willful men chasing illusions. But in the wake of the massacre, the death of Gemayel, the resurgence of Syria, and the Reagan peace plan, the profound lesson was that there were limits to military power. Israel could not thrive in the region by force alone.

TWELVE

Protecting the Ruling Elite

Shimon Peres was blunt in describing how he felt in late 1986 about turning over the Israeli government to his Likud rival, Yitzhak Shamir, a man he detested.

"I'll make him swallow toads and snakes and scorpions," Peres told one confidant. "What did you think—that I would cooperate with Shamir?"[1]

But just days before Peres made the final decision to vacate the prime minister's office and return to the Foreign Ministry, the chiefs of the intelligence services came to him with some troubling news: a technician from the Dimona nuclear complex had left the country and was believed to be peddling his knowledge, along with photographs, of Israel's secret atomic bomb program to the foreign news media.

The technician's name was Mordechai Vanunu, and soon Peres, Shamir, and Rabin all were seated around a table with the chiefs of Mossad, Shabak, military intelligence, and the atomic energy agency.

Over the next few weeks, the three Israeli leaders—rivals who had battled each other viciously in public—worked closely together behind closed doors to supervise a squad of Mossad agents that fanned out across Europe, located Vanunu in the center of London, threw an attractive female agent in his path, and enticed him on a romantic Roman holiday, where her Mossad colleagues jabbed Vanunu with a tranquilizing needle and bundled him out to sea off the coast of Italy.

An Israeli naval vessel, possibly a submarine, transported him back to Israel for trial and imprisonment.

The case was a sensation primarily because the *Sunday Times* of London was able to report, based on Vanunu's information, that Israel's stockpile of nuclear weapons now totaled about one hundred atomic war-heads.[2]

The real threat for Israel was that exposure of its atomic capabilities would force the Jewish state to admit openly and for the first time that for more than twenty years it had lied to a succession of American presidents and to the international community about what it had been doing at Dimona. Israel's credibility was at the heart of the "special relationship" President Kennedy had described to Golda Meir. Now, in Peres's final days as prime minister, his pledge to Kennedy that Israel would not be the first country in the Middle East to introduce nuclear weapons was about to be unmasked as false.

Even worse, exposure might also renew proliferation pressures among the Arab states and Iran to develop their own nuclear deterrent forces as a counter to Israel's. If Israel was allowed to have nukes, why shouldn't they? the Arabs and Iranians might ask. This was the paradox at the heart of Israel's nuclear policy: it had no ambivalence about being a nuclear power—only about being *seen* as a nuclear power.

The urgent question of what to do fused the interests of the country's ruling elite, which feared an international scandal. While the rivalries within Israel were real and, at times, heated, there were limits to how far any leader could go in seeking to discredit or overthrow another without risking exposure of politically explosive secrets that each felt bound to protect.

In conducting research for this book, I spoke with Shabtai Shavit, one of the senior Mossad officers in 1986 who supervised the Vanunu recovery operation. The case marked the first time that Shavit had worked closely with the "political echelon," as he called it—Peres, Shamir, and Rabin—and he marveled at how cooperatively they made decisions, orchestrated events, controlled the news media, and shaped a propaganda line that allowed Israel to continue its posture of nuclear "ambiguity," while also standing mute as the foreign press conveyed irrefutable evidence that Israel had become the sixth-largest member of the nuclear club.

"It was a rather intimate relationship," said Shavit, describing a multi-agency operation that involved the military, the intelligence services, the navy, the justice ministry, and the atomic energy chiefs.

The intensely partisan jousting that marked the day-to-day political relations among the leaders disappeared in the private council to which they repaired to manage the crisis and control information.

After the *Sunday Times* published its article, one of the most sensitive decisions was whether to simply assassinate Vanunu.

"The easiest thing to do would have been to kill him," Shavit said. "The newspaper, until the last second, was hesitating because they were not sure it was not a hoax, so it would have been easy to kill him."

But as only Peres, Rabin, and Shamir knew, the military and intelligence establishments were in the midst of covering up a high-level decision to execute two Palestinian militants following their arrest in a 1984 terrorist attack. Peres feared another scandal, this time involving the assassination of a Jew. He decided to bring Vanunu home alive.

The Vanunu case showed the seamless fusion at the top of a military society, where the political echelon, in this case a former chief of staff (Rabin), a former Mossad officer (Shamir), and a former defense minister (Peres), reverted to combat mode to manage a crisis secretly and wholly independent of democratic review.

During Peres's premiership, the two-headed government "handled" three major scandals, and each crisis made clear that the ruling elite and the military establishment ran the country, often with little regard for the rule of law, especially when Israel's interests were threatened by scandal or crisis.

The first arose from the Bus 300 affair.

In April 1984, Shamir was in the final days of his premiership after Begin's resignation. Four Palestinian militants hijacked Bus No. 300 on its regular route from Tel Aviv south to Ashkelon. Forty-one passengers were on board and the militants hoped to trade them for five hundred Palestinian prisoners in Israeli jails. Israeli security forces quickly caught up with the bus after it veered into Gaza. A shoot-out ensued, and an Israeli commando team under General Yitzhak Mordechai freed the hostages. Two of the PLO militants were killed, but the army unit captured two others and turned them over to internal security agents of the Shabak.

Ehud Yatom, the owlish-looking thirty-six-year-old chief of Shabak's operations branch, put the two Palestinian prisoners in a van. They had been badly beaten. Yatom later described them as "two sacks of potatoes."

"We put them in our van and then I received instructions from [Shabak chief] Avraham Shalom to kill them, so I killed them." He picked up a large stone. "I crushed their skulls. Believe me, there was no need for too much of an effort. They were already finished."[3] No one in Israel knew these facts, and it would take years for them to fully emerge because top Shabak officials covered up the extrajudicial murders of the two hijackers. When it became known that press photographers had seen the two militants alive after the battle, Shabak officials told an internal inquiry that the army commandos under Mordechai had beaten the men to death. Mordechai and his men were forced to stand trial based on evidence fabricated by Shabak senior officers.

In the Bus 300 affair, the military-intelligence establishment was not monolithic except at the top; within the ranks, it had proved that it was possible for one powerful component, in this case the Shabak, to lie, perjure, and shift blame to the military out of self-preservation.

Finally, in late 1985, Shabak's deputy director broke ranks with Shalom and revealed the fact of the killings to Peres, by then prime minister. Peres shared the sensational revelation with a very small circle and, by his actions, it was clear that his overarching impulse, shared by Rabin and Shamir, was to cover up the murders, pardon the officers involved, and protect the military and intelligence establishments and the political elite overseeing them.

Censors were dispatched to keep the story out of the press. One newspaper was shut down for violating the ban. The *New York Times* correspondent David K. Shipler was upbraided by the Israeli Press Office for reporting on the case. Peres fired an attorney general to prevent a prosecution; he orchestrated pardons for the Shabak agents and kept any formal criminal charge from reaching the prime minister's office.

True to form, Rabin, Peres, and Shamir circled the wagons to protect the prime minister.

Peres performed like a party boss, investing his entire government in the cover-up. On May 30, 1986, he brought Shalom to his home along with the senior Labor ministers in the government. According to Peres's biographer Michael Bar-Zohar, "Shalom maintained that he had acted 'on the authority and with the permission' of Prime Minister Yitzhak Shamir.

Now he felt the ministers were forsaking him. He suddenly broke down and started to cry."[4]

Bar-Zohar wrote also that Peres's participation in the cover-up and pardon of the Shabak chiefs, while "clumsy and lame," actually "served Israel's security by preventing the washing of dirty laundry in public." But this conclusion hardly addresses the real quandary that Peres faced. It was inevitable that the laundry was going to be prominently displayed. Yatom confessed his role in the murders publicly in a 1996 interview. He said he was still troubled by what he had done.

Peres's only alternative was to put his Shabak chief on trial, where Israelis would be confronted with testimony that Shamir himself, on the telephone or in person, had uttered the words "kill them," testimony that would expose Shamir to international condemnation and possible criminal charges. It was bad enough that Shamir had come to office from the Mossad and, before that, the Stern Gang underground with its history of involvement in assassinations and bank robberies. But to be accused—as a sitting prime minister—of ordering the extrajudicial murder of Palestinians engaged in politically motivated violence against the occupation of Palestinian lands would cut so deeply into Israel's standing in the world as to be intolerable.

The nightmare for Peres was that he might be blamed for bringing down a cataclysm that could sweep both him and Shamir from office. The impulse to cover up and lie—both to the Israelis and to the world—was the same that had motivated Sharett in the Lavon Affair: fear of the abyss, of delegitimization.

The fear was real, yet irrational.

The truth was that Peres would have garnered respect and admiration from many quarters for taking a moral stand against the killings. Some critics would have recoiled at how there was no real difference between the military and intelligence establishments and the government, as was often the case. But the real victim in the Bus 300 affair was the rule of law.

The second scandal that drew Peres, Rabin, and Shamir together was a case of insidious espionage. In 1985, U.S. officials discovered that Jonathan Pollard, a navy analyst inside the Pentagon, was an Israeli spy. Pollard, an American Jew who seemed motivated by money as much as any sympathy for the Jewish state, had turned over thousands of pages of top secret documents to his Israeli handler in exchange for $20,000 in cash and jewelry, plus a hefty monthly retainer.

The spying operation was run out of a secretive unit within Israel's Ministry of Defense, which functioned as a separate intelligence agency whose mission was to acquire weapons and technology. Peres had set up the Scientific Liaison Unit in the 1950s, and its agents had run guns and purchased or stolen weaponry and high-technology components, including technology for Israel's nuclear weapons program.

Under Rabin, the unit was run by Rafael Eitan (not Raful, the former chief of staff, but a former Mossad officer known as Rafi, a veteran of many covert operations, including the abduction of Adolf Eichmann from Argentina). Rafi Eitan was a notorious figure in Israel and the United States: as a young saboteur in the Jewish underground, he had crawled through sewer pipes to blow up the British radar installation on Mount Carmel; as a Mossad operative in the 1960s, he turned up—in the guise of a Ministry of Defense chemist—at a sensitive U.S. nuclear facility that subsequently reported two hundred pounds of highly enriched uranium missing and possibly diverted to Israel.

The revelation that Eitan had been running an agent inside the U.S. government was potentially catastrophic. What kind of country spied on its most powerful ally, its vital source of financial support, weapons, and deterrent power? Rabin was Eitan's boss, and so the first thing he and Peres had to do was to make a plausible case that the spying operation was somehow an accident and that no senior Israeli leader knew of or condoned it.

In the insular world of the Israeli military establishment, this was not a credible assertion, if for no other reason than that Rabin had made his reputation as the defense chief who read every internal communiqué and knew the details of Israel's relations with Washington like no other Israeli.

In public, Peres reacted to Pollard's arrest by saying, "Spying on the United States stands in total contradiction to our policy." Within the U.S. intelligence community, almost no one believed him. The Israelis were forced to return the documents, and Peres and Rabin submitted to an investigation by the Knesset's Foreign Affairs and Defense Committee, then chaired by Abba Eban, the former foreign minister.[5]

Once again, crisis—or, to put it more precisely, the revelation of how the military elite really operated—brought Peres, Rabin, and Shamir together.

They met daily in the prime minister's office to manage the blowback from Washington and to try to convince the Americans that they were not to blame. Within a week, the three leaders and the Knesset committee almost certainly fabricated the report asserting that Rafi Eitan had been running a "rogue" intelligence operation that had "misinterpreted" the strict government guidelines against carrying out espionage inside the United States. Peres's spokesman, Nachman Shai, called in Thomas L. Friedman, the *New York Times* bureau chief, and provided an exclusive briefing on the findings that the whole affair had been "a sincere mistake."[6]

It would take more than a year for the Knesset subcommittee charged with a thorough review of the episode to state the obvious: for Rabin's account to be believed, one would have to envision an Israeli defense minister who, for fourteen months, watched an increasing volume of "particularly sensitive" top secret American documents arrive on his desk from Rafi Eitan's Scientific Liaison Unit and not inquire whether someone was violating the state ban on espionage against Israel's most important patron.[7]

In a U.S. court, Pollard drew a life sentence for espionage. But Peres, Rabin, and Shamir survived the crisis, because neither Israel nor the United States wanted the Pollard affair to dampen a secret and joint special operation that was under way at the time.

In late 1985, a few months before Pollard's espionage was detected, President Reagan had given his approval for a clandestine operation in which the United States would ship arms to Iran via the Israeli military, an operation that made the Pollard affair pale by comparison and that came to be known as the Iran-contra affair. Reagan and his closest advisers convinced themselves that a group of moderate clerics in Tehran were willing to work behind the scenes to gain the release of American hostages in Lebanon and improve relations between the Reagan White House and key figures inside the revolutionary government of the Ayatollah Ruhollah Khomeini.[8]

The arms-for-hostages trade represented an act of desperation by the Reagan White House to win the release of American hostages who were chained to radiators in Beirut's dark basements. But the sale of weapons to Iran also served as a means to generate off-the-books cash that the United States could funnel to the anti-Sandinista guerrillas in Nicaragua, whose funding through the CIA had been cut off by a skeptical Congress.

Israel had received its first secret request to help fund the contras earlier, in 1984, but Shamir, then prime minister, sent word to the White House through David Kimche that he was not able to help.[9]

By the time Peres came to office as prime minister, the Americans had found a different source of secret funding. Reagan's men had persuaded Saudi Arabia's King Fahd to make monthly covert payments to the contras, tilting the balance of power in the region as the Arabs carried more and more weight helping to defeat the Soviet occupation of Afghanistan.[10]

After the Pollard affair, Peres was eager to get Israel back into the game as Washington's indispensable ally. Israeli businessmen, most of them working with the knowledge of their government, had been supplying spare parts and munitions to Iran as part of the secret arms trade in the Middle East, but Iranian commanders needed missiles to stop Iraqi tanks and aircraft. The Israelis presented the new idea of quietly shipping American-made missiles from the Israeli arsenal to Tehran, missiles that would then be replaced with new ones shipped from the United States.

As defense minister, Rabin was in favor of working clandestinely with Washington to sell arms to Khomeini's regime. Rabin understood the dynamics of the arms trade. If Washington was shipping large quantities of TOW antitank missiles and Hawk air-defense missiles to a militant Islamic state that was the byword for anti-Americanism, how could Washington turn down even bigger arms requests from Israel, its democratic friend?

Mossad had developed useful relationships in Iran. Kimche, still director general of the Israeli Foreign Ministry, traveled to Washington and, in private conversations with Reagan's national security adviser, Robert McFarlane, made the case that Khomeini could be toppled by powerful rivals within the religious hierarchy.[11]

When the Iran-contra saga was exposed, at first through leaks to newspapers, then via harried White House briefings and tortured acknowledgments, the whole tawdry story of McFarlane's clandestine visit to Tehran, carrying a cake, acting out an espionage drama that fell flat on its face when the Iranians were caught off guard, left the Reagan administration looking inept.[12] But the greater shock—after it all settled in—was that the United States and Israel together had been arming a Middle Eastern power deeply hostile to Israel. Suddenly, Israel's claim to perpetual vulnerability in the region looked like a cover—even a lie.

Once again, Peres, Rabin, and Shamir worked closely together behind the scenes to mask the extent of Israel's involvement in the American scandal and protect its own military and intelligence establishments.

This was the backdrop to the struggle between Peres and Shamir. Together with Rabin, all three faced intense political crises that threatened to end their careers and discredit the political order that held them in place. These were not the intrigues of an embattled democracy; these were the covert machinations of a *chekist* apparat caught out while exploiting the special relationship with Washington to gain advantage over the Arabs.

The intensely partisan veneer that marked the day-to-day public exchanges among Shamir, Peres, and Rabin faded as each man worked his own channels to cover up wrongdoing that might be devastating at home or cause a rupture with Washington. Here was an example of the military culture suspending truth and accountability in a unilateral arrogation of power that Israelis had learned to expect. Since Ben-Gurion's time, Israelis had come to understand that deception was a necessary element in a military society.

So when leaders were caught selling weapons to an implacable enemy, or spying on the country's most intimate ally, the national impulse was to embrace a narrative of rationalization—true or not—that the weapons sold were not so good, that Israel got better and more weapons in return, that Israel's leaders earned some credit from Washington by trying to help, and that the Americans would come to understand that Pollard's spying was an innocent mistake among friends.

THIRTEEN

Intifada: The Intimate Enemy Awakes

At the main crossing coming out of the Gaza Strip, the traffic jam was just tuning up one morning in December 1987: honking horns, revving engines, drivers shouting and gesturing. The sun rose through the haze over the Negev Desert to illuminate thousands of Palestinians packed into buses, taxis, and private cars queued up to pass the Israeli army checkpoint before heading for day jobs in the kitchens, farms, and factories of Israel.

Into this dissonance, an Israeli truck intruded, veering off the road and crashing into the line of Palestinian cars, touching off a chaotic scene of rescue, calls for ambulances, and cries for the dead.

Four Palestinians died. It seemed clearly an accident, perhaps through carelessness or lack of sleep, but the deaths triggered an outpouring of frustration and rage. The funeral processions in Gaza turned to riot, and when an Israeli army patrol entered the Jabaliya refugee camp as a show of force, a mob of angry Palestinian youths began hurling stones at the soldiers. The Israelis gave chase but were quickly surrounded by more stone-throwing teenagers, some of whom lobbed Molotov cocktails at the vehicle. Gunfire rang out as the soldiers fired into the crowd, killing a fifteen-year-old boy.

That was the beginning of the intifada, a spontaneous uprising of young Palestinians who had lived their entire lives under Israeli occupation. They wrapped their checkered kaffiyehs around their heads so the Shabak agents could not identify them and took up their slings, like young Davids, and let fly their anger against the steel of the Israeli army.

Columns of smoke rose from the refugee camps of Gaza where young militants piled up car and truck tires in the middle of intersections and set them on fire to block the army and enforce a general strike meant to prevent tens of thousands of Palestinian workers from commuting to Israel for work.

"Kill us all! . . . Kill us all!" the brazen youngsters screamed at Israeli soldiers day after day. "Come and kill us all or get out!"

Jacob Peri was the Shabak's deputy director when the first Palestinians rioted. He went straight to Prime Minister Yitzhak Shamir with a recommendation to make a strong showing of Israeli military force in Gaza and the West Bank to quell the outbreak. Shamir said he would consider it but did not act. Day after day, the rioting continued. Rabin was in the United States, where he told American officials that he planned to "crush" the lawlessness as soon as he returned.[1]

Peri was a politically astute domestic intelligence man. He had spent most of his life chasing, interrogating, imprisoning, and killing Palestinian militants. He believed that he understood the Palestinians, their strengths and weaknesses; he spoke their language, and he had lived among them when he was studying Arabic as a young recruit into the service. He was a committed Zionist and did not have any trouble sleeping at night, but he was also more pragmatic than some of his political masters about how to deal with "the intimate enemy," as the Palestinians were sometimes called.

By 1987, Peri quickly came to the conclusion that the intifada was not the work of the PLO; it was a spontaneous outburst, though words seemed insufficient in Peri's view to describe the origins of the rebellion in Palestinian society.

"You have to understand that since 1967 a whole generation of Palestinians was raised, educated, suppressed, arrested—you name it—by Israel," he told me. "There was a tone of despair, lack of hope, anger at having no way out, no direction—and it just burst out."[2]

Here was a problem that could not be solved by military means.

Almost everything about the new conflict refused to conform to the army's assumptions for how to overcome a challenge to state security. A new generation of Palestinians, those who had grown up with nothing to lose, were determined to risk the only asset they possessed—their lives—to confront their occupier.

The prime minister and his defense minister dismissed the tire-burning mobs in the Palestinian camps as rabble that would succumb to overwhelming Israeli force. Rabin returned from Washington and told reporters that the violence was being instigated by Syria and Iran, though he knew that this was not the case. At first, Rabin could not bring himself to admit that the Palestinians were wielding a power with which the Israeli army, with all of its might, could not cope. Everything that life in uniform had taught Rabin had led him to respect military power. Nasser had had an army. The king of Jordan had an army. It had crushed the Palestinians during Black September. That's what nation-states did. They contested for power and deterred their enemies with military might. The Palestinians had no army and, as a consequence, Rabin seemed to have little respect for them.

Rabin told his wife, Leah, that Israel had faced many challenges in its short history, but "the intifada is not one of them."[3] Then he issued orders to use "might, force and beatings" to quell the disturbances. Soon Gaza's Shifa Hospital was full of thirteen- and fourteen-year-old boys whose arms had been snapped by Shabak agents acting on orders to get brutal in the face of daily rioting.

"Break their bones," Rabin was said to have muttered, though he later denied it.[4]

When Shimon Peres called on the government to undertake a political initiative that might give the Palestinians hope for greater self-rule, Shamir scowled. "These bloody attacks must not be linked to political solutions," he said.

Shamir attacked Peres as "a defeatist with a scalpel who wants to put Israel on the operating table so he can give away Gaza today, Judea and Samaria tomorrow and the Golan Heights after that."[5]

But unlike Shamir, Rabin looked at the intifada as a realist, and after ninety days of unrelenting rebellion, of worldwide astonishment that the Palestinian people were taking their fate into their own hands for the first time since 1948, Rabin turned on a dime and began speaking about "the need for a policy that stands on two legs, military and political."[6]

So policy in the territories needed a political side: that was the real breakthrough for a sabra raised on the certainty of military force.

"I've learned something in the past two and a half months," Rabin told Labor Party leaders in Tel Aviv. "You can't rule by force over one and a half million Palestinians."[7]

Rabin called upon the members of his own party, but also the leaders on the right, to consider the national predicament. How could the dream of Greater Israel, if ever fulfilled, bring security? Security was the cornerstone of everything the Israelis hoped for.

"What would we do with all the Palestinians?" he asked. To those who said they should be "transferred" in another forced expulsion, Rabin said Israelis could not contemplate such an act. "Transfer so far has only been done to Jews, we should not forget that. If we make [the Palestinians] citizens, they will have 25 to 30 seats in the Knesset. If we don't we shall be a racist state, not a Jewish one."[8]

Though Rabin and Shamir stood for different visions of the future, they shared a basic caution, and it soon became apparent that Arafat and the PLO were laying claim to leadership of the intifada, as was Sheikh Ahmed Yassin, the spiritual leader of Hamas, the Islamic renaissance movement in Gaza.

The Dimona nuclear reactor is a half hour's drive through the Negev southeast of Beersheba, which in Hebrew means "seven wells." During World War I, the British forces under General Edmund Allenby broke the Turkish line at Beersheba with one of the last successful cavalry charges in British military history.

The nuclear complex is located a short distance from the town of Dimona, where many of the plant's technicians and scientists live. A CIA station chief in the 1960s was once detained for driving through Dimona and writing down in his notebook the names on the mailboxes. He thereafter was referred to as "the bastard."[9]

In March 1988, PLO guerrillas infiltrated the Negev near the Dimona reactor and hijacked a bus full of working mothers, three of whom died in a shoot-out with Israeli commandos who stormed the vehicle. Rabin asked his security chiefs for their recommendation. Jacob Peri had just become chief of the Shabak. Ehud Barak was deputy chief of staff, Amnon Lipkin-Shahak was director of military intelligence, and Nahum Admoni was chief of the Mossad. Shabtai Shavit was his deputy.

"Abu Jihad was the architect of terror activities at that time," Lipkin-Shahak said later. "When the [PLO] team infiltrated from the Egyptian border and took the bus full of [women] hostage, we were around the bus before our attack and we could hear them shouting, 'Abu Jihad sent us to kill you!' "[10] To Lipkin-Shahak, this was a good enough reason to kill Abu Jihad. He says today that Abu Jihad was targeted for assassination not because he was Arafat's envoy to the young Palestinians running the intifada. He was targeted, Lipkin-Shahak insists, because he was Arafat's military strategist and operational commander.

Yet it was an election year in Israel. The military elites were competing. Both Shamir and Rabin hoped (for these reasons) to burnish their credentials as Mr. Security: Shamir because he hoped to fend off another challenge by Peres, and Rabin because he hoped to weaken Peres so Rabin could lead the party in his stead.

The plot to assassinate Arafat's right-hand man was undertaken at a moment when the confidence of Israel's military elite had been shaken by four straight months of Palestinian violence, strikes, and economic turmoil. Sabra militarism was still the most quenching tonic against the unease. Arafat was calling the uprising "the blessed intifada." And though Rabin understood that for the first time in his life he was up against an enemy that he could not defeat by force, he and Shamir reached for a military option to resuscitate the plummeting morale of the army—and thus of the public.

Shamir and Rabin assigned the task to Sayeret Matkal. The commando team was assembled by Moshe "Boogie" Ya'alon, a tenacious special forces officer who had fought in the Yom Kippur War. Mossad activated its network in Tunis to set up the surveillance and ground transportation to Abu Jihad's villa in the fashionable suburb of Sidi Bou Said. Naval commandos landed from the sea and an aerial command post circled near the Tunisian coastline with Ehud Barak aboard to supervise the team.

The assassination of Abu Jihad was the kind of martial display that created a sensation, especially in Israel, where amazing feats by special forces always energized public opinion as if they were the Olympics. The tabloids were full of details about how it happened: Abu Jihad appeared at the top of a staircase wielding a pistol but went down in a hail of bullets. His corpse showed sixty gunshot wounds. The assassination triggered intensified rioting in Gaza and the West Bank where the IDF moved in to quell the violence begotten by its own violence and killed dozens of young Palestinians.[11]

To protect the sensibilities of the Tunisian government, Israel stood mute on whether it was responsible for the hit. But anyone connected to the media and the security establishment knew that Boogie Ya'alon had headed the team, that Ehud Barak circled above in the airborne command post, and that a Mossad agent, a tall woman, taped the killing, producing a video, which was almost certainly screened for Shamir, Rabin, and the trusted inner circle of the military and ruling elite.

Days later, Rabin went on *Nightline* and told Ted Koppel, "I am ready to negotiate" with the PLO, but, he added, not until the PLO renounced its covenant to destroy Israel.[12]

Rabin relentlessly employed the military in a campaign that seemed timed to boost his political prospects. Two weeks after the killing of Abu Jihad, he dispatched more than one thousand Israeli troops into Lebanon with tanks and armored personnel carriers. He did not inform the cabinet in advance. He barely notified Shamir, who said later of the operation that he had been "unaware of its scope." Peres learned about it from news reports. Rabin claimed that he was operating within government guidelines in the war against terrorist organizations, but many Israelis saw a political purpose.[13]

Once across the border, the Israeli incursion force had raced to the Hezbollah stronghold at Maidoun near the southern end of the Bekáa Valley, part of the logistical base for the Shiite militia. Hezbollah was holding Western hostages in these strongholds, and Rabin may have launched the raid in hopes of freeing the American military officer Lieutenant Colonel William R. Higgins, who had been kidnapped from the UN observer force in Lebanon. Higgins was a high-profile target, having served in Washington as military aide to Defense Secretary Caspar Weinberger.[14]

To understand Rabin, it was necessary only to see how assiduously he was struggling to buck up the morale of the military establishment even as he began to question his long-held assumptions about the Palestinians. And, of course, he was trying to improve his election prospects.

But Rabin's attempt to rescue Higgins, if that is what it was, failed, and Israel's isolation seemed only to deepen.

George Shultz, the American secretary of state, on a swing through the Middle East to see if there was any chance for diplomatic advance, delivered a valediction that struck Rabin as dire, even if he was beginning to agree with it. "The continued occupation of the West Bank and the Gaza

Strip, and the frustration of Palestinian rights, is a dead-end street," he said. "The belief that this can continue is an illusion."[15]

Shimon Peres led the Labor Party into the elections in the fall of 1988 on a platform calling for negotiations with Jordan and a clear vision that peace could be achieved only by giving up land for a Palestinian homeland.

A new face in the Likud camp answered back.

It was Benjamin Netanyahu, the younger brother of the dead hero of the Entebbe raid. Speaking with a thoroughly American accent from his schooling outside Philadelphia and at MIT, Netanyahu radiated the energy and intelligence of a rising generation of right-wing sabras coming out of the army.

"The whole question in this election is whether or not we should give up what we already have," the youthful Netanyahu told a cheering crowd of Israeli settlers perched behind barbed wire and armed guards in the West Bank. "It's very simple: are we going to be here, or is the PLO? Is it going to be Yasser Arafat and George Habash, or settlers and the IDF?"[16]

Netanyahu's strong message helped to reinvigorate the right, but others were less sure. The November election failed to break the national stalemate. Likud's share of Knesset seats dropped from forty-one to forty, but Labor dropped from forty-four to thirty-nine, giving Shamir the right to form a government.

Raful Eitan, the chief of staff forced into retirement after the Lebanon War, won two seats for his Tzomet (Crossroads) Party, and another retired general, Rehavam Ze'evi, famously known as Gandhi, won two seats for his Molodet (Homeland) Party. Both openly advocated the expulsion of the Palestinian population from the West Bank and Gaza. Eitan had criticized Shamir's government for not cracking down harder on the intifada, saying that he would have put "a bullet in the head of every stone thrower."[17]

These were the maximalist sentiments arrayed against Peres and the so-called peace camp.

Peres's failure to make a stronger showing at the polls enabled Shamir to prevent him from returning as foreign minister. In the new national unity government, Peres accepted the finance minister's post. Rabin returned as defense minister while Shamir chose the hard-line Likudnik Moshe Arens as foreign minister.

The election of George H. W. Bush in the United States brought a new Republican administration to power, one experienced in the Middle East and determined to break the deadlock. Arab leaders had helped to orchestrate a statement from the PLO renouncing terrorism. This breakthrough created a new sense of momentum. The PLO, after decades of violence, was beginning to see a diplomatic path toward its goals.

But the Palestinian uprising simply would not subside, and neither Shamir nor Rabin could quell the violence.

The statistics were grim.

By early 1989, some 350 Palestinians had been killed, 20,000 wounded, and another 20,000 imprisoned. The Israeli army had blown up 157 Palestinian houses and sealed another 54 where a family member was suspected of being connected to the underground leadership of the uprising. When Shamir went to visit the troops near Nablus in February, one soldier looked up plaintively and said, "Mr. Prime Minister, to achieve order in the casbah I have to act brutally toward people free of crime. I feel humiliated by this behavior. The situation has become a catastrophe. It's breaking us and strengthening the Arabs."[18]

Shamir had no answer other than that soldiers had to follow orders. Sharon and other cabinet ministers on the right increasingly called for military action to put down the revolt, but the chief of staff, Dan Shomron, and his director of military intelligence, Lipkin-Shahak, said there was no viable military strategy.

"There is no such thing as eradicating the uprising, because in its essence it expresses the struggle of nationalism," Shomron said. When Lipkin-Shahak was asked who was in charge of the intifada in 1989, he answered, "The PLO," only to set off denunciations that he was giving legitimacy to Arafat.[19]

Yet a new generation of senior officers was rising in the military establishment, and many of them, like Rabin, had begun to recognize the irrepressible nature of Palestinian aspirations, against which military force could not prevail. And, of course, such thinking was anathema to men such as Sharon, Eitan, Ze'evi, Netanyahu, and Ya'alon. A new battleground was taking shape within the military establishment—how to perceive the intimate enemy.

―――――――

Rabin had to come up with something.

In January 1989, he presented a four-point plan that called for the cessation of violence followed by Palestinian elections and then negotiations with new Palestinian leaders over autonomy and a "final status" for the territories. The right wing howled that Rabin was trying to give away the Land of Israel. Arens came up with a rival plan, which also called for Palestinian elections but limited self-rule. In May, Shamir floated his own plan in advance of his first trip to Washington to meet President Bush.

Shamir called his ministers together and asked them what he should tell Bush, and when it was Arens's turn to speak, the foreign minister said, "They are going to play hardball with us, and if they feel that they have the political backing for it they will try to cut our balls off without mercy."[20]

The prime minister just sat there flushed with rage. He clenched his fists and cut Arens off. "If there is one thing I cannot stand, it is fear!"

Courage in the face of adversity was part of Shamir's code, as if he were a son of Archidamus in Sparta, admonishing his men that true soldiers do not ask how many the enemy are, or how strong they are—only *where* they are.

What Shamir was looking for that spring was a strategy to hold the new Bush administration at bay. Shamir had very little room to maneuver. Every time he entered the Knesset chamber to parley with the leading lights of his party, there sat Sharon and his chorus of nationalistic deputies who pounced on any concession to the rioting Palestinians as if Shamir did not have the gumption to stand up to the rabble.

He had gone to Washington with a minimalist's peace plan that would not bring peace, and all he really managed to do was convince Bush and James A. Baker III, the tough-minded secretary of state, that Israel was in the grip of a dysfunctional government: too hard-line, too defensive, and too much in the thrall of the settler movement.

The best thing about Shamir's government was that it had kept Rabin at defense, which prevented Sharon and the other right-wing generals in the Knesset from pushing through reckless schemes of Arab expulsion that were circulating in the face of the intifada.

The Middle East was changing rapidly. The end of the Iran-Iraq War had ushered a new Arab leader onto the world stage. Saddam Hussein emerged from the war with the most powerful army in the region, more than fifty divisions, four thousand tanks, French and Soviet warplanes, Soviet Scud missiles, and an arsenal of chemical weapons that had been used to devastating effect on Iranian troops and on the Kurdish population of northern Iraq.

Saddam saw himself as the Arab Caesar. He had successfully defended the eastern flank of the Arab world against the Shiite hordes that Khomeini had hurled across the desert to threaten Arabia. Yet Saddam nurtured towering grievances. He believed the Arabs owed him their allegiance; he wanted his debts forgiven; and he saw both Israel and the United States as obstacles to his ambition to dominate the region.

He had never forgotten that Israel had bombed the Osirak reactor in 1981; he saw Israeli power as an extension of American power in the Middle East. And he could never forget that the Americans had betrayed him in the Iran-contra affair by feeding intelligence about his forces to the ayatollahs.

No one had seen Saddam coming. Both the CIA and the Mossad believed that Iraq was exhausted and bankrupt after eight years of war with Iran and that Saddam would moderate his butchery and join Egypt and Saudi Arabia as an American ally. The end of the cold war was supposed to usher in an era of peacemaking, of negotiation and reconciliation. The Americans were talking about a new world order. Everyone was wrong about Saddam. He stood before his Arab peers in Amman in early 1990 and said, defiantly, "There is no place among the ranks of the good Arabs for the faint-hearted who would argue that, as a superpower, the United States will be the decisive factor and others have no choice but to submit."[21]

On April 1, Saddam stoked the already high morale among his army officers by telling them that Iraq stood ready to confront any rival, including Israel, and if Israel dared again to bomb Iraq as it had in 1981, "By God, we will make the fire eat up half of Israel if it tries to do anything against Iraq."

His words reverberated as a new alarm through Western capitals.[22]

The following month, Saddam hosted the Arab leaders in Baghdad and asserted that Israel was seeking to reconstitute a Hebrew empire from the Nile to the Euphrates River. He postured himself as the guardian of the Palestinian people and lavished tens of millions of dollars on the PLO, putting an executive jet at Arafat's disposal and sending massive amounts of aid to Palestinian refugees. Every Palestinian family who had lost a son in the intifada received money from Saddam.

To cap the summit, a PLO faction funded by Iraqi intelligence carried out a brazen commando raid against an Israeli army base near Tel Aviv. Israeli security forces detected and intercepted the squad, and though the commandos failed to reach their target, Saddam had made his point: he was now the supreme commander of Arab militarism. The festering sore of Palestinian suffering under occupation was a ready club for any Arab dictator to seize and swing against the "imperialists" and the "colonialists."

As Saddam's power dawned, Israel's political stability collapsed. Peres tried to bring down the unity government, but Shamir preempted him, firing the rebellious finance minister. The Labor Party brought a no-confidence motion that passed sixty to fifty-five and dissolved the government coalition.

In the wake of the dissolution, Shamir and Sharon engaged in shouting matches over who was in charge of the Likud Party.

Sharon's delegates chanted, "Arik! Arik!" and Shamir demanded to know, "Do I speak for the party or not? Who is representing the Likud, me or some minister?"[23]

At the core of this struggle was the fundamental question of whether Shamir's government, or any other, could sit down at a peace conference and give the Palestinians what most of the rest of the world believed they deserved: their own homeland. Four decades after the Israelis had gotten theirs, a strong martial impulse was still preventing a prime minister from fulfilling the promise that Zionism had originally offered to the Arabs: a shared sovereignty in the Holy Land.

In truth, Shamir wanted no part in the peace process. He wanted to complete his premiership having prevented any loss of Israeli territory. But as a pragmatist, he understood the importance of keeping diplomacy in motion if only to prevent it from reaching a conclusion, and thus Shamir, an aficionado of political tradecraft, danced a duet with the new Bush administration, allowing both Rabin and Peres to engage Washington because it was good for Israel's image but preventing them from bringing any proposal for serious peace negotiations to fruition. In that sense, Shamir saw himself as a tough and effective Zionist because the struggle between the left and right in Israel had come down to the question of the nature of Zionism. Was it more important to fulfill the Zionist destiny of seizing as much of the Land of Israel as was possible with might and force? Or was it more important, as Zionists, to live on the land with the Arabs, ending the isolation of the people that had dwelled alone?

Sabras stood on both sides of this question.

During Shamir's tenure, the novelist Amos Oz went out into the hinterlands and compiled a kind of oral history about the tone of the national conversation, and he found the right bitterly jingoistic, as if "there is some ancient, mysterious curse of fate because of which we are doomed to eternal conflict with an inimical, alien world, no matter what we do, and therefore we had perhaps better slough off the image of the 'nice Jewish boy' and become big bad wolves for a change—they are not going to love us anyway, but maybe they will fear us."[24]

It is also certain that Sharon did not think Shamir was going to give away the West Bank or Gaza, but for Sharon—and younger political acolytes such as Benjamin Netanyahu—whipping up political hysteria over the prospect of a "PLO terrorist state" next door to Israel was the staple of right-wing politics. Sharon judged that his path back to power could be cleared only by attacking the vacillations of the centrists, who feared international opprobrium, whereas Sharon did not. Sharon knew that no matter how deeply he had been tarred by Sabra and Shatila and the whole Lebanon fiasco, many Israelis still admired his fearlessness, his instinct to charge, and his confidence that there is always a military solution to any security threat.

Though the peace camp was growing, there was still no countervailing institution strong enough to overcome security-based fears in Israel, or to offer an alternative to the sabra concept of deterrence based on excessive retaliation. The nascent Peace Now movement bespoke the anguish of many that peace had failed to take hold. But the movement had no strategy for how to sustain a negotiating track with the Arabs when some new terrorist act or threat rattled the psychological foundations of the country. The politics of retribution was ingrained in the national character. Generations of army officers had been indoctrinated with the notion that deterrence was crucial to survival and retribution was integral to deterrence.

The Israeli army operated on these reflexive impulses, which were reinforced by the news media, whose front pages and editorials often stoked nationalistic rhetoric, fear, and emotionalism in a cocktail, the effects of which could not easily be overcome by reason.

The arrival of Saddam Hussein as a brutal conqueror with hegemonic ambitions set off alarms in Israel and incited new fears that another Nasser had come to plague the Israelis. Saddam's bid for power was sudden and shocking, in part because he was scouring Europe for nonconventional weapons that could magnify the geographic reach of his army.

Shamir authorized Mossad to disrupt Saddam Hussein's shopping spree. It is believed that in March 1990, Mossad assassinated Gerald Bull, a Canadian American engineer who was assisting the Iraqis in improving the performance of their Scud missiles. Bull was also building a massive "supergun" for Iraq—a cannon several hundred feet in length capable of firing a projectile as large as an automobile into space or against targets thousands of miles distant. Bull had been warned about his work for Iraq and, clearly, Israel could have pursued any number of pathways to shut down his project using legal means, or to sabotage it covertly. But Shamir in all likelihood had decided to deal with him just as Ben-Gurion had dealt with the German scientists who were helping Nasser in the early 1960s.

On the evening of March 22, Bull was returning to his apartment in Brussels when an unidentified assassin appeared and raised a silenced pistol to put five bullets in his chest and head. The assassin fled undetected. Israel was officially silent, but many European intelligence officials suspected that Israel had murdered the scientist to send a warning to Western companies: Israel's government would resort to murder to stanch the flow of sophisticated weaponry to Saddam Hussein's military establishment.[25]

The assassination did little to deter the Iraqi leader.

Iraqi intelligence continued to recruit scientists to improve the performance of the Soviet-made ballistic missiles. Saddam bellowed defiance to the West. For the Palestinian youth manning the barricades of Gaza and the West Bank with stones and burning tires, Saddam's voice was a call to arms against the status quo of American power and Israeli militarism. He promised riches and protection to those who followed him, and when he sent his army into Kuwait in August 1990, neighboring Jordan and the PLO pinned themselves to his coattails.

The Iraqi invasion of Kuwait triggered a long counterwar to destroy Saddam Hussein, and from the outset, the Israeli security establishment was determined to play a role against such a bitter enemy who had threatened the destruction of Israel many times.

With the Iraqi army uncoiled across the Kuwaiti landscape all the way to the Saudi border, Saddam became the region's central power—he had the largest army, and he had oil reserves to rival those of Saudi Arabia, which lay almost defenseless on his southern flank. It was Saddam against the world and, for all of Israel's self-regard as a strategic power, the Jewish state could not devise a leading role for itself in mobilizing the region against this new tyrant. Sharon had once lectured Ronald Reagan about Israel's ability to defend the region, to protect Saudi Arabia and its oil reserves, but the Jewish state was humbled by the sheer mass of the Iraqi army. There was no strategic role for Israel's vaunted army.

Indeed, the crisis with Iraq accentuated Israel's isolation.

Decades of militarism had left Israel with no constructive role alongside the Arabs and Iranians, who were facing a regional catastrophe of the first order: Saddam rampant on a field of weaklings.

American leadership was the only option, and yet the real test of the crisis would be whether Israel could cooperate by staying out of the fight altogether. The Bush administration assembled a fragile coalition of Arab and Western powers to confront Saddam. The Iraqi leader did all he could to turn the battle into an Arab-Israeli match, calculating that, if Israel joined the fray, the White House would never be able to keep Syria, Egypt, and Saudi Arabia in the coalition because Arab leaders could not be seen to be fighting alongside Israel.

Shamir teetered precariously. George H. W. Bush and other Western leaders explained to him the stakes if Israel entered the war: the U.S.-led coalition would splinter. Shamir countered by pointing out the danger to his government if Saddam scored a direct hit on Tel Aviv or any other city with his missiles, killing dozens or hundreds of Israelis. If Jews were dying, how long could he withstand the pressure for retribution? No one knew the tipping point, but they knew Shamir: when the moment came, Shamir would act with little warning.

When America and its allies launched their massive counterattack to drive Saddam's army out of Kuwait in January and February 1991, the on-slaught against Israel began, too. Saddam's Scud missiles streaked across the desert and exploded in fireballs as they reentered the atmosphere at seventeen thousand miles per hour. Some broke up under the heat of re-entry; some were intercepted by American Patriot missiles. There were few casualties. Israel had never witnessed anything like it: sirens blaring, high-ways jammed with families fleeing the dense neighborhoods of Tel Aviv and Haifa for Jerusalem, where Saddam would not dare strike. Israelis strapped gas masks on children and lined "safe rooms" with plastic and duct tape to keep deadly gases out. Missile debris was raining down on Is-raeli neighborhoods night after night, inciting panic. Moshe Arens, the de-fense minister, pressed Shamir to send the air force into the Iraqi desert to take out the Scud launchers, but the American war commander, Norman Schwarzkopf, insisted that his forces were doing everything possible to find and destroy them.

From the outset, there was a strong push from the right, led by Arens, to enter the war to attack into western Iraq and clean out the Scud launch-ing zones. Arens's advocacy put Dan Shomron, the chief of staff, and his deputy, Ehud Barak, in a tough position. In a matter of weeks, Arens was due to make his recommendation on who would succeed Shomron as chief of the army. Here Barak, the politician in uniform, stayed close to Arens and became an advocate for entering the war.[26]

Shomron, however, was not persuaded that the Israeli air force and Sayeret Matkal could operate in the Iraqi desert; he was not convinced they could find the Scuds or protect themselves from Iraqi or Jordanian attack. Shomron broke with Arens and took the position that Shamir was correct in keeping the Israeli military out of the fight.

Shamir went personally to the large air force base near Beersheba to meet with the F-15 and F-16 pilots who were pressing their superiors to let them enter the war to take out the Scud launchers.

Shamir told them he had two questions. "Can you promise me that af-ter the government will let you fly to Iraq and do what you want to do, that after that not one Scud missile will penetrate the air space of Israel?"

The pilots were silent.

Shamir asked his second question: "If during the American campaign an Israeli pilot is shot down and then he is paraded on television all over the world, is that good or bad for me?"[27]

To Arens and the militarists in Shamir's cabinet, nothing was as important as Israeli self-reliance. Israel had to defend itself or "deterrence" would collapse. These same arguments had been used to overpower Eshkol in 1967.

Shamir's tough stand against his own political base and against a substantial war lobby in the military establishment was a remarkable feat of restraint. His innate caution overcame his ideology. The Persian Gulf War, for Israel's right wing, was an opportunity to overthrow the Jordanian monarch and drive the Palestinians out of the West Bank into Jordan. This was the Sharonist dream that had seduced many Israelis, but Shamir was not willing to risk war or break with the United States over Jabotinskyian dreams that he might have shared.

Pragmatism won out.

Israel—and Shamir—survived the war with minimum damage from Iraqi Scuds. But the experience intensified Shamir's resistance to the peace agenda, and so he had to be pushed and cajoled to attend the Madrid Peace Conference, which Bush had promised to the Arabs who had joined the coalition against Saddam.

Hosted by President Bush and Mikhail Gorbachev, the conference convened in the fall of 1991 as the era of two superpowers was ending. Gorbachev had survived a coup attempt in August, and the Soviet empire would cease to exist by the end of the year.

Some Israelis disparaged Madrid as nothing more than visible payback from Bush to the Arabs, devoid of meaningful political content. But here was Yitzhak Shamir sitting among the Arab leaders, the first time any Israeli prime minister had done so, with pomp and pageantry provided by Spain's royal family.

To the cynics who doubted peace was ever possible, Bush asked, "Who, two years ago, would have predicted that the Berlin Wall would come down?" Or that the cold war "would come to a peaceful end?"[28]

Shamir spoke to the Arabs in words that had a hard, metallic edge. "We are the only people who have lived in the Land of Israel without interruption for 4,000 years. We are the only people, except for a short Crusader kingdom, who have had an independent sovereignty in this land. We are the only people for whom Jerusalem has been a capital. We are the only people whose sacred places are only in the Land of Israel."[29]

He showed no recognition of the competing national narrative in the Holy Land, that of the Palestinians, and by the time Shamir returned home, it was plain that he was incapable of extending a hand of accommodation.

Instead, he made another offer of limited autonomy, which the Palestinians could only refuse. It was this offer, however paltry by any standard, that nonetheless emboldened a right-wing uprising within Shamir's party that brought down his government.

Sharon was the instigator.

Raful Eitan, the former chief of staff, had weakened Shamir's coalition in December 1991 with his resignation. In January 1992, Yuval Ne'eman, a physicist who had worked on the atom bomb project and then entered politics, claimed that Shamir had put Israel on the path to creating a Palestinian state. He pulled his Tehiya (Revival) Party out of the government. He was followed by Rehavam Ze'evi, the former general, who wanted to expel Palestinians to Jordan.

"The government deserves to die," Ze'evi declared in the well of the Knesset, "because of two unpardonable sins. Not putting the intifada down for 49 months and the fact that this government is intent on pursuing the policy of autonomy, which puts the whole state of Israel in grave danger."[30]

Shamir had little with which to rally his party, but within weeks of his government's collapse, with elections looming, he approved a major military operation to assassinate Sheikh Abbas al-Musawi, the leader of Lebanon's Hezbollah, or Party of God, which had waged a covert war against the American, French, and Israeli forces during the long Lebanon debacle.

The attack did not come out of the blue. It followed an infiltration raid by Palestinian militants against an Israeli military post where three soldiers were hacked to death with machetes as they slept. Under Israeli military doctrine, it may have been a given that there would have to be a response, but the decision to decapitate the leadership of the dominant political party in the volatile Shiite region of Lebanon was a fateful one.[31]

The military establishment had crossed a new threshold.

Since Ben-Gurion's time, Israeli leaders had been extremely wary of proposals to assassinate Arab leaders. After all, if leaders are killed, who is there to negotiate with? And how can it be known who will rise after such a decapitation? Begin had been the first to break the unwritten injunction when he sent Mossad and military intelligence into Beirut to kill Arafat in his "bunker." That effort failed, but the precedent had been set. Increasingly, the rising generation of Israeli military commanders, Ehud Barak most prominently, saw personal and institutional advantage in hitting prominent targets in spectacular operations. It created a sensation of Israeli military power in the region, it was a potent morale booster at home, and it buttressed the army's bureaucratic weight in the competition for budget resources in the Knesset. Any concerns about violations of international law or the Geneva Conventions were enveloped in a skein of Israeli counterarguments on the rights of states to proactive defense, especially against nonstate paramilitaries that hid among civilians and waged guerrilla war.

Barak oversaw the planning of the Musawi hit.

Helicopter gunships equipped with precision missiles swept across southern Lebanon on the morning of February 16. Musawi was traveling by motorcade with his wife, son, and bodyguards. The gunships caught the Hezbollah leader by surprise, firing missiles into the vehicles and incinerating him, his family members, and four others.

And for the military establishment, there was a political component to any spectacular strike: the public liked it; the tabloids lionized the pilots and praised the intelligence assets that tracked the target and the technology wielded against an enemy who lurked over the horizon.

Musawi and his family were buried at a large funeral ceremony by an emotional throng—tens of thousands of Shiites blanketing the dusty hillside in the Bekáa Valley. The voices of Hezbollah's imams called out the grievances deeply embedded in the Shiite psyche, where martyrdom in the face of overwhelming odds was the very essence of a noble spirit. Hassan Nasrallah, Hezbollah's hard-line adjutant under Musawi, now stood as Musawi's successor and told the faithful that it was possible to avenge the death of their leader because the Israelis lived in a culture that worshipped "the preservation of life," while "our point of departure is the preservation of principle and sacrifice" at all costs.

Just as the grandson of the Prophet Mohammed raged into battle against overwhelming forces at Karbala in the seventh century, Nasrallah and the other speakers vowed that Hezbollah would show the same courage in standing up for the righteous and the dispossessed.

It did not take long.

A month later and seven thousand five hundred miles away in the Argentinean capital of Buenos Aires, which hosts a large Jewish population, a Ford truck loaded with more than two hundred pounds of explosives rolled up to the Israeli embassy and detonated its cargo to devastating effect. The explosion destroyed the embassy, killing 29 people and wounding more than 240 as it shredded walls and trees, wrecking a nearby Catholic church and school, where children were lacerated by flying glass.[32]

It was the deadliest attack ever on an Israeli mission abroad. It was followed two years later, in July 1994, by an even more powerful truck bomb that destroyed the Jewish Community Center in Buenos Aires, killing 100 people and wounding 250. It took years of investigation to piece together all of the evidence, but Argentinean police authorities, assisted by other Western and Israeli intelligence officials, came to the conclusion that Hezbollah, assisted by Iran, had mounted both attacks, leaving the question begging as it had been since Sharett first posed it in a similar context: What good had come from Israel's decision to kill Hezbollah's leader?[33]

The logic that had been employed to justify the Musawi assassination was never put on trial. No Israeli military commander stood to point out that deterrence had failed, that the decision to decapitate Hezbollah had given rise to a more brazen and radicalized successor, willing to strike in any corner of the globe where Israelis might be vulnerable. No director of military intelligence stood to point out that from the perspective of the impoverished Shiites of Lebanon, Israel had come first as a liberator to free them from the grip of the PLO ministate in Lebanon but then turned into a destroyer whose artillery and tanks killed thousands of innocent civilians, leveled whole villages, and treated the Shiites as an enemy. The logic of war thus dictated that the Shiites would look to Syria and Iran for aid and solidarity, and a powerful new force arose to confront Israeli militarism.

In the wake of the carnage against Jews in Argentina, it was possible to feel the sense of doom that washed over Israelis when they looked at the array of new enemies rising from the ashes of previous wars. Who had awakened the Shiites of Lebanon? Israeli intelligence was quick to blame the Ayatollah Khomeini and his Revolutionary Guard who sought to galvanize Shiites everywhere as a fifth column against the West and its allies. But it was impossible to negate the destructive impact of Israel's serial invasions of its northern neighbor, especially the devastating and unnecessary war of 1982.

FOURTEEN

Peace Strategy: The New Yitzhak

The Israelis were calling it one of the most important elections in the country's forty-four-year history.

"Israel is waiting for Rabin," campaign posters shouted from telephone poles. The slogan paraphrased the old ditty from the Six-Day War: "Nasser is waiting for Rabin." It was a reminder that Rabin was a military hero whose army had defeated the Arabs.

But what Israelis were really waiting for was an end to the political paralysis that had frozen the national agenda for eight years.

The election of June 1992 established the power of the peace movement in Israel for the first time, and the fact that Rabin was its candidate—instead of Peres—showed that the country was ready to take risks for peace as long as the decision making was in the hands of a trusted icon of the military establishment.

Shamir had tried everything to stave off Rabin's return: he called Rabin "a failure as prime minister" the first time around; Shamir's campaign aides mocked Rabin's bouts of hard drinking, comparing him to Russia's Boris Yeltsin. And they dredged up his "nervous breakdown" on the eve of war in 1967.[1]

"We need a clear-headed prime minister," read the signs sticking up from Likud campaign crowds.[2]

But Shamir's suffocating refusal to put forward any proposal that might advance the peace agenda, his contentious relationship with President Bush and James Baker—plus high unemployment, which pushed new immigrants into the Labor Party camp—persuaded most Israelis that Rabin understood the future, whereas Shamir was stuck in the past.

For the first time in his life, Rabin projected an aura of boldness and self-assurance about putting the country on the right path, and when he spoke, still in his plodding way, the whiskey baritone was so deep that one observer said it "seemed to rumble up from somewhere around his socks."[3]

Going into the campaign, he had told his Labor Party colleagues that "should I form the next Israeli government, I undertake to reach an agreement with the Palestinians in the territories over the establishment of an autonomy within 6 to 9 months. After the agreement with the Palestinians, we shall reach agreement with Jordan and then with Syria."[4]

The *New York Times* columnist William Safire, a self-described "right-wing hawk" in the pro-Israel camp, had journeyed to Tel Aviv to interview both candidates. He pronounced that "I like and respect both Yitzhaks" but added that he was "leery of the lefties hiding behind Rabin" who opposed settlements that were designed to prevent the establishment of a Palestinian state. To Safire, this was "the slippery slope to a PLO state."[5]

Rabin was not exactly grasping to return to power. He had turned seventy in March.

He told friends that it wasn't his "obsession" to become prime minister again "but only an option," and for some reason his simple approach—it was time to make peace—connected him with an electorate eager for change.

Still, it was a campaign for two old fighters. Shamir, at seventy-seven, still believed in the long struggle with the Arabs. He remained wary of peace and spoke instead of the virtues of war: "We still need this truth today," he told a Stern Gang reunion, "the truth of the power of war, or at least we need to accept that war is inescapable, because without this, the life of the individual has no purpose and the nation has no chance of survival."[6]

Shamir echoed Jabotinsky and Ben-Gurion, men who understood that a military society cannot stay mobilized without the constant affirmation of threat, men distrustful of peace because peace undermined the organizing principle of the warrior enterprise. What was Sparta without war?

Yet the Israelis—and many sabras within the military establishment—turned Shamir out and gave the election to Rabin in a landslide, not because the martial impulse had dissipated but because Rabin and the generals of Peace Now had persuaded them that the end of the cold war had opened a window. Who knew how long it would remain open? Iran or a resurgent

Iraq could threaten the future, but Rabin thought Israel had a decade or more to make peace with Syria, Jordan, and the Palestinians, and that such a peace might fortify the region to withstand the rise of a new threat.

After the election, Shamir admitted to an interviewer from the right-wing newspaper *Ma'ariv* that all of the peace proposals he had floated as prime minister were fraudulent. His "moderation" as prime minister was merely tactical. The goal had always been, and still was, the seizure of the lands that had been designated for a Palestinian homeland.

"It pains me greatly that in the coming four years, I will not be able to expand the settlements in Judea and Samaria and to complete the demographic revolution in the Land of Israel," Shamir said. "I would have carried on autonomy talks for ten years, and meanwhile we would have reached half a million people in Judea and Samaria."[7]

Israelis were as surprised by Shamir's candor as by the cynicism underlying his remarks, but he had revealed a hard-line Zionist code that many liberal Zionists rejected. The problem with Shamir, and Begin before him, was the failure to see what even Jabotinsky might have seen: that the majority of the Arabs had come to accept Israel as a fact, as the king of Saudi Arabia had said to Ronald Reagan, and this created opportunities for negotiation and compromise.

The country was poised for a great contest over peace, but it was impossible to see how it would unfold, other than, as Rabin said, "It will get ugly."

When he presented his government in July, Rabin told the Israeli people that they no longer need regard themselves as "a people that dwells alone.

"We must overcome the sense of isolation that has held us in thrall for almost half a century" and "join the international movement toward peace, reconciliation and cooperation."[8]

He told an American interviewer that the lesson of the Persian Gulf War was that, "for obvious reasons, the U.S. does not want Israel's help" in Middle Eastern wars. But in the struggle against Islamic fundamentalism, Israel could help.

"The more the U.S. can say it is bringing peace to the area—assisted by Israel acting in its own interests—the more Israel will serve the mutual interest in creating stability and leaving less room for extremists."[9]

Rabin, the self-educated thinker, stood before the Knesset on July 13, 1992, as the first Israeli prime minister since Sharett to break with the Ben-Gurion line of interminable war with the Arabs. He had begun to free himself of his long-held view that opposed negotiating with the PLO, although he still preferred to do so indirectly. He had come to believe that a powerless people, the Palestinians, had power—not the military variety, but power nonetheless, and their aspirations could not be extinguished.

"What can we do?" he asked one American and then answered his own question: "Peace you don't make with friends, but with very unsympathetic enemies. I won't try to make the PLO look good. It was an enemy, it remains an enemy, but negotiations must be with enemies."[10]

But the truth was that Rabin didn't know how to open the kind of discreet channels to the Palestinian leadership that would be necessary to make peace. He had no institutional reservoir for diplomacy that he could activate. The only diplomatic game in play was the desultory talks in Washington that had been organized by the Americans after Madrid. And they were going nowhere.

Rabin's only creative ally for diplomacy was Peres, but Rabin had taken him off the field.

"Rabin made Shimon foreign minister in charge of cocktails," one aide explained. "He took away from him the relations with the United States and the peace negotiations. Peres accepted that, because this is Peres: between being out and being in—even humiliated—he'll always be in."[11]

Rabin even dictated a memo that enshrined the limits of Peres's authority. He would not be involved in relations with Syria, Jordan, Lebanon, or the Palestinians.

Those who knew Peres also knew that these restrictions could not last.

The military establishment refused to stay on the sidelines.

It was the nature of Ehud Barak as chief of staff to see himself as the indispensable intellect in the national security realm. He had trained for leadership his entire life. Short of stature, Barak had a powerful and compact frame. He had been well educated, attending Stanford University in California, but at home he spoke Hebrew like a patriarch. Some of his obsessions seemed strange—lock picking and clock repair—but he also played concert piano and read broadly. Barak was fascinated with time, schedules, and the plotting of strategy by laying out a precise sequence of actions and anticipated reactions as if life imitated clockwork. It seemed that Barak looked at the world as a place where events, if planned and executed with discipline and courage, could change history, and Barak regarded himself, even as a young man, as a historic figure—a young Ben-Gurion, a visionary.

His friends called him Napoleon.

In late 1992, in the wake of the Persian Gulf War, Barak was searching for the means to reestablish the primacy of the Israeli army in the Middle East. And from this ferment emerged the idea of assassinating Saddam Hussein. Barak would succeed where America had failed—and stun the world.[12]

Operation Bramble Bush was one of the most important and most covered up episodes of Barak's career, for everything about the aborted plan to kill the Iraqi leader occurred under his supervision.

"There was an idea to build capabilities to operate in Iraq in order to hit Saddam Hussein," explained Amnon Lipkin-Shahak when I met him in Tel Aviv. He had served as Barak's deputy chief of staff.[13]

"For the Israelis, Saddam was still the representative of evil and someone with whom we had an open account," he added.

The Iraqi leader had become the main enemy due to the size of his army, and also because he had fired thirty-nine Scud missiles at Israel.

His containment had been relegated to American and British warplanes running no-fly zones while UN inspectors sniffed out the remnants of Iraq's nuclear, chemical, and biological warfare programs.

Barak, however, believed that Saddam would rebuild his arsenal and come after Israel once again. He wanted to demonstrate that Israeli special forces, using precision weapons, could infiltrate Iraq and lay a high-tech ambush to kill Saddam and then escape without a trace.

Aharon Ze'evi Farkash, who headed the Israeli agency that intercepts communications around the world, recalled that the intelligence chiefs "foresaw the difficulties" of leaving Saddam in power over the long term. "It would be very difficult to have early warning [about surprise attacks]," he said. Israel needed 100 percent assurance that Saddam could not acquire a nuclear weapon "because you cannot allow one bomb" in the hands of a dictator who had fired dozens of Scud missiles at Israel during the war.

To prevent this from happening, "maybe the best way is to disappear"—he paused—"to change the leader," Farkash said. "These are things you can do with fingerprints or without fingerprints, and the problem is to do things without fingerprints—I call it the 'undercover new war' that is crucial for every democratic state: to have a capacity to do things without taking responsibility."[14]

On October 2, 1992, Barak and the intelligence chiefs presented Rabin with a plan to kill the Iraqi leader. Rabin "went into the tiniest details," according to Major Nadav Ze'evi, a military intelligence officer involved in the planning. A month later, on November 5, Barak staged an invitation-only dress rehearsal for the performance of a lifetime—the killing of the dictator who had eluded the mighty American-led coalition. The Israeli army, which had been forced to sit out the Persian Gulf War, would deliver the final, devastating blow.

Operation Bramble Bush had the potential to propel Barak toward the kind of global notoriety that clinches a political career. And with Rabin and Peres both in their seventies, the fifty-year-old Barak was ever mindful that his performance at the top of the military establishment was an audition for the more visible career that awaited the country's most decorated uniformed officer.

The guest list for the dress rehearsal remains secret.

"It was basically a show for the generals," said Major Ze'evi.[15]

Rabin had told Barak that he wanted a 98 percent certainty of success before he would approve the dangerous operation.

Saddam's father-in-law, Khairallah Tulfah, lay dying.

Tulfah had raised Saddam, and Saddam had married Tulfah's daughter, Sajida. With the family elder near death, Israeli intelligence believed that Saddam would attend the funeral at a small cemetery at al-Awja, Saddam's ancestral village outside Tikrit. A mixed force of Israeli commandos and weapons specialists was on standby to infiltrate two teams, one to set up a surveillance on the road Saddam often used and the other a dozen miles back and ready to fire guided missiles that would home on the targeting beacon focused on Saddam's vehicle. The teams would then make their way to drop zones and escape in unmarked aircraft.

At the sprawling Tse'elim military base in the Negev Desert, Barak arrived by helicopter to play master of ceremonies. He was accompanied by the director of military intelligence, General Uri Saguy, and General Amiram Levine, who was in charge of the exercise. The guests assembled. In the distance, Israeli commandos dressed in Iraqi military uniforms played the roles of Saddam and his entourage.

The faux Saddam, played by a commando named Eyal Katvan, came across the horizon in his vehicle. The strike team acquired its target from their hiding places and—*whoosh*—from nowhere, a missile streaked across the desert.[16]

Suddenly there was an explosion. There was not supposed to be an explosion.

A live missile had mistakenly been fired and struck with deadly accuracy, killing five Sayeret Matkal commandos and wounding five others. A cry went up for medics, and the VIP assembly disappeared in a rush of vehicles, exiting the base as the dead and wounded were collected from the field. Katvan—playing Saddam—survived with leg injuries.

Barak did not stay on the field.

He did not rush to comfort the wounded soldiers, mourn the dead, or greet the devastated families. Barak looked out at the mayhem caused by the accident, then he turned and boarded his helicopter, putting as much distance as he could between himself and the disaster.

The military censor, who operated under Barak's command, kept tight rein on information, specifically forbidding the Israeli press from reporting that Barak and Saguy had been present. Disinformation was fed to the foreign press that the special forces unit was testing a possible operation against Hezbollah in Lebanon. Yet a wide swath of the public soon knew what the "training accident" was all about and that Barak's behavior had been criticized by those who had observed him leave the scene in haste.[17]

In a country where every soldier judges his commanders by their actions on the field, Barak's behavior, however defensible, reflected poorly. Some called him a coward.

Rabin escaped all criticism. It had been Barak's show. The prime minister's aides hastened to brief those who needed to know that the operation had not been presented to him for final approval. These statements protected Rabin, who in fact had urged Barak to perfect the assassination plan so it would have the highest certainty for success. Why wouldn't Rabin have wanted to deliver the head of Saddam Hussein to the outgoing Bush administration and the incoming Clinton administration? It would have been a sensation.

Instead, Rabin and Barak were left with ashes. The plan to assassinate Saddam was deferred indefinitely as investigations ensued. When censorship was finally lifted after Saddam's capture in 2003, the military writer for *Ma'ariv*, Ben Caspit, suggested that Barak had been driven by "megalomania, audacity [and] arrogance" for undertaking the assassination of an Arab leader as "late compensation" for the Scud strikes of 1991.[18]

But Barak was operating under Rabin's supervision and the support of the military establishment. The very audacity that Operation Bramble Bush displayed proved that the military elite was still in charge of national policy, despite Rabin's new ambition on the peace front, where audacity was definitely missing.

The Clinton administration, just sworn in, was pushing for peace between Israel and Syria because Damascus commanded the last Soviet-equipped army still parked on Israel's border. Clinton's aides thought Rabin had miscalculated by focusing on the Palestinians first and by committing himself to a "politically dangerous deadline"—concluding peace within nine months.

Rabin had only three months left on that nine-month clock and no real plan for action.[19]

His more immediate problem was Hamas, the Islamic extremist group based in the Gaza Strip and run—from prison—by Sheikh Ahmed Yassin, a paraplegic preacher. As a potential rival to the PLO in Gaza, Yassin's movement and its charitable network had been encouraged over the years by Israeli intelligence, but the flirtation had ended in 1989 when Hamas militants kidnapped and murdered two Israeli soldiers and hid their bodies to trade for the release of Hamas prisoners. The army and the Shabak intelligence service arrested more than three hundred Hamas members and charged Yassin with organizing the attacks. A military court sentenced the wheelchair-bound cleric to life in prison.

The problem was that Hamas and other extremist groups, such as Islamic Jihad, also based in Gaza, refused to call a cease-fire in the ongoing intifada. Attacks against Israeli soldiers and civilians continued, making it difficult for Rabin to build the political momentum for peace.

As chief of staff, Barak began to agitate for a new strategy: a large-scale deportation of top Hamas officials as a means to destabilize the organization. The idea was that in the wake of a terrorist attack, a dramatic expulsion of Palestinians would not only reestablish "deterrence," it might also decapitate the whole Hamas structure. Rounding up hundreds of top clerics, organizers, and neighborhood chiefs and dumping them across a border in the midst of winter would be a devastating blow, Barak reasoned. Let them sleep under the stars on the freezing slopes of Lebanon. *That* would have a chilling effect—literally so—on future violence.[20]

When Rabin entered office, he had quietly canceled Shamir's last deportation order against twelve militants accused of "inciting terrorism," because the United Nations condemned the practice as a violation of the Fourth Geneva Convention, which protects people living under occupation from expulsion.

Shamir, back on the opposition benches in parliament, rose to condemn Rabin for "steadily appeasing terrorism."

In early December, a car carrying Hamas militants pulled up beside an Israeli patrol in Gaza and opened fire, killing three soldiers. Another Hamas cell operating inside Israel near the Ben Gurion International Airport kidnapped an Israeli border policeman, Sergeant Major Nissim Toledano, as he left his house for work.

His body, bound and bearing stab wounds, was dumped in the West Bank the next day. The brazenness of Toledano's kidnapping and the many wounds on his mutilated corpse incited public opinion, and the calls for retribution overwhelmed Rabin.

Barak stood poised to strike.

Over the next twenty-four hours, more than four hundred Hamas leaders were rounded up, blindfolded and handcuffed, and herded into buses, where they sat for an entire day while the Israeli Supreme Court weighed the legality of the anticipated action. When the five-to-two decision came down in support of the government, the Palestinians were dumped at gunpoint in the middle of the night in freezing conditions and forced to march toward the Lebanese army checkpoint across the northern border. The large-scale expulsion triggered waves of protest around the world; Rabin came under attack again for his iron-fisted approach.

Rabin's allies said the prime minister had faced a horrible choice: "do nothing, do this, or do something worse."

Rabin told foreign journalists, "You have to bear in mind that we are fighting Islamic fundamentalist groups that are trying to kill Palestinians, Israelis and the peace."[21]

Suddenly the prime minister, who had made such an eloquent commitment to peace, was reverting to the brutish stereotype of Sharon.

Barak's impulse to dazzle with bold military feats had led only to condemnation and criticism. The notion that mass deportation—the Israelis called it "temporary removal"—would weaken Hamas proved wrong. The Hamas leadership, living in tents on the rocky Lebanese terrain, held court before the international press as the UN Security Council—the United States included—voted unanimously to "strongly condemn" Israel's act.

The truth was, neither Rabin nor Barak understood how to engage Israel's enemies. All they had marshaled in their first year was an array of military options and little else, and they were headed toward failure when Peres and his brain trust of young diplomats started plotting to intervene.

Rabin had another terrible problem, which he really did not want the world to know of.

Mossad officials had detected a massive breach of security: an Israeli businessman, a former decorated soldier named Nahum Manbar, had secretly sold Iran a full production line—twenty-four truckloads of equipment—to manufacture chemical weapons.

In the age of WMD and the threat from revolutionary Iran, about which Rabin had preached so forcefully to so many foreign leaders, Israel was now guilty—not as a government, but guilty nonetheless—of arming Tehran with some of the most deadly gases known to science. Both the American CIA and British MI6 were picking up the telltales of Manbar's activities and were enraged that the Israeli intelligence services seemed unable or unwilling to throw a net over this rogue operator and bring him in for "discipline."

By April 1993, Manbar had shipped the production line for mustard gas and the nerve agents sarin and tabun for a fee of $16 million. He signed a new contract to provide the production line for VX gas, the binary chemical warfare agent that was far more deadly and that would magnify the power of Iran's military several times over.[22]

Shabtai Shavit, one of the intelligence community's experts on Iran, was serving as Mossad chief. He had run Mossad's Caesarea Division in charge of assassination and other special operations. He was a calculating veteran who had lived a life of tradecraft so ingrained that he still burned his sensitive correspondence in the barbecue pit on his patio. Shavit was a cautious intelligence bureaucrat in the best sense of the term: he avoided conflict with the other intelligence chiefs and exhorted his staff to focus on future threats, such as Iran, in a methodical manner.

As Mossad's boss, Shavit had gone to the prime minister on only one or two occasions to resolve a conflict.

The Manbar case was one of them.

The problem for Shavit was that Manbar was playing the "system" so cleverly that Shavit could not get agreement among the chiefs of the three intelligence services to arrest him and bring him to justice.

Jacob Peri, the chief of Shabak, liked Manbar and was protecting him because Manbar had established key contacts in the upper echelons of Iran's Revolutionary Guard and Ministry of Defense. His "customer" for the chemical warfare production line was Dr. Majid Abbasfour, president of Iran's Special Industries Group and a high-level official in the Ministry of Defense.

For Shavit, however, Manbar's actions threatened to undermine Western security. How could Israel raise the alarm over Iran's secret nuclear ambitions while an Israeli businessman and former military officer was secretly providing some of the very weapons of mass annihilation that caused so much concern? And for some insane reason, the Israeli military and intelligence establishments—those sabra tough guys—could not reach a consensus that Manbar was a danger.[23]

Manbar came from the mother's milk of the Israeli kibbutz movement and the military elite, one intelligence chief explained to me. He fought in both the Six-Day and Yom Kippur wars. He trained Israeli military officers at the national academy. His record as a businessman was dicey; he had gone bankrupt in the 1980s and was forced to leave the country, but he made his way back to notoriety in Israel through his sponsorship of a prominent national basketball team.

Though Shavit chaired the committee of intelligence chiefs, Peri's views carried great weight. Peri had helped Rabin and Shamir clean up the Bus 300 affair; he had advised Rabin all through the intifada and had supported Rabin's conclusion that there was not a military solution to the Palestinian conflict. Peri could be found on many Saturday afternoons sharing a whiskey with the prime minister, and Rabin had entrusted Shabak with one of the most sensitive intelligence projects—the search for a missing Israeli pilot named Ron Arad, whose plane had been shot down over Lebanon in October 1986.

Arad had been riding the rear seat in an F-4 Phantom on a strike mission against Shiite militant targets when an errant bomb detonated just after its release, disabling the warplane. Both airmen ejected and the pilot was soon rescued, leaping up to grab the landing skids of a Cobra attack helicopter that carried him to safety, but Arad was captured by Shiite Amal forces. Israeli intelligence believed that he had been traded to the Iranian Revolutionary Guard in the Bekáa Valley.

It was Peri's job to find Ron Arad to satisfy the Israeli public's demand that no soldier, or his remains, be left behind.[24]

Manbar was clever.

Israeli businessmen, especially former military officers like Manbar, had wide latitude to deal with pariah regimes as long as they kept Israel's national interests in mind and checked in with the intelligence agencies when they intruded into sensitive areas. Manbar told his Shabak control officer that he was selling Iran spare parts and industrial equipment. He never mentioned chemical warfare agents. And to keep the heat off his business activities, he promised to deliver information on Arad. He passed along rumors, straws in the wind, and Peri, who had so few real sources inside Iran, was desperate to keep Manbar in play.[25]

Mossad was more in touch with reality. When Shavit learned from indignant Western intelligence officials that Manbar was trading chemical weapons technology, he went to Rabin and sounded an initial alarm. But Rabin and the military establishment were slow to act, in part because Peri opposed interference. He suggested that Manbar get a warning.[26]

In late May 1993, Mossad tracked Manbar to Vienna, where he was meeting Abbasfour to sign new contracts and to receive information from Iran about where Ron Arad was being held. Abbasfour walked into Manbar's room and demanded to know why two Israeli agents had followed his car to the meeting.

"I don't understand you Israelis," he said. "After all you promised me that they know about our meeting."[27]

Manbar also was upset. He told his guest to wait in the room and then took the elevator to the lobby, where he confronted the young Mossad officers.

"Who do you think you are? Big heroes?" He spoke to them in Hebrew.

They pretended not to take notice. One of them was reading a newspaper.

"You're nobodies. Get out of here!" Manbar shouted.[28]

Still no reaction. Manbar came forward aggressively, picked up the sugar dish on their table, and dumped the contents into the cup of coffee on the table. Then he wheeled and walked away.

Their cover blown, the Mossad officers retreated to the street, where they mounted a motorcycle and waited for Abbasfour to leave the hotel. When the Iranian official and his driver lurched into traffic, the Mossad men followed. A driving rain pelted the Mossad team. The black Iranian sedan followed a route to deliver Abbasfour to a safe house in the Vienna suburbs. The two vehicles entered an underpass, and when they emerged, the motorcycle lost control and went down, right into the path of another car. Both Mossad riders were killed.

Efraim Halevy, Shavit's deputy, was on duty when word came in to headquarters. The trauma of losing two of its officers engaged in surveillance of a suspected traitor infuriated the entire Mossad and military intelligence community. Shavit returned to the prime minister with a strong recommendation to bring Manbar to justice.[29]

Yet Rabin still did not act to arrest Manbar.

He directed the intelligence chiefs to send an emissary to the wayward officer with a stern warning. In November 1993, Brigadier General Avi Cohen delivered the message in person to Manbar: he was to desist from dealing with Iran in chemical agents or face prosecution. Yet the damage was done, and it would take four more years before Manbar was arrested, and only after Mossad agents working on several continents stitched together the complete record of each of his transactions, building a case that documented the movement of chemicals, the transfer of funds—all the evidence the Israeli attorney general would need to mount a prosecution.

Manbar was tried and convicted in 1998 in a secret court proceeding. He was sentenced to sixteen years in prison.* Many of the details of what he sold to Iran, especially related to VX gas technology, remain secret. The self-protective ruling elite tied off the knot in their own way. Israel has never offered a full accounting of the case to the international community.[30]

Nor has Ron Arad, or his body, been found.

---

* Manbar was released from prison on October 31, 2011, after having served more than fourteen years of his sixteen-year sentence. He agreed to accept a number of restrictions that would extend his probation indefinitely, including bans on travel, contact with foreign citizens, interviews with the news media, or any business activity connected to the arms trade.

FIFTEEN

Oslo: Wary Generals Waging Peace

It took a pair of Israeli academics, Yair Hirschfeld and Ron Pundak—both peace activists—to open a circuit. They met in London in January 1993 and laid the groundwork, without really understanding how it might proceed, for the first real peace process between Israelis and Palestinians.

Strangely, London, long after the days of empire, was still a crossroads of the Middle East, a convenient venue for clandestine meetings with the PLO, which, for Israelis, were still illegal—regarded as treason by some—until the law was amended in early 1993.

Hirschfeld and Pundak represented a generational movement in Israel that rejected a perpetual military orientation for the Jewish state. They were more interested in conflict resolution and the structures of peace. Hirschfeld taught Middle Eastern history at the University of Haifa, and Pundak, after a stint in the army and Israeli intelligence, had earned a doctorate at the University of London's School of Oriental and African Studies. He worked briefly for *Ha'aretz* but was hungry for a career with greater impact than journalism when he fell in with Hirschfeld and the "lefties" around Shimon Peres.

In London, they found their way to Ahmed Qurei, a finance minister of the PLO and close to Arafat. They proposed a secret dialogue that would put on the table the kinds of compromises that would be necessary to make peace, compromises that could not be broached in the formal negotiations in Washington, now suspended because of Rabin's mass expulsion of Hamas leaders from Gaza.

Secrecy was everything. Any leak to the news media that suggested

Israel might make a deal with the PLO would set off a storm and might land Hirschfeld and Pundak in jail.

But Qurei, also known as Abu Ala'a, had shown a willingness to take the talks forward. The Israeli academics shared their secret and their enthusiasm with Yossi Beilin, the director general of the Israeli Foreign Ministry and a member of Peres's inner circle. Rabin liked to refer to Beilin as Peres's "poodle," which hurt Beilin with the military establishment, but in truth, Beilin was a relentless advocate for engaging the Arabs.

Beilin was visiting London on official business. He met privately with Hirschfeld and Pundak and approved their plan for an informal dialogue—one step removed from the Foreign Ministry—to probe how a deal with the PLO might be structured.

Peres and Rabin were briefed on the secret talks, but in the wake of the Hamas expulsions and UN condemnations, neither man had great expectations. The talks moved to secret venues in the Norwegian woods around Oslo, where Norway's foreign minister, Johan Jørgen Holst, and his envoy, Terje Rød-Larsen, who personified Norway's special commitment to peacemaking, nurtured what soon progressed into a full-blown negotiation.

By May, Rabin and Peres learned that the Oslo channel had the full backing of Arafat; now they had to decide whether to commit the government of Israel to take over the negotiations. They were going to have to trust each other, even though both men were drenched in mutual enmity.

"Once Oslo brought them together, they were able to harness and focus their efforts," Pundak told me in an interview. "It was connected to their age and to the understanding that this might be, psychologically, their last big project."

Peres would have to restrain his instinct for self-promotion; Rabin would have to restrain his impulse to share the secret with the generals who might seek to smother the negotiations with security concerns because the PLO was still the enemy.[1]

From May to August, the secret Oslo channel went "live" as a formal negotiation between Israel and the PLO. Hirschfeld and Pundak moved into support roles as Uri Savir, a senior Foreign Ministry official, flew in to take control of the Israeli delegation. For the first time in his life, Rabin put a significant amount of trust in Shimon Peres, as both men supervised the final negotiations.

And then something remarkable happened: the secret negotiations succeeded in producing a blueprint for how to conclude peace, and the news burst into the public realm. Rabin and Peres, stunned by the profound implications of the steps they committed the Jewish state to take, stood as the first Zionist leaders to reach an accommodation with the local Arab population of the Holy Land. Two communities that had been at war almost continuously since the 1920s moved to the verge of peaceful coexistence. And it seemed nothing would have been possible had not Rabin and Peres—these two sons of the founding political and military establishment—put away their poisonous rivalry in order to let something extraordinary occur.

The Oslo process immediately created a governing Palestinian authority under the PLO in Gaza. The concept was simple: Palestinian rule would expand, the Israeli occupation would retreat, setting the stage for "final status" negotiations within five years.

No one used the term "Palestinian state," but such a state was the inescapable endpoint of the negotiations.

The news broke on the Israeli army radio, then Israeli TV. Blindsided by the breakthrough, Ehud Barak was shocked and offended; the right wing was in uproar.

Rabin's decision to withhold the secret of the Oslo negotiations from the most prominent members of the military establishment surprised and angered many of them. Efraim Halevy, who was deputy Mossad director, found it hard to believe that Rabin had lied to him for months, denying the existence of a channel as Mossad was picking up rumors of peace talks in Norway. But the reason for his secrecy was self-evident, for as soon as the news broke, the opposition took aim at him with venomous attacks.

"Mr. Prime Minister, there have been examples in this century when heads of state have gone crazy," Benjamin Netanyahu said in parliament. "Chamberlain acted with blatant stupidity when he believed the liar Hitler and that is exactly what you are doing. . . . You are far worse than Chamberlain. You are endangering the security and freedom of your own people. In this case you are giving credence to the liar Arafat."[2]

Raful Eitan accused Rabin of signing a pact "with the greatest murderer of Jews since Hitler."[3]

But Rabin held firm. He still owned the loyalty of most Israelis who, for the first time since Anwar Sadat had come to Jerusalem sixteen years earlier, saw the peace process taking place. They were captivated by the drama of seeing Israel's leaders on the South Lawn of the White House, shaking hands with President Clinton and Yasser Arafat. They took pride in the Nobel Peace Prizes shared by Rabin, Peres, and Arafat.

Arafat, who had spent most of his life as a hunted guerrilla leader and the face of terror to Israelis, stood before the world as a new statesman anointed by the great powers, the United Nations, and the Nobel committee. Yet for all the pomp, the Palestinians living under occupation got little relief from their grim existence.

The roadblocks, the closures, the destitute economy, especially in Gaza, and the heavy presence of the Israeli army all remained—and as time went on, the delays in fulfillment of the promises of Oslo, the setbacks, and the vicious acts of violence on both sides proved more destabilizing than ever.

"The residents of the territories discovered nothing had changed on the Israeli side," said Shlomo Gazit, the former military intelligence chief who had been the first administrator of the West Bank and Gaza after they were seized in 1967. "Instead of . . . confidence building measures, both sides descended into an ugly and demagogic battle of declarations, while attempting to establish new facts to strengthen their hands towards the final settlement talks."[4]

Some of the sabras of the officer corps resisted the concept of a permanent peace with Arafat.

Colonel Shaul Arieli, head of a "peace" directorate within the general staff, observed, "Though we asked ourselves what shape peace would take, the military continued to think in terms of war. Officers were unable to understand that the whole idea was that we were moving into a state of peace, and that peace would bring security. They wanted to establish a framework which would give us security as though there were no peace. This was unacceptable to our adversaries and rightly so."[5]

Barak told Rabin that, as chief of staff, he wanted to go before the cabinet and present a dissenting view: the Oslo agreement was a giant "Swiss cheese" with so many "security loopholes" that it represented a danger to the state of Israel, he said.[6]

Uri Saguy, the military intelligence chief, saw Rabin on the morning of the breakthrough announcement. "I told Mr. Rabin, 'You are not in a position to have any final agreement vis-à-vis the Palestinians.'" For Saguy it was a mistake "to [defer] the core problems [of Jerusalem, refugees, settlements, and borders]" over the five years of implementation—saving them for the "final status" negotiations—while building up a Palestinian Authority that could make no promises to its people.[7]

But Rabin, wielding his authority, led the army into this new endeavor. He put army officers—not diplomats—in charge of negotiating the first security arrangements that would provide for Arafat's return to Gaza and the setting up of a Palestinian Authority headquarters in Gaza and Jericho. Most of these officers had spent their lives fighting Arabs. Yet human contact had the same transformative effect as it had when Sadat came to Israel a generation earlier.

Lipkin-Shahak, in line to become chief of staff, was assigned to meet with Nabil Shaath, a beefy and articulate PLO negotiator who had traveled broadly and who held degrees in law and economics from the University of Pennsylvania. The two men developed close bonds, but Lipkin-Shahak was embarrassed when his private meetings were targeted for front-page coverage in the right-wing Israeli press with photos showing the general and the PLO man strolling arm in arm on the beach wearing informal Arab gowns, or gallabayas. Their point was clear: he had gone native. The general looked like a pawn of the Arabs.

Jacob Peri, the chief of the Shabak intelligence service, also began clandestine meetings with Arafat and his top aides after Oslo and he, too, soon developed strong personal bonds. The first time Peri flew to Tunis to meet with Arafat, he took along the radio that he had kept in his office since 1967 when, as a young Shabak officer on the West Bank, he had chased Arafat from hideout to hideout trying to arrest or kill him. The radio was war booty, taken from a room Arafat had vacated moments before Shabak agents burst in.

Peri presented Arafat with the radio, a symbolic gesture meant to convey that the era of "the hunt" was over.[8]

The opponents of Oslo soon resorted to violence.

The first salvo came from an enraged Israeli army physician, an American-born settler from Brooklyn named Baruch Goldstein. On

February 25, 1994, he strode into the Mosque of Abraham in Hebron on the West Bank and leveled an automatic weapon at hundreds of Palestinian worshippers engaged in morning prayers. In the ensuing spray of gunfire, thirty-one Palestinians were killed before others rushed Goldstein and beat him to death with a fire extinguisher.

The Hebron massacre, as it was called, broke the positive psychology of Oslo.

Rabin felt he had no choice but to slap a curfew on Hebron, sending troops into its center and into other Palestinian cities to contain demonstrations in which dozens more Palestinians died.

Arafat asked indignantly how the Israelis could punish the Palestinians for what Goldstein had perpetrated, but Rabin just wanted to restore order. He understood that he was at war—not with these rioting Palestinian children but with the Jewish settler movement, which was so threatened by his commitment to give up the West Bank and Gaza that it was engaged in its own civil uprising. Hard-line sabras were joining in.

Rabin told the Knesset that he was "shamed" that an army officer—"a degenerate murderer"—had brought disgrace on Israel and on the army that protected the Jewish state. He said that Goldstein was a man who "grew in a swamp whose murderous sources are found here, and across the sea; they are foreign to Judaism," adding, "To him and to those like him we say: you are not part of the community of Israel."[9]

But of course Goldstein *was* part of the community of Israel. He had served in the army. He knew what he was doing. His act of terror demonstrated that any fanatic—right-wing Israeli or Palestinian militant—could explode the peace process.

Arafat was under assault from his own people because Oslo had done so little to change anything. And Goldstein's deed gave Palestinian radicals—especially Hamas—the righteous cause they needed to exploit Palestinian anger.

Hamas had named its underground terrorist wing the Izzedine al-Qassem Brigades in memory of the Arab outlaw who had terrorized the British army in the 1930s. Now an electrical engineer named Yahya Ayyash was perfecting an instrument that Israelis had never imagined could penetrate the army's bands of steel. Within weeks of Goldstein's rampage, Ayyash carefully fitted a 1987 Opel sedan with seven gas cylinders, five antipersonnel grenades, and more than one thousand nails for a new kind of low-tech weapon in an asymmetrical war. He placed the lethal payload in the hands of a nineteen-year-old Hamas volunteer, Raed Zaqarna. On April 6, 1994, Zaqarna drove the car to Afula, an agricultural town in Galilee just north of the West Bank, and there he pulled in front of a city bus as it was loading Israeli schoolchildren and detonated the load.

The fireball entered the bus through the windshield, peeling back the roof like a can of sardines; the wall of shrapnel and nails did its work, shredding the driver, killing seven passengers, and wounding forty-four.[10]

The wave of Palestinian retribution continued.

The next day, Hamas militants gunned down an Israeli hitchhiker near Ashdod in the south, and a week after the Afula attack, another suicide bomber struck on a bus at Hadera, north of Tel Aviv. He detonated a five-pound explosive pack as the bus got under way. Six people were killed and thirty injured. Israelis recoiled at how effortlessly the Islamic extremists of Gaza had found an effective new weapon—operated by suicidal young men—that could reach the intimacy of Jewish neighborhoods in a country defended by the mightiest army in the region. What had peace with the Palestinians wrought?

Rabin knew that the military establishment was deeply conflicted.

Many of the generals and intelligence chiefs had dedicated their professional lives to the destruction of the PLO. Most of all, Barak was conflicted, but in a speech to the army, he tried to articulate the basis of loyalty. "The IDF does not determine policies," he said. "The duty and responsibility of the IDF vis-à-vis the political echelon is to make clear, in advance, loudly and clearly, what is the security reality that is going to emerge as a result of the agreement."

His words sounded like a complaint. After all, Rabin did not give him the opportunity to express the army's concerns in advance of Oslo.

"We should be careful to avoid taking positions, and we should not make manipulative use of the sensitive and central security issue in Israeli existence," he added.

But the army had to take positions every day. It had to pronounce on which countries posed the greatest threat, which weapons were needed for future combat, and which Israeli national policies might influence events most constructively.

"We have to be very cautious not to steer the government or to put pressure on an elected government toward policies that are different from its own," Barak continued, a statement that seemed naïve at best in a society so enveloped by the military institution.

"The government is empowered to do things which some of us, as individuals, may view as bad. Our responsibility is to carry out the government's instructions in the best possible way, to execute what has been agreed upon, and not to reach a situation whereby we try—knowingly or otherwise—to dictate to the government the nature of the political arrangement."[11]

Barak's declaration would echo again and again, but the manifest reality was that the military establishment's opinion on security matters loomed so large that only a prime minister of Rabin's stature stood a chance of countering its influence.

If it took a Nixon to go to China, who but Rabin could have taken Arafat as a partner?

The threat to peace drew Rabin closer to the Palestinian leadership, and to Arafat personally, in part because the Israeli leader had seen how profoundly Arafat's leadership was shaken by Baruch Goldstein's rampage in Hebron. At the same time, he saw how flummoxed Arafat was by the Islamic opposition of Hamas and its terrorist cells. To the Hamas leadership, peace with the Jewish state was inconsistent with the restoration of Islamic rule in Palestine.

Rabin broadened the diplomatic outreach that fall, asking American secretary of state Warren Christopher to open a negotiating channel with Syria's Hafez al-Assad.

And initially, Rabin entrusted Peres with a peace mission to King Hussein. But Peres could not suppress the urge to brag in front of newsmen that he was a maestro of secret diplomacy.

After a series of private meetings with the Jordanian king, Peres strolled into the prime minister's outer office in Jerusalem one afternoon in early November—just six weeks after the Oslo Accords—and all but announced to reporters a new breakthrough with Jordan. Peres pompously instructed the journalists to "put November 3rd in your calendars as an historic date.

All that's needed is a pen to sign it." His remarks triggered instant news that peace with Jordan was at hand, infuriating King Hussein, who had yet to prepare his own people on the final compromises that were needed for a peace treaty with the Jewish state. Peres's indiscretion cost Rabin a year, and as a result, Rabin cut Peres out of the loop by turning the negotiations over to Mossad's Halevy, who enjoyed a strong confidential bond with the king.[12]

Nine weeks after the Hebron massacre, Israeli and PLO negotiators concluded the Gaza-Jericho pact that put the Palestinian Authority on its feet and set the stage for Arafat's return to his homeland. He made the crossing from Egypt into Gaza on July 1, 1994, and the Palestinians—more than one hundred thousand of them—greeted him ecstatically. They raised PLO or Hamas banners over every house and lamppost. The extravaganza—in which the aging guerrilla leader stooped to kiss the earth—seemed to mute the opposition and the naysayers.

Three weeks later, King Hussein and Rabin flew to Washington to declare before Congress and on the lawn of the White House that Jordan and Israel had reached a framework for a treaty that would end the state of war. The momentum for peace seemed unstoppable.

In October, President Clinton was on his way to the Holy Land to celebrate all that had been accomplished. But in advance of his arrival, Palestinian gunmen went on a shooting spree in Jerusalem, killing two and wounding twelve. Hamas militants kidnapped an Israeli soldier, Nachshon Wachsman, and demanded that Israel release Sheikh Yassin, the Hamas leader, from prison along with hundreds of other Palestinians. Rabin and Arafat both called Wachsman's mother and promised to do everything they could to win his release, but the clock was ticking on a four-day deadline set by the kidnappers.

The intelligence service located the hideout where Wachsman was being held near Ramallah. Rabin sent in a Sayeret Matkal commando team. The commandos went in shooting on October 14, killing three terrorists but not before Wachsman was executed and Captain Nir Poraz, one of the Israeli officers, was mortally wounded in the firefight.

The failed rescue hurt Rabin, not because he had used force but because he had used force and failed. If a state organized around the military could not execute a rescue, what was the point? Someone had to take the blame, and Rabin had never shirked stepping up to take responsibility.

Israelis grieved at military funerals, then Hamas struck again, this time in the center of Tel Aviv: a suicide bomber named Salah Sawi blew himself up on a bus near Dizengoff Square, killing twenty-four people and wounding dozens more.

By the time Clinton and all the other dignitaries arrived for Arafat's investiture, Rabin had closed the Gaza Strip, shutting in tens of thousands of workers who had jobs on the Israeli side. Gaza's economy slumped 25 percent. Rioting broke out at the crossing points. Half of Gaza's workers were unemployed, and the territory seethed with discontent. Palestinians asked: What has come from peace?

Rabin declared before the Knesset that Israel was in a state of war against "extremist Islam the enemy of peace . . . and the enemy of the Jews which threatens the peace of our country." He told Clinton that the Islamic terror wave "also threatens the peace of your country" and "it threatens the regimes of moderate Arab rulers and the peace of the world." Rabin then declared, "Iran is leading this terrorism."[13]

Iran had little to do with the violence wrought by Hamas, but Rabin was in the throes of a dark strategic vision, as he explained to former president Nixon, who stopped through for a visit: Iran was exporting Islamic revolution using cold war tactics "similar to those of the Soviet Union's infamous Comintern before World War II."[14]

Rabin explained to Nixon that Iran was demanding loyalty not to Iran but to an Islamic empire as in the days of the Prophet, and this simple call to a heroic past carried a broad appeal that washed across national boundaries.

As veterans of the cold war, Rabin and Nixon saw the threat from Islamic extremism through the same lens. And however one rationalized its provenance, violent extremism was on the rise within the fabric of Islam.

Arafat was not willing to confront Hamas with the force needed to end the suicide campaign. Hadn't the Israelis tried and failed before him? Sheikh Yassin and hundreds of his supporters were already in jail. What good had it done?

One of Peres's confidants argued that Israel should downplay the terrorist attacks; treat them the way the British treated the violence perpetrated by the Irish Republican Army—with a stiff upper lip—viewing the phenomenon as an aberration from the fringe and not as a war.[15]

But the martial impulse for retribution was deeply embedded. The military establishment was impelled to develop the military options to strike a counterblow, and each time Rabin showed restraint, it seemed to weaken him.

The opposition was portraying the prime minister as if he were a Nazi. Ultra-Orthodox rabbis labeled him a traitor—a betrayer of Jews—someone who could be killed for his "crimes" against his people. Carmi Gillon, the Shabak chief, tried to tamp down the hate speech, but right-wing politicians said he was intruding into the political sphere. Israel's tabloid press screamed the news of every incident of terror, and Rabin could do little to control the frenzy without suspending democratic rule and free speech. He railed against the press barons, pointing out that the headlines about terror attacks were bigger than the headlines that had announced the Six-Day War.

The violence threw a pall over the ceremony that Rabin and King Hussein had carefully planned to celebrate the signing of the Israeli-Jordanian peace treaty. But they went ahead, flying out to the sandstone contours of the Wadi Arava just north of Aqaba to declare the completion of their work.

Peace with Jordan was bittersweet.

At the beginning of 1995, Rabin and Peres went forward with Oslo II negotiations to extend Palestinian authority over the Arab cities in the West Bank in preparation for the first democratic elections for a Palestinian government.

Rabin's administration announced a three-year plan to build thirty-one thousand new Israeli housing units around Jerusalem. These were the Palestinian lands that Israel—Oslo or no Oslo—wanted to annex in advance of the final status negotiations to make Jerusalem an eternally Jewish capital. Arafat cried foul. He protested in a personal meeting with Rabin, who relented, pledging to Arafat that he would freeze construction. Still, the housing binge showed how even Rabin was maneuvering to improve his bargaining position for the "final status" negotiations that were to begin in 1996.

Hamas and Islamic Jihad were determined to explode the peace, and the relentlessness with which they staged their assault on Israeli society betrayed a strong militant character intrinsic to the Palestinian community as well.

Working together for the first time with bombs supplied by Ayyash, the militant groups dispatched a team to a highway junction north of Tel Aviv at a place called Beit Lid, where a huge crowd of soldiers jostled on the pavement every week for seats on buses heading north toward their units.

On the morning of January 22, 1995, a young militant named Anwar Soukar, who had been mingling with the soldiers, feigned illness by dropping to his knees at a telephone stand. When a group of soldiers gathered around him, Soukar reached into his pack and triggered a foot-long cylinder, eight inches in diameter, filled with TNT and nails. The horrible blast ripped the young people asunder. Most were eighteen to twenty-one years old.

Emergency crews rushed to the scene and began treating the wounded and collecting the dead. But then Salah Shaaker, a second bomber, took advantage of the mayhem. He walked into the junction and detonated another bomb.

Twenty-one Israelis now lay dead and nearly seventy wounded.

The intelligence services found a third bomb that was to have been used by yet another suicide volunteer. They surmised that his task was to kill Rabin and other senior political figures when they arrived on the scene. But he failed to reach the junction. Police studied the explosive device and mapped Ayyash's signature circuitry.

Sheikh Yassin, as it happened, was just a few hundred feet away, at Ashmoret Prison, which is located at the junction. The sound of the blasts thundered through the facility, and prison guards feared that Hamas was mounting a rescue attempt. They rushed Yassin from the day room into a cell and locked down the prison.

Rabin tried to appear calm in the crisis, but the Beit Lid bombing shook the foundations of his peace strategy. He and the whole sabra ruling class of Israel had spent a lifetime believing that a strong military was the ultimate guarantor of national security, and now, the advent of the suicide bomber threatened to turn the doctrine on its head.

Just as there had been no effective military response to children hurling stones during the intifada, there could be no effective response to the insidious tactic of young men determined to explode themselves like some kind of human cruise missile operating in slow motion.

If Rabin had begun to harbor doubts about whether he had taken the country down the wrong path, this would have been the moment when the specter of failure began to gnaw at him. He called in the Americans and told them to inform Arafat that all talks were suspended and that nothing would move forward until the PLO chairman got a grip on security and on his own people.

Rabin looked at the Palestinian leadership and thought about the chaos that had confronted Israelis when they were setting up the Jewish state. There was an important parallel: Ben-Gurion had faced competing Jewish militias, terrorist cells such as the Stern Gang and the Irgun. It was uncertain that the government could impose central authority until Ben-Gurion had given the orders that were passed down to a young Yitzhak Rabin to attack the *Altalena*, the ship that was carrying Menachem Begin and his Irgun fighters to land their own weapons on a Tel Aviv beach.

"Peace will not be possible until Arafat has his own *Altalena*," Rabin told the Americans, expecting that they would pass on this stern admonition to bring discipline to the Palestinian ranks, even if it meant civil war for Arafat. He would have to set his own Fatah forces against Hamas to show them that the Palestinian Authority was unifying military power.[16] He also asked the army to look into the possibility of building a separation wall to protect Israelis from the new suicide weapon. If he couldn't defeat it, perhaps he could isolate it.

In public, Rabin tried to project the stoicism that was a hallmark of his character. He invented an aphorism to describe his plight, which seemed borrowed from Ben-Gurion, who had tried to buck up his people in 1939 when the British issued a "white paper" to slow Jewish immigration. Ben-Gurion had said, "We will fight with the British against Hitler as if there was no white paper; we will fight the white paper as if there were no war."

Rabin adapted the sentiment to his predicament, telling the Knesset that he would pursue peace as if there were no terrorism, and he would fight terrorism as if there were no peace.[17]

Arafat struggled to end the bloodletting, but he simply was not strong enough to overcome the bonfire of religious idealism that was fueling the radicals. In April, six more Israeli soldiers were killed when Hamas rigged two exploding cars at Kfar Darom.

Yet amazingly, Rabin kept the peace process on track through a hot summer in which suicide bombers struck at Ramat Gan in late July and in Jerusalem in late August, killing a total of ten more Israelis and wounding more than a hundred. When Rabin arrived on the scene of the Ramat Gan bombing on the edge of Tel Aviv, he and the chief of staff, Lipkin-Shahak, were berated by angry Israelis.

Negotiations with the Palestinians—over extending the powers of Arafat's authority—had to be moved from the Tel Aviv area to Taba in the far south because right-wing Israeli protestors were becoming increasingly abusive and threatening. In August, the right-wing newspaper *Ma'ariv* bore the headline "Security Around Rabin Is Heightened. The Shabak Fears an Assassination."

In tumultuous negotiating sessions, Israeli generals demanded more security concessions, but Arafat shouted back, "I am not your slave!" He demanded more power and respect for a proposed Palestinian police force, the closest thing to a Palestinian army. He didn't get it.

At one point, Peres himself confronted the military officers on the Israeli negotiating team. They opposed allowing Arafat's security forces to move into Hebron, where a group of Israeli settlers was a constant source of friction.

"What gall!" Peres shouted at the military men. "You want 150,000 Hebronites to remain under our control because of 400 Jews? . . . I'm telling you that we can break Arafat, if that's what you want. But then we'll be left with Hamas, an intifada, and terror."[18]

In such an atmosphere, the Oslo II agreement was completed at the end of September. It provided for the withdrawal of the Israeli army from the populated parts of the West Bank and Gaza so that the Palestinian Authority could call elections and stand up a government.

The so-called Interim Agreement that was Oslo II was a major step for both sides, for it showed that two years on, Oslo was working despite the threatening rhetoric emanating from the Israeli right and the terror campaign being waged by Hamas and Islamic Jihad.

The Israelis and Palestinians were poised between two worlds, trying to cross from one to the other. The former was marked by hatred, enmity, war, and separation of peoples, and the new world was an inchoate realm of coexistence, not exactly the federation of Semitic peoples that the early Zionists envisioned, for no one could imagine Israeli settlers and religious Jews ever being reconciled with Palestinians. Peace had yet to be defined, and neither Rabin nor Peres had the rhetorical skill to define it in terms that the military establishment, as the guardian of the state, could absorb. Peres had begun to talk about a new Middle East in which investment, tourism, and new technologies could knit the region back together, but his words floated unrealistically through the impoverished warrens of Gaza and the West Bank refugee camps where the lives of radicalized Palestinian youth had seen no improvement.

On the day that Rabin took the Oslo II accord to the Knesset for approval, the streets of Jerusalem filled with tens of thousands of protesters, to whom Benjamin Netanyahu shouted the slogans of the right: Rabin had committed an "act of surrender," he said. The new accord was "a danger to the existence of the state of Israel." That evening, a mob rushed Rabin's Cadillac, and one of the rioters ripped the ornament off the hood.[19]

"If we managed to get Rabin's Cadillac emblem, we can get Rabin," a young man bragged to newsmen.

Within the military establishment, some officers began to question Arafat's sincerity about long-term peace.

Moshe Boogie Ya'alon, the young commando who in 1988 had led the team that killed Abu Jihad in Tunisia, had risen to be director of military intelligence. Ya'alon had been in office only two months when he surprised Rabin by saying, "Mr. Prime Minister, I have to give you a strategic early warning. I don't see any sign for reconciliation on the Palestinian side."[20]

Ya'alon came from a Labor Party family near Haifa, but he had spent his military career fighting Arabs and targeting Palestinian militants or their leaders for assassination. Ya'alon was among those officers who were not emotionally suited to engaging an enemy they had demonized all their life. His idealism led him to the most hard-line position: that the Palestinians had not really changed. The world for Ya'alon was a place where facts were judged with brutal simplicity. Palestine was an enemy, not a neighbor, and that was that.

"Actually, I didn't have to use my sophisticated intelligence sources," Ya'alon told me in an interview. "I just had to listen to Arafat, to his rhetoric. I had to look at the Palestinian textbooks, which I did, or to walk into the Palestinian classes, which I also did. I went to Nablus and Ramallah, and I was shocked. I realized that Arafat—at the beginning I was not sure; it was a long process to realize it—that Arafat didn't want to conclude a final settlement based on the two-states-for-two-peoples principle, recognizing Israel as a Jewish state. He was not ready to do it."

According to Ya'alon's account of this conversation, Rabin looked at him and replied that he might be right, but what was more important was helping Arafat to stand up his government, call elections and—with the prestige of presidential office and consolidated power—take firm control so he could defeat the virulent strain of extremism that opposed a two-state solution and called for the destruction of the Zionist state and the restoration of Islamic rule in Palestine.

Ya'alon, whose mandate it was to look at Israel's strategic position, had missed the fundamentals that Rabin understood more viscerally as a commander. Instead of looking at the big-picture task of helping Arafat become a statesman for the first time in his life, Ya'alon was down in the weeds reading the transcriptions of Arafat speeches, playing "gotcha" over rhetoric, school texts, and what any teacher might say in the classroom about thirty years of Israeli occupation. He was missing the contradictions of politics. Ya'alon's approach was essentially negative: he had fallen into the psychological trap—the belief that people cannot change, that peace is therefore impossible, and that the only thing that works is a lethal and effective prophylactic of separation and overwhelming force.

"Rabin asked me what do I recommend and I said, 'I recommend to stop the whole peace process and to put an ultimatum to Arafat demanding that he arrest the terrorists, stop the violence, but first of all to stop the peace process, the redeployments, to stop everything until he will prove to us that he was going to eliminate the terror capabilities.'"[21]

This was the essence of Ya'alon's approach: there could be no peace until the Palestinians were pristine. They did not deserve peace until their society was completely transformed.

Rabin understood Boogie Ya'alon. The younger man, a sabra whom Rabin respected for his energy and courage, was still at the beginning of an intellectual process that Rabin had passed through during a half century as a soldier, and now as a statesman. And Rabin was learning remarkably fast toward the end. He and Peres drew closer not just because their fates were intertwined but also because they could see that civil conflict among the Jews was enveloping Israel and, therefore, the fate of the country was in the balance as profoundly as it had ever been.

"Though they were never really friends," Leah Rabin wrote later, "destiny had thrown them together."[22]

Unlike Ya'alon, Rabin and Peres understood that there were no clean lines in statecraft. A calculated risk for peace was just that: anything could happen, contradictory behavior was part of the norm, while patience, restraint, and good intelligence were essential. The task of leaders—Israeli and Palestinian—was to hold back the onslaught of doubt, naysaying, and extremism while pushing and dragging both communities across the fulcrum where each new action could tip the process in the right direction despite the negative gravity trying to pull it back.

Rabin had not gone pacifist. While he was cutting Arafat all the slack that he could manage, Rabin secretly authorized a large Mossad operation to go after Fathi Shiqaqi, the founder of Islamic Jihad. Shiqaqi, forty-four, bragged in an interview with *Time* magazine that the Beit Lid bombing that had killed twenty-one soldiers the previous January "gives satisfaction to our people." Israel's military establishment wanted him dead. The public and the army wanted retribution. National morale was sagging. That's why Rabin approved the plan to kill the Islamic Jihad leader in a bold stroke.[23]

Shiqaqi came from a prominent Palestinian family. His brother, Khalil, was a well-known academic and public opinion pollster in Nablus. Fathi had joined the Muslim Brotherhood as a young medical student but had been frustrated by its moderation. He was among the first jihadists to rationalize suicide as an acceptable form of resistance to the occupation. Jailed and later deported from the West Bank, Shiqaqi had quickly found support from Hezbollah in Lebanon and, from there, he moved to Damascus to establish the external headquarters of Palestinian Islamic Jihad.

Mossad had reported to Rabin that the Oslo process had driven the extremists toward greater levels of cooperation, and Shiqaqi had helped to forge the alliance with Hamas and its bomb maker, Ayyash. In the *Time* interview, Shiqaqi admitted that Islamic Jihad carried out the double bombing at Beit Lid junction, though he was not asked about the third bomb that was found at the scene and was believed to have been prepared to kill Rabin.[24]

On October 26, Shiqaqi was in Malta, the Mediterranean island state that lies between Libya and Italy. He had been to visit Colonel Muammar el-Qaddafi, the Libyan leader, who provided funding to Islamic Jihad and many other terrorist organizations. Shiqaqi was headed back to Damascus when the Mossad contingent that had put the Diplomat Hotel under surveillance caught sight of him and sent in a two-man shooting team on a motorcycle. It was over in seconds: a blaze of gunfire; the shooters had a contraption attached to their guns to catch the spent shell casings so there would be no evidence to examine. They sped away as Shiqaqi expired on the pavement with multiple gunshot wounds to the head. Some reports indicated that the assassins caught a speedboat out to sea, where they were picked up by a larger vessel, perhaps an Israeli submarine.

The tabloids feasted on the red meat of retribution. Rabin, always elated by an Israeli military success, scheduled a private reception for the Mossad team, where he could congratulate them and toast their success. But Rabin did not live to host the celebration.

The prime minister was making his way to his Cadillac in Tel Aviv's central square on the night of November 4. It was late, but the sidewalks were still swarmed with Israelis. Rabin had appeared with Peres and other prominent figures at a national rally for peace that drew tens of thousands of people. At the end, they had joined hands and sung the "Song of Peace." Rabin's staff had typed out the lyrics on a piece of paper because he could never remember them, but he had stuffed the paper in his breast pocket.

Through the crowd walked a young man with a gun, a right-wing extremist, Yigal Amir, a law student born in Herzliya, north of Tel Aviv. Amir was just another version of Baruch Goldstein, who had opened fire in Hebron in 1994, only Amir turned his weapon on the leader of the Jewish state. Given all the hate speech and incitement that the Israelis had tolerated that summer, it was not surprising that an impressionable mind like Amir's had been turned to thoughts of assassination. The police found a copy of *Day of the Jackal* on his bookshelf.

Amir approached the prime minister from the rear, sidestepping Rabin's security detail. He fired three shots into Rabin's back. The prime minister went down. Guards pushed him into his car and raced to nearby Ichilov Hospital. Rabin died on the surgeon's table.

The act seemed to take the air away from the Jewish state.

Amir had taken to heart the rabbinical denunciations aimed at Rabin and at the Oslo Accords. He decided that God would reward the person who killed this heretical prime minister who was threatening to turn over the hills of Judea and Samaria to the Palestinians for their state. (Amir was caught at the scene. He was tried, convicted, and sentenced to life plus fourteen years in prison.)

The world stood in noiseless shock. No prime minister had invested as much in peace. No prime minister had shown the capacity to move the military establishment constructively onto a new path. Not since Moshe Sharett's death had a figure so central to reconciliation with the Arabs been unhorsed so abruptly, leaving the country to wonder who would carry the burden.

In a military society, violence had been turned self-destructively against the state, not as national suicide but as a decapitation meant to force a change in national strategy, a change in course.

SIXTEEN

Bibi Against the Military Elite

Rabin's death allowed all the world to believe for a little while that Israel was wholly on the road to peace—that the country was not riven by discord and violence. Rabin's peace offensive had deeply divided the sabra military establishment between advocates for negotiation and peace and skeptics who were pushing for a return to a hard militarist approach to the Arabs.

All eyes shifted to Shimon Peres, who assumed the premiership as the ranking Labor Party minister under Rabin. Surrounded and consoled by Western and even Arab leaders, embraced by Bill Clinton and blessed by Leah Rabin to pick up the mantle that could be placed only on his shoulders, Peres held himself out to his people with all the humility he could muster and all the vanity he could not suppress.

To the U.S. Congress, onto whose podium Peres strode to be anointed in the capital of Israel's greatest ally, Peres said, "In my country I have shouldered almost every responsibility. I have tasted almost every title. I have served almost in every position. Today, I wish only one thing: to bear the burden of peace-making."[1]

Yet Israelis knew that Peres had a limited amount of time to demonstrate unambiguously that he could lead a country whose electorate—for more than a decade—had refused to grant him the vote of confidence he now effortlessly conferred upon himself.

Partnered with Rabin, Peres's reputation had improved, but there was no underestimating the corrosive effect of Peres on his own as a leader, especially since the army and the military establishment had never accepted him as one of their own. And many generals undoubtedly hoped that Ehud Barak would soon be circling Peres like a shark.

The period of mourning and introspection that unified the country after the assassination would not last. Many Israelis took satisfaction that the extreme right was under investigation for inciting Amir to murder. And even politicians such as Netanyahu, who had called Rabin a traitor, were on the defensive because Leah Rabin made it clear that she blamed all the clarions of the right who baited the violent impulses of the Israeli fringe. She refused to shake Netanyahu's hand at the funeral.[2]

So Peres had benefited from these currents and, after huddling with his advisers and consulting the Americans, he decided that he would make a grand play for peace with Syria because Hafez al-Assad was primed. His eldest son, Basil, had been killed in a car accident on the Beirut-Damascus highway, forcing the elder Assad to contemplate his own mortality. Striking a deal with the Israelis for peace might help ensure a stable transition for Assad's second son, Bashar, who would now take over upon Assad's death.

For Assad, it all depended on whether Peres would honor the commitment Rabin had made—privately to the Americans—that he was prepared to return all of the Golan Heights in exchange for a full peace with Syria.

From the outset, however, Peres seemed to lack the political courage to make a frontal assault on those Israelis who would most strenuously resist peace with Syria: the settlers of the Golan. For three decades, settlers had been clearing boulder-strewn slopes on the Golan Heights for agriculture and erecting a landscape of tourism that had made many of them wealthy. A generation of Israelis had grown up trekking across the promontory, basking on verandas where they enjoyed soaring views of Galilee and the Jordan Valley.

"The Golan Heights is the only mountain we have," Peres declared in Washington. "I am not prepared to give it away for skim milk."[3]

Peres told the Americans, using one of his clever aphorisms, that he was prepared to lose the Golan or lose the elections, "but not both."[4] What he really needed, he explained, was a Sadat-like bit of theater to capture the public imagination, to dazzle the political realm. His big idea was to get on an airplane with Bill Clinton and fly to Damascus and, like Sadat, make a pitch for reconciliation. Assad would not dare shoot them down, he reasoned.

But even the Americans knew that Assad would never agree to an Israeli "stunt." The Arabs did not trust Peres. As far as they were concerned, he would seize all of the glory and publicity from a trip to Damascus, but when it was time to deliver—by evacuating the Golan and returning the land to Syria based on the 1967 border—Peres would freeze, or feint, or run for cover. Assad was a master of maneuver, and he knew a maneuverer when he saw one.

The conversation between the Americans and Peres took place on a Sunday afternoon in late November 1995 after Dennis Ross, the American envoy, reported that he had met in Tel Aviv with Lipkin-Shahak, the chief of staff, Boogie Ya'alon, the chief of military intelligence, and Dany Yatom, who had been Rabin's military secretary. These chiefs of the military establishment were less than enthusiastic about engaging Assad after Rabin's death, which could mean only that they were concerned that Peres did not possess the gravitas to carry the country into a deal with its most devious enemy, especially since the Americans had already shared with Assad Rabin's pledge about giving up the Golan.[5]

Without Rabin, without strong political leadership by a trusted figure who had worn the uniform, the center of gravity on national security policy would shift back to the army, which was the repository of doubt and suspicion over Syrian intentions; it was also a repository of doubt about the Palestinians, especially Arafat, and those doubts would surface soon enough. The army's institutional interests were taking over by default because Peres simply did not have the credibility to overcome them. It was as if, without Rabin in charge, going for peace was a far too risky business.

The doubts about Peres incited almost immediate competition from Barak, who had resigned from the army at the beginning of the year to join Rabin's cabinet as minister of interior. Before he had shed his uniform, Barak had gone on television to confront the whispering campaign over how he had acted that day when the errant missile killed five Sayeret Matkal commandos at Tse'elim. Barak had given a good performance, recounting a career of heroism in combat that had made him the most decorated soldier in the IDF. He had met the courage standard of a tough sabra, charging into machine-gun fire and looking into "the whites of their eyes." How could a man who had seen the "whites of their eyes"—he repeated the phrase—be accused of acting cowardly?[6]

Barak had put the matter to rest so well that when Peres took over the government and reshuffled ministers, he nixed the suggestion that Barak should be elevated to defense minister. That would have established Barak as a powerful rival to the prime minister, so Peres kept the Defense Ministry for himself—he would be prime minister and defense minister—and offered Barak the Foreign Ministry, knowing that diplomacy was Barak's weakest suit. In cabinet meetings, Peres would sit there as a Nobel Peace Prize winner, as the architect of Oslo, as a friend of Clinton and an intimate of world leaders. Barak could not compete with those credentials. And besides, it would be good for Peres when the little Napoleon embarrassed himself now and again.

One of Barak's first diplomatic appearances was in Barcelona at a gathering of Mediterranean nations. When the conference debated how to express its support for Palestinian rights, Barak went up to Javier Solana, the Spanish foreign minister, and said, "Ehud Barak is my name, and I want to be prime minister of Israel one day. I can't go back to my country with a declaration containing a paragraph enshrining the principle of land in exchange for peace and recognizing the Palestinians' right to self-determination." Barak was hypersensitive to how he would be perceived.[7]

The Palestinians held their first democratic elections in January 1996. Arafat won the overwhelming mandate from his people, the mandate that Rabin had expected would strengthen the Palestinian leader in the struggle against extremists.

The Israeli army pulled out of Nablus, Ramallah, and Bethlehem. A new Palestinian police force took to the streets, but in Gaza, the UN coordinator for the territory, Terje Rød-Larsen, the Norwegian diplomat, warned that the strip was a powder keg due to soaring unemployment. Israeli factories and farms had begun to replace Palestinians with foreign workers. Separation was the new paradigm, the only way Israelis felt they could stop the suicide bombers.

It was in this critical transition to Palestinian rule that the Israeli military establishment struck a blow that had unintended consequences.

The Shabak had suffered a grievous public indictment for failing to protect Rabin from an assassin's bullet. Carmi Gillon, the Shabak chief, was losing his job as the official scapegoat for failure. An investigation had shown not only lax personal security around Rabin, but one of Shabak's undercover informants knew Amir, knew that he was dangerous and had expressed a desire to kill the prime minister. But the warning had not been passed on. Shabak's threat surveillance had been proved to be if not incompetent, then negligent.

In his final days, Gillon believed the agency had caught a break. Shabak agents in Gaza had discovered the hiding place of the Hamas "engineer," Ayyash. During the hunt for Ayyash, Gillon had told Arafat that he ought to arrest the bomb maker and put him on trial, but Arafat insisted that Ayyash had fled the country. "He is in Sudan!" Arafat protested. This proved untrue.

Arafat's security chief for Gaza, Mohammed Dahlen, strongly urged Shabak not to kill Ayyash because he had become a hero of the angry and unemployed youth there. Dahlen believed that Fatah could keep Ayyash under control.

"We are going to cooperate with you only as long as we believe that this process, the peace process, will bring us an end of the occupation and a Palestinian state alongside Israel," Dahlen told them, adding, "The moment that we and our people will not believe, forget about us."[8]

But Shabak had just lost a prime minister. Gillon was eager for any success. Despite the cautionary warnings, he went to Peres with a recommendation to assassinate Ayyash. He did not have to sell very hard. Killing Ayyash was the kind of bold stroke that Peres, too, needed; it would burnish his credentials as Mr. Security, win him support in the defense establishment, and buck up a demoralized country. He approved the hit.[9]

Shabak had an informant close to Ayyash.

The Israeli agents were able to infiltrate a telephone with plastic explosive in the handset at the home of one of Ayyash's relatives. All the Shabak agents had to do was place a call at the designated moment, and when Ayyash answered the phone, they pushed a button. On January 5, the phone rang at the home of Ayyash's uncle in Beit Lahiya. Ayyash picked up.

"The Israelis blew his head off," said Stanley Moskowitz, the CIA station chief. The explosion killed Ayyash as swiftly and as brutally as his bombs had killed more than 50 Israelis and wounded 340.[10]

When the word went out that Ayyash was dead, more than one hundred thousand Gazans turned out for the funeral, including the leaders of Arafat's Fatah movement in Gaza, who felt they had no choice but to honor a fallen warrior against occupation. Ayyash had given the dispossessed of Gaza a sense of potency seldom felt. To make up for what they lacked in American arms, gunships, and F-16s, Ayyash had given them a primitive weapon that could be wielded by pious youth ready to trade life itself to show their intolerance for what fate had dealt them.

Peres—and more pointedly Gillon, the intelligence community, and the military elite—completely misperceived the impact of the assassination. Ami Ayalon, a decorated naval commando and former chief of the navy, walked into Shabak's headquarters to take over from Gillon after the assassination only to reap the whirlwind.

"When I became the director, we had probably the highest wave of violence ever," Ayalon said. "In less than two weeks we lost 54 people in our streets and 215 wounded in terror actions—in Dizengoff Square [Tel Aviv], Jerusalem twice, and Ashkelon."[11] The scenes of blood-drenched streets and of rabbis peeling body parts from twisted metal and masonry profoundly affected Israelis. The four suicide attacks demonstrated that Ayyash's primitive skills were transferable, yet Gillon's enthusiasm to assassinate him at a time when Gazans were pressurized by blockade, high unemployment, and the illusion of peace was ill conceived. The Israeli security services, like the army, were dedicated to deterrence, and yet killing the most infamous bomb maker had failed to deter the Hamas leadership from going on the attack with the inventory of suicide bomb vests Ayyash had left behind.

Neither Peres nor the military establishment had been able to overcome the impulse to strike at Ayyash, though the logic behind the assassination was so apparently flawed: killing the man would not kill the knowledge or the ardor with which it had been passed on and was now being wielded. Ayyash's designs for efficient, low-tech bomb-delivery systems were easily disseminated in handmade manuals.

And again, the question stood: Why didn't they just arrest him? If Ayyash's hiding place was so well known to Shabak that it could infiltrate a bomb to kill him, Shabak agents could just as easily have moved in and seized the bomb maker and put him on trial for the Beit Lid attack and the other acts of terror that killed so many civilians. But there was no glory in police work. The drama, and the emotive release, came from blowing Ayyash's head off.

For anyone focused on the peace process, however, a different reality was becoming apparent. Ayalon said that soon after taking over the internal security command, he noticed the correlation between hope and terror. It was possible to reduce and contain the terror wave incited by the Islamic fringe only when the peace process was showing the tangible progress that came from good-faith negotiations. Three years after Oslo, the Gaza economy was a wreck; Israeli closures and checkpoints were on the rise across the West Bank as a stifling perimeter around the emerging Palestinian polity. Hamas's strategy to undermine Arafat and the peace process was calibrated to magnify the growing sense of Palestinian disillusionment.

With Rabin gone, the doubts about Arafat came rushing back to the fore. Young Likud politicians were promoting the analysis that Arafat wanted his PLO state so that he could continue his war to destroy the Jewish state from closer range. Ya'alon, the military intelligence chief, and other like-minded analysts in the system were building a case that "Arafat was cheating us."

Benny Begin, the science minister and late prime minister's son, believed that Arafat was operating the "theory of stages," seeking a foothold in the Holy Land from which to carry on the war. Netanyahu highlighted the same danger in his book *Fighting Terrorism*.[12] Peres went to meet Arafat after the Palestinian elections in January. He took Ya'alon along to present the list of terror suspects that Israel wanted arrested. Backing up Ya'alon was Avi Dichter, in charge of the Shabak operations in Gaza.

The first name on the "wanted" list was Mohammed Dieff, a PLO militant believed to be plotting revenge strikes after the killing of Ayyash.

Ya'alon told Peres that they should press Arafat hard.

"Peres called me in to brief Arafat about the terrorists that we demanded to be arrested and about Mohammed Dieff's intentions," Ya'alon told me. When Dieff's name came up, Arafat turned to his security chief and asked, "Mohammed *shoo* [what]?"—pretending not to recognize it.

"I knew that Arafat knew Mohammed Dieff," Ya'alon said. "Arafat met personally with him three days before on the twenty-first of January. We knew it. And he pretended not knowing him."

This was proof to Ya'alon that Arafat was a liar. He was cheating Israel, just as he had when he made his fabled return to Gaza. Ya'alon explained that Israeli intelligence learned that the PLO leader had smuggled heavy weapons and a known terrorist into the territory in his car.

"Arafat was sitting on him in his car to hide him at the crossing point and the car was full of weapons, which were forbidden according to Oslo,"

Ya'alon said. "He brought RPGs [rocket-propelled grenade launchers]. Now we know it."[13]

Yet despite Ya'alon's dissatisfaction, Arafat *did* respond.

In early 1996, Palestinian police arrested hundreds of Hamas and Islamic Jihad militants and confiscated caches of weapons and bomb-making materials. The extensive crackdown impressed both Israeli and U.S. intelligence officials.

Mohammed Dahlen told George Tenet, the CIA director, that Hamas suicide bombers were taking their orders from the Hamas directorate based in Amman, Jordan. The Americans passed this information to Jordanian intelligence.

Yet for all the pressure on the terrorist underground, Peres's political standing was still under assault following the Hamas bombing spree. Israelis felt unsafe.

President Clinton tried to resuscitate Peres and the peace camp. The Americans convened the Summit of Peacemakers in March 1996, hosted by Egypt's Hosni Mubarak in Sharm el-Sheikh, and attended by leaders from fourteen Arab states.

Peres was portrayed as a statesman by the Israeli news media. He evoked the pain that had convulsed the Israelis: "Nine days ago, on the eve of the festival of Purim, two twelve-year-old boys went to celebrate at the Tel Aviv Mall. Yovav Levy and Kobi Zaharon were best friends. They had the innocence and the freshness of youth. Kobi studies in a class for gifted children. Yovav excelled at football. Their whole future was before them. Yet, in a split second, it came to an end at the hands of a crazed terrorist, a living bomb."[14]

The truth was that Peres had lost control of events.

He could not unwind the coil of anger that was propelling Hamas. Gaza was a prison of Israeli closures; the prosperity of the previous decade had evaporated.

An Arafat aide, Hassan Asfour, explained how the hothouse of Gaza was working against them. "After the outrage of the suicide bombings, people in Gaza shouted: 'Yes to peace, no to terrorism!' Then, after the tightening of the closure, they shouted: 'Yes to peace, no to terror, no to closure!' And now, with the deterioration in the economic situation, they are crying: 'No to occupation, no to closure!' Before long, these shouts could turn into 'No to peace!' "[15]

But the Israelis, even those who could absorb this message, were unable to break out of the cycle of retribution. When a roadside bomb went off on April 8 in the Lebanese village of Barashit, killing a fourteen-year-old Arab boy and injuring three of his friends, no one was sure who had planted the device. Hezbollah blamed it on Israel and loosed dozens of Katyusha rockets across the border, injuring a half dozen Israelis. Separately, Hezbollah ambushed an outpost and killed an Israeli soldier.

If Rabin had been alive, he might have been able to contain the outcry. He might have been able to restrain the impulse for retribution. But Peres was simply not strong enough and instead of showing any restraint, he launched a war reflexively—fortress Israel reverting to type.

Operation Grapes of Wrath was an offensive designed by Ehud Barak, though he was no longer in uniform. Just as he had exhorted Rabin four years earlier to engage in mass expulsions to break the leadership strength of Hamas, Barak—now foreign minister—convinced Peres that the Israeli army could use its massive firepower to create a refugee crisis in Lebanon that would deliver a strategic result.

The idea was to unleash a broad bombing and artillery attack across southern Lebanon, setting up a refugee wave that would choke the roads and highways leading to Beirut, threatening humanitarian disaster and panicking the Lebanese government. This would force Syria to respond by reining in Hezbollah and restoring quiet in the security zone north of Israel's border, where Hezbollah was firing rockets and sending out raiding parties.[16]

Peres had already made the decision to call for early elections.

When he launched his sixteen-day war to stampede the civilian population of Lebanon and degrade the country's infrastructure, he and his political advisers believed he needed an unassailable mandate to move forward on the peace front, and the person standing in the way of his goal was Netanyahu, the leader of the invigorated Israeli right wing.

Operation Grapes of Wrath was designed to show that Peres had a firm hand on security. It was as if he felt he had to destroy the peace process in order to save it.

But no battle plan is immune from surprise.

On April 18, Israeli artillery gunners targeted—mistakenly, they said—a UN refugee center at Kana and slaughtered a hundred civilians—women, children, and the elderly—in an inferno of shrapnel and explosion.

Peres went into shock. The entire edifice of his peace offensive, so eloquently proclaimed before the U.S. Congress, succumbed to the gravitational pull of war. Peres froze, as he often did when under attack. Instinctively, he defended the IDF and absorbed the blows of international condemnation of his miniwar, which was criticized as collective punishment against a civilian population. Day after day, Israeli bombers struck power plants, villages, and infrastructure targets, stoking the humanitarian crisis that Barak and the military had hoped for.[17]

Peres was less in command than he was a spectator.

And as he had in the past when he was in trouble, he flew off to Washington to meet with President Clinton, diverting attention from the storm. Clinton deliberately muted U.S. criticism of the Kana massacre because he was desperate to help Peres win the coming election.

Netanyahu was hammering Peres with an effective slogan: "There is no peace; there is no security; there is no reason to vote for Peres!"[18]

That's how he summed it up to a swelling base of supporters, who saw a former Sayeret Matkal officer whose brother had died leading the Entebbe raid, whose father imbibed the tough catechism of Jabotinsky, and whose voice sounded distinctly American, as if he controlled the wellspring of Jewish support abroad.

Netanyahu courted the religious vote by asserting that Peres had a secret plan to divide Jerusalem, and his campaign slogan exuded that hard nationalistic cant—"Bibi is good for the Jews"—implying that Peres had lost his perspective in trying to please the Arabs.[19]

But the Israeli Arabs, who represented a sizable and crucial voting bloc for the Labor Party, had fallen out of love with Peres after the Kana disaster and after the grim accounting from Operation Grapes of Wrath. As many as 500,000 Arab civilians had been put to flight. The Israeli air force flew more than 1,100 bombing missions, and the army fired more than 25,000 artillery shells during the campaign, killing more than 150 Lebanese and destroying more than 2,000 Arab homes. The IDF had needlessly targeted roads, bridges, and power plants that would take years and hundreds of millions of dollars to repair or replace. Not since the Lebanon War of

1982—Sharon's war—had the Israeli army and air force so enthusiastically engaged in an exercise of mass destruction of an Arab state. The Israeli Arabs asked themselves how they could vote for Peres, a reborn militarist whose talk of peace had led to so much blood.

One of Peres's aides, looking out at the images of smoldering villages, said, "The peace camp just lost the elections."[20]

More crucially, the leader of the peace camp had lost his way; he had sought to flex the army's muscle for political gain and didn't understand until it was too late that the army—Barak and the sabras of the military establishment—did not have a solution for defeating Hezbollah or for negotiating peace in the region. What they had were military options and a militarist's approach to foreign policy: if you hit the enemy long and hard enough, he will surrender or be deterred.

Rabin's breakthrough had been to see the flaw in that logic.

On May 29, 1996, Peres went to bed thinking he had won the election. He awoke to discover that Netanyahu had stolen his victory on the strength of a mere twenty-nine thousand votes out of nearly three million cast.

The Arab Israelis had abandoned the Labor Party, preferring to stay home rather than to ratify the massacre at Kana. Peres lost despite the pleas from Leah Rabin that her husband's death not be in vain. Peres's supporters had even put up posters of the smirking Rabin assassin, Amir, and asked voters to "wipe that smile off his face."

But Netanyahu was the only candidate smiling. The brash scion of the right stepped into the prime minister's office with a mandate from his bloc to demolish the peace process as a threat to Israel's very existence. The Americans could see the Rabin architecture buckling. At a minimum, the world was in for a long stall by a young and inexperienced politician.

Netanyahu's view of the Palestinians was far harsher than it was prudent to admit. Much later, speaking candidly to a sympathetic audience when he thought the microphone was turned off, Netanyahu said that when it came to Palestinians, it was necessary to "beat them up, not once, but repeatedly; beat them up so it hurts badly, until it's unbearable." If Washington opposed Israeli policies, American public opinion could be "moved"—manipulated—and his mandate as prime minister, as he saw it, was to halt the progress of the Oslo Accords. "I'm going to interpret the accords in such a way that would allow me to put an end to this galloping forward to the '67 borders."[21] That might mean transferring 2 percent of the land in order to keep the rest, an option that had been promoted by Netanyahu's grandfather.

Arafat was morose, his voice barely audible when friends and colleagues called to express condolences over the election results. Arafat understood that in order to hold on to his relationship with Clinton, he would have to do business with Netanyahu, but few Palestinians had any illusions about the hard-line ideology that Netanyahu represented.

Some Israeli intelligence officials later reflected that it was during this spring of 1996, in the wake of Netanyahu's election, the Hamas bombings, the Gaza closures, and the Grapes of Wrath campaign, that Arafat changed. He realized that he, too, had been cheated and that a significant portion of his people looked to him to bring the war back to the Israelis in order to force them to end the occupation and pave the way for Palestinian statehood.

"Maybe [Arafat] understood that he took the wrong decision in signing the Oslo agreement," said Aharon Ze'evi Farkash. Or maybe Netanyahu's determination to bury Oslo motivated Arafat to put his armor back on.[22]

Arafat had undertaken the most extensive crackdown on Hamas ever in March and April. He had convened the Palestinian Council, which, as promised, had voted overwhelmingly to strike the language from its covenant that called for the destruction of Israel. And what was the result? Peres unleashed hell against Arabs in Lebanon and Netanyahu took over the prime minister's office.

Just before Peres cleaned out his desk, he told Arafat that the Israeli army could not withdraw from Hebron, the largest Palestinian city in the southern Judean Hills.

This was how the content of peace had drained away.

Hard-liners filled out Netanyahu's cabinet. Sharon was back. David Levy, a leader of the Moroccan Jewish community, became minister of foreign affairs. It wasn't so much a united Likud as a collection of rivals from the right replacing the collection of rivals from the left.

Syria's propagandists offered a snarky caricature, observing that Netanyahu's cabinet was "dominated by rabbis, generals, racists, mass murderers, and advocates of transfer." And from the rostrum of the Knesset, Peres, sounding somewhat smug, observed that Netanyahu's platform was a jumble of contradictions that would undermine the search for peace.

Yet Netanyahu projected supreme self-confidence. He stood for Israel as a military state without illusions, which was ironic given that he lacked the extensive battle experience of Rabin or the savvy of the sabras.

"Leaders must have the courage to do what is required even in the face of the most stinging criticism," Netanyahu wrote a year before winning the election. "Courageous action is in itself the best answer to the inevitable slings that the small-minded heap upon the statesman facing great odds."[23] His favorite office portrait was of Churchill.

From the beginning, Netanyahu was more isolated than many Israelis understood. The army's loyalty—and much of the country's—still belonged to Rabin. Even Barak, now sitting on the opposition benches in the Knesset, seemed to have a greater influence on the generals—many of whom he had promoted. After all, Barak had been Netanyahu's commander in Sayeret Matkal, and among sabras, Netanyahu was never going to overcome Barak's view of him as a subordinate.

There was an iconic image that many Israelis remembered that spring. It was from 1972, when Ehud Barak, having led the successful storming of a hijacked Sabena airliner on the runway outside Tel Aviv, stood on the wing of the aircraft and triumphantly raised his weapon. Barak's silhouette was the very picture of heroism, and many Israelis remembered that Netanyahu had also been on that rescue mission, but he went out on a stretcher, embarrassed to have been accidentally shot in the leg by one of his own men.

Barak had delivered the eulogy at Jonathan Netanyahu's funeral in 1976. Bibi may have served in the "unit," but he had never proved himself as a military leader the way his brother and Barak had. For Bibi to succeed as prime minister, he would have to outmaneuver the generals who had taught him much of what he knew about strategy and tactics.

It didn't take long for Netanyahu to prove how ineffectual a leader he really was.

He went to Washington and displayed an almost insufferable arrogance at the White House, lecturing President Clinton to the point that Clinton complained that "he thinks he is the superpower and we are here to do whatever he requires."[24] To some extent, it worked.

After Netanyahu returned home, he lit the fuse of his first big crisis, plotting—without consulting the military establishment—to open a long-closed tunnel from the Hasmonean era (c. 140 B.C.) in the Old City of Jerusalem. Every square inch of stone in the Old City is a battleground of religion and history. Intelligence chiefs had counseled against opening the Hasmonean Tunnel, warning that it would incite religious and nationalistic paranoia among the Palestinians, who believed the Israelis wanted to dig under the Temple Mount to destabilize the grand mosques of Islam or otherwise improve the Israeli claim to the uncharted areas of the foundations of King Solomon's Temple, where the Ark of the Covenant once rested in an inner chamber referred to as the Holy of Holies.

But Netanyahu, working secretly with Jerusalem's mayor, Ehud Olmert, went ahead against the caution of the military and intelligence establishment. Work began in the dead of night on September 24, 1996, and when the city woke up to the excavation, rioting erupted that overwhelmed the Palestinian police. The army was suddenly called in to put down the violence, which spread across the West Bank.

A senior Shabak officer, Israel Hasson, saw the young Palestinians charging the army positions with stones, only to be shot down. He turned to the general in charge and said, "This has to be stopped right away because we're attacking the honor of the Palestinian Authority. They are not just going to stand there and they might return fire with real bullets. Then the whole area will go up in flames."[25]

It soon did.

Dozens of Palestinians were killed as the death toll climbed to eighty, with more than twelve hundred wounded. Seventeen Israeli soldiers died because, for the first time, Palestinian policemen turned their guns on Israeli soldiers firing on stone-throwing youngsters. The army sent tanks to restore order, but tanks on the West Bank was a terrible image for peace.

The Hasmonean Tunnel debacle set off alarms about the character of Netanyahu as a leader.

The military command was flabbergasted. How could an Israeli prime minister light such a fuse without consulting the army, which is in charge of security in the occupied territories? Netanyahu had been reckless by any accounting, but he feigned innocence: he had just been following the recommendations of municipal authorities, he said. The deadly clashes and days of riot instantly destroyed hard-earned trust; Arafat and his men assumed the worst about Netanyahu's intentions.

The most profound consequence was that the army felt that it had been so ill prepared for the violence that it began planning how to conduct full-scale warfare within the intimate confines of Jerusalem and the West Bank. The Palestinian police were now armed, and it was no longer a war of stones but a shooting war. Out of this planning process came a contingency plan called Operation Field of Thorns, which called for the use of early and massive force to quell any large-scale Palestinian uprising. Here was the army making policy that no prime minister could easily challenge because the army's mandate was to minimize casualties.

Arafat also developed a new military option. As a result of the suicide bombings at the beginning of the year, Clinton had signed a presidential finding to authorize the CIA to undertake the training of Palestinian security forces so they could detect and disrupt the Hamas underground.

The new CIA station chief, Stanley Moskowitz, had been dispatched in 1996 to improve the terror-fighting ability of the Palestinians. CIA director George Tenet and Moskowitz came ashore as supportive allies, but what they found was near total disillusionment in the Israeli army and among Palestinian security forces.

"The Palestinians believed in the peace process, but they did not believe in Bibi," said Ami Ayalon, the Shabak chief. "They knew that Bibi was cheating them, but they believed in the American president, and so America became part of the process after September 1996."[26]

Moskowitz said he found Arafat "hyperventilating" because the Israeli army had "slaughtered" a number of his men, employing heavy machine guns against Palestinian policemen with light weapons.[27]

"'This will not happen again,'" he quoted Arafat as saying. Moskowitz said Arafat was "more determined to get heavy weaponry." The Palestinian leader was going for a military option, too. The younger Fatah commanders on the West Bank, such as Marwan Barghouti, also emerged from the clashes of late 1996 convinced that the only way to win concessions from Netanyahu was by force.

In this toxic climate, Netanyahu lost the respect of his military chiefs. Lipkin-Shahak, the chief of staff, had been deeply affected by Rabin's death, and Netanyahu's peremptory style in the prime minister's chair worried him. The defense minister, Yitzhak Mordechai, a highly decorated paratrooper commander (who had been falsely accused and acquitted in the Bus 300 affair), also expressed private doubts about the young Netanyahu. He was too rash, too erratic, and too subject to intimidation by Sharon.

The army's commitment to the peace process, always shaky, was breaking down.

Intelligence analysts increasingly questioned Arafat's commitment to peace. A leading skeptic was Boogie Ya'alon, who, after serving as Rabin's director of military intelligence, now headed the Central Command in charge of the West Bank.

Ya'alon developed a theory that Israel would have to defeat Palestinian militancy in a perpetual "low-intensity conflict." Operation Field of Thorns, the plan to reinvade the West Bank, was part of this new thinking. The idea was to shut down a new intifada with a sudden, massive, and focused show of force, with an emphasis on putting snipers at key choke points to eliminate militant leaders.[28]

The first signs that the generals were plotting against Netanyahu came in November 1996, when Major General Oren Shachor, who was Ya'alon's superior as the overall coordinator in the occupied territories, was photographed holding clandestine meetings with Peres and, on other occasions, with Yossi Sarid of the left-wing Meretz Party.

The tabloids trumpeted the "plot," and soon Shachor retired from the army and announced he was entering politics to fight Netanyahu and his policies.

"There is an atmosphere of acute paranoia and witch hunting on the part of the prime minister, directed at the IDF's higher echelons," he said publicly, adding that Netanyahu's actions were pushing both him and Lipkin-Shahak into politics.[29]

Other signs of turmoil appeared.

A senior Mossad case officer, Yehuda Gil, was charged in September 1996 with fabricating intelligence that Syrian dictator Hafez al-Assad had given up hope of peace and was preparing for war. It had taken months to conduct a counterespionage operation to determine whether the source of Gil's information, reportedly a high-level Syrian official, actually existed. The motive for Gil's treasonous actions appeared to be a kind of "detonator" strategy—to goad the Israeli military establishment into a destructive war that would postpone, indefinitely, any chance of returning the Golan Heights.[30]

Deciding the fate of Hebron, the city of Abraham and resting place for the patriarchs of three religions, seemed beyond mortal capability.

Under pressure from the Americans, Netanyahu and the Palestinians went ahead with negotiations to add Hebron to the territory under the control of the Palestinian Authority, but the negotiations only showed how little Netanyahu was willing to give. The right-wing members of his cabinet threatened to resign if Israel withdrew from the city. And true to form, the day after the cabinet ratified the Hebron accord on January 15, 1997, Benny Begin walked out on Netanyahu, sending a strong signal that the right was prepared to bring down the government if more "concessions" to Arafat were made.

Netanyahu protested incoherently, "We are not leaving Hebron, we are redeploying from Hebron." But everyone knew that the army was turning the city over to the Palestinians.[31]

Then, as if to demonstrate that what Israel had given up in Hebron it would seize elsewhere, Netanyahu sent bulldozers to a hilltop between Jerusalem and Bethlehem to break ground on a large new settlement called Har Homa. The Americans were angered, the Palestinians enraged. Jibril Rajoub, the head of West Bank security for Arafat, pronounced that Har Homa would "lead to the clinical death of the Oslo process."[32] Marwan Barghouti told the Americans that Fatah could not compete with the extremist organizations that were preaching to Palestinian youth that Oslo was a betrayal.

Netanyahu had sent in the bulldozers, proclaiming that "the battle for Jerusalem has begun" and, three days later, Hamas dispatched one of its suicide bombers to a popular outdoor café in Tel Aviv, where he detonated a bomb vest studded with nails. Four people died and forty were injured. The Apropo Café bombing was unconnected to Arafat, who telephoned Netanyahu and President Ezer Weizman to express his condolences. But Netanyahu blamed Arafat directly and accused him of "giving a green light" to Hamas to strike.

What was truly astounding was the blatancy of Netanyahu's false accusation, and it prompted a response from the military establishment. General Amos Gilad, a top military analyst, told reporters that the prime minister had seriously overstated the case.

"We never said Yasser Arafat gave the green light," Gilad clarified. The "green light" was inferred by the Islamists "on the basis of a general feeling, statements that had been heard and so on" after the bulldozers had started work at Har Homa. Gilad added that Israeli intelligence had noted a more "intensive effort on the part of the Palestinian Authority to prevent terrorism" because Arafat "realizes today that terrorism and the peace process can't [co]exist."[33]

The truth in this case did not seem to deter Netanyahu; he needed Arafat more as an enemy than as a partner; *that* would justify his lack of fulfillment on the peace front; *that* would keep the Americans from applying pressure. After the Apropo Café bombing, Netanyahu ordered a new closure of the Palestinian territories. Demonstrations broke out in Hebron, Bethlehem, Jenin, and the Gaza Strip. Arafat warned of an "explosion."

The only images were negative: the bulldozers at Har Homa and angry faces of Palestinians behind Israeli barriers and checkpoints.

At the Labor Party convention in May 1997, Barak replaced Peres as chairman. Barak pushed through a motion to amend the party platform to recognize for the first time a Palestinian right to statehood, which was still anathema to the Likud.

"Israel cannot afford and should not try to govern over another people," Barak said, calling for national separation between Israelis and Palestinians, a solution that would provide greater security and fulfill national aspirations in both camps. He said Israel did not need or desire "apartheid" rule, or the kind of ethnic suppression that the world had witnessed in Bosnia.[34]

As Labor pulled together, Likud pulled apart.

Dan Meridor, one of Likud's young princes, resigned as finance minister in June, citing views irreconcilable with Netanyahu's. Meridor's father, like Netanyahu's father, had been part of Jabotinsky's inner circle in the 1930s, and Meridor's desertion over the Hebron agreement was a serious blow. When the right-wing parties brought a no-confidence motion in the Knesset, Netanyahu survived by a vote of fifty-five to fifty. His rivals were gaining strength.

In a television interview on the one-year anniversary of taking office, Netanyahu boasted that he was delivering peace with security. He claimed that he had put an end to the Palestinian "game of tipping a wink to Hamas and Islamic Jihad and telling them that they may go ahead and blow up buses in Israeli cities." Now they knew that they "will not get off scot free," he said.[35]

Two days later, on July 30, Hamas replied to Netanyahu's boast by sending two suicide bombers into Jerusalem's busy Machane Yehuda market, setting off bomb vests that silenced the everyday bustle with a consuming blast, which killed 16 Israelis and wounded more than 170. Hamas waited a little more than four weeks and then struck again at almost the same spot outside the Jerusalem market. Three suicide bombers returned to mingle in the crowd of shoppers and trigger three explosions in a deadly sequence, which killed 7 people and injured 200. The honey-colored stones of the market were smeared with blood.

The city of peace was under siege.

One of the victims, Smadar Elhanan, age thirteen, was the granddaughter of Matti Peled, a retired major general who campaigned tirelessly for peace with the Palestinians.[36] Smadar's mother, Nurit, had gone to Jerusalem high school with Netanyahu. In such a small country, connections of youth, school, and army joined Israelis in every event. Nurit took the opportunity of her daughter's death to rebuke her classmate, the prime minister.

"Israel is raising terrorists," she wrote, in a letter released to the press. "My daughter's death is the direct result of the humiliation inflicted on Palestinians. . . . We invented the suicide bombers. They are sacrificing themselves because we have made their lives valueless in their own eyes."[37]

Even though it was a view from the left, Nurit's complaint poked a finger into the wound that many Israelis were nursing. The triumphalism of 1967, the arrogance that had turned a transitory conquest into a conversion scheme—the dream of Greater Israel—was a tragic mistake. Barak's warning of "apartheid" was not an exaggeration. Apartheid was coming. Without a two-state solution, there was going to be a single cruel and repressive state where the Arabs would be a brutalized underclass, whether they lived in Haifa or Ramallah. The truth was that the unceasing military occupation was a curse.

In the Israeli army, every officer is drilled in one basic doctrine: always attack.

Desperate for some success, Netanyahu ordered up a major commando operation into southern Lebanon to blow up a Hezbollah headquarters. The navy's Shayetet 13 unit sent sixteen commandos into enemy territory on September 8, 1997, and within a few hours more than half of them were dead, killed in a cascade of improvised explosive devices placed so expertly that it appeared the team's movements had been detected by Hezbollah in advance.

An unmanned drone that was deployed to support the commandos mistakenly broadcast unencrypted video of the Israeli ground movements, which Hezbollah commanders possibly intercepted in setting their trap.

Three large IEDs erupted when the commandos came within range. Only five of the sixteen survived. The army sent in reinforcements to recover the shell-shocked soldiers as Hezbollah declared a victory. The deaths of eleven commandos, highly trained young men who represented the best and brightest of Israeli society, cut Netanyahu deeply. Israelis were quick to question the competence and execution of the raid, and during a summer of suicide bombing madness, Netanyahu was still standing there before his people with no plan to end it.[38]

He soon tried again. He told Mossad director Dany Yatom and other intelligence chiefs that he wanted to strike dramatically at the Hamas leadership in retribution for the two dozen dead Israelis and more than three hundred wounded by suicide bombings that summer. Yet after the loss of the navy team in Lebanon, he wanted something less risky. That ruled out striking the Hamas headquarters in Damascus. It also ruled out an attack on Gaza because that might set off the same riotous reaction that had followed the assassination of Ayyash.

This was the logic that spawned the Khaled Meshal affair, the aborted attempt by a team of Mossad agents to kill the Hamas political director in Jordan with an exotic toxin.

There was no risk in dispatching a Mossad team across the river; Israel and Jordan had established diplomatic relations. But the folly of the Mossad plan was Yatom's belief that he could pull off a "silent execution" by jumping a well-known figure in broad daylight on a public street, jabbing him behind the ear with an injector that had to be held in a cloth so as not to contaminate its handler, and then escape undetected. Did Yatom and Netanyahu, who reviewed the plan in detail, believe that King Hussein would allow an Israeli prime minister to abuse diplomatic privilege with a high-profile assassination in the heart of the Jordanian capital?

It was only later, after the botched assassination and the arrest of two Mossad officers caught after a wild chase through the streets of Amman, and after King Hussein, furious over the affront to Jordan, telephoned President Clinton to complain about Netanyahu's invasion of Jordanian territory to commit murder, and after the king threatened to tear up the Israeli-Jordanian peace treaty and put the Mossad men on trial for attempted murder and espionage, that someone asked the critical question: Why had the Mossad ignored the Hamas offer of a truce?

Sheikh Yassin, sitting in prison, had begun talking about a thirty-year *hudna*, or cease-fire, one in which Hamas would continue to work for an Islamic state but would coexist with Israel if Israel agreed to return Arab lands and move forward with Palestinian statehood.

In late September, after the last suicide bombing at the Machane Yehuda market, senior Hamas officials had met with King Hussein and asked him to transmit their offer of a truce to Israeli officials. He did, sending the message through Mossad.

The one person who asked why this offer was ignored was Efraim Halevy, the former deputy Mossad director, who was called back urgently from his new post as ambassador to the European Union to help Netanyahu handle the Meshal disaster. Halevy asked the question not because he was an impulsive leftist but because he was a hardened realist like Rabin. He had no trouble hitting Hamas hard to deter further suicide attacks. But Halevy had absorbed the lesson that Rabin had painfully learned: one must engage the enemy, as an enemy, to make peace.

The offer of a thirty-year truce was peace by another name. Who knew if the Hamas offer would last? Who knew if war with Hamas would return? The important thing was to recognize opportunities and exploit them.

"We will never know if this method [force] of dealing with them was the only valid one, for there was never a discussion of their offer of a truce at the time it could have been operative," Halevy later wrote.[39]

It was not Halevy's style to criticize, but that was his meaning. The military establishment had failed to recognize a significant opportunity. Sharett had said that peace had to be pursued constantly and relentlessly, but no institution was carrying the torch.

The likely truth was that Netanyahu was not interested in exploring a truce as much as he was in scoring political points with a high-profile strike that would convince voters that he—like his brother before him—had the kind of military weight that would be able to deliver the security that Israelis craved after all the bloodshed.

The Khaled Meshal affair ended badly for Netanyahu: the British-run *Economist* put him on its cover with the headline "Serial Bungler."[40]

Halevy proved to be the silent hero of the episode, for he had convinced his former colleagues at Mossad that the only effective move they could make was one that would make King Hussein look good. They should release the Hamas leader, Sheikh Yassin, and turn him over to King Hussein. Thus the king could be persuaded to release the jailed Mossad men and allow the rest of the Mossad team, still trapped in Jordan, to come home.[41]

In the days that followed, Yassin's life sentence was commuted and he returned to a hero's welcome in Gaza. Mossad recovered its embarrassed officers trapped or jailed in Jordan. The episode spurred Lipkin-Shahak, the chief of staff, to write in *Ma'ariv* that there is no military solution to some conflicts, and that the "list of graves" on the Israeli and Palestinian sides would grow longer until there was peace.[42]

These thoughts weighed heavily on the Israelis in 1997, because at the beginning of the year, two large transport helicopters ferrying troops into the south Lebanon security zone collided in a fireball that killed more than seventy soldiers and crewmen. The accident devastated national morale, deepening the sense of failure over the policies that had driven Israel into Lebanon in 1982.

Lipkin-Shahak's candor as chief of staff provoked the hard-liners to respond. Raful Eitan, the former chief of staff who had planned the Lebanon War with Sharon, shot back that the military establishment could not shirk its responsibilities by "tossing the problem over to the political branch and saying 'solve it [because] we have no solution.' . . . Such words must not be heard coming from the mouths of military people," Eitan admonished.[43]

There always was a military solution, Eitan believed.

But Lipkin-Shahak responded that it was incumbent upon the generals to advise civilians on the consequences of military power. He reminded Eitan that the 1982 invasion of Lebanon had reached Beirut, but it had not achieved it goals; the PLO was not destroyed, the Shiite Muslims of south

Lebanon were radicalized, and Israel was forced to occupy a security zone to protect its northern border from enemies supported by Iran.

And what about the intifada? Lipkin-Shahak asked. It had raged from 1987 until 1993. "Why did it end?" the general asked pointedly. The answer was obvious: it ended because Rabin extended his hand to the Palestinians for negotiations on peace and homeland, giving them a political horizon.

The general's message was a rebuke not just to Eitan but also to Netanyahu himself, for Lipkin-Shahak ended his essay by saying that the intifada would have gone on for years were it not for Rabin. The lesson of Oslo, he said, was that "it is the political echelon's responsibility to take the bull by the horns" to make peace.[44]

But Netanyahu was not listening.

It was clear that after little more than a year in office, Netanyahu's "peace and security" government had failed to deliver either. He had shaved back Oslo's commitment to turn over more land to the Palestinian Authority, so much so that the Palestinians felt betrayed; any Palestinian state that would have emerged under Netanyahu's conceptualization would have been the "Bantustan" that Arafat feared. It would have comprised about 36 percent of the West Bank and Gaza; it would have been surrounded by Israeli settlements that would have stifled its economic viability.

More and more Netanyahu relied on Ariel Sharon, his foreign minister, for delaying tactics, but every increment of Netanyahu's decline seemed to enhance Sharon's stature. It is difficult for Westerners to understand how isolated an embattled prime minister stands in Israel. His ministers owe their loyalty to party factions or religious icons. The most powerful ministers of defense and foreign affairs are often party rivals who can't be trusted. Ambition to replace the sitting prime minister colors every action. Sensitive information shared with a minister is frequently leaked to the press to undermine the leader. And the military looms over all.

A tiny staff served the prime minister and was driven by the urgent need to bolster his image through constant briefings for major newspaper and television correspondents, to whom the prime minister's actions could be spun in the most favorable light. No independent policy staff served the prime minister, though Netanyahu created a national security council when he realized that the military establishment was losing confidence in his judgment.

The army served as the dominant think tank, assessing and judging threats, and offering—inescapably—political and military options because it was impossible to separate the two. There was no competing think tank—in Mossad or the Ministry of Foreign Affairs—to step back and analyze the trajectory of peace, to try to better understand the growing power of the Islamic fringe, or to examine how the strictures of occupation were turning Palestinians against peace. The system remained skewed to maximize the role of the generals judging their own performance and in shaping the policy debate.

Netanyahu rebelled against putting his fate in the hands of his former military superiors because they were out to orchestrate his failure. He had Sharon on his right, Barak on his left, and a defense establishment that he did not trust. And the feeling was mutual.

Almost no one in Israel knew that for much of 1997, Netanyahu had been secretly conducting diplomacy with Syria using the American businessman Ronald Lauder as his envoy. Working through a foreign emissary gave Netanyahu deniability and reduced the threat that his own foreign minister, David Levy, who opposed making any concessions to Syria, would discover the talks. Netanyahu's motivation in probing Syria was mysterious. His coalition opposed compromise with Assad, and so Netanyahu may have thought that even the appearance of progress on the peace front might divert some of the criticism over his broader failure.[45]

When Levy discovered in early 1998 that he had been kept in the dark about the Syrian talks, he resigned. As Netanyahu's political base weakened, he told the Americans that he could not transfer 13 percent of additional territory to the Palestinians as he had promised. Clinton envoy Dennis Ross protested, but Netanyahu upbraided him: "Screw up your courage! Act like a superpower and tell them [the Palestinians] this is it."[46]

The outburst was telling, for one of Netanyahu's character traits was that he deflected pressure by attacking his critics, a trait straight out of his military training, which demanded that any attack be met by counterattack.

Many Israelis had begun to smell the panic. Netanyahu lurched from one crisis to the next. In March 1998, more than fifteen hundred officers, including eighty-two retired generals, issued a letter calling on Netanyahu to abandon the right wing's obsession with settlements and expansion, which could only lead to an apartheid rule over 2.5 million Palestinians.

"A government that prefers maintaining settlements beyond the Green Line [1967 boundaries] to solving the historic conflict and establishing normal relations in our region will cause us to question the righteousness of our path."[47]

Netanyahu later acknowledged that the goal *was* to create a Palestinian "Bantustan." He was convinced that Israel could impose a final settlement in which the Palestinian entity—he could never say state—would achieve permanent status on less than 40 percent of the land. If he succeeded, the Zionist enterprise, which had taken 78 percent of historic Palestine (not counting Jordan), would take 60 percent of what remained.[48]

Netanyahu believed in that inequity.

Meanwhile, Arafat seemed to understand Rabin's dictum that the Palestinians needed their own *Altalena* episode to restore discipline. With the help of George Tenet and the CIA, Arafat signed a new memorandum of understanding that called for a more robust Palestinian crackdown against Hamas and other extremists. The Americans and most of the Israeli security establishment believed that Palestinians were making progress.

Arafat ordered the arrest in April 1998 of Abdel Aziz Rantissi, the Gazan pediatrician and Hamas cofounder. Rantissi's arrest served as a warning to Sheikh Yassin that he, too, could return to prison. Vice President Al Gore visited Jerusalem in May and declared that the peace process had reached a "critical moment." First Lady Hillary Clinton told an interviewer that the only solution that made sense in the Holy Land was a Palestinian state.[49]

President Clinton, in trying to save himself in the Monica Lewinsky affair, dragged Netanyahu to the Wye Plantation near Washington to restart negotiations with Arafat. On the table were the final and stalled land transfers under Oslo and the release of Palestinian prisoners. They could then move to the "permanent status" talks for statehood. Netanyahu arrived at Wye as if under close supervision from his cabinet. Accompanying him were Sharon, serving as foreign minister, and Yitzhak Mordecai, the defense minister. On the Chesapeake shore, the Israelis engaged in a cynical and protracted series of unpleasant encounters that seemed less about peace than about plugging for "trophies" that could be held up to hard-line constituencies at home as evidence that they were conceding nothing to the Palestinians.

Netanyahu, in front of Clinton, suggested to Arafat that he assassinate one of the Palestinian police chiefs that the Israelis suspected of having ties to militants. Clinton displayed outrage, but both sides knew he was desperate for progress. Netanyahu pressed the Americans to release the convicted spy Jonathan Pollard as a trophy that Netanyahu could take home to trump the blowback over any territorial concessions he made to Arafat.

The Wye Agreement would have propelled a strong and willing Israeli prime minister into final negotiations for Palestinian statehood, but Netanyahu proved neither strong nor willing. He brought home, to a surly government, an agreement that called for additional land transfers to the Palestinians. He failed to win Pollard's release.

Arafat came home from Wye trying to look pristine to the Americans. He subjected Sheikh Yassin to months of house arrest and tightened the security crackdown.

The Israeli cabinet voted eight to four to ratify the Wye accord, though all of Netanyahu's Likud Party ministers abstained, signaling that he had lost his own party.

In the Middle East, paralysis can be the thing that incites anarchy, and while Netanyahu seemed deadlocked within his own coalition, the re-arrest of Sheikh Yassin triggered a response from Hamas, whose militants attempted to blow up a busload of Israeli schoolchildren; Islamic Jihad militants mounted a bombing attack in Jerusalem, wounding twenty people; in Lebanon, Hezbollah staged an ambush and killed seven Israeli soldiers.

Netanyahu suspended the Wye Agreement, angering Clinton.

He relented only after weeks of pressure from Washington, and the Israeli army began finally to pull back under the Wye guidelines in November

1998. Netanyahu refused, however, to release hundreds of Palestinian prisoners whose freedom had been promised at Wye.

The reversal made Arafat look weak on the Palestinian street; Edward Said, the acclaimed Palestinian academic at Columbia University in New York, observed that no national liberation movement had surrendered quite so much and so pathetically as the PLO, which had signed peace accords and gotten less than a Bantustan.[50]

"Unlike [Nelson] Mandela, who never abandoned the principles and the goal of his struggle," Said wrote in the newspaper *al-Hayat*, "Arafat and the people who follow him have trampled on principle, sold out on commitment, and emptied language of any connection with political truth."[51]

Five years after Oslo, there was no Palestinian state; there was no "permanent status" negotiation under way; the promised transfers of land had been delayed, deferred, and diminished so that the Palestinians looked around and saw themselves still surrounded, still humiliated by restrictions on their movement, still repressed by an all-powerful neighbor with limitless military power and a strong faction of Arab-hating settlers and militants maneuvering to keep them down.

Oslo's architects were either dead or out of power.

Arafat threatened to declare independence for his Palestinian state and seek world recognition unless Netanyahu moved.

And so Clinton's trip to Gaza in December 1998 was designed to help get something going.

He came by helicopter to herald the realization of Palestinian nationalism.

"I am profoundly honored to be the first American president to address the Palestinian people in a city governed by Palestinians," Clinton said warmly to the throng gathered near the sea and waving PLO and Hamas banners.

And he seemed to admonish Netanyahu. "I want the people of Israel to know that for many Palestinians, 5 years after Oslo, the benefits of this process remain remote; that for too many Palestinians lives are hard, jobs are scarce, prospects are uncertain, and personal grief is great." He talked about "losses suffered from violence, the separation of families, the restrictions on the movement of people and goods.

"I understand your concerns about settlement activity, land confiscation, and home demolitions," Clinton continued, but he implored the Palestinians to stick with the process even when they felt there were "a hundred good reasons to walk away."[52]

He praised Arafat and pledged hundreds of millions of dollars for development of the Palestinian economy, and he drove with Hillary Clinton to cut the ribbon at the site of the Gaza International Airport, a facility that promised the ultimate freedom, connecting Palestinians with the rest of the world.

It wasn't until this extraordinary scene of American affirmation unfolded—the leader of the free world conferring legitimacy on Palestinian statehood and Arafat's leadership—that Netanyahu, Sharon, and the other guardians on the right realized they had made a serious mistake.

They believed they had won a great concession at Wye when Arafat agreed to convene the Palestinian National Council in Gaza to declare the Palestinian covenant null and void on the subject of Israel's destruction. They wanted the world to witness the Palestinians voting down the old covenant while pledging peace and coexistence for two states.

Yet what the world saw was a great act of empathy on the dusty landscape of the Gaza Strip: the American president celebrating the fulfillment of Palestinian national rights. The Palestinian Authority now had a capital, a flag, an international airport, and a security force of thirty-five thousand men, many of them trained by the CIA.

Clinton's celebrity on the Palestinian street was a sensation of personal charisma and moral exhortation. And when he spoke, the Palestinians heard the voice of a friend.

Netanyahu, trapped in his own political circumstances, suspended the Wye Agreement again a week after Clinton returned to Washington to launch a bombing campaign against Iraq and face impeachment from the House of Representatives in the Monica Lewinsky affair.

Both leaders were in dire straits, but Netanyahu's ship had already taken on too much water. The Israeli leader simply couldn't hold his coalition together over the concessions he had made. The final seams that had been holding back the deluge burst and Netanyahu's coalition collapsed. The Knesset voted eighty-one to twenty for new elections and set a date for May 1999.

The foundation for peace that Rabin had laid was in shambles.

Lipkin-Shahak and a host of generals formed a centrist party to help weaken the Likud. Yitzhak Mordecai, the defense minister, quit the government and joined.

The military establishment turned against Netanyahu so thoroughly that the tone was mutinous: a dangerous prevaricator had to be driven from office, hopefully by democratic means.

Mordechai confronted Netanyahu during a televised debate in April. "You are utterly devoid of honesty, decency and integrity," he told the prime minister in front of a national audience. "You know that I stood in the way of certain things because they would have plunged the country into a very different situation from what we have today. . . ."

Netanyahu, deeply wounded, lashed out. "You have no ideals, no message to send. You're motivated by hate and the defense of your own personal interests."[53]

To add water to Netanyahu's ship, the generals whispered to the news media examples of his recklessness. He had wanted to kidnap one of Arafat's top security officers by infiltrating secret agents into the Palestinian self-rule zone. The Shabak chief, Ami Ayalon, had told the prime minster, "You're crazy. That would lead to a break with the Palestinian Authority."

There were rumors that Netanyahu had made intemperate comments in private about employing Israel's nuclear arsenal against Syria during a period of tension.[54]

Was he so reckless and desperate that he would drag the country to the brink of massive regional war to save his political skin?

More than anything, it was the military establishment that overthrew Benjamin Netanyahu. He had held himself out as the epitome of sabra strength and competence, but he was found seriously wanting by the army and the country, which was still torn between Rabin's legacy and the onslaught of suicide bombing.

Some one hundred generals joined the new party that Lipkin-Shahak and Mordechai had founded, or they signed up with Ehud Barak and the Labor Party. And though the election season was filled with images of former generals jumping into the political arena, it soon became clear that the one who had the strongest chance was Barak, in part because he had so easily eclipsed Peres in assuming the mantle of Mr. Security. The strategic importance of peace was back in the campaign because, it was widely assumed, Barak and the other generals who had served under Rabin were the embodiment of his ideals. During the campaign, Barak's name became synonymous with hope.

Mordechai threw his support behind Barak, and Netanyahu was turned out of office in what seemed like a democratic coup—orchestrated by the military elite.[55]

SEVENTEEN

Barak: The Arrogance of Power

Ehud Barak waited until 3:00 a.m. on election night before stepping out onto the floodlit platform overlooking the central square in Tel Aviv, where the peace movement had been born and where Rabin had been murdered. Almost defiantly his words rang out: "The time for peace has come."

He had told the Israelis that he would "storm the citadels of peace" to reach a reconciliation with the Arabs, and now when the Israelis voted him into office with a landslide victory over Netanyahu he spoke righteously about his strategic commitment—Rabin's commitment. But there was a hard, metallic edge to the words. This national hero standing before the cheering masses was no peace strategist. He was a military man, a warrior deeply imbued with the concept of victory and deeply resistant to making concessions. Peace was his new battlefield.

He did not evoke the "Song of Peace" or extend his hand to Arafat.

He would fight for peace, although "not peace from a position of weakness, but peace in strength and security; not peace by giving up security, but peace that will bring security. . . . We will move quickly toward a separation from the Palestinians by drawing four lines in the sand," he told the crowd. The first line: "once and for all a united Jerusalem, under our sovereignty, as the eternal capital of Israel." The second line: "in no case will we withdraw to the 1967 borders." The third line: "no foreign army on the west bank of the Jordan," and the fourth: Israeli sovereignty would be expanded to accommodate the settlers of the West Bank.[1]

This was not peacemaking. This was more "separation" and "expansion," as if in defiance of the Oslo Accords. This was antagonism toward withdrawal to the 1967 lines. Where was Rabin's oration of peace, of ending the mind-set of a people that dwells alone?

In the night air, electrified by flashbulbs and jubilation, most Israelis heard what they wanted to hear, but the Palestinians, taking it all in on their televisions, privately recoiled, for they had heard what the man said. Barak's "lines in the sand" suggested that the Palestinians were no longer a partner, that they had been downgraded to the status of potential enemy.

Lipkin-Shahak, who had fought alongside Barak in war, heard those words and wondered why Barak would make such a mistake.[2] What was the point of drawing lines in the sand? he asked.

Desperate for progress, the peace camp saw Barak as its new leader and expected him to embrace Arafat and rebuild all that had been torn down by Netanyahu since Rabin's death.

But that was not Barak.

He was wary of the elders of his own party. He refused to give either Shimon Peres or Yossi Beilin, the architects of Oslo, key posts in his government. He flattered Ariel Sharon, if only to keep him at bay; he brought the former Likud minister David Levy back as foreign minister and gave key cabinet posts to the leaders of the settler movement: Natan Sharansky, the former Russian dissident, and Yitzhak Levy of the National Religious Party.

In other words, Barak pandered to the same hard-right constituencies as Netanyahu did in order to reach a parliamentary majority. Barak would need a majority to make peace, but the political majority he assembled in the Knesset would keep him from making peace in the same way the facts on the ground were working against him. The population of Israeli settlers in the occupied Palestinian territories had doubled since the Oslo Accords. More than fifty-four thousand acres of Palestinian land had been confiscated between 1993 and 1999, the bulk of it under Netanyahu.[3] The army and the settlers—using security as a pretext—had imposed new restrictions on Palestinian movement with roadblocks and checkpoints. Agreements on water sharing, trade, and economic development—all signed since Oslo—had not been implemented. Palestinian unemployment was over 25 percent.

In these circumstances, the Palestinian leadership distrusted Israel so much that when Barak tried to sweep Arafat off his feet with a proposal to freeze all prior agreements and begin immediate negotiations on "permanent status," Arafat did not hesitate.

No! said Arafat. "The two have to be done at the same time: implementing Wye and the other accords, and beginning negotiations on the permanent status."

The two men held their first meeting at the edge of Gaza, in a small utility room at the Erez Crossing.

Barak cajoled. "If we haven't reached an agreement in six months, we can go back to the implementation of the Wye River Accord and the interim accord."[4]

But Arafat dug in. He had no reason to trust Barak. "My mind is made up. Implement Wye right away! It's an agreement that Netanyahu made."

That was true. But Barak seemed taken aback by Arafat's resistance. Barak wanted to command the political realm. He wanted his cabinet, and Arafat, to follow a new political script as his commandos followed the scripts of his daring military operations. Barak was not accustomed to the backslapping and arm-twisting of retail politics. He had been a military man all his life. When people failed to respond to his command, he just got angry.

Arafat's chief negotiator, Saeb Erekat, and Mohammed Dahlen, Arafat's security chief for Gaza, asked Barak's aides how Barak could come into office on a peace platform and then act as though he could not move politically—like Netanyahu—for fear of setting off a storm in his coalition.

"We have no more leeway," Erekat told Barak's men. "Palestinian society has lost all hope for peace. Over the past years it has been literally suffocated and humiliated."[5]

The Palestinians simply wanted Barak to make a tangible gesture, to give life to all the fine words about storming the citadel. But Barak, for the first time in his life, was learning that it was one thing to imagine bold political moves that dazzled the electorate and united the country, but it was another thing to persuade the ministers of his new government to follow him.

It turned out that Barak knew almost nothing about how to lead a government. His secretive and egocentric character collided with reality. He trusted no one. He shared more information with Bill Clinton than with his ministers. He kept people waiting—important people—for hours. He did very little touring around the country to shore up his base, and when he did, he invariably antagonized his constituents by showing up late or speaking to them in condescending terms.

In the army, he had issued orders and executed perfectly timed plans, but politics was different and Barak had no time for politics. He was obsessed with time: he had less than two years to transform the Middle East before Iraq or Iran became a nuclear power, putting the Israeli electorate back into a defensive crouch; he had fifteen months to conclude peace with the Palestinians—not fourteen—because, he calculated, the U.S. Congress would not be willing to spend the billions necessary to support Middle East peace after the 2000 elections.

Barak had promised during the campaign that he would withdraw from Lebanon in twelve months, which meant that peace with Syria had to be synchronized so Damascus would have a strong incentive to restrain Hezbollah as Israeli forces made their departure.

Barak designed time lines as if politics could be choreographed. When events did not unfold according to his script, he blamed anyone but himself. He telephoned Bill Clinton two to three times a day, sensing that Clinton needed a success in the Middle East so badly that Barak was effectively in charge of the relationship, and Barak loved the idea of stage-managing Clinton's diplomacy.

It took weeks for Barak to understand that the Palestinians were not going to go along with his attempt to renege on agreements already signed by Netanyahu's government. When Barak and Arafat finally came to terms in September 1999, Barak agreed to complete the land transfers and begin final status negotiations on Palestinian statehood. The goal was to complete them in twelve months. But no sooner had they agreed than Barak lurched in another direction.

In October, he announced to parliament that the "decisive hour to achieve peace with Syria has come."[6]

The Palestinians stood dumbfounded. Barak had just declared the decisive hour to make peace with *them*. He could not do both at once. Either track—Syrian or Palestinian—would entail a huge political struggle. Barak refused to admit that he was downgrading the Palestinian track, but as

Dennis Ross observed, Barak's duplicity was ingrained. He would publicly embrace one approach but privately and impulsively veer onto the course of less resistance.

The Palestinian track thus slowed to a crawl. Barak feared opening up the big issues—Jerusalem, borders, and the right of return—because each of these would detonate in the Knesset. Barak's heroic vision for peace evaporated because in his first step beyond the threshold, he did not know how to find his footing on a political field where compromise was essential to success. As weeks and then months went by, he failed to appoint a negotiator to meet with the Palestinians.

No wonder that Boogie Ya'alon started thinking about the consequences of failure. Ya'alon, who commanded the occupation army of the West Bank and Gaza, was now one of the leading skeptics of peace. If Barak failed to deliver a final accord with the Palestinians within twelve months, "I realized that . . . Arafat might initiate a terror war against Israel." Ya'alon made the argument within the chain of command that "we have to be prepared" because Arafat was an unreconstructed guerrilla leader in search of "the last battle" to force the creation of the Palestinian state.[7]

The second possibility, Ya'alon reiterated, was that Arafat was not even interested in the "two states for two peoples" solution that Rabin had embraced. Instead, Arafat would carry on the battle to destroy the Jewish state.

Boogie Ya'alon's deeply ingrained suspicions did not represent the mainstream in the military establishment, but Ya'alon was a formidable figure in the army and a contender to become deputy chief of staff.

It was easy for Barak to rationalize that Syria was the more important citadel. Assad had an army. The Palestinians did not.

Israeli prime ministers were among the select allies for whom the White House had installed secure telephone lines. Still calling Clinton almost every day, in late 1999, Barak convinced the president to write a letter to Hafez al-Assad, encouraging him to enter negotiations for peace. Clinton did so right away.

It took a month for Assad to reply.

The Syrian leader demanded a full return of the Golan Heights and a permanent border that would touch the eastern shoreline of the Sea of Galilee. Barak was rattled by Assad's claim to the sea boundary. Galilee was Israel's national water supply. No way, Barak said, could he allow Syrian access.

Barak told Clinton that the only thing that would "shock" Assad into making peace on more accommodating terms was a surprise presidential visit to Damascus by Clinton himself. He was grasping, like Peres before him, for political theatrics that might crack the masonry of resistance.

Clinton was spared the risky journey when Assad agreed, in a meeting with Secretary of State Madeleine Albright, to formal resumption of Israeli-Syrian peace talks. Albright had worn a lion brooch to flatter Assad—his name means "lion" in Arabic—but flattery was not necessary. Assad said he was ready to conclude peace with Israel, and that in itself was a historic development. The venue was Washington, and Assad sent his foreign minister, Farouk al-Sharaa, with a mandate to make a deal. Barak sent Uri Saguy, former director of military intelligence, an expert on Syria. But Barak had poorly prepared the Knesset, which mustered only 47 votes out of 120 when Barak sought his own mandate for the negotiations. Sharon accused Barak of offering to give up the Golan "without demanding anything in return."

Amazingly, the negotiators, in a relatively short span of time, overcame all of the major obstacles to reaching a peace agreement, according to Saguy.

The only problem was that Barak was not ready; the master of timing needed more time.

He had not prepared the public. He had envisaged a climactic negotiation between himself and Assad in the spring of 2000, a heroic drama in which he, playing the leading role, would energize public opinion and trump the naysayers of his coalition government.

Instead, the Israeli tabloids raised all the questions of what "full peace" with Syria would mean. Israelis could not imagine coming down from Golan without getting anything in return. A prominent writer wondered aloud whether Assad would "fax" a peace treaty to Israel—in other words, that relations would continue to be frigid.

Uri Saguy, who came from one of the oldest sabra families in northern Palestine, a major general who had commanded the Golani Brigade, fighting on the Golan Heights in both the 1967 and 1973 wars, was astounded when he realized that Barak was losing his nerve.

"Tell me," Barak asked him during one private conversation about the nearly completed treaty, "do you think it will be accepted?"

"Yes!" Saguy responded.

"Why?" Barak asked.

"Because it's beyond belief! You and I both know what peace with Syria means."[8]

Saguy explained that Assad had obviously calculated that it was safer for him to make peace than to die without making it. With peace, Assad could leave a legacy that could be defended. It would protect his son Bashar from the hard-liners who might oppose peace when Assad was gone.

Peace would remove the last major threat of war on Israel's borders; it would mean that Hezbollah and the Palestinian radicals who called Damascus their home would lose their base from which to wage war on the Jewish state. Peace with Syria would lead to peace with Lebanon and the pacification of the entire northern sector; it would open the Levantine coastline where it would be possible for the first time in a half century to rent a car in Aleppo, in northern Syria, and drive unhindered all the way to Cairo and the pyramids.

Barak asked Saguy to help him convince key right-wing ministers, among them Natan Sharansky and Yitzhak Levy of the National Religious Party.

Sharansky was asking, "Why should Israelis give up the Golan Heights?"

"It's up to you," Saguy replied.

Sharansky was a Russian immigrant, a former dissident who had suffered in the Soviet gulag. He had arrived long after the Israelis had fought and died to secure the state.

Giving up the Golan Heights meant "a different relationship with our neighbors," Saguy continued.

Sharansky mocked him. "You are a very bad businessman." Israel could simply hold on to the former Syrian territory. The world would not end.

"Anatoly, how many times have you been on the Golan Heights? Once, twice . . . ?" Saguy asked him. "I spent many years there, I know almost every rock. I lost many friends there. But you were not there when I was there in 1967. And I know it is unfair, but where were you in 1973?"

"I was in a Soviet jail," Sharansky retorted.

"Okay, so let's agree that I cannot understand what it means to be put in a Soviet jail, but you don't understand what it means to fight on the Golan Heights. Is it fair, Anatoly?"[9]

The two men had laughed, each failing to convince the other, but for the general who was in charge of the Syrian negotiations, the conversation demonstrated how little Barak had done to shape opinion on the right. Sharon, Sharansky, and the others wanted some additional "payment" for leaving the Golan. That was their idea of good "business." Peace was not enough.

Public opinion polls in Israel showed that a majority favored the peace but only 13 percent supported a total withdrawal from the Golan. The polling data seemed to have negated Barak's whole approach, and when he flew to Washington that winter to ink the deal, he literally froze on his airplane. Martin Indyk, one of Clinton's assistants for Middle East policy, had to coax him off the aircraft.[10]

When he succeeded, the Syrian foreign minister, Farouk al-Sharaa, wanted to know whether Barak was ready to do what Rabin had promised: to withdraw from all Syrian land to the lines of 1967.

Barak refused to give him a straight answer. He used the Americans—Clinton and his envoy Dennis Ross—to delay and obfuscate because, he said, the Israelis needed to see him putting up a fight.

The climactic moments came at Shepherdstown, West Virginia, where Clinton brought Barak and Sharaa back together just after the millennial celebration of the New Year in 2000. Clinton had tried to push Barak to the finish line by laying out a draft treaty with bracketed language on the final items that needed resolution. Clearly a treaty was within reach. Assad sent private messages to the White House and to Barak that it was time to stop prevaricating over how to draw the border. They could do it in secret, Assad suggested, in one marathon session, and then announce that they had reached an agreement.

At dinner, Sharaa wheeled on Barak and demanded clarity: Would he reaffirm Rabin's pledge to withdraw to the 1967 lines?

Barak just smiled. He could not bring himself to close the deal.[11]

Clinton, Ross, Saguy—no one could understand Barak's obsessive logic or his inability to compromise with Assad.

Saguy later said the dinner "was very sad."

Sharaa turned to Barak and said, "You broke your promise . . . I failed my president. I was fooled or cheated by you. I told my president that there was a chance for peace . . . I came here determined to move. I had a mandate to reach an agreement. Now I'll have to go back and report that we got nothing . . . Nothing. This was an opportunity!"[12]

Saguy believed that Sharaa was right, but no one could tell Barak anything. He just sat there smirking.

"You're a great general in front of the Israeli public," Sharaa continued, "but not in front of us. You've misled me and I misled my president."[13]

In the midst of the Syrian drama, Barak seemed unaware that the Palestinians were completely turning their backs, writing him off as another Israeli leader with whom they could not do business.

The most serious warning came from the Shabak chief, Ami Ayalon. He went to see Barak in January 2000, right after Barak had returned from that dispiriting last supper with Clinton and the Syrian foreign minister, and told the prime minister that he wanted to resign.

"Stay until September and we shall have a peace treaty [with the Palestinians]," Barak entreated him.

"No, forget it, you will not have a peace treaty," Ayalon replied.

Barak asked him to explain.

"Because you lost him. You lost your partner." Ayalon was talking about Arafat. "He lost his street. He does not represent the Palestinian people anymore. If he will sign something that they cannot live with, they will kill him. So this is what you lost in your first six months."

"You are naïve," Barak replied. "I will give him an offer he will not refuse."

"Ehud, you do not understand. No matter what you will offer him, if he does not believe you, he will not work with you. He will go to war; he will go back to Tunisia; he will start the whole revolution from the beginning. If you lose him as a partner, if you lose his confidence, you will have no deal."[14]

Barak waved him off; he did not believe him. But Ayalon's judgment was widely shared among those in the defense establishment who felt the pulse of the Palestinian community.

"Of all our prime ministers, Barak is the one who least understood the Palestinians," observed Uri Savir, the diplomat who had helped to complete the original Oslo Accords.[15]

Barak's spokesman and political adviser, Gadi Baltiansky, agreed. Barak, he said, was what the Russians called a *chekist*, a security man. He had spent a minimal amount of time in his life trying to understand his Palestinian "enemies"—only how to defeat them.

"He was a soldier. He didn't learn the Arab mentality; he was not interested in that," said Baltiansky. "He didn't want to make peace with the Arabs because they deserve a Palestinian state, or because they have their national aspirations. He doesn't care about it. He doesn't believe in the Arabs at the end of the day—like Sharon in many ways—but he believes in his own power. He never trusted Arafat. He trusted Assad more, although he never, of course, met him. But he had a kind of confidence that with Assad you can have a deal; with Arafat, with the Palestinians, no—not unless the Americans will guarantee and if the IDF is the warranty."[16]

In truth, Barak was like the early Rabin.

The only thing he respected was power, and the Palestinians had none. Thus he could not take Arafat seriously, nor could he offer him the measure of respect that Arafat demanded and that Rabin had afforded him as a partner in the peace negotiations. Ahmed Qurei, who had conducted the Oslo negotiations under Arafat, said of Barak, "Even if it is not his intention, Barak exudes contempt and arrogance."[17]

Sharansky once told Dennis Ross that he had no objections to most of Barak's initiatives in the spring of 2000, but because he usually heard about them from the Americans or from the newspapers, he deeply resented Barak's exclusionary and peremptory style.

Ayalon was particularly bitter.

He and his senior aide, Yossi Ginnosar, whose job it was to maintain the discreet channels to the Palestinian leaders, had worked hard to persuade Arafat to keep faith in Barak.

In submitting his resignation, Ayalon rebuked Barak: "Ginnosar and I had a hard time getting the Palestinians to trust you. Now it's all no good." Barak had misjudged not only the Palestinians; the Israelis, too, were turning on him. "If you think you can evacuate ten thousand [settlers] from the Golan—which will take you to the brink of civil war—and then evacuate tens of thousands of others from Judea-Samaria, then you don't understand anything about the reality in Israel."[18]

There was so much Barak did not understand. "He fixed on a certain concept of reality and if things did not work out, there was something wrong with reality, or the space-time continuum was out of whack," explained Alon Pinkas, a diplomat who served both Peres and Barak.[19]

Even after Barak's terrible performance with the Syrians at Shepherdstown, he still believed that he could maneuver Assad into a deal.

But it would fall to President Clinton to share the risk of failure.

The terms of the draft treaty that had been prepared for the Shepherdstown summit had leaked to the Israeli news media and set off a volcanic reaction that magnified the contradictory feelings Israelis held about peace with Syria.

Barak convinced Clinton to telephone Assad in early March and tell him that Barak was willing to put a "fantastic offer" on the table. It all came down to where to draw the boundary along the Sea of Galilee, which at one time had been ten meters back from the shore. Barak's "fantastic" offer was to push the Syrians six hundred meters back from the water's edge.

Assad showed up in Geneva with an entourage of one hundred aides and took over one of the luxury hotels. On the plane in from Damascus, he had told his aides that he doubted anything would come from the meeting.

Indeed, Clinton showed up with a bad case of diarrhea, and then right before he went in to see Assad, Barak called with his "final" terms, which were so disappointing to Clinton that he wondered why he had come.

But Clinton and Assad never got to Barak's bottom line.

When Clinton opened by telling Assad that Barak was willing to withdraw to a "commonly agreed border," Assad grew cantankerous.

"If he wants sovereignty over the water then he doesn't want peace!" Assad said.

Everyone in the room knew that Assad's outburst was contrived. Sharaa had essentially agreed that Syria could live with the old boundary just off the shoreline, but now he, too, protested.[20]

Clinton pleaded that Barak was struggling politically at home.

"That's Barak's problem," Assad fired back. "We're here to reach a just peace, and a just peace means we get the land that we had in 1967, and in 1967 I, along with my officers, were swimming in the lake. So don't tell me that Israel wants a strip along the lake."

Clinton was crestfallen and struggling for composure. Assad was smiling.

"Look, you and I are friends, but there's not gonna be a deal if I don't get to run my feet in the lake."

Clinton was shaken. The Israelis groaned at failure, but there had been nothing heroic in Barak's methods. His obsessions made him a terrible statesman; his arrogance and disdain for retail politics made him an ineffectual politician. Barak saw himself as a Ben-Gurion, but he lacked Ben-Gurion's capacity to dominate the government.

Barak had tried so hard to win the approval of Sharansky and Sharon that he had alienated Arafat and Assad. If he had taken Peres or Yossi Beilin into his confidence, perhaps he might have developed a broader set of options. But Barak stood alone as the architect of his own failure.

The disaster on the Syrian front prompted Barak to shift the focus of his premiership back to the promise, made during the campaign, to bring the army home from Lebanon. Shaul Mofaz, the chief of staff, thought it was a terrible idea. He warned Barak that Hezbollah would regard Israeli withdrawal as surrender. Withdrawal would undermine Israeli deterrence. Hezbollah would choose its moment and then unleash a new war against the northern border. Publicly, Mofaz was stoic, telling his commanders that the army could not choose its own missions, but he resisted Barak at every turn and relented only under duress.

The pullout began in May 2000, with Barak declaring, "From now on, the government of Lebanon is accountable for what takes place within its territory."

When Hezbollah saw the Israeli tanks and artillery pulling back in a cloud of dust, its leaders staged a "victory parade" in the Lebanese town of Bint Jbeil, where Hassan Nassrallah, Hezbollah's secretary general, delighted thousands of his followers: "My dear brothers, I say this to you: with all of its atomic weapons, Israel is weaker than cobwebs!"[21]

Palestinians saw an invidious comparison between their circumstances and Hezbollah's.

The Lebanese militants had used violence and terror against Israel and they got 100 percent of their territory back. The Palestinians had chosen a path of negotiation; they had arrested and imprisoned hundreds of their own militants. Yet Israel refused to leave the West Bank and Gaza, or return to the 1967 lines. Israel wanted to annex as much as 15 percent of the West Bank to absorb its major settlement blocs, with the IDF staying in the Jordan Valley in perpetuity, thus surrounding the Palestinians and strangling their state. What good had come from a peaceful approach? Marwan Barghouti, the street-savvy Arafat aide on the West Bank, preached that the Israelis responded only to violence. Here was the evidence.

The withdrawal from Lebanon did not trigger the war that Mofaz had envisaged, but Hezbollah stockpiled thousands of rockets in caves and villages across southern Lebanon, powerful rockets that could reach Haifa and Hadera north of Tel Aviv. They would be ready for war at any time.

Barak was now down to one negotiating track—the Palestinians.

His government was flying apart. The left-wing secular Meretz Party could not abide staying in a government with the ultra-Orthodox Shas Party. The National Religious Party was threatening to pull out if Barak transferred three Arab villages around Jerusalem to the Palestinian Authority, a gesture of good faith that Arafat had asked of Barak. From the opposition benches, Sharon shouted that if the government turned over the village of Abu Dis to the Palestinian Authority, the Palestinians could climb onto the rooftops and fire their weapons into Jerusalem.

Barak had no answers.

He told the Americans that with regard to the Palestinian track, he could not imagine how he would survive politically if he opened up Jerusalem for negotiation, and yet the Americans told him that they could not imagine "permanent status" negotiations without putting Jerusalem on the table.

But if he did nothing, he would most certainly fail and his government would collapse. He telephoned the White House and told Clinton that the only way to achieve a breakthrough was for the president of the United States to summon the parties for a climactic summit.

And it was at this moment, almost imperceptible to the Americans, that the Israeli military establishment began to turn against peace as a strategic objective. A sizable faction began to coalesce around the notion that Barak would never be able to meet the Palestinians' terms and, therefore, Arafat would launch a war.

The first and most influential person to signal this warning was Boogie Ya'alon, but he was soon joined by Amos Gilad, head of the assessments branch of the army. Gilad was a powerful intellect within the intelligence community, and by May 2000 he was standing up in every government meeting he could get into to say that Barak would not be able to reach a peace agreement unless he was willing to withdraw to the 1967 lines, divide Jerusalem, and acknowledge a right of return for Palestinians. Less than that the Palestinians would never accept.

Barak could not refute Gilad's assessment without admitting that he was contemplating dividing Jerusalem and giving the Palestinians nearly 100 percent of the West Bank and Gaza. Even a hint that such concessions were under consideration would have brought down the government, which made Gilad's vocal assertions a political act. This was a military, not a diplomatic, mind-set. The important implication of the army's assessment was that Arafat would put up a maximalist front at any summit; Barak would never be able to meet his demands and, when the negotiations collapsed, some kind of violence would ensue—perhaps Arafat would launch a war. This was the impulse that made negotiations so difficult: if you believe always that your neighbor is readying for war, you will never make peace.

It must have seemed to Barak that there was only one way out.

He would force Arafat into a final negotiation and see if he was willing to make peace, and if he was not, the failure of the negotiation would unmask "the true face" of the Palestinian leader—that he was not capable of making peace.

This is how the stage was set for the Camp David summit: the military establishment had forced a prime minister into a corner in which he expected Arafat to accept whatever terms Barak thought the Israeli parliament might accept at that moment, or else be declared an outlaw. Barak's logic was more akin to forcing a surrender than making peace with his enemy.

Gadi Baltiansky, the only one of Barak's advisers who had the courage to challenge the muddled thinking of the prime minister, asked—on the night before they left for Camp David—"Why are you going for all or nothing?"

Baltiansky pointed out that if they failed at Camp David, that did not mean peace was not possible. There could be a follow-on summit to keep the momentum going. But Barak looked at him and took a pencil, placing its point on a piece of paper and holding it vertically with his thumb.

"'You see this pencil? I am now holding this pencil. Either we sign the peace treaty, or I leave it, and if I leave it, everything falls down and collapses. That's it.'

"This was the state of his mind," Baltiansky said.

It was more than all or nothing. If there was no agreement, Barak explained that the strategy would be to declare that there was no partner. That was the "unmasking" strategy. If Barak was to face voters in the next election, he had to give an accounting to the public, Baltiansky explained: "Either I have an agreement or I don't, and if I don't, I have to blame the other side: I can't say it's my fault. I have to say that they [the Palestinians] didn't mean it from the beginning and everything was a game, a fake, the entire Oslo process since 1993."[22]

The Palestinians feared that Camp David would be a trap.

Clinton needed a deal to save his presidency (sullied by Lewinsky and impeachment), and Barak needed a deal to save his premiership. It fell to Clinton to persuade Yasser Arafat that if he came to Camp David, he would not be blamed for failure.

The Palestinians countered that they needed a few more months of secret negotiations to close the gap between the sides on the major issues—Jerusalem, refugees—but Clinton and Barak felt that they were out of time. So the Camp David summit went forward in a funk of ill will.

Barak had failed to transfer the three villages he promised; he released only three Palestinian prisoners.

A White House aide, Rob Malley, reported that in Arab capitals, Arafat was saying he "has lost all trust in Ehud Barak."

What made Arafat go ahead, according to Sandy Berger, the national security adviser, was the president. Arafat put his faith in Clinton.[23]

The summit was a disaster of poor timing and even poorer preparation. And when it failed, Clinton did blame Arafat. He told the news media that Barak had made historic concessions. He had tried harder than Arafat.

Arafat came out of the thirteen-day negotiation embittered. "Barak treated me like a slave," he complained to Madeleine Albright. It was an exaggeration, but it reflected his mood.[24]

"Barak really did have several personality defects, which led to his downfall in the end," Shlomo Ben-Ami, one of Barak's negotiators at Camp David, said later. Ben-Ami had urged Barak to try to build a "more personal and empathetic approach" to Arafat, and Barak seemed to listen, but he did nothing.

"He expected his interlocutors to fall in with his wishes, according to the scenario that he had prepared for himself and for them, and when this did not happen, he tended to lose his composure, to entrench himself deeply in his positions, thus, in effect, helping to block the dynamics of negotiation."[25]

Yoram Peri, the Rabin aide who closely observed Barak, said that his behavior "typified the working style of the security-culture school." Barak was patronizing to Arafat because that was the history of the army during the decades of occupation: the strong dictated to the weak in a take-it-or-leave-it manner.

Rumors of what had been offered to the Palestinians raked public sensibilities in Israel.

Arafat was saying publicly that the Arab parts of Jerusalem should become the capital of the Palestinian state. Arafat had said he could not accept Israeli sovereignty over the plaza where the al-Aqsa mosque and the Dome of the Rock stood. The Noble Sanctuary—or Temple Mount—whatever your religion, was the key.

It was clear to Israelis that Barak had opened the question of Jerusalem at Camp David and was now maneuvering to reassure all sides that he knew what he was doing. When Sharon decried the results without knowing the specifics, Barak called him from New York. Barak said he was laying a trap for Arafat—to unmask him if necessary—and that he might need to form a government of national unity with Sharon and the Likud.

This was certainly music to Sharon's ears.

"Ehud, I'm ready to help you. If you get out of this trap now, I promise I will never use it against you, but you must get out." The "trap," as Sharon saw it, was creating a Palestinian state, or ever sharing Jerusalem. Sharon accelerated his efforts to close the door that Barak had opened.[26]

Sharon called Uri Dan in late September and told him that he had a plan to stop Barak from surrendering any part of the Old City. He would stage a walkabout in the Muslim sanctuary on the Temple Mount, and though it was a highly provocative act in a time of high tension, no one really tried to stop him.[27]

The Palestinians claimed that they appealed to Barak and to the Americans to block Sharon, who was targeting any compromise on Jerusalem by asserting his right to walk on the plaza at the heart of the Old City, where conspiracy-minded Arabs feared an alleged Israeli plot to tear down the mosques and to build the Third Temple.

Barak could have stopped him, but he was not about to antagonize Sharon. Instead, he gave Sharon the green light to go up to the Temple Mount with one thousand police as his escort. Sharon stirred the magma of Palestinian fear and suspicion and seemed surprised when flames shot out. Young Palestinians screamed at the sight of Sharon outside their mosques. They rioted, pelted Israeli police with stones, and took withering fire in return.

Looking back at that crucial moment, Efraim Halevy said that no one who served in Barak's government at the time really knows why he approved Sharon's visit, except that political considerations were paramount. Barak knew that it might induce the explosion of rioting that occurred; his intelligence agencies had been warning for months that violence could erupt if Camp David failed and if September 13—Barak's one-year deadline for peace with the Palestinians—passed without producing a state.

"The air was rife with tension," Halevy told me. "So you can say that the Temple Mount was a mistake, but you can also say that if it hadn't been there, that something else would have ignited the storm. It would have happened anyway—there would have been an outbreak for another reason."[28]

Perhaps so, but Israeli and American leaders bore the responsibility for letting Sharon, of all people, swagger onto the plaza of the mosques and reignite the war fever that had been rising over dashed hopes and seething anger since Camp David.

The clash ignited the Al-Aqsa Intifada, more deadly and destructive than either side could imagine. The army under Mofaz and Ya'alon sprang into action.

In the space of a few weeks, as the massive outbreak of violence cascaded across the West Bank, the Israeli army unleashed Operation Field of Thorns, its plan to hit the Palestinians with overwhelming force.

It was later reported that one million bullets were fired by Israeli Defense Forces against the Palestinians. Boogie Ya'alon explained that Israeli commanders had prepared the killing zones so carefully that the snipers actually used an economy of fire to fell the Palestinian activists who rushed into the streets and organized the rock throwing and sniping from the Palestinian side. When I went to meet Ya'alon at his home in Modi'in, he smiled when he heard my description of the Palestinian complaint that so many young militants were killed by a single bullet to the head. What did they expect? Ya'alon asked. "We were well prepared for such a scenario. In this kind of arena, we had snipers and special soldiers to observe the [Palestinian] activists, to identify them, and to direct the snipers to hit them." When a Palestinian militant would stick out his head, an Israeli sniper was waiting to shoot him. Hence the proliferation of head wounds, Ya'alon explained.[29]

The big accusation, however, was that Arafat had ordered the war. It wasn't true, as all later reconstructions confirmed, but it didn't matter.

All it took was for a handful of key figures in the military establishment to say it—and the Israeli press to magnify—and it became fact: Arafat had planned the new uprising. Here was the "unmasking": supposedly Arafat had duped Barak just as he had duped Rabin before him. Stan Moskowitz, the CIA station chief, called it "one of the most successful bits of agitprop by the Israelis—that [Arafat] had it all planned."[30]

Inside the military, Ya'alon believed it—because he had predicted it. Amos Gilad shouted down other analysts, asserting that Arafat had never wanted peace.

"The defense establishment sold us a story, describing the intifada as a planned and coordinated move of the Palestinian leadership," said Ami Ayalon, the former Shabak chief. "Accordingly, the IDF used snipers, backed up by legal approval granted on the basis of those intelligence descriptions, killing both armed men and civilians and escalating the conflict."[31]

Many Israelis could not understand how the militarist impulse came rushing voraciously back to undermine everything that had been achieved on the peace side of the ledger.

Shaul Mofaz, the chief of staff, Ya'alon, and Amos Gilad were now like a tag team. They attended critical government meetings asserting that Arafat was not a partner. They shouted down dissenters. The senior ranks of the military had adopted a blatantly political and propagandistic narrative that supported Barak's "conception"—stated at the outset of Camp David—that if Camp David failed, they would "unmask" Arafat and blame him.

Lieutenant Colonel Ephraim Lavie, who headed the Palestinian desk in the military intelligence directorate, knew that Arafat had not planned the outbreak of violence. But Arafat would be forced to join it. Palestinians were dying in such disproportionate numbers that Arafat had no choice.[32]

Barak was trapped between war and peace, between Sharon and Arafat.

"It was a terrible period of time," Baltiansky recalled. "For Barak, who always knew what he wanted, suddenly everything collapsed. He realized that he does not have peace with Syria; he doesn't have an agreement with the Palestinians. Instead he has an intifada, and he doesn't know which way to turn. He was cornered by two approaches: one told him to continue to negotiate with the Palestinians, and the other one said, you have no partner, make a government with Sharon and go for a war with the Palestinians—Arafat is your enemy."[33]

And here is what no Israeli has been able to admit about the travesty of governance that occurred in late 2000: the military establishment saw that Barak was a failed politician, that Sharon was in charge of the Likud, and that the Likud had the loyalty of the one million Russians and the parties on the right.

"They smelled the weakness of Barak," said Lipkin-Shahak, speaking of the army and the defense establishment. "Barak had practically no co-alition, and they decided"—he meant the generals—"that security should be done in the way they believed it should be done." It wasn't a putsch, but Barak was no longer in control of the military. A good example was Arafat's request to reopen the Palestinian airport in Gaza, which had been damaged by the IDF at the start of the Al-Aqsa Intifada. Lipkin-Shahak received Barak's approval and conveyed the order to the army that it be done, and the army reported back that it had complied with the order.[34]

But the airport did not reopen because the army, after withdrawing from the terminal, set up a roadblock on the only road leading to the terminal and refused to let anyone enter, thus subverting the prime minister's order.

Boogie Ya'alon, the deputy chief of staff, was driving the military response, which was overkill, and this was inflaming the Palestinians to even greater acts of defiance and violence. Ephraim Sneh, the son of one of the army's founders and a senior aide to Barak, told the besieged prime minister that "from the chief of the general staff to the last sergeant at the roadblocks, not one of them carries out your policy." The army had become a wrecking crew.[35]

"The reaction of the army to the intifada was much tougher than our intention," said Yossi Beilin. The idea that massive fire would shut down the intifada quickly proved fallacious. "What happened was that the Israeli overreaction in September, October, November 2000 just ignited even the more moderate Palestinians to use suicide bombers. I think that otherwise it wouldn't have happened. It was not a government resolution. This was the military."[36]

The military had abandoned peace as its strategic objective. At the Shabak, the agency most attuned to the Palestinians, Avi Dichter replaced Ami Ayalon.

Dichter was not interested in understanding the enemy. He was interested in defeating the enemy. He canceled the agency's long-standing contract with Dr. Matti Steinberg, the internal Arafat biographer. And he started building a new force of Shabak special units for reconnaissance, information collection, and assassination.

The symbolism heralded a massive reordering of priorities. The Rabin era was dead. Sharon very possibly would be the next prime minister. The army understood that. The generals had turned on Netanyahu because he was reckless, and now they were turning on Barak because he was weak.

And what was most appalling was that Mofaz and Ya'alon were at war based on their assessment that Arafat and the Palestinians were incapable of making peace, a view not supported by their own intelligence professionals.

The Americans seemed to be oblivious of these destructive currents. Neither Clinton nor his principal aides saw that Israel—the Israel of Rabin—was changing dramatically. Rabin's calculated risk for peace had been judged a failure. If there was no strategic basis for peace, there could only be a basis for war. The military establishment was leading the civilian government.

The American ambassador, Dan Kurtzer, reported in private conversations that he thought Ya'alon was calling the shots, hammering the Palestinians even as Barak was trying to get the violence down and keep channels open to the Palestinian leadership.

"I'm apprehensive of Ya'alon," Kurtzer said. "He's one of the two people in charge, and it's petrifying."[37]

With America diverted by the election deadlock between Al Gore and George W. Bush, Barak, in December 2000, tendered his resignation and called for early elections. Netanyahu was preparing to challenge Sharon for the leadership of the Likud, and Barak believed Sharon would be an easier opponent because his brutal past turned out voters to stop him. A national election was set for February 2001.

Barak's last chance for political survival was Bill Clinton—and Yasser Arafat. In his arrogance, Barak conveyed the sense of *après moi le déluge*, just as Ben-Gurion had. The old warrior had warned in his letters to world leaders in 1963 that after his death, the state of Israel might cease to exist. Now Barak warned that if the country failed to support his last-ditch effort to reach an agreement with the Palestinians, it could mean that "our peace agreement with the Egyptians and the Jordanians will be severely cracked, and may collapse."[38]

After dozens of behind-the-scenes negotiating sessions that fall, Clinton called in the Palestinians and the Israelis in late December and read out his "parameters" for a peace agreement that would establish a Palestinian state. The Clinton parameters, though launched into the gale of violence that was roiling the Holy Land, demonstrated how far both the Palestinians and Israelis had come. There on paper was a Palestinian state on nearly 100 percent of the West Bank and Gaza, there was Jerusalem as the capital for both states, and there were the roughed-out compromises for refugees and the division of the Old City. Though there was still work to be done to narrow the gaps, in more than fifty years of conflict since the 1947 UN partition resolution, the two sides had never come so close. More than anything, the Clinton initiative showed that it could be done. Yet the promising moment arrived at a time when both sides were under maximum pressure to delay, leaving Clinton with no time and no leverage to close a deal.

Sharon reemerged with a vengeance as Barak's support disintegrated. Ehud Olmert, the mayor of Jerusalem, said Barak "is working to dismantle the state of Israel."

When Barak brought in his military chiefs to discuss the Clinton parameters, Mofaz was beside himself. He said Clinton's ideas constituted "a danger to the state." He then went public, telling *Ha'aretz* that while peace was still important to the army, Clinton's notion of giving up 95 percent of the West Bank and ending the occupation "will destroy the peace agreement and present a significant threat to Israel."

His logic was so distorted that Barak had looked at his chief of staff and said, "Shaul, you don't really think that Israel cannot exist without ruling over the Palestinian people, but that's the conclusion that arises from your comments."[39]

Also, the violence genie was out of the bottle.

The Palestinians were hitting hard and the Israeli army was hitting back harder, much harder. Terje Rød-Larsen, the UN coordinator for the Middle East who had done so much to support the Oslo process, issued a report stating that in addition to the high death toll among Palestinians, the Israeli army had destroyed nearly five hundred Palestinian homes, businesses, and mosques in October and November. Seventy orchards had been razed and the suffocating siege made it impossible for hundreds of thousands of Palestinians to return to their jobs. Unemployment was 40 percent and two hundred thousand had lost their main source of income in the space of a few months.[40]

Barak hoped that some miracle would save him, that Clinton would convince Arafat to accept some formula that would allow Barak to call a national referendum on peace. But the political career of the military legend was coming to an end because he could command neither the army nor the people.

Napoleon's long winter was over.

EIGHTEEN

Sharon: The Last Campaign Against Arafat

Miraculously, the old warhorse had resuscitated himself. Not even the stain of the Sabra and Shatila massacres had prevented it.

Arik Sharon—seventy-two years old, emphatically obese, argumentative, manipulative, and so deeply duplicitous that almost nothing he said could be taken at face value—made a surprising comeback, defying the polls and the pundits, because, it seemed, he was seen by a majority of the populace as supremely resolute in the face of the mayhem that was engulfing the country.

When in doubt, the thinking went, rely on the military, and Sharon symbolized the return of the ultimate warrior to lead the military in putting down the violence, restoring security, and taking action against Arafat, against Hamas and, for many, against Palestinian statehood and giving up the Golan.

Sharon came with an inchoate desire to hit harder than Barak had dared, to strike at Arafat, his old nemesis, to destroy him for good if that were possible, and thus Sharon seemed to offer the Israelis what they most wanted: crude and brutal reassurance against the next suicide bomber.

The Israelis more than anything wanted separation from the Palestinians and, while many hated to admit it, they wanted Sharon's clenched fist.

One columnist called him "the club in the closet."

The peace camp had splintered with recriminations. Many Israelis sought to affix blame—to Rabin, Barak, Hamas, or Arafat. All that most Israelis knew for certain was that the PLO, after Oslo, had been invited into the national living room for a peace parley that was to have created a Palestinian state, but instead the whole thing had devolved into a bloody urban war. Who knew whether Baruch Goldstein or Ayyash the engineer was more to blame? Retribution had overtaken every other impulse.

Now Sharon had been handed the opportunity of a lifetime.

Both Clinton and Barak blamed Arafat for the collapse of Clinton's eleventh-hour peace effort. And the incoming president, George W. Bush, was no Arafat admirer. When Sharon entered the White House for his first visit, the tone had changed.

Bush was almost fawning before the legendary general, who had once given Governor Bush a helicopter tour of the Holy Land. The president pledged that he would do anything—use force if necessary—to protect the Jewish state. The visit went so well that Sharon declared, upon his return, that "Arafat is the biggest obstacle to peace. I've been saying that for 20 years and nobody believed me. Now they do."[1]

The army was also tilting in Sharon's direction. Ya'alon had moved up to be deputy chief of staff and teamed with Shaul Mofaz; the two generals had taken a brutal approach toward the Palestinian uprising. This was the kind of military prescription that Sharon could endorse, only he wanted more. He had no qualms about the rising Palestinian death toll; he had no reservations about increasing the numbers of targeted assassinations. He told his military and intelligence chiefs that he was prepared to use artillery against Palestinian civilians to reestablish order.[2]

He pounded the table in the prime minister's conference room, saying, "This is war!"

Two weeks after he was sworn in, Sharon approved a robust war plan, putting his stamp on policy. Its goal was "to prevent Palestinians from attaining objectives through violent means."[3]

Mofaz reportedly ordered his regional officers—in an off-the-record session—to kill ten Palestinians a day in their respective areas, a quota that would require seventy killings across the command regions.[4]

When Major General Yitzhak Eitan, the head of the army that oversaw the West Bank, demanded that Mofaz put the order in writing, the chief of staff refused. Eitan told his officers they could ignore the order.

Mofaz then declared that the Palestinian Authority was "becoming a terrorist entity." He cited an intelligence report that Arafat, in meeting with his security chiefs, had asked, "Why aren't there more dead Israelis?" The smoking gun, Mofaz asserted, was Arafat exhorting his chiefs with the words "You know what to do."

But Sharon did not need Mofaz to tell him that Arafat was the enemy. "We will demand of the Palestinians that they renounce violence, terror, incitement, and of the Palestinian Authority that they fulfill their obligations and combat terrorism directed against Israel, its citizens and soldiers," he said in his inaugural address.[5]

Sharon's landslide victory had come without separate elections for parliament. He formed a broad national unity government with the Labor Party, inviting Peres to become foreign minister. Peres convened top diplomats and intelligence officials to debate the question of Arafat.

"All the top diplomats thought we should ignore him, he is a lost cause, he is not an appropriate partner because he went back to the armed struggle; he cheated us," recalled Alon Liel, the former director general of the Foreign Ministry.

Peres listened to all of them and then he summed up the meeting: "I heard you all. I want the following line: Arafat is a partner, we don't have anyone else." So there was still a voice for peace, but only one.[6]

Sharon's policy was to be polite to Peres and then ignore him.

The first diplomatic feeler from Arafat's camp called for reciprocal gestures toward a cease-fire. But Sharon was not interested. He demanded a complete cessation of violence on the Palestinian side.

Instead, the violence just spiraled up.

Whatever restraints Arafat had earlier imposed were removed. Fatah's Tanzim militants under Marwan Barghouti went on the offensive, as did Hamas.

On June 1, 2001, a suicide bomber reached the Tel Aviv waterfront where hundreds of young people—many of them Russian—were lined up to enter the Dolphinarium Disco. The explosion killed 21 and wounded 120.

Arafat was in Moscow. He accused Mossad of setting off the bomb. Halevy could not believe his ears, and Arafat's accusation hardened attitudes on the Israeli side.

Sharon demanded "10 days of quiet" before he would consider pulling the army back.[7]

Avi Dichter recommended the assassination of more Palestinian militants and, in August, Sharon approved sending an Apache helicopter to Ramallah to fire a missile into the office of Abu Ali Moustafa, head of the Popular Front for the Liberation of Palestine. Moustafa died in a fireball.

When the news reached Mossad headquarters, Halevy was alarmed.

Was Israel going to assassinate the very people with whom it would have to negotiate peace? Halevy agreed that Moustafa certainly had blood on his hands, but the assassination was "a deviation" carried out without any discussion "about the real implications of the fact that you're suddenly going to take out the political leadership."

Dichter argued, "They are all the same; they are all involved," but Halevy was concerned that "somehow or another I have to have an address on the other side" when the time came for negotiation.[8] And what was the point, Halevy asked, of killing a leader if the one who follows is worse?

Sharon did not allow himself to be troubled by these questions. Robust military assault was the policy.

Israeli snipers gunned down Hamas commanders in Nablus, along with civilian bystanders, including two children. Hamas retaliated by sending a suicide bomber into Jerusalem to blow up the Sbarro pizzeria on the afternoon of August 9, killing 15 people, including 7 children, and wounding 130.

Arab satellite stations beamed out images of Israeli soldiers beating or shooting Palestinian civilians, bulldozing olive groves, and blowing up the homes of the families of militants.

By late summer, Saudi Arabia's ruler, Crown Prince Abdullah, became so agitated by the images of repression that he threatened to break relations with the United States if Bush did not get Sharon under control. The Saudi leader's stern message to Bush set off panic in the White House.

Abdullah called home his ambassador to Washington, Prince Bandar bin Sultan, and told him that Bush "was just diddling us" with promises to restore the peace process in the Middle East. The president was not trying to play the honest broker. "He is one hundred percent with Sharon!" Abdullah complained.

"You tell him right now that I don't want to have anything to do with him or with America," the Saudi leader said.[9]

Out of this tumult came a surprising response from Bush.

He told his advisers that he would go before the United Nations and declare an American commitment to a Palestinian state.

Yet Bush had no plan for how to accomplish Palestinian statehood. He had laid no foundation; he certainly had not consulted Sharon, or Arafat. The new administration seemed bereft of ideas on how to actually proceed. George Tenet, the CIA director, privately approached Halevy that August and told him that Bush had no clue how to move forward in the Middle

East. Tenet's message was that if the Israelis knew how to end the violence and get back to a negotiating track, now was the time to unveil a plan.[10]

That was where things stood on September 11, 2001.

Al-Qaeda's terror attacks against America incited deep anxiety in Israel: Would the United States—in an attempt to mollify Muslim rage over the plight of the Palestinians—bring pressure on Sharon to return to the peace table?

Sharon could not imagine himself sitting with Arafat, so he went public with his own narrative.

"There is no good terror and no bad terror," he told American Jewish leaders. The war on terror, he said, should be waged against all terrorist groups, and "the organization that is led by Arafat" was no different from Osama bin Laden's.

"This is a war between good and evil," Sharon told the Knesset on September 16. "We must remember it was Arafat who—dozens of years ago—legitimized the hijacking of planes. It was Palestinian terrorist organizations who began to dispatch suicide terrorists."[11]

Bush and his advisers debated whether the president should go ahead with a major address on Palestinian statehood. On October 2, the president told reporters that a Palestinian state had always been part of his vision of the Middle East, and he was considering how to build support for such a policy.[12]

Two days later, in Jerusalem, Sharon called on the Western democracies, particularly "the leader of the free world: do not repeat the dreadful mistake of 1938, when enlightened European democracies decided to sacrifice Czechoslovakia for a 'convenient temporary solution' to Hitler's aggression.

"Do not try to appease the Arabs at our expense," Sharon said, as "this is unacceptable to us. Israel will not be Czechoslovakia. Israel will fight terrorism."[13]

The Americans were indignant, but they backed off. Bush dropped the speech.

Instead, Secretary of State Colin Powell was designated to deliver an address, but the White House so feared a negative reaction from Israel's supporters in Congress that Powell found himself fighting Condoleezza Rice, the national security adviser, just to clear an unremarkable text for delivery at the University of Louisville in November. The much anticipated speech left no discernible imprint.

In Israel, Peres went to Sharon to get approval to open a cease-fire negotiation with Arafat. "You can meet with Arafat as much as you want," Sharon told Peres's chief of staff, but, Sharon added, the army was going to send tanks into Gaza the next day to keep the war going because Hamas had attacked a border post.

"We can't allow them to screw us like that," Sharon shouted.[14]

Peres sat there, unable to confront Sharon, unable to make the case that Sharon's application of unceasing military force was doomed to fail when there was an obvious negotiating path.

Here was the tragedy of Sparta.

In a society so consumed by a military orientation, no one from the founding generation was left to stand up to a figure like Sharon. Peres had promised to do so, but he could not abide confrontation and was no match for Sharon in any case, because he had never worn the uniform.

The signs of military futility were everywhere as violence begat more violence.

On October 17, a PFLP hit team slipped quietly into Jerusalem on a retribution mission over the assassination of Moustafa in August. The gunmen walked into the Hyatt Hotel on Mount Scopus overlooking the Old City, took the elevator to the eighth floor, and waited for Rehavam Ze'evi, Gandhi, the ex-general who now served as Sharon's tourism minister. As he was returning to his room, two men stepped forward with silenced guns and shot him in the head and neck. He died on the spot.

Gandhi was two years older than Sharon and was a veteran of the 1948 war. It was Gandhi whom Dayan dispatched in 1956 to warn Sharon against entering the Mitla Pass. They went back a long way, and Sharon read out a stirring eulogy at his funeral.

In his old age, Gandhi had become an ultranationalist. As the founder of the Molodet Party, he ran on a platform of ethnic purging—transferring Palestinians across the Jordan River. He had publicly called on Sharon to disband the Palestinian Authority and to assassinate Arafat.

"It's not murder to get rid of potential terrorists," he had told a British interviewer a few months before his death. "Each one eliminated is one less terrorist for us to fight."[15]

Shortly before his death, he had announced that he and Avigdor Lieberman were going to resign their ministerial posts over the government's decision to pull the army out of two neighborhoods in Hebron.

No one could get the war under control. A climactic cascade of Palestinian bombings in December 2001 prompted the Israeli cabinet to declare Arafat "irrelevant" as a political leader.

Arafat, Sharon said, "is guilty of everything that is happening here."[16]

The army blew up Arafat's personal helicopters, bombed his offices into rubble, and sent bulldozers to gouge holes in the runway at Gaza International Airport.

Under heavy pressure, Arafat tried to rein in his own forces. On December 17, he went before his people and called for a complete cessation of violence—a "halt to all operations, especially suicidal operations, which we have always condemned."

He put the Hamas leader, Sheikh Yassin, back under house arrest, and Palestinian police arrested hundreds of militants including suspects on Israel's "most wanted" list.

But Sharon offered nothing in return.

He demanded seven days of absolute calm and refused to start counting the days until the Palestinians turned over Gandhi's murderers, who had given themselves up and were being held in Palestinian jails.

General Amos Malka, the director of military intelligence who was among the candidates to become chief of staff, mocked Arafat's speech at a news conference, calling it a "charade."

"Arafat is not built for historical compromise with Israel," Malka said in an interview shortly after. "He is not built to achieve a political settlement in which he accepts Israel's existence as a Jewish state with secure borders for any length of time."[17]

Malka parroted the language of Ya'alon and Mofaz. It was not based on professional intelligence assessment; it was the army's political line, the same one that Barak had ordained on the eve of the Camp David summit.

Arafat may have been a flawed character. But for more than a decade he had pushed and hauled the hard-liners of the PLO to engage Israel on the political front, to trade militancy for diplomacy as long as there was an Israeli prime minister willing to work for a two-state solution. But Arafat had to ask: What was his obligation under Sharon, who offered nothing to the Palestinians but a suffocating level of oppression and a rejection of Oslo? Sharon believed that Oslo was a historic mistake. And Arafat saw no reason to keep the peace that was no peace.

The flaw in the Israeli military analysis was that the army could not admit that its own actions since Oslo had contributed to the violence; it could not acknowledge that Netanyahu had worked to dismantle Rabin's legacy or that the army had protected and enabled the settler movement. In short, it could not admit that Israel's political leaders had made a peace deal that the military state had no intention of keeping.

Sharon's approach was similar to Shamir's a decade earlier: to give up nothing, to buy time, to make life miserable for the Palestinians so that they might remain submissive or, better still, migrate to other lands. The military establishment, which was seeing an increase in the number of religious Jews with a strong affinity for the settler movement entering the army, was becoming an accomplice in this strategy.

In early 2002, Peres argued that Sharon had to offer the Palestinians some political horizon in order to reduce the violence. Peres and Ahmed Qurei, who had negotiated the Oslo Accords, reached an agreement whereby the Palestinians would consent to a cease-fire, the collection of weapons, and the arrest of militants. In return, Israel would within two months formally recognize a Palestinian state, one defined provisionally by the areas that had been turned over to the Palestinian Authority prior to the outbreak of hostilities in September 2000.

After that, final status negotiations would resume to define permanent borders of the Palestinian state. Needless to say, Sharon treated the proposal with scorn, saying it was "in absolute contradiction" to his policy.[18]

Sharon was ready with a different kind of surprise.

At the same moment that Peres was offering a path to negotiation,

Israeli commandos boarded a cargo ship in the Red Sea carrying arms from Iran bound for Arafat's security organs. The *Karine A* was loaded with machine guns, RPGs, and three thousand pounds of C-4 explosive, enough for three hundred suicide bomb vests.

Arafat denied any connection with the ship. Israeli intelligence, however, had documents to prove Arafat was involved, and the CIA seemed to agree. Arafat had arranged the shipment through Hezbollah intermediaries.

Here was a gift for Sharon, delivered with exquisite timing.

It should have been no surprise that Arafat's security organizations were trying to arm themselves in the midst of an all-out war, but following Arafat's December speech, the blatancy of exposure and the illicit nature of the Palestinian supply line struck a heavy blow to Arafat's credibility, a final blow, perhaps, with the Americans.

Farkash, the incoming director of military intelligence, told *Ma'ariv* that "Arafat has not made a strategic decision to come to an agreement. Without terrorism, he would not be on the map."

The intelligence chief's assessment was strikingly negative. He stated unconditionally that "it will not be possible to come to an agreement with Arafat."[19]

This was exactly what Sharon wanted to hear. Farkash's language was not the neutral syntax of professional intelligence but rather the didactic cant of a military elite straining to declare the political track bankrupt.

Arafat's appeal to his people ushered in a period of calm nonetheless.

The daily toll of Palestinian attacks went nearly to zero for three weeks. Still, Sharon did not respond. The quiet begged the question: Was Israel willing to do anything at all for peace?

The answer was supplied by the new chief of Shabak, Avi Dichter.

Dichter came in with a plan to assassinate Ra'ad Karmi, a militant leader of Fatah's underground Tanzim organization in the West Bank city of Tulkarem. Karmi had not been active for six months, so there was no urgent requirement to move against him. But the Shabak had put Karmi's girlfriend under surveillance and found that he was visiting her almost every day by the same path.

By all accounts it was Dichter who proposed an anonymous assassination.

Shabak agents suggested planting an explosive, which could be remotely triggered, on the rocky path Karmi followed. *Boom!* As when a tree falls in the forest, there would be no fingerprints. Israel would deny responsibility.

At risk, of course, was the de facto cease-fire. Sharon knew it. It was absurd that Israel would not be blamed in the highly charged atmosphere that prevailed.

Farkash advised against the hit. Just because Shabak had the operational capability of killing someone didn't mean they should do it, he said. There were political risks.[20]

Sharon, not unexpectedly, rejected Farkash's dissent. It seemed entirely reasonable to Sharon to orchestrate an anonymous explosion on a hillside in Tulkarem to kill a Tanzim leader. He approved the hit.

On January 14, Ra'ad Karmi walked into a blast of deadly shrapnel. The West Bank erupted. Eight weeks of vicious internal violence followed, the worst that Israel had ever experienced. Karmi's funeral was a day of rage on the streets of Tulkarem and most other Palestinian cities.

There was no more talk of de-escalation. A squad of Fatah militants from the al-Aqsa Martyrs Brigades opened fire on a bat mitzvah ceremony in Hadera, killing six people and wounding thirty-five.

In Jerusalem's quiet Rehavia neighborhood, a bomber walked into Café Moment, just down the street from the prime minister's office, and blew himself up at ten thirty on a Saturday night, killing eleven. Another bomber blew up a bus on the road to Nazareth, killing seven, including four soldiers. Gunmen shot their way into Tel Aviv restaurants or picked off settlers driving on roads in the West Bank.

Karmi's "anonymous" assassination proved to be anything but. The defense minister, Ben-Eliezer, was so eager to take credit that he confided the truth to journalists, who trumpeted the news.[21]

Marwan Barghouti vented his exasperation to a reporter for Israel's largest daily newspaper. He said that Fatah, Hamas, and Islamic Jihad all had agreed to honor Arafat's call for a cessation of violence.

"There was a cease-fire for twenty-three days," Bargouti asserted. "But then you killed Karmi. What's next? Within six months, the situation will be very bad, on your side as well. On ours it already is."[22]

When Dichter looked back, all he could say was that he wished he had killed Karmi sooner.

"Look, the filthiest job on earth is the one I did. Even Israeli politicians have to work hard to match the level of filth I'm used to." Karmi had to die, Dichter said. "It was our duty to deter [our enemies], to get into their guts, physically, by all means necessary, and in the event that we can't, drop a bomb."[23]

Sharon agreed. For the first time in his political career, it seemed as if there were no real constraints on him in the war to destroy Arafat.

The only member of the Bush administration who seemed to question Sharon's approach was Secretary of State Colin Powell, who told Congress, "If you declare war on the Palestinians and think you can solve the [Israeli-Palestinian] problem by seeing how many Palestinians can be killed—I don't know if that leads you anywhere."[24]

Within the military establishment, even an incipient rise in the number of conscientious objectors did not faze Sharon. Fifty-one officers and soldiers signed an open letter refusing to serve the "mission of occupation and oppression," as they called it. "We shall not continue to fight beyond the 1967 borders in order to dominate, expel, starve and humiliate an entire people." The number of objectors swelled beyond the scale of the Lebanon War.[25]

The wave of blood crested on Passover. A bomber descended on Netanya and walked self-consciously into the dining room of the Park Hotel. Hundreds of gray-haired ladies were gathered with children and family. He pulled the trigger on his detonator. The building convulsed, the force of the explosion consuming and shredding guests with fire and debris.

The Netanya bombing killed 30 and wounded 250 in scenes of carnage that tipped Sharon and the military establishment across a new threshold.

Though Hamas claimed responsibility, Arafat and the Palestinian Authority were the target of Sharon's retribution. He ordered a full-scale reoccupation of the West Bank and Gaza, to destroy the "infrastructure" of terror. It was an invasion the likes of which had not been seen even in the Six-Day War.

On Good Friday, thousands of Israeli troops in mechanized formations moved into the territories in an operation the Israeli army called Defensive Shield. Merkava tanks rolled up to the edge of Arafat's compound in Ramallah, blasted through the walls, and then started pulverizing building after building with tank fire until Arafat was holed up with the remnants of his government and security force in a confined space with a single toilet.

Farkash had consulted three staff psychiatrists, working under contract with military intelligence, about how far the army should go in stripping Arafat of his "honor," meaning the trappings of power. The army destroyed Arafat's world until the psychiatrists judged that he was at his psychological limit: in their view, on the brink of personal and physical collapse.

More than two thousand Palestinians were arrested and nearly five hundred killed in the onslaught. Farkash appeared at a news conference and told reporters that among those arrested and charged with multiple counts of terrorism was Marwan Barghouti.

"He is the commander of the Al Aqsa Martyrs Brigade which is the Fatah terrorist arm," Farkash told them. He alleged that Barghouti "apparently coordinated with [Arafat] the terrorist activities," making Arafat complicit in directing terror.[26]

"The direct link between the Palestinian Authority and Arafat personally, in assisting and encouraging terrorism has been proven beyond any doubt," Farkash said. The chief of staff, Mofaz, stated publicly that the army's position was that Arafat should be expelled. Others called for assassination, but Sharon had promised Bush that he would not harm Arafat.

In Washington, Netanyahu bragged to an audience that he had told Sharon, "Get rid of Arafat! Get rid of him! Get rid of that regime! And America will understand, and many in America will support you."[27]

Sharon summoned his intelligence chiefs to a cabinet meeting and demanded that they advise him on the spot whether to expel Arafat. The chiefs were Halevy (Mossad), Dichter (Shabak), and Farkash (military intelligence). Each told Sharon that he could not recommend expelling Arafat, and each went away wondering whether Sharon had politicized the intelligence services in this public confrontation to back down Netanyahu and those who were demanding expulsion.

Sharon may have saved Arafat's skin, but it was a temporary ploy. Sharon was moving toward a new strategy: "regime change."

In the era of George W. Bush, regime change was the preferred euphemism for the violent overthrow of rogue states. Israel's ruling elite was no less ambitious. The military and intelligence chiefs came to Sharon after the Netanya bombing with a plan to shunt Arafat aside, paving the way for the appointment of a prime minister with whom the world might do business.

One of the chief advocates of this plan was Mossad's Halevy.

A clear-eyed analyst, Halevy had grown up in England during the world war. Among his distant cousins was Isaiah Berlin, the Oxford University philosopher. For the entirety of his career in intelligence, Halevy had maintained an abiding revulsion for Arafat, whom he had met as a young man.

The enmity went back to 1956, when Halevy, as a student at Hebrew University, had led the Israeli delegation to the International Union of Students convention in Prague, where Arafat led the Palestinian delegation.

The young firebrand from Cairo University had put the plight of the Palestinian people on the agenda. From the podium, Arafat had shouted out the vitriol of youthful recrimination against the Jews, decrying the injustice that had been inflicted upon his people and attacking the legitimacy of the Zionist state.

Halevy, pinned by curiosity and anger, was aware that he could not remain inert in the face of Arafat's attack. Halevy stood, bringing all of his delegates to their feet and, according to Halevy, many other delegates as well. They turned their backs on Arafat and stalked out of the auditorium. He refused to return to the hall until the Israeli delegation was granted a right of reply to Arafat's attack on the Jewish state, which Halevy delivered the next day.[28]

As a Mossad officer, Halevy had been fighting Arafat and the PLO ever since and had spent most of his life seeking to undermine European sympathy and American support for the Palestinian cause.

The plan to sideline Arafat would require the blessing of Bush and Tony Blair, the British prime minister. And it would need some sort of Palestinian acquiescence.

Sharon dispatched Halevy secretly in May to Qatar in the Persian Gulf to meet with the PLO elder Mahmoud Abbas—Abu Mazen—who agreed to speak with Arafat about how such a move could end the war with Sharon.

"A responsible Palestinian Authority that can advance the cause of peace should not be dependent on the will of one man," Sharon told an audience in Washington.[29]

Bush agreed. He and Blair were preparing for war against Saddam

Hussein. Calling for Arafat's removal would change the subject in the Middle East in a useful way.

The president stepped before news reporters in Washington on June 24, 2002, and said, "Peace requires a new and different Palestinian leadership, so that a Palestinian state can be born. I call on the Palestinian people to elect new leaders, leaders not compromised by terror."

It was a stealthy victory for Sharon, or so it seemed.

He had undermined Arafat so thoroughly that the old guerrilla leader would never fully recover. The Palestinian issue was going to be sidelined indefinitely under the rubric of reform and preparation for a post-Arafat era. All of the urgency drained out of the Middle East peace process, and the great powers turned toward war to topple Saddam Hussein.

Oslo was a receding memory. Powell drafted a holding strategy called the "road map" to improve security and confidence-building measures under the aegis of a "quartet"—the United States, Russia, the United Nations, and the European Union. But Sharon was in charge.

The sidelining of Arafat coincided with the ascension of Boogie Ya'alon as chief of staff of the Israeli armed forces, and he immediately set the tone for delegitimizing the Palestinian Authority.

"The present Palestinian leadership does not recognize the existence of Israel," he told a conference of rabbis. "The Palestinian danger to Israel constitutes a threat of cancerous dimensions and character that must be eliminated, must be fought to the death."

The Palestinians were out "to cause the Israeli public to lose its morale and to drag its political leadership into decisions like unilateral withdrawal from the territories, which would in effect be surrender to terror."[30]

One Israeli columnist admonished Ya'alon for his language: "A Jew should not forget the people who termed his people a cancerous element. He is expected to remember them day and night, to sear their horrible image in his mind and to strive wholeheartedly to have nothing to do with them."

The cancer that was *really* threatening Israel, he added, was "the cancer of occupation and brutalization, the cancer of ignorant racism, the cancer of Neanderthal militarism."[31]

Israeli intelligence services excelled at penetrating Palestinian militant groups. After Bush's speech, Israeli air force commanders were keen to demonstrate how precision-guided bombs could be ideal tools for targeted assassinations. Shabak agents in Gaza pinpointed the location of one of the most notorious Hamas commanders, Salah Shehadeh. Sharon wanted him killed, but the question was, how? The air force argued that precision-guided bombs were clean and neat from a military perspective. Their use did not risk the lives of Israeli soldiers.

Sharon was persuaded. He authorized a plan to drop a one-ton bomb on Shehadeh's apartment building, which was located in a densely populated section of Gaza City.

Just before the operation got the final go-ahead, Sheikh Yassin went public with a proposed cease-fire. He called on Sharon to pull the army out of Palestinian areas that had been invaded after the Passover bombing; he called for an end to house demolitions and assassinations. "Once the occupation and all those measures against our people stop, we are ready to study totally stopping martyrdom operations, in a positive way," he said.[32]

The offer was conditional, but it was nonetheless significant, according to a number of Israeli officials. The question for Sharon was whether to pass up an opportunity to kill Shehadeh and explore a new modus vivendi with Hamas.

The two-thousand-pound bomb that pierced the darkness just before midnight on July 22—gliding down on an invisible stream of satellite data—was Sharon's response. The twelve-foot-long explosive, released by an American-made F-16, entered the building like a meteor; the blast shook the neighborhood and completely destroyed the apartment house, killing Shehadeh, his wife, and one of their daughters. It also killed thirteen others, including ten children who were sleeping in the building or in adjoining houses, where walls buckled and collapsed under the force of the concussion.

The shock over the death of so many children incited public opinion in Israel and internationally. The secretary-general of the United Nations, Kofi Annan, decried Israel's lack of regard for "the loss of innocent life." The disillusionment of the peace camp was signified by the high-profile resignation of Dalia Rabin, the daughter of the late prime minister. She had been serving in the national unity government as deputy defense minister.

In leaving, she charged that Sharon was destroying her father's life's work.

Sharon was unfazed. He telephoned Uri Dan, a friendly journalist in New York, after the bombing, waking him at 1:00 a.m. to say, "We have just liquidated a murderer in Gaza. Write an article for your newspaper."[33]

The air force commander Major General Dan Halutz responded defiantly to criticism: "There is no clean war. I don't know anyone who can handle a clean war." Those Palestinians like Shehadeh, "who want to murder children in Israel should take into account that their own children might get killed," and he added, bitterly, that "the leftists who claim that the pilots are committing war crimes should be the ones to be judged."[34]

Asked how a pilot feels when he drops a bomb into a civilian neighborhood, Halutz replied, "What do I feel when I drop a bomb? I feel a light bump in the plane, as a result of the release. A second later, it passes, and that is all. That is what I feel."*

Sheikh Yassin vowed revenge: "The only worthy course left is holy war."

Hamas unleashed another series of suicide attacks in late 2002 and then resumed after a brief truce in 2003. Hamas volunteers blew up buses in Jerusalem on June 11 and August 19, 2003, killing forty Israelis and wounding more than two hundred. In a small country, every attack detonates on the Israeli psyche like an atomic weapon.

The death toll of the Al-Aqsa Intifada climbed to eleven hundred Israeli soldiers and civilians; the Palestinian death toll was far higher, at fifty-five hundred.

When journalists asked Hamas commanders how they justified sending suicide bombers against Israeli civilians, they replied that if they had American F-16s or helicopter gunships, they would use them instead.

If the casualty rates were converted to make them proportionate to the U.S. population, it would be as if 58,000 Israelis had died and 383,000 Palestinians; thus the pain and anger in each society was vast and extreme.

The Labor Party pulled out of Sharon's coalition in November 2002 and forced him to advance elections to January 2003.

The U.S.-led invasion of Iraq was only weeks away. Israel stood more isolated than ever under Sharon, who won the January election in another

---

* He later apologized for the remark, stating that he did not intend it as a display of callousness for the loss of innocent lives.

landslide, this time against Amram Mitzna, the progressive mayor of Haifa. Mitzna, a former general, tried unsuccessfully to remobilize the peace camp and revitalize the Labor Party, but he failed miserably as Israelis issued a strong vote of confidence for Sharon.

Likud took thirty-eight seats to Labor's nineteen. Sharon brought Mofaz into his government as defense minister.

Arafat, abandoned by many of his own followers, relinquished some political power. Mahmoud Abbas became the first prime minister of the Palestinian Authority. Arafat remained as president, in charge of thirty-five thousand Palestinian police.

In that first heady summer after America's successful entry into Baghdad, Arafat's decision to hand over powers to Abbas was a giant step toward the reforms that Sharon and the Americans were demanding. Washington wanted to reward the Palestinians. Abbas was invited to the White House, and Bush called a peace summit in the Jordanian port of Aqaba to build on the victory over Saddam.

With Arafat offstage, Abbas denounced the violence that had been the hallmark of PLO doctrine under his predecessor.

"There will be no military solution to this conflict, so we repeat our renunciation, a renunciation of terror against the Israelis wherever they might be. Such methods are inconsistent with our religious and moral traditions and are dangerous obstacles to the achievement of an independent, sovereign state we seek. . . . The armed intifada must end," he declared, "and we must use and resort to peaceful means in our quest to end the occupation and the suffering of Palestinians and Israelis."[35]

Sharon, too, dropped his bellicose front: "It is in Israel's interest *not* to govern the Palestinians but for the Palestinians to govern themselves in their own state," he said. Sharon still insisted on his preconditions. "There can be no peace," he added, "without the abandonment and elimination of terrorism, violence, and incitement." Nevertheless, Sharon employed the language of hope. He was willing to "reassure our Palestinian partners that we understand the importance of territorial contiguity in the West Bank, for a viable Palestinian state." It was as if Sharon was reading Palestinian talking points.[36]

Yet Sharon's veneer of conciliation masked a deeper skepticism that the Palestinians could ever meet his expectations.

The problem was that Hamas was still at war, and Sharon refused to allow his intelligence services to open a negotiating channel with Hamas to explore Sheikh Yassin's notion of a thirty-year truce.

Just days after the summit, four Israelis were killed in a shoot-out near Gaza. Sharon ordered a helicopter missile strike on Sheikh Yassin's deputy, Abdel Aziz Rantissi, but the missile missed its mark and instead killed a Palestinian woman and her three-year-old daughter.

Bush, for the first time, said he was "troubled" by Sharon's continued heavy reliance on military options.

Hamas hit back with a suicide bomber dressed as an ultra-Orthodox Jew, who killed seventeen people on a bus in Jerusalem. Israeli security services assassinated the Islamic Jihad leader in Hebron in August 2003, and five days later, a suicide bomber blew up a bus full of Jews returning from the Western Wall. Twenty-three died. Sharon sent the air force to kill the Hamas spokesman, Ismail Abu Shanab, incinerating his car on a Gaza street.

That's when Shabak agents picked up a profoundly sensitive bit of intelligence. The entire Hamas leadership, the "dream team," as Dichter called it, was going to meet on September 6. The venue was the top floor of a three-story apartment building.

Dichter argued for a massive strike with another two-thousand-pound bomb, but Sharon and the military establishment were concerned about collateral damage after the Shehadeh hit. "They decided to scale it down and opted for a smaller bomb instead of the one that would have eradicated everyone without a shadow of doubt," Dichter said later.[37]

The fallback was a five-hundred-pound bomb, which should have delivered a sufficient blast, but when the Hamas leaders arrived, they decided to meet on the ground floor of the building. The smaller bomb destroyed the upper floors, but Yassin and the others were able to dive for cover and survive the attack.[38]

Sharon was exasperated.

The violence and political stasis finally drove four former chiefs of the Shabak—Avraham Shalom, Jacob Peri, Ami Ayalon, and Carmi Gillon—in November 2003 to issue a strong rebuke against the military establishment's simplistic and brutal approach.

Sharon had put the country "on the road to catastrophe," the former chiefs said. He would fail unless he offered the Palestinians some "political horizon" in exchange for ending the violence.

Speaking to editors of *Yedioth Ahronoth*, the largest newspaper, Ami Ayalon, the Shabak chief under Barak, asked, "Imagine that Avi Dichter would come tomorrow and say that we should drop an atom bomb on Gaza. So because it is a recommendation of the most crucial [intelligence agency], it would be done?"[39]

Avraham Shalom, who ran Shabak from 1980 until 1986, added, "We must once and for all admit that there is another side . . . that it is suffering, and that we are behaving disgracefully. Yes, there is no other word for it: disgracefully. . . . We have turned into a people of petty fighters using the wrong tools."[40]

Carmi Gillon said Sharon's focus on only fighting terror was a mistake.

"It was not a mistake," interjected Shalom. "It is an excuse. An excuse for doing nothing."

"Terror," Shalom said, "is not thwarted with bombs or helicopters, but rather quietly," without the "element of vindictiveness" that was so apparent under Sharon.

Rarely had the security establishment, especially such an impressive phalanx of Shabak directors, so vocally and vociferously turned on a prime minister. Jacob Peri, who ran Shabak under Shamir and Rabin, made a recommendation that all the other chiefs joined enthusiastically: "If the state of Israel were to get up tomorrow morning and leave the Gaza Strip and Gush Katif [a settlement in Gaza], and really and truly begin to dismantle illegal settlements, then I tend to believe, based on longstanding acquaintance with our future dialogue partners—that the Palestinians would come to the negotiating table."

Disengagement as a national strategy burst into the public consciousness because Sharon's government was at a complete dead end, bereft of ideas and resistant to dialogue.

Unwilling to negotiate with the Palestinians and unable to destroy their leadership, Sharon seized upon the idea of disengaging from the Palestinians altogether, fencing off all of Gaza and leaving the Gazans to "boil by themselves" (in Jacob Peri's words) in a shattered economy. Suddenly, this unilateral act of disengagement seemed an ideal solution to Sharon and a large part of his political base. While some saw it as a trick to turn Gaza into a huge open-air prison, others saw it as the ultimate respite. The Israelis would be a people that dwelled alone once again, but at least the gates would be closed and heavily fortified. On the other side of the wall, the Palestinians could create a provisional government that, someday in the distant future, might prove worthy of statehood. That was how many Israelis rationalized it.

A day after the Shabak chiefs had blasted Sharon's policies, Ehud Olmert, one of Sharon's closest Likud allies, told *Ha'aretz* that "in the absence of a negotiated agreement—and I do not believe in the realistic prospect of an agreement—we need to implement a unilateral alternative."[41]

Two days after Olmert's interview, Sharon traveled to Rome and met secretly with Elliot Abrams, Bush's aide on the Middle East, and conveyed the outline of a disengagement plan.

Sharon told Abrams that Israel had come to a dead end. The Palestinians, even in the best of circumstances, could not exert control over their most ardent religious elements, and therefore, the terrorism would never end. Sharon wanted to try disengagement, because that at least would freeze relations with the Palestinians; it would put the political process in "formaldehyde," and the Palestinians would understand that they could not come back to the table until they were ready to become as Finland was to Russia, subservient and docile.

"This is the significance of what we did, of freezing the political process," Sharon's chief of staff, Dov Weisglass, said later. "And when you freeze that process you prevent the establishment of a Palestinian state and you prevent a discussion about the refugees, the borders and Jerusalem."[42]

After months of laying the political groundwork, Sharon stated publicly in May 2004 that he had embraced the idea.

"To keep 3.5 million people under occupation is bad for us and them. This can't continue endlessly. Do you want to remain forever in Ramallah, Jenin and Nablus?"[43]

Disengagement and formaldehyde. This was the old warrior's solution.

NINETEEN

At Wit's End: Killing the Paraplegic Preacher

With America supporting him, Sharon astounded the country with his announcement in December 2004 that he would pull the army out of Gaza after nearly forty years of occupation. He vowed to remove the eight thousand Israeli settlers living there and warned the Palestinians not to treat the withdrawal as a victory.

This decision put Sheikh Yassin's life in jeopardy.

Yassin, a gentle-looking man with a snowy beard and an elfin smile, addressed God from a wheelchair instead of prostrating himself on the ground in the traditional manner because he had been paralyzed at the age of fourteen in a wrestling accident. It was almost unimaginable that this fragile and infirm cleric, whose vision was failing and whose muscles were frozen irreparably by spinal cord trauma, was nonetheless at war with the state of Israel, a war in which Yassin, a profoundly nonviolent man for most of his life, incited the most atrocious acts of violence perpetrated against Israeli civilians and soldiers.

Disengagement might lionize Yassin and Hamas, just as Israel's withdrawal from Lebanon in 2000 had lionized Hezbollah, prompting its leaders to declare victory over the Jewish state. Withdrawal from Gaza could incite a similar reaction from Hamas. So Israel's military establishment focused on how to prevent Hamas from thinking or acting as if it had won.

Yassin, born in 1937 during the British Mandate in Palestine, seemed oblivious of the danger. His family had been chased by the War of 1948 from a farming village near what is now the Israeli city of Ashkelon into Gaza's refugee warrens. Soon thereafter, Yassin's catastrophic injury changed the young man's focus to a life of books and ideas, and after schooling in Gaza under Egyptian rule, he briefly attended university in Cairo, but his poor health and paralysis forced his return to Gaza, where he taught Arabic in a primary school.[1]

His education had introduced him to the Muslim Brotherhood, the religious society founded in 1928 by the Egyptian schoolteacher Hassan al-Banna. The brotherhood promoted Islamic revival as well as government based on the Koran, which threatened Egypt's secular president, Gamal Abdel Nasser, who suppressed its activities. The movement thrived nonetheless in an Islamic society where Nasser's secularism could never fully overpower religious tradition.

Yassin was known for ferocity of spirit; he exuded religious piety and demonstrated keen organizational skills, deploying Hamas to deliver charitable aid to the poor. This made Yassin popular in religiously conservative Gaza. And though he had served nearly a decade in Israeli prisons for exhorting his followers to violence against the occupation, Yassin also evinced a strong pragmatic streak. He had formulated several proposals for a long-term truce—*hudna*—with Israel if the Israelis agreed to end the occupation.

While in prison, Yassin developed an improbable relationship with a Jewish rabbi, Menachem Froman, a founding member of the Israeli settler movement Gush Emunim.

Froman came to believe that the source of Yassin's hatred for the Jewish state was a deep cultural resentment that could be ameliorated over time: "For me," Froman said during an interview at his home in the West Bank settlement Tekoa, "it is because the Israelis are a knife in the Islamic heart.[2]

"Israel for the Muslims is the most extreme expression of American and Western arrogance," he continued. "Americans and Europeans established Israel in order to show how successful a Western state can be and to show them [the Arabs] what a low position they are in." Froman tried but failed to convince Israeli authorities that Yassin was someone with whom they could establish a rapport to negotiate peace.

The Israelis were debating whether Sharon's disengagement would weaken or invigorate Hamas, or whether it would just turn Gaza into a prison, when Yassin stepped up the pressure.

He authorized the dispatch of a female suicide bomber. It was the first time that Hamas had done so. Reem Riyashi, a young mother in her twenties and a member of Hamas, said goodbye to her two children and walked to one of the crossings between Gaza and Israel, a checkpoint called Magen 12. Passing through a metal detector, she triggered the alarm. Asked whether she was carrying a weapon or anything metal, she replied that she had a surgical plate in her leg.

A female Israeli soldier escorted her to an office to examine her, but before she could do so, Riyashi set off the explosive device under her clothing, blowing out windows and walls and killing four Israelis, including the young woman who was to examine her.

Hours later, Israel's deputy defense minister, Ze'ev Boim, who had taken the place of Dalia Rabin, went on Israeli Army Radio to say that "Sheikh Yassin is marked for death, and he should hide himself deep underground" because "we will find him in the tunnels, and we will eliminate him."[3]

Journalists asked Sheikh Yassin whether he was alarmed by the threat. Pausing outside a mosque, he told journalists that "death threats do not frighten us, because we are in search of martyrdom."[4]

At the Directorate of Military Intelligence on the northern outskirts of Tel Aviv, Major General Farkash's aides brought him transcripts of Yassin's remarks where he stated that "Hamas views women as a reserve force. . . . When the military wing of the Hamas saw it necessary to use a woman to carry out an attack, it did so."

Farkash said that the suicide bombing carried out by Riyashi marked the first time that the intelligence agencies got "hard evidence" that Yassin was personally involved in dispatching the human bomb carriers.

"I was convinced," Farkash told me. He took his recommendation to assassinate Yassin to Ya'alon and Mofaz, and finding them in agreement, they went to Sharon.

The nagging question for the Israeli military commanders was whether the elimination of Sheikh Yassin might trigger an even more violent spasm of terror against Israelis, but this was not a crucial consideration for Sharon, who believed in meeting violence with greater violence.

Avi Dichter, the Shabak chief, also favored killing Yassin. Dichter was a firm believer in "mowing the grass." That's how he referred to killing Palestinian militants.

"This was the view," explained Farkash. "All the time we have to mow the grass—all the time—and then the leaders with experience will die, and the others will be without experience, and finally the 'barrel of terror' [a Dichter analogy] will be drained."

The debate over "mowing the grass" had been reported in the Hebrew-language press. It embarrassed Sharon because it displayed the simplistic brutality at the core of Israeli military policy.

The debate revealed, however, that the military technocrats lived in an insular world where the metrics of success were one-dimensional: How well did various applications of lethal force work? The military technocrats lacked the aptitude or affinity for diplomacy. And when they argued among themselves over providing the Palestinians with some political horizon, their efforts were either cast aside by Sharon or abandoned because no Israeli political or military leader since Rabin could withstand the cries for retribution that arose after each act of terror. Rabin had withstood these cries, saying that he would pursue peace as if there were no terror, and fight terror as if there were no peace. But Rabin was dead.

"I told [Dichter] that always the bottom [of the barrel] will be there," said Farkash, "and even if you are cutting down thousands [of Palestinians], always we will have fifty to two hundred people that are part of our [target] list that we have to kill.

"I know that Sharon didn't like this argument between the head of the Shabak and myself about the bottom of the barrel of terror," Farkash added. And so Sharon would say to both intelligence chiefs, "You don't have to discuss this in the media."[5]

The moral objections to targeted assassinations in Israel had lessened as the violence escalated. Even the Ministry of Foreign Affairs, which bore the brunt of international condemnation over assassinations, stood mute.

Alon Liel, a former director general of the Israeli Foreign Ministry, explained the weak hand with which nonmilitary advisers played in their discussions with their uniformed counterparts.

According to Liel, the military men would lecture Israeli diplomats, "Look, we are in a battle every year for our budget, we have to take credit [for assassinations] because we have a lot of criticism from the public about whether we are doing enough to kill these guys, so we don't care about the world, we care about our budget next year. We will get our budget only if we deliver security. You care about the world; you go sell the world what you want to sell them. We have to see to it that next year, we have enough ammunition, and enough airplanes. . . ."[6]

Whatever debate was still under way about Sheikh Yassin was rapidly brought to a close after the explosions on March 14, 2004, at Ashdod Port. Two eighteen-year-old Palestinians from the Jabaliya refugee camp in Gaza had sealed themselves up with explosives behind a false wall of a shipping container that then passed through Israeli checkpoints to reach the loading terminal at Ashdod. Once within the perimeter of the port, the young men broke free from the container and exploded themselves near groups of Israeli civilian employees. One of the blasts killed five people instantly and blew the roof off of a machine shop. In all, ten people were killed and sixteen injured. Both Hamas and Arafat's Fatah claimed responsibility for the operation, which demonstrated that both organizations were competing to show the Arabs that they were struggling to defeat Sharon's plan to wall off their territory.

Just after daybreak on March 22, 2004, Yassin was preparing for morning prayers at a mosque on a dusty street in Gaza City when his son, Mohammed, mentioned reports of an Israeli reconnaissance aircraft spotted nearby.

The old man dismissed the information and spoke of God's will: "To him we belong and to him we return."

The recommendation had originated with Farkash, the chief of military intelligence.

On that cool morning, Sheikh Yassin was wheeled to his car for the short ride to the mosque, where he and his bodyguards entered the sanctuary. Overhead, a loudspeaker was calling the faithful to sunrise prayers with the mantra of a Muslim morning: "In the name of God, the merciful and the compassionate . . ."

A Hellfire missile travels at just under one thousand miles per hour, or Mach 1.3, and so from the moment the Israeli pilot pressed the launch button in his American-made attack helicopter hovering just out of small-arms range above the Gaza Strip, there was barely an instant of cognition between the depression of the thumb, the whooshing sound of rocket ignition, the slight shudder of the helicopter as it let go its projectile, and the explosion on the ground. The five-foot-long missile, because it outpaces the speed of sound, arrived at the target in muted surprise, exploding in a fireball of concussion that drowned the senses and enveloped Yassin and his bodyguards as they wheeled the cleric from the portal of the mosque back toward the waiting car.

The flash and intense heat seared clothing and flesh; the red-hot shrapnel severed arms and legs; the sheikh's wheelchair was disassembled by the force and the whole bloody mass of twisted flesh and metal was slammed to the pavement by the shock wave. One Hellfire missile, with its eighteen-pound high-explosive charge sealed in a casing designed to penetrate tank armor and incinerate a crew, would have been more than enough, but, because an earlier attempt to kill Sheikh Yassin had failed, the Israeli military commander in charge of the assassination team had authorized three Hellfires for the attack. The resulting inferno killed not only the sheikh and his bodyguards but also nine other people who were standing nearby or coming out of the mosque.

In dying, Sheikh Yassin experienced what his bomb makers had inflicted on hundreds of Israeli civilians—women, children, and elderly Jews—and some Israeli Arabs who had been unlucky enough to be riding a bus, or walking through a market when a Hamas bomber appeared.

The explosions awakened Gaza. The cry went out that Israel had murdered Yassin. Sharon rushed to address his Likud Party deputies at the Knesset, calling Yassin "one of Israel's greatest enemies" and "the greatest arch-murderer of Palestinian terrorism" who sought to "kill Jews everywhere and eliminate . . . Israel." Sharon congratulated the combined team of intelligence and air force officers who carried out the operation.[7]

The IDF issued a statement to the news media acknowledging that Yassin had been killed by the state of Israel, describing him as "the authorizing and initiating authority for all Hamas terrorist attacks emanating from the West Bank and Gaza Strip."

A month later, in April 2004, Sharon ordered the assassination of Abdel Aziz Rantissi, the Gaza pediatrician who cofounded Hamas. Rantissi was in his car with two bodyguards when a Hellfire missile soundlessly entered through the roof of the vehicle and exploded.

Rabbi Froman was saddened. He went to Gaza after the death of Yassin and met with Hamas officials. "I haven't killed Ahmed Yassin," he told them. "It was not my deed."

When I visited Froman's home in Tekoa and asked him how he felt about the killing, he said simply, "If Israel is not going to accept being attacked for years and believes that Hamas is not a partner for peace, then Israel has to fight, including killing the leader of Hamas."

But "my whole point," he concluded, "is that there is another way."[8]

The assassination of Sheikh Yassin and the decapitation of Hamas in 2004 did not bring an end to terrorism emanating from the Gaza Strip. Most of the world understood what Ariel Sharon and many of the men at the top of the Israeli military would never understand: there was no military solution in Gaza or the West Bank.

Sheikh Yassin was one of hundreds of Palestinian militants targeted for assassination during Sharon's premiership in what seemed like an orgy of killing on both sides, but the state-sanctioned murder of this old cleric who had been calling out for martyrdom seemed to reflect Sharon's profound exasperation. The brutal application of military force, which was the hallmark of Sharon's approach, was failing him.

The more Sharon slashed at the Palestinians with all of the tools of the army and the intelligence services, the more the suicide bombers, the gunmen, and the kidnappers kept coming. All attempts to persuade Sharon to open a channel for negotiation had proved futile. Israelis were falling deeper and deeper into a state of helplessness. After three years in office, Sharon's strategy seemed no more sophisticated than increasing gradations of scorched earth. By 2004 it was apparent that Israel under Sharon was sputtering grotesquely without any path to a solution.

Since he was a teenager in the Jewish underground, Sharon had lived by a unitary code in the conflict with the Arabs: hit hard, take few prisoners, and never compromise. As a seventy-four-year-old politician, the target of multiple corruption investigations, reviled by many as the spoiler of peace, Sharon nonetheless stood as no prime minister before him: the quintessential standard bearer of Israeli militarism. And yet the man who believed that every security threat could be defeated by military means and that the only valid response to terrorism was war, had reached his wit's end: state-directed violence had become as trivial and banal as the assassination of a paraplegic preacher.

Sharon could easily have sent soldiers to arrest the cleric: Yassin was not in hiding or on the run, and Israel had arrested him before. And when the deed was done, when Yassin was incinerated by missiles fired from a multimillion-dollar bird of prey hovering over the squalor of Gaza, there was something obscenely excessive about it all. What did Yassin's death really achieve, other than confirming the truism that a long line of even more militant Hamas leaders would replace him? Where was Sharon taking the country?

For Sharon, there was nothing left but war, or disengagement, or both.

He deluded himself that this decapitation of Hamas would somehow restore "deterrence."

"We eliminated the leaders of Hamas—Yassin and Rantissi—and other terrorist heads when the time was right," Sharon told his favorite propagandist, Uri Dan. "The same principle goes for Yasser Arafat. We will treat him like the others. I see no difference between him and Yassin: they both murder Jews.

"For Arafat," he continued, "we will choose the time that suits us best. Everyone will receive his due."[9]

Arafat's time came sooner than anyone expected. He fell seriously ill after dinner one evening in October 2004 and was flown to France, where his immune system rapidly collapsed. He died on November 11 at a military hospital of an undiagnosed illness. His death raised questions whether he had been assassinated by an exotic and undetectable pathogen.

"I don't know what happened," Farkash, the intelligence chief, told me. "We decided not to be involved [investigating] the pathology because in any case we knew they would blame us." So Israel's intelligence community took the position it did not want to know who or what killed its most important adversary. All they knew was that it came at a good time, because Arafat stood as an obstacle to change in the Palestinian territories.

Sharon went forward with disengagement in 2005. The separation wall in the West Bank went forward, too—with many legal challenges and some adjustments to its route, but it rose over the landscape nonetheless. Sharon spent an inordinate amount of time arguing with Ya'alon, his chief of staff, who opposed disengagement as a form of surrender. Sharon arranged for Ya'alon's early retirement.

The old warrior was in flight from corruption investigations that would force his son, Omri, to resign from the Knesset and plead guilty to taking kickbacks. It turned out that millions had been paid to the Sharon family in alleged bribes, and the investigation might well have reached Sharon personally had he not suffered a massive stroke in early January 2006 that left him in a vegetative state.

Sharon's collapse drew more expressions of shock than regret. Reviled and feared for most of his life, Sharon lay comatose, unwilling, it seemed, to surrender even to death.

In a valedictory interview, Ya'alon said he saw no end to the Israeli-Palestinian dispute in his lifetime. "We must recognize that we are destined to remain a warring society," he said, and the Jewish state "is fated to live by the sword for a long time."[10]

TWENTY

Olmert: Putting Lebanon Back Twenty Years

Economically, the Jewish state was roaring. "Disengagement" and "security" didn't play well in the Western press, but they apparently were good for business, even as the peace process sputtered.

The coastal strip north of Tel Aviv was a new Silicon Valley, with many companies listed on America's Nasdaq stock exchange; the real estate market along the Mediterranean rivaled Manhattan for luxury and high prices. Boardwalks and bistros lined the seafront, and thousands of young professionals enjoyed the café and discotheque society of Tel Aviv nights. It was as if they had created their own bubble as a prophylaxis against the unease.

Half the country was on the new six-lane freeways pursuing the new affluence, and half the country was at the beach. Young Israelis lived completely separate lives from young Palestinians; it was illegal for Israelis to visit the occupied territories except on the segregated bypass roads on which settlers traveled to their outposts. The Palestinian existence was being—if not erased—transported to a less visible zone behind a concrete curtain whose sickening profile on the biblical landscape evoked Northern Ireland during the Troubles or Berlin during the cold war.

The country had gone through ten straight years of suicide bombers and low-intensity war with the Palestinians.

And the founding generation was coming to an end, so many Israelis were asking: Who would lead?

By the time Sharon slipped into insentience in early 2006, Israel's leadership class resembled a fractured and self-absorbed community whose constituent parts were tethered, blindly, it seemed, to religious, ethnic, or nationalist affiliations.

The only institution in Israeli life that served as a repository of national self-confidence was the military establishment, especially the army, but it, too, was riven with ideological wedges.

Sharon's deputy prime minister, Ehud Olmert, the popular former mayor of Jerusalem and a sabra of the right, stepped forward to grasp the reins of government, but there was little certainty that Olmert possessed what the country needed.

Under Sharon, Olmert's role was that of a weather vane, broaching controversial subjects such as the disengagement from Gaza, enabling Sharon to read the feedback from the news media, from the army, and from other important constituencies.

In his final months, Sharon had formed a new political party, Kadima (Forward), to jettison the Likud and the opposition that had formed around Benjamin Netanyahu, his younger rival.

Netanyahu pilloried Sharon: "[He] has abandoned the way of Likud and chosen another way, the way of the left."[1]

He accused Sharon, of all people, of surrendering to the Palestinians. "Sharon gave and gave and gave some more, and the Palestinians got more and more and more," Netanyahu shouted out to his party. "And what did we get in return? The answer is: Nothing, nothing and nothing."[2]

The truth was Sharon had left the country perilously adrift. The Gaza disengagement was merely a military quarantine of Gaza's 1.4 million Arabs for an indefinite period. Like many a prime minister before him, Sharon had bought time.

In January 2006, the Palestinian elections delivered a sweeping victory to Hamas, throwing much of the world into a quandary over how to support Palestinian democracy when an avowed terrorist movement had swept the field by democratic means, not terrorism. Islamic radicals had taken 76 out of 120 seats in the Palestinian parliament, leaving the party of Arafat, Fatah, with 43.*

---

*Fatah had allowed multiple candidates to run in many districts, whereas Hamas aggregated its votes behind a single candidate in each district. The result made Hamas look disproportionately strong, and its victory threw the Palestinian camp into turmoil with spasms of armed conflict.

Olmert knew that he could never command the military establishment like Sharon. Olmert was an affable apparatchik of the right wing. He had been a minister of trade, a minister of health; he had crusaded against organized crime. He and Sharon had entered the Knesset together in 1973 and so Olmert could fall back on his many years of experience, but he was never going to be more than a transitional figure heavily reliant on the military establishment.

Born in 1945 in Nahalat Jabotinsky, a district in northern Israel populated by former fighters for the Irgun underground, Olmert had grown up in the bosom of right-wing politics. His family had fled Ukraine early in the twentieth century as revolutionary forces were sweeping the Russian empire, but they got only as far as China, where Olmert's father, Mordechai, a devotee of Jabotinsky's Revisionist Party, built the Betar youth chapter in the Manchurian city of Harbin.

The family finally reached Palestine in 1933. Mordechai joined the Irgun to help drive the British out of Palestine. After statehood in 1948, his sons—including Ehud—became part of the generation of Israeli youth divorced from the political mainstream, where Ben-Gurion and the Mapai dominated. In 1963, Olmert reported for his military service, but he barely served. Inducted into the Thirteenth Regiment of the elite Golani Brigade, Olmert was deemed unfit for combat duty due to preexisting injuries, which he has always refused to specify.

He entered Hebrew University, where he read law and joined a small right-wing political group allied with Menachem Begin's Herut Party. At the age of twenty-one, Olmert gained national notoriety when he stood up at a party conference and called on Begin to resign over Herut's poor showing in the 1965 elections, triggering a near riot in the hall as delegates surged forward to physically remove the obstreperous young man. It was said that Begin himself protected Olmert at the podium, and six years later, Olmert became the youngest Israeli to win a seat in the Knesset.

Unlike most Israeli men his age, Olmert did not return to the army in 1967 to fight in the Six-Day War; four years later, in 1971, he sought to burnish his military record by taking officer training, but when the Yom Kippur War broke out in 1973, Olmert was not assigned a combat role. He was dispatched as a correspondent by an army magazine to Sharon's headquarters in Sinai, where he joined other journalists, such as Uri Dan of *Ma'ariv*, to construct the heroic narrative of Sharon as commander of the "Likud

Division" fighting its way across the Suez Canal. It was the closest Olmert ever came to combat.

Still, many Israelis had come to admire Olmert, in part for his long service as mayor of Jerusalem (1993–2003) and also for his pragmatic approach to government. His wife, Aliza, and most of his five children, were far more liberal than he was—they supported Palestinian statehood and an end to the occupation—and that was generally known. Thus Olmert's management of the political contradictions within his family struck a chord with the public, where many families were similarly divided.

But the military establishment was hardly in awe of Ehud Olmert.

When Olmert led Sharon's Kadima Party into the March 2006 elections, many Israelis may have felt they had little choice but to vote for a continuation of Sharon's policies as the old warhorse lay in a coma. It was either Olmert or Amir Peretz, the come-from-nowhere Labor Party boss whose Moroccan ancestry, political skills, and dovish views had propelled him to the top of the Labor establishment. He had ousted Shimon Peres and fought off a challenge from Ehud Barak. (Peres quit the Labor Party and joined Sharon and Olmert in the new Kadima Party.)

Among the stragglers in the balloting was Netanyahu, demonstrating that Israelis did not yet see him as fit to return to high office.

Could civilians actually run the Jewish state?

What emerged that spring was a government of neophytes.

Olmert—over the objections of military chiefs—appointed Amir Peretz minister of defense, putting a civilian with scant experience in charge of the military establishment. It was as if the generals had been expelled from the cabinet room for the first time since 1967.

Tzipi Livni took over Israeli diplomacy as minister of foreign affairs. Livni was a novelty: not since Golda Meir had a woman risen to such high office. A child of prominent right-wing Irgun fighters, Livni had served in Paris as a Mossad officer from 1980 to 1984. Here was a woman of the intelligence establishment, a sabra who had worked undercover in Europe, a follower of Sharon who had broken with Likud's dream of Greater Israel, and who had helped to formulate the Gaza disengagement plan. And, with all of her right-wing credentials, she was also suspected of being a pragmatic centrist who was interested in returning to the negotiating table with the Palestinians.

"I want things to happen, especially when it comes to the Israeli-Palestinian conflict," she told an interviewer. With regard to the Arabs, she said, "Each of us can live with our narrative, so long as we are pragmatic when it comes to the land." She said that she still believed in Israel's right to all of biblical Israel, but she also believed in compromise. "We cannot solve who was right or wrong in 1948 or decide who is more just. The Palestinians can feel justice is on their side, and I can feel it is on my side. What we have to decide about is not history but the future."[3] Hers was a fresh voice, perhaps profoundly so, but there was a reticence in Livni, an uptightness that was palpable and that could be deadly for a politician. Her friends wondered whether this shy and intense daughter of extremists had the charisma or the fire for leadership—and the guile for politics.

Olmert presented his government to the public on May 4, 2006, and by the end of the month, the military situation on Israel's northern border had deteriorated. Hezbollah had so expanded its deployment of militants armed with missiles and other weapons smuggled in from Iran and Syria that its commanders had grown overconfident, seemingly oblivious of Israel's red lines.

Hezbollah chief Hassan Nasrallah bragged that "all of Israel is in our range—ports, military bases, factories—everything is in our range" and with a "huge" arsenal of "quality weapons," he added, Hezbollah could rain down "thousands of rockets" on Israeli cities in any offensive.

The Israeli military was under the command of General Dan Halutz, the former air force chief who had perfected the use of precision bombs to assassinate Palestinian militant leaders. Halutz was born in Tel Aviv to a family of Sephardic Jews. Farsi was spoken at home because Halutz's father had emigrated from Iran (his mother was Iraqi). Sharon had rewarded Halutz by elevating him to be chief of staff in 2005, passing over the army's candidate, Gabi Ashkenazi, a sabra who fought in Sinai in 1973 and who had commanded the Golani Brigade.

Olmert hadn't been in office even two months when he faced his first crisis. Hezbollah and Hamas had been employing hit-and-run tactics to strike at Israeli army patrols and, in June, Hamas fighters succeeded in tunneling across the Gaza perimeter to an Israeli tank position. They struck with rocket-propelled grenades and rifle fire, killing two Israeli soldiers and capturing a third, Gilad Shalit. They dragged the twenty-year-old corporal to a Gaza hideout, where he was held hostage for five years while his freedom was the subject of protracted negotiations. (He was finally released in October 2011 in a prisoner exchange.)

Next to strike was Hezbollah in the north, staging rocket attacks on several villages as a prelude to an ambush on an Israeli patrol, where Hezbollah fighters killed three soldiers and carried off two other Israelis, Ehud Goldwasser and Eldad Regev, who were either mortally wounded or dead. After the Israelis discovered that their patrol was missing, a Merkava tank force burst across the border to rescue the soldiers, only to be destroyed by a large land mine that killed all four Israeli crew members. A fifth soldier on the rescue team also died before commanders called off the operation.

The loss of so many soldiers sickened Israelis and made them yearn for revenge. General Halutz arrived in the prime minister's office with plans for a large-scale reprisal—not on Hezbollah, but on Lebanon more broadly.

Both the civilian and military leadership were untested and unprepared. Peretz was poorly equipped even to understand how much the combat readiness of the IDF had been degraded by extended deployments and garrison duty in the Palestinian territories. The generals complained, just before they were called upon to mobilize, that the IDF had become a "hollow" and "mediocre" army. As one general explained in private to the prime minister, "Here and there are islands of excellence," but the main force was "a sea of mediocrity."[4]

Olmert was out to become Mr. Security with a muscular show of force. "The events of this morning cannot be considered a terrorist strike," he told journalists. "They are the acts of a sovereign state that has attacked Israel without cause. The Lebanese government, which Hezbollah is part of, is trying to upset regional stability. . . . We will not give in to the blackmail or negotiate with terrorists on any aspect of the lives of IDF soldiers."[5]

Halutz arrived with plans "to put Lebanon back twenty years" with a massive bombing campaign. "We have to put out the lights in Lebanon," he told Peretz in a meeting with the chiefs of staff. "We can shut off their electricity for a year."

Olmert was all in.

The Mossad chief, Meir Dagan, wanted a bombing campaign against Syria, but the consensus was to strike and to strike big, and to do so quickly before pressure from Washington or European diplomacy could intervene to prevent a full measure of revenge.

It was as if the genome of Ben-Gurion and Dayan was coiled in each of them. The militarist impulse did not allow any discussion of alternatives. When Tzipi Livni questioned the scale of the military operation, beginning with the massive bombing strike on Beirut's Dahia neighborhood where Hezbollah was headquartered, Olmert tuned her out.

"When I began speaking, the prime minister started talking with the chief of staff or someone. I held my tongue," Livni recalled in testimony after the war.

Livni glared at Olmert until he noticed.

"Go ahead," the prime minister said.

"I want you to hear me out," Livni replied sharply.

"I'm listening to every word you say, to every vibration," Olmert replied.

Livni made the point that "the operation will not end by military means. Hezbollah will not willingly get up and leave. Goals must be set. The operation won't bring the soldiers back. The solution can only be a political one."[6]

But no one was having it. Livni "came away feeling that the IDF officers and Olmert were impatient and anxious to get on with the bombing."

Lebanon was so weakened by earlier invasions that the central government no longer controlled most of its territory. Syria's army had pulled out of Lebanon during the Cedar Revolution of 2005, triggered by the assassination of Rafik Hariri, the architect of Lebanon's restoration during the 1990s. His attempts to disarm Lebanon's militia forces had largely succeeded, with one exception: Hezbollah. Its well-armed military, backed by Iran's Revolutionary Guard and Syrian intelligence, still reigned in the southern half of the country.

In thirty-four days, the military rampage that came to be called the Second Lebanon War put a million Lebanese to flight, killed more than one thousand civilians, and wounded four thousand more. When Hezbollah responded with missile strikes into Israel, setting off a general panic, Halutz reportedly ordered the air force to flatten ten multistory apartment buildings in Beirut for every Hezbollah rocket fired into Israel.[7]

The Israeli air force and artillery batteries destroyed more than sixteen thousand homes, commercial structures, major roads and bridges, schools, ports, and two hospitals. One errant Israeli bomb struck an apartment building in Qana on July 30, the same town where errant artillery fire had slaughtered one hundred civilians in 1996. This time, twenty-eight civilians died, more than half of them children.[8]

Though Israeli air force planes destroyed Hezbollah's most advanced missiles, all of them hidden in residential structures and capable of striking major Israeli cities, Hezbollah lashed out with waves of rocket fire into Israel, killing 43 people, nearly half of them Israeli Arabs, and forcing 350,000 people to evacuate their homes and hide in bomb shelters. Hezbollah's advanced weapons included sea-skimming antiship missiles, one of which killed four Israeli sailors on the INS *Hanit* off Beirut.

Olmert's spirits lifted when major voices in the Arab world condemned Hezbollah—Iran's ally and stalking horse—for provoking an all-out war that would only ravage Lebanon.

Jordan's king Abdullah II and Egypt's president Hosni Mubarak criticized Hezbollah for "irresponsible and escalatory acts." Saudi Arabia's foreign minister, Saud al-Faisal, said Hezbollah's actions were "dishonorable," adding, "They will put the region back years and are utterly unacceptable."[9]

Washington seemed to be applauding Israel when Condoleezza Rice, the national security adviser, declared "this is no time for a cease-fire" as Israeli warplanes and bombers continued to streak north.

Olmert, the rare Israeli with absolutely no military experience, stood as a tribune of war before his people. "There are moments in the life of a nation when it is compelled to look directly into the face of reality and say, 'No more!'" he told the deputies.

From the opposition benches, Netanyahu exhorted the prime minister to greater levels of violence: "Fight them—smash them!"[10]

A week into the war, some of Olmert's advisers began to ask where it would lead. Perhaps it was time, some suggested, to declare victory and withdraw, leaving the Arabs to blame Hezbollah for reckless provocation.

But Olmert was soaring on the adrenaline of the campaign. He consulted some of his most trusted friends in the security establishment because the next big decision was whether to launch a ground war into

Lebanon to consolidate the gains of the air force and clean out the under-ground warehouses and tunnel networks that Hezbollah used to carry on its guerrilla attacks. Many of Olmert's advisers warned of the dangers of ground operations. Some told him to quit while he was ahead.

The former Shabak chief Jacob Peri received a telephone call from Olmert at the crucial moment of decision. Peri believed that he had con-vinced the prime minister that the ground war would be a mistake. The army was not performing well; the air force campaign was turning Lebanon into a humanitarian nightmare. It was time to get out.[11]

"I told him that we should stop," Peri told me. He advised Olmert, "We should come to a cease-fire. You made enough failures and the street is angry."

After the conversation, Peri went home for an afternoon nap. "I was sure that everything was okay, and then I woke up and opened the televi-sion, we [the army] are inside [Lebanon]."[12]

Invading Lebanon again proved disastrous for Israel and for Olmert. Hezbollah fighters, though outgunned, held a remarkable advantage on their home turf, where they laid ambushes, resupplied themselves from hidden tunnel networks, and took advantage of the "hollow" Israeli army that was short of equipment and ill prepared for ground combat opera-tions that had been ordered up too hastily to succeed.

Prominent figures, including the writers Amos Oz, A. B. Yehoshua, and David Grossman, publicly beseeched Olmert to conclude a cease-fire. Two days after their statement, Grossman's son, Uri, was killed when a Hezbol-lah missile struck his tank in southern Lebanon. In all, nearly 120 Israeli soldiers lost their lives in a war of choice that did not achieve its objectives. Soon after the UN cease-fire was put in place on August 14, 2006, Boogie Ya'alon, the former chief of staff who had followed the war from Washington where he was spending the summer at a pro-Israel think tank, called on Olmert to resign, accusing the prime minister of laying on a poorly planned offensive in the last two days of the war for "political spin" at the cost of thirty-three soldiers' lives.

"You don't send soldiers to carry out a futile mission after the political outcome has already been set," Ya'alon told *Ha'aretz*. "It had no substan-tive security-political goal, only a spin goal. It was meant to supply the missing victory picture.

"This is not the way to go to war," Ya'alon continued. "Going to war was scandalous, and he [Olmert] is directly responsible for that. . . . He was warned and he did not heed the warnings. Therefore, he must resign."[13]

Olmert's decision making not only enraged Ya'alon; it also irritated the Americans, who, according to Ya'alon, wanted Israel to exploit the opportunity of the war to strike Damascus and topple Assad so as to undermine Iran's most important ally. Ya'alon passed on the message, but Olmert heeded the advice of his own security establishment: removing Assad would only lead to dangerous instability and would likely usher in an even more radical regime.

In the end, the Knesset demanded a review of the war, which was conducted by a commission chaired by retired justice Eliyahu Winograd, whose blistering report emerged the following spring. It concluded that Israel had initiated a war without preparing "a detailed, comprehensive and authorized military plan." Olmert, his cabinet, and the military chiefs had failed to first "consider the whole range of options" short of war, and the overall leadership failure "reflects weakness in strategic thinking" at the top. Olmert was charged with serious failure of "judgment, responsibility and prudence."[14]

In a military culture, no condemnation could cut deeper.

Dan Halutz was the first high-level casualty for having sold the public a phony vision of a massive air campaign erasing Hezbollah from the political map. Already reeling from accusations that he had traded on inside government information to protect his own assets—selling off stocks on the eve of the war—Halutz resigned in January 2007, and Gabi Ashkenazi came out of retirement to take the post that Sharon had denied him.

Halutz's resignation was soon followed by Amir Peretz's. The feckless defense minister had never overcome a photograph snapped while he was reviewing military maneuvers with binoculars whose lens caps were still attached. His departure paved the way for Ehud Barak to return to the government as minister of defense.

Tzipi Livni, the most prominent cabinet member who had pressed Olmert to consider options short of war, called on the prime minister to resign, a step that could have catapulted her into the prime minister's office, though she said, incongruously, that was not her aim.

But even after the Winograd findings shredded the prime minister's standing before the public and took his popularity rating to 3 percent, Olmert clung to power.

Corruption investigations into whether he had steered contracts and accepted illicit funds gained momentum, but still he held on. More than one hundred thousand Israelis flooded Rabin Square in Tel Aviv in May 2007 calling for the government to step down in the wake of the Winograd Commission findings. Uzi Dayan—nephew of Moshe Dayan and a former national security adviser—told the crowd that the time had come for all Israelis to say, "Enough!"[15]

But Olmert dared the political establishment to bring him down. That would open a path for Netanyahu's return. Public opinion polls showed him leading the pack of political figures who were circling Olmert's political carcass.

Netanyahu preened in the Knesset. "As a result of the last war, it seems to many of our enemies that a weak hand grasps the Sword of David," he said, playing on the military metaphor to remind voters that he had served in "the unit" while Olmert avoided combat in Israel's wars.[16]

How could the public and the military establishment, which had so thoroughly rejected Netanyahu as a reckless and failed leader, restore him as a favorite to return to the prime minister's office? Part of the answer lay in the fact that Netanyahu was winning public approval by default; the more Olmert's political coalition crumbled, the more Netanyahu benefited by holding that familiar position on the Israeli right where a warrior figure could galvanize the large right-wing base of the electorate by hectoring the government for weakness and hesitation. Sharon had made no less a comeback. Netanyahu was vying for the mantle of Sharon as a sabra who knew how to fight, how to influence Washington, how to tame the domestic economy, and how to stiff-arm the Arabs. With Olmert discredited, and Livni unwilling or unable to project herself as a national leader, Netanyahu was the beneficiary of political convergence: religious Jews, Russian immigrants, and right-of-center parties disenchanted with what they perceived as the serial failures of the peace camp and, now, the failure of Olmert.

For all the reasons that Netanyahu was ascending, Ehud Barak, by contrast, was still confined in the political wilderness. He may have been the most hated politician in Israel.

Though Barak had wrested control of the Labor Party from Amir

Peretz, the party of Ben-Gurion cast the weakest shadow in its long history. Only Barak's vanity could imagine a path back to power. The new Barak had even less of a common touch than the old one. He returned to government as a man of conspicuous wealth. Where had it come from? Israelis asked. Barak had spent his life in the army, and then in government service, yet he wanted the public to believe that a short stint in the private sector had made him rich. He and his new wife moved into a high-rise luxury apartment that cost millions of dollars. In a country that had been founded by European Socialists, Barak's wealth raised questions. Israelis recalled that White House transcripts released in 2001 documented that Barak had sought a pardon from Bill Clinton for the fugitive financier and oil trader Marc Rich.

Amnon Lipkin-Shahak, the former chief of staff who knew Barak as well as any Israeli, said that for many, just to live as Barak did in a gilded tower forty stories above the modest masonry apartments of the working class was to live "in a bubble" like someone "not really in touch with the Israeli public."[17]

Nonetheless, Olmert needed Barak. He was still Israel's most decorated soldier. The Israeli public didn't like him, but the military establishment made up Barak's core competence, and the military needed rebuilding after the Lebanon debacle. The public accepted the logic of Olmert's reliance on Barak's management skill. He could return as Mr. Security, but that seemed the extent of it.

For Olmert, there was another benefit: Barak had been Netanyahu's commander in "the unit," Sayeret Matkal, and therefore Barak's presence in the cabinet shielded Olmert from Netanyahu's stinging criticism of his incompetence in the military realm.

Yet the addition of Barak did little to reverse Olmert's descent. The only thing that was preventing Olmert's rivals from bringing down the government was the fear of Netanyahu's return. The political barons who had joined Olmert and who had rallied to Sharon's Kadima Party banner did not want to fail. Many saw Olmert as the lesser evil.

And so Olmert stretched his collapsing premiership month after month, hoping that he could pull some rabbit out of the hat that might save him. He had tried war, and so he turned to peace.

In early 2007, Olmert embraced the Saudi peace initiative, which was the land-for-peace formula first proposed in March 2002; he praised King Abdullah of Saudi Arabia and said he was ready to meet and negotiate with the Arab leaders.

"As a young politician, I voted against the return of Sinai and peace with Egypt," Olmert wrote in 2007 in an essay in the *Guardian* of London. "I was mistaken."

The new Olmert, he said, would "not hesitate to take bold initiatives to advance peace, even if they require heavy concessions."[18] He opened secret negotiations with Syria, which he had long avoided because of resistance from George W. Bush's administration, where regime change was the favored policy. Olmert hoped that he could convince Bashar al-Assad to pick up the deal that his father had almost accepted in 2000.

It was difficult to read whether Olmert had reached an epiphany in his personal and political life—he was confronting the onset of prostate cancer—or whether he was merely searching for some triage that would breathe life back into his political corpse. He began to speak with a less strident voice about the big issues of war and peace with the Arabs, and he seemed to question whether militarism had set the country on a course that would leave the Jewish state in control of a Palestinian population larger than its own.

The nightmare of a binational state was that Israel would either have to grant all of the Palestinians citizenship and lose its Jewish identity, or it would have to subjugate them in perpetuity in an apartheid arrangement. Olmert was only the latest secular nationalist to wake up to this dark vision. Whether or not his political conversion was genuine, it added to the sense of desperation that he must do what was necessary to stay in power, to block Netanyahu's return, and to fight for a reconciliation with the Arabs, a momentous step for which, he said, he was ready.

Olmert's weakness left him few prospects to advance. If he truly offered a land-for-peace deal to the Arabs, one that would divide Jerusalem and establish a Palestinian state, his government coalition would collapse, pulled down by the extreme right and religious parties that rejected compromise, especially over Jerusalem.

The Palestinians understood this. They also had made peace more complicated.

In June 2007, Hamas went to war to purge its rival, Fatah, from all government institutions in the Gaza Strip. Hamas militants overran Fatah's bases, blew up Fatah's headquarters in the Khan Yunis refugee camp, and arrested many of its security forces.

As Arafat's political heir, Mahmoud Abbas was devastated by Hamas's show of strength. Central authority lay in tatters. Abbas's own home in Gaza was surrounded. Only the West Bank remained under his control. Gaza, for the first time, was fully in Hamas's hands, and its leaders called out for solidarity with jihadists across the region.

They asked for financial assistance from Iran and smuggled weapons into the territory from wherever they could find them. Israel's military establishment looked in shock at what Sharon's disengagement plan had spawned.

The Israelis started calling Gaza Hamastan.

TWENTY-ONE

War (on Syria) War (on Gaza) War (on Iran?)

For months Olmert had been sitting on a secret that his Mossad director had brought to him with all the gravity that the military and intelligence establishments could convey: Syria was building a nuclear reactor.

The most dangerous Arab regime in the Middle East was in the midst of a secret program to become the first Arab nuclear power. The construction site, on a bluff overlooking the Euphrates River near the Turkish border, had been photographed by Israeli intelligence. The CIA, apparently, was unaware of the facility.[1]

North Korean technicians had been detected in Syria. Mossad agents had purloined detailed photographs, perhaps from a laptop computer, showing interior and exterior views of the reactor. Its design appeared to be identical to a North Korean facility at Yongbyon, which produces plutonium for nuclear weapons.

Israel was already facing what some considered an existential threat from the burgeoning nuclear industry in Iran, which it suspected of conducting secret research on atomic weapons.

Now Syria was building a plutonium production reactor which, if fueled and operated, could begin producing weapons-grade fissile material, assuming that was Syria's intention, within a few years.

Not since Begin's decision to bomb Iraq's Osirak reactor in 1981 had Israel faced such direct challenges to its nuclear exclusivity in the Middle East.

Another complicating factor was that Olmert was engaged in secret peace negotiations with Syria using Turkish diplomats as intermediaries.

In April and again in June 2007, after meeting with his intelligence chiefs, Olmert made public statements indicating that Israel was calibrating its policy toward Syria with great caution.

"Israel does not want war with Syria and we need to be careful to avoid a scenario of miscalculations that could cause the security situation to worsen," Olmert said.[2] The news media believed that Olmert was speaking in generalities about the secret peace talks and their prospects for success. But Olmert was engaged in a very complex scheme that combined coercion and diplomacy.

When his Mossad chief, Meir Dagan, informed him of the Syrian reactor in the desert, Olmert and the military establishment had to consider their options. Should Israel expose the reactor and seek UN action to dismantle it? Should the Israeli air force destroy the reactor? Should Olmert ask the United States to destroy it?

Israel's deliberations on these questions remain secret, but Olmert's actions suggest that he and the military hoped to use the Syria crisis to draw the United States into a larger scheme against both Syria and Iran.

Olmert dispatched a confidential report on the Syrian reactor to the White House in June. He followed up with a secure telephone call to President Bush.

"George, I'm asking you to bomb the compound," Olmert said, explaining in a subsequent call that "this is something that hits at the very serious nerves of this country." It was an "existential" threat.[3]

It is not clear whether Bush understood all the ramifications of Olmert's request.

For more than a year, Vice President Dick Cheney had been pressing Bush to consider bombing Iran's nuclear facilities. Cheney had worried aloud to an old friend, Prince Bandar bin Sultan of Saudi Arabia, that Bush might be "losing his nerve" to use force in the Middle East.[4]

In the telephone call with Olmert, Bush, by his own account, showed no curiosity why Israel, which had acted alone in 1981 to destroy Iraq's Osirak reactor, now wanted the United States to take the lead in bombing a Syrian reactor, which had no apparent source of fuel and which the CIA judged not to be an urgent threat to anyone.

Was this Olmert and the military establishment drawing America into a joint enterprise—a strike on Syria that would be a dress rehearsal for an attack on Iran? I put that question to Olmert through his spokesman after he left office and I am still waiting for an answer.

By 2007, Israel's military elite had come to the conclusion that a preemptive strike on Iran was crucial to thwart Iranian nuclear ambitions. But the military also believed the operation was too large, too complex, and too risky for Israel to undertake alone.

Israeli policy focused on convincing the United States to lead the international community in sanctioning Iran and, if that did not work, to strike Iran militarily in order to degrade its nuclear industry. Indeed, Bush had tasked the Pentagon in 2006 to study options for such a military assault on Iran.[5]

In reliving the summer of 2007, Bush makes no reference to how the threats from the Syrian and Iranian nuclear programs were joined at the moment he found himself on the secure line with Olmert.

Bush explains that he ordered a full review of the Syrian reactor by CIA director Michael Hayden. CIA analysts quickly concluded that the reactor was constructed, like its North Korean template, to produce plutonium for nuclear weapons. The CIA could find no uranium fuel source for the reactor, and no plutonium separation facility. On that basis and, with an abundance of caution, Hayden told the president that the CIA had "low confidence" the Syrian reactor was part of a nuclear weapons program.[6]

After the CIA's disastrous manipulation of intelligence prior to the Iraq invasion, Hayden's caution was understandable, though his logic was distorted to allow Bush to step back from what would have been a highly controversial military operation at a time when the United States remained bogged down in Iraq. (What would Hayden have said about Israel's Dimona reactor in 1960?)

Dick Cheney pressed Bush to bomb the reactor, but Bush begged off, telling Olmert, "I cannot justify an attack on a sovereign nation unless my intelligence agencies stand up and say it's a weapons program." Bush decided on a diplomatic option to "expose the facility and demand that Syria shutter and dismantle it under the supervision of the IAEA."[7]

Yet Bush never explains what happened to this diplomatic option, or why he did not insist that Israel hold in abeyance any military planning to give diplomacy a chance. Bush recounts that he did not give Israel a green light, but how else could Olmert read Bush's unwillingness to insist on a diplomatic track?

The Israeli military establishment followed the logic that if it "walked like a duck," there was no question about Syria's intentions, even if those intentions were not yet fully realized.

At home, Olmert faced another daunting obstacle.

Barak questioned the wisdom of mounting a major bombing raid on Syria without a parallel diplomatic strategy to prevent Damascus from retaliating. An act of war so blatant might trigger a massive response, not only from Syria but also from Hezbollah, which was sitting on thousands of rockets aimed at Israel, putting more than a million Israelis in the line of fire. An attack might also provoke Iranian reprisals against Israeli embassies and other targets around the world.

In an interview in 2009, I asked Barak about his reported opposition to Olmert's plan to attack Syria. He hedged his answer carefully because Israel had yet to publicly acknowledge the raid.

"I made a point that we should not rush into an operation before thinking of all the consequences and preparing ourselves slowly for every implication," Barak told me. "If you want to execute a certain operation, and make sure it's done in a way that will not impose a war, a regional war, we have to think, slowly, what it means to shape an operation in a way that will not make the rest of the cascade automatic."

Barak told me he was thinking of the Second Lebanon War and how blatant militarism without any diplomatic component had spun out of control. Barak, who had designed so many grand military exercises that had gone awry, was saying that he had tried to impress upon Olmert that they should strike Syria in a manner that left Assad his dignity as well as a diplomatic option to continue the secret peace talks.

"I insisted on never embarrassing Bashar," Barak said. "We are strong enough to destroy this regime in Syria, or to defeat it militarily," but the point was that Barak believed, and apparently so did Olmert, that it was possible to carry out the act of war in such a way that Assad could ignore it, pretend that it did not occur. Deniability was critical, and to create deniability it was essential that Israel avoid crowing over its attack.

After sharing the evidence on the Syrian reactor with the United States and Great Britain, Olmert and his military high command believed that there was a reasonable chance that Bashar al-Assad would suffer the blow in silence.

On the night of September 5, 2007, a flight of American-made F-15s took off from the Ramat David Air Base south of Haifa and flew a diversionary route west over the Mediterranean before turning north and east to enter Syrian airspace in the early morning hours of September 6. They made a run toward the remote Syrian desert, where they loosed a spray of two-thousand-pound bombs to penetrate the concrete shell of the reactor containment building and destroy the reactor within.

The Israeli jets then banked toward Turkish airspace, where they dropped their spare fuel tanks in an act that roiled the Turkish military. Olmert telephoned Turkish prime minister Recep Tayyip Erdogan and revealed what had just occurred. Olmert asked Erdogan to call Assad and explain to him that Israel would not tolerate a nuclear power on its northern flank. At the same time, he made clear that Israel had no further aggressive intentions toward Damascus. Indeed, Olmert was still interested in concluding peace with Syria.

The morning after the attack, rumors were rampant. Syria reported an incursion of its airspace but nothing else. Commentators speculated that Israel had bombed a suspect facility, but Olmert slapped state censorship on Israeli news media.

Bush wanted to trumpet the news as a means to further isolate Syria.

"Olmert told me he wanted total secrecy," Bush recounted. "He wanted to avoid anything that might back Syria into a corner and force Assad to retaliate." Bush did not mention the Israeli-Syrian negotiations.

Israel went to extraordinary lengths to limit news of its attack on Syria.

As a result, some experts outside the government had bruising encounters with the Israeli military censor. One of the experts invited by the news media to comment about the raid was Alon Liel, the former director general of the Foreign Ministry and a former ambassador to Turkey. Liel had been instrumental in opening the secret talks with Syria that Olmert's government had taken over. Though not privy to military information, Liel had his own sources.

"The morning after the attack, I was on the radio," Liel explained to me. "I said, 'This was an Israeli attack.'" He said he had been told by Turkish diplomats that the Israeli jets had dropped their spare fuel tanks over Turkey after bombing the reactor.

"The Turks told me, 'It's on our soil and it was not coordinated with us. You penetrated our skies!'

"They were furious."

Within a matter of minutes after Liel made these comments on the air, "I got a phone call from the censor," he said. "He told me, 'Look, I know you are an expert, but you don't know if we attacked or not; you don't know if it was our planes, and I ask you not to speak about it.'

"I told him, 'Look, I am a private person: I left the government many years ago; I am a university guy, you cannot tell university people what to say.'"

But the censor admonished him. "No, no. These days you are not a private person." Liel digested the threat. If he defied the censor, he could be arrested; he could lose his teaching position or face other sanctions. This was the security state enforcing discipline, suspending the right of free expression. There was no civilian review of the military censor's power; the censor reported to the minister of defense and the chief of staff. And in this instance, they took their orders from the prime minister.

Liel was supposed to go on TV that evening. "I called the interviewer, and I told him I cannot speak under such a threat from the censor."[8]

Syria did not launch a retaliatory war in response to Israel's 2007 attack. It took six months for the truth to emerge about the Israeli military operation and the intelligence on which it was based. The CIA produced a video for the U.S. Congress and briefed key members in April 2008.

Many countries privately cheered Israel's destruction of the nascent Syrian nuclear program. But at what cost? Was it in the interest of the region and the international community for Israel to act as the hegemonic military power, leveling a rival's illicit nuclear site without relying on the United Nations or the IAEA, which is charged with preventing proliferation?

As President Kennedy had done during the Cuban missile crisis, Israel could have gone before the UN Security Council or the IAEA to demand that Syria dismantle the reactor.

The great powers could have called Assad's regime into the dock for attempting to further destabilize the Middle East by seeking to acquire nuclear weapons. A strong intervention by the international community might well have strengthened the institutions charged with preventing proliferation and demonstrated to the Israelis that unilateral militarism need not be the first resort.

Diplomacy carried no downside risk. If the international community had failed to force Syria to destroy the reactor, the unilateral military option would still be available, as it was for Kennedy when he made plans in October 1962 to invade Cuba if its nuclear missile sites were not dismantled.

Israel would have garnered great credit for investing in diplomacy. But Olmert, a child of the Irgun, a product of the militarism that had shaped his father's generation and his own, was incapable of overcoming the inertial power of that culture. The generals had declared the Syrian reactor an existential threat and demanded action. Barak's cautionary advice did not amount to opposition as much as it helped to refine an operational plan that sought to avoid a full-scale war.

Despite the heavy hand of censorship, the popular reaction in Israel to the surprise attack on Syria was rhapsodic. The IDF once again stood as the guardian of the nation, protecting the Jewish state from the nightmare of a Syrian atomic bomb.

But for the Arabs, many of whom feared a Syrian regime allied with Iran and armed with a nuclear weapon, the worse outcome was Israel's unprovoked demonstration of its power. It was deeply humiliating for the Arabs that the Jewish state—financed and armed to a great extent by American governments—had become the regional policeman. Some asked: Is this what Israel's contribution to the Middle East had come to—the arbitrary and unbridled use of military power to keep the Arabs down?

Many sabras asked themselves how militarism was a viable long-term strategy.

"We are becoming more aggressive," lamented Uri Saguy, the retired major general who had commanded the Golani Brigade and had served as Rabin's director for military intelligence. Saguy was a sixth-generation sabra, an olive farmer from the coastal plain north of Haifa.

I spoke with Saguy as he was serving as a back-channel adviser on Syria to Gabi Ashkenazi, the chief of staff, and to Ehud Barak. Saguy knew Barak's limitations; he had watched Barak fail in the Syrian negotiations of 1999 and 2000. Still, as an expert, Saguy was a tireless advocate of peace with Syria.

Unfortunately, he added, "we are only relying upon our military capability. We can take care of terrorist activity, that's true, but we cannot solve the Palestinian issue by using only our military force. It's not enough." Saguy's generation, those old soldiers who had come up under Rabin, had lost the capacity to influence the military establishment they had helped to build or the government that seemed firmly in the grasp of a coalition of right-wing parties buttressed by ultra-Orthodox sects and a strong Russian-speaking voting bloc.

One of the emerging power brokers in Israel was Avigdor Lieberman, a beefy Russian immigrant who had attached himself and his Yisrael Beiteinu (Israel Is Our Homeland) Party to Netanyahu during the 1990s.

Born in 1958 in Moldova, Lieberman arrived in Israel in 1978, served as a corporal in the artillery corps of the IDF, and then devoted himself to building a political base among the one million Russians who were flooding into Israel in the post-Soviet exodus. The arrival of the Russian-speaking population profoundly changed the politics of Israel. The typical Russian immigrant favored liberal social policies that benefited the immigrant class, but on security issues and relations with the Arabs, the Russian community favored a hard line that was anti-Arab, at times blatantly racist, and generally unaccommodating.

In launching his party, which quickly became one of the largest political blocs in the electorate, Lieberman opposed any land-for-peace deal with the Palestinians. Instead, he spoke the language of Arab expulsion. He called his party "a national movement with a clear vision to follow in the brave path of Ze'ev Jabotinsky," the founder of Revisionist Zionism.

Never had Israel fielded such an array of political parties so hostile to the peoples of the region. A large fraction of sabras who were secular, humanist, and willing to make peace with the Arabs under favorable conditions were deeply troubled by the shift to the right.

Amos Elon, the *Ha'aretz* journalist and historian who had chronicled the Zionist state almost from its inception, abandoned Israel altogether and moved to Tuscany in 2004. For Elon, the rise of the settler movement and the messianic triumphalism of the Six-Day War—"a victory worse than defeat," he called it—had changed the character of the Jewish state. His decision to emigrate touched off a national debate. What did it mean that such a bright light could leave his homeland?

Elon talked about his disillusionment. He had been among the first to warn that the neocolonialism of the Greater Israel advocates would come to ruin. "Nothing has changed here for the past forty years," he told one of his colleagues at *Ha'aretz*. "The solutions were already known back then"—Israel would have to give back the land in order to achieve peace. "I realized I was saying the same thing again and again. I began to bore myself," Elon concluded. He simply said farewell.

The successful attack on Syria's nuclear reactor inspired an even bolder concept among the generals—war on Iran to destroy its evolving nuclear complex.

The development of a potential nuclear threat from revolutionary Iran emerged in 2002 and 2003, but its foundation lay in the era of Shah Mohammad Reza Pahlavi, when Iran had first shown an interest in becoming a nuclear power.

Wedged between the Arab world and the nuclear giants Russia, China, and India (and, soon, Pakistan), Iran would inevitably seek atomic weapons to deter its enemies and extend its hegemony over the Persian Gulf.

For Israel's military establishment, the loss in 1979 of the shah as a powerful ally in the Muslim world had been a painful blow.

Rabin was the first Israeli leader to warn that the rise of the Islamic Republic of Iran would become Israel's greatest challenge. And within a decade of that warning, Israeli and Western intelligence agencies had detected a uranium enrichment program that was going to put Iran in position, sooner or later, to produce the fissile material needed to fabricate an atomic bomb.

One of the leading analysts on Iran is the former Mossad chief Shabtai Shavit, who cut his teeth in espionage as a young Farsi-speaking operative in Iran running agents into Iraq from Abadan, the giant refinery town in southwestern Iran. Shavit worked undercover in what was then a British-run city. Shavit's wife also spoke Farsi and accompanied him on his assignment.

Many Israeli intelligence insiders credit Shavit for shifting the focus of the intelligence community to Iran, and his assessment reflects the deep pessimism about the Tehran regime within the military and intelligence establishments. I spoke to him at his home north of Tel Aviv.

"It may be Machiavellian," Shavit told me, "but the most stable global era was the cold war. Global deterrence was achieved only when the two superpowers reached mutual assured destruction capability. They realized that if you shoot first you are going to be annihilated anyhow. This conviction meant stability and deterrence of the cold war."

However, Shavit added, "we cannot and should not make comparisons between the global cold war concept of deterrence and the present-day Iran concept" due to the "religious parameters in the equation," meaning that Iran, as a theocracy, puts decision making in the hands of an "infallible" spiritual leader, Ayatollah Ali Khamenei.

"The decision is taken by one person whom everyone believes has got a direct line with God Almighty," he pointed out.

The Shiites, Shavit continued, want to return to an imperial Islamic past, a world ruled by a Muslim caliphate, which will come to pass when the Twelfth Imam, the Hidden Imam, reappears. "Muslims need to do what is needed to make him reappear," Shavit said, and "only after a global [war] on the scale of Armageddon" can this happen.

Here was the logic underlying one of the core assessments inside the Israeli intelligence establishment. As a Mossad chief who advised prime ministers on what to do about Iran, Shavit explained how the worst-case scenario comes to dominate national thinking.

The Ayatollah Khamenei, he said, is a messianic ideologue. "A guy like this who believes in the fate of history—with his finger on the nuclear trigger—once he acquires the capability, is he going to use it? I have no answer and no one I have spoken with could give me an answer."

I pointed out to Shavit that Khamenei's mentor, the Ayatollah Khomeini, acted rationally in the long Iran-Iraq War (1980–88).

Shavit countered that Khomeini ended the war only after sending hundreds of thousands of teenage volunteers—the *baseej*—to their certain death in battles they could not win. To Shavit, Iran's ayatollahs did not value life. They would do what is necessary, he said, to bring on the global conflagration in which the Hidden Imam will emerge to rebuild the Islamic empire.

"As a practitioner," Shavit said, "I have to come to my political leadership and recommend what to do. Can I afford to give a recommendation based on a working assumption that is less than worst case?"

His words made me think of Dayan and the intelligence chiefs under Ben-Gurion. They, too, had reached for the worst-case assessment of Nasser's intentions in the 1950s, which undermined the efforts of Moshe Sharett to open secret negotiations in Paris to reach an accommodation with Egypt.

"Israel cannot afford except to prepare itself according to the worst-case scenario," Shavit said, leveling his gaze to emphasize the point. "If they [Iran] acquire it [the bomb], they will use it. Okay, maybe they will use coercion first, or other steps in between, but they would not hesitate to use it. Iran is eighty million now, and for them to absorb a nuclear strike is not too high a price for achieving their religious goals.

"This is the nature of the threat, and the world is doing next to nothing," Shavit complained. "My concern," he added, "especially after the strike in Syria, is that people will say, 'What the heck? Let Israel take care of it.'"

And here is where Shavit, like most other Israeli intelligence chiefs, came to his most uncomfortable analytical point—Israel was poorly positioned to attack Iran for a host of reasons, not least that such an attack would trigger a regional war that would be devastating to Israel and the West.

"I believe that if Israel were to undertake it, we would face insurmountable obstacles," he said. Only America could lead the international community to do the right thing, in his view.

He had convinced himself that deterrence would not work; diplomacy would not work. The only thing that mattered was the worst-case view that Iran's ayatollahs were in the grip of a messianic, apocalyptic vision, and if they managed to fabricate an atomic bomb, they would launch it against Israel knowing that a retaliatory strike from Israel would annihilate millions of Iranians.

In December 2006, Olmert had said publicly that he could not rule out the possibility of an attack on Iran's nuclear complex. Key members of Kadima, Mofaz included as the Iranian-born former chief of staff, also warned publicly that if Iran did not forswear nuclear weapons, it would be subject to attack. Barak flew to Washington to negotiate the upgrading of Israel's air force so that if the day came, the Israeli military would be equipped with deep-penetration bombs and other hardware necessary to carry out a long-range bombing mission against Iran. The Israeli air force subsequently carried out a massive air force exercise over the Mediterranean to simulate an attack on Iran.[9]

Barak over time became the strongest advocate for keeping a military option on the table for an Israeli strike on Iran. When I went to interview

Barak in 2008, he invited me to his luxury apartment nearly forty stories above Tel Aviv, where he looked out on the panorama of Israel's heavily populated coastline toward Haifa. He wanted to talk about Iran and the strength of the Persian culture. He didn't believe that Khomeini's Islamic revolution would prevail over time

"This was a nation that was there from the dawn of history with a great tradition and heritage, and my instinct tells me that during the third generation"—in other words, the grandchildren of the 1979 generation that fomented the Iranian Revolution—they "will throw [the ayatollahs] out, like Russians did to the Communists.

"This revolution will be toppled by its own people," he said.

It was not well known, but Barak had served in Iran in 1972 as a young captain in the army, most likely part of the contingent of Israeli special forces who entered northern Iraq to train the Kurds as part of the shah's covert operation to put pressure on Saddam Hussein.

As a military man, Barak looked out at the world and saw the convergence of three large threats: terrorism fomented by Islamic extremism, proliferation of nuclear weapons, and reckless behavior by rogue states such as North Korea. Barak was not one to dawdle talking about diplomacy or about "soft" power or past efforts to formulate rapprochement with states such as Iran.

"I can hardly see any stable world order if Iran turns nuclear," Barak said. "Not because they will immediately drop a bomb on a neighbor. Too many neighbors are nuclear and they fully understand what might follow. But because it will be the end of any antiproliferation regime. If Iran will turn nuclear, we can end up with a nuclear Saudi Arabia" or a nuclear Egypt or a nuclear Turkey.

His big nuclear worry was the clandestine delivery of a crude nuclear explosive in a shipping container that could detonate at a major Israeli port, or in Rotterdam, the major oil port on Europe's coast, or in the United States.

My interview with Barak took place shortly after Barack Obama and John McCain had been nominated to represent their parties in the presidential election of 2008. By then, Barak had met with both of them.

"I told McCain and Obama, and earlier Bush and even his father and Cheney at that time—for years I am arguing—that we are in a way in a major historical struggle against a triad of challenges [terror, proliferation, and rogue states].” And when it came to Iran, Barak said he was pressing for more robust sanctions backed up by the threat of a military strike.

There was little room for diplomacy in Barak's world. As Gadi Baltiansky had said, Barak was not interested in the Arab or Muslim worlds, except to prevail over them strategically. He had the mind of a *chekist*.

“I told [Obama and McCain] very honestly that we do not remove any option from the table, and when we say it, we mean it,” he said. “I didn't try to pretend that there is a decision [to bomb Iran] or a date, or a way by which it will be executed, but when we say we don't remove any option from the table, we just mean it.”

The military and intelligence chiefs knew that Israel's only chance to head off Iran's nuclear project in the long run was to galvanize the international community against it, but Israel remained largely isolated. More than ever it needed a visionary leader to make the case that a line had to be drawn in Iran. And Olmert, who would soon be under indictment, was never going to be that leader.

On a trip to Germany on December 11, 2006, Olmert had stumbled badly by admitting that Israel, like Russia, China, and the United States, possessed nuclear weapons. The Jewish state had never made such an admission publicly and Olmert was embarrassed because in flubbing his lines, he reminded Israelis how Eshkol had not seemed fit to serve as commander in chief on the eve of the Six-Day War. Olmert was snakebit as a leader. He could not articulate Israel's national strategy. He seemed ever the amateur, a front man with a chamber of commerce grin.

In September 2007, Israel's attorney general announced he was opening yet another criminal investigation over the favorable financing under which Olmert had purchased his home in Jerusalem. This was followed by allegations that Olmert had taken envelopes stuffed with cash totaling $150,000 from an American Jewish supporter, Morris Talansky, and Talansky later testified about what he had done.

Olmert responded by working even more intensely for a breakthrough with the Palestinians. He had help from Secretary of State Condoleezza Rice and President Bush, both of whom seemed as desperate as Olmert to shore up their own legacies on the peacemaking side of the ledger.

At Annapolis, Maryland, in late November 2007, the Americans helped to orchestrate the drafting and signing of a short text setting out terms to open negotiations on Palestinian statehood. With fanfare, Olmert and Mahmoud Abbas, the Palestinian leader, ratified the text and, in the weeks and months that followed, Olmert tried repeatedly to close the gaps that had frustrated Clinton in the final days of his presidency when he had proposed a set of "parameters" for a deal on Palestinian statehood to Arafat and Barak, who was then prime minister.

Olmert hoped—naïvely, given his precarious legal circumstance—that he could strike a bargain that would astound the world and somehow overcome the state prosecutors who were pursuing him.

But Olmert's diplomacy produced no result. It seemed as if all of the momentum in Israel belonged to the military and intelligence establishments, which were waging a new kind of war in the Middle East.

If there was one militant in the world whom both Israel and the United States wanted dead, it was forty-five-year-old Imad Mughniyeh, the Hezbollah underground commander who for almost twenty-five years had the blood of hundreds of Americans, Israelis, and Arabs on his hands. A Shiite from Beirut's suburbs, Mughniyeh had come of age during the Israeli invasion of Lebanon; he had trained with Arafat's Force 17 brigade.

After the PLO left Beirut, he had migrated into the Iranian-backed Shiite militias, where he had soon established himself as an effective agent of terror against the West.

Mughniyeh was believed to be the mastermind of the truck-bombing spree of 1983 that killed dozens of American diplomats, 59 French peacekeepers, and 240 American marines; his guerrillas in Beirut had kidnapped Westerners and chained them to radiators or tortured them to death.

Only Osama bin Laden had killed more Americans.

Mughniyeh recruited suicide bombers—young Shiite men willing to die behind the wheel of a car or truck loaded with explosives—and he would launch them like human torpedoes at Western and Israeli targets, including the devastating strike on the Israeli army headquarters in Tyre in November 1983, where twenty-nine Israelis died.

Over the years, Mughniyeh had changed his profile, perhaps with cosmetic surgery. One photograph revealed him in military fatigues, bespectacled and with a thoughtful countenance. He was heavier than he had appeared in grainy photos circulated during the 1980s. A beard covered his ample jowls under a military cap. He would be difficult to pick out of a crowd on the streets of South Beirut.

In early 2008, Mughniyeh came under surveillance in Damascus by intelligence agents possibly recruited by the Israelis. Damascus was lethal territory for Mossad. Ever since the capture and execution of Mossad spy Eli Cohen in the 1960s, the agency had been reluctant to operate its own officers inside Syria. It seems more likely that Mossad had established a network of Syrian Druze, Kurd, or Arab agents who could track Mughniyeh.

Yet the provenance of the operation remained murky for the obvious reason that sources and methods were being protected. Some reports suggested that Mughniyeh was attending a reception at the residence of the Iranian ambassador to Syria; others said he was meeting with Syrian intelligence chiefs at a headquarters in the same fashionable suburb of Damascus. Whatever Mughniyeh was doing there, when he left the meeting between 10:30 and 11:00 p.m., he got into his Mitsubishi Pajero without suspecting that he was in danger. Just then, the driver's-side headrest exploded.[10]

The force of the blast hurled Mughniyeh's body out of the car. He was dead when he hit the pavement.

"The resistance has lost one of its pillars," said Sheikh Mohammed Hussein Fadlallah, the leading Shiite cleric of Beirut, who was once considered to be Hezbollah's spiritual leader.

Many Israelis believed that Mossad was behind the operation and that Israel was waging a new-style war, the kind that endeavored not to leave Israeli fingerprints. This was the kind of war about which Avi Dichter, the former Shabak chief, and Aharon Ze'evi Farkash, the former military intelligence chief, had spoken—anonymous assassination and silent, untraceable acts of war.

Only months later, in August, a Syrian general was assassinated by a sniper firing from the deck of a yacht off the Syrian coastal city of Tartus. Brigadier General Mohammed Suleiman was said to have been in charge of supplying Hezbollah with modern weapons. Again, Israeli intelligence was suspected, but Olmert's government remained officially silent.[11]

Meir Dagan, the Mossad director who had gained his reputation as a clever and brutal operator under Sharon during the 1970s in the Gaza

Strip, suddenly was in the national spotlight. The Israeli press hinted that Dagan had been tasked not only to wage war against Hezbollah and Hamas but also to open a new front against Iran in an effort to disrupt Tehran's bid to become a nuclear power.

Olmert was going down like the *Titanic*, bow first but in a drama of gradual inundation that carried long into the political night. There was frantic chamber music on deck and much scurrying about in search of lifeboats— and a paucity of valor.

The prime minister had announced in July 2008 that he would give up the chairmanship of Kadima and step aside so a new party leader could form a government, a step that short-circuited any requirement for new elections. If it worked, it would keep Netanyahu at bay.

On September 17, Kadima's delegates were set to make their choice. The day before the vote, Olmert summoned Mahmoud Abbas secretly to the prime minister's residence in Jerusalem. Olmert spread out a map of Israel, the West Bank, and Gaza. He said he was putting an offer of Palestinian statehood on the table that was new and historic.

Under the terms he proposed, Israel would withdraw from all but 6.3 percent of the West Bank. The Palestinian state would receive an equivalent amount of land from Israel as compensation for the 6.3 percent Israel retained. To join the West Bank and Gaza Strip, Israel would build a twenty-five-mile tunnel through the Negev Desert.

The capital of Palestine would be the Arab portion of Jerusalem, but the Old City, including the sacred mosques of the Noble Sanctuary and Temple Mount, would be governed under an international consortium. Five thousand displaced Palestinians would be allowed to return to Israel proper. The rest would move to the Palestinian state or take compensation and relocate elsewhere.[12]

Abbas stared across the table at Olmert, who was trying to conceal the desperation he must have felt. His premiership was in its final hours. Even a peace agreement with Abbas might not save him; indeed, it might lead to a government collapse and a rejection of the terms Olmert had offered. The thin reed that Olmert was grasping was his belief that an Olmert-Abbas accord would render the world awestruck, that the Bush administration would immediately embrace it, and that the seismic magnitude of peace would overpower the poisonous politics of the right wing and create a centrist, pro-peace majority where none had existed since Rabin's time.

Olmert could even call a special election to ratify peace.

Abbas sat there silently, evaluating where he and Olmert stood.

When he spoke, he told the Israeli leader that he could not decide immediately. The gaps were still large and questions hung in the air about a myriad of details. Abbas needed time.

"I told him he was making a historic mistake," Olmert later wrote.

Abbas repeated that he needed time to consult.

"No," Olmert said, perhaps surprising his guest with his bluntness. "Take the pen and sign now. You will never get a more fair or just offer."

Still nothing.

"Even in another fifty years there will not be a government in Israel that will offer you what I offered," Olmert insisted.

The irony was that Olmert's government was not making the offer, only a prime minister so weakened by failure and persistent allegations of corruption that his political obituary was nearly set in type. The offer was conveyed in private because Olmert's terms for peace were toxic to his coalition. Uprooting Jewish settlers and dividing Jerusalem was anathema to the Shas Party, whose leader, Eli Yishai, had put Olmert on notice that he would bring down any government that tried to divide Jerusalem.

The next day, all eyes turned to Tzipi Livni, who narrowly prevailed in the vote by Kadima's seventy thousand party members. She defeated Shaul Mofaz, the former chief of staff, and she trounced Avi Dichter, Sharon's favorite Shabak chief, who had elevated assassination to an art form.

But it was not Livni's destiny to lead the Jewish state, not yet, in any case. Her very interest in peace with the Palestinians contributed to her failure to form a viable coalition that could muster 61 votes in the 120-member Knesset. The Shas Party wanted her word never to divide Jerusalem. Livni refused to tie her own hands in advance.

After weeks of negotiations, only deadlock was apparent. New national elections would have to be called for early 2009. Kadima's sabras could put it off no longer. They would have to face Netanyahu in a national contest.

Livni's failure provided another reprieve for Olmert.

He was now a caretaker prime minister until a new government could be formed after elections in February 2009, five months hence. Seldom had a foundering hulk tarried so long above the waves. Olmert had wanted to go out as a peacemaker, but his final months were another buildup for war.

The Hamas takeover of Gaza had put the militant heirs of Sheikh Ahmed Yassin under great pressure. Many Gazans chafed at Hamas's harsh treatment of Fatah loyalists. Hamas fundamentalism was not popular. Hamas's rocket war on the Israelis seemed counterproductive. The projectiles had virtually no military utility. In thousands of firings over seven years, Hamas had killed a dozen Israelis. Still, the rocketeers got on the news almost every night. They caused scenes of panic at Israeli elementary schools, day-care centers, hospitals, and markets in the towns just beyond Gaza's frontier.

In June 2008, Hamas's leaders had agreed to a cease-fire. The pact was informal, brokered through the Egyptians, but it held for months, giving respite to the Israelis living near the perimeter of Gaza. Then Barak approved an incursion into Gaza on November 4, which undermined the calm. Israeli military bulldozers burst across the Gaza frontier to shut down a tunnel complex that provided an infiltration route for militants seeking to kill or abduct Israeli soldiers. The incursion touched off a firefight in which a Hamas fighter was killed. A spokesman for the group called the raid a "massive breach of the truce," and Hamas launched dozens of rockets and mortars into the Israeli Negev in retaliation.

Israel responded with air strikes, one of which killed five more Hamas fighters.

"They cannot leave us drowning in blood while they sleep soundly in their beds," the Hamas spokesman told journalists.[13]

The confrontation with Hamas took place on a political stage where Olmert, Barak, Livni, and Mofaz took increasingly militant positions, and as Netanyahu, speaking from the opposition bench of the Knesset, ridiculed them for failure.

It was a political climate predisposed to war, and Hamas relished the prospect of a clash.

One final spark came from Khaled Meshal, the Hamas leader in Damascus. He abruptly called off further negotiation to restore the truce. A new wave of Hamas rocket fire arched out of Gaza.

On December 25, 2008, Olmert issued a final warning. Appearing on al-Arabiya, the Arabic-language satellite channel, he said, "I am telling them now, it may be the last minute, I'm telling them, 'Stop it. We are stronger.' "[14]

It was the kind of statement Rabin might once have made when he believed that the only thing that mattered was military power, and since the Palestinians had none, their resistance could be crushed.

The war on Gaza commenced two days later.

It began with an air campaign of one hundred warplanes and attack helicopters striking a single target each in the span of 220 seconds just before noon on December 27.[15]

Gaza thundered with deafening percussion. Buildings dissolved in explosions whose shock waves leveled everything in a blast radius that numbed the senses of civilians running for cover. A great convection of smoke, ash, and human anguish rose darkly from the southern horizon as millions of Israelis went about their business a half hour away from the war zone. Thirty minutes after the opening wave, another sixty aircraft hit sixty additional targets, and the waves just kept coming. In the opening day of the war, 230 Palestinians were killed and more than 700 injured, one of the deadliest death tolls for a single day since 1948.[16]

Forty Hamas police cadets were killed when their graduation ceremony was targeted with a massive bomb strike. Over the next three weeks, as President-elect Obama and the rest of the world looked on, the Israeli military destroyed four thousand buildings and killed hundreds of Hamas militants in a campaign that enjoyed wide support at home.

Israeli ground forces rolled into the strip on January 3 and fought running battles into the neighborhoods of Gaza City until January 17, when Olmert declared a unilateral cease-fire, saying that Israel's military objectives had been met. With Gaza flattened, Israel had made its point of intolerance for rocket attacks.

The truth was, no one in the Israeli leadership wanted the war to carry on into the inauguration ceremonies in the United States. Hamas and Gaza's civilian population had absorbed a devastating blow. Much of the international community was appalled by Israel's use of disproportionate force.

Cries of massacre and excessive force went up in the Arab world and among human rights organizations. Israelis countered tenaciously that they had had no choice but to defend their civilian population from the continual stream of rockets and mortars being fired from Gaza. No country could tolerate an adjoining frontier being used to send rockets into schools and playgrounds. Hamas replied that it had no choice but to attack Israel in response to economic embargo, the closure of its territory, and frequent Israeli attacks that caused widespread Palestinian suffering. No people could tolerate asphyxiation by a neighboring oppressive power that had carried out a forty-year occupation. Israel countered that Hamas was a terrorist state, dedicated to Israel's destruction. . . . It just went on and on.

Israel's war on Gaza was another war of choice, but what did it change? Many Israelis convinced themselves that Hamas had been taught a lesson, but Hamas staged only a tactical retreat, as Hezbollah had, taking its time to rearm and to rebuild its networks, preparing to fight another day.

The Gaza War was Olmert's last act.

Another militant sabra had hit the wall after a binge of violence, only to discover, too late, that accommodation with the Arabs was possible for a strong prime minister willing to rebuild the coalition for peace. Olmert never really had a chance. He failed the test of leadership in the conduct of the Second Lebanon War, and he seemed to be failing the test of personal integrity amid the skein of corruption indictments that enveloped him. (On July 12, 2012, Olmert was acquitted of corruption charges in two major cases. He was convicted of a lesser charge of "breach of trust" in a third and was still facing charges that he accepted bribes, while serving as mayor of Jerusalem, in connection with a major residential project.)

His premiership would not be remembered for any milestone of diplomacy, even though he had envisioned himself greeting the king of Saudi Arabia and other Arab heads of state in a new dawn of negotiation that would also bring to life a Palestinian state. He simply could not move the Israelis where he wanted them to go.

The Zionist movement had survived the onslaught of world wars, the Holocaust, and clashes of ideology, but in the modern era of statehood, Israel seemed incapable of fielding a generation of leaders who could adapt to the times, who were dedicated to ending the occupation and, thus, their isolation, or to changing the paradigm of military preeminence.

The great training ground of the twentieth century on which Chaim Weizmann, Ben-Gurion, Sharett, Eshkol, and Meir had shaped their ideology of Jewish nationhood, of democratic governance and integration with other Semitic peoples, seemed lost to the second and third generations. Engagement had been one of the touchstones of the Zionist mainstream, but it had been all but abandoned. The rise of Israeli militarism overtook every competing sentiment, contributing to a radicalization of the Arabs. The cold war and Islamic resurgence did the rest.

Israel stood alone as a regional superpower, a fortress of martial capability, but the Israelis were powerless to influence the region to which they had made a great migration during the twentieth century and where, in a new century, a broad new political awakening was afoot.

Notes

Acknowledgments

Index

Notes

Prologue: Murder in Tehran

1. Initial confusion over the identity and the profession of the murdered scientist took several days to clear. The dead man was first identified as a nuclear scientist and a university professor. It was ultimately established that he was, instead, Darioush Rezaeinejad, a graduate student in electrical engineering at Khajeh Nasir University. The semi-official Fars News Agency reported two days after the killing that Rezaeinejad was a researcher whose work was devoted to the electronic switches that could be used in nuclear weapons. The agency said there was no evidence linking Rezaeinejad to nuclear weapons design, but the agency speculated that "all the scientists whose works are being guessed to be used in a weapons project will be placed in the assassination list of Western and Israeli intelligence organizations." The Fars News Agency later deleted the portion of its online article that stated that Rezaeinejad's work on electronic switches was applicable to nuclear weapons. Also, in the wake of this shooting, Iran's Revolutionary Guard Corps announced that it would undertake the protection of key scientists since it was obvious that they were being targeted by foreign intelligence organizations.
2. Scott Peterson, "Another Iranian Scientist Killed: Part of 'Covert War'?" *Christian Science Monitor*, January 11, 2012.
3. Jeffrey Goldberg, "Netanyahu to Obama: Stop Iran—Or I Will," *The Atlantic*, March 31, 2009.
4. Western intelligence agencies believed Israel had launched the first known cyber-attack on Iran's nuclear facilities by employing a computer virus known as the Stuxnet worm. The virus compromised the control systems at the Natanz enrichment plant where Roshan had worked, causing malfunctions that damaged hundreds of centrifuges. See William J. Broad, John Markoff, and David E. Sanger, "Israeli Test on Worm Called Crucial in Iran Nuclear Delay," *New York Times*, January 11, 2011.
5. Ronen Bergman, "Will Israel Attack Iran?" *New York Times*, January 29, 2012.
6. See, for instance, Ken Dilanian, "U.S. Does Not Believe Iran Is Trying to Build

Nuclear Bomb," *Los Angeles Times*, February 23, 2012; also, James Risen and Mark Mazzetti, "U.S. Agencies See No Move by Iran to Build a Bomb," *New York Times*, February 24, 2012. Iran may have continued to conduct secret research related to nuclear weapons design after 2003, but this was still the subject of investigation by the International Atomic Energy Agency and Western intelligence services. See IAEA Report by the Director General to the IAEA Board of Governors, "Implementation of the NPT Safeguards Agreement and Relevant Provisions of Security Council Resolutions in the Islamic Republic of Iran," November 8, 2011.

7. Ben Caspit, "The Polish Poet and the Art of Assassination," interview with Avi Dichter [Hebrew; trans. Gilad Halpern], *Ma'ariv*, June 10, 2005.

8. Shlomo Gazit, interview with the author, May 5, 2008.

9. Brigadier General Michael Herzog, interview with the author, March 5, 2009.

10. *Bahad 1*, documentary, Scorpion TV, London, 2010.

11. Reuven Merhav, interview with the author, November 22, 2008.

1. Ben-Gurion: The Origins of Militarism

1. Ben-Gurion suffered from Ménière's disease, an affliction of the inner ear. He was also prone to bouts of depression and, at times of great stress, acute illnesses marked by fever.

2. Gabriel Sheffer, *Moshe Sharett: Biography of a Political Moderate* (New York: Oxford University Press, 1996), p. 830.

3. David Ben-Gurion, *My Talks with Arab Leaders* (New York: Third Press, 1973).

4. Mordechai Bar-On, interview with the author, March 3, 2009; Avi Shlaim, *The Iron Wall: Israel and the Arab World* (New York: Norton, 2000), p. 140; Sheffer, *Moshe Sharett*, pp. 826–27.

5. The Sharett line was articulated in response to pressure from the Eisenhower administration to refrain from retaliatory operations. Sharett defined Israel's defense and foreign policy thus: "Israel's policy is not aimed at achieving a decisive military victory"; rather it was aimed at reducing tension on its borders through political means. See Sheffer, *Moshe Sharett*, p. 732.

6. In the fall of 1953, Sharett observed a stark change in Lavon's outlook. He began talking about the need for "strong nerves" and "toughness" to overcome international condemnation of Israel's illicit military actions. Sharett, in his personal diary, lamented the fact that he was losing an ally owing to "the basic transformation that has occurred in the mode of thinking and inclinations of this talented and wise person, who has tasted control over the most powerful establishment in Israel: the IDF." Moshe Sharett, Personal Diary, October 18, 1953, pp. 49–50, The Moshe Sharett Heritage Society, Tel Aviv; also Sheffer, *Moshe Sharett*, p. 688.

7. Sharett, Personal Diary, p. 639; Sheffer, *Moshe Sharett*, p. 767. Lavon sets forth his theory of continual conflict and confrontation in his memoir, *In the Paths of Reflection and Struggle* [Hebrew] (Tel Aviv, 1968). See also Lavon's private comments to Mapai's Central Committee: "I cannot say: I do not want war. I say: I want it, and I

wish there was a situation in which there were no Englishmen and no Americans, and there were only us and the Arabs, and we could do that." Protocol of the Central Committee, April 15, 1954, cited in Shlaim, *The Iron Wall*, p. 100.

8. In his diary, Sharett said Lavon had proposed "the Satanic doctrine of setting the Middle East on fire, stirring up war, organizing bloody coups, striking targets belonging to the Powers, desperate and suicidal acts." Sharett, Personal Diary, October 1, 1955, cited in Martin Van Creveld, *Moshe Dayan* (London: Weidenfeld & Nicolson, 2004), p. 77.

9. Sheffer, *Moshe Sharett*, p. 752.

10. In its dispatch from Cairo, the *New York Times* reported that the Gaza raid "could easily lead to an outbreak of full-scale hostilities." Robert C. Doty, "Egyptians Assert Israelis Slew 37 in Gaza Attacks," *New York Times*, March 1, 1955.

11. *New York Times*, "The Gaza Incident," editorial, March 4, 1955.

12. Keith Kyle, *Suez: Britain's End of Empire in the Middle East* (New York: St. Martin's Press, 1991), pp. 56–82; Abba Eban, *Personal Witness: Israel Through My Eyes* (New York: Putnam, 1992), p. 245; Wilbur Crane Eveland, *Ropes of Sand* (New York: Norton, 1980), pp. 157–59.

13. The Israeli historian Benny Morris observed, "There is no knowing whether, had Israel pursued the negotiations with Jordan, Syria [and Egypt] with greater vigor and a more conciliatory spirit, peace treaties would have resulted or whether, if signed they would not rapidly have unraveled. What is certain is that the patterns of enmity that have characterized Israeli-Arab relations ever since crystallized and consolidated during those early post-1948 years." Benny Morris, *Israel's Border Wars, 1949–1956* (New York: Oxford University Press, 1993), p. 426.

14. Vladimir (Ze'ev) Jabotinsky, "The Iron Wall (We and the Arabs)," *Jewish Herald* (South Africa), November 26, 1923.

15. Efraim Halevy, interview with the author, September 11, 2008.

16. Moshe Dayan, *Living with the Bible* (New York: William Morrow, 1976), p. 127.

17. Ibid., p. 128.

18. Anita Shapira, *Yigal Allon, Native Son: A Biography*, trans. Evelyn Abel (Philadelphia: University of Pennsylvania Press, 2008), p. 92.

19. Yaël Dayan, *My Father, His Daughter* (New York: Farrar, Straus and Giroux, 1985), p. 75.

20. Moshe Dayan, *Living with the Bible*, p. 130.

21. Yaël Dayan, *My Father, His Daughter*, p. 106.

22. Rami Tal, "Moshe Dayan: Repentance" [Hebrew; trans. Gilad Halpern], *Yedioth Aharonoth*, April 27, 1997.

23. Nahum Goldmann, *The Autobiography of Nahum Goldmann—Sixty Years of Jewish Life*, trans. Helen Sebba (New York: Holt, 1969), p. 289.

24. Menachem Begin, *The Revolt* (New York: Nash Publishing, 1977 [1951]), p. xxv.

25. Michael Bar-Zohar, *Shimon Peres: The Biography* (New York: Random House, 2007), pp. 40–41.

26. Sheffer, *Moshe Sharett*, p. 830; Shlaim, *The Iron Wall*, p. 140.

27. Avner Cohen, *Israel and the Bomb* (New York: Columbia University Press, 1998), p. 42.

28. Michael Karpin, *The Bomb in the Basement: How Israel Went Nuclear and What That Meant for the World* (New York: Simon & Schuster, 2006), p. 22.

29. Goldmann, *Autobiography*, pp. 290–93.

30. From an interview by Michael Brecher, quoted in Ya'akov Sharett, "A Dove Among Hawks: Moshe Sharett—The Political Tragedy of an Israeli Leader," *Midstream*, May 1, 2004.

31. Goldmann, *Autobiography*, pp. 290–93.

32. Sharett, "A Dove Among Hawks."

33. In the most exhaustive study of Arab infiltration, Benny Morris concludes that "though there were some terroristic and politically motivated infiltrations, which increased over the early and mid-1950s, Israeli statistics and Arab evidence . . . show that the vast bulk of the infiltration, 90 percent and more, through 1949–56, was economically or socially motivated. Most of the infiltrators came to retrieve possessions and crops and, thereafter, to steal. A small proportion engaged in smuggling. More crossed the border to resettle in their former villages and towns or to visit relatives or just to look at their former homes and lands." Morris, *Israel's Border Wars*, p. 428.

34. Benny Morris attempts to explain Israeli policy in the 1950s: "The IDF's shoot-to-kill orders, minings, expulsion operations and retaliatory strikes all, to one degree or another, involved state-authorized or, at least, permitted killing of unarmed civilians. Together they reflected a pervasive attitude among the Israeli public that Arab life was cheap (or that only Jewish life was sacred)." Ibid., p. 178.

35. Lt. Gen. Sir John Bagot Glubb, *A Soldier with the Arabs* (New York: Harper, 1957), p. 247; Morris, *Israel's Border Wars*, pp. 170–73.

36. Benny Morris, *Righteous Victims: A History of the Zionist-Arab Conflict 1881–2001* (New York: Vintage Books, 2001), p. 275.

37. Shlaim, *The Iron Wall*, p. 39; Morris, *Righteous Victims*, p. 265.

38. Morris, *Righteous Victims*, pp. 263–65; Shlaim, *The Iron Wall*, pp. 45–47; also Farah Sudki, "The Story of Nouran and Husni al-Zaim," *Forward Magazine*, November 2008.

39. Kati Marton, *A Death in Jerusalem: The Assassination by Jewish Extremists of the First Arab-Israeli Peacemaker* (New York: Pantheon, 1994), pp. 209, 253.

40. Tal, *Moshe Dayan*. Dayan, in two interviews granted after he was forced to resign in the wake of the Agranat Commission findings on the failures leading up to the 1973 Yom Kippur War, acknowledged that Israel had carried out what was then a secret strategy of provocation and creeping expansion beyond the 1949 Armistice lines. The 1976 interviews were held for twenty years before they were published. Among other things, Dayan said, "For a long time we thought we could redraw the armistice lines with lower-scale operations than full-fledged war. In other words, capture a piece of land and hold on to it until the enemy gives up. There was certainly a degree of naivety on our part, but you must remember that we were inexperienced."

41. A description of the genesis of Unit 101 can be found in Shabtai Teveth, *Moshe Dayan: The Soldier, the Man, the Legend* (Boston: Houghton Mifflin, 1972), p. 209.

42. David Ben-Gurion, diary entries August 11 and 15, 1953, cited in Morris, *Righteous Victims*, p. 280.

43. Moshe Sharett, Personal Diary, October 14, 1953, p. 37.

44. Ibid., p. 39.

45. Ibid., October 18, 1953, pp. 49–50.

46. Gadi Bloom and Nir Hefez, *Ariel Sharon: A Life* (New York: Random House, 2006), p. 58.

47. Ibid, p. 59; Ariel Sharon with David Chanoff, *Warrior: An Autobiography* (New York: Simon & Schuster, 1989), pp. 90–91.

48. Sharon and Chanoff, *Warrior*, p. 91.

2. The Destruction of Israel's Second Prime Minister

1. Sheffer, *Moshe Sharett*, p. 683.

2. Ibid., p. 715; Shlaim, *The Iron Wall*, p. 105.

3. Ze'ev Schiff, *A History of the Israeli Army* (London: Sidgwick & Jackson, 1987), pp. 46–57.

4. Sheffer, *Moshe Sharett*, p. 720.

5. Avner Yaniv, *Dilemmas of Security, Politics, Strategy, and the Israeli Experience in Lebanon* (New York: Oxford University Press, 1987), pp. 32–35.

6. Dayan published in early 1955 a spirited defense of Israel's militarism in America's leading foreign policy journal, *Foreign Affairs*. He blamed the violence on Arab intransigence, official threats against Israel by Arab leaders, and constant harassment from Arab marauders. "It has been asserted quite wrongly," he wrote, "that this infiltration is conducted primarily by refugees. The nightly incursions into Israeli territory, which in most cases show careful planning, are not the work of destitute refugees but of highly trained gunmen acting on paramilitary lines." But the most revealing aspect of the article was that while Dayan at home had just completed a year of aggressive cross-border raids aimed at provoking a war with the Arabs, he now proclaimed that Israel had done no such thing: "Israel has no aggressive designs against her neighbors. If she had, she could have had many opportunities in recent years, when Arab states were weakened by internal disturbances and coups d'état. There has been a scrupulous abstention by Israel from exploiting these instabilities." Major-General Moshe Dayan, "Israel's Border and Security Problems," *Foreign Affairs*, January 1955, pp. 250–67.

7. Steven L. Spiegel, *The Other Arab-Israeli Conflict: Making America's Middle East Policy from Truman to Reagan* (Chicago: University of Chicago Press, 1985), p. 54.

8. Sheffer, *Moshe Sharett*, pp. 738–39; Shlaim, *The Iron Wall*, p. 108.

9. Morris, *Israel's Border Wars*, p. 417.

10. Ben-Gurion's concept was for Jewish dominion over any part of the biblical Land of Israel that Jews were willing to settle with agriculture, industry, and investment so long as they did not encroach on the already settled Arab population. With this approach, he believed that there was room for millions of Jews to bring their skills

from Europe and other parts of the world and build a large and vibrant state that would also lift the Arab population. "Palestine is not capable of absorbing large additional immigration except through the methods adopted by the Jews, i.e., the expenditure of large sums of capital and much enterprise on the improvement of the soil, irrigation, the creation of new industries, etc.," he stated to an emissary from the king of Saudi Arabia in May 1937. See Ben-Gurion, *My Talks with Arab Leaders*, pp. 42–54, 127–40.

11. Sheffer, *Moshe Sharett*, pp. 750–66; Moshe Dayan, *Story of My Life* (New York: William Morrow, 1976), pp. 144–45, 227; Shlaim, *The Iron Wall*, pp. 110–12; Bar-Zohar, *Shimon Peres*, pp. 93–94.

12. Gideon Rafael, *Destination Peace: Three Decades of Israeli Foreign Policy—A Personal Memoir* (New York: Stein and Day, 1981), p. 37.

13. "Syrian Airliner Seized by Israel," *New York Times*, December 13, 1954; Sheffer, *Moshe Sharett*, p. 774.

14. The American passenger was Ralph K. Hansen from Wayne, New Jersey. He disputed Israeli statements that the plane had been flying over a forbidden area of Israel's coastline. See "Syrian Plane and 4 Released by Israel," *New York Times*, December 15, 1954.

15. Rafael, *Destination Peace*, p. 38.

16. Sheffer, *Moshe Sharett*, p. 761; Shlaim, *The Iron Wall*, pp. 119–20.

17. Sheffer, *Moshe Sharett*, p. 774.

18. Rafael, *Destination Peace*, p. 41; Sheffer, *Moshe Sharett*, p. 781.

19. See "Israel Now Seeks Arms Tie to West," *New York Times*, February 2, 1955.

20. Shlaim, *The Iron Wall*, p. 125.

21. Sharon and Chanoff, *Warrior*, p. 108.

22. Morris, *Israel's Border Wars*, p. 344. Sharett considered Operation Black Arrow his "greatest failure as prime minister" (Sheffer, *Moshe Sharett*, p. 787). Benny Morris pointed out that the IDF, in assessing the raid, failed to understand its profound impact on Nasser, and that Egyptian defense policy "would henceforth focus on Israel and the need to confront (and perhaps destroy) the Jewish state" (*Israel's Border Wars*, p. 345).

23. Sheffer, *Moshe Sharett*, p. 789.

24. Mordechai Bar-On interview; Sharon and Chanoff, *Warrior*, pp. 111–13.

25. Sheffer, *Moshe Sharett*, pp. 788–89.

26. Ibid.

27. Shlaim, *The Iron Wall*, p. 125.

28. Humphrey Trevelyan, *Middle East in Revolution* (New York: Macmillan, 1970), p. 31.

29. Kennett Love, *Suez: The Twice-Fought War* (New York: McGraw-Hill, 1969), p. 225.

30. Sheffer, *Moshe Sharett*, p. 793.

31. Ibid., p. 797.

32. Morris, *Israel's Border Wars*, p. 348n52.

33. Sheffer, *Moshe Sharett*, p. 801; Shlaim, *The Iron Wall*, pp. 135–36.

34. From David Ben-Gurion's Independence Day address, May 14, 1955, cited in Cohen, *Israel and the Bomb*, p. 42.
35. Sharett, Personal Diary, May 26, 1955, cited in Shlaim, *The Iron Wall*, p. 133.
36. Moshe Dayan, *Diary of the Sinai Campaign* (New York: Harper & Row, 1966), pp. 12–13.
37. Mordechai Bar-On interview.
38. Shlaim, *The Iron Wall*, p. 146.
39. Ibid., p. 148.
40. Sharon and Chanoff, *Warrior*, 122.
41. Eban, *Personal Witness*, p. 245.
42. Ibid., p. 249; Mordechai Bar-On interview; Sharon and Chanoff, *Warrior*, pp. 125–26.
43. Shlaim, *The Iron Wall*, p. 151.
44. Sheffer, *Moshe Sharett*, p. 848.
45. Rafael, *Destination Peace*, p. 48; Sheffer, *Moshe Sharett*, p. 849.
46. Shlaim, *The Iron Wall*, p. 153.
47. Sheffer, *Moshe Sharett*, p. 849.
48. Rafael, *Destination Peace*, p. 48.
49. Sharon and Chanoff, *Warrior*, p. 128.
50. Shlaim, *The Iron Wall*, p. 154.
51. Michael Bar-Zohar, *Spies in the Promised Land: Iser Harel and the Israeli Secret Service*, trans. Monroe Stearns (Boston: Houghton Mifflin, 1972), p. 151.
52. Ben-Gurion, *My Talks with Arab Leaders*, pp. 271, 273.
53. Ibid., p. 281.
54. Sheffer, *Moshe Sharett*, p. 853.
55. Ben-Gurion, *My Talks with Arab Leaders*, p. 318.
56. Ibid., p. 319.
57. Shlaim, *The Iron Wall*, p. 155.
58. United Nations Security Council Resolution no. 111, January 19, 1956.
59. Document #1773, March 8, 1956, Presidential Papers of Dwight David Eisenhower.
60. Chester L. Cooper, *The Lion's Last Roar: Suez, 1956* (New York: Harper & Row, 1978), p. 86.
61. Bar-Zohar, *Shimon Peres*, p. 122.
62. Morris, *Israel's Border Wars*, pp. 387–88.
63. Bar-Zohar, *Shimon Peres*, p. 126.
64. Shlaim, *The Iron Wall*, p. 164.
65. Bar-Zohar, *Shimon Peres*, pp. 209–10.
66. Sheffer, *Moshe Sharett*, p. 875.
67. *Ha'aretz*, June 15, 1956, cited ibid., p. 878.

3. Suez Crisis: Ben-Gurion Goes to War

1. Mordechai Bar-On interview; Mordechai Bar-On, *The Gates of Gaza: Israel's Road to Suez and Back* (New York: St. Martin's Press, 1994), pp. 169–70; Keith Kyle, *Suez* (New York: St. Martin's Press, 1991), p. 117.

2. Eban, *Personal Witness*, p. 352.
3. Shlaim, *The Iron Wall*, p. 166.
4. Shimon Peres, *Battling for Peace: A Memoir* (New York: Random House, 1995), p. 106.
5. Sharon and Chanoff, *Warrior*, p. 129.
6. Ibid., pp. 129–30.
7. Ibid., pp. 136–39; Yehuda Ben Meir, *Civil-Military Relations in Israel* (New York: Columbia University Press, 1995), p. 130.
8. Michael Bar-Zohar, *Ben-Gurion: A Biography* (New York: Delacorte, 1979), p. 236; Moshe Dayan, *Story of My Life*, pp. 177–78.
9. Bar-Zohar, *Shimon Peres*, p. 150.
10. Moshe Dayan, *Story of My Life*, p. 178–84; Shlaim, *The Iron Wall*, pp. 171–78; Bar-Zohar, *Shimon Peres*, p. 152.
11. Bar-Zohar, *Shimon Peres*, p. 151.
12. Mordechai Bar-On interview.
13. Sharon and Chanoff, *Warrior*, p. 142.
14. Uri Dan, *Ariel Sharon: An Intimate Portrait* (New York: Palgrave Macmillan, 2006), p. 23.
15. Reuven Merhav interview.
16. Sharon and Chanoff, *Warrior*, p. 147.
17. Meron Rapoport, "Into the Valley of Death," *Ha'aretz Daily*, February 7, 2007.
18. Reuven Merhav, communication to the author, August 24, 2009.
19. James Reston, "Capital Softens Mideast Position," *New York Times*, November 4, 1956; Dov Tamari, interview with the author, February 24, 2009.
20. *Ha'aretz Daily*, October 29, 2006.
21. Dov Tamari interview.
22. Michael Brecher, *Decisions in Israel's Foreign Policy* (New Haven, CT: Yale University Press, 1974), p. 283.
23. Mordechai Bar-On interview.
24. Moshe Dayan, *Story of My Life*, p. 202.
25. Eban, *Personal Witness*, p. 275.
26. Moshe Dayan, *Story of My Life*, p. 210.
27. Shlaim, *The Iron Wall*, p. 181.
28. Bar-Zohar, *Shimon Peres*, p. 160.
29. Abba Eban, *An Autobiography* (New York: Random House, 1977), p. 229.
30. Yoram Peri, *Generals in the Cabinet Room: How the Military Shapes Israeli Policy* (Washington, D.C.: U.S. Institute of Peace Press, 2006), p. 160.
31. Yaacov Herzog, *A People That Dwells Alone* (London: Weidenfeld & Nicolson, 1975), p. 247.
32. Bar-Zohar, *Shimon Peres*, p. 211.
33. Sharon and Chanoff, *Warrior*, p. 157.
34. Ibid. Margalit Sharon, in the days before her death in 1962, confided to a friend that "her life had become miserable as a result of her all-consuming suspicion of a liai-

son between her sister [Lily] and her husband." Driving from Jerusalem to Tel Aviv, she veered into the path of an oncoming truck and died of her injuries. See Uzi Benziman, *Sharon—An Israeli Caesar* (New York: Adama Books, 1985), p. 92. Ben-Gurion was rumored to have carried on a long affair with Rivka Katznelson, the editor of the monthly magazine of the Histadrut, as well as a series of other women over the years. And Golda Meir was said to have had affairs with David Remez and Zalman Shazar, Israel's third president. See Elinor Burkett, *Golda* (New York: Harper, 2008), pp. 67–68.

35. Spiegel, *The Other Arab-Israeli Conflict*, pp. 78–80.
36. Radio and Television Address to the American People on the Situation in the Middle East, February 20, 1957, Presidential Papers of Dwight David Eisenhower.
37. Eban, *Personal Witness*, pp. 280–81; Richard B. Parker, ed., *The Six-Day War: A Retrospective* (Gainesville: University Press of Florida, 1996), pp. 122, 131.
38. Eban, *Personal Witness*, p. 280.
39. Mordechai Bar-On interview.
40. Yaël Dayan, *My Father, His Daughter*, p. 135.
41. Anthony Nutting, *Nasser* (New York: Dutton, 1972), pp. 192–95.

4. Israel as "Detonator"

1. Sam Pope Brewer, "Beirut Welcomes Marines; Second Contingent Ashore," *New York Times*, July 16, 1958.
2. Dwight D. Eisenhower, *Waging Peace: The White House Years, a Personal Account 1956–1961* (Garden City, NY: Doubleday, 1965), p. 274.
3. Ibid., p. 271.
4. Ibid., p. 276.
5. Ibid., p. 277.
6. "Ben-Gurion Warns on Carving Israel," *New York Times*, July 30, 1958.
7. In October 1958, Golda Meir discussed Israel's arms needs in Washington. Dulles told her that "events have brought the U.S. and Israel closer together." He added that Eisenhower's dispatch of nineteen thousand troops to Lebanon "made it clear that if Israel should be the victim of unprovoked aggression to extinguish its sovereignty, our response would be just as good as it was in the Lebanese case. This should add to Israel's sense of security and act as a deterrent to Israel's enemies." Meir thanked Dulles for stating plainly that the United States would assist Israel "in case of an attack," but she said the fifty-five Centurion tanks coming from Britain were not enough. Israel needed one thousand tanks, and she pointed out that surplus American Patton tanks were in Italy and France if Washington would only release them. Dulles said that America had just made "important exceptions to our policy of not being a major supplier of arms to Israel," but the basic policy had not changed. Memcon, Dulles-Meir, October 2, 1958, National Security File, History, Vol. XII, LBJ Library, Austin, Texas.
8. A great deal of scholarship has focused on the question of when the United States

began helping Israel to acquire arms. But Ben-Gurion's diary makes clear that after Golda Meir and Shimon Peres lobbied John Foster Dulles for arms in 1958, the Eisenhower administration said no, again, to "direct" arms sales, but yes to an indirect and clandestine method for supporting Israeli purchases of arms in Britain and elsewhere. Ben-Gurion's entries in late 1958 refer to Dulles's counteroffer of $38 million in food aid that Israel could effectively use for any purpose because the State Department granted an exemption to the requirement of making food purchases in the United States with the allotted funds. Hence, food aid dollars helped to purchase British Centurion tanks. Eisenhower made one further exception in approving the direct sale of one thousand recoilless rifles to the IDF, a significant step for improving the firepower of the Israeli infantry. See David Ben-Gurion, diary [Hebrew; trans. Omri Sender], October 18, 1958, Ben-Gurion Archives, Sde Boker; also, Warren Bass, *Support Any Friend* (New York: Oxford University Press, 2003), p. 151.

9. Moshe Dayan, *Avnei Derekh* [Hebrew], p. 356, cited in Yaniv, *Dilemmas of Security*, p. 301n.

10. Bar-Zohar, *Shimon Peres*, pp. 168–69.

11. In his diary, Sharett was more cutting, writing that Ben-Gurion's appetite for conquest "grows with the eating. At first, it was said that we had entered the fray [the Suez War] and conquered what we conquered in order to root out nests of murderers and destroy the bases of their senders. Now, though, we have already invaded not only Sinai but the recesses of primeval history and we have forged a new Torah to prove that this territory [Sinai] is fundamentally ours. If these islands belong to the Jewish people from ancient times, why should the lot of Mount Sinai itself be any less? But Mount Sinai is ours, so what about the great river, the Euphrates?" Quoted in Uri Ben-Eliezer, *The Making of Israeli Militarism* (Bloomington: Indiana University Press, 1998), p. 221.

12. Moshe Sharett, Address to Mapai Party at Beit Berl, October 2, 1957, English translation published in the *Jerusalem Post*, October 18, 1966.

13. Teveth, *Moshe Dayan*, p. 294.

14. Cohen, *Israel and the Bomb*, pp. 58–59; Shlaim, *The Iron Wall*, p. 205.

15. Bar-Zohar, *Shimon Peres*, p. 220.

16. Amos Elon, interview with the author, September 26, 2005.

17. In her memoir, Yaël Dayan revealed that in November 1953, a series of articles appeared in an Israeli magazine touching on sensitive issues, such as the Qibya massacre and Pinhas Lavon, the controversial defense minister. "Some clues concerning a security leak had led the Intelligence Service to me," she said. She was interrogated repeatedly over the course of several days, including by her uncle, Ezer Weizman. Moshe Dayan was in New York at the United Nations, helping Abba Eban defend Israel from international condemnation. Dayan refused to come home early to rescue his fourteen-year-old daughter from the Shabak interrogations. When he finally reached home, "he kissed me warmly, as we hadn't seen each other for a long while, and then he slapped my face, so hard I was almost thrown across the room." *My Father, His Daughter*, pp. 98–99.

18. Dan, *Ariel Sharon*, p. 26.

19. Sharon and Chanoff, *Warrior*, p. 525.

20. Uri Bar-Joseph, "Rotem: The Forgotten Crisis on the Road to the 1967 War," *Journal of Contemporary History* 31, no. 3 (1996): 547–66.

21. Yitzhak Rabin, *The Rabin Memoirs* (Berkeley: University of California Press, 1996), p. 56.

22. Memorandum of Conversation, Eisenhower–Ben-Gurion, National Security File, History (of 1967 War), Vol. XIII, LBJ Library.

23. Ibid.

24. Bar-Zohar, *Shimon Peres*, p. 231; Cohen, *Israel and the Bomb*, pp. 65–75.

25. Bar-Zohar, *Shimon Peres*, p. 231.

26. Ibid., p. 233.

27. Chronology of Israel Assurances of Peaceful Uses of Atomic Energy, National Security File, Robert W. Komer, Box 30, LBJ Library.

28. Ben-Gurion diary, September 26, 1960, cited in Bar-Zohar, *Shimon Peres*, p. 237.

29. Amos Elon, "A Very Special Relationship," *New York Review of Books*, January 15, 2004.

30. Ibid.; Cohen, *Israel and the Bomb*, p. 102.

31. Cohen, *Israel and the Bomb*, p. 103.

32. Ibid., p. 107; Bass, *Support Any Friend*, p. 199.

33. Memorandum, "The French-Israeli Relationship," January 26, 1961, CIA document collection released under the Freedom of Information Act, CIA FOIA website.

34. Memorandum of Conversation, Kennedy–Ben-Gurion, May 30, 1961, National Security File, History, Vol. XII, LBJ Library.

35. Ibid.; Karpin, *The Bomb in the Basement*, p. 193.

36. Bass, *Support Any Friend*, p. 56; Karpin, *The Bomb in the Basement*, p. 194.

37. Stewart Steven, *The Spy-Masters of Israel* (New York: Macmillan, 1980), p. 145; Ian Black and Benny Morris, *Israel's Secret Wars: A History of Israel's Intelligence Services* (New York: Grove Atlantic, 1991), p. 196.

38. Memorandum of Conversation, Kennedy–Meir, December 27, 1962, National Security File, History, Vol. XII, LBJ Library.

39. Ibid.

40. Steven, *The Spy-Masters of Israel*, pp. 140–55.

41. Bar-Zohar, *Shimon Peres*, p. 268.

42. Shlaim, *The Iron Wall*, p. 214.

43. Bar-Zohar, *Shimon Peres*, p. 249.

5. The Rise of the Generals

1. Jay Walz, "Nasser Presses Arab River Plan," *New York Times*, January 14, 1964.

2. Jay Walz, "Nasser Receives Hussein in Cairo; New Ties Hinted," *New York Times*, January 13, 1964.

3. Shlaim, *The Iron Wall*, p. 229.

4. Eshkol, born in 1895 near Kiev, immigrated in 1915. During World War I, he joined the Poalei Yehuda Foundation, which sought to provide welfare to farmers who suffered hardship as a result of the war. In 1917, he enlisted in the Jewish Legion of the British army. During the 1948 War of Independence, Eshkol was part of the Haganah senior command, in charge of procuring equipment and supplies to keep Israeli troops in the field. He was the first director general of the Ministry of Defense, where he served for one year, and he was finance minister from 1951 to 1963.

5. Descriptions of the *Altalena* incident can be found in Moshe Dayan, *Story of My Life*, p. 73; Ezer Weizman, *The Battle for Peace* (New York: Bantam Books, 1981), pp. 213–14; Robert Slater, *Rabin of Israel* (New York: St. Martin's Press, 1993), pp. 75–76.

6. The politicization of the military was apparent when, in 1953, Mapam demanded that officers affiliated with its political movement be allowed to return to military service as part of the negotiations between Mapam and Mapai to join in coalition. Moreover, Ben-Gurion offered to restore Yigal Allon as head of the Southern Command in exchange for the support of Ahdut Ha'avoda (Labor Unity) for war against Egypt. Yoram Peri, *Between Battles and Ballots: Israeli Military in Politics* (New York: Cambridge University Press, 1983), p. 123.

7. Dennis Ross, *The Missing Peace: The Inside Story of the Fight for Middle East Peace* (New York: Farrar, Straus and Giroux, 2004), p. 209.

8. Yitzhak Rabin, *Memoirs*, p. 58.

9. Ibid., p. 60.

10. Bar-Zohar, *Shimon Peres*, p. 265.

11. Cohen, *Israel and the Bomb*, p. 162.

12. Ibid., p. 163.

13. Kennedy's advisers may already have assumed that Eshkol was deceiving them. On November 8, 1965, Dean Rusk cabled the U.S. embassy in Paris, stating that "the possibility of an Israeli-French nuclear weapons arrangement must seriously be considered." He asked for stepped-up intelligence collection in France, adding, "It is difficult to avoid the conclusion" that Israel, at a minimum, is "preserving the nuclear option" at this time. National Security File, Komer, Box 30, LBJ Library.

14. Cohen, *Israel and the Bomb*, p. 168.

15. Bass, *Support Any Friend*, p. 237.

16. Robert Komer Memorandum to President Johnson, February 27, 1964, National Security File, LBJ Library.

17. Cohen, *Israel and the Bomb*, p. 204.

18. Hedrick Smith, "Arab Water Plan Backed at Parley," *New York Times*, September 12, 1964.

19. "Syria Charges Lag by Arabs on Israel," *New York Times*, January 14, 1965.

20. Bar-Zohar, *Shimon Peres*, p. 271.

21. For Dayan's attitude toward following Ben-Gurion into opposition, see Yaël Dayan, *My Father, His Daughter*, p. 166.

22. "Espionage: The Murder of Mehdi Ben Barka," *Time*, December 29, 1975; Black and Morris, *Israel's Secret Wars*, pp. 202–205; Steven, *The Spy-Masters of Israel*, pp. 198–

202. The *New York Times* carried a lengthy investigative article, disclosing details, rumors, and allegations about the Ben Barka assassination and the top secret investigation it had triggered within the upper reaches of the Israeli government. The *Times* disclosed that the Israeli military censor had intercepted queries from the newspaper's headquarters in New York asking about the case, and in one instance, the *Times* acknowledged receiving a message from the Israeli military censor stating, "Censor not permitting further reply to your . . . query." The *Times* reported that Shmuel Mor and Maxim Gilan, editors of the Israeli magazine *Bul*, were arrested on December 11, 1966. They were convicted in secret of violating state security and sentenced to one-year prison terms (they were released in April 1967). Their colleagues were threatened with arrest if they discussed the secret proceedings. "Two Israeli Editors Sentenced on Security Charges," February 19, 1967.

23. "Two Israeli Editors Sentenced on Security Charges," *New York Times*, February 19, 1967.

24. Bar-Zohar, *Shimon Peres*, p. 273.

25. Karpin, *The Bomb in the Basement*, p. 259.

26. Ibid., p. 276.

27. Project Icarus, as Amit's overture to Nasser later came to be called, was first discussed by his senior staff at his home in Ramat Gan. Nachik Navot, then the chief of staff for Amit, took notes at the session. Nachik Navot, interview with the author, April 21, 2008. See also Shlaim, *The Iron Wall*, p. 226.

28. Memorandum, Komer to Johnson, February 8, 1966, National Security File, Komer, Box 6, LBJ Library.

29. Memorandum of Conversation, Gazit–Heywood Stackhouse and William R. Crawford, Jr., March 19, 1964, National Security File, Komer, Box 12, LBJ Library.

30. Gunther E. Rothenberg, *The Anatomy of the Israeli Army* (New York: Hippocrene, 1979), pp. 119–20.

31. Michael B. Oren, *Six Days of War: June 1967 and the Making of the Modern Middle East* (New York: Ballantine, 2003), p. 30.

32. Slater, *Rabin of Israel*, p. 116.

33. Oren, *Six Days of War*, p. 35.

34. Parker, *The Six-Day War*, pp. 67–69.

35. Ibid., p. 42, and chronology.

6. Six-Day War: The Military Revolts

1. "Text of Nasser's Speech on the Blockade of Aqaba," *New York Times*, May 26, 1967.

2. Parker, *The Six-Day War*, p. 59.

3. James Feron, "Eshkol Urges Mutual Troop Pullback," *New York Times*, May 23, 1967.

4. "Text of Nasser's Speech on the Blockade of Aqaba."

5. Donald Janson, "Nixon Asks Action on Mideast Peace," *New York Times*, May 23, 1967.

6. Felix Blair, Jr., "Eisenhower Is Cool to a Unilateral Step," *New York Times*, May 25, 1967.

7. Yitzhak Rabin, *Memoirs*, p. 76; Slater, *Rabin of Israel*, p. 126.

8. Bar-Zohar, *Shimon Peres*, p. 280.

9. Yitzhak Rabin, *Memoirs*, p. 77.

10. Oren, *Six Days of War*, p. 90.

11. Ibid.

12. The preparations for a nuclear warning shot in the event of an Egyptian break-through have never been officially acknowledged by the Israeli government, but key figures have referred to the debate and planning for such a demonstration of Israeli nuclear capability. Michael Bar-Zohar, a biographer of Ben-Gurion and Peres, wrote that Peres had the idea of carrying out a widely publicized nuclear test as a way of preventing the war, but Eshkol rejected it. However, Eshkol seemed interested in holding a couple of crude nuclear devices in reserve as a fail-safe. See Bar-Zohar, *Shimon Peres*, pp. 283–84. One of Israel's top nuclear scientists, Munya Mardor, wrote in his diary that his teams were working around the clock on "a weapons system," which he could not name, but it has been said by other officials to refer to these crude atomic weapons. Avner Cohen, a leading expert on Israel's nuclear complex, also refers to this episode in *The Worst-Kept Secret: Israel's Bargain with the Bomb* (New York: Columbia University Press, 2010), p. 72. Eshkol's stormy relationship with the Israeli nuclear establishment is covered in Karpin, *The Bomb in the Basement*, pp. 260–67.

13. Yitzhak Rabin, *Memoirs*, p. 81.

14. Ibid., p. 83; Slater, *Rabin of Israel*, p. 129.

15. Cable, State to US Embassy Israel, Johnson to Eshkol, May 17, 1967, National Archives, Central Files, 1967–9, Pol, Arab-Israeli.

16. Yitzhak Rabin, *Memoirs*, p. 85; Oren, *Six Days of War*, p. 99.

17. Yitzhak Rabin, *Memoirs*, p. 87.

18. National Security File, History (of 1967 War), Vol. II, LBJ Library.

19. Moshe Dayan, *Story of My Life*, p. 265.

20. Presidential Diary, Message to Eshkol, May 27, 1967, LBJ Library.

21. Ami Gluska, *Eshkol, Give the Order! Israel's Army Command and Political Leadership on the Road to the Six-Day War, 1963–67*, trans. Omri Sender (Tel Aviv: MOD, Ma'arachot, 2005), p. 347; Ze'ev Schiff, "1967—The Generals in the Eyes of the Government" [Hebrew], *Ha'aretz*, June 6, 1997.

22. Miriam Eshkol, interview with the author, December 1, 2005; Tom Segev, *1967: Israel, the War, and the Year That Transformed the Middle East* (New York: Metropolitan Books, 2007), p. 291.

23. Moshe Dayan, *Story of My Life*, p. 266.

24. Oren, *Six Days of War*, p. 132.

25. CIA Report, 1630 Hours, National Security File, History (of 1967 War), Vol. X, LBJ Library.

26. CIA Report, 0900 Hours, ibid.

27. Moshe Dayan, *Story of My Life*, p. 267.

28. Memorandum, [Walt] Rostow to Johnson, re: Eshkol letter attached, National Security File, History (of 1967 War), Vol. III, LBJ Library.

29. Oren, *Six Days of War*, p. 138.

30. Yitzhak Rabin, *Memoirs*, pp. 94–95.

31. Memorandum, Rostow, May 31, 1967, National Security File, History (of 1967 War), Vol. III, LBJ Library; Eban, *Personal Witness*, p. 400.

32. A draft maritime declaration was cabled to American embassies around the world just before midnight on May 31, 1967. Walt Rostow also reported to the president that at the United Nations, the U.S. delegation presented an interim resolution calling for Security Council endorsement of U Thant's appeal to the Arabs and Israelis to forgo belligerence and for further diplomatic and UN efforts to resolve the crisis. National Security File, History (of 1967 War), Vol. III, LBJ Library.

33. Telegram, Robert B. Anderson to President Johnson and Secretary Rusk, Foreign Relations of the United States (FRUS), Vol. XIX, Document 129; also Parker, *The Six-Day War*, p. 212.

34. Yitzhak Rabin, *Memoirs*, p. 95.

35. Memorandum, Helms to Johnson, June 2, 1967, private collection of Robert McNamara.

36. Ibid.

37. Bar-Zohar, *Shimon Peres*, p. 282.

38. Meir Amit, interview with the author, November 17, 2005; Memorandum, Helms to Johnson, June 2, 1967.

39. General Earle G. Wheeler, chairman of the Joint Chiefs of Staff, told President Johnson on May 26 that Egypt had moved 50,000 troops into Sinai and organized them into two defensive lines. Israel was at the same time mobilizing 160,000 ground troops. Wheeler said that based on the Pentagon's assessment, Israel could remain mobilized for two months without harming its economy, whereas Egypt could probably sustain its deployment for only one month. See Memorandum for the Record, FRUS, Vol. XIX, pp. 140–46; Memorandum for the Record, "Meeting on the Arab-Israeli Crisis," May 26, 1967, National Security File, History (of 1967 War), Vol. II, LBJ Library.

40. Memorandum, Helms to Johnson, June 2, 1967.

41. On the day of Amit's return to Israel, Earle Wheeler wrote a detailed memorandum to Robert McNamara, stating that a combined U.S.-British naval task force could "demonstrate US intent to ensure the right of free passage in international waters in the Straits of Tiran and the Gulf of Aqaba." In order to forestall any possibility of a large-scale Egyptian counterstrike, Wheeler recommended a thirty-six-day preparation period to deploy forces that could prevail in any circumstance. Memorandum, Wheeler to McNamara, June 2, 1967, National Security File, History (of 1967 War), Vol. III, LBJ Library.

42. CIA Report, re: Order of Battle: "The UAR has used mustard, phosgene and a type of nerve gas in aerial attacks in Yemen in the past few years, and also has some capability in ground chemical munitions. We have no information on the size of UAR stocks. . . . Israel probably has some offensive CW capability themselves." National Security File, History (of 1967 War), Vol. III, LBJ Library.

43. Bar-Zohar, *Shimon Peres*, p. 283.

44. Yaël Dayan, *My Father, His Daughter*, p. 177.

45. Oren, *Six Days of War*, p. 157; Moshe Dayan, *Story of My Life*, pp. 277–79.

46. Moshe Dayan, *Story of My Life*, pp. 277–79.

47. Ibid.

48. Yaël Dayan, *My Father, His Daughter*, p. 180.

49. In his June 3, 1967, letter to Eshkol, Johnson reiterated the need for Israeli restraint. He said that the United States was "vigorously" pursuing measures "to assure that the Strait and the Gulf remain open to free and innocent passage of the vessels of all nations." Johnson admitted that Israel's "liaison and communication" with the Sixth Fleet "can be improved" and added, "We have completely and fully exchanged views with General Amit." Presidential Diary, LBJ Library.

50. Cable, Ambassador Barbour to Johnson, June 5, 1967, at 0948 Hours. National Security File, History (of 1967 War), Vol. XV, LBJ Library. Also, at 1019 hours on June 5, Johnson received a letter from Eshkol, stating, "After weeks in which our peril has grown day by day, we are now engaged in repelling the aggression which Nasser has been building up against us." FRUS, Arab-Israeli Crisis and War, 1967, Vol. XIX, pp. 302–303.

51. Cable, Ambassador Barbour to Johnson, June 5, 1967.

52. Johnson, writing in his memoir, expressed "a deep feeling of sympathy for Israel and its people," but added, "Nonetheless, I have never concealed my regret that Israel decided to move when it did." He pointed out that by June 4, eight maritime countries (the United States, Britain, Australia, Netherlands, Iceland, Belgium, New Zealand, and Israel) had agreed to support a strong declaration in support of freedom of navigation. Five others, he said (West Germany, Argentina, Portugal, Canada, and Panama), were close to joining the action. Lyndon Baines Johnson, *The Vantage Point: Perspectives of the Presidency 1963–1969* (New York: Holt, Reinhart, 1971), pp. 296–97.

53. Segev, *1967*, p. 367.

54. Hilary Appelman, "Blow Up the Dome of the Rock!" Associated Press, December 31, 1997. Narkiss, who led the Israeli army's capture of the Old City, told the story of Rabbi Goren's statements in an interview with *Ha'aretz* in May 1997, but he stipulated that the story not be published until he and Goren were dead. Goren died in 1994 and Narkis on December 17, 1997.

55. Yaël Dayan, *My Father, His Daughter*, p. 185.

56. Ibid.

57. Tal, "Moshe Dayan: Repentance."

58. Miriam Eshkol interview.

59. Radio traffic between Israeli air controllers released during investigations showed conclusively that Shmuel Kislev, the chief air controller in the Kirya, or military command center, identified the ship as "possibly American" early in the attack, and that one of the pilots read out the *Liberty*'s hull markings in English. Egypt did not use English hull markings. Yet despite these prominent red flags, the attack contin-

ued. See A. J. Cristol, *The "Liberty" Incident* (Washington, D.C.: Brassey's, 2002), pp. 218–19. Secretary of State Dean Rusk, in a formal note to the Israelis, said, "At the time of the attack, the USS *Liberty* was flying the American flag and its identification was clearly indicated in large white letters and numerals on its hull. It was broad daylight and the weather conditions were excellent. Experience demonstrates that both the flag and the identification number of the vessel were readily visible from the air. . . . In these circumstances, the later military attack by Israeli aircraft on the USS *Liberty* is quite literally incomprehensible." FRUS, 1964–68, Arab-Israeli Crisis and War, 1967, Vol. XIX, p. 424. See also James Scott, *The Attack on the "Liberty": The Untold Story of Israel's Assault on a U.S. Spy Ship* (New York: Simon & Schuster, 2009), p. 159; testimony of Richard Helms in Parker, *The Six-Day War*, pp. 278–79.

60. Oren, *Six Days of War*, p. 278.
61. Yitzhak Rabin, *Memoirs*, p. 116.
62. Shlaim, *The Iron Wall*, p. 248.
63. Oren, *Six Days of War*, p. 280.
64. Ibid., p. 292.
65. Moshe Arens, interview with the author, June 13, 2006.

7. War as Policy: Nasser and the PLO

1. Amos Eiran, who was an intimate of Yitzhak Rabin's, said, "Johnson had around him a number of Jewish operators. He preferred, as far as I could judge, to conduct his relations [with Israel] through his Jewish friends and the Jewish friends wanted very much to have it that way as well." Amos Eiran, interview with the author, November 29, 2005. Johnson told his national security advisers that it was "important for everyone to know that the US is not for aggression. We are sorry this has taken place." He added that by the time they got through all the festering problems, "we are going to wish the war had not happened." Memorandum for the Record, National Security Council Meeting, June 7, 1967, 12:05 p.m., National Security File, History (of 1967 War), Vol. XI, LBJ Library.

2. A CIA report sent to the president early in the morning of June 9 stated that Israel's demand that the Arabs enter into immediate peace negotiations as the price of getting their lands back "isn't as simple as it sounds. Mere recognition of Israel, even tacitly through direct negotiations, would be an extremely bitter pill for the Arabs to swallow, and they can be expected to stall and hedge as long as is possible before capitulating to that extent." CIA Report, National Security File, History (of 1967 War), Vol. XI, LBJ Library.

3. Shlomo Gazit, *Trapped Fools: Thirty Years of Israeli Policy in the Territories* (London: Frank Cass, 2003), pp. 138–39.

4. Most telling was Israel's claim that the resolution had succeeded in preventing the UN declaration from requiring withdrawal from all territories. Negotiators had used the phrase "withdrawal . . . from territories occupied in the recent conflict"

instead of "from *the* territories occupied. . . ." Israelis argued that the UN resolution allowed for negotiated changes in the armistice lines that had served as borders up until the outbreak of war in 1967.

5. Eban, *Personal Witness*, p. 460.

6. Shlomo Gazit, then a senior official in the IDF intelligence branch, drafted a peace proposal that called for the creation of a Palestinian state in the West Bank and Gaza Strip, and for making Jerusalem an open city with independent status, like the Vatican. Gazit was part of a group of senior intelligence officials assigned to provide Eshkol and the Israeli cabinet with options in the days after the war. David Kimche of Mossad and Rehavam Ze'evi were also part of this effort. Gazit's recommendation went to Eshkol, Dayan, Rabin, and Meir, but no discussion was held and no action was taken, presumably because any suggestion of giving up the West Bank and Jerusalem would have triggered a political storm that would have destabilized the triumphal spirit that followed the cease-fire. Professor Arye Naor, a biographer of Menachem Begin, said that when Begin heard that Eshkol was receiving various recommendations to establish a Palestinian "autonomy" in the West Bank, he protested that "this would eventually lead to a Palestinian state." Because Begin was still a member of the National Unity government, Eshkol was loath to antagonize him. Stated simply, Gazit said, "Those people were in a terrible euphoria." Gazit, *Trapped Fools*, p. 142; interviews with Shlomo Gazit, November 6, 2005; David Kimche, April 24, 2008; Arye Naor, September 17, 2008.

7. Yoram Peri, a longtime political adviser to Yitzhak Rabin, wrote that due to the nerve-racking "waiting period" that preceded the war, "the government perceived itself as inferior to the General Staff, not only in military issues, but also in political ones. While the generals for their part felt that they had the right to determine such matters." Peri quoted Chaim Bar-Lev as saying, "The war put the generals in a different light in the eyes of the civilian public . . . as those who had something to say and whose opinions the public wanted to know. . . . It also gave the IDF the feeling that it had contributed in the political sphere." Peri, *Between Battles and Ballots*, p. 95.

8. Peri, *Generals in the Cabinet Room*, p. 228.

9. Amir Oren, *Ha'aretz*, April 2004 interview, quoted ibid.

10. Jacob Peri, interview with the author, August 27, 2008.

11. Muki Betser with Robert Rosenberg, *Secret Soldier: The True Life Story of Israel's Greatest Commando* (New York: Atlantic Monthly Press, 1996), pp. 1–24; Muki Betser, interview with the author, March 1, 2009.

12. Andrew Gowers and Tony Walker, *Arafat: The Biography* (London: Virgin Books, 1994), pp. 53–56; Mohammed Heikal, *Road to Ramadan* (New York: Times Books, 1975), p. 66; Efraim Halevy, *Man in the Shadows* (New York: St. Martin's Press, 2006), p. 123; Saïd K. Aburish, *Arafat: From Defender to Dictator* (New York: Bloomsbury, 1998), pp. 81–83.

13. Yaël Dayan, *My Father, His Daughter*, p. 197.

14. Burkett, *Golda*, p. 231.

15. "The Guerrilla Threat in the Middle East," *Time*, December 13, 1968.

16. Robert B. Semple, Jr., "Nixon Stresses Commitment to Israel," *New York Times*, September 9, 1968.

17. Ben Meir, *Civil-Military Relations in Israel*, p. 130.

18. Moshe Dayan, *Avnei Derekh*, pp. 544–45, cited in Yaniv, *Dilemmas of Security*, pp. 32–35.

19. "U.S. Protests Raid in Strong Terms," *New York Times*, December 29, 1968.

20. Harry McPherson, interview with the author, January 26, 2006.

21. FRUS, Vol. XX, 1964–68, Arab-Israeli Dispute, 1967–68, Doc. No. 316.

22. Moshe Dayan, *Living with the Bible*, p. 218.

23. Israel Tal, who commanded the tank forces that overran el-Arish in northern Sinai, went on to develop the Merkava tank for Israel. For his life's work as a tank warfare strategist, Tal is enshrined as one of the five great armor commanders at the Patton Museum of Cavalry and Armor at Fort Knox, Kentucky. Tal reportedly was jealous that Sharon received more acclaim for his armored thrust through central Sinai. Sharon's complex-maneuver warfare in 1967 is still highlighted in Israeli military studies. Mordechai Bar-On and Dov Tamari interviews.

24. His explanation incited much comment, such as this one from a prominent news editor: "From where does Arik Sharon get his pretension that he is the one to judge what is for the good of the state?" Quoted in Peri, *Between Battles and Ballots*, p. 118.

25. Sharon and Chanoff, *Warrior*, pp. 221–27.

26. Gluska, *Eshkol, Give the Order!*, p. 336.

27. Sharon and Chanoff, *Warrior*, p. 233.

28. Efraim Halevy, interview with the author, September 24, 2008.

29. Yitzhak Rabin, *Memoirs*, p. 152.

30. Ibid.

31. Memorandum, Helms to Nixon, September 24, 1969, "The Situation in the Middle East," and Memorandum, Kissinger to Nixon, September 25, 1969, "The Israeli Position—[redacted title]," National Archives, Mandatory Review Release, November 2007.

32. The Israeli military historian Martin Van Creveld wrote, "The main proponent of engaging in 'strategic' bombing was not Dayan but Rabin. . . . Rabin's goal was to bring down Nasser by showing the Egyptian people that their entire country was wide open to attack." Van Creveld, *Moshe Dayan*, p. 147.

33. Spiegel, *The Other Arab-Israeli Conflict*, p. 185; Yitzhak Rabin, *Memoirs*, p. 156. Nixon had created a special committee of top advisers to recommend what he should do about Israel's nuclear program, which was preparing at least ten atomic bombs for deployment on medium-range ballistic missiles. The members of the committee were Henry Kissinger, David Packard, Elliot Richardson, Richard Helms, and Earle Wheeler. In the summer of 1969, the committee presented the president with a range of options meant to apply pressure on Israel to prevent it from declaring itself a nuclear power or deploying nuclear weapons. Even if Israel decided to secretly possess atomic bombs, the committee concluded this also would increase the danger of war in the Middle East. Summing up, Kissinger wrote, "What this means is

that, while we might ideally like to halt actual Israeli possession, what we really want at minimum may be just to keep Israeli possession from becoming an established international fact." No record exists of Nixon taking any action. He did not, as some advisers recommended, withhold the sale of F-4 Phantom jets to force Israel to either halt its bomb-making effort or put its nuclear program under international supervision. Israel, however, perhaps with some private coaching from Washington, adopted a policy of "ambiguity" about its nuclear weapons program by never acknowledging its existence in public statements. See Memorandum for the President, undated, Henry Kissinger, Nixon National Security File, Mandatory Review Release, November 2007.

34. Yitzhak Rabin, *Memoirs*, p. 157.
35. Ibid., p. 158; Shlaim, *The Iron Wall*, p. 292.
36. Heikal, *Road to Ramadan*, p. 92; Richard B. Parker, *The Politics of Miscalculation in the Middle East* (Bloomington: Indiana University Press, 1993), pp. 141–43.
37. Heikal, *Road to Ramadan*, pp. 85–88; also Richard B. Parker, ed., *The October War: A Retrospective* (Gainesville: University Press of Florida, 2001), p. 107.
38. Yitzhak Rabin, *Memoirs*, p. 171.
39. A very disparaging account of Goldmann's mission can be found in Burkett, *Golda*, pp. 278–80; see also Shlaim, *The Iron Wall*, p. 294.
40. Eban, *Personal Witness*, p. 488; Yitzhak Rabin, *Memoirs*, p. 175.
41. Yitzhak Rabin, *Memoirs*, p. 175.
42. Eban, *Personal Witness*, p. 488.
43. UN Security Council Resolution 242, November 22, 1967, called for "withdrawal of Israeli armed forces from territories occupied in the recent conflict," as well as recognition of the right of every state in the area "to live in peace within secure and recognized boundaries free from threats or acts of force." It affirmed the necessity "for guaranteeing freedom of navigation through international waterways in the area" and "for achieving a just settlement of the refugee problem."
44. Henry Kissinger, *The White House Years* (Boston: Little, Brown, 1979), pp. 600–31.
45. Sharon and Chanoff, *Warrior*, p. 247.
46. *Sunday Times* (London), June 15, 1969.
47. In February 1969, a month after his inauguration, Nixon received a memorandum from Secretary of Defense Melvin Laird saying that the Pentagon "was persuaded" that "Israel is developing both nuclear weapons and strategic missiles at a rapid pace and may have both this year." By the end of 1970, Israel was expected to have a total force of twenty-four to thirty surface-to-surface Jericho missiles, ten of which were programmed for nuclear warheads. See documents attached to Memorandum for the President (July 1969), Henry Kissinger, Nixon National Security File, Mandatory Review Release, November 2007.
48. Shlaim, *The Iron Wall*, p. 315.
49. Teveth, *Moshe Dayan*, p. 292; Yaël Dayan, *My Father, His Daughter*, p. 204.
50. Yaël Dayan, *My Father, His Daughter*, p. 201.
51. Sharon and Chanoff, *Warrior*, pp. 250–51.

52. Ibid.

53. Gaza residents remember the Bulldozer in Phil Reeves, "Sharon's Return Puts Wreckage Street in Fear," *Independent* (London), January 21, 2001.

54. Sharon and Chanoff, *Warrior*, pp. 260–62.

55. Memorandum of Conversation, Allon–Rockefeller, March 10, 1971, National Archives, Nixon National Security Files.

56. Memorandum of Conversation, Meir–Rockefeller, March 10, 1971, National Archives, Nixon National Security Files.

57. Eban, *Personal Witness*, pp. 504–505; Peri, *Generals in the Cabinet Room*, p. 157; Yitzhak Rabin, *Memoirs*, p. 197.

58. Memorandum of Conversation, Meir–Barbour, March 23, 1971, National Archives, Nixon National Security Files; see also Craig A. Daigle, "The Russians Are Going: Sadat, Nixon and the Soviet Presence in Egypt 1970–1971," *Middle East Review of International Affairs* 8, no. 1 (March 2004): 1–15.

59. Yitzhak Rabin, *Memoirs*, p. 196.

60. Peri, *Between Battles and Ballots*, p. 97; Gazit, *Trapped Fools*, p. 65.

61. Yitzhak Rabin, *Memoirs*, p. 205.

62. Ibid., p. 210.

63. Mahmoud Riad, *The Struggle for Peace in the Middle East* (New York: Quartet Books, 1981), p. 230; Heikal, *Road to Ramadan*, pp. 171–84; Parker, *The Six-Day War*, p. 48.

64. Muki Betser interview.

65. Betser and Rosenberg, *Secret Soldier*, pp. 138–42, 144–45.

66. Abu Iyad with Eric Rouleau, *My Home, My Land: A Narrative of the Palestinian Struggle* (New York: Times Books, 1981), p. 116.

67. Terence Smith, "Israel Vows Wide Fight on Guerrillas," *New York Times*, September 13, 1972.

68. Betser records that during the send-off at Haifa pier on April 9, General Elazar stood with General Eli Zeira and exhorted the team to success. "We've got to kill those bastards," Elazar said. Betser raised his hand. "Did you say kill?" he asked. Until that moment, Betser said, they had planned the operation as a kidnapping, to take the Black September leaders back to Israel and put them on trial. "We practiced to take them prisoner, tying their hands and feet and carrying them back home with us," Betser said. At that moment, Dado Elazar looked at Zeira and then turned back to the commando team: "Yes. Kill them," the chief of staff said. Betser and Rosenberg, *Secret Soldier*, pp. 165–66.

69. Ibid., p. 170.

8. The High Price of Militarism: Yom Kippur

1. President Johnson played host to "Lt. and Mrs. Ashraf Marwan" on September 13, 1966. Johnson had invited the couple in an August 23, 1966, letter to Mona's father. Confidential File, Box 12, LBJ Library. After Marwan's death in London in suspicious

circumstances on June 27, 2007, a number of investigations into his secret life were opened, but none has come to any public conclusion. His family reported that Marwan had completed a tell-all memoir, but at the time of his death, the manuscript went missing from his London apartment. On May 10, 2009, the U.S. television show *60 Minutes* examined the extensive record of Marwan's Mossad contacts. "Was the Perfect Spy a Double Agent?," produced by Ira Rosen with Steve Kroft as correspondent.

2. Former chief of military intelligence Aharon Ze'evi Farkash said in an interview that he produced a scholarly study from all intelligence sources of the run-up to the 1973 war, including from captured Egyptian files and communications intercepts. "On May 10, we began to see that maybe on the 16th or 17th it will be the beginning of this maneuver and that May 19 was the D-day. It was easier to cross the canal in May due to the flow of water. We called for a few reserve forces [to be mobilized] and the intelligence said that this is going to be war. But suddenly, everything stopped. Why? Because of Brezhnev and Nixon. Brezhnev stopped the Syrians and the Egyptians, and told them this is impossible for us because of détente and the summit in Washington in May [sic] 1973." Aharon Ze'evi Farkash, interview with the author, September 25, 2008.

3. Bernard Gwertzman, "Overseas Criticism on Watergate Mild," *New York Times*, May 17, 1973.

4. Henry Tanner, "Sadat Appeals to Soviet," *New York Times*, May 2, 1973.

5. Sharon and Chanoff, *Warrior*, pp. 269–71.

6. Ibid., p. 230.

7. Memorandum of Conversation, Kissinger–Ardeshir Zahedi, August 13, 1973, Nixon National Security Files, National Archives.

8. Anatoly Dobrynin, *In Confidence: Moscow's Ambassador to America's Six Cold War Presidents* (New York: Times Books, 1995), p. 293.

9. Tanner, "Sadat Appeals to Soviet."

10. Aharon Ze'evi Farkash interview.

11. Memorandum for the President's Files, June 23, 1973, Nixon National Security Files, National Archives.

12. Gazit, *Trapped Fools*, pp. 256–57.

13. Ibid.

14. Heikal, *Road to Ramadan*, p. 20.

15. After declaring that there was no Palestine, Dayan went on to say, "I should have said I'm sorry, but I'm not sorry. There are Palestinians, and there was a country named Palestine. That Palestine was divided between Israel and Jordan, so there are Palestinian people but there is not any Palestinian state. The country called Palestine vanished in 1948." Jerrold Schecter, "Israel: Waiting in the Wings," *Time*, July 30, 1973.

16. Shlaim, *The Iron Wall*, p. 317.

17. Ibid.; Gazit, *Trapped Fools*, pp. 257–58.

18. Sharon and Chanoff, *Warrior*, pp. 275–87.

19. The internecine struggle in the Jewish community was a dominant theme in Sha-

ron's life; indeed, it was the story of his life. Sharon was deeply marked by the many conflicts fostered by his strong-willed father in the agricultural moshav where Sharon grew up. The disputes were over crops and agricultural techniques, but they were waged with so much rancor, stubbornness, and acrimony that the village seemed to be at war with Sharon's family, causing much consternation for the young Sharon. "My father was never one to get out of a hurricane's path for any reason, and here his deepest principles were at issue," Sharon wrote. "First and last he was a Jewish nationalist. The idea of Jews fighting each other while the community as a whole was struggling for existence went against the marrow of his bones." Sharon seems to have conflated the struggle in his village with the larger ideological conflict that racked the Jewish community as Ben-Gurion faced off with Jabotinsky and the Revisionists over basic Zionist goals and principles. "The Mapai membership closed ranks behind their leaders, focusing a consuming hatred toward Jabotinsky's 'revisionists.' It was a hatred that penetrated every corner of the Jewish community, stigmatizing the revisionists as assassins [in the death of Chaim Arlosoroff], enemies of the Jewish people, illegitimate Zionists whose methods made them anathema. Like the rest of the country, Kfar Malal was swept by violent emotions." Sharon concluded this description by saying, "Like Jabotinsky's followers themselves, he [his father] and my mother were branded. For a time the hatred in the village was palpable." Ibid., pp. 25–26.

20. Dan, *Ariel Sharon*, p. 54.

21. Ibid., p. 295.

22. Muki Betser interview.

23. Nicholas Veliotes, Oral History, January 29, 1990, pp. 29–30, Association for Diplomatic Studies and Training, Arlington, VA.

24. For a detailed study of the intelligence failure, see Uri Bar-Joseph, *The Watchmen Fell Asleep: The Surprise of Yom Kippur and Its Sources* (Albany: State University of New York Press, 2005).

25. Van Creveld, *Moshe Dayan*, p. 177. Other details about Zeira's failure to activate the bugging system and his duplicity over that failure were provided by a senior military intelligence officer who cannot be named because the matter is still classified and the officer would be subject to sanction.

26. Parker, *The October War*, pp. 87–88; Aharon Ze'evi Farkash interview.

27. A number of experts in Israeli nuclear matters allude to this nuclear alert, but declassified U.S. government files shed no light on the protocols Golda Meir followed in preparing for the worst case. The most recent speculative account appears in Cohen, *The Worst-Kept Secret*. White House files indicate clearly that the CIA had documented a small but potent Israeli arsenal of more than ten serviceable nuclear weapons by the early 1970s, so it is logical that this arsenal was activated as a contingency to prevent an Israeli military collapse. Regarding Dayan's state of gloom, the Israeli journalist Amos Elon stated that the editor of *Davar*, the Mapai-backed newspaper, burst into tears when she heard Dayan express his fear that Egyptian forces might break through on the southern front and overrun Israel. General Avraham

Adan says that it was Dayan's statement to the editors—that he was going to repeat his pessimistic projection on television in order to "play straight with the people"— that prompted the journalists to appeal to Meir to prevent it. General Aharon Yariv appeared in his stead. This example of self-censorship revealed a deeply ingrained impulse for propaganda within the Israeli media, demonstrating a preference for broad national deception on security grounds, a practice that had been fostered since Ben-Gurion's time, when newspaper editors were suborned to share the responsibility of keeping state secrets about Dimona, reprisal raids, and sensitive intelligence operations.

28. An authoritative account of the opening days of the war can be found in Avraham (Bren) Adan, *On the Banks of the Suez: An Israeli General's Personal Account of the Yom Kippur War* (Novato, CA: Presidio Press, 1980).

29. Meir was critical of her own performance. When Elazar pressed for a call-up of reserves on October 5, she refused. "That Friday morning I should have listened to the warnings of my own heart and ordered a call-up. For me, that fact cannot and never will be erased . . . and I shall have to live with that terrible knowledge for the rest of my life." Golda Meir, *My Life* (New York: Putnam, 1975), p. 425.

30. Peri, *Between Battles and Ballots*, p. 257; Ben Meir, *Civil-Military Relations in Israel*, p. 66.

31. Burkett, *Golda*, p. 337; Motti Ashkenazi wrote a gripping remembrance of the battle for Budapest, "Just a Scared Soldier," *Jerusalem Post*, October 3, 2003.

32. Muki Betser interview.

33. Meir, *My Life*, p. 458.

9. Rabin: From General to Prime Minister

1. Terence Smith, "Ben-Gurion Bier Viewed by 200,000," *New York Times*, December 3, 1973.

2. Terence Smith, "Knesset Endorses Rabin as Premier," *New York Times*, June 4, 1974.

3. "Israeli Premier Wins Vote Over U.S.-Egyptian Accord," United Press International, June 19, 1974.

4. Slater, *Rabin of Israel*, pp. 213–19; Yitzhak Rabin, *Memoirs*, p. 240; Bar-Zohar, *Shimon Peres*, p. 301.

5. In his memoir, Abba Eban skewered Rabin as a militarist during his ambassadorship in Washington. "A study of his cables to Jerusalem showed periods of thoughtfulness and moderation interrupted by sudden outbursts of aggressiveness." Eban quoted Gideon Rafael, his deputy, as saying that Rabin once confronted Joseph Sisco with a proposal "that the Israeli Army might have to march on Cairo." Rabin implied that it was a sign of possible assent that Sisco "did not fall from his chair." Eban, *Personal Witness*, p. 567.

6. Spiegel, *The Other Arab-Israeli Conflict*, p. 232.

7. David Holden, "'Hero of the Crossing,' They Shout, 'Where Is Our Breakfast?'" *New York Times*, June 1, 1975.

8. Ibid.

9. Gazit, *Trapped Fools*, p. 265; Peri, *Generals in the Cabinet Room*, p. 169; Bar-Zohar, *Shimon Peres*, p. 308; Ben Meir, *Civil-Military Relations in Israel*, p. 116.

10. Gazit, *Trapped Fools*, p. 265; Ben Meir, *Civil-Military Relations in Israel*, p. 116.

11. Slater, *Rabin of Israel*, p. 237.

12. Bar-Zohar, *Shimon Peres*, p. 311.

13. Ibid.

14. Sharon and Chanoff, *Warrior*, pp. 346–47.

15. Speech by Yasser Arafat, General Assembly of the United Nations, 29th Session, November 13, 1974.

16. Jacob Peri, interview with the author, September 23, 2008.

17. David Kimche's association with the Lebanon project is well known among the military and political elites of Israel. Among those I interviewed to understand Kimche's influence were Shabtai Shavit, Efraim Halevy, Reuven Merhav, Nachik Navot, Avi Primor, and Kimche himself. He told me before he died that he had considered writing a more detailed account of the Lebanon tragedy than the summary treatment rendered in his book *The Last Option: After Nasser, Arafat and Saddam Hussein: The Quest for Peace in the Middle East* (New York: Scribner, 1991), but had not found the time.

18. Kimche, *The Last Option*, p. 143.

19. Peres, *Battling for Peace*, p. 195; Bar-Zohar, *Shimon Peres*, p. 305.

20. Shlaim, *The Iron Wall*, p. 344.

21. Yitzhak Rabin, *Memoirs*, p. 282.

22. Muki Betser interview; Betser and Rosenberg, *Secret Soldier*, pp. 326–28.

23. Muki Betser interview.

24. Slater, *Rabin of Israel*, p. 253; Yitzhak Rabin, *Memoirs*, p. 289.

25. Yitzhak Rabin, *Memoirs*, p. 291.

26. Leah Rabin revealed a much more calculating perspective on her husband's decision, suggesting that he left office in order not to take the blame for the coming Labor Party defeat and to preserve a chance at political comeback down the road. Leah Rabin, *Our Life, His Legacy* (New York: G. P. Putnam's Sons, 1997), p. 171.

27. Alon Liel, interview with the author, April 23, 2008.

28. Jimmy Carter explained his viewpoint to me in an interview. "Before I became president, I knew that I wanted to make a major effort towards Middle East peace, and I had seen what had happened in the past. We had four wars, between Israel and Egypt primarily, in the last twenty-five years, all of them very devastating wars. And I knew that I had to take a balanced position, so-called, which is inimical to American supporters of Israel; the word 'balanced' means 'unbalanced.' And I think it was March, just within two months after I became president I called for a Palestinian homeland. [There] was an outpouring of criticism, but I was a brand-new president then, and I think a lot of the Israeli supporters in our country thought that I was just naïve and didn't quite know what was going on. But it was that approach, in my own not completely unbiased opinion, that made it possible for me to be successful later

on at Camp David, because I had to protect Palestinian rights as I dealt with Sadat because that was one of the two requirements that he had in reaching any sort of agreement." Interview with the author, April 28, 2006. See also Yitzhak Rabin, *Memoirs*, p. 299.

10. Begin: A Peace to Enable War

1. Marvine Howe, "Arabs Say the Vote Is a Blow to Peace," *New York Times*, May 19, 1977.
2. Sources on Begin include Menachem Begin, *The Revolt* (New York: Nash Publishing, 1977); Amos Perlmutter, *The Life and Times of Menachem Begin* (Garden City, NY: Doubleday, 1987); J. Bowyer Bell, *Terror out of Zion: Irgun Zvai Leumi, LEHI, and the Palestine Underground 1929–1949* (New York: St. Martin's Press, 1977); Eitan Haber, *Menachem Begin: The Legend and the Man* (New York: Delacorte, 1978).
3. "No Victors in Israel," editorial, *New York Times*, May 19, 1977.
4. Colin Shindler, *The Triumph of Military Zionism: Nationalism and the Origins of the Israeli Right* (London: I. B. Taurus, 2006), pp. 14–17.
5. William E. Farrell, "Begin Takes Office After 8-Hour Debate," *New York Times*, June 21, 1977.
6. Arye Naor, interview with the author, September 17, 2008.
7. Moshe Dayan, *Breakthrough: A Personal Account of the Egypt-Israel Peace Negotiations* (New York: A. A. Knopf, 1981), p. 4.
8. Begin was speaking on ABC-TV's *Issues and Answers* program. See "Begin Bars Return to '67 Borders," *New York Times*, May 23, 1977.
9. Weizman, *The Battle for Peace*, p. 20.
10. Ezer Weizman, *On Eagles' Wings: The Personal Story of the Leading Commander of the Israeli Air Force* (New York: Macmillan, 1976), p. 74.
11. Gazit, *Trapped Fools*, p. 81.
12. Ben Meir, *Civil-Military Relations in Israel*, p. 147.
13. "Sadat Rules Out Ties in a Pact with Israel," *New York Times*, July 2, 1977.
14. Bernard Gwertzman, "U.S. Calls on Israel to Quit Some Lands in All the Sectors," *New York Times*, June 28, 1977.
15. Weizman, *The Battle for Peace*, p. 19.
16. Moshe Dayan, *Breakthrough*, pp. 38–54; William B. Quandt, *Camp David: Peacemaking and Politics* (Washington, D.C.: Brookings Institution, 1986), p. 110; Shlaim, *The Iron Wall*, p. 358.
17. Riad, *The Struggle for Peace in the Middle East*, p. 306; Peri, *Generals in the Cabinet Room*, p. 164.
18. Jehan Sadat, *A Woman of Egypt* (New York: Simon & Schuster, 1987), p. 378.
19. Anwar Sadat, *In Search of Identity: An Autobiography* (New York: Harper & Row, 1977), p. 309.
20. Anwar Sadat, Transcript of Address to the Knesset, *New York Times*, November 21, 1977.

21. Weizman, *The Battle for Peace*, p. 33.

22. Ibid., p. 145.

23. Sharon and Chanoff, *Warrior*, p. 365.

24. Ibid., pp. 370–71.

25. "Begin Bars Return to '67 Borders."

26. Tamar S. Hermann, *The Israeli Peace Movement: A Shattered Dream* (New York: Cambridge University Press, 2009), p. 89.

27. Henry Kamm, "Begin Hints Strongly at Reprisal for Attack in Which 46 Perished," *New York Times*, March 13, 1978. See also Isabel Kershner, "Palestinians Honor a Figure Reviled in Israel as a Terrorist," *New York Times*, March 11, 2010.

28. Weizman, *The Battle for Peace*, p. 273; Jimmy Carter, *The Blood of Abraham: Insights into the Middle East* (Boston: Houghton Mifflin, 1986), pp. 96–97; Jimmy Carter, *Keeping Faith* (New York: Bantam Books, 1982), p. 310.

29. Shlomo Nakdimon, *First Strike: The Exclusive Story of How Israel Foiled Iraq's Attempt to Get the Bomb* (New York: Summit Books, 1997), pp. 92–95; Sharon and Chanoff, *Warrior*, pp. 381–82; Shlaim, *The Iron Wall*, p. 386.

30. Slater, *Rabin of Israel*, p. 305.

31. Moshe Dayan, *Breakthrough*, pp. 153–54.

32. Major-General Avraham Tamir, *A Soldier in Search of Peace: An Inside Look at Israel's Strategy in the Middle East* (New York: Harper & Row, 1988), p. 41.

33. Sharon and Chanoff, *Warrior*, p. 402.

34. Israel's hypersensitivity about the PLO was intense. During Gerald Ford's administration, Kissinger had pledged that the United States would not deal with the PLO until it renounced terrorism. The State Department enforced a ban against diplomats even meeting with the PLO. The obsessive monitoring of these restrictions had forced Carter in August 1979 to fire Andrew Young, his UN ambassador, for holding conversations with Arafat's representative in New York.

35. Steven, *The Spy-Masters of Israel*, pp. 281–93; Black and Morris, *Israel's Secret Wars*, pp. 275–77.

36. Sharon and Chanoff, *Warrior*, p. 426.

37. Ben Meir, *Civil-Military Relations in Israel*, pp. 40–41.

38. Weizman, *The Battle for Peace*, p. 229.

39. Moshe Dayan, *Breakthrough*, pp. 304–305.

40. Carter, *Keeping Faith*, pp. 494–95.

41. Sharon and Chanoff, *Warrior*, p. 427.

42. Avi Primor, a career diplomat, had been in trouble with Dayan when Kimche rescued him. In the early 1970s, Primor had been press spokesman at the Israeli embassy in Paris. He had raised questions about an alleged demand by Dayan for $15,000 in cash for an interview with French television. Primor had written to Dayan, criticizing the practice of demanding fees for interviews, and leaked the letter to the Israeli press, triggering a Knesset inquiry. Dayan never forgave him for impugning his reputation, and when Begin appointed Dayan foreign minister, suddenly he was Primor's boss and Primor was certain that his career was over. Then

Kimche had come calling, looking for an experienced hand to teach the Lebanese Phalange how to take over their country. Dayan approved the transfer, saying simply, "By all means." Avi Primor, interview with the author, February 25, 2009.

43. Ibid.

44. Interviews with Shabtai Shavit (April 25, 2008), Efraim Halevy, Reuven Merhav, and Nachik Navot. My request to Kimche to address his dispute with Hofi was under discussion when he fell ill in 2009. Hofi declined my request.

45. Weizman, *The Battle for Peace*, p. 113.

46. Shlaim, *The Iron Wall*, p. 383.

47. "The Architect of Toughness," *Time*, May 3, 1982.

48. David Ivry, interview with the author, May 6, 2008.

49. Ben Meir, *Civil-Military Relations in Israel*, p. 138; Shlaim, *The Iron Wall*, p. 386.

50. Matti Golan, *The Road to Peace: A Biography of Shimon Peres* (New York: Warner Books, 1989), p. 204.

51. Ibid., p. 203.

52. Dan Margalit, *Ha'aretz*, May 13, 1981, cited in Yaniv, *Dilemmas of Security*, p. 82. See also Ze'ev Schiff and Ehud Ya'ari, *Israel's Lebanon War* (New York: Simon & Schuster, 1984), p. 25.

53. Howard Teicher and Gayle Radley Teicher, *Twin Pillars to Desert Storm* (New York: William Morrow, 1993), pp. 118, 121–22, 143; Sharon and Chanoff, *Warrior*, p. 428.

54. Yoram Peri, *Between Battles and Ballots: Israeli Military in Politics* (New York: Cambridge University Press, 1983), p. 267.

55. Kimche, *The Last Option*, p. 139.

56. Israel received seventy-five F-16s in the summer of 1980 and was able to employ this superior technology fighter-bomber against the Iraqi reactor. David Ivry interview.

57. Translated text of Peres letter in Perlmutter, *The Life and Times of Menachem Begin*, p. 364; Ben Meir, *Civil-Military Relations in Israel*, p. 142; Golan, *The Road to Peace*, pp. 206–207.

58. Aluf Ben, "Olmert's Gamble," *Ha'aretz*, October 18, 2006.

59. Shlaim, *The Iron Wall*, p. 387.

60. Dan, *Ariel Sharon*, p. 90.

61. General Avraham Tamir wrote that after Sharon took over the Defense Ministry, "the air force resumed bombing PLO positions in Lebanon on a more intensive scale than before. The new policy was that the PLO should be subjected to continuous attack at times and places of Israel's choosing, instead of in reprisal for specific acts of terrorism." The climax of this offensive came on July 17 with an air attack on PLO headquarters. "What came as a shock to Israel," Tamir wrote, "was the PLO reaction to these bombings. Israeli towns and villages in the border areas came under artillery and rocket fire" lasting twelve days. Tamir, *A Soldier in Search of Peace*, p. 116.

62. Sharon and Chanoff, *Warrior*, pp. 432–36.

63. Tamir, *A Soldier in Search of Peace*, p. 116.

64. Yaniv, *Dilemmas of Security*, p. 20.

65. Arye Naor interview.

66. Teicher and Teicher, *Twin Pillars to Desert Storm*, pp. 155–58.

67. Alexander M. Haig, Jr., *Caveat: Realism, Reagan and Foreign Policy* (New York: Macmillan, 1984), pp. 326–27.

68. Yaël Dayan, *My Father, His Daughter*, p. 210.

69. Ibid.

70. Weizman, *The Battle for Peace*, p. 114.

71. Shlaim, *The Iron Wall*, p. 393.

72. Samuel Lewis, interview with the author, March 15, 2006.

73. Sharon and Chanoff, *Warrior*, pp. 436–37.

74. Ben Meir, *Civil-Military Relations in Israel*, p. 151; Shlaim, *The Iron Wall*, p. 397.

75. Schiff and Ya'ari, *Israel's Lebanon War*, pp. 65–66.

76. Sharon and Chanoff, *Warrior*, pp. 437–42.

77. Nachik Navot interview.

78. Sharon and Chanoff, *Warrior*, p. 442; Nachik Navot interview.

79. Sharon and Chanoff, *Warrior*, p. 443.

80. Ibid., p. 445; Yaniv, *Dilemmas of Security*, p. 302n43.

81. Tamir, *A Soldier in Search of Peace*, pp. 60–61.

82. Shlaim, *The Iron Wall*, p. 399.

83. Tamir, *A Soldier in Search of Peace*, p. 124; Schiff and Ya'ari, *Israel's Lebanon War*, p. 53.

84. Ben Meir, *Civil-Military Relations in Israel*, pp. 154–55.

85. *Yedioth Ahronoth*, May 14, 1982, cited in David Hirst, *Beware of Small States: Lebanon, Battleground of the Middle East* (New York: Nation Books, 2010), p. 134.

86. Sharon and Chanoff, *Warrior*, pp. 447–50.

87. Gowers and Walker, *Arafat*, p. 192; Lawrence Joffee, "Obituary: Shlomo Argov," *Guardian*, February 25, 2003.

88. Shlaim, *The Iron Wall*, p. 405.

11. The Sabra Caesar: Sharon in Lebanon

1. Two senior officials described Israeli intentions thus: "As the military infrastructure of the PLO grew in strength, it became increasingly clear to Israel's political and defense establishment that [the Israeli] army would sooner or later have to destroy it." See Kimche, *The Last Option*, p. 143. "A further consideration was that a crippling blow to the PLO in Lebanon would diminish its influence in the West Bank and Gaza, and thus strengthen Israel's hold on these occupied territories." See Tamir, *A Soldier in Search of Peace*, p. 116.

2. Yaniv, *Dilemmas of Security*, p. 307n21.

3. Arye Naor interview.

4. Hirst, *Beware of Small States*, p. 135.

5. Dan, *Ariel Sharon*, pp. 101–102.

6. Sharon and Chanoff, *Warrior*, p. 479.

7. Slater, *Rabin of Israel*, p. 230.

8. Ronald Reagan, *The Reagan Diaries* (New York: HarperCollins, 2007) p. 98; Dan, *Ariel Sharon*, p. 105.

9. *Ma'ariv*, July 17, 1982, cited in Yaniv, *Dilemmas of Security*, p. 288n3.

10. Mohamed Heikal, *Secret Channels: The Inside Story of Arab-Israeli Peace Negotiations* (London: HarperCollins, 1996), p. 356.

11. Gowers and Walker, *Arafat*, p. 202.

12. Oriana Fallaci, "Interview with Ariel Sharon: 'If the Syrians Don't Move, We Don't . . .'" *Times* (London), August 30, 1982.

13. Gowers and Walker, *Arafat*, p. 203.

14. Shabtai Shavit interview.

15. Sharon and Chanoff, *Warrior*, p. 497.

16. Kimche, *The Last Option*, p. 157.

17. "Excerpts from Interview with Begin," *New York Times*, August 29, 1982; Ariel Sharon, "Gains from the War in Lebanon," *New York Times*, August 29, 1982.

18. Howard M. Sachar, *A History of Israel: From the Rise of Zionism to Our Time*, 3rd ed. (New York: Knopf, 2007), pp. 911–12; Kimche, *The Last Option*, pp. 157–58; Schiff and Ya'ari, *Israel's Lebanon War*, pp. 234–36.

19. Shlaim, *The Iron Wall*, p. 415.

20. "Excerpts from Interview with Begin."

21. Colin Shindler, *Land Beyond Promise: Israel, Likud and the Zionist Dream* (London: I. B. Taurus, 1995), p. 150.

22. One of the most chilling documents to emerge in the reconstruction of the massacre was a memorandum of conversation from the September 16, 1982, meeting of Sharon, Eitan, Saguy, and the American diplomats Morris Draper and Samuel Lewis. Draper expressed shock and surprise when he was informed that IDF was about to allow the Phalange militia into West Beirut where the IDF had taken up positions. After a testy exchange, Eitan told the Americans, "Let me explain to you. Lebanon is at a point of exploding into a frenzy of revenge. No one can stop them. Yesterday we spoke with the Phalange about their plans. They don't have a strong command. . . . They're obsessed with the idea of revenge. You have to know the Arabs well to sense something like that. . . . I'm telling you that some of their commanders visited me and I could see in their eyes that it's going to be a relentless slaughter. A number of incidents already happened today, and it's a good thing we were there, rather than the Lebanese army, to prevent it from going further." Schiff and Ya'ari, *Israel's Lebanon War*, pp. 259–60.

23. Nachik Navot interview.

24. David K. Shipler, "Pullout Opposed, Cabinet Leaves Open the Possibility of Holding an Internal Inquiry," *New York Times*, September 22, 1982.

25. Sharon and Chanoff, *Warrior*, p. 513.

26. Ibid., p. 510.

27. Report of the Kahan Commission, February 8, 1983, available from the Council on Foreign Relations.

28. Ibid.

29. Sharon and Chanoff, *Warrior*, pp. 35, 522.
30. Ibid.
31. On December 4, 1983, two U.S. navy combat planes were shot down during a bombing run against Syrian air defense sites in Lebanon. One pilot, Lieutenant Mark Lange, was killed, and another was rescued. Lange's weapons officer, Lieutenant Robert Goodman, was captured and held by Syria until being released by President Hafez al-Assad to the Reverend Jesse Jackson on January 3, 1984.
32. Arye Naor interview.
33. David K. Shipler, "Begin Announces He Plans to Quit as Israeli Premier," *New York Times*, August 29, 1983.
34. Slater, *Rabin of Israel*, p. 320.
35. Interview with Yitzhak Rabin, *Time*, February 11, 1985.
36. Ibid.
37. Efraim Halevy interview.

12. Protecting the Ruling Elite

1. Bar-Zohar, *Shimon Peres*, p. 415.
2. Peter Hounam, "Revealed: The Secrets of Israel's Nuclear Arsenal," *Sunday Times* (London), October 5, 1986.
3. John Daniszewski, "Confession of a Killing in Cold Blood Chills Israel," *Los Angeles Times*, July 27, 1996.
4. Bar-Zohar, *Shimon Peres*, p. 375.
5. Thomas L. Friedman, "'Shocked' Israel Investigates Charge by U.S. of Espionage," *New York Times*, November 25, 1985.
6. Slater, *Rabin of Israel*, p. 327.
7. Ibid., p. 328.
8. Lawrence E. Walsh, *Firewall: The Iran-Contra Conspiracy and Cover-up* (New York: Norton, 1997), pp. 37–47.
9. Teicher and Teicher, *Twin Pillars to Desert Storm*, p. 301.
10. Prince Bandar bin Sultan, interview with the author, August 2006.
11. Robert C. McFarlane with Zofia Smardz, *Special Trust* (New York: Cadell & Davies, 1994), pp. 19–21.
12. Bernard Gwertzman, "McFarlane Took Cake and Bible to Teheran, ex-C.I.A. Man Says," *New York Times*, January 11, 1987.

13. Intifada: The Intimate Enemy Awakes

1. Jacob Peri interview.
2. Ibid.
3. Slater, *Rabin of Israel*, p. 331.
4. Gazit, *Trapped Fools*, pp. 292–312; Eitan Haber, interview with the author, November 21, 2005.

5. Shlaim, *The Iron Wall*, p. 452.
6. Yitzhak Rabin, *Memoirs*, p. 355.
7. Slater, *Rabin of Israel*, p. 341.
8. Ibid.
9. John Hadden, interview with the author, April 5, 2006.
10. Amnon Lipkin-Shahak, interview with the author, September 4, 2008.
11. Dan Raviv and Yossi Melman, *Every Spy a Prince: The Complete History of Israel's Intelligence Community* (Boston: Houghton Mifflin, 1990), pp. 391–97; Ephraim Kahana, *Historical Dictionary of Israeli Intelligence* (Lanham, MD: Scarecrow Press, 2006), pp. 2–3.
12. Slater, *Rabin of Israel*, p. 343.
13. Ben Meir, *Civil-Military Relations in Israel*, p. 61.
14. Joel Brinkley, "Lebanon Battle Stirring Doubts in Israel," *New York Times*, May 6, 1988; Efraim Inbar, *Rabin and Israel's National Security* (Washington, D.C.: Woodrow Wilson Center Press, 1999), p. 111.
15. Robert Pear, "Shultz, in Warning to Israel, Says Occupation Is 'Dead-End Street,'" *New York Times*, June 6, 1988; Gowers and Walker, *Arafat*, p. 267.
16. Joel Brinkley, "A Divided Electorate Ponders Which Israel Is the Right One," *New York Times*, October 2, 1988.
17. Azmy Bishara, "Israel Faces the Uprising: A Preliminary Assessment," *Middle East Report* 157 (March–April 1989): 6–14.
18. Anthony Lewis, "Israel Against Itself," *New York Times*, February 12, 1989.
19. Ibid.
20. Moshe Arens, *Broken Covenant: American Foreign Policy and the Crisis Between the U.S. and Israel* (New York: Simon & Schuster, 1995), pp. 53–54.
21. Gowers and Walker, *Arafat*, p. 297.
22. Alan Cowell, "Iraq Chief, Boasting of Poison Gas, Warns of Disaster If Israelis Strike," *New York Times*, April 3, 1990.
23. Joel Brinkley, "Sharon Resigns from Israeli Cabinet," *New York Times*, February 13, 1990.
24. Amos Oz, *In the Land of Israel* (New York: Vintage Books, 1984), p. 146.
25. Linden MacIntyre, "Murdered by the Mossad?" *The Fifth Estate*, Canadian Broadcasting Corp., February 12, 1991.
26. Amnon Lipkin-Shahak interview.
27. Dov Tamari interview.
28. "The Middle East Talks: Excerpts from Speeches in Madrid," *New York Times*, October 31, 1991.
29. Ibid.
30. Slater, *Rabin of Israel*, p. 373.
31. Clyde Haberman, "Israelis Kill Chief of Pro-Iran Shiites in South Lebanon," *New York Times*, February 17, 1992.
32. Nathaniel C. Nash, "At Least 6 Die as Blast Destroys Israel's Embassy in Buenos Aires," *New York Times*, March 18, 1992.

33. Aharon Ze'evi Farkash, an Israeli intelligence chief, said, "We made a few mistakes. [Hassan] Nasrallah is worse than Abbas Musawi." See also Ze'ev Schiff, "How Iran Planned the Buenos Aires Blast," *Ha'aretz*, March 18, 2003.

14. Peace Strategy: The New Yitzhak

1. William Safire, "Israel: Rabin Redux," *New York Times*, June 4, 1992.
2. Clyde Haberman, "Rabin Invokes Old Victory to Seek a New One in Israeli Election Campaign," *New York Times*, May 21, 1992.
3. Ibid.
4. Slater, *Rabin of Israel*, pp. 387–88.
5. Safire, "Israel: Rabin Redux."
6. Shlaim, *The Iron Wall*, p. 501.
7. Daniel Williams, "Shamir Tells of Plan to Stall Talks," *Los Angeles Times*, June 27, 1992.
8. Address to the Knesset by Prime Minister Rabin Presenting His Government, July 13, 1992, Israel Ministry of Foreign Affairs.
9. Leslie H. Gelb, "America in Israel," *New York Times*, June 15, 1992.
10. Ross, *The Missing Peace*, p. 93.
11. Bar-Zohar, *Shimon Peres*, p. 426.
12. Greg Myre, "The Struggle for Iraq: The Iraqi Leader: '92 Israeli Plan to Kill Hussein Is Reported," *New York Times*, December 17, 2003.
13. Amnon Lipkin-Shahak interview.
14. Aharon Ze'evi Farkash interview.
15. Richard H. Curtiss, "Israel's Botched Assassination Attempt Surfaces After Saddam Hussein's Capture," *Washington Report on Middle East Affairs*, March 2004, p. 22.
16. Ben Lynfield, "Planned to Assassinate Saddam with Rocket," *Scotsman*, December 17, 2003.
17. Clyde Haberman, "Scandal Embroils the Israeli Army," *New York Times*, November 23, 1992.
18. Agence France-Presse, "Israel Reveals Post Gulf War Plan to Assassinate, Shelved After Drill Blunder," DefenceTalk, December 16, 2003, accessed February 29, 2012, www.defencetalk.com/israel-reveals-post-war-plan-to-assassinate-shelved-after -drill-blunder-2074.
19. Martin Indyk, *Innocent Abroad: An Intimate Account of American Peace Diplomacy in the Middle East* (New York: Simon & Schuster, 2009), p. 26.
20. Ben Meir, *Civil-Military Relations in Israel*, p. xiii.
21. Clyde Haberman, "400 Arabs Ousted by Israel Are Mired in Frozen Limbo," *New York Times*, December 19, 1992.
22. Shabtai Shavit, interview with the author, September 15, 2008.
23. Ibid.
24. Jacob Peri interview.
25. Dvorah Chen, Israeli prosecuting attorney, interview with the author, March 7, 2009.

26. Jacob Peri interview.

27. Reuven Pedatzur, "They Just Don't Give up, Those Mossad Guys," *Ha'aretz*, July 5, 2007.

28. Ibid.

29. Efraim Halevy interview.

30. *State of Israel v. Nahum Manbar*, Court of Criminal Appeals, Supreme Court, December 5, 2000 [Hebrew; trans. Gilad Halpern], previous judgment June 17, 1998, Tel Aviv District Court. See also Ronen Bergman, *The Secret War with Iran* (New York: Free Press, 2008), pp. 302–15.

15. Oslo: Wary Generals Waging Peace

1. Uri Savir, interview with the author, November 21, 2005; also Uri Savir, *The Process: 1,100 Days That Changed the Middle East* (New York: Random House, 1998), pp. 25–26.

2. Yossi Beilin, *The Path to Geneva* (New York: Akashic Books, 2004), p. 54.

3. Shlaim, *The Iron Wall*, p. 521.

4. Gazit, *Trapped Fools*, pp. 314, 321.

5. Peri, *Generals in the Cabinet Room*, p. 222.

6. Ibid., p. 64.

7. Uri Saguy, interview with the author, September 10, 2008.

8. Jacob Peri interview.

9. Excerpts from Rabin Speech to Parliament, *New York Times*, March 1, 1994.

10. Clyde Haberman, "Arab Car Bomber Kills 8 in Israel, 44 Are Wounded," *New York Times*, April 7, 1994.

11. Peri, *Generals in the Cabinet Room*, p. 25.

12. Shlaim, *The Iron Wall*, p. 540; Bar-Zohar, *Shimon Peres*, p. 455; Halevy, *Man in the Shadows*, p. 89.

13. Prime Minister Rabin's Speech in the Knesset [during visit of President Bill Clinton], October 27, 1994, Israel Ministry of Foreign Affairs.

14. Richard Nixon, *Beyond Peace* (New York: Random House, 1994), p. 145.

15. Savir, *The Process*, pp. 149–51.

16. Ross, *The Missing Peace*, p. 94.

17. Shlaim, *The Iron Wall*, p. 23.

18. Savir, *The Process*, pp. 201–204.

19. Ibid., pp. 248–55.

20. Moshe Ya'alon, interview with the author, August 28, 2008.

21. Ibid.

22. Leah Rabin, *Rabin: Our Life, His Legacy*, p. 260.

23. Laura Marlowe, "Interview with a Fanatic," *Time*, February 6, 1995.

24. Joel Greenberg, "Islamic Group Vows Revenge for Slaying of Its Leader," *New York Times*, October 30, 1995.

16. Bibi Against the Military Elite

1. Serge Schmemann, "In Congress, Peres Again Appeals to Syria for a Mideast Peace," *New York Times*, December 13, 1995.

2. Naomi Segal, "Holder of Slain Spouse's Torch, Peace Advocate Leah Rabin Dies," Jewish Telegraphic Agency, November 17, 2000.

3. Schmemann, "In Congress . . ."

4. Steven Erlanger, "Peres Under Pressure to Call an Early Election in Israel," *New York Times*, January 19, 1996.

5. Ross, *The Missing Peace*, p. 227.

6. Gadi Baltiansky, interview with the author, February 23, 2009.

7. Charles Enderlin, *Shattered Dreams: The Failure of the Peace Process in the Middle East, 1995–2002*, trans. Susan Fairfield (New York: Other Press, 2002), pp. 19–20.

8. Ami Ayalon, interview with the author, September 6, 2008.

9. Shlaim, *The Iron Wall*, p. 556.

10. Stanley Moskowitz, interview with the author, August 31, 2005.

11. Ami Ayalon interview.

12. Benjamin Netanyahu, *Fighting Terrorism: How Democracies Can Defeat the International Terrorist Network* (New York: Farrar, Straus and Giroux, 1995), p. 101.

13. Moshe Ya'alon interview.

14. Shimon Peres, Text of Address to Summit of Peacemakers, March 13, 1996, Israel Ministry of Foreign Affairs.

15. Savir, *The Process*, pp. 293–97.

16. Shlaim, *The Iron Wall*, p. 560.

17. Enderlin, *Shattered Dreams*, p. 38.

18. Savir, *The Process*, p. 303.

19. Ibid., pp. 305–308.

20. Enderlin, *Shattered Dreams*, p. 39.

21. Netanyahu's remarks were reported on Israeli television in mid-July 2010 and on Internet sites around the world. The remarks were transcribed from a videotape of Netanyahu's meeting in Ofra in 1999 with a group of settlers. Netanyahu did not dispute the accuracy or the context of his remarks.

22. Aharon Ze'evi Farkash interview.

23. Netanyahu, *Fighting Terrorism*, p. 148.

24. Ross, *The Missing Peace*, p. 261.

25. Enderlin, *Shattered Dreams*, p. 56.

26. Ami Ayalon interview.

27. Stanley Moskowitz interview.

28. Peri, *Generals in the Cabinet Room*, pp. 97, 124.

29. Ibid., pp. 86–87.

30. Ze'ev Schiff, "The Intelligence That Gil Passed On: The Syrians Will Attack on the Golan," *Ha'aretz*, December 8, 1997; see also Shlaim, *The Iron Wall*, p. 592.

31. Shlaim, *The Iron Wall*, p. 580.

32. Enderlin, *Shattered Dreams*, p. 68.

33. Ibid., p. 70.

34. Shlaim, *The Iron Wall*, p. 583.

35. Ross, *The Missing Peace*, p. 353.

36. See Joseph Finklestone, "Obituary: General Matti Peled," *Independent*, March 16, 1995.

37. Enderlin, *Shattered Dreams*, p. 73.

38. According to several authoritative accounts, Hezbollah successfully intercepted the unencrypted video footage from Israeli UAV drones that mapped the area of the raid. Hezbollah was able to infer from the video footage what route the commandos would follow and mined the area, according to both Hezbollah and Israeli experts. See Yaakov Lappin, "Nasrallah Recalls '97 Shayetet to 'Deflect Pressure,'" *Jerusalem Post*, November 8, 2010.

39. Halevy, *Man in the Shadows*, p. 166.

40. *The Economist*, October 9, 1997.

41. Efraim Halevy interview.

42. Peri, *Generals in the Cabinet Room*, p. 84.

43. Ibid.

44. Ibid.

45. Indyk, *Innocent Abroad*, pp. 246–47.

46. Ross, *The Missing Peace*, p. 391.

47. *Yedioth Aharonoth*, March 8, 1998; Arieh O'Sullivan, "1,554 Ex-Officers Sign Ad Urging Peace, Not Settlements," *Jewish Weekly*, March 13, 1998.

48. Yossi Beilin notes that "a senior source" in Netanyahu's office was quoted as saying that "the prime minister's strategic goal was achieved: the Oslo process was halted." Beilin, *The Path to Geneva*, p. 69.

49. "Hillary Clinton Supports a Palestinian State," *New York Times*, May 8, 1998.

50. Edward W. Said, *The End of the Peace Process: Oslo and After* (New York: Vintage Books, 2001), p. 188.

51. Ibid., p. 68.

52. Bill Clinton, Remarks to the Members of the Palestinian National Council and Other Palestinian Organizations, Gaza City, December 14, 1998, *Public Papers of the Presidents of the United States*, William J. Clinton.

53. Enderlin, *Shattered Dreams*, p. 105.

54. The rumors of Netanyahu's remarks about Israel's possible use of its nuclear forces against Syria were reported to the author by an Israeli academic.

55. Any vestige of the old doubts about Barak's lack of courage was swept away by a state comptroller's report in March. The official review stated that Barak's behavior during the 1992 accident that killed five Sayeret Matkal commandos was not cowardly or inappropriate. See Patrick Cockburn, "Barak Cleared over Botched Assassination," *Independent*, March 11, 1999.

17. Barak: The Arrogance of Power

1. Enderlin, *Shattered Dreams*, p. 112.
2. Clayton E. Swisher, *The Truth About Camp David: The Untold Story About the Collapse of the Middle East Peace Process* (New York: Nation Books, 2004), p. 16; Amnon Lipkin-Shahak interview.
3. Swisher, *The Truth About Camp David*, p. 23.
4. Enderlin, *Shattered Dreams*, p. 116.
5. Ibid., p. 118.
6. Gilead Sher, *Within Reach: The Israeli-Palestinian Peace Negotiations, 1999–2001* (New York: Routledge, 2006), p. 15.
7. Moshe Ya'alon interview.
8. Uri Saguy interview; Enderlin, *Shattered Dreams*, p. 118.
9. Uri Saguy interview.
10. Indyk, *Innocent Abroad*, pp. 245–51.
11. Ross, *The Missing Peace*, pp. 565, 589.
12. Ahron Bregman, *Elusive Peace: How the Holy Land Defeated America* (New York: Penguin Books, 2005), p. 48.
13. Ibid.
14. Ami Ayalon interview.
15. Enderlin, *Shattered Dreams*, p. 136.
16. Gadi Baltiansky interview.
17. Beilin, *The Path to Geneva*, p. 126.
18. Enderlin, *Shattered Dreams*, p. 136.
19. Alon Pinkas, interview with the author, November 7, 2005.
20. Bregman, *Elusive Peace*, pp. 59–60.
21. Amos Harel and Avi Issacharoff, *34 Days: Israel, Hezbollah, and the War in Lebanon* (New York: Palgrave Macmillan, 2008), p. 38.
22. Gadi Baltiansky interview.
23. Enderlin, *Shattered Dreams*, pp. 164–65.
24. Shlomo Ben-Ami, *A Front Without a Rearguard: A Voyage to the Boundaries of the Peace Process* [Hebrew] (Tel Aviv: Miskal-Yedioth Ahronoth Books, 2004), p. 473.
25. Ibid.
26. Dan, *Ariel Sharon*, p. 177.
27. Ibid., p. 157.
28. Efraim Halevy interview.
29. Moshe Ya'alon interview.
30. Stanley Moskowitz interview.
31. Peri, *Generals in the Cabinet Room*, p. 101.
32. Ephraim Lavie, interview with the author, March 4, 2009; also correspondence with Lavie.
33. Gadi Baltiansky interview.
34. Amnon Lipkin-Shahak interview.

35. Peri, *Generals in the Cabinet Room*, pp. 106–107.
36. Yossi Beilin interview.
37. Raviv Drucker and Ofer Shelah, *Boomerang: The Leadership Failure During the Second Intifada* [Hebrew; trans. Gilad Halpern] (Tel Aviv: Keter Publishing, 2005), p. 73.
38. Jane Perlez, "Clinton Presents a Broad New Plan for Mideast Peace," *New York Times*, December 25, 2000.
39. Peri, *Generals in the Cabinet Room*, p. 104.
40. Enderlin, *Shattered Dreams*, p. 325.

18. Sharon: The Last Campaign Against Arafat

1. Drucker and Shelah, *Boomerang*, pp. 87–98.
2. Aharon Ze'evi Farkash interview.
3. Peri, *Generals in the Cabinet Room*, p. 127.
4. Drucker and Shelah, *Boomerang*, pp. 55–57.
5. Inauguration Speech of Prime Minister Ariel Sharon in the Knesset, March 7, 2001, Israel Ministry of Foreign Affairs.
6. Alon Liel interview.
7. See Jane Perlez, "Bush and Sharon Differ on Ending Violence," *New York Times*, June 27, 2001.
8. Efraim Halevy interview.
9. Interview with a senior official who was present during the crown prince's audience with the ambassador.
10. Efraim Halevy interview. Also Halevy, *Man in the Shadows*, p. 207.
11. Ariel Sharon, Speech in the Knesset, September 16, 2001, Prime Minister's Office.
12. Julian Borger, "U.S. Backs State for Palestine," *Guardian*, October 3, 2001.
13. Statement by Israeli Prime Minister Ariel Sharon, Jerusalem, October 4, 2001, Israel Ministry of Foreign Affairs.
14. Drucker and Shelah, *Boomerang*, pp. 140–46.
15. Suzanne Goldenberg, "Far-Right Leader Who Fell Victim to His Own Ideas," *Guardian*, October 18, 2001.
16. "Excerpts from Talk by Sharon," *New York Times*, December 4, 2001.
17. Statement to *Ma'ariv*, cited in Peri, *Generals in the Cabinet Room*, p. 113.
18. Stan Goodenough, "Peres Wants Palestine," *Israel Insider*, January 2, 2002.
19. Statement to *Ma'ariv*, cited in Peri, *Generals in the Cabinet Room*, p. 113.
20. Aharon Ze'evi Farkash interview.
21. Drucker and Shelah, *Boomerang*, pp. 175–83.
22. Ibid., pp. 166–74.
23. Ben Caspit, "The Polish Poet and the Art of Assassination" [Hebrew; trans. Gilad Halpern], *Ma'ariv*, June 10, 2005.
24. Robin Wright, "Powell Criticizes Israeli Strategy," *Los Angeles Times*, March 7, 2002.
25. Peri, *Generals in the Cabinet Room*, p. 186.

26. Briefing by Major General Aharon Zeevi Farkash, April 16, 2002, Israel Ministry of Foreign Affairs.

27. Mark Matthews, *Lost Years: Bush, Sharon and the Failure in the Middle East* (New York: Nation Books, 2007), p. 210.

28. Efraim Halevy interview.

29. Todd S. Purdum with Steven Erlanger, "Sharon, and Arab Officials, Press White House on Mideast," *New York Times*, May 6, 2002.

30. Yair Sheleg, "Ya'alon: Palestinian Threat Is Cancerous," *Ha'aretz*, August 26, 2002.

31. B. Michael, *Yedioth Ahronoth*, cited in Peri, *Generals in the Cabinet Room*, p. 141.

32. Reuters, July 22, 2002.

33. Dan, *Ariel Sharon*, p. 207.

34. *Seven Days* (Supplement), *Ha'aretz*, August 23, 2002, cited in Peri, *Generals in the Cabinet Room*, p. 181; see also Vered Levy Barzilai, "The High and the Mighty," *Ha'aretz*, August 21, 2002.

35. Final Statements at Conclusion of the Middle East Peace Summit at Aqaba, June 4, 2003, Israel Ministry of Foreign Affairs.

36. Ibid.

37. Chemi Shalev, "I Don't Feel I've Given Enough" [Hebrew; trans. Gilad Halpern], *Yisrael Hayom*, September 17, 2010.

38. Moshe Ya'alon, "The Rules of War," *Washington Post*, August 3, 2006.

39. Alex Fishman and Sima Kadmon, "We Are Seriously Concerned About the Fate of the State of Israel," *Yedioth Ahronoth*, November 14, 2003.

40. Ibid. Also Molly Moore, "Ex–Security Chiefs Turn on Sharon," *Washington Post*, November 15, 2003.

41. Matthews, *Lost Years*, p. 347.

42. Ari Shavit, "Top PM Aide: Gaza Plan Aims to Freeze the Peace Process," *Ha'aretz*, October 6, 2004. Sharon was also able to extract a major concession from George W. Bush, who had proclaimed publicly in April that "it is unrealistic to expect" that Israel would ever give up the "major population centers" it had established in the occupied West Bank and that the Palestinian right of return could apply only to a Palestinian state.

43. Matthews, *Lost Years*, p. 244.

19. At Wit's End: Killing the Paraplegic Preacher

1. On Sheikh Yassin's life, see David Hirst, "Obituary: Sheikh Ahmed Yassin," *Guardian*, March 23, 2004; Andrew Higgins, "How Israel Helped to Spawn Hamas," *Wall Street Journal*, January 24, 2009; Beverley Milton-Edwards and Stephen Farrell, *Hamas: The Islamic Resistance Movement* (Cambridge: Polity Press, 2010).

2. Rabbi Menachem Froman, interview with the author, March 7, 2009.

3. Joel Leyden, Israel News Agency, March 22, 2004.

4. "Sheikh Yassin Denies Attack Role," BBC, January 16, 2004.

5. Aharon Ze'evi Farkash interview.

6. Alon Liel interview.
7. "Israel Defiant over Yassin Killing," BBC News, March 22, 2004.
8. Rabbi Menachem Froman interview.
9. Dan, *Ariel Sharon*, p. 234.
10. Peri, *Generals in the Cabinet Room*, p. 250.

20. Olmert: Putting Lebanon Back Twenty Years

1. Greg Myre, "Netanyahu to Challenge Sharon; Move Could Force Election," *New York Times*, August 31, 2005.
2. Steven Erlanger, "Ex-Rival Now Trying to Position Himself as Heir Apparent," *New York Times*, January 10, 2006.
3. Roger Cohen, "Israel Is Growing Steadily More Prosperous—and Less Secure," *New York Times*, July 8, 2007.
4. Harel and Issacharoff, *34 Days*, p. 72.
5. Greg Myre and Steven Erlanger, "Clashes Spread to Lebanon as Hezbollah Raids Israel," *New York Times*, July 13, 2006.
6. Harel and Issacharoff, *34 Days*, p. 100.
7. Yaakov Katz, "High-ranking Officer: Halutz Ordered Retaliation Policy," *Jerusalem Post*, July 24, 2006. After a high-ranking Israeli air force officer told journalists that Halutz had issued the order to destroy ten buildings in Beirut for every Katyusha strike against Haifa, the IDF spokesman suggested that reporters had misquoted the officer, but later withdrew this assertion. A second statement from the spokesman said that the officer was wrong in claiming that Halutz had issued such a directive.
8. "Mideast War, by the Numbers," Associated Press, August 17, 2006.
9. Hassan M. Fattah, "Israel Bombards Lebanon After Hezbollah Hits Haifa with Missiles," *New York Times*, July 17, 2006; also, Harel and Issacharoff, *34 Days*, p. 103.
10. Harel and Issacharoff, *34 Days*, p. 107.
11. Jacob Peri interview.
12. Ibid.
13. *Ha'aretz*, September 15, 2006.
14. Winograd Commission, Interim Report, Israel Ministry of Foreign Affairs, April 30, 2007; Winograd Commission, Final Report, Council on Foreign Relations, January 30, 2008.
15. "Uzi Dayan: Rally Aims to Send Gov't Clear Message," *Jerusalem Post*, May 3, 2007.
16. Steven Erlanger and Isabel Kershner, "Protesters Gather to Urge Olmert to Resign," *New York Times*, May 3, 2007.
17. Amnon Lipkin-Shahak interview.
18. Ehud Olmert, "1967: Israel Cannot Make Peace Alone," *Guardian*, June 6, 2007.

21. War (on Syria) War (on Gaza) War (on Iran?)

1. George W. Bush recounts in his memoir that he learned of the Syrian reactor from "a foreign intelligence partner," presumably Israel, in the spring of 2007. George W. Bush, *Decision Points* (New York: Crown, 2010), p. 420.

2. Ian Black, "Olmert Calls for Peace with Syria as Rumors Grow of Secret Talks," *Guardian*, June 7, 2007.

3. Bush, *Decision Points*, p. 421.

4. Prince Bandar bin Sultan interview.

5. Bush, *Decision Points*, p. 417.

6. A senior U.S. intelligence official who gave a White House briefing on the Syrian reactor said that his "assessment" was that "the reactor was planned to be part of a weapons program." But the lack of physical evidence—the missing plutonium separation facility—had resulted in Hayden's decision to express the "low confidence" view to Bush. See Bob Woodward, "The Lesson Cheney Didn't Learn," *Washington Post*, September 12, 2011.

7. Bush, *Decision Points*, p. 421.

8. Alon Liel interview.

9. Aluf Benn, "Washington Parks Israeli Plan for Attack on Iran's Nuclear Facilities," *Ha'aretz*, August 25, 2008.

10. Uzi Mahnaimi, Hala Jaber, and Jon Swain, "Israel Kills Terror Chief with Headrest Bomb," *Sunday Times* (London), February 17, 2008.

11. Nicholas Blanford, "The Mystery Behind a Syrian Murder," *Time*, August 7, 2008.

12. The account of the Olmert-Abbas meeting was published in Hebrew by Olmert in a memoir excerpted in *Yedioth Ahronoth* in January 2011. See Matti Friedman, "In Memoirs, Ex–Israeli PM Regrets Failure of Peace Talks," Associated Press, January 28, 2011.

13. Rory McCarthy, "Gaza Truce Broken as Israeli Raid Kills Six Hamas Gunmen," *Guardian*, November 5, 2008.

14. "Olmert Delivers 'Last Minute' Warning to Gaza," Associated Press, December 25, 2008.

15. "In Gaza, Both Sides Reveal New Gear," *Defense News*, January 5, 2009.

16. Nidal al-Mughrabi, "Israel Kills Scores in Gaza Air Strikes," Reuters, December 27, 2008.

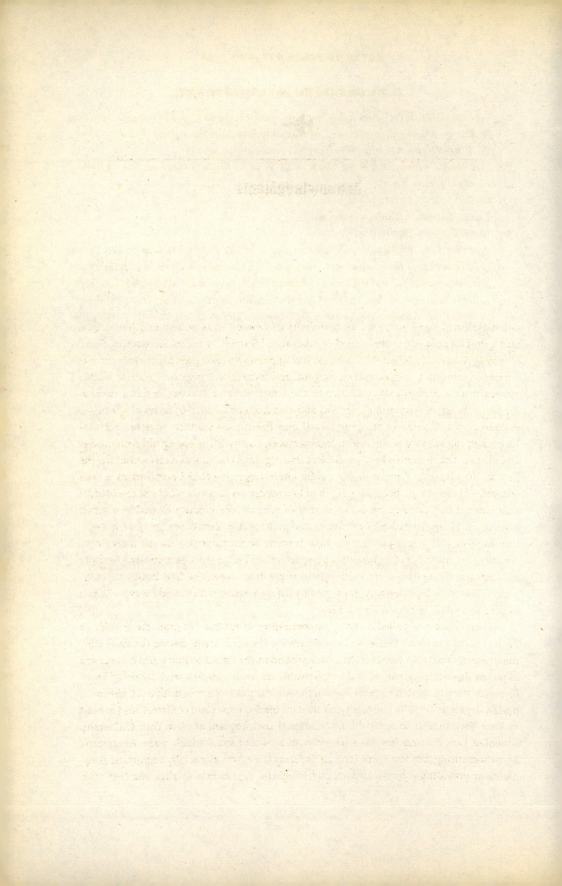

Acknowledgments

Gilad Halpern, a graduate of City University of London in sociology and journalism and a Ph.D. candidate at the School for Advanced Studies in Social Sciences in Paris, served as research assistant for this book. It is impossible to overstate his contribution as a partner, a thinker, and a creative, diligent, and focused investigator. He came to this project from a background of service in the Israeli Defense Forces (he was a combat medic in the 433rd Armored Regiment) and also from an admirable series of volunteer assignments as diverse as bringing Israeli and Palestinian students together for dialogue, helping migrant workers find legal services, and assisting young ultra-Orthodox Israelis to make their own lifestyle choices. His rigorous training as a researcher for the British Broadcasting Corporation's public affairs program *HARDtalk* and as a staff writer for Ha'aretz.com brought a depth of knowledge and experience about the Middle East conflict that elevated his status to that of brilliant collaborator as well as a gifted researcher. He translated Hebrew books and articles that were never going to make it into English within our publication time frames; he accompanied me on interviews, contributing his thoughts, questions, perspective, and experience generously, candidly and, always, thoughtfully. He made useful suggestions when the first draft was completed. This work is profoundly imprinted by his association with it, and I was fortunate to have shared the experience with him.

When Gilad was pulled away by opportunities to resume his graduate studies in Paris, I turned to Omri Sender to help me review the manuscript during the final editing process. Omri also comes from a background in the Israeli military and had served as an invaluable, imaginative, and indefatigable research assistant on *A World of Trouble*, my history of American presidents in the Middle East. After the military, Omri took his law degree at Tel Aviv University, clerked on the Supreme Court of Israel, and moved to New York in 2011 to enter the international law program at New York University School of Law. *Fortress Israel* is a narrative of a culture about which many Americans know something, but few know intimately. Thus Omri was a crucially important commentator providing rigorous, smart, and insightful suggestions to align the text with the historical and contemporary Israeli reality. I am most grateful to him. Any flaws or mistakes are wholly my responsibility.

My exposure to Israel's military culture began in the 1980s when I was a young correspondent based in Cairo for the *Washington Post*. But the inspiration for this book really took shape during the years I was traveling back and forth to Tel Aviv to interview Israeli political figures and the military and intelligence chiefs for *A World of Trouble*. My Israeli "base" has been the home of Igal and Raya Tabori, who pulled me into their family, doctored me when I fell ill, consoled me when my brother, Michael, passed away during one trip in 2008, and invited me to countless Sabbath dinners that helped me understand the wild diversity of opinions that inhabit Israeli families. In 2011, a hiking accident in India claimed the life of the Taboris' eldest daughter, Einat, a promising medical student, and so I have dedicated this book to the memory of my brother and their daughter.

When the manuscript was in production, I asked a number of people to read and comment on it, including one of my oldest references on the Middle East, Douglas Roberts, who reads more broadly every morning on the Middle East than anyone else I know, and not just because he helps to oversee National Public Radio's reporting from the region. Philip Wilcox, the former U.S. consul general in Jerusalem, also provided useful suggestions and observations, as did several friends in Washington and in Israel.

I am grateful to all of those who devoted their time and intellectual energy to this long inquiry. The Moshe Sharett Heritage Society, especially Yaakov Sharett and Yoram Sharett, the son and grandson of the second prime minister, were most helpful in providing assistance and photo resources, as was the staff of the Government Press Office in Jerusalem. Lori Wiener, a photo editor in Arlington, Virginia, who has now assisted me on two books, did a wonderful job of culling images from archives around the world.

I have been fortunate for more than a decade to be represented by the Bernstein dynasty. Robert L. Bernstein, the former Random House chairman and founder of Human Rights Watch, has guided and advised me on writing projects since our first meeting in China in the early 1990s. He has slowly handed me down to Peter Bernstein, whose long career as executive editor of *U.S. News & World Report* and as a publisher of Times Books/Random House has rendered him irreplaceable as a literary adviser, agent, and friend.

At Farrar, Straus and Giroux, I am grateful to Jonathan Galassi for his fearless independence in guiding a storied institution into a new era of ideas, contention, and wonder. His greatest contribution to this work was in assigning Paul Elie, a senior editor, to shepherd the manuscript from first to final draft, providing brilliant insight and reinforcement at every step. The final production was managed with great skill by Ileene Smith, the new executive editor, and Mareike Grover, the production editor, with guidance from Jeff Seroy, the head of publicity, all ably assisted by Karen Maine, Daniel Gerstle, and Brian Gittis.

Sustaining me throughout this process, and in everything else, was Linda Catherine Tyler, who has shared sorrow, joy, and adventure with me for forty years.

Index

A NOTE ABOUT THE AUTHOR

Patrick Tyler worked for twelve years at the *Washington Post* before joining the *New York Times* in 1990 as a military analyst, and later as a foreign correspondent in Beijing, Moscow, Baghdad, and London. He also served as chief correspondent in Washington, D.C. Tyler is the author of *Running Critical: The Silent War, Rickover, and General Dynamics*; *A Great Wall: Six Presidents and China* (which won the 2000 Lionel Gelber Prize); and *A World of Trouble: The White House and the Middle East—from the Cold War to the War on Terror*. He and his wife live in Washington, D.C.